After receiving feedback on my books I have compiled this alphabetical Index to assist researchers. This index is a supplement to my book: 1930 Population Census of Guam: Transcribed (ISBN 978-0-9851257-1-4).

This Index is the intellectual property of Bernard T. Punzalan (author, publisher and principal investigator) of the Chamorro Roots Genealogy Project™ (www.chamorroroots.com). No part of this Index may be reproduced or transmitted in any form or by any means, electronic or mechanical, including photocopying, recording, or by any information storage and retrieval system, without the written permission of the author. I would appreciate your support to this because all proceeds generated from the Chamorro Roots Genealogy Project are used to maintain and enhance the website, subscriptions and expenses for public presentations.

Si Yu'os Ma'ase,

Bernard Punzalan

INDEX
1930 Population Census of Guam: Transcribed

[blank], -pg. D-8-50
[illegible], [illegible] D -pg. D-13-20
[illegible], Howard W -pg. D-13-18
[illegible], Keith Q -pg. D-13-20
Abarguza, Pacifico -pg. D-1-56
Abtue, Joseph W -pg. D-13-9
Acfalle, Albert A -pg. D-7-15
Acfalle, Ana A -pg. D-9-28
Acfalle, Ana C -pg. D-6-37
Acfalle, Ana C -pg. D-9-5
Acfalle, Ana C -pg. D-9-9
Acfalle, Ana M -pg. D-9-4
Acfalle, Andrea C -pg. D-9-21
Acfalle, Andrea M -pg. D-9-4
Acfalle, Antonia R -pg. D-9-14
Acfalle, Blaz C -pg. D-9-21
Acfalle, Carmelo C -pg. D-9-21
Acfalle, Carmelo M -pg. D-9-17
Acfalle, Carmelo R -pg. D-9-23
Acfalle, Carmen A -pg. D-7-14
Acfalle, Carmen C -pg. D-6-29
Acfalle, Carmen R -pg. D-9-23
Acfalle, Concepcion B -pg. D-10-22
Acfalle, Concepcion C -pg. D-6-29
Acfalle, Consolacion C -pg. D-6-37
Acfalle, Crecencia L -pg. D-11-13
Acfalle, Crecencia L -pg. D-11-14
Acfalle, Delfina B -pg. D-10-22
Acfalle, Dimas A -pg. D-9-28
Acfalle, Dolores M -pg. D-6-28
Acfalle, Dominga B -pg. D-7-14
Acfalle, Dorothy R A -pg. D-1-60
Acfalle, Emiterio C -pg. D-9-9
Acfalle, Estefania L -pg. D-11-14
Acfalle, Fausto C -pg. D-9-23
Acfalle, Felicidad A -pg. D-1-60
Acfalle, Felicita A -pg. D-7-15
Acfalle, Felipe C -pg. D-9-14
Acfalle, Felix C -pg. D-9-5
Acfalle, Francisca C -pg. D-6-29
Acfalle, Francisca R -pg. D-9-23
Acfalle, Francisco A -pg. D-7-15
Acfalle, Francisco A -pg. D-11-9
Acfalle, Geronimo SN -pg. D-6-37
Acfalle, Gregorio M -pg. D-6-28
Acfalle, Ignacio C -pg. D-10-23
Acfalle, Isabel C -pg. D-9-21
Acfalle, Isabel C -pg. D-9-21
Acfalle, Isabel Q -pg. D-9-5
Acfalle, Jesus B -pg. D-9-9
Acfalle, Jesus B -pg. D-10-22
Acfalle, Jesus C -pg. D-6-29
Acfalle, Jesus C -pg. D-13-21
Acfalle, Joaquin A -pg. D-6-29
Acfalle, Jose A -pg. D-5-56
Acfalle, Jose A -pg. D-9-28
Acfalle, Jose B -pg. D-10-22
Acfalle, Jose B -pg. D-11-13
Acfalle, Jose C -pg. D-9-5

Acfalle, Jose M -pg. D-9-4
Acfalle, Jose O -pg. D-11-14
Acfalle, Josefina A -pg. D-1-60
Acfalle, Juan B -pg. D-9-4
Acfalle, Juan C -pg. D-9-5
Acfalle, Juan N -pg. D-7-19
Acfalle, Julia B -pg. D-9-2
Acfalle, Julia T -pg. D-7-21
Acfalle, Margarita C -pg. D-6-37
Acfalle, Maria B -pg. D-10-22
Acfalle, Maria M -pg. D-6-28
Acfalle, Maria T -pg. D-7-21
Acfalle, Miguel M -pg. D-9-4
Acfalle, Natividad M -pg. D-11-12
Acfalle, Nicolas A -pg. D-9-28
Acfalle, Nieves C -pg. D-10-24
Acfalle, Petra C -pg. D-9-21
Acfalle, Prudencio B -pg. D-9-2
Acfalle, Ramon R -pg. D-9-23
Acfalle, Rita M -pg. D-6-29
Acfalle, Rosa B -pg. D-10-22
Acfalle, Rosalia M -pg. D-6-28
Acfalle, Rosalia Q -pg. D-6-28
Acfalle, Santiago A -pg. D-1-53
Acfalle, Tomasa B -pg. D-7-14
Acfalle, Tomasa R -pg. D-9-14
Acfalle, Trinidad M -pg. D-9-4
Acfalle, Vicente B -pg. D-6-29
Acfalle, Vicente M -pg. D-9-5
Acfalle, Vicente R -pg. D-9-23
Achaigua, Consolacion Q -pg. D-3-50
Achaigua, Dolores C -pg. D-5-82
Achaigua, Esperanza A -pg. D-3-47
Achaigua, Felix S -pg. D-13-30
Achaigua, Maria -pg. D-3-50
Achaigua, Maria L -pg. D-3-50
Achaigua, Pedro -pg. D-3-50
Acosta, Ana H -pg. D-5-94
Acosta, Antonia A -pg. D-4-24
Acosta, Antonio B -pg. D-11-3
Acosta, Beatris D -pg. D-2-12
Acosta, Concepcion -pg. D-5-94
Acosta, Concepcion R -pg. D-2-34
Acosta, Dolores -pg. D-5-94
Acosta, Felipe M -pg. D-4-54
Acosta, Felisa -pg. D-5-94
Acosta, Felix -pg. D-5-94
Acosta, Isabel A -pg. D-2-50
Acosta, Isabel LG -pg. D-2-10
Acosta, Joaquin A -pg. D-2-12
Acosta, Joaquin C -pg. D-2-50
Acosta, Joaquin D -pg. D-2-51
Acosta, Joaquina -pg. D-5-94
Acosta, Jose -pg. D-5-94
Acosta, Jose V -pg. D-4-54
Acosta, Juan M -pg. D-3-44
Acosta, Juan S -pg. D-5-94
Acosta, Manuel -pg. D-5-94
Acosta, Manuel S -pg. D-5-94

Acosta, Maria -pg. D-5-94
Acosta, Maria LG -pg. D-2-10
Acosta, Maria P -pg. D-2-51
Acosta, Mariano C -pg. D-2-10
Acosta, Mariano S -pg. D-5-94
Acosta, Miguel C -pg. D-5-94
Acosta, Pedro A -pg. D-2-34
Acosta, Ramon S -pg. D-5-94
Acosta, Rosa P -pg. D-4-54
Acosta, Rosa R -pg. D-2-34
Acosta, Rosa V -pg. D-2-25
Acosta, Rosario -pg. D-3-53
Acosta, Vicenta S -pg. D-5-94
Ada, Agnes P -pg. D-4-88
Ada, Agueda M -pg. D-5-59
Ada, Ana C -pg. D-1-17
Ada, Ana M -pg. D-5-59
Ada, Antonio C -pg. D-1-17
Ada, Antonio F -pg. D-2-78
Ada, Antonio Q -pg. D-2-78
Ada, Antonio S -pg. D-4-95
Ada, Candelaria C -pg. D-4-63
Ada, Carmen H -pg. D-4-63
Ada, Delia -pg. D-3-60
Ada, Elvira -pg. D-3-61
Ada, Felis C -pg. D-4-63
Ada, Herman -pg. D-3-60
Ada, Herminia -pg. D-3-60
Ada, Ignacio F -pg. D-4-95
Ada, Jesus M -pg. D-5-59
Ada, Jesus Q -pg. D-2-78
Ada, Joaquin S -pg. D-4-95
Ada, Joaquina M -pg. D-5-59
Ada, Jose -pg. D-3-60
Ada, Jose C -pg. D-1-17
Ada, Jose M -pg. D-3-60
Ada, Jose M -pg. D-5-59
Ada, Jose Q -pg. D-2-78
Ada, Juan -pg. D-3-61
Ada, Lydia -pg. D-3-60
Ada, Manuel -pg. D-13-21
Ada, Margarita Q -pg. D-2-78
Ada, Maria -pg. D-3-61
Ada, Maria A -pg. D-3-17
Ada, Maria M -pg. D-1-17
Ada, Maria M -pg. D-1-17
Ada, Maria M -pg. D-5-59
Ada, Maria P -pg. D-4-88
Ada, Maria Q -pg. D-2-78
Ada, Maria T -pg. D-3-60
Ada, Mariano Q -pg. D-2-78
Ada, Nicolas B -pg. D-9-15
Ada, Pedro M -pg. D-4-88
Ada, Pedro T -pg. D-8-44
Ada, Pilar H -pg. D-4-63
Ada, Ramon M -pg. D-5-59
Ada, Regino M -pg. D-1-17
Ada, Rosa C -pg. D-3-57
Ada, Rosa M -pg. D-5-59

INDEX
1930 Population Census of Guam: Transcribed

Ada, Rosalia Q -pg. D-2-78
Ada, Severina H -pg. D-4-63
Ada, Vicente B -pg. D-1-17
Ada, Winifred H -pg. D-4-63
Adamos, Ana LG -pg. D-4-74
Adamos, Ireneo -pg. D-13-34
Adamos, Pablo LG -pg. D-4-74
Adams, Henry F -pg. D-13-2
Adams, Henry F -pg. D-13-3
Adams, Philip C -pg. D-13-3
Adams, Robert L -pg. D-13-4
Adams, Sarah J -pg. D-13-2
Adriano, Joaquin G -pg. D-2-14
Adriano, Jose G -pg. D-2-28
Adriano, Jose U -pg. D-2-28
Adriano, Maria C -pg. D-2-70
Adriano, Maria G -pg. D-2-14
Adriano, Maria U -pg. D-2-28
Adriano, Roberta U -pg. D-2-28
Afaisen, Ana D -pg. D-8-21
Afaisen, Ana SN -pg. D-8-41
Afaisen, Antonio N -pg. D-8-23
Afaisen, Catalina D -pg. D-8-21
Afaisen, Cristina D -pg. D-8-21
Afaisen, Dolores M -pg. D-8-5
Afaisen, Ignacia D -pg. D-8-21
Afaisen, Jesus A -pg. D-5-25
Afaisen, Joaquin SN -pg. D-8-20
Afaisen, Jose D -pg. D-8-21
Afaisen, Juan D -pg. D-8-21
Afaisen, Manuel M -pg. D-8-5
Afaisen, Maria C -pg. D-8-23
Afaisen, Maria D -pg. D-8-20
Afaisen, Maria D -pg. D-8-21
Afaisen, Paz M -pg. D-8-5
Afaisen, Ramon A -pg. D-5-25
Afaisen, Regina A -pg. D-5-25
Afaisen, Rita SN -pg. D-8-21
Afaisen, Santiago -pg. D-8-20
Afaisen, Susana T -pg. D-5-86
Afaisen, Susana T -pg. D-8-20
Afaisen, Vicenta N -pg. D-8-22
Aflague, Alexander J -pg. D-4-77
Aflague, Alfonso C -pg. D-4-19
Aflague, Ana A -pg. D-10-5
Aflague, Ana C -pg. D-1-50
Aflague, Ana C -pg. D-1-51
Aflague, Ana C -pg. D-3-60
Aflague, Ana R -pg. D-3-60
Aflague, Ana S -pg. D-7-3
Aflague, Ana V P -pg. D-1-61
Aflague, Antonia C -pg. D-2-81
Aflague, Antonio S -pg. D-7-19
Aflague, Concepcion LG -pg. D-3-25
Aflague, Concepcion S -pg. D-13-43
Aflague, Dolores C -pg. D-3-49
Aflague, Dolores SM -pg. D-1-58
Aflague, Dolores T -pg. D-7-19
Aflague, Elsie A -pg. D-10-5

Aflague, Enrique SM -pg. D-1-58
Aflague, Eugenia C -pg. D-1-51
Aflague, Eugenia J -pg. D-4-76
Aflague, Felipe -pg. D-3-60
Aflague, Fermin -pg. D-3-25
Aflague, Francisca G -pg. D-1-58
Aflague, Francisco A -pg. D-10-5
Aflague, Francisco S -pg. D-1-58
Aflague, Francisco T -pg. D-4-20
Aflague, Fructoso SM -pg. D-1-58
Aflague, Helen J -pg. D-4-77
Aflague, Ignacio P -pg. D-1-61
Aflague, Inocencio S -pg. D-4-76
Aflague, Inocencio SM -pg. D-1-58
Aflague, Isabel P -pg. D-1-61
Aflague, Jesusa A -pg. D-10-5
Aflague, Joaquin G -pg. D-1-58
Aflague, Jose -pg. D-3-50
Aflague, Jose -pg. D-13-34
Aflague, Jose P -pg. D-1-61
Aflague, Josefina SM -pg. D-1-58
Aflague, Joseph J -pg. D-4-77
Aflague, Juan -pg. D-3-60
Aflague, Juan S -pg. D-13-33
Aflague, Juan T -pg. D-7-19
Aflague, Lawrence J -pg. D-4-77
Aflague, Lorenzo S -pg. D-10-5
Aflague, Manuel G -pg. D-1-58
Aflague, Maria C -pg. D-1-51
Aflague, Maria C -pg. D-3-60
Aflague, Norberto G -pg. D-1-58
Aflague, Pilar SM -pg. D-1-58
Aflague, Reguberto -pg. D-3-60
Aflague, Ricardo G -pg. D-1-58
Aflague, Rita -pg. D-3-68
Aflague, Rita G -pg. D-1-58
Aflague, Rosa A -pg. D-3-68
Aflague, Rosa SM -pg. D-1-58
Aflague, Rosa SM -pg. D-1-58
Aflague, Rosario -pg. D-3-60
Aflague, Simeon -pg. D-3-60
Aflague, Tomas SM -pg. D-1-58
Aflague, Vicenta C -pg. D-3-60
Aflague, Vicenta S -pg. D-3-50
Aflague, Vicente C -pg. D-1-51
Aflague, Vicente T -pg. D-1-50
Aflague, Wilfred J -pg. D-4-77
Aflleje, Ana C -pg. D-7-7
Aflleje, Ana T -pg. D-7-3
Aflleje, Andres -pg. D-13-21
Aflleje, Angelina L -pg. D-10-19
Aflleje, Antonina N -pg. D-7-9
Aflleje, Antonio T -pg. D-7-3
Aflleje, Antonio T -pg. D-7-15
Aflleje, Beatrice N -pg. D-7-9
Aflleje, Carlos T -pg. D-7-11
Aflleje, Catalina T -pg. D-10-26
Aflleje, Cristina N -pg. D-7-9
Aflleje, Dolores G -pg. D-7-15

Aflleje, Francisco N -pg. D-7-9
Aflleje, Isabel T -pg. D-10-26
Aflleje, Jesus T -pg. D-7-11
Aflleje, Jesusa T -pg. D-10-26
Aflleje, Joaquin -pg. D-7-22
Aflleje, Joaquina T -pg. D-7-3
Aflleje, Jose F -pg. D-7-7
Aflleje, Jose G -pg. D-7-15
Aflleje, Jose T -pg. D-7-3
Aflleje, Jose T -pg. D-7-11
Aflleje, Jose T -pg. D-7-11
Aflleje, Josefa P -pg. D-7-22
Aflleje, Juan -pg. D-13-28
Aflleje, Juan P -pg. D-7-3
Aflleje, Juana T -pg. D-10-26
Aflleje, Judit A -pg. D-7-15
Aflleje, Lourdes N -pg. D-7-9
Aflleje, Magdalena C -pg. D-7-7
Aflleje, Marcela T -pg. D-7-15
Aflleje, Maria C -pg. D-10-30
Aflleje, Maria L -pg. D-10-19
Aflleje, Maria L -pg. D-10-19
Aflleje, Maria N -pg. D-7-9
Aflleje, Maria T -pg. D-7-3
Aflleje, Maria T -pg. D-7-11
Aflleje, Maria T -pg. D-7-11
Aflleje, Maria T -pg. D-10-26
Aflleje, Maria T -pg. D-10-27
Aflleje, Maximo -pg. D-10-30
Aflleje, Natividad G -pg. D-7-15
Aflleje, Nicolasa P -pg. D-7-6
Aflleje, Regina T -pg. D-7-3
Aflleje, Rita I -pg. D 10-19
Aflleje, Rita T -pg. D-7-3
Aflleje, Rosa C -pg. D-7-7
Aflleje, Rosa L -pg. D-10-19
Aflleje, Rosario C -pg. D-7-7
Aflleje, Teresa G -pg. D-7-15
Aflleje, Vicente -pg. D-7-11
Aflleje, Vicente L -pg. D-10-19
Aflleje, Victoria A -pg. D-7-15
Agoun, Joaquin T -pg. D-13-27
Aguajlo, Ana C -pg. D-2-12
Aguajlo, Ana P -pg. D-2-42
Aguajlo, Ana S -pg. D-2-33
Aguajlo, Antonia S -pg. D-2-32
Aguajlo, Carmen A -pg. D-5-81
Aguajlo, Catalina C -pg. D-2-12
Aguajlo, Concepcion C -pg. D-2-12
Aguajlo, Delfina S -pg. D-2-33
Aguajlo, Emilia C -pg. D-5-79
Aguajlo, Francisco C -pg. D-2-12
Aguajlo, Ignacia C -pg. D-2-12
Aguajlo, Jose C -pg. D-5-80
Aguajlo, Juan A -pg. D-2-42
Aguajlo, Juan S -pg. D-2-16
Aguajlo, Maria -pg. D-5-81
Aguajlo, Maria C -pg. D-2-12
Aguajlo, Maria P -pg. D-2-16

Aguajlo, Miguel M -pg. D-5-81
Aguajlo, Pedro C -pg. D-5-80
Aguajlo, Pedro S -pg. D-2-33
Aguajlo, Rita M -pg. D-5-81
Aguajlo, Vicente A -pg. D-5-81
Agualo, Alejandro C -pg. D-10-30
Agualo, Jose C -pg. D-10-30
Agualo, Luis S -pg. D-1-53
Agualo, Miguel C -pg. D-10-30
Agualo, Santiago T -pg. D-7-23
Aguero, Amparo C -pg. D-5-58
Aguero, Felisa T -pg. D-12-12
Aguero, Felix Q -pg. D-12-12
Aguero, Francisco T -pg. D-4-92
Aguero, Jesus SN -pg. D-12-12
Aguero, Joaquin SN -pg. D-5-55
Aguero, Jose A -pg. D-2-64
Aguero, Jose SN -pg. D-12-8
Aguero, Juan A -pg. D-5-58
Aguero, Juan SN -pg. D-4-92
Aguero, Juan T -pg. D-4-92
Aguero, Maria SN -pg. D-12-12
Aguero, Maria T -pg. D-4-92
Aguero, Oliva T -pg. D-12-8
Aguero, Pedro T -pg. D-12-12
Aguero, Remedios T -pg. D-12-8
Aguero, Soledad T -pg. D-12-12
Aguero, Tomas T -pg. D-12-8
Aguero, Vicente SN -pg. D-12-12
Aguero, Vicente T -pg. D-12-8
Aguigui, Ana P -pg. D-2-51
Aguigui, Ana SN -pg. D-6-15
Aguigui, Ana T -pg. D-9-3
Aguigui, Antonia C -pg. D-1-67
Aguigui, Antonia C -pg. D-6-9
Aguigui, Antonio C -pg. D-6-7
Aguigui, Balbino G -pg. D-6-32
Aguigui, Beatrise T -pg. D-6-4
Aguigui, Benidicto SN -pg. D-6-7
Aguigui, Bienvenida T -pg. D-9-2
Aguigui, Carmen G -pg. D-6-37
Aguigui, Carmen T -pg. D-9-2
Aguigui, Delfina T -pg. D-9-2
Aguigui, Delores G -pg. D-6-32
Aguigui, Dionicio C -pg. D-6-8
Aguigui, Dolores SN -pg. D-11-2
Aguigui, Elias SN -pg. D-11-3
Aguigui, Enrique C -pg. D-6-9
Aguigui, Enrique C -pg. D-11-8
Aguigui, Felix B -pg. D-6-32
Aguigui, Felix T -pg. D-9-2
Aguigui, Francisca B -pg. D-6-32
Aguigui, Francisco A -pg. D-6-37
Aguigui, Guadalupe A -pg. D-11-51
Aguigui, Guadalupe SN -pg. D-6-15
Aguigui, Herbert J -pg. D-6-15
Aguigui, Ignacio B -pg. D-9-2
Aguigui, Isabel T -pg. D-6-4
Aguigui, Isabel T -pg. D-9-2

Aguigui, Joaquin SN -pg. D-6-4
Aguigui, Joaquina T -pg. D-6-4
Aguigui, Jose R -pg. D-6-5
Aguigui, Jose T -pg. D-9-3
Aguigui, Josefa C -pg. D-6-9
Aguigui, Josefa R -pg. D-6-5
Aguigui, Josefina SN -pg. D-6-15
Aguigui, Juan A -pg. D-1-53
Aguigui, Juan SN -pg. D-11-2
Aguigui, Juan T -pg. D-6-4
Aguigui, Juana C -pg. D-6-7
Aguigui, Luis P -pg. D-2-51
Aguigui, Luis SN -pg. D-6-9
Aguigui, Luisa C -pg. D-6-8
Aguigui, Manuel SN -pg. D-6-15
Aguigui, Maria C -pg. D-6-7
Aguigui, Maria C -pg. D-6-9
Aguigui, Maria G -pg. D-6-32
Aguigui, Maria T -pg. D-6-4
Aguigui, Maria T -pg. D-9-2
Aguigui, Milagro C -pg. D-6-7
Aguigui, Pedro N -pg. D-9-3
Aguigui, Rosalia G -pg. D-6-37
Aguigui, Rosalia T -pg. D-6-4
Aguigui, Rosalia T -pg. D-9-2
Aguigui, Santos A -pg. D-8-38
Aguigui, Trinidad C -pg. D-6-9
Aguigui, Vicente C -pg. D-6-8
Aguigui, Vicente SN -pg. D-11-2
Agulto, Ana C -pg. D-11-19
Agulto, Antonio P -pg. D-11-18
Agulto, Consuelo C -pg. D-3-63
Agulto, Emilia P -pg. D-11-18
Agulto, Jesusa C -pg. D-11-19
Agulto, Juan M -pg. D-11-18
Agulto, Magdalena C -pg. D-11-19
Agulto, Pedro P -pg. D-11-18
Aguon, Agueda A -pg. D-9-33
Aguon, Ana A -pg. D-9-32
Aguon, Ana B -pg. D-9-44
Aguon, Ana F -pg. D-8-19
Aguon, Ana M -pg. D-9-39
Aguon, Ana P -pg. D-4-124
Aguon, Ana Q -pg. D-9-32
Aguon, Ana S -pg. D-2-65
Aguon, Ana S -pg. D-9-45
Aguon, Andrea S -pg. D-2-65
Aguon, Angela B -pg. D-9-44
Aguon, Angelina M -pg. D-7-19
Aguon, Antonia C -pg. D-4-100
Aguon, Antonio C -pg. D-6-29
Aguon, Antonio I -pg. D-4-81
Aguon, Antonio I -pg. D-5-64
Aguon, Antonio R -pg. D-9-40
Aguon, Asuncion C -pg. D-9-32
Aguon, Atanacio M -pg. D-9-38
Aguon, Baldovino Q -pg. D-9-32
Aguon, Barcelisa M -pg. D-4-28
Aguon, Benito C -pg. D-6-29

Aguon, Bernadita G -pg. D-12-18
Aguon, Bernadita M -pg. D-9-38
Aguon, Blandina S -pg. D-2-65
Aguon, Brigida Q -pg. D-9-36
Aguon, Calistra T -pg. D-9-34
Aguon, Candelaria L -pg. D-5-14
Aguon, Carlos C -pg. D-6-29
Aguon, Carmen C -pg. D-5-14
Aguon, Catalina C -pg. D-5-14
Aguon, Catalina F -pg. D-12-17
Aguon, Celestino -pg. D-3-21
Aguon, Clotilde S -pg. D-4-53
Aguon, Concepcion -pg. D-7-19
Aguon, Concepcion C -pg. D-8-40
Aguon, Concepcion F -pg. D-8-19
Aguon, Concepcion M -pg. D-4-28
Aguon, Concepcion M -pg. D-8-45
Aguon, Concepcion M -pg. D-9-38
Aguon, Concepcion O -pg. D-1-30
Aguon, Concepcion S -pg. D-4-53
Aguon, Concepcion V -pg. D-2-65
Aguon, Consuelo Q -pg. D-9-32
Aguon, Cristina A -pg. D-9-33
Aguon, Cristobal SN -pg. D-1-24
Aguon, Damiana C -pg. D-3-21
Aguon, Delfina T -pg. D-9-34
Aguon, Delores C -pg. D-6-29
Aguon, Dolores C -pg. D-4-100
Aguon, Dolores C -pg. D-9-21
Aguon, Dolores F -pg. D-8-19
Aguon, Dolores L -pg. D-4-95
Aguon, Dolores L -pg. D-5-14
Aguon, Dolores S -pg. D-10-12
Aguon, Eduardo -pg. D-3-51
Aguon, Emilia Q -pg. D-9-39
Aguon, Eufracia C -pg. D-4-109
Aguon, Faustina C -pg. D-9-21
Aguon, Felicidad O -pg. D-1-30
Aguon, Felipe R -pg. D-9-33
Aguon, Felipe V -pg. D-2-65
Aguon, Felix -pg. D-3-14
Aguon, Felix C -pg. D-5-14
Aguon, Felix D -pg. D-3-13
Aguon, Fidela SN -pg. D-1-24
Aguon, Francisco -pg. D-3-64
Aguon, Francisco A -pg. D-9-32
Aguon, Francisco C -pg. D-5-14
Aguon, Francisco C -pg. D-6-29
Aguon, Francisco L -pg. D-1-25
Aguon, Francisco L -pg. D-12-17
Aguon, Francisco LG -pg. D-4-5
Aguon, Francisco M -pg. D-10-11
Aguon, Francisco S -pg. D-2-65
Aguon, Francisco S -pg. D-10-11
Aguon, Genoveva I -pg. D-3-13
Aguon, Gregorio -pg. D-3-21
Aguon, Gregorio SN -pg. D-1-24
Aguon, Gregorio T -pg. D-9-34
Aguon, Guadalupe G -pg. D-4-124

Aguon, Guardalupe B -pg. D-9-44
Aguon, Ignacio I -pg. D-4-124
Aguon, Ignacio O -pg. D-1-30
Aguon, Ignacio O -pg. D-12-18
Aguon, Ignacio Q -pg. D-9-32
Aguon, Ignacio T -pg. D-5-10
Aguon, Isabel A -pg. D-9-33
Aguon, Isabel C -pg. D-4-109
Aguon, Isabel C -pg. D-4-109
Aguon, Isabel F -pg. D-8-19
Aguon, Jesus B -pg. D-4-95
Aguon, Jesus C -pg. D-4-109
Aguon, Jesus F -pg. D-8-19
Aguon, Jesus G -pg. D-12-18
Aguon, Jesus L -pg. D-1-25
Aguon, Jesus L -pg. D-11-41
Aguon, Jesus L -pg. D-13-28
Aguon, Jesus P -pg. D-5-19
Aguon, Jesus S -pg. D-2-65
Aguon, Joaquin C -pg. D-4-109
Aguon, Joaquin C -pg. D-8-40
Aguon, Joaquin C -pg. D-8-40
Aguon, Joaquin LG -pg. D-1-30
Aguon, Joaquin M -pg. D-4-28
Aguon, Joaquin Q -pg. D-9-32
Aguon, Joaquin Q -pg. D-9-39
Aguon, Joaquin S -pg. D-2-65
Aguon, Joaquina B -pg. D-9-33
Aguon, Joaquina C -pg. D-8-40
Aguon, Joaquina C -pg. D-9-21
Aguon, Joaquina F -pg. D-5-46
Aguon, Joaquina Q -pg. D-9-36
Aguon, Joaquina SN -pg. D-1-24
Aguon, Joaquina T -pg. D-9-34
Aguon, Jose A -pg. D-9-32
Aguon, Jose A -pg. D-9-33
Aguon, Jose A -pg. D-9-40
Aguon, Jose B -pg. D-9-44
Aguon, Jose C -pg. D-4-6
Aguon, Jose C -pg. D-4-100
Aguon, Jose C -pg. D-5-14
Aguon, Jose C -pg. D-8-40
Aguon, Jose C -pg. D-9-21
Aguon, Jose E -pg. D-6-30
Aguon, Jose G -pg. D-12-18
Aguon, Jose L -pg. D-12-18
Aguon, Jose L -pg. D-13-28
Aguon, Jose M -pg. D-4-28
Aguon, Jose M -pg. D-11-12
Aguon, Jose O -pg. D-12-18
Aguon, Jose P -pg. D-4-124
Aguon, Jose P -pg. D-5-14
Aguon, Jose P -pg. D-5-20
Aguon, Jose Q -pg. D-8-45
Aguon, Jose Q -pg. D-9-31
Aguon, Jose Q -pg. D-9-45
Aguon, Jose T -pg. D-1-25
Aguon, Jose T -pg. D-4-37
Aguon, Jose T -pg. D-7-23

Aguon, Jose T -pg. D-12-18
Aguon, Jose V -pg. D-2-65
Aguon, Jose V -pg. D-4-100
Aguon, Josefa -pg. D-3-14
Aguon, Josefa C -pg. D-4-109
Aguon, Josefa L -pg. D-4-95
Aguon, Josefina C -pg. D-1-65
Aguon, Juan A -pg. D-9-33
Aguon, Juan A -pg. D-9-35
Aguon, Juan A -pg. D-9-40
Aguon, Juan C -pg. D-1-65
Aguon, Juan C -pg. D-4-109
Aguon, Juan C -pg. D-4-109
Aguon, Juan C -pg. D-7-19
Aguon, Juan C -pg. D-8-40
Aguon, Juan F -pg. D-8-19
Aguon, Juan L -pg. D-4-95
Aguon, Juan L -pg. D-12-18
Aguon, Juan M -pg. D-3-21
Aguon, Juan M -pg. D-9-39
Aguon, Juan M -pg. D-11-12
Aguon, Juan N -pg. D-7-19
Aguon, Juan P -pg. D-5-13
Aguon, Juan Q -pg. D-9-39
Aguon, Juan S -pg. D-4-124
Aguon, Juan S -pg. D-10-11
Aguon, Juan SN -pg. D-1-24
Aguon, Juan T -pg. D-1-24
Aguon, Juan T -pg. D-4-5
Aguon, Juan T -pg. D-8-19
Aguon, Juan U -pg. D-3-51
Aguon, Juana C -pg. D-9-32
Aguon, Julia F -pg. D-12-17
Aguon, Julian IG -pg. D 4 5
Aguon, Juliana M -pg. D-4-79
Aguon, Justo C -pg. D-9-32
Aguon, Librada C -pg. D-9-36
Aguon, Lorenzo Q -pg. D-11-12
Aguon, Lucas I -pg. D-9-33
Aguon, Luis L -pg. D-12-17
Aguon, Luis P -pg. D-5-19
Aguon, Luis S -pg. D-10-11
Aguon, Luisa C -pg. D-5-14
Aguon, Luisa T -pg. D-1-57
Aguon, Magdalena A -pg. D-9-40
Aguon, Magdalena M -pg. D-4-79
Aguon, Magdalena N -pg. D-7-19
Aguon, Magdalena T -pg. D-7-10
Aguon, Manuel -pg. D-3-64
Aguon, Manuel -pg. D-11-19
Aguon, Manuel B -pg. D-9-44
Aguon, Manuel M -pg. D-11-12
Aguon, Manuel T -pg. D-12-21
Aguon, Marcela C -pg. D-5-14
Aguon, Maria -pg. D-3-21
Aguon, Maria -pg. D-3-64
Aguon, Maria B -pg. D-9-44
Aguon, Maria C -pg. D-1-65
Aguon, Maria C -pg. D-4-95

Aguon, Maria C -pg. D-4-100
Aguon, Maria C -pg. D-5-14
Aguon, Maria C -pg. D-9-36
Aguon, Maria F -pg. D-12-17
Aguon, Maria G -pg. D-4-124
Aguon, Maria L -pg. D-4-95
Aguon, Maria LG -pg. D-4-5
Aguon, Maria M -pg. D-4-28
Aguon, Maria M -pg. D-8-45
Aguon, Maria N -pg. D-7-19
Aguon, Maria O -pg. D-12-18
Aguon, Maria P -pg. D-5-19
Aguon, Maria Q -pg. D-9-32
Aguon, Maria Q -pg. D-9-36
Aguon, Maria Q -pg. D-9-39
Aguon, Maria S -pg. D-9-45
Aguon, Maria T -pg. D-1-61
Aguon, Maria T -pg. D-9-34
Aguon, Mariano A -pg. D-3-55
Aguon, Mariano T -pg. D-7-10
Aguon, Martina C -pg. D-4-109
Aguon, Maximo C -pg. D-9-33
Aguon, Milagro Q -pg. D-9-45
Aguon, Nicolas C -pg. D-1-65
Aguon, Pedro -pg. D-3-14
Aguon, Pedro -pg. D-3-21
Aguon, Pedro C -pg. D-4-53
Aguon, Pedro C -pg. D-9-21
Aguon, Pedro F -pg. D-12-17
Aguon, Pedro N -pg. D-7-19
Aguon, Pedro S -pg. D-2-65
Aguon, Pedro T -pg. D-1-25
Aguon, Pedro T -pg. D-12-17
Aguon, Purdiria T -pg. D-12-18
Aguon, Ramon -pg. D-3-21
Aguon, Ramon C -pg. D-8-40
Aguon, Ramon O -pg. D-1-30
Aguon, Ramon P -pg. D-4-124
Aguon, Ramon P -pg. D-5-19
Aguon, Remedios S -pg. D-3-64
Aguon, Remedios S -pg. D-4-53
Aguon, Rita C -pg. D-9-21
Aguon, Rita F -pg. D-12-17
Aguon, Rita O -pg. D-12-18
Aguon, Rita U -pg. D-3-51
Aguon, Roman V -pg. D-2-65
Aguon, Rosa -pg. D-3-14
Aguon, Rosa A -pg. D-9-32
Aguon, Rosa B -pg. D-9-44
Aguon, Rosa F -pg. D-8-19
Aguon, Rosa F -pg. D-12-17
Aguon, Rosa I -pg. D-5-40
Aguon, Rosa M -pg. D-4-28
Aguon, Rosa S -pg. D-2-65
Aguon, Rosa S -pg. D-4-53
Aguon, Rosa T -pg. D-8-9
Aguon, Rosa V -pg. D-4-100
Aguon, Rosario S -pg. D-4-34
Aguon, Rosauro M -pg. D-2-65

Aguon, Rufina S -pg. D-10-11
Aguon, Sabina A -pg. D-9-40
Aguon, Sabina I -pg. D-4-81
Aguon, Sabina I -pg. D-5-64
Aguon, Santiago Q -pg. D-9-21
Aguon, Santiago T -pg. D-7-10
Aguon, Segundo C -pg. D-4-109
Aguon, Simeon C -pg. D-1-65
Aguon, Simon C -pg. D-9-32
Aguon, Soledad M -pg. D-11-12
Aguon, Soledad O -pg. D-1-30
Aguon, Teresa C -pg. D-8-40
Aguon, Teresa LG -pg. D-4-5
Aguon, Tomas S -pg. D-4-53
Aguon, Tomasa A -pg. D-4-101
Aguon, Tomasa O -pg. D-12-17
Aguon, Venancio T -pg. D-12-17
Aguon, Vicenta C -pg. D-8-40
Aguon, Vicenta M -pg. D-4-28
Aguon, Vicente A -pg. D-9-32
Aguon, Vicente C -pg. D-4-100
Aguon, Vicente C -pg. D-4-100
Aguon, Vicente C -pg. D-5-14
Aguon, Vicente C -pg. D-8-40
Aguon, Vicente C -pg. D-9-21
Aguon, Vicente C -pg. D-9-36
Aguon, Vicente F -pg. D-8-19
Aguon, Vicente L -pg. D-1-25
Aguon, Vicente L -pg. D-4-95
Aguon, Vicente L -pg. D-12-17
Aguon, Vicente M -pg. D-11-12
Aguon, Vicente P -pg. D-5-19
Aguon, Vicente R -pg. D-9-44
Aguon, Vicente S -pg. D-3-64
Aguon, Vicente S -pg. D-4-53
Aguon, Vicente S -pg. D-10-11
Aguon, Vicente T -pg. D-4-28
Aguon, Vicente T -pg. D-4-81
Aguon, Vicente T -pg. D-5-64
Aguon, Virginia -pg. D-3-21
Ahlam, Carmen D -pg. D-4-22
Ahlam, Francisco D -pg. D-4-22
Ahlam, Josefina D -pg. D-4-22
Ahlam, Leon D -pg. D-4-22
Ahlam, Maria D -pg. D-4-22
Ahlam, Pilar D -pg. D-4-22
Alcantara, Antonia B -pg. D-6-6
Alcantara, Benita I -pg. D-6-6
Alcantara, Eugenia I -pg. D-6-6
Alcantara, Francisco B -pg. D-6-6
Alcantara, Francisco I -pg. D-6-6
Alcantara, Joaquin S -pg. D-11-18
Alcantara, John T -pg. D-11-18
Alcantara, Luis S -pg. D-11-50
Alcantara, Maria I -pg. D-6-6
Alcantara, Maria S -pg. D-11-50
Alcantara, Priscilla T -pg. D-11-18
Alcantara, Soledad T -pg. D-11-18
Aldan, Antonio N -pg. D-4-36

Alexanders, Roy T -pg. D-13-35
Alicto, Felix C -pg. D-2-3
Alicto, Melchor C -pg. D-2-3
Alicto, Natividad C -pg. D-2-3
Alicto, Pedro C -pg. D-2-3
Alig, Jose T -pg. D-8-50
Allen, Harold Q -pg. D-13-21
Allison, Frederick -pg. D-13-39
Alton, J A -pg. D-13-44
Alvarez, Agripina C -pg. D-2-64
Alvarez, Concepcion R -pg. D-1-33
Alvarez, Jose G -pg. D-2-20
Alvarez, Juan SA -pg. D-2-64
Alvarez, Maria C -pg. D-2-64
Alvarez, Maria R -pg. D-1-33
Alvarez, Rufina SA -pg. D-2-64
Alvarez, Soledad G -pg. D-2-20
Amber, Lovell H -pg. D-13-21
Anderson, Ana P -pg. D-11-20
Anderson, Antonia P -pg. D-5-42
Anderson, Antonio -pg. D-3-22
Anderson, Antonio D -pg. D-11-44
Anderson, Antonio Q -pg. D-3-56
Anderson, Antonio Q -pg. D-5-71
Anderson, Arthur -pg. D-3-26
Anderson, Arthur G -pg. D-3-26
Anderson, Asuncion L -pg. D-11-2
Anderson, Asuncion M -pg. D-11-2
Anderson, Aurelia -pg. D-3-22
Anderson, Barbara -pg. D-3-56
Anderson, Beatrice -pg. D-3-62
Anderson, Chester E -pg. D-13-14
Anderson, Concepcion D -pg. D-11-44
Anderson, Dolores -pg. D-3-61
Anderson, Donald W -pg. D-13-4
Anderson, Engracia P -pg. D-3-16
Anderson, Estefania -pg. D-3-22
Anderson, Felix A -pg. D-11-20
Anderson, Felix LG -pg. D-11-20
Anderson, Feliza A -pg. D-11-20
Anderson, Francisco -pg. D-3-56
Anderson, Francisco B -pg. D-3-61
Anderson, Francisco Q -pg. D-3-61
Anderson, Frank -pg. D-13-26
Anderson, George -pg. D-3-26
Anderson, George -pg. D-13-9
Anderson, Gertrudes D -pg. D-11-44
Anderson, Henry -pg. D-3-26
Anderson, Isabel A -pg. D-11-20
Anderson, Isabel D -pg. D-11-44
Anderson, Jesus A -pg. D-11-20
Anderson, Joaquin -pg. D-3-61
Anderson, Joaquin M -pg. D-3-22
Anderson, Joaquina -pg. D-3-56
Anderson, Joaquina M -pg. D-3-56
Anderson, Joaquina M -pg. D-5-71
Anderson, John -pg. D-3-26
Anderson, John H -pg. D-13-9
Anderson, Jose -pg. D-3-22

Anderson, Jose -pg. D-3-61
Anderson, Jose A -pg. D-11-20
Anderson, Jose C -pg. D-11-2
Anderson, Jose L -pg. D-11-2
Anderson, Josefa -pg. D-3-61
Anderson, Josefa -pg. D-3-61
Anderson, Josefa -pg. D-3-61
Anderson, Josefina -pg. D-3-22
Anderson, Joseph -pg. D-3-26
Anderson, Juan -pg. D-3-56
Anderson, Juan -pg. D-3-62
Anderson, Juan -pg. D-5-71
Anderson, Juan -pg. D-13-28
Anderson, Juan L -pg. D-11-2
Anderson, Leo -pg. D-13-4
Anderson, Leon Q -pg. D-5-42
Anderson, Lillian -pg. D-3-26
Anderson, Lourdes -pg. D-3-56
Anderson, Magdalena -pg. D-3-56
Anderson, Manuela L -pg. D-11-2
Anderson, Margarita -pg. D-3-56
Anderson, Maria -pg. D-3-22
Anderson, Maria -pg. D-3-56
Anderson, Maria -pg. D-3-61
Anderson, Maria D -pg. D-11-44
Anderson, Mariano LG -pg. D-11-20
Anderson, Matilde -pg. D-3-61
Anderson, Odon -pg. D-3-22
Anderson, Pedro M -pg. D-3-56
Anderson, Pedro M -pg. D-5-71
Anderson, Rafael -pg. D-3-56
Anderson, Ramon -pg. D-3-61
Anderson, Ramona -pg. D-3-56
Anderson, Ramona -pg. D-5-71
Anderson, Rita -pg. D-3-56
Anderson, Rita -pg. D-5-71
Anderson, Rosa C -pg. D-3-26
Anderson, Rosa D -pg. D-11-44
Anderson, Rosalina C -pg. D-11-2
Anderson, Rosario -pg. D-3-22
Anderson, Soledad -pg. D-3-61
Anderson, Thomas P -pg. D-11-20
Anderson, Tomas -pg. D-3-61
Anderson, Tomasa LG -pg. D-3-22
Anderson, Vicenta LG -pg. D-11-20
Anderson, Vicenta R -pg. D-1-36
Angoco, Agustin C -pg. D-4-7
Angoco, Ana A -pg. D-7-21
Angoco, Ana G -pg. D-4-15
Angoco, Ana M -pg. D-4-14
Angoco, Ana T -pg. D-4-16
Angoco, Concepcion T -pg. D-4-16
Angoco, Dionicia S -pg. D-4-17
Angoco, Dolores D -pg. D-4-16
Angoco, Engracia A -pg. D-7-21
Angoco, Felix S -pg. D-4-17
Angoco, Jesus D -pg. D-4-16
Angoco, Joaquin T -pg. D-4-16
Angoco, Joaquin T -pg. D-4-16

Angoco, Jose M -pg. D-4-15
Angoco, Juan T -pg. D-4-16
Angoco, Librada S -pg. D-4-17
Angoco, Manuel D -pg. D-4-16
Angoco, Manuel M -pg. D-11-37
Angoco, Manuela M -pg. D-4-14
Angoco, Maria A -pg. D-7-21
Angoco, Maria S -pg. D-4-17
Angoco, Mariano A -pg. D-4-9
Angoco, Pedro A -pg. D-4-14
Angoco, Ramona D -pg. D-4-16
Angoco, Rosa T -pg. D-4-16
Angoco, Santiago D -pg. D-4-16
Angoco, Teresa S -pg. D-4-16
Angoco, Tomasa A -pg. D-7-21
Angoco, Vicenta D -pg. D-4-16
Angoco, Vicente D -pg. D-7-21
Angoco, Vicente M -pg. D-4-15
Anthony, John P -pg. D-13-4
Apuron, Ana S -pg. D-1-2
Apuron, Francisca T -pg. D-3-22
Apuron, Ignacia R -pg. D-3-23
Apuron, Manuel T -pg. D-1-2
Apuron, Severino R -pg. D-3-23
Apuron, Simon T -pg. D-3-22
Aquiningoc, Albano F -pg. D-1-13
Aquiningoc, Alice Q -pg. D-9-31
Aquiningoc, Amparo P -pg. D-11-9
Aquiningoc, Ana D -pg. D-11-30
Aquiningoc, Ana Q -pg. D-9-31
Aquiningoc, Ana W -pg. D-11-34
Aquiningoc, Antonia C -pg. D-6-3
Aquiningoc, Antonio A -pg. D-11-30
Aquiningoc, Antonio T -pg. D-11-40
Aquiningoc, Caridad M -pg. D-11-32
Aquiningoc, Carmen Q -pg. D-9-31
Aquiningoc, Dolores P -pg. D-11-9
Aquiningoc, Dolores Q -pg. D-9-31
Aquiningoc, Dormitila C -pg. D-6-3
Aquiningoc, Felicidad Q -pg. D-9-31
Aquiningoc, Francisco -pg. D-11-45
Aquiningoc, Francisco A -pg. D-11-23
Aquiningoc, German M -pg. D-11-32
Aquiningoc, Grabiel P -pg. D-11-9
Aquiningoc, Isabel C -pg. D-6-3
Aquiningoc, Isabel M -pg. D-1-17
Aquiningoc, Isabel M -pg. D-11-32
Aquiningoc, Jesus C -pg. D-11-45
Aquiningoc, Jesus F -pg. D-1-14
Aquiningoc, Jesus R -pg. D-11-45
Aquiningoc, Joaquin T -pg. D-13-26
Aquiningoc, Jose -pg. D-13-26
Aquiningoc, Jose B -pg. D-6-3
Aquiningoc, Jose C -pg. D-11-37
Aquiningoc, Jose P -pg. D-11-10
Aquiningoc, Jose Q -pg. D-9-31
Aquiningoc, Josefa F -pg. D-1-13
Aquiningoc, Juan B -pg. D-11-40
Aquiningoc, Juan F -pg. D-1-13

Aquiningoc, Juan Q -pg. D-9-31
Aquiningoc, Juana C -pg. D-11-29
Aquiningoc, Julia C -pg. D-6-3
Aquiningoc, Lydia C -pg. D-6-3
Aquiningoc, Magdalena W -pg. D-11-34
Aquiningoc, Manuel A -pg. D-9-31
Aquiningoc, Manuel C -pg. D-11-32
Aquiningoc, Maria C -pg. D-11-23
Aquiningoc, Maria C -pg. D-11-29
Aquiningoc, Maria C -pg. D-11-31
Aquiningoc, Maria F -pg. D-1-13
Aquiningoc, Maria M -pg. D-11-32
Aquiningoc, Maria Q -pg. D-9-31
Aquiningoc, Maria R -pg. D-11-45
Aquiningoc, Mariano C -pg. D-11-29
Aquiningoc, Nicolas C -pg. D-11-29
Aquiningoc, Rosalia C -pg. D-11-23
Aquiningoc, Rosario C -pg. D-11-37
Aquiningoc, Ruth P -pg. D-11-10
Aquiningoc, Susana P -pg. D-11-9
Aquino, Ana M -pg. D-3-4
Aquino, Antonia C -pg. D-5-18
Aquino, Artemio -pg. D-3-4
Aquino, Gregorio C -pg. D-5-18
Aquino, Jesus C -pg. D-4-82
Aquino, Jose C -pg. D-4-82
Aquino, Jose C -pg. D-5-18
Aquino, Juan C -pg. D-3-4
Aquino, Maria C -pg. D-5-18
Aquino, Maria C -pg. D-5-75
Aquino, Matias C -pg. D-5-18
Aquino, Ramon C -pg. D-5-18
Aquino, Roman -pg. D-3-4
Aquino, Rosario C -pg. D-5-18
Aquino, Rufina C -pg. D-5-18
Arceo, Amalia G -pg. D-5-88
Arceo, Ana G -pg. D-4-70
Arceo, Antonia -pg. D-3-42
Arceo, Brigida -pg. D-3-42
Arceo, Carmen S -pg. D-6-37
Arceo, Dolores -pg. D-5-79
Arceo, Felicita -pg. D-3-42
Arceo, Felicita S -pg. D-3-40
Arceo, Francisco C -pg. D-2-42
Arceo, Francisco F -pg. D-2-25
Arceo, Francisco G -pg. D-4-70
Arceo, Francisco S -pg. D-2-42
Arceo, Gregorio C -pg. D-13-28
Arceo, Guadalupe G -pg. D-4-70
Arceo, Guadalupe N -pg. D-11-41
Arceo, Henry -pg. D-3-42
Arceo, Ignacio -pg. D-2-25
Arceo, Ignacio C -pg. D-5-79
Arceo, Jesus G -pg. D-4-70
Arceo, Jose -pg. D-5-79
Arceo, Jose B -pg. D-4-70
Arceo, Jose C -pg. D-5-88
Arceo, Jose F -pg. D-2-25
Arceo, Jose G -pg. D-4-70

Arceo, Jose I -pg. D-5-11
Arceo, Jose M -pg. D-11-41
Arceo, Josefa S -pg. D-3-42
Arceo, Josefina F -pg. D-2-25
Arceo, Juan F -pg. D-2-25
Arceo, Lidia C -pg. D-3-53
Arceo, Lucia -pg. D-3-42
Arceo, Maria -pg. D-3-42
Arceo, Maria A -pg. D-11-41
Arceo, Maria C -pg. D-3-41
Arceo, Maria C -pg. D-12-19
Arceo, Maria F -pg. D-2-25
Arceo, Maria F -pg. D-2-25
Arceo, Maria G -pg. D-4-70
Arceo, Maria S -pg. D-2-42
Arceo, Natividad N -pg. D-11-41
Arceo, Nicolasa -pg. D-3-41
Arceo, Regina C -pg. D-5-79
Arceo, Remedio -pg. D-3-42
Arceo, Rosa -pg. D-3-42
Arceo, Rosalia G -pg. D-4-70
Arceo, Rosario -pg. D-3-41
Arceo, Tomas F -pg. D-2-25
Arceo, Vicente G -pg. D-4-70
Arceo, William S -pg. D-2-42
Archerman, Charles F -pg. D-13-35
Arnold, Frank L -pg. D-4-26
Arola, Joseph L -pg. D-13-21
Arriola, Antonio F -pg. D-1-13
Arriola, Consolacion C -pg. D-2-63
Arriola, Felomina C -pg. D-2-63
Arriola, Francisco C -pg. D-2-12
Arriola, Francisco R -pg. D-2-62
Arriola, Isabel S -pg. D-6-22
Arriola, Joaquin C -pg. D-2-12
Arriola, Jose A -pg. D-2-57
Arriola, Jose A -pg. D-5-52
Arriola, Jose Q -pg. D-6-22
Arriola, Josefa C -pg. D-2-62
Arriola, Juana A -pg. D-2-56
Arriola, Juana F -pg. D-1-13
Arriola, Magdalena S -pg. D-4-28
Arriola, Margarita A -pg. D-11-18
Arriola, Pedro E -pg. D-11-19
Arriola, Ramona R -pg. D-2-62
Arriola, Rosa F -pg. D-11-10
Arriola, Simona M -pg. D-1-4
Arriola, Soledad C -pg. D-2-12
Arriola, Soledad S -pg. D-6-22
Arriola, Vicente R -pg. D-1-4
Arriola, Vicente T -pg. D-2-12
Arroyo, Brigidio -pg. D-13-34
Arroyo, Olivia U -pg. D-4-22
Artero, Antonio C -pg. D-1-15
Artero, Consulasion C -pg. D-1-15
Artero, Eugenia V -pg. D-1-16
Artero, Isabel C -pg. D-1-15
Artero, Jesus C -pg. D-1-16
Artero, Jesus V -pg. D-1-16

Artero, Jose C -pg. D-1-16
Artero, Maria C -pg. D-1-15
Artero, Pascual C -pg. D-1-15
Artero, Pascual S -pg. D-1-15
Artero, Pedro V -pg. D-1-16
Asano, Ignacio F -pg. D-1-24
Asano, Isabel F -pg. D-1-24
Asano, Jose F -pg. D-1-24
Asano, Maria F -pg. D-1-23
Asano, Oliva F -pg. D-1-24
Asano, Rita F -pg. D-1-24
Asano, Vicente F -pg. D-1-24
Asano, Yoshijiro -pg. D-1-23
Asanoma, Ana C -pg. D-8-29
Asanoma, Francisco C -pg. D-8-29
Asanoma, Jose C -pg. D-8-29
Asanoma, Josefa C -pg. D-8-30
Asanoma, Maria C -pg. D-8-29
Asanoma, Sabina C -pg. D-8-29
Asanoma, Tito K -pg. D-8-29
Ascan, James -pg. D-13-35
Asuncion, Andres SL -pg. D-5-99
Asuncion, Apolonia R -pg. D-2-47
Asuncion, Baltazara M -pg. D-5-99
Asuncion, Manuel B -pg. D-2-47
Asuncion, Maria -pg. D-5-99
Asuncion, Natividad R -pg. D-2-47
Asuncion, Nieves P -pg. D-5-41
Asuncion, Vicente B -pg. D-5-41
Asuncion, Vicente M -pg. D-5-99
Atao, Ana M -pg. D-5-6
Atao, Dolores A -pg. D-5-6
Atao, Juan A -pg. D-5-6
Atchinson, Wallace J -pg. D-13-35
Atoigue, Alejandrina M -pg. D-4-91
Atoigue, Ana A -pg. D-3-57
Atoigue, Ana L -pg. D-5-98
Atoigue, Ana Q -pg. D-5-78
Atoigue, Antonia T -pg. D-1-48
Atoigue, Antonio A -pg. D-5-85
Atoigue, Antonio T -pg. D-1-48
Atoigue, Asuncion T -pg. D-1-48
Atoigue, Brigida F -pg. D-4-93
Atoigue, Carmen T -pg. D-5-82
Atoigue, Dolores B -pg. D-3-63
Atoigue, Dolores P -pg. D-8-42
Atoigue, Emeliana O -pg. D-2-79
Atoigue, Engracia O -pg. D-2-80
Atoigue, Eufrasia A -pg. D-2-33
Atoigue, Felipe M -pg. D-2-79
Atoigue, Flora M -pg. D-4-91
Atoigue, Francisco P -pg. D-8-42
Atoigue, Francisco Q -pg. D-5-79
Atoigue, Francisco T -pg. D-8-42
Atoigue, Isabel O -pg. D-2-80
Atoigue, Jesus -pg. D-5-98
Atoigue, Jesus A -pg. D-4-8
Atoigue, Jesus L -pg. D-5-92
Atoigue, Jesus P -pg. D-8-42

Atoigue, Jesusa O -pg. D-2-80
Atoigue, Joaquin A -pg. D-5-82
Atoigue, Joaquin C -pg. D-3-57
Atoigue, Joaquin C -pg. D-5-92
Atoigue, Joaquin M -pg. D-12-15
Atoigue, Joaquina E -pg. D-5-84
Atoigue, Joaquina P -pg. D-1-19
Atoigue, Jose -pg. D-3-63
Atoigue, Jose -pg. D-5-82
Atoigue, Jose P -pg. D-8-42
Atoigue, Jose R -pg. D-12-11
Atoigue, Jose U -pg. D-4-91
Atoigue, Josefa U -pg. D-4-93
Atoigue, Juan -pg. D-3-63
Atoigue, Juan M -pg. D-5-82
Atoigue, Juan M -pg. D-12-15
Atoigue, Juan SN -pg. D-5-82
Atoigue, Magdalena -pg. D-5-82
Atoigue, Maria -pg. D-3-57
Atoigue, Maria A -pg. D-2-33
Atoigue, Maria H -pg. D-12-16
Atoigue, Maria M -pg. D-4-91
Atoigue, Maria O -pg. D-2-80
Atoigue, Maria U -pg. D-4-93
Atoigue, Nicolas A -pg. D-4-8
Atoigue, Oliva A -pg. D-4-8
Atoigue, Pablo A -pg. D-5-91
Atoigue, Pedro M -pg. D-4-8
Atoigue, Regina P -pg. D-8-42
Atoigue, Rita T -pg. D-1-48
Atoigue, Rosa -pg. D-3-52
Atoigue, Rosa M -pg. D-12-15
Atoigue, Rosario A -pg. D-2-33
Atoigue, Teodora A -pg. D-4-8
Atoigue, Teresa T -pg. D-1-48
Atoigue, Tomas M -pg. D-12-21
Atoigue, Vicente -pg. D-5-79
Atoigue, Vicente A -pg. D-1-23
Atoigue, Vicente L -pg. D-5-92
Atoigue, Vicente M -pg. D-12-15
Atoigue, Vincente U -pg. D-13-32
Auger, Thomas C -pg. D-13-19
Austin, Harold N -pg. D-13-19
Avilla, Arthur -pg. D-13-45
Awls, Harold P -pg. D-13-45
Babauta, Alberto A -pg. D-6-16
Babauta, Amable M -pg. D-6-4
Babauta, Amparo M -pg. D-6-23
Babauta, Ana A -pg. D-6-29
Babauta, Ana A -pg. D-9-37
Babauta, Ana C -pg. D-5-43
Babauta, Ana C -pg. D-9-9
Babauta, Ana C -pg. D-9-43
Babauta, Ana C -pg. D-11-22
Babauta, Ana E -pg. D-9-9
Babauta, Ana S -pg. D-5-22
Babauta, Angel B -pg. D-9-26
Babauta, Angelina C -pg. D-5-43
Babauta, Angelina T -pg. D-9-27

Babauta, Antonia A -pg. D-11-22
Babauta, Antonia R -pg. D-6-35
Babauta, Antonio A -pg. D-6-6
Babauta, Antonio B -pg. D-5-55
Babauta, Antonio B -pg. D-11-10
Babauta, Antonio C -pg. D-5-43
Babauta, Antonio C -pg. D-6-7
Babauta, Antonio C -pg. D-10-18
Babauta, Antonio D -pg. D-10-18
Babauta, Antonio M -pg. D-6-5
Babauta, Antonio R -pg. D-11-34
Babauta, Benito A -pg. D-6-38
Babauta, Benjamin T -pg. D-6-10
Babauta, Brigida T -pg. D-6-21
Babauta, Candelario C -pg. D-5-43
Babauta, Carlina C -pg. D-5-43
Babauta, Carmen C -pg. D-11-22
Babauta, Carmen C -pg. D-11-34
Babauta, Carmen C -pg. D-11-43
Babauta, Carmen S -pg. D-6-28
Babauta, Carmen T -pg. D-6-21
Babauta, Catalina R -pg. D-11-28
Babauta, Concepcion C -pg. D-3-49
Babauta, Concepcion Q -pg. D-8-43
Babauta, Consolacion C -pg. D-10-18
Babauta, Consolacion C -pg. D-11-3
Babauta, Delores S -pg. D-6-8
Babauta, Dionisio C -pg. D-6-12
Babauta, Dolores Q -pg. D-8-43
Babauta, Dolores T -pg. D-6-10
Babauta, Domingo O -pg. D-6-38
Babauta, Elena C -pg. D-9-9
Babauta, Faustino B -pg. D-9-4
Babauta, Felistina Q -pg. D-9-40
Babauta, Felix C -pg. D-11-22
Babauta, Felix SN -pg. D-6-11
Babauta, Felix SN -pg. D-11-50
Babauta, Florence C -pg. D-11-35
Babauta, Florencia A -pg. D-9-37
Babauta, Florentina Q -pg. D-9-45
Babauta, Fortunato J -pg. D-5-22
Babauta, Francisco C -pg. D-10-18
Babauta, Francisco L -pg. D-6-21
Babauta, Francisco Q -pg. D-8-43
Babauta, Francisco R -pg. D-6-9
Babauta, Francisco R -pg. D-6-40
Babauta, Francisco S -pg. D-6-9
Babauta, Francisco SN -pg. D-6-11
Babauta, Gregorio M -pg. D-6-4
Babauta, Ignacia B -pg. D-6-9
Babauta, Ignacia T -pg. D-6-10
Babauta, Ignacio G -pg. D-9-40
Babauta, Ignacio G -pg. D-9-45
Babauta, Ignasia S -pg. D-6-40
Babauta, Jesus A -pg. D-6-29
Babauta, Jesus A -pg. D-9-33
Babauta, Jesus C -pg. D-9-9
Babauta, Jesus C -pg. D-11-22
Babauta, Jesus C -pg. D-11-35

INDEX
1930 Population Census of Guam: Transcribed

Babauta, Jesus L -pg. D-6-14
Babauta, Jesus T -pg. D-6-21
Babauta, Joaquin B -pg. D-6-9
Babauta, Joaquin C -pg. D-11-22
Babauta, Joaquin S -pg. D-6-28
Babauta, Joaquina A -pg. D-9-37
Babauta, Joaquina B -pg. D-6-9
Babauta, Joaquina S -pg. D-5-22
Babauta, Joaquina SN -pg. D-6-12
Babauta, Jose A -pg. D-6-16
Babauta, Jose A -pg. D-9-37
Babauta, Jose B -pg. D-6-6
Babauta, Jose C -pg. D-6-12
Babauta, Jose C -pg. D-11-22
Babauta, Jose G -pg. D-6-13
Babauta, Jose G -pg. D-9-43
Babauta, Jose L -pg. D-6-32
Babauta, Jose P -pg. D-6-11
Babauta, Jose Q -pg. D-8-43
Babauta, Jose R -pg. D-6-4
Babauta, Jose S -pg. D-5-22
Babauta, Jose S -pg. D-6-8
Babauta, Josefa A -pg. D-6-16
Babauta, Josefa R -pg. D-11-28
Babauta, Juan A -pg. D-6-6
Babauta, Juan B -pg. D-6-29
Babauta, Juan C -pg. D-6-29
Babauta, Juan C -pg. D-6-32
Babauta, Juan C -pg. D-11-22
Babauta, Juan G -pg. D-9-37
Babauta, Juan M -pg. D-6-4
Babauta, Juan N -pg. D-9-27
Babauta, Juan S -pg. D-5-22
Babauta, Juan S -pg. D-11-22
Babauta, Juan SN -pg. D-3-49
Babauta, Juana A -pg. D-6-6
Babauta, Julita C -pg. D-5-43
Babauta, Justina C -pg. D-11-22
Babauta, Lagrimas A -pg. D-9-37
Babauta, Luisa C -pg. D-5-43
Babauta, Manuel A -pg. D-6-6
Babauta, Manuel R -pg. D-6-35
Babauta, Manuel R -pg. D-11-28
Babauta, Manuel S -pg. D-6-9
Babauta, Margarita T -pg. D-9-27
Babauta, Maria A -pg. D-6-6
Babauta, Maria A -pg. D-6-16
Babauta, Maria A -pg. D-6-38
Babauta, Maria A -pg. D-9-37
Babauta, Maria C -pg. D-6-29
Babauta, Maria C -pg. D-6-32
Babauta, Maria C -pg. D-11-22
Babauta, Maria C -pg. D-11-34
Babauta, Maria M -pg. D-6-23
Babauta, Maria Q -pg. D-9-45
Babauta, Maria Q -pg. D-9-45
Babauta, Maria S -pg. D-5-22
Babauta, Maria S -pg. D-6-40
Babauta, Mariano S -pg. D-6-8

Babauta, Natividad S -pg. D-6-8
Babauta, Nieves M -pg. D-6-23
Babauta, Pedro C -pg. D-6-8
Babauta, Pedro C -pg. D-6-12
Babauta, Pedro M -pg. D-6-36
Babauta, Ramona C -pg. D-3-63
Babauta, Ramona P -pg. D-8-43
Babauta, Remedios A -pg. D-6-16
Babauta, Rita C -pg. D-6-29
Babauta, Rita C -pg. D-11-22
Babauta, Robinio G -pg. D-9-37
Babauta, Rosa A -pg. D-6-6
Babauta, Rosa C -pg. D-6-29
Babauta, Rosa G -pg. D-6-13
Babauta, Rosa Q -pg. D-9-45
Babauta, Rosalia Q -pg. D-8-43
Babauta, Rosalia S -pg. D-6-8
Babauta, Rosario T -pg. D-6-10
Babauta, Santiago C -pg. D-6-28
Babauta, Serafin C -pg. D-11-22
Babauta, Serafin S -pg. D-6-8
Babauta, Soledad C -pg. D-6-7
Babauta, Teodora SN -pg. D-6-11
Babauta, Vicenta N -pg. D-9-26
Babauta, Vicente A -pg. D-9-37
Babauta, Vicente B -pg. D-6-9
Babauta, Vicente B -pg. D-6-23
Babauta, Vicente C -pg. D-11-37
Babauta, Vicente L -pg. D-6-16
Babauta, Vicente R -pg. D-11-22
Babauta, Vicente S -pg. D-5-22
Babauta, Vicente T -pg. D-6-10
Badey, George F -pg. D-13-36
Bair, Ernest O -pg. D 13 45
Baker, Clyde C -pg. D-13-10
Balajadia, Agapito R -pg. D-4-119
Balajadia, Ana S -pg. D-12-3
Balajadia, Antonio I -pg. D-12-4
Balajadia, Anunciacion Q -pg. D-4-124
Balajadia, Catalina I -pg. D-12-3
Balajadia, Cecilia P -pg. D-12-2
Balajadia, Cornelia I -pg. D-12-3
Balajadia, Elisa I -pg. D-12-4
Balajadia, Emiliana P -pg. D-12-15
Balajadia, Felicita G -pg. D-4-124
Balajadia, Felix S -pg. D-12-3
Balajadia, Fermin P -pg. D-12-15
Balajadia, Jesus G -pg. D-4-124
Balajadia, Jesus I -pg. D-12-4
Balajadia, Jesus S -pg. D-12-3
Balajadia, Joaquin G -pg. D-4-124
Balajadia, Joaquin J -pg. D-12-2
Balajadia, Jose G -pg. D-4-119
Balajadia, Jose I -pg. D-12-4
Balajadia, Jose J -pg. D-12-3
Balajadia, Jose P -pg. D-12-2
Balajadia, Juan G -pg. D-4-124
Balajadia, Juan I -pg. D-12-15
Balajadia, Juan P -pg. D-12-2

Balajadia, Luis LG -pg. D-4-125
Balajadia, Manuel I -pg. D-12-3
Balajadia, Maria R -pg. D-4-119
Balajadia, Maria S -pg. D-12-3
Balajadia, Olivia G -pg. D-4-124
Balajadia, Pedro I -pg. D-12-11
Balajadia, Pedro P -pg. D-12-2
Balajadia, Pilar I -pg. D-12-4
Balajadia, Priscilla Q -pg. D-4-124
Balajadia, Remedios P -pg. D-12-2
Balajadia, Rita T -pg. D-7-12
Balajadia, Roman I -pg. D-12-4
Balajadia, Romana I -pg. D-12-4
Balajadia, Rosa B -pg. D-12-11
Balajadia, Rosa G -pg. D-4-124
Balajadia, Rosa P -pg. D-12-11
Balajadia, Susana P -pg. D-12-2
Balajadia, Tomas P -pg. D-12-11
Balajadia, Vicenta R -pg. D-12-11
Balajadia, Vicente M -pg. D-12-3
Balajadia, Vicente P -pg. D-12-2
Baleto, Andrea -pg. D-11-47
Baleto, Antonio P -pg. D-11-10
Baleto, Encarnacion P -pg. D-11-10
Baleto, Engracia P -pg. D-11-2
Baleto, Francisco C -pg. D-11-2
Baleto, Jesus C -pg. D-11-10
Baleto, Jose C -pg. D-11-10
Baleto, Maria C -pg. D-11-10
Baleto, Maria C -pg. D-11-10
Baleto, Maria P -pg. D-11-10
Baleto, Sebastian -pg. D-11-9
Baleto, Vicente B -pg. D-11-10
Baleto, Vicente C -pg. D-11-10
Baleto, Vicente P -pg. D-11-10
Ballard, Albert G -pg. D-13-10
Balletti, Herbert C -pg. D-13-14
Bamba, Amalia C -pg. D-5-23
Bamba, Ana S -pg. D-4-125
Bamba, Antonio S -pg. D-4-125
Bamba, Concepcion C -pg. D-5-23
Bamba, Concepcion S -pg. D-4-125
Bamba, Federic -pg. D-3-51
Bamba, Felisa -pg. D-3-51
Bamba, Francisco B -pg. D-2-42
Bamba, George -pg. D-3-51
Bamba, Jesus B -pg. D-4-125
Bamba, Jesus M -pg. D-3-51
Bamba, Jorge C -pg. D-5-23
Bamba, Jose B -pg. D-2-36
Bamba, Jose B -pg. D-3-51
Bamba, Jose B -pg. D-5-23
Bamba, Jose G -pg. D-3-51
Bamba, Juan A -pg. D-5-22
Bamba, Leon C -pg. D-5-23
Bamba, Magdalena S -pg. D-4-125
Bamba, Magdalena S -pg. D-4-125
Bamba, Maria B -pg. D-4-125
Bamba, Maria C -pg. D-5-23

Bamba, Maria S -pg. D-5-22
Bamba, Nicolas C -pg. D-5-23
Bamba, Rita C -pg. D-5-23
Bamba, Rita M -pg. D-3-51
Bamba, Roberto R -pg. D-3-51
Bamba, Rosa B -pg. D-2-42
Bamba, Rosalia R -pg. D-3-51
Bamba, Rosemary -pg. D-2-43
Bamba, Vicente -pg. D-3-51
Bamba, Vicente SA -pg. D-5-22
Barasley, Talph F -pg. D-13-36
Barbour, James -pg. D-12-21
Barbour, Maria C -pg. D-12-21
Barcinas, Amelia V -pg. D-4-110
Barcinas, Ana C -pg. D-9-19
Barcinas, Andriano B -pg. D-8-37
Barcinas, Antonio T -pg. D-9-3
Barcinas, Dolores T -pg. D-9-3
Barcinas, Francisco A -pg. D-6-5
Barcinas, Gabriel C -pg. D-9-13
Barcinas, Gertrudes T -pg. D-9-11
Barcinas, Ignacio -pg. D-13-33
Barcinas, Ignacio T -pg. D-9-3
Barcinas, Inigo C -pg. D-9-19
Barcinas, Issac R -pg. D-8-37
Barcinas, Jesus C -pg. D-9-11
Barcinas, Joaquin A -pg. D-6-5
Barcinas, Joaquin C -pg. D-9-19
Barcinas, Joaquin T -pg. D-9-3
Barcinas, Jose A -pg. D-6-5
Barcinas, Jose C -pg. D-9-5
Barcinas, Jose D -pg. D-8-37
Barcinas, Jose S -pg. D-9-19
Barcinas, Jose T -pg. D-9-3
Barcinas, Juan A -pg. D-6-5
Barcinas, Juan D -pg. D-6-5
Barcinas, Juan S -pg. D-9-3
Barcinas, Magdalena D -pg. D-8-37
Barcinas, Maria B -pg. D-8-37
Barcinas, Martin C -pg. D-9-19
Barcinas, Mercedes D -pg. D-8-37
Barcinas, Pedro B -pg. D-9-14
Barcinas, Pedro T -pg. D-9-3
Barcinas, Pilar T -pg. D-4-110
Barcinas, Rita A -pg. D-6-5
Barcinas, Tomas C -pg. D-9-19
Barcinas, Tomas G -pg. D-9-16
Barcinas, Tomasa T -pg. D-9-3
Barnes, Russell M -pg. D-13-10
Barnes, Thomas N -pg. D-13-36
Barney, Charlie N -pg. D-13-41
Barnham, Minnie -pg. D-1-7
Baroski, Wilbert C -pg. D-13-36
Barries, Jose G -pg. D-13-34
Barton, Lawrence K -pg. D-13-33
Basa, Jesus -pg. D-3-2
Basa, Joaquin C -pg. D-3-2
Basa, Josefa D -pg. D-3-2
Batten, Sam -pg. D-13-36

Battles, Marvin S -pg. D-13-10
Bautista, Alfonsina -pg. D-4-12
Bautista, Ana A -pg. D-2-35
Bautista, Ana A -pg. D-5-90
Bautista, Ana L -pg. D-5-84
Bautista, Antonio -pg. D-5-83
Bautista, Antonio C -pg. D-5-83
Bautista, Antonio L -pg. D-12-17
Bautista, Enrique C -pg. D-2-26
Bautista, Francisco B -pg. D-5-34
Bautista, Ignacio C -pg. D-2-26
Bautista, Isabel C -pg. D-2-26
Bautista, Jesus -pg. D-5-83
Bautista, Jose -pg. D-5-90
Bautista, Jose A -pg. D-2-35
Bautista, Jose C -pg. D-2-26
Bautista, Jose S -pg. D-2-34
Bautista, Juan -pg. D-5-90
Bautista, Juan A -pg. D-2-35
Bautista, Juan S -pg. D-8-48
Bautista, Leocadio -pg. D-13-30
Bautista, Luis P -pg. D-4-12
Bautista, Manuel S -pg. D-2-35
Bautista, Manuel S -pg. D-5-90
Bautista, Manuela P -pg. D-5-89
Bautista, Maria -pg. D-5-90
Bautista, Maria A -pg. D-2-35
Bautista, Maria C -pg. D-2-26
Bautista, Maria S -pg. D-2-34
Bautista, Matias -pg. D-5-83
Bautista, Pablo C -pg. D-2-26
Bautista, Pedro L -pg. D-5-84
Bautista, Rosa C -pg. D-2-26
Bautista, Rosa G -pg. D-4-12
Bautista, Rosa L -pg. D-5-83
Bautista, Rosario C -pg. D-2-26
Bautista, Vicente C -pg. D-5-89
Bautista, Vicente S -pg. D-2-34
Bautista, Vicente S -pg. D-12-17
Bayona, Antonio B -pg. D-4-31
Bayona, Antonio M -pg. D-4-31
Bayona, Candido M -pg. D-4-31
Bayona, Catalina I -pg. D-4-31
Bayona, Desiderio B -pg. D-4-32
Bayona, Fabiana M -pg. D-4-31
Bayona, Jose I -pg. D-4-31
Bayona, Juan I -pg. D-4-31
Bayona, Rosa G -pg. D-4-31
Bayona, Rosalia M -pg. D-4-31
Bayona, Teodora M -pg. D-4-31
Baza, Adela C -pg. D-12-5
Baza, Agustin U -pg. D-5-4
Baza, Ana C -pg. D-2-26
Baza, Ana C -pg. D-4-99
Baza, Ana G -pg. D-12-9
Baza, Ana M -pg. D-12-9
Baza, Antonio C -pg. D-2-55
Baza, Barcelisa C -pg. D-4-41
Baza, Beatris C -pg. D-12-4

Baza, Carmen C -pg. D-12-5
Baza, Concepcion A -pg. D-9-29
Baza, Concepcion G -pg. D-12-9
Baza, Dolores A -pg. D-9-29
Baza, Dolores G -pg. D-5-86
Baza, Dolores SA -pg. D-2-46
Baza, Elizabal A -pg. D-2-6
Baza, Emeterio A -pg. D-2-6
Baza, Enrique C -pg. D-12-4
Baza, Enrique C -pg. D-12-5
Baza, Felisa C -pg. D-2-55
Baza, Francisca SA -pg. D-2-46
Baza, Francisco LG -pg. D-2-15
Baza, Gloria C -pg. D-12-5
Baza, Gregorio C -pg. D-12-5
Baza, Ignacia B -pg. D-1-33
Baza, Isabel LG -pg. D-2-15
Baza, Jesus A -pg. D-9-29
Baza, Jesus C -pg. D-4-99
Baza, Jesus C -pg. D-12-4
Baza, Jesus C -pg. D-12-9
Baza, Jesus LG -pg. D-2-15
Baza, Jose A -pg. D-9-29
Baza, Jose B -pg. D-1-27
Baza, Jose C -pg. D-1-53
Baza, Jose C -pg. D-1-58
Baza, Jose C -pg. D-2-55
Baza, Jose C -pg. D-9-23
Baza, Jose C -pg. D-12-5
Baza, Jose C -pg. D-12-5
Baza, Jose LG -pg. D-2-15
Baza, Jose T -pg. D-9-29
Baza, Juan B -pg. D-1-33
Baza, Juan C -pg. D-4-99
Baza, Juan C -pg. D-12-5
Baza, Juan G -pg. D-12-9
Baza, Juan SA -pg. D-2-46
Baza, Juana C -pg. D-12-5
Baza, Julia C -pg. D-12-4
Baza, Julia SA -pg. D-2-46
Baza, Luis C -pg. D-2-55
Baza, Luis M -pg. D-2-55
Baza, Luisa -pg. D-9-6
Baza, Magdalena SA -pg. D-2-46
Baza, Manuel C -pg. D-2-14
Baza, Manuela C -pg. D-12-5
Baza, Margarita C -pg. D-12-9
Baza, Margarita M -pg. D-12-9
Baza, Maria -pg. D-9-6
Baza, Maria A -pg. D-1-33
Baza, Maria A -pg. D-9-29
Baza, Maria B -pg. D-1-33
Baza, Maria C -pg. D-2-55
Baza, Maria C -pg. D-4-99
Baza, Maria C -pg. D-12-5
Baza, Maria C -pg. D-12-5
Baza, Maria G -pg. D-12-9
Baza, Maria LG -pg. D-2-14
Baza, Maria P -pg. D-4-99

Baza, Maria SA -pg. D-2-46
Baza, Maria SA -pg. D-2-46
Baza, Pedro T -pg. D-4-40
Baza, Pedro T -pg. D-9-6
Baza, Pilar C -pg. D-12-4
Baza, Ramon C -pg. D-5-86
Baza, Ramon C -pg. D-9-6
Baza, Ramon G -pg. D-12-9
Baza, Ramon S -pg. D-12-4
Baza, Ramona C -pg. D-1-28
Baza, Rita M -pg. D-12-9
Baza, Rosa A -pg. D-9-29
Baza, Rosa B -pg. D-1-33
Baza, Rosa C -pg. D-2-55
Baza, Rosa C -pg. D-12-4
Baza, Rosa T -pg. D-9-6
Baza, Rosario C -pg. D-12-5
Baza, Rosario LG -pg. D-2-15
Baza, Soledad C -pg. D-4-41
Baza, Telefaro C -pg. D-12-5
Baza, Teleforo Q -pg. D-12-9
Baza, Teresa C -pg. D-12-4
Baza, Tito C -pg. D-12-4
Baza, Vicente C -pg. D-4-99
Baza, Vicente C -pg. D-12-5
Baza, Vicente C -pg. D-12-9
Baza, Vicente S -pg. D-12-4
Baza, Vicente U -pg. D-2-46
Baza, Virginia C -pg. D-12-5
Baza, Visitacion A -pg. D-9-29
Bealer, Ernest -pg. D-13-39
Beaton, Frank E -pg. D-13-19
Bebich, Michael S -pg. D-13-35
Becael, Ralph J -pg. D-13-35
Beckers, Ralph Γ pg. D-13-35
Begona, Jesus -pg. D-1-56
Behind, Gerst -pg. D-13-34
Bell, Ana J -pg. D-3-73
Bell, Henry -pg. D-3-73
Belosers, Bernard -pg. D-13-36
Benabente, Carmen D -pg. D-8-4
Benabente, Edita D -pg. D-8-4
Benabente, Enrique R -pg. D-8-3
Benabente, Francisca D -pg. D-8-4
Benabente, Maria D -pg. D-8-4
Benavente, Agripina S -pg. D-5-23
Benavente, Alvina L -pg. D-2-70
Benavente, Ana B -pg. D-3-61
Benavente, Ana G -pg. D-5-27
Benavente, Ana L -pg. D-2-70
Benavente, Ana Q -pg. D-5-24
Benavente, Ana Q -pg. D-5-33
Benavente, Antonia Q -pg. D-5-32
Benavente, Antonio A -pg. D-2-50
Benavente, Asuncion R -pg. D-2-38
Benavente, Carmen G -pg. D-2-8
Benavente, Carmen U -pg. D-2-29
Benavente, Cecilia Q -pg. D-5-24
Benavente, Cristobal D -pg. D-2-22

Benavente, Dolores D -pg. D-5-25
Benavente, Dolores G -pg. D-5-34
Benavente, Dolores P -pg. D-12-14
Benavente, Dolores Q -pg. D-12-12
Benavente, Elena C -pg. D-5-27
Benavente, Eloi Q -pg. D-5-32
Benavente, Eugenio A -pg. D-2-50
Benavente, Felipe C -pg. D-2-40
Benavente, Felix R -pg. D-5-44
Benavente, Francisca SA -pg. D-5-44
Benavente, Francisco C -pg. D-12-21
Benavente, Grabiela G -pg. D-5-27
Benavente, Grabiela T -pg. D-5-41
Benavente, Ignacia G -pg. D-5-35
Benavente, Ignacio G -pg. D-2-29
Benavente, Ignacio M -pg. D-2-40
Benavente, Ignacio T -pg. D-5-41
Benavente, Isabel G -pg. D-5-36
Benavente, Jesus G -pg. D-5-27
Benavente, Jesus G -pg. D-5-36
Benavente, Jesus H -pg. D-2-15
Benavente, Jesus R -pg. D-12-12
Benavente, Jesus S -pg. D-5-23
Benavente, Jesus SA -pg. D-5-44
Benavente, Joaquin A -pg. D-2-70
Benavente, Joaquin A -pg. D-5-59
Benavente, Joaquin G -pg. D-5-27
Benavente, Joaquin G -pg. D-5-35
Benavente, Joaquin M -pg. D-5-23
Benavente, Joaquin R -pg. D-2-38
Benavente, Joaquin S -pg. D-5-23
Benavente, Jose B -pg. D-5-37
Benavente, Jose G -pg. D-2-70
Benavente, Jose G pg. D-5-34
Benavente, Jose G -pg. D-5-35
Benavente, Jose L -pg. D-2-70
Benavente, Jose Q -pg. D-5-27
Benavente, Jose S -pg. D-5-23
Benavente, Jose SA -pg. D-5-44
Benavente, Jose U -pg. D-2-29
Benavente, Josefa C -pg. D-5-16
Benavente, Josefa D -pg. D-5-25
Benavente, Josefa G -pg. D-5-34
Benavente, Josefa M -pg. D-2-40
Benavente, Josefina Q -pg. D-5-33
Benavente, Juan A -pg. D-2-50
Benavente, Juan C -pg. D-2-50
Benavente, Juan D -pg. D-5-33
Benavente, Juan G -pg. D-5-35
Benavente, Juan M -pg. D-2-40
Benavente, Juan Q -pg. D-5-32
Benavente, Juan Q -pg. D-5-33
Benavente, Julia G -pg. D-5-36
Benavente, Juliana Q -pg. D-5-32
Benavente, Justo B -pg. D-5-25
Benavente, Lourdes Q -pg. D-5-33
Benavente, Manuel Q -pg. D-5-32
Benavente, Manuel T -pg. D-5-32
Benavente, Manuel U -pg. D-2-29

Benavente, Manuela G -pg. D-5-35
Benavente, Maria A -pg. D-2-50
Benavente, Maria G -pg. D-5-27
Benavente, Maria G -pg. D-5-35
Benavente, Maria G -pg. D-5-36
Benavente, Maria L -pg. D-2-70
Benavente, Maria Q -pg. D-5-24
Benavente, Maria Q -pg. D-5-32
Benavente, Maria Q -pg. D-5-33
Benavente, Maria SA -pg. D-5-44
Benavente, Maria SA -pg. D-5-44
Benavente, Maria SN -pg. D-5-6
Benavente, Maria U -pg. D-2-29
Benavente, Mariano G -pg. D-5-35
Benavente, Nicolasa Q -pg. D-12-12
Benavente, Nieves L -pg. D-2-70
Benavente, Pedro G -pg. D-5-35
Benavente, Pedro M -pg. D-5-34
Benavente, Pedro SA -pg. D-5-44
Benavente, Ramon Q -pg. D-5-32
Benavente, Ramon Q -pg. D-12-12
Benavente, Rita G -pg. D-5-36
Benavente, Rita Q -pg. D-5-24
Benavente, Rita S -pg. D-5-23
Benavente, Rosa G -pg. D-5-36
Benavente, Rosa R -pg. D-2-38
Benavente, Rosalia G -pg. D-5-27
Benavente, Rufina G -pg. D-5-36
Benavente, Sisto Q -pg. D-5-32
Benavente, Teresa Q -pg. D-5-32
Benavente, Tomas Q -pg. D-5-32
Benavente, Veronica SA -pg. D-5-44
Benavente, Viconta G -pg. D-5-27
Benavente, Vicente A -pg. D-2-38
Benavente, Vicente B -pg. D-5-35
Benavente, Vicente G -pg. D-5-36
Benavente, Vicente M -pg. D-5-27
Benavente, Vicente R -pg. D-12-14
Benavente, Vicente S -pg. D-5-23
Benavente, Vicente SA -pg. D-5-44
Benavente, Virginia L -pg. D-2-70
Benevente, Ana C -pg. D-2-6
Benevente, Candaleria C -pg. D-2-6
Benevente, Francisco C -pg. D-2-6
Benevente, Jose C -pg. D-2-6
Benevente, Jose R -pg. D-2-6
Benevente, Juan C -pg. D-2-7
Benevente, Maria C -pg. D-2-6
Benevente, Rosalia C -pg. D-2-6
Benevente, Tomasa C -pg. D-2-6
Benito, Barbara P -pg. D-4-21
Benito, Beatrice P -pg. D-4-21
Benito, Joseph P -pg. D-4-21
Benito, Margarita P -pg. D-4-21
Benito, Pedro R -pg. D-4-21
Benito, Roy P -pg. D-4-21
Benjamin, Alexander -pg. D-13-21
Bennett, Basil H -pg. D-13-4
Bennett, Charles E -pg. D-13-19

Bennett, Robert P -pg. D-13-19
Bennette, Maurices O -pg. D-13-10
Bennington, James W -pg. D-13-45
Bera, Martin W -pg. D-13-40
Bernard, Emma M -pg. D-7-23
Bernard, Richard F -pg. D-13-21
Bernardo, Ana Q -pg. D-4-52
Bernardo, Artemeo Q -pg. D-4-52
Bernardo, Concepcion C -pg. D-4-52
Bernardo, Guilliermo C -pg. D-4-52
Bernardo, Guilliermo T -pg. D-4-52
Bernardo, Joaquin C -pg. D-4-40
Bernardo, Jose Q -pg. D-4-52
Bernardo, Josefa LG -pg. D-4-40
Bernardo, Maria Q -pg. D-4-52
Bernardo, Mariana Q -pg. D-10-32
Bernardo, Pedro C -pg. D-4-52
Bernardo, Rosario C -pg. D-4-52
Bernardo, Tomas C -pg. D-4-40
Berrings, Yancey A -pg. D-13-41
Best, Hazel B -pg. D-3-73
Best, William A -pg. D-13-31
Beuna, Ana T -pg. D-2-26
Beuna, Victoria T -pg. D-2-26
Bicio, Pete P -pg. D-13-4
Bien, Dave -pg. D-13-14
Bird, Emily S -pg. D-13-4
Bird, Franklin A Jr -pg. D-13-45
Bird, Mary M -pg. D-13-4
Bird, Samuel K -pg. D-13-4
Birdrell, Donald T -pg. D-13-19
Bishop, Dewey C -pg. D-13-40
Bishop, Vernin E -pg. D-13-10
Bitanga, Anatalio A -pg. D-4-69
Bitanga, Fermin LG -pg. D-4-69
Bitanga, Francisca LG -pg. D-4-69
Bitanga, Inocensio LG -pg. D-4-69
Bitanga, Jose LG -pg. D-4-69
Bitanga, Maria C -pg. D-4-69
Bitanga, Vicente LG -pg. D-4-69
Bixby, Robert -pg. D-13-19
Blai, Anthony C -pg. D-13-21
Blaire, Ebmey R -pg. D-13-4
Blanco, Delfina F -pg. D-2-50
Blanco, Felipe P -pg. D-2-50
Blanco, Francisco M -pg. D-6-20
Blanco, Joaquina F -pg. D-2-50
Blanco, Rita M -pg. D-6-20
Blanco, Vicente F -pg. D-2-50
Blankowski, Helen K -pg. D-7-21
Blankowski, Regina -pg. D-7-21
Blanks, Hugh A -pg. D-13-39
Blanks, Loela E -pg. D-11-5
Blanten, Gus -pg. D-13-36
Blas, Adam C -pg. D-4-121
Blas, Ana -pg. D-5-75
Blas, Ana A -pg. D-2-41
Blas, Ana A -pg. D-10-26
Blas, Ana C -pg. D-1-6

Blas, Ana C -pg. D-1-6
Blas, Ana L -pg. D-7-5
Blas, Angustia L -pg. D-7-6
Blas, Antonia B -pg. D-1-29
Blas, Antonia L -pg. D-7-5
Blas, Antonia M -pg. D-10-26
Blas, Antonia R -pg. D-1-23
Blas, Antonio L -pg. D-5-2
Blas, Antonio R -pg. D-2-42
Blas, Asencsion R -pg. D-1-23
Blas, Barbara C -pg. D-1-6
Blas, Beatriz R -pg. D-1-23
Blas, Carmen -pg. D-5-76
Blas, Carmen A -pg. D-2-41
Blas, Carmen B -pg. D-1-29
Blas, Carmen P -pg. D-1-11
Blas, Catalina A -pg. D-4-15
Blas, Concepcion C -pg. D-1-43
Blas, Concepcion U -pg. D-1-32
Blas, Consolacion A -pg. D-10-26
Blas, Cornelia R -pg. D-1-34
Blas, Dolores C -pg. D-1-61
Blas, Dolores C -pg. D-1-61
Blas, Dolores C -pg. D-5-2
Blas, Dolores T -pg. D-1-23
Blas, Dolores U -pg. D-1-32
Blas, Domingo -pg. D-10-8
Blas, Domingo C -pg. D-3-8
Blas, Domingo C -pg. D-5-84
Blas, Emilia G -pg. D-10-2
Blas, Esperanza C -pg. D-1-61
Blas, Estella G -pg. D-1-23
Blas, Felicita -pg. D-3-7
Blas, Flora U -pg. D-1-32
Blas, Francisca C -pg. D-1-61
Blas, Francisco -pg. D-5-76
Blas, Francisco A -pg. D-10-26
Blas, Francisco B -pg. D-5-47
Blas, Francisco C -pg. D-3-7
Blas, Francisco R -pg. D-1-34
Blas, Francsico R -pg. D-2-41
Blas, Gregorio F -pg. D-2-41
Blas, Guido F -pg. D-5-7
Blas, Heyne B -pg. D-1-32
Blas, Ignacio A -pg. D-10-26
Blas, Jesus A -pg. D-4-15
Blas, Jesus C -pg. D-2-50
Blas, Jesus F -pg. D-5-75
Blas, Jesus R -pg. D-1-23
Blas, Jesus R -pg. D-2-42
Blas, Jesus S -pg. D-4-121
Blas, Jesusa C -pg. D-4-121
Blas, Joaquin B -pg. D-4-15
Blas, Joaquin C -pg. D-1-6
Blas, Joaquin F -pg. D-1-23
Blas, Joaquin T -pg. D-1-43
Blas, Joaquina L -pg. D-7-5
Blas, Joaquina R -pg. D-1-34
Blas, Jose -pg. D-3-7

Blas, Jose -pg. D-5-76
Blas, Jose A -pg. D-2-41
Blas, Jose A -pg. D-4-15
Blas, Jose A -pg. D-5-2
Blas, Jose A -pg. D-7-5
Blas, Jose A -pg. D-10-26
Blas, Jose B -pg. D-1-31
Blas, Jose C -pg. D-1-61
Blas, Jose C -pg. D-5-5
Blas, Jose F -pg. D-5-7
Blas, Jose G -pg. D-1-23
Blas, Jose R -pg. D-2-42
Blas, Jose T -pg. D-5-7
Blas, Josefa A -pg. D-10-26
Blas, Josefa B -pg. D-1-29
Blas, Josefa C -pg. D-3-7
Blas, Josefa P -pg. D-1-11
Blas, Josefa R -pg. D-2-41
Blas, Josefina -pg. D-3-7
Blas, Josefina B -pg. D-1-29
Blas, Josefina M -pg. D-3-26
Blas, Juan -pg. D-5-76
Blas, Juan B -pg. D-1-32
Blas, Juan C -pg. D-1-6
Blas, Juan C -pg. D-1-61
Blas, Juan C -pg. D-1-61
Blas, Juan L -pg. D-7-5
Blas, Juan M -pg. D-5-5
Blas, Lagrimas R -pg. D-2-41
Blas, Lorenzo L -pg. D-7-5
Blas, Lourdes C -pg. D-3-7
Blas, Macarina A -pg. D-2-41
Blas, Manuel A -pg. D-5-55
Blas, Manuel C -pg. D-1-6
Blas, Manuel C -pg. D-4-121
Blas, Maria A -pg. D-2-41
Blas, Maria A -pg. D-5-55
Blas, Maria B -pg. D-3-7
Blas, Maria C -pg. D-1-6
Blas, Maria C -pg. D-1-43
Blas, Maria G -pg. D-1-23
Blas, Maria G -pg. D-10-2
Blas, Maria M -pg. D-4-15
Blas, Maria M -pg. D-5-5
Blas, Maria M -pg. D-10-8
Blas, Maria M -pg. D-10-27
Blas, Maria P -pg. D-1-11
Blas, Maria R -pg. D-1-23
Blas, Maria R -pg. D-2-42
Blas, Mariano -pg. D-5-76
Blas, Mariano G -pg. D-2-18
Blas, Mariano R -pg. D-2-41
Blas, Matias P -pg. D-3-8
Blas, Matilde A -pg. D-5-55
Blas, Mercedes A -pg. D-2-41
Blas, Miguel C -pg. D-3-8
Blas, Natividad C -pg. D-1-6
Blas, Natividad P -pg. D-1-11
Blas, Pedro C -pg. D-1-43

Blas, Ramon -pg. D-5-76
Blas, Ramona C -pg. D-4-121
Blas, Rebeca B -pg. D-1-29
Blas, Rebeca C -pg. D-1-29
Blas, Regina R -pg. D-2-41
Blas, Rita B -pg. D-1-31
Blas, Rita G -pg. D-10-2
Blas, Rosa B -pg. D-1-29
Blas, Rosa C -pg. D-4-121
Blas, Rosa R -pg. D-2-41
Blas, Rosa U -pg. D-1-32
Blas, Rosalia A -pg. D-4-15
Blas, Rosalia R -pg. D-1-34
Blas, Rosalia R -pg. D-2-42
Blas, Rosario G -pg. D-10-2
Blas, Rosario R -pg. D-2-41
Blas, Soledad A -pg. D-5-55
Blas, Soledad M -pg. D-5-5
Blas, Teresa -pg. D-5-76
Blas, Teresa C -pg. D-1-61
Blas, Tomas C -pg. D-4-121
Blas, Tomas C -pg. D-5-19
Blas, Tomas R -pg. D-1-34
Blas, Tomasa E -pg. D-5-2
Blas, Trinidad A -pg. D-5-55
Blas, Trinidad C -pg. D-4-121
Blas, Trinidad M -pg. D-5-75
Blas, Vicenta M -pg. D-5-5
Blas, Vicente -pg. D-10-2
Blas, Vicente C -pg. D-1-6
Blas, Vicente G -pg. D-10-2
Blasiar, Caroline H -pg. D-1-8
Blasingame, Fred -pg. D-13-14
Blaslar, Arthur F -pg. D-13-21
Blaz, Alice A -pg. D-1-24
Blaz, Alvina -pg. D-3-61
Blaz, Ana A -pg. D-2-48
Blaz, Ana E -pg. D-1-30
Blaz, Ana G -pg. D-1-8
Blaz, Ana G -pg. D-1-8
Blaz, Ana I -pg. D-4-72
Blaz, Ana M -pg. D-2-75
Blaz, Angelina E -pg. D-1-30
Blaz, Angustia -pg. D-3-61
Blaz, Antonia B -pg. D-5-90
Blaz, Antonia F -pg. D-2-76
Blaz, Antonia G -pg. D-1-8
Blaz, Antonio B -pg. D-4-120
Blaz, Antonio C -pg. D-1-30
Blaz, Antonio I -pg. D-4-73
Blaz, Antonio LG -pg. D-4-90
Blaz, Antonio O -pg. D-4-98
Blaz, Antonio P -pg. D-4-73
Blaz, Antonio R -pg. D-2-70
Blaz, Apolonia T -pg. D-2-55
Blaz, Asuncion M -pg. D-2-8
Blaz, Atanacio P -pg. D-4-73
Blaz, Benjamin -pg. D-3-61
Blaz, Blanche -pg. D-5-90

Blaz, Brigida -pg. D-3-49
Blaz, Carmen B -pg. D-3-61
Blaz, Carmen F -pg. D-2-76
Blaz, Catalina S -pg. D-2-48
Blaz, Concepcion C -pg. D-2-24
Blaz, Consulo M -pg. D-2-8
Blaz, de Caseda -pg. D-4-51
Blaz, Dolores C -pg. D-2-24
Blaz, Dolores S -pg. D-2-48
Blaz, Dolores S -pg. D-2-48
Blaz, Dominga O -pg. D-4-98
Blaz, Efigenia -pg. D-3-49
Blaz, Elena P -pg. D-4-73
Blaz, Ememterio -pg. D-3-49
Blaz, Enrique D -pg. D-12-14
Blaz, Esperanza G -pg. D-2-45
Blaz, Eva -pg. D-3-61
Blaz, Felisa I -pg. D-4-72
Blaz, Fermina U -pg. D-2-57
Blaz, Fidela -pg. D-3-49
Blaz, Francisca S -pg. D-2-48
Blaz, Francisco A -pg. D-13-28
Blaz, Francisco B -pg. D-4-72
Blaz, Francisco C -pg. D-4-75
Blaz, Francisco C -pg. D-4-109
Blaz, Francisco C -pg. D-12-14
Blaz, Francisco F -pg. D-4-120
Blaz, Francisco G -pg. D-1-8
Blaz, Francisco S -pg. D-2-48
Blaz, Francisco S -pg. D-2-48
Blaz, Gregorio B -pg. D-1-24
Blaz, Henry -pg. D-3-61
Blaz, Ignacia A -pg. D-2-48
Blaz, Ignacia S -pg. D-2-48
Blaz, Ignacio A -pg. D-10-24
Blaz, Ignacio F -pg. D-4-121
Blaz, Isabel G -pg. D-1-8
Blaz, Isabel G -pg. D-2-45
Blaz, Isabel G -pg. D-2-46
Blaz, Jesus B -pg. D-2-67
Blaz, Jesus C -pg. D-2-24
Blaz, Jesus E -pg. D-1-30
Blaz, Jesus F -pg. D-4-121
Blaz, Jesus G -pg. D-1-8
Blaz, Jesus L -pg. D-2-69
Blaz, Jesus P -pg. D-4-73
Blaz, Jesus S -pg. D-2-48
Blaz, Jesusa F -pg. D-2-76
Blaz, Jesusa R -pg. D-2-70
Blaz, Jesusa S -pg. D-2-48
Blaz, Joaquin A -pg. D-2-48
Blaz, Joaquin E -pg. D-1-30
Blaz, Joaquin G -pg. D-1-8
Blaz, Joaquina U -pg. D-2-57
Blaz, Jose -pg. D-13-32
Blaz, Jose -pg. D-13-34
Blaz, Jose A -pg. D-1-24
Blaz, Jose B -pg. D-3-49
Blaz, Jose B -pg. D-4-72

Blaz, Jose Blaz -pg. D-13-26
Blaz, Jose C -pg. D-1-8
Blaz, Jose C -pg. D-2-24
Blaz, Jose E -pg. D-1-30
Blaz, Jose F -pg. D-2-48
Blaz, Jose F -pg. D-2-76
Blaz, Jose G -pg. D-1-8
Blaz, Jose L -pg. D-2-69
Blaz, Jose O -pg. D-4-98
Blaz, Jose P -pg. D-4-98
Blaz, Jose U -pg. D-2-57
Blaz, Josefa A -pg. D-2-48
Blaz, Josefa F -pg. D-2-75
Blaz, Josefa I -pg. D-4-72
Blaz, Josefina M -pg. D-2-8
Blaz, Josefina P -pg. D-4-73
Blaz, Juan A -pg. D-1-24
Blaz, Juan A -pg. D-2-45
Blaz, Juan A -pg. D-2-75
Blaz, Juan G -pg. D-2-46
Blaz, Juan S -pg. D-2-76
Blaz, Juana F -pg. D-2-76
Blaz, Julia F -pg. D-4-120
Blaz, Julia P -pg. D-4-73
Blaz, Juliana A -pg. D-1-24
Blaz, Lorenzo L -pg. D-2-8
Blaz, Lorenzo M -pg. D-2-8
Blaz, Lourdes G -pg. D-2-46
Blaz, Luis A -pg. D-2-47
Blaz, Mabel -pg. D-5-90
Blaz, Magdalena I -pg. D-4-72
Blaz, Magi M -pg. D-2-8
Blaz, Manuel A pg. D-1-25
Blaz, Manuel A -pg. D-4-108
Blaz, Maria -pg. D-3-61
Blaz, Maria A -pg. D-1-25
Blaz, Maria A -pg. D-2-48
Blaz, Maria A -pg. D-2-75
Blaz, Maria D -pg. D-12-14
Blaz, Maria E -pg. D-1-30
Blaz, Maria F -pg. D-2-76
Blaz, Maria F -pg. D-4-120
Blaz, Maria G -pg. D-1-8
Blaz, Maria G -pg. D-2-45
Blaz, Maria L -pg. D-2-69
Blaz, Maria LG -pg. D-3-21
Blaz, Maria M -pg. D-2-8
Blaz, Maria M -pg. D-2-8
Blaz, Maria O -pg. D-3-47
Blaz, Maria O -pg. D-4-98
Blaz, Maria P -pg. D-4-73
Blaz, Maria P -pg. D-4-75
Blaz, Matilde A -pg. D-1-25
Blaz, Matilde G -pg. D-1-8
Blaz, Matilde O -pg. D-4-98
Blaz, Nicolasa O -pg. D-3-49
Blaz, Nicolasa S -pg. D-4-108
Blaz, Pedro F -pg. D-2-76
Blaz, Pedro G -pg. D-1-8

Blaz, Pedro S -pg. D-2-48
Blaz, Ramon F -pg. D-2-75
Blaz, Ramon T -pg. D-4-109
Blaz, Regina T -pg. D-4-76
Blaz, Rita C -pg. D-2-24
Blaz, Rita L -pg. D-2-69
Blaz, Roman F -pg. D-2-76
Blaz, Rosa A -pg. D-2-48
Blaz, Rosa B -pg. D-4-109
Blaz, Rosa S -pg. D-2-48
Blaz, Rosalia S -pg. D-2-48
Blaz, Tomasa I -pg. D-4-72
Blaz, Tomasa M -pg. D-2-8
Blaz, Trinidad A -pg. D-1-25
Blaz, Trinidad B -pg. D-4-109
Blaz, Vicente F -pg. D-2-48
Blaz, Vicente S -pg. D-2-48
Blaz, Victoria F -pg. D-2-76
Blaz, Vincente C -pg. D-13-27
Blonkowski, John J -pg. D-13-21
Blouin, William -pg. D-13-21
Bojra, Juan M -pg. D-13-21
Bollerud, Irene -pg. D-13-19
Bond, Clayton T -pg. D-13-15
Bonistsorn, Annie E -pg. D-13-19
Bontugan, Antonio C -pg. D-5-6
Bontugan, Francisca F -pg. D-5-6
Bontugan, Josefa C -pg. D-5-16
Bontugan, Juan C -pg. D-5-16
Bontugan, Regina C -pg. D-5-16
Books, Wayd L -pg. D-13-15
Boorman, Thomas T -pg. D-13-4
Borband, Elmber F -pg. D-13-22
Bordallo, Alfredo T -pg. D-1-10
Bordallo, Baltazar B -pg. D-6-2
Bordallo, Baltazar J -pg. D-4-91
Bordallo, Barbara L -pg. D-4-91
Bordallo, Carlos E -pg. D-3-28
Bordallo, Carlos P -pg. D-3-28
Bordallo, Concepcion T -pg. D-1-10
Bordallo, Enesta P -pg. D-3-28
Bordallo, Erwin B -pg. D-3-28
Bordallo, Irene D -pg. D-4-91
Bordallo, Josefina P -pg. D-4-91
Bordallo, Ricardo J -pg. D-4-91
Bordallo, Richard C -pg. D-3-28
Bordallo, Rita P -pg. D-6-3
Bordallo, Sylvia L -pg. D-4-91
Bordallo, Tomas A -pg. D-1-10
Bordor, Henry F -pg. D-13-41
Borja, Adriano C -pg. D-4-72
Borja, Agustina S -pg. D-2-31
Borja, Alberto -pg. D-3-19
Borja, Ana I -pg. D-2-74
Borja, Ana I -pg. D-5-67
Borja, Ana LG -pg. D-4-43
Borja, Ana M -pg. D-2-84
Borja, Ana M -pg. D-4-98
Borja, Ana M -pg. D-11-14

Borja, Ana O -pg. D-2-68
Borja, Ana P -pg. D-5-99
Borja, Ana Q -pg. D-4-70
Borja, Ana S -pg. D-11-7
Borja, Ana S -pg. D-11-45
Borja, Andrea S -pg. D-11-7
Borja, Andres C -pg. D-11-3
Borja, Ann T -pg. D-2-33
Borja, Antonia G -pg. D-9-10
Borja, Antonia Q -pg. D-11-26
Borja, Antonio -pg. D-5-67
Borja, Antonio -pg. D-11-15
Borja, Antonio A -pg. D-6-19
Borja, Antonio A -pg. D-11-51
Borja, Antonio B -pg. D-2-73
Borja, Antonio B -pg. D-5-60
Borja, Antonio C -pg. D-11-8
Borja, Antonio M -pg. D-6-19
Borja, Antonio Q -pg. D-1-40
Borja, Antonio S -pg. D-10-35
Borja, Antonio T -pg. D-2-84
Borja, Asuncion A -pg. D-6-19
Borja, Beatrice G -pg. D-4-94
Borja, Bernadita S -pg. D-4-97
Borja, Candelaria M -pg. D-5-93
Borja, Carlo -pg. D-5-92
Borja, Carlos M -pg. D-4-118
Borja, Carmen N -pg. D-11-4
Borja, Carridad LG -pg. D-4-43
Borja, Catalina -pg. D-3-19
Borja, Catalina -pg. D-5-67
Borja, Celestina C -pg. D-4-72
Borja, Concepcion G -pg. D-4-94
Borja, Consuelo M -pg. D-4-106
Borja, Cresencia Q -pg. D-1-40
Borja, Daniel M -pg. D-11-14
Borja, Demetrio G -pg. D-4-95
Borja, Dolores A -pg. D-11-50
Borja, Dolores C -pg. D-9-13
Borja, Dolores C -pg. D-11-3
Borja, Dolores F -pg. D-5-11
Borja, Dolores M -pg. D-11-45
Borja, Dolores S -pg. D-4-97
Borja, Emeliana S -pg. D-2-49
Borja, Felipe LG -pg. D-4-72
Borja, Felix B -pg. D-4-98
Borja, Filomena Q -pg. D-5-55
Borja, Francisca -pg. D-3-19
Borja, Francisca C -pg. D-3-19
Borja, Francisca D -pg. D-5-45
Borja, Francisco -pg. D-5-76
Borja, Francisco B -pg. D-2-74
Borja, Francisco C -pg. D-4-70
Borja, Francisco C -pg. D-4-104
Borja, Francisco C -pg. D-5-29
Borja, Francisco M -pg. D-11-46
Borja, Francisco N -pg. D-11-4
Borja, Francisco S -pg. D-2-31
Borja, Francisco S -pg. D-4-97

Borja, Francisco S -pg. D-5-88
Borja, Francisco S -pg. D-10-36
Borja, Francisco S -pg. D-11-45
Borja, Gertrudes Q -pg. D-2-83
Borja, Grabela L -pg. D-2-49
Borja, Gravela L -pg. D-2-33
Borja, Gravela T -pg. D-2-33
Borja, Gregorio A -pg. D-11-51
Borja, Gregorio C -pg. D-2-31
Borja, Gregorio C -pg. D-5-29
Borja, Gregorio M -pg. D-11-14
Borja, Gregorio S -pg. D-11-7
Borja, Hermanigilda S -pg. D-4-61
Borja, Ignacia B -pg. D-5-37
Borja, Ignacia G -pg. D-1-40
Borja, Ignacia R -pg. D-4-55
Borja, Ignacio M -pg. D-5-93
Borja, Ignacio M -pg. D-11-14
Borja, Ignacio Q -pg. D-1-39
Borja, Ignacio S -pg. D-5-3
Borja, Ignacio T -pg. D-4-97
Borja, Isabel L -pg. D-5-15
Borja, Isabel M -pg. D-11-45
Borja, Isabel M -pg. D-11-45
Borja, Isabel S -pg. D-4-48
Borja, Jesus -pg. D-3-12
Borja, Jesus A -pg. D-6-19
Borja, Jesus C -pg. D-4-70
Borja, Jesus C -pg. D-4-72
Borja, Jesus M -pg. D-2-84
Borja, Jesus M -pg. D-11-46
Borja, Jesus O -pg. D-2-83
Borja, Jesus Q -pg. D-11-26
Borja, Jesus S -pg. D-2-31
Borja, Jesus T -pg. D-2-49
Borja, Jesusa G -pg. D-4-95
Borja, Joaquin -pg. D-3-19
Borja, Joaquin D -pg. D-5-12
Borja, Joaquin G -pg. D-1-40
Borja, Joaquin L -pg. D-5-91
Borja, Joaquin M -pg. D-4-98
Borja, Joaquin S -pg. D-5-12
Borja, Joaquin T -pg. D-4-98
Borja, Joaquin T -pg. D-11-50
Borja, Joaquina S -pg. D-4-48
Borja, Jorge -pg. D-5-91
Borja, Jose A -pg. D-6-19
Borja, Jose B -pg. D-1-40
Borja, Jose B -pg. D-2-73
Borja, Jose B -pg. D-4-106
Borja, Jose B -pg. D-5-45
Borja, Jose C -pg. D-1-26
Borja, Jose C -pg. D-5-29
Borja, Jose D -pg. D-5-12
Borja, Jose D -pg. D-5-45
Borja, Jose D -pg. D-5-55
Borja, Jose F -pg. D-5-11
Borja, Jose L -pg. D-2-49
Borja, Jose L -pg. D-2-58

Borja, Jose M -pg. D-2-84
Borja, Jose M -pg. D-11-46
Borja, Jose M -pg. D-13-28
Borja, Jose P -pg. D-5-56
Borja, Jose Q -pg. D-4-70
Borja, Jose Q -pg. D-11-26
Borja, Jose R -pg. D-4-55
Borja, Jose R -pg. D-5-67
Borja, Jose S -pg. D-4-98
Borja, Jose S -pg. D-11-45
Borja, Jose T -pg. D-2-19
Borja, Jose V -pg. D-2-9
Borja, Josefa B -pg. D-5-37
Borja, Josefa LG -pg. D-4-43
Borja, Josefa LG -pg. D-4-79
Borja, Josefa S -pg. D-2-31
Borja, Josefina G -pg. D-4-94
Borja, Josefina M -pg. D-4-118
Borja, Juan B -pg. D-2-74
Borja, Juan C -pg. D-2-31
Borja, Juan C -pg. D-4-72
Borja, Juan C -pg. D-9-10
Borja, Juan C -pg. D-11-3
Borja, Juan M -pg. D-4-55
Borja, Juan O -pg. D-5-74
Borja, Juan P -pg. D-5-56
Borja, Juan Q -pg. D-5-55
Borja, Juan S -pg. D-2-73
Borja, Juan S -pg. D-4-48
Borja, Juan S -pg. D-4-97
Borja, Juan S -pg. D-4-97
Borja, Juan S -pg. D-11-3
Borja, Juan T -pg. D-8-12
Borja, Juan W -pg. D-9-13
Borja, Iuana C pg. D-3-62
Borja, Julia C -pg. D-4-72
Borja, Julian A -pg. D-11-50
Borja, Lorenzo L -pg. D-2-56
Borja, Lorenzo L -pg. D-3-19
Borja, Lucas C -pg. D-11-8
Borja, Lucas T -pg. D-11-14
Borja, Luis A -pg. D-11-26
Borja, Luis G -pg. D-3-49
Borja, Luis Q -pg. D-1-26
Borja, Luisa -pg. D-5-67
Borja, Magdalena M -pg. D-5-93
Borja, Manuel -pg. D-3-19
Borja, Manuel -pg. D-10-35
Borja, Manuel A -pg. D-11-51
Borja, Manuel B -pg. D-2-73
Borja, Manuel G -pg. D-4-94
Borja, Manuel L -pg. D-4-118
Borja, Manuel M -pg. D-11-8
Borja, Manuel S -pg. D-5-11
Borja, Manuel S -pg. D-10-36
Borja, Maria -pg. D-5-67
Borja, Maria -pg. D-5-92
Borja, Maria A -pg. D-6-19
Borja, Maria B -pg. D-2-73

Borja, Maria B -pg. D-2-74
Borja, Maria B -pg. D-5-37
Borja, Maria C -pg. D-1-26
Borja, Maria C -pg. D-2-25
Borja, Maria C -pg. D-2-31
Borja, Maria C -pg. D-4-72
Borja, Maria C -pg. D-5-67
Borja, Maria C -pg. D-5-76
Borja, Maria C -pg. D-11-3
Borja, Maria D -pg. D-5-12
Borja, Maria F -pg. D-5-11
Borja, Maria G -pg. D-1-40
Borja, Maria G -pg. D-1-51
Borja, Maria L -pg. D-4-118
Borja, Maria M -pg. D-4-118
Borja, Maria M -pg. D-4-118
Borja, Maria M -pg. D-5-27
Borja, Maria O -pg. D-3-12
Borja, Maria P -pg. D-5-55
Borja, Maria Q -pg. D-11-26
Borja, Maria R -pg. D-4-55
Borja, Maria R -pg. D-5-15
Borja, Maria S -pg. D-2-31
Borja, Maria S -pg. D-4-48
Borja, Maria S -pg. D-10-35
Borja, Maria S -pg. D-11-7
Borja, Maria SN -pg. D-2-9
Borja, Maria T -pg. D-2-19
Borja, Maria C M -pg. D-2-84
Borja, Mariano A -pg. D-6-19
Borja, Mariano C -pg. D-11-3
Borja, Mariano R -pg. D-5-27
Borja, Martina A -pg. D-6-19
Borja, Matilde S pg. D-1-59
Borja, Natividad D -pg. D-5-45
Borja, Nicolasa C -pg. D-5-29
Borja, Nicolasa S -pg. D-5-88
Borja, Nieves D -pg. D-5-12
Borja, Paulino B -pg. D-5-67
Borja, Paz -pg. D-3-49
Borja, Paz C -pg. D-3-49
Borja, Pedro C -pg. D-2-31
Borja, Pedro C -pg. D-4-72
Borja, Pedro G -pg. D-1-40
Borja, Pedro I -pg. D-2-74
Borja, Pedro M -pg. D-4-98
Borja, Pedro Q -pg. D-5-55
Borja, Pilar O -pg. D-11-32
Borja, Rafael N -pg. D-11-4
Borja, Rafael T -pg. D-11-4
Borja, Ramon F -pg. D-5-11
Borja, Ramon S -pg. D-5-15
Borja, Rita C -pg. D-11-13
Borja, Rita M -pg. D-11-43
Borja, Rita S -pg. D-11-7
Borja, Rosa A -pg. D-6-19
Borja, Rosa B -pg. D-4-98
Borja, Rosa B -pg. D-5-37
Borja, Rosa C -pg. D-1-26

Borja, Rosa C -pg. D-9-17
Borja, Rosa D -pg. D-5-91
Borja, Rosa I -pg. D-2-74
Borja, Rosa S -pg. D-4-98
Borja, Rosalina Q -pg. D-4-70
Borja, Rosario D -pg. D-5-12
Borja, Rosario M -pg. D-4-118
Borja, Rosario T -pg. D-2-19
Borja, Rufina -pg. D-5-92
Borja, Saturnina M -pg. D-5-93
Borja, Soledad B -pg. D-5-37
Borja, Soledad M -pg. D-2-84
Borja, Soledad M -pg. D-11-45
Borja, Susana Q -pg. D-1-40
Borja, Toribia -pg. D-5-92
Borja, Trinidad -pg. D-5-92
Borja, Trinidad M -pg. D-4-118
Borja, Vicenta C -pg. D-11-8
Borja, Vicenta F -pg. D-5-11
Borja, Vicenta S -pg. D-4-97
Borja, Vicente -pg. D-5-67
Borja, Vicente B -pg. D-2-31
Borja, Vicente C -pg. D-5-29
Borja, Vicente C -pg. D-9-10
Borja, Vicente C -pg. D-11-3
Borja, Vicente D -pg. D-5-12
Borja, Vicente G -pg. D-1-40
Borja, Vicente I -pg. D-5-76
Borja, Vicente M -pg. D-4-48
Borja, Vicente M -pg. D-4-118
Borja, Vicente M -pg. D-11-45
Borja, Vicente O -pg. D-5-74
Borja, Vicente S pg. D-2-31
Borja, Vicente S -pg. D-11-7
Borja, Vicente T -pg. D-11-7
Borosee, William A -pg. D-13-41
Borrow, Curtis W -pg. D-13-36
Bourne, Dana H -pg. D-13-10
Bowdre, Paul A -pg. D-13-10
Boyle, Howard R -pg. D-13-4
Bradley, Anne W -pg. D-13-31
Bradley, Josephine W -pg. D-13-31
Bradley, Sue Worthingtno -pg. D-13-31
Bradley, Sue Worthingtno -pg. D-13-31
Bradley, William W Jr -pg. D-13-31
Brady, John A -pg. D-1-21
Brady, Mary R -pg. D-1-21
Brady, Thomas J Jr -pg. D-13-31
Branches, Frances E -pg. D-13-5
Brandt, Lorenzo I -pg. D-13-36
Brat????, Dale ? -pg. D-13-10
Brennan, Thomas P -pg. D-13-5
Brocker, Edward W -pg. D-13-10
Broll, Isadore -pg. D-13-21
Bronning, Lewis J -pg. D-13-10
Broski, Elden J -pg. D-13-36
Broste, Ida E -pg. D-13-19
Brown, Charle D -pg. D-13-10
Brown, Charles S -pg. D-1-57

Brown, Emma S -pg. D-1-57
Brown, Frank -pg. D-1-57
Brown, Helen S -pg. D-1-57
Brown, Raymond L -pg. D-13-40
Brown, Teodora S -pg. D-1-57
Brudere, Charles -pg. D-13-15
Brummond, Alice E -pg. D-10-5
Brummond, Emily M -pg. D-10-5
Brummond, Euthorpea E -pg. D-10-5
Bryan, Harry C -pg. D-13-36
Bryan, Williams ? -pg. D-13-5
Bryant, Welles Y -pg. D-13-45
Bryce, Bascorn D -pg. D-13-44
Buckley, Harriet M -pg. D-7-23
Buckner, Walter C -pg. D-13-5
Bugbee, Beatrice V -pg. D-11-27
Buinie, Arthur W -pg. D-13-15
Bukikosa, Joaquina C -pg. D-4-78
Bukikosa, Jose C -pg. D-4-78
Bukikosa, Manuel C -pg. D-4-78
Bukikosa, Maria B -pg. D-4-61
Bukikosa, Sacarias -pg. D-13-34
Bumps, Arthur E -pg. D-13-15
Burke, Ralph A -pg. D-13-45
Burnbee, Alvin R -pg. D-13-39
Burnham, Harry J -pg. D-13-32
Burns, Florence V -pg. D-13-10
Burtrow, Joseph H -pg. D-13-39
Bush, William A -pg. D-13-45
Bushell, Alfred -pg. D-13-34
Butler, Beatrice -pg. D-3-30
Butler, Benjamin -pg. D-3-30
Butler, Berry P -pg. D-3-31
Butler, Chester C -pg. D-3-30
Butler, Clara -pg. D-3-30
Butler, Dorthy -pg. D-3-31
Butler, Henry R -pg. D-4-82
Butler, Ignacia B -pg. D-3-30
Butler, James -pg. D-3-30
Butler, Margarita R -pg. D-4-82
Butler, Nellie R -pg. D-4-82
Butler, Robert R -pg. D-4-82
Butler, Tomas R -pg. D-4-82
Butler, William R -pg. D-4-82
Butterfield, Willis A -pg. D-13-15
Button, Bruce E -pg. D-4-26
Byrando, Everette J -pg. D-13-5
Cabe, Antonio D -pg. D-4-33
Cabe, Nicolasa D -pg. D-4-33
Cabo, Angel D -pg. D-4-115
Cabo, Dolores T -pg. D-4-115
Cabo, Jose D -pg. D-4-115
Cabo, Manuela D -pg. D-4-115
Cabrera, Ana C -pg. D-1-35
Cabrera, Ana D -pg. D-3-42
Cabrera, Ana Q -pg. D-10-23
Cabrera, Benita -pg. D-3-42
Cabrera, Concepcion C -pg. D-1-45
Cabrera, Concepcion M -pg. D-2-56

Cabrera, Delfina T -pg. D-2-40
Cabrera, Dolores C -pg. D-1-35
Cabrera, Enrique V -pg. D-1-35
Cabrera, Enriqueta B -pg. D-8-50
Cabrera, Francisco C -pg. D-1-45
Cabrera, Ignacio M -pg. D-3-4
Cabrera, Isabel -pg. D-3-42
Cabrera, Jesus -pg. D-3-42
Cabrera, Jesus C -pg. D-1-35
Cabrera, Jesus C -pg. D-1-45
Cabrera, Jose C -pg. D-1-35
Cabrera, Jose D -pg. D-10-23
Cabrera, Jose M -pg. D-2-56
Cabrera, Jose Q -pg. D-10-23
Cabrera, Josefa B -pg. D-8-50
Cabrera, Juan B -pg. D-8-50
Cabrera, Juan D -pg. D-8-50
Cabrera, Juan M -pg. D-2-56
Cabrera, Juan T -pg. D-2-40
Cabrera, Julia B -pg. D-8-50
Cabrera, Maria -pg. D-3-4
Cabrera, Maria -pg. D-3-42
Cabrera, Maria C -pg. D-1-35
Cabrera, Maria C -pg. D-3-4
Cabrera, Maria M -pg. D-2-56
Cabrera, Maria Q -pg. D-10-23
Cabrera, Maria Q -pg. D-10-23
Cabrera, Maria T -pg. D-2-39
Cabrera, Mariano T -pg. D-2-40
Cabrera, Pilar Q -pg. D-10-23
Cabrera, Rosa M -pg. D-2-56
Cabrera, Rosalia C -pg. D-1-35
Cabrera, Rosario M -pg. D-2-56
Cabrera, Soledad -pg. D-3-42
Cabrera, Vicente -pg. D-3-4
Cabrera, Vicente C -pg. D-1-45
Cady, Willam H -pg. D-13-46
Cafy, Ora E -pg. D-1-55
Cafy, Phyllis G -pg. D-1-55
Cafy, Robert A -pg. D-1-55
Calens, William P -pg. D-13-36
Calesqa, Pablo -pg. D-13-21
Call, Donald M -pg. D-13-15
Calls, Ora E -pg. D-13-5
Calvo, Ana A -pg. D-4-110
Calvo, Angelina T -pg. D-4-110
Calvo, Antonia B -pg. D-5-68
Calvo, Antonio -pg. D-5-68
Calvo, Antonio A -pg. D-5-51
Calvo, Antonio B -pg. D-4-114
Calvo, Augusto -pg. D-5-68
Calvo, Beatriz -pg. D-5-68
Calvo, Carlos T -pg. D-4-110
Calvo, Clotilde T -pg. D-4-110
Calvo, Eduardo T -pg. D-3-47
Calvo, Eluterio -pg. D-3-45
Calvo, Felix -pg. D-3-45
Calvo, Felix P -pg. D-5-68
Calvo, Felix V -pg. D-4-114

Calvo, Fermin -pg. D-5-68
Calvo, Fidela -pg. D-5-68
Calvo, Flora T -pg. D-4-110
Calvo, Gregorio A -pg. D-5-51
Calvo, Gregorio LG -pg. D-5-51
Calvo, Gregorio P -pg. D-4-114
Calvo, Herminia T -pg. D-4-109
Calvo, Isabel S -pg. D-3-45
Calvo, Ismael T -pg. D-4-109
Calvo, Jacinto -pg. D-5-68
Calvo, Jacinto A -pg. D-4-110
Calvo, Jesus -pg. D-5-68
Calvo, Jose -pg. D-3-32
Calvo, Juana -pg. D-3-45
Calvo, Leon P -pg. D-3-32
Calvo, Manuel A -pg. D-5-51
Calvo, Maria A -pg. D-5-51
Calvo, Maria A -pg. D-5-51
Calvo, Maria LG -pg. D-3-32
Calvo, Pedro A -pg. D-5-51
Calvo, Pilar -pg. D-3-45
Calvo, Ramon P -pg. D-3-45
Calvo, Regina T -pg. D-4-109
Calvo, Ricardo T -pg. D-4-110
Calvo, Rita A -pg. D-5-51
Calvo, Rufo -pg. D-3-45
Calvo, Tomas A -pg. D-4-109
Calvo, Trinidad T -pg. D-4-109
Calvo, Vicente -pg. D-4-114
Calvo, Vicente -pg. D-5-68
Camacho, Abraham C -pg. D-4-74
Camacho, Aduardo M -pg. D-1-13
Camacho, Aleandra -pg. D-1-5
Camacho, Alfonso M -pg. D-1-27
Camacho, Amparo A -pg. D-2-10
Camacho, Ana A -pg. D-2-10
Camacho, Ana A -pg. D-2-10
Camacho, Ana A -pg. D-11-25
Camacho, Ana B -pg. D-12-11
Camacho, Ana C -pg. D-1-68
Camacho, Ana C -pg. D-2-40
Camacho, Ana C -pg. D-10-6
Camacho, Ana G -pg. D-2-61
Camacho, Ana G -pg. D-4-84
Camacho, Ana M -pg. D-1-13
Camacho, Ana M -pg. D-1-27
Camacho, Ana M -pg. D-1-27
Camacho, Ana M -pg. D-2-68
Camacho, Ana M -pg. D-4-99
Camacho, Ana S -pg. D-1-33
Camacho, Ana S -pg. D-2-67
Camacho, Ana S -pg. D-11-12
Camacho, Ana SN -pg. D-1-24
Camacho, Andres Q -pg. D-2-58
Camacho, Antonia A -pg. D-1-61
Camacho, Antonia B -pg. D-2-42
Camacho, Antonia C -pg. D-5-60
Camacho, Antonia G -pg. D-4-88
Camacho, Antonia LG -pg. D-2-73

Camacho, Antonia S -pg. D-11-12
Camacho, Antonio -pg. D-3-74
Camacho, Antonio C -pg. D-2-40
Camacho, Antonio M -pg. D-4-84
Camacho, Antonio M -pg. D-10-31
Camacho, Antonio M -pg. D-11-30
Camacho, Atanasio R -pg. D-4-84
Camacho, Barbara C -pg. D-4-74
Camacho, Beatrice C -pg. D-1-29
Camacho, Beatrice C -pg. D-11-34
Camacho, Bidad A -pg. D-4-35
Camacho, Brigida C -pg. D-10-6
Camacho, Buenaventuro C -pg. D-4-74
Camacho, Candaleria R -pg. D-2-21
Camacho, Carlos E -pg. D-4-92
Camacho, Carlos G -pg. D-4-88
Camacho, Carlos M -pg. D-4-94
Camacho, Carmen C -pg. D-1-29
Camacho, Carmen C -pg. D-1-34
Camacho, Carmen P -pg. D-1-29
Camacho, Carmen R -pg. D-4-84
Camacho, Catalina E -pg. D-4-92
Camacho, Cecilio G -pg. D-1-53
Camacho, Cecilio M -pg. D-4-99
Camacho, Clotilde C -pg. D-10-6
Camacho, Columbina E -pg. D-4-92
Camacho, Concepcion C -pg. D-2-67
Camacho, Concepcion C -pg. D-3-72
Camacho, Concepcion G -pg. D-4-84
Camacho, Concepcion M -pg. D-4-93
Camacho, Concepcion R -pg. D-4-84
Camacho, Concepcion S -pg. D-1-33
Camacho, Consolacion Q -pg. D-2-58
Camacho, Crispina E -pg. D-4-92
Camacho, Cristina C -pg. D 4-74
Camacho, David R -pg. D-2-54
Camacho, Delores A -pg. D-13-43
Camacho, Dolores C -pg. D-5-7
Camacho, Dolores C -pg. D-11-21
Camacho, Dolores G -pg. D-11-11
Camacho, Dolores M -pg. D-1-13
Camacho, Dolores M -pg. D-11-30
Camacho, Dolores M -pg. D-11-30
Camacho, Dolores R -pg. D-4-28
Camacho, Dorothy C -pg. D-11-21
Camacho, Edward M -pg. D-4-99
Camacho, Edwardo G -pg. D-4-88
Camacho, Eliza S -pg. D-4-69
Camacho, Emelia R -pg. D-2-54
Camacho, Emeteria LG -pg. D-2-73
Camacho, Emma G -pg. D-11-15
Camacho, Enrique -pg. D-5-58
Camacho, Enrique G -pg. D-13-28
Camacho, Enrique M -pg. D-2-73
Camacho, Estella S -pg. D-4-69
Camacho, Felicidad -pg. D-3-63
Camacho, Felicita C -pg. D-5-7
Camacho, Felicita G -pg. D-4-84
Camacho, Felisa G -pg. D-4-84

Camacho, Felix A -pg. D-1-60
Camacho, Felix G -pg. D-2-61
Camacho, Felix M -pg. D-4-88
Camacho, Fidela M -pg. D-11-30
Camacho, Filomenia C -pg. D-4-74
Camacho, Filomina LG -pg. D-2-73
Camacho, Florencia C -pg. D-4-74
Camacho, Florentina A -pg. D-11-13
Camacho, Francisca M -pg. D-1-13
Camacho, Francisca P -pg. D-12-10
Camacho, Francisca T -pg. D-4-74
Camacho, Francisco B -pg. D-12-6
Camacho, Francisco C -pg. D-5-60
Camacho, Francisco G -pg. D-11-11
Camacho, Francisco L -pg. D-1-25
Camacho, Francisco M -pg. D-1-27
Camacho, Francisco M -pg. D-4-74
Camacho, Francisco M -pg. D-4-94
Camacho, Francisco S -pg. D-1-33
Camacho, Francisco SN -pg. D-1-25
Camacho, Gaily C -pg. D-11-21
Camacho, Gregorio C -pg. D-1-34
Camacho, Gregorio R -pg. D-4-84
Camacho, Gregorio S -pg. D-1-33
Camacho, Gregorio SN -pg. D-1-24
Camacho, Guadalupe -pg. D-3-72
Camacho, Guillermo S -pg. D-11-35
Camacho, Hediliza E -pg. D-4-92
Camacho, Higinio -pg. D-3-74
Camacho, Ignacia C -pg. D-4-35
Camacho, Ignacio -pg. D-3-74
Camacho, Ignacio G -pg. D-4-84
Camacho, Ignacio L -pg. D-4-93
Camacho, Ignacio M pg. D-4-93
Camacho, Ignacio R -pg. D-8-16
Camacho, Irene Q -pg. D-2-58
Camacho, Ireneo S -pg. D-4-69
Camacho, Isabel D -pg. D-1-26
Camacho, Isabel M -pg. D-2-68
Camacho, Isidora E -pg. D-4-92
Camacho, Jesus -pg. D-3-72
Camacho, Jesus -pg. D-3-74
Camacho, Jesus A -pg. D-11-13
Camacho, Jesus C -pg. D-1-29
Camacho, Jesus C -pg. D-2-42
Camacho, Jesus C -pg. D-5-48
Camacho, Jesus G -pg. D-4-84
Camacho, Jesus M -pg. D-1-13
Camacho, Jesus M -pg. D-2-68
Camacho, Jesus M -pg. D-4-94
Camacho, Jesus M -pg. D-11-30
Camacho, Jesus P -pg. D-3-74
Camacho, Jesus R -pg. D-4-28
Camacho, Jesus S -pg. D-1-33
Camacho, Jesus SN -pg. D-1-25
Camacho, Jesus SN -pg. D-1-65
Camacho, Jesusa O -pg. D-12-6
Camacho, Joaquin -pg. D-3-63
Camacho, Joaquin C -pg. D-10-6

Camacho, Joaquin F -pg. D-4-84
Camacho, Joaquin M -pg. D-4-93
Camacho, Joaquin M -pg. D-4-99
Camacho, Joaquin M -pg. D-10-31
Camacho, Joaquin O -pg. D-5-3
Camacho, Joaquina -pg. D-4-126
Camacho, Joaquina C -pg. D-1-34
Camacho, Jose -pg. D-3-72
Camacho, Jose -pg. D-3-74
Camacho, Jose -pg. D-13-21
Camacho, Jose A -pg. D-1-65
Camacho, Jose C -pg. D-2-40
Camacho, Jose C -pg. D-2-40
Camacho, Jose C -pg. D-2-67
Camacho, Jose C -pg. D-5-7
Camacho, Jose C -pg. D-5-48
Camacho, Jose C -pg. D-5-60
Camacho, Jose C -pg. D-11-12
Camacho, Jose C -pg. D-11-25
Camacho, Jose D -pg. D-1-24
Camacho, Jose G -pg. D-2-61
Camacho, Jose G -pg. D-2-68
Camacho, Jose G -pg. D-4-84
Camacho, Jose G -pg. D-11-11
Camacho, Jose M -pg. D-1-13
Camacho, Jose M -pg. D-1-17
Camacho, Jose M -pg. D-4-74
Camacho, Jose M -pg. D-4-92
Camacho, Jose M -pg. D-4-93
Camacho, Jose O -pg. D-1-26
Camacho, Jose O -pg. D-4-28
Camacho, Jose O -pg. D-12-6
Camacho, Jose Q pg. D-2-58
Camacho, Jose Q -pg. D-11-15
Camacho, Jose R -pg. D-2-21
Camacho, Jose R -pg. D-2-21
Camacho, Jose R -pg. D-11-40
Camacho, Jose S -pg. D-1-38
Camacho, Jose S -pg. D-1-68
Camacho, Jose S -pg. D-13-30
Camacho, Jose SN -pg. D-1-25
Camacho, Jose SN -pg. D-1-29
Camacho, Jose SN -pg. D-1-65
Camacho, Josefa A -pg. D-1-60
Camacho, Josefa A -pg. D-1-60
Camacho, Josefa C -pg. D-11-25
Camacho, Josefa G -pg. D-2-61
Camacho, Josefa G -pg. D-2-61
Camacho, Josefa P -pg. D-12-10
Camacho, Josefa R -pg. D-4-84
Camacho, Josefa S -pg. D-11-12
Camacho, Josefina G -pg. D-4-88
Camacho, Josefina LG -pg. D-2-73
Camacho, Josefina M -pg. D-2-68
Camacho, Josefina O -pg. D-12-6
Camacho, Juan B -pg. D-5-41
Camacho, Juan C -pg. D-1-34
Camacho, Juan C -pg. D-11-34
Camacho, Juan D -pg. D-11-30

Camacho, Juan F -pg. D-4-99
Camacho, Juan G -pg. D-4-84
Camacho, Juan G -pg. D-4-88
Camacho, Juan G -pg. D-11-11
Camacho, Juan LG -pg. D-2-73
Camacho, Juan P -pg. D-2-16
Camacho, Juan R -pg. D-4-28
Camacho, Juan S -pg. D-1-34
Camacho, Juana G -pg. D-2-61
Camacho, Juana Q -pg. D-2-58
Camacho, Julita S -pg. D-11-12
Camacho, Leonora S -pg. D-11-40
Camacho, Lourdes P -pg. D-12-10
Camacho, Lourdes S -pg. D-4-69
Camacho, Luis C -pg. D-2-54
Camacho, Luis G -pg. D-4-88
Camacho, Luis P -pg. D-2-69
Camacho, Luis S -pg. D-7-3
Camacho, Manuel -pg. D-11-12
Camacho, Manuel C -pg. D-11-11
Camacho, Manuel G -pg. D-4-84
Camacho, Manuel M -pg. D-1-27
Camacho, Manuel M -pg. D-4-93
Camacho, Manuel SN -pg. D-1-27
Camacho, Manuela C -pg. D-1-34
Camacho, Manuela S -pg. D-1-33
Camacho, Maria -pg. D-3-72
Camacho, Maria -pg. D-3-74
Camacho, Maria A -pg. D-11-13
Camacho, Maria B -pg. D-12-11
Camacho, Maria C -pg. D-1-29
Camacho, Maria C -pg. D-2-21
Camacho, Maria C -pg. D-4-74
Camacho, Maria C -pg. D-5-7
Camacho, Maria C -pg. D-7-21
Camacho, Maria G -pg. D-2-61
Camacho, Maria G -pg. D-4-84
Camacho, Maria LG -pg. D-2-73
Camacho, Maria M -pg. D-1-13
Camacho, Maria M -pg. D-1-13
Camacho, Maria M -pg. D-4-94
Camacho, Maria M -pg. D-4-99
Camacho, Maria M -pg. D-10-31
Camacho, Maria O -pg. D-1-30
Camacho, Maria O -pg. D-12-6
Camacho, Maria R -pg. D-1-26
Camacho, Maria R -pg. D-2-21
Camacho, Maria R -pg. D-2-54
Camacho, Maria S -pg. D-1-33
Camacho, Maria S -pg. D-4-69
Camacho, Maria S -pg. D-11-40
Camacho, Maria S -pg. D-11-40
Camacho, Maria SN -pg. D-1-65
Camacho, Mariana P -pg. D-3-63
Camacho, Mariano R -pg. D-1-26
Camacho, Matilde M -pg. D-4-99
Camacho, Matilde S -pg. D-4-69
Camacho, Mendiola A -pg. D-13-34
Camacho, Miguel B -pg. D-5-61

Camacho, Monica M -pg. D-10-31
Camacho, Nicolasa M -pg. D-10-31
Camacho, Nicolasa R -pg. D-4-84
Camacho, Nuncia E -pg. D-4-92
Camacho, Olfa -pg. D-3-72
Camacho, Olimpia O -pg. D-5-47
Camacho, Pablo S -pg. D-11-12
Camacho, Pedro -pg. D-3-72
Camacho, Pedro -pg. D-3-74
Camacho, Pedro A -pg. D-2-10
Camacho, Pedro C -pg. D-1-68
Camacho, Pedro D -pg. D-4-92
Camacho, Pedro M -pg. D-1-13
Camacho, Pedro M -pg. D-4-69
Camacho, Pedro M -pg. D-4-99
Camacho, Pedro O -pg. D-12-6
Camacho, Pedro SN -pg. D-1-25
Camacho, Pilar -pg. D-3-72
Camacho, Pilar M -pg. D-4-93
Camacho, Rafael M -pg. D-10-31
Camacho, Raimundo D -pg. D-4-92
Camacho, Ramon C -pg. D-1-34
Camacho, Ramon O -pg. D-12-6
Camacho, Ramon SN -pg. D-1-65
Camacho, Ramona G -pg. D-2-61
Camacho, Remedio -pg. D-3-72
Camacho, Remedios R -pg. D-2-54
Camacho, Rita C -pg. D-2-40
Camacho, Rita C -pg. D-4-35
Camacho, Rita C -pg. D-11-34
Camacho, Rita M -pg. D-4-74
Camacho, Rita M -pg. D-4-108
Camacho, Rita T -pg. D-11-35
Camacho, Roman E -pg. D-4-92
Camacho, Rosa C -pg. D-5-60
Camacho, Rosa G -pg. D-11-15
Camacho, Rosa O -pg. D-5-47
Camacho, Rosa R -pg. D-2-54
Camacho, Rosa R -pg. D-4-84
Camacho, Rosa S -pg. D-1-33
Camacho, Rosa T -pg. D-1-17
Camacho, Rosalia -pg. D-3-72
Camacho, Rosalia C -pg. D-11-34
Camacho, Rosario B -pg. D-12-11
Camacho, Rosario C -pg. D-1-34
Camacho, Rosario M -pg. D-4-93
Camacho, Rosario O -pg. D-5-47
Camacho, Rosario S -pg. D-1-33
Camacho, Severino C -pg. D-4-74
Camacho, Sigena D -pg. D-4-92
Camacho, Silvestre A -pg. D-4-35
Camacho, Simeon R -pg. D-4-84
Camacho, Soledad A -pg. D-11-30
Camacho, Teodora C -pg. D-8-16
Camacho, Teresa B -pg. D-2-36
Camacho, Thomas C -pg. D-11-34
Camacho, Thomas M -pg. D-11-30
Camacho, Thomas S -pg. D-11-30
Camacho, Thomas T -pg. D-11-35

Camacho, Tomasa B -pg. D-2-69
Camacho, Tomasa S -pg. D-4-69
Camacho, Trinidad C -pg. D-1-16
Camacho, Ursula C -pg. D-11-34
Camacho, Vicenta C -pg. D-1-34
Camacho, Vicenta C -pg. D-5-60
Camacho, Vicenta R -pg. D-1-26
Camacho, Vicente A -pg. D-2-10
Camacho, Vicente A -pg. D-4-35
Camacho, Vicente C -pg. D-1-29
Camacho, Vicente C -pg. D-2-58
Camacho, Vicente C -pg. D-2-61
Camacho, Vicente C -pg. D-8-17
Camacho, Vicente D -pg. D-2-10
Camacho, Vicente D -pg. D-4-92
Camacho, Vicente M -pg. D-1-13
Camacho, Vicente O -pg. D-12-6
Camacho, Vicente P -pg. D-1-16
Camacho, Vicente P -pg. D-12-10
Camacho, Vicente Q -pg. D-2-58
Camacho, Vicente R -pg. D-4-84
Camacho, Vicente R -pg. D-5-7
Camacho, Vicente S -pg. D-12-10
Camacho, Victoriano P -pg. D-3-72
Camacho, Vincente -pg. D-13-28
Camacho, Zoilo LG -pg. D-2-73
Campbell, Harold D -pg. D-13-2
Campbell, Harold D -pg. D-13-2
Campbell, Marilyn D -pg. D-13-2
Campbell, Mildred F -pg. D-13-2
Campbell, Nancy J -pg. D-13-2
Campos, Antonia R -pg. D-3-72
Campos, Antonio -pg. D-3-72
Campos, Dominga G -pg. D-3-68
Campos, Elisa -pg. D-3-72
Campos, Joaquina A -pg. D-3-47
Campos, Jose -pg. D-3-72
Campos, Juan -pg. D-3-72
Campos, Maria -pg. D-3-73
Campos, Ramon -pg. D-3-72
Candan, Clifford K -pg. D-13-19
Candaso, Amanda D -pg. D-9-20
Candaso, Antonio T -pg. D-9-19
Candaso, Brigida D -pg. D-9-19
Candaso, Carmen D -pg. D-9-19
Candaso, Consolacion T -pg. D-9-18
Candaso, Dolores D -pg. D-9-19
Candaso, Felipe D -pg. D-9-19
Candaso, Felix D -pg. D-9-19
Candaso, Jesus T -pg. D-9-18
Candaso, Jose D -pg. D-9-19
Candaso, Jose T -pg. D-9-19
Candaso, Maria D -pg. D-9-19
Candaso, Maria D -pg. D-9-19
Candaso, Rosa D -pg. D-9-19
Candaso, Vicenta D -pg. D-9-20
Candaso, Vicente T -pg. D-9-18
Cani, Manuel C -pg. D-3-55
Cani, Maria C -pg. D-3-56

Cann, Dorothy B -pg. D-4-95
Cann, George R -pg. D-4-95
Carbuillido, Benjamin R -pg. D-6-11
Carbuillido, Catherine R -pg. D-6-11
Carbuillido, Elmer R -pg. D-6-11
Carbuillido, Rosa R -pg. D-6-11
Carbullido, Agnes B -pg. D-11-8
Carbullido, Albert Edw T -pg. D-6-5
Carbullido, Ana C -pg. D-6-13
Carbullido, Ana C -pg. D-10-4
Carbullido, Ana M -pg. D-6-3
Carbullido, Antonio P -pg. D-6-5
Carbullido, Aurelia B -pg. D-11-8
Carbullido, Baltasar B -pg. D-11-8
Carbullido, Baltasar P -pg. D-11-8
Carbullido, Charles B -pg. D-11-8
Carbullido, Clotilde C -pg. D-6-13
Carbullido, Concepcion C -pg. D-6-13
Carbullido, Consolasion C -pg. D-6-12
Carbullido, Delfina B -pg. D-11-8
Carbullido, Edward B -pg. D-11-8
Carbullido, Edward C -pg. D-6-13
Carbullido, Enriqueta T -pg. D-6-5
Carbullido, Evelyn T -pg. D-6-5
Carbullido, Felicita C -pg. D-6-13
Carbullido, Felix -pg. D-13-34
Carbullido, Felix T -pg. D-6-5
Carbullido, Felominia B -pg. D-6-10
Carbullido, Francis C -pg. D-6-13
Carbullido, Francisco M -pg. D-6-9
Carbullido, Frank C -pg. D-6-13
Carbullido, Fransisco A -pg. D-6-14
Carbullido, Helen C -pg. D-10-4
Carbullido, Hilda T -pg. D-6-5
Carbullido, Ignacio M pg. D-6-5
Carbullido, Jesus B -pg. D-6-5
Carbullido, Jesus C -pg. D-6-4
Carbullido, Joaquin C -pg. D-6-13
Carbullido, Joaquin P -pg. D-6-10
Carbullido, Jose B -pg. D-6-3
Carbullido, Jose M -pg. D-6-9
Carbullido, Josefa C -pg. D-6-4
Carbullido, Josefina C -pg. D-6-13
Carbullido, Juan -pg. D-13-28
Carbullido, Junior C -pg. D-6-13
Carbullido, Luis A -pg. D-6-14
Carbullido, Luis B -pg. D-6-10
Carbullido, Luisa M -pg. D-6-8
Carbullido, Magdalena S -pg. D-6-5
Carbullido, Manuela C -pg. D-6-13
Carbullido, Maria C -pg. D-6-13
Carbullido, Maria M -pg. D-6-9
Carbullido, Maria T -pg. D-6-5
Carbullido, Martina A -pg. D-6-14
Carbullido, Mildred C -pg. D-6-13
Carbullido, Remedios M -pg. D-6-8
Carbullido, Rita M -pg. D-6-4
Carbullido, Rosa C -pg. D-6-13
Carbullido, Ruth C -pg. D-10-4

Carbullido, Soledad M -pg. D-6-9
Carbullido, Trinidad C -pg. D-6-13
Carbullido, Vicente C -pg. D-6-14
Cardese, William -pg. D-13-22
Carlide, Charles H -pg. D-13-32
Carlyle, Bessie E -pg. D-1-10
Carring, Chelaca M -pg. D-13-34
Carrol, Anna M -pg. D-4-108
Carrol, Anna S -pg. D-4-108
Carrol, John J -pg. D-4-108
Carrol, Thomas -pg. D-4-108
Carroll, John J -pg. D-13-31
Carroll, Luis R -pg. D-13-10
Carroll, William H -pg. D-13-36
Caruso, Mario -pg. D-13-40
Carver, George A -pg. D-13-18
Casablanca, Robert -pg. D-13-44
Casaott, Elvis C -pg. D-13-41
Caseda, Bernabe -pg. D-1-56
Caspers, Frank A -pg. D-13-4
Caspers, Mary A -pg. D-13-4
Castro, Amalia -pg. D-3-9
Castro, Amalia Q -pg. D-8-43
Castro, Ana A -pg. D-2-84
Castro, Ana B -pg. D-2-67
Castro, Ana B -pg. D-5-13
Castro, Ana C -pg. D-4-64
Castro, Ana C -pg. D-8-44
Castro, Ana C -pg. D-9-10
Castro, Ana LG -pg. D-2-51
Castro, Ana LG -pg. D-8-20
Castro, Ana M -pg. D-3-29
Castro, Ana M -pg. D-13-43
Castro, Ana P -pg. D-2-17
Castro, Ana P -pg. D-8-38
Castro, Ana R -pg. D-6-2
Castro, Ana S -pg. D-1-38
Castro, Ana S -pg. D-5-89
Castro, Ana S -pg. D-6-26
Castro, Ana SN -pg. D-1-66
Castro, Ana T -pg. D-4-78
Castro, Angela P -pg. D-3-26
Castro, Angelina T -pg. D-7-11
Castro, Angusta Q -pg. D-2-33
Castro, Angustia C -pg. D-8-44
Castro, Antonia B -pg. D-2-53
Castro, Antonia LG -pg. D-3-55
Castro, Antonia LG -pg. D-8-20
Castro, Antonia T -pg. D-4-78
Castro, Antonio I -pg. D-4-78
Castro, Antonio P -pg. D-11-37
Castro, Antonio T -pg. D-10-16
Castro, Anunsia T -pg. D-7-11
Castro, Asencion C -pg. D-1-70
Castro, Asuncion R -pg. D-6-17
Castro, Atanacio P -pg. D-8-39
Castro, Atanacio P -pg. D-8-42
Castro, Brigida -pg. D-3-35
Castro, Caridad -pg. D-3-15

Castro, Carmen R -pg. D-6-17
Castro, Concepcion B -pg. D-2-67
Castro, Concepcion B -pg. D-5-13
Castro, Concepcion C -pg. D-1-23
Castro, Concepcion C -pg. D-4-47
Castro, Concepcion C -pg. D-5-16
Castro, Concepcion C -pg. D-8-47
Castro, Concepcion C -pg. D-8-47
Castro, Concepcion C -pg. D-11-22
Castro, Concepcion G -pg. D-8-44
Castro, Concepcion I -pg. D-4-72
Castro, Concepcion R -pg. D-1-44
Castro, Consalacion R -pg. D-3-40
Castro, Consalacion V -pg. D-4-63
Castro, Consolacion C -pg. D-8-44
Castro, Cristina T -pg. D-7-11
Castro, Cristobal N -pg. D-8-25
Castro, David C -pg. D-9-10
Castro, Delfina -pg. D-3-55
Castro, Delfina C -pg. D-8-47
Castro, Delfina S -pg. D-1-38
Castro, Dolores -pg. D-5-87
Castro, Dolores C -pg. D-6-2
Castro, Dolores C -pg. D-8-44
Castro, Dolores M -pg. D-2-27
Castro, Dolores S -pg. D-1-41
Castro, Dolores W -pg. D-4-89
Castro, Dominga B -pg. D-8-43
Castro, Dorothea R -pg. D-1-44
Castro, Edward G -pg. D-8-44
Castro, Elena G -pg. D-8-44
Castro, Eliza A -pg. D-8-20
Castro, Emilia -pg. D-3-41
Castro, Engracia LG -pg. D-2-51
Castro, Enrique -pg. D-3-41
Castro, Enrique M -pg. D-4-89
Castro, Enrique P -pg. D-8-38
Castro, Enrique S -pg. D-4-56
Castro, Esperanza S -pg. D-1-64
Castro, Esther C -pg. D-8-47
Castro, Evelyna V -pg. D-4-64
Castro, Felix -pg. D-3-29
Castro, Felix -pg. D-3-41
Castro, Felix P -pg. D-4-47
Castro, Felix P -pg. D-4-53
Castro, Felix R -pg. D-5-46
Castro, Feliza S -pg. D-1-67
Castro, Fernando A -pg. D-5-61
Castro, Florencia C -pg. D-1-23
Castro, Florentina C -pg. D-9-10
Castro, Francisco A -pg. D-3-16
Castro, Francisco B -pg. D-2-53
Castro, Francisco C -pg. D-8-8
Castro, Francisco F -pg. D-2-74
Castro, Francisco P -pg. D-4-52
Castro, Francisco Q -pg. D-2-33
Castro, Francisco R -pg. D-1-44
Castro, Francisco R -pg. D-2-51
Castro, Francisco S -pg. D-11-10

Castro, Francisco T -pg. D-7-11
Castro, Francisco W -pg. D-4-47
Castro, Gertrudes LG -pg. D-8-20
Castro, Gertrudes M -pg. D-1-63
Castro, Gloria N -pg. D-8-25
Castro, Gregorio C -pg. D-1-70
Castro, Gregorio LG -pg. D-2-51
Castro, Herman V -pg. D-4-64
Castro, Honedina -pg. D-3-9
Castro, Ignacio C -pg. D-8-44
Castro, Ignacio J -pg. D-5-86
Castro, Ignacio L -pg. D-1-63
Castro, Ignacio P -pg. D-8-44
Castro, Ignacio T -pg. D-7-11
Castro, Isabel -pg. D-5-88
Castro, Jesus -pg. D-5-88
Castro, Jesus B -pg. D-2-53
Castro, Jesus B -pg. D-5-13
Castro, Jesus C -pg. D-1-33
Castro, Jesus C -pg. D-2-53
Castro, Jesus C -pg. D-9-10
Castro, Jesus C -pg. D-13-28
Castro, Jesus D -pg. D-2-82
Castro, Jesus LG -pg. D-8-25
Castro, Jesus P -pg. D-8-38
Castro, Jesus P -pg. D-8-43
Castro, Jesus S -pg. D-1-63
Castro, Jesus SN -pg. D-1-66
Castro, Jesus SN -pg. D-5-25
Castro, Jesus T -pg. D-10-16
Castro, Jesus M -pg. D-5-88
Castro, Joaquin C -pg. D-8-44
Castro, Joaquin LG -pg. D-8-20
Castro, Joaquin O -pg. D-5-58
Castro, Joaquina -pg. D-3-41
Castro, Joaquina C -pg. D-1-60
Castro, Joaquina P -pg. D-4-52
Castro, Joaquina R -pg. D-2-53
Castro, Joaquina S -pg. D-1-63
Castro, Joaquina SN -pg. D-5-25
Castro, Jose -pg. D-3-9
Castro, Jose -pg. D-3-41
Castro, Jose A -pg. D-1-67
Castro, Jose A -pg. D-8-20
Castro, Jose B -pg. D-2-53
Castro, Jose B -pg. D-2-67
Castro, Jose B -pg. D-5-13
Castro, Jose C -pg. D-1-23
Castro, Jose C -pg. D-1-38
Castro, Jose C -pg. D-1-70
Castro, Jose C -pg. D-4-63
Castro, Jose C -pg. D-5-62
Castro, Jose C -pg. D-6-17
Castro, Jose C -pg. D-8-42
Castro, Jose C -pg. D-8-44
Castro, Jose C -pg. D-9-10
Castro, Jose D -pg. D-2-82
Castro, Jose D -pg. D-8-20
Castro, Jose F -pg. D-3-26

Castro, Jose G -pg. D-3-55
Castro, Jose G -pg. D-8-44
Castro, Jose L -pg. D-8-42
Castro, Jose LG -pg. D-1-53
Castro, Jose LG -pg. D-8-20
Castro, Jose M -pg. D-1-63
Castro, Jose M -pg. D-5-89
Castro, Jose P -pg. D-4-56
Castro, Jose P -pg. D-8-43
Castro, Jose R -pg. D-6-17
Castro, Jose R -pg. D-11-10
Castro, Jose R -pg. D-12-19
Castro, Jose S -pg. D-1-64
Castro, Jose S -pg. D-1-67
Castro, Jose S -pg. D-4-56
Castro, Jose S -pg. D-4-56
Castro, Jose T -pg. D-7-11
Castro, Jose T -pg. D-10-16
Castro, Josefa C -pg. D-3-16
Castro, Josefa C -pg. D-9-10
Castro, Josefa G -pg. D-2-52
Castro, Josefa S -pg. D-5-89
Castro, Josefa T -pg. D-4-78
Castro, Josefa M T -pg. D-7-11
Castro, Josefina -pg. D-3-41
Castro, Juan B -pg. D-2-53
Castro, Juan B -pg. D-5-13
Castro, Juan B -pg. D-8-43
Castro, Juan C -pg. D-1-33
Castro, Juan C -pg. D-1-60
Castro, Juan C -pg. D-1-70
Castro, Juan C -pg. D-2-52
Castro, Juan C -pg. D-2-74
Castro, Juan C -pg. D-3-29
Castro, Juan C -pg. D-7-11
Castro, Juan D -pg. D-2-82
Castro, Juan F -pg. D-2-74
Castro, Juan H -pg. D-4-89
Castro, Juan P -pg. D-2-82
Castro, Juan P -pg. D-8-38
Castro, Juan Q -pg. D-2-33
Castro, Juan R -pg. D-5-37
Castro, Juan R -pg. D-6-2
Castro, Juan S -pg. D-1-38
Castro, Juan S -pg. D-12-18
Castro, Juan S -pg. D-13-34
Castro, Juan SN -pg. D-5-25
Castro, Juan T -pg. D-10-16
Castro, Juana M -pg. D-2-26
Castro, Juana R -pg. D-8-46
Castro, Julia C -pg. D-8-44
Castro, Julia LG -pg. D-2-52
Castro, Julita -pg. D-3-9
Castro, Julita B -pg. D-5-13
Castro, Leocadio -pg. D-3-55
Castro, Leonardo F -pg. D-2-74
Castro, Leonicio I -pg. D-4-36
Castro, Leonora C -pg. D-1-23
Castro, Librada M -pg. D-2-27
Castro, Librada P -pg. D-8-39

Castro, Librada P -pg. D-8-39
Castro, Lourdes LG -pg. D-2-51
Castro, Lourdes T -pg. D-7-11
Castro, Lucas R -pg. D-2-33
Castro, Lucia C -pg. D-1-23
Castro, Luis P -pg. D-5-13
Castro, Luis R -pg. D-5-23
Castro, Manuel B -pg. D-2-53
Castro, Manuel C -pg. D-4-64
Castro, Manuel P -pg. D-4-52
Castro, Manuel R -pg. D-5-58
Castro, Manuel S -pg. D-1-63
Castro, Manuela D -pg. D-2-82
Castro, Marcos A -pg. D-1-62
Castro, Margarita -pg. D-8-20
Castro, Margarita LG -pg. D-2-52
Castro, Margarita P -pg. D-4-47
Castro, Margarita S -pg. D-6-26
Castro, Maria -pg. D-5-87
Castro, Maria B -pg. D-2-53
Castro, Maria B -pg. D-2-53
Castro, Maria B -pg. D-5-13
Castro, Maria C -pg. D-1-23
Castro, Maria C -pg. D-1-33
Castro, Maria C -pg. D-3-9
Castro, Maria C -pg. D-3-15
Castro, Maria C -pg. D-5-23
Castro, Maria C -pg. D-5-58
Castro, Maria C -pg. D-8-44
Castro, Maria C -pg. D-9-10
Castro, Maria F -pg. D-2-74
Castro, Maria F -pg. D-5-39
Castro, Maria G -pg. D-2-74
Castro, Maria I -pg. D-4-36
Castro, Maria L -pg. D-8-7
Castro, Maria LG -pg. D-2-51
Castro, Maria M -pg. D-4-89
Castro, Maria N -pg. D-8-25
Castro, Maria P -pg. D-4-47
Castro, Maria P -pg. D-4-53
Castro, Maria P -pg. D-8-42
Castro, Maria Q -pg. D-2-27
Castro, Maria R -pg. D-1-44
Castro, Maria R -pg. D-2-53
Castro, Maria R -pg. D-6-17
Castro, Maria S -pg. D-1-38
Castro, Maria S -pg. D-11-10
Castro, Maria SN -pg. D-5-25
Castro, Maria T -pg. D-10-16
Castro, Maria T -pg. D-12-8
Castro, Maria U -pg. D-2-53
Castro, Mariano C -pg. D-1-33
Castro, Mariano C -pg. D-2-66
Castro, Mariano LG -pg. D-2-17
Castro, Matilde B -pg. D-2-53
Castro, Mercedes L -pg. D-3-37
Castro, Miguel S -pg. D-5-87
Castro, Natividad -pg. D-3-55
Castro, Natividad M -pg. D-8-8

Castro, Nicolas M -pg. D-5-88
Castro, Nieves R -pg. D-2-53
Castro, Ojenia R -pg. D-1-44
Castro, Pedro -pg. D-3-15
Castro, Pedro C -pg. D-1-44
Castro, Pedro D -pg. D-5-25
Castro, Pedro Q -pg. D-2-27
Castro, Pedro S -pg. D-1-70
Castro, Pedro SN -pg. D-5-25
Castro, Pedro T -pg. D-10-16
Castro, Pilar S -pg. D-1-38
Castro, Rafael -pg. D-3-55
Castro, Ramon C -pg. D-4-47
Castro, Ramon O -pg. D-9-10
Castro, Ramon S -pg. D-1-38
Castro, Ramon S -pg. D-1-66
Castro, Ramona -pg. D-5-87
Castro, Regina -pg. D-3-8
Castro, Regina M -pg. D-4-89
Castro, Remedios C -pg. D-5-23
Castro, Rita B -pg. D-2-67
Castro, Rita C -pg. D-4-64
Castro, Rita C -pg. D-8-44
Castro, Rita C -pg. D-8-44
Castro, Rita I -pg. D-3-29
Castro, Rita M -pg. D-5-87
Castro, Rita N -pg. D-8-25
Castro, Rodolfo V -pg. D-4-63
Castro, Roman P -pg. D-8-39
Castro, Rosa B -pg. D-3-8
Castro, Rosa L -pg. D-11-24
Castro, Rosa LG -pg. D-2-44
Castro, Rosa P -pg. D-10-11
Castro, Rosa S -pg. D-4-56
Castro, Rosa T -pg. D-10-16
Castro, Rosalina C -pg. D-8-47
Castro, Rosario C -pg. D-1-23
Castro, Rufina SN -pg. D-5-25
Castro, Santiago -pg. D-3-37
Castro, Santiago C -pg. D-2-27
Castro, Santiago M -pg. D-4-89
Castro, Santiago R -pg. D-6-17
Castro, Saturnina T -pg. D-10-16
Castro, Soledad C -pg. D-11-37
Castro, Sylvia Maria -pg. D-1-12
Castro, Teresa C -pg. D-13-43
Castro, Teresa Q -pg. D-2-33
Castro, Theresa R -pg. D-6-17
Castro, Tomas LG -pg. D-2-51
Castro, Tomas R -pg. D-6-2
Castro, Trinidad C -pg. D-1-33
Castro, Trinidad L -pg. D-1-63
Castro, Trinidat -pg. D-3-8
Castro, Veronica S -pg. D-6-26
Castro, Vicenta B -pg. D-5-13
Castro, Vicenta C -pg. D-1-23
Castro, Vicenta C -pg. D-5-23
Castro, Vicenta S -pg. D-1-41
Castro, Vicenta S -pg. D-5-88

Castro, Vicente B -pg. D-12-8
Castro, Vicente C -pg. D-1-33
Castro, Vicente C -pg. D-3-8
Castro, Vicente C -pg. D-5-23
Castro, Vicente C -pg. D-8-47
Castro, Vicente C -pg. D-9-10
Castro, Vicente G -pg. D-8-44
Castro, Vicente I -pg. D-3-29
Castro, Vicente I -pg. D-5-39
Castro, Vicente L -pg. D-8-20
Castro, Vicente M -pg. D-1-63
Castro, Vicente P -pg. D-5-16
Castro, Vicente P -pg. D-8-44
Castro, Vicente R -pg. D-1-44
Castro, Vicente S -pg. D-5-89
Castro, Vicente S -pg. D-6-26
Castro, Virginia P -pg. D-8-38
Castro, Virginia R -pg. D-1-44
Cato, Paul D -pg. D-13-22
Caye, Maurice -pg. D-13-5
Celes, Brigida T -pg. D-4-9
Celes, Guadalupe T -pg. D-4-9
Celes, Jesus T -pg. D-4-9
Celes, Joaquin I -pg. D-4-71
Celes, Jose I -pg. D-4-9
Celes, Jose T -pg. D-4-9
Celes, Juan T -pg. D-4-9
Celes, Nieves T -pg. D-4-9
Cepeda, Agnes G -pg. D-5-9
Cepeda, Alfredo C -pg. D-1-7
Cepeda, Amanda -pg. D-3-13
Cepeda, Ana A -pg. D-4-82
Cepeda, Ana B -pg. D-1-32
Cepeda, Ana C -pg. D-1-38
Cepeda, Ana C -pg. D-1-64
Cepeda, Ana C -pg. D-5-9
Cepeda, Ana C -pg. D-8-15
Cepeda, Ana F -pg. D-4-78
Cepeda, Ana L -pg. D-4-103
Cepeda, Andrea Q -pg. D-8-32
Cepeda, Antonia C -pg. D-8-15
Cepeda, Antonia M -pg. D-1-18
Cepeda, Antonio M -pg. D-1-18
Cepeda, Barcelisa A -pg. D-4-81
Cepeda, Carmen -pg. D-3-13
Cepeda, Charlie F -pg. D-1-18
Cepeda, Dolores -pg. D-3-48
Cepeda, Dolores F -pg. D-4-78
Cepeda, Dolores T -pg. D-8-28
Cepeda, Emeliana G -pg. D-5-9
Cepeda, Esperanza -pg. D-3-55
Cepeda, Ester T -pg. D-8-28
Cepeda, Evelia -pg. D-3-48
Cepeda, Feleberto T -pg. D-8-28
Cepeda, Francisca P -pg. D-5-62
Cepeda, Francisca Q -pg. D-4-66
Cepeda, Francisco -pg. D-3-13
Cepeda, Francisco C -pg. D-4-103
Cepeda, Francisco C -pg. D-5-9

Cepeda, Francisco F -pg. D-4-78
Cepeda, Francisco S -pg. D-10-18
Cepeda, Gloria -pg. D-3-48
Cepeda, Gregoria C -pg. D-8-32
Cepeda, Ignacia A -pg. D-4-81
Cepeda, Ignacia M -pg. D-1-18
Cepeda, Ignacio -pg. D-3-13
Cepeda, Isabel C -pg. D-4-78
Cepeda, Isabel P -pg. D-5-62
Cepeda, Jesus -pg. D-3-13
Cepeda, Jesus -pg. D-3-55
Cepeda, Jesus M -pg. D-5-9
Cepeda, Jesus Q -pg. D-5-34
Cepeda, Jesus S -pg. D-4-74
Cepeda, Joaquin C -pg. D-4-74
Cepeda, Joaquin C -pg. D-8-28
Cepeda, Joaquin Q -pg. D-4-66
Cepeda, Joaquina B -pg. D-5-7
Cepeda, Joaquina M C -pg. D-1-6
Cepeda, Jose -pg. D-3-13
Cepeda, Jose -pg. D-3-55
Cepeda, Jose -pg. D-4-81
Cepeda, Jose B -pg. D-13-22
Cepeda, Jose C -pg. D-1-31
Cepeda, Jose C -pg. D-1-64
Cepeda, Jose C -pg. D-4-76
Cepeda, Jose M -pg. D-5-9
Cepeda, Jose P -pg. D-5-62
Cepeda, Jose S -pg. D-3-13
Cepeda, Jose SN -pg. D-4-63
Cepeda, Josefa B -pg. D-1-32
Cepeda, Josefa D -pg. D-1-61
Cepeda, Josefina -pg. D-3-13
Cepeda, Josefina R -pg. D-4-102
Cepeda, Juan -pg. D-3-55
Cepeda, Juan C -pg. D-1-32
Cepeda, Juan C -pg. D-4-62
Cepeda, Juan C -pg. D-4-66
Cepeda, Juan C -pg. D-12-19
Cepeda, Juan M -pg. D-4-66
Cepeda, Juan M -pg. D-4-102
Cepeda, Juan Q -pg. D-4-66
Cepeda, Juan S -pg. D-5-62
Cepeda, Juan S -pg. D-10-18
Cepeda, Juana G -pg. D-5-9
Cepeda, Julia C -pg. D-5-9
Cepeda, Leon M -pg. D-1-18
Cepeda, Leonila -pg. D-3-13
Cepeda, Lourdes C -pg. D-4-74
Cepeda, Lourdes C -pg. D-4-76
Cepeda, Magarita S -pg. D-10-18
Cepeda, Manuel -pg. D-10-18
Cepeda, Manuel B -pg. D-1-32
Cepeda, Manuel S -pg. D-10-18
Cepeda, Marcela C -pg. D-1-64
Cepeda, Maria -pg. D-3-13
Cepeda, Maria -pg. D-3-48
Cepeda, Maria A -pg. D-4-81
Cepeda, Maria A -pg. D-5-34

Cepeda, Maria B -pg. D-3-48
Cepeda, Maria C -pg. D-3-13
Cepeda, Maria C -pg. D-3-55
Cepeda, Maria C -pg. D-4-76
Cepeda, Maria L -pg. D-4-103
Cepeda, Maria M -pg. D-1-18
Cepeda, Maria P -pg. D-5-62
Cepeda, Maria R -pg. D-1-31
Cepeda, Maria S -pg. D-4-75
Cepeda, Maria T -pg. D-8-28
Cepeda, Milagro A -pg. D-5-34
Cepeda, Natibida M -pg. D-1-18
Cepeda, Natividad G -pg. D-5-9
Cepeda, Nicolasa C -pg. D-5-9
Cepeda, Nieves M -pg. D-4-52
Cepeda, Pancracio M -pg. D-1-18
Cepeda, Pancracio M -pg. D-5-50
Cepeda, Paz R -pg. D-1-31
Cepeda, Pedro -pg. D-3-55
Cepeda, Pedro -pg. D-13-30
Cepeda, Pedro F -pg. D-4-78
Cepeda, Pedro LG -pg. D-1-6
Cepeda, Pedro S -pg. D-10-18
Cepeda, Ramona SN -pg. D-4-62
Cepeda, Rita Q -pg. D-4-66
Cepeda, Rita S -pg. D-10-18
Cepeda, Rosa A -pg. D-4-82
Cepeda, Rosa B -pg. D-1-32
Cepeda, Rosa C -pg. D-5-9
Cepeda, Rosa Q -pg. D-4-66
Cepeda, Rosa R -pg. D-4-102
Cepeda, Rosa T -pg. D-8-28
Cepeda, Teresa C -pg. D-8-15
Cepeda, Tomas A -pg. D-4-81
Cepeda, Tomas C -pg. D-4-75
Cepeda, Trinidad -pg. D-3-13
Cepeda, Trinidad Q -pg. D-4-66
Cepeda, Vicenta C -pg. D-4-74
Cepeda, Vicente -pg. D-3-55
Cepeda, Vicente C -pg. D-1-6
Cepeda, Vicente C -pg. D-8-15
Cepeda, Vicente LG -pg. D-4-90
Cepeda, Vicente M -pg. D-1-18
Cepeda, Vicente R -pg. D-1-31
Cepeda, Vicente S -pg. D-5-7
Cepeda, Virginia -pg. D-3-55
Cepedes, Crecencia S -pg. D-2-22
Cepedes, Gregorio S -pg. D-2-22
Cepedes, Josefa S -pg. D-2-22
Cepedes, Leopaldo S -pg. D-2-22
Cepedes, Samuel S -pg. D-2-22
Certeza, Agapito Q -pg. D-10-20
Certeza, Atanasio Q -pg. D-10-19
Certeza, Delfin Q -pg. D-10-20
Certeza, Evelino Q -pg. D-10-20
Certeza, Gabriel A -pg. D-10-19
Certeza, Javier Q -pg. D-10-20
Certeza, Maria Q -pg. D-10-19
Chaco, Ana B -pg. D-6-12

Chaco, Ana C -pg. D-6-10
Chaco, Antonio C -pg. D-6-25
Chaco, Antonio Q -pg. D-6-9
Chaco, Antonio R -pg. D-6-30
Chaco, Asuncion S -pg. D-6-8
Chaco, Beatrice R -pg. D-6-10
Chaco, Carmen R -pg. D-6-37
Chaco, Cary C -pg. D-6-12
Chaco, Concepcion A -pg. D-6-25
Chaco, Dolores C -pg. D-6-12
Chaco, Engracia C -pg. D-6-30
Chaco, Felipe Q -pg. D-6-12
Chaco, Francisco C -pg. D-6-10
Chaco, Francisco R -pg. D-6-12
Chaco, Frank C -pg. D-6-12
Chaco, Graciosa C -pg. D-6-12
Chaco, Guadalupe A -pg. D-6-25
Chaco, Ignasio L -pg. D-6-16
Chaco, Jesus C -pg. D-6-10
Chaco, Jesus C -pg. D-6-30
Chaco, Jesus R -pg. D-6-10
Chaco, Jesus S -pg. D-6-8
Chaco, Joaquin A -pg. D-6-25
Chaco, Joaquin R -pg. D-13-28
Chaco, Joaquina R -pg. D-6-37
Chaco, Jose Q -pg. D-6-37
Chaco, Jose R -pg. D-6-9
Chaco, Juan C -pg. D-6-12
Chaco, Juan R -pg. D-13-28
Chaco, Manuel A -pg. D-6-25
Chaco, Manuel Q -pg. D-6-10
Chaco, Margarita L -pg. D-6-16
Chaco, Maria C -pg. D-6-30
Chaco, Maria R -pg. D-6-10
Chaco, Mariano Q -pg. D-6-16
Chaco, Mercedes C -pg. D-6-16
Chaco, Milagro R -pg. D-6-9
Chaco, Regina R -pg. D-6-10
Chaco, Slate C -pg. D-6-12
Chaco, Soledad A -pg. D-6-25
Chaco, Soledad R -pg. D-6-10
Chaco, Sylvia S -pg. D-6-8
Chaco, Tomas R -pg. D-6-37
Chaco, Vicente R -pg. D-6-9
Chaco, Victoriana LG -pg. D-6-12
Champaco, Ana E -pg. D-9-25
Champaco, Ana M -pg. D-9-29
Champaco, Ana T -pg. D-10-3
Champaco, Antonio C -pg. D-9-26
Champaco, Asuncion M -pg. D-9-29
Champaco, Dolores E -pg. D-9-24
Champaco, Felicita C -pg. D-9-25
Champaco, Isabel T -pg. D-9-29
Champaco, Jesus C -pg. D-9-5
Champaco, Joaquina E -pg. D-11-32
Champaco, Jose E -pg. D-9-24
Champaco, Jose M -pg. D-9-29
Champaco, Jose T -pg. D-10-3
Champaco, Josefina T -pg. D-10-3

Champaco, Juan C -pg. D-9-24
Champaco, Juan C -pg. D-9-26
Champaco, Luisa A -pg. D-2-70
Champaco, Maria C -pg. D-9-14
Champaco, Maria M -pg. D-9-29
Champaco, Mariano M -pg. D-9-29
Champaco, Pedro E -pg. D-9-29
Champaco, Rosa T -pg. D-10-3
Champaco, Rosalia M -pg. D-9-29
Champaco, Vicente M -pg. D-9-29
Champaco, Vincente A -pg. D-13-28
Chance, Hannah -pg. D-4-87
Chance, Harriet C -pg. D-4-87
Chance, Harry -pg. D-4-87
Chance, Harry P -pg. D-4-87
Chance, John W -pg. D-4-88
Chance, Martha -pg. D-4-88
Chance, Rosa C -pg. D-4-88
Chance, Rosario -pg. D-4-87
Chance, Woodrow -pg. D-4-87
Chandler, Evedine J -pg. D-4-97
Chandler, Frederick N -pg. D-4-97
Chandler, Frederick O -pg. D-4-97
Chandler, Harriet O -pg. D-4-97
Chandler, Isabel O -pg. D-4-97
Charfauros, Ana B -pg. D-6-11
Charfauros, Andres C -pg. D-11-17
Charfauros, Angelina D -pg. D-6-25
Charfauros, Antonio B -pg. D-6-25
Charfauros, Antonio C -pg. D-9-40
Charfauros, Arthur L -pg. D-9-5
Charfauros, Baldobino D -pg. D-4-105
Charfauros, Barbara L -pg. D-9-5
Charfauros, Carlos A -pg. D-1-66
Charfauros, Carlota C -pg. D-9-39
Charfauros, Carmela B -pg. D-6-13
Charfauros, Carmen B -pg. D-6-11
Charfauros, Carmen C -pg. D-1-70
Charfauros, Carmen SN -pg. D-6-24
Charfauros, Edward B -pg. D-11-4
Charfauros, Emma C L -pg. D-9-5
Charfauros, Felix B -pg. D-6-11
Charfauros, Felix C -pg. D-9-40
Charfauros, Felix L -pg. D-6-39
Charfauros, Francisco -pg. D-4-38
Charfauros, Francisco M -pg. D-6-35
Charfauros, Francisco N -pg. D-6-6
Charfauros, Fransisco SN -pg. D-6-24
Charfauros, George L -pg. D-9-5
Charfauros, Ignasia N -pg. D-6-6
Charfauros, Ignasio N -pg. D-6-6
Charfauros, James B -pg. D-6-24
Charfauros, Jesus A -pg. D-6-19
Charfauros, Jesus B -pg. D-6-11
Charfauros, Jesus B -pg. D-6-13
Charfauros, Jesus C -pg. D-9-39
Charfauros, Joaquin A -pg. D-1-65
Charfauros, Joaquin C -pg. D-9-40
Charfauros, Joaquin L -pg. D-6-17

Charfauros, Joaquin N -pg. D-6-6
Charfauros, Joaquin T -pg. D-11-51
Charfauros, Joaquina L -pg. D-9-5
Charfauros, Jose A -pg. D-6-8
Charfauros, Jose C -pg. D-9-39
Charfauros, Jose C -pg. D-11-17
Charfauros, Jose F -pg. D-11-5
Charfauros, Jose L -pg. D-6-31
Charfauros, Jose M -pg. D-6-35
Charfauros, Jose N -pg. D-6-6
Charfauros, Josefa C -pg. D-9-40
Charfauros, Joseph B -pg. D-11-4
Charfauros, Juan B -pg. D-6-11
Charfauros, Juan B -pg. D-6-24
Charfauros, Juan B -pg. D-11-5
Charfauros, Juan C -pg. D-6-35
Charfauros, Juan L -pg. D-1-53
Charfauros, Juan S -pg. D-6-22
Charfauros, Juan T -pg. D-9-39
Charfauros, Juana SN -pg. D-6-24
Charfauros, Louise L -pg. D-9-5
Charfauros, Lucia C -pg. D-9-21
Charfauros, Lydia B -pg. D-6-12
Charfauros, Manuel -pg. D-9-5
Charfauros, Manuel S -pg. D-6-22
Charfauros, Marcela M -pg. D-6-35
Charfauros, Margarita A -pg. D-2-55
Charfauros, Maria B -pg. D-6-13
Charfauros, Maria C -pg. D-9-39
Charfauros, Maria C -pg. D-11-17
Charfauros, Maria L -pg. D-3-63
Charfauros, Maria M -pg. D-6-35
Charfauros, Maria SN -pg. D-6-24
Charfauros, Maria SN -pg. D-6-24
Charfauros, Maria T -pg. D-9-43
Charfauros, Mariana A -pg. D-1-65
Charfauros, Mariano A -pg. D-6-24
Charfauros, Mariano F -pg. D-6-6
Charfauros, Pedro C -pg. D-6-12
Charfauros, Ramon A -pg. D-1-65
Charfauros, Ramon T -pg. D-6-31
Charfauros, Regina C -pg. D-3-63
Charfauros, Rita S -pg. D-4-105
Charfauros, Rita T -pg. D-6-31
Charfauros, Rosa B -pg. D-6-24
Charfauros, Rosa B -pg. D-11-4
Charfauros, Teodora F -pg. D-11-5
Charfauros, Tomas C -pg. D-6-24
Charfauros, Vicente B -pg. D-6-25
Charfauros, Victoria M -pg. D-6-35
Charfauros, Vinancio B -pg. D-6-11
Charfauros, Virginia B -pg. D-6-12
Charfauros, William L -pg. D-9-5
Charfauros, Antonio B -pg. D-6-14
Charfauros, Consalasion C -pg. D-6-14
Charfauros, Ignasio C -pg. D-6-14
Charfauros, Luis A -pg. D-6-14
Charfauros, Luis B -pg. D-6-14
Charfauros, Rosa C -pg. D-6-14

Chargualaf, Adela SN -pg. D-8-18
Chargualaf, Agustin M -pg. D-4-58
Chargualaf, Alice C -pg. D-9-15
Chargualaf, Ana -pg. D-3-52
Chargualaf, Ana A -pg. D-6-34
Chargualaf, Ana A -pg. D-9-17
Chargualaf, Ana A -pg. D-10-2
Chargualaf, Ana L -pg. D-8-7
Chargualaf, Ana R -pg. D-5-42
Chargualaf, Ana R -pg. D-5-42
Chargualaf, Ana T -pg. D-7-12
Chargualaf, Angel -pg. D-3-2
Chargualaf, Angelina -pg. D-11-7
Chargualaf, Angelina C -pg. D-9-22
Chargualaf, Antonia C -pg. D-4-58
Chargualaf, Antonia Q -pg. D-9-14
Chargualaf, Antonio -pg. D-3-2
Chargualaf, Antonio -pg. D-5-56
Chargualaf, Antonio S -pg. D-7-9
Chargualaf, Augustin T -pg. D-6-34
Chargualaf, Barsalisa T -pg. D-2-55
Chargualaf, Bernadita C -pg. D-4-58
Chargualaf, Candelaria N -pg. D-9-26
Chargualaf, Carlos -pg. D-3-14
Chargualaf, Carmela S -pg. D-7-8
Chargualaf, Carmen M -pg. D-8-6
Chargualaf, Cecilia -pg. D-3-25
Chargualaf, Consolacion C -pg. D-10-3
Chargualaf, Consolacion S -pg. D-11-26
Chargualaf, Crecencio M -pg. D-9-17
Chargualaf, Cristina T -pg. D-8-37
Chargualaf, Dimas B -pg. D-9-27
Chargualaf, Dolores M -pg. D-8-30
Chargualaf, Dolores R -pg. D-3-25
Chargualaf, Dolores S -pg. D-7-8
Chargualaf, Dolores T -pg. D-7-18
Chargualaf, Domitila M -pg. D-8-30
Chargualaf, Ediviges M -pg. D-8-30
Chargualaf, Eduardo C -pg. D-10-3
Chargualaf, Elias C -pg. D-4-103
Chargualaf, Eliza A -pg. D-9-18
Chargualaf, Encarnacion T -pg. D-7-18
Chargualaf, Enrique C -pg. D-10-2
Chargualaf, Esperanza -pg. D-10-2
Chargualaf, Estefania SN -pg. D-8-28
Chargualaf, Eugenio C -pg. D-7-12
Chargualaf, Eulogio P -pg. D-5-41
Chargualaf, Florentina T -pg. D-8-23
Chargualaf, Francisco C -pg. D-9-15
Chargualaf, Francisco M -pg. D-8-23
Chargualaf, Francisco M -pg. D-8-30
Chargualaf, Francisco Q -pg. D-7-8
Chargualaf, Francisco R -pg. D-3-14
Chargualaf, Francisco S -pg. D-7-9
Chargualaf, Frank T -pg. D-2-55
Chargualaf, Froilan M -pg. D-8-6
Chargualaf, Genoveba C -pg. D-6-18
Chargualaf, Germonimo T -pg. D-9-7
Chargualaf, Gertrudes C -pg. D-4-103

Chargualaf, Gregorio C -pg. D-4-16
Chargualaf, Ignacio C -pg. D-6-6
Chargualaf, Inigo C -pg. D-9-25
Chargualaf, Isabel D -pg. D-8-6
Chargualaf, Isabel LG -pg. D-5-38
Chargualaf, Jacobo B -pg. D-9-26
Chargualaf, Jesus -pg. D-7-9
Chargualaf, Jesus M -pg. D-8-23
Chargualaf, Jesus M -pg. D-8-30
Chargualaf, Jesusa C -pg. D-9-15
Chargualaf, Joaquin C -pg. D-3-52
Chargualaf, Joaquina F? -pg. D-11-3
Chargualaf, Joaquina S -pg. D-7-8
Chargualaf, Jose -pg. D-3-14
Chargualaf, Jose A -pg. D-6-34
Chargualaf, Jose B -pg. D-6-29
Chargualaf, Jose M -pg. D-8-18
Chargualaf, Jose N -pg. D-8-6
Chargualaf, Jose R -pg. D-3-2
Chargualaf, Jose R -pg. D-3-25
Chargualaf, Jose S -pg. D-7-8
Chargualaf, Jose SN -pg. D-5-41
Chargualaf, Jose SN -pg. D-8-28
Chargualaf, Jose T -pg. D-8-23
Chargualaf, Jose T -pg. D-8-30
Chargualaf, Jose T -pg. D-9-7
Chargualaf, Jose T. -pg. D-8-50
Chargualaf, Josefa M -pg. D-8-32
Chargualaf, Josefa T -pg. D-8-23
Chargualaf, Josefina C -pg. D-6-18
Chargualaf, Josefina T -pg. D-2-55
Chargualaf, Juan B -pg. D-9-17
Chargualaf, Juan C -pg. D-6-18
Chargualaf, Juan C -pg. D-10-3
Chargualaf, Juan N -pg. D-8-18
Chargualaf, Juan P -pg. D-5-41
Chargualaf, Juan R -pg. D-5-42
Chargualaf, Juan R -pg. D-5-42
Chargualaf, Juan L -pg. D-6-19
Chargualaf, Julia -pg. D-3-14
Chargualaf, Juliana T -pg. D-9-7
Chargualaf, Julita R -pg. D-5-42
Chargualaf, Justo C -pg. D-4-58
Chargualaf, Justo Q -pg. D-7-18
Chargualaf, Justo T -pg. D-8-35
Chargualaf, Lorenza A -pg. D-9-18
Chargualaf, Lorenzo P -pg. D-5-41
Chargualaf, Lucas M -pg. D-8-7
Chargualaf, Lucia M -pg. D-8-25
Chargualaf, Luis M -pg. D-8-18
Chargualaf, Magdalena I -pg. D-3-2
Chargualaf, Manuel SN -pg. D-5-38
Chargualaf, Manuela A -pg. D-9-17
Chargualaf, Margarita C -pg. D-10-3
Chargualaf, Maria -pg. D-3-2
Chargualaf, Maria A -pg. D-9-15
Chargualaf, Maria C -pg. D-3-14
Chargualaf, Maria C -pg. D-4-58
Chargualaf, Maria C -pg. D-6-18

Chargualaf, Maria C -pg. D-9-15
Chargualaf, Maria L -pg. D-4-108
Chargualaf, Maria M -pg. D-8-30
Chargualaf, Maria S -pg. D-7-9
Chargualaf, Maria SN -pg. D-8-18
Chargualaf, Maria T -pg. D-7-18
Chargualaf, Mariano B -pg. D-9-14
Chargualaf, Mariano T -pg. D-9-7
Chargualaf, Natividad C -pg. D-9-25
Chargualaf, Nicolas A -pg. D-9-17
Chargualaf, Pedro C -pg. D-4-58
Chargualaf, Pedro SN -pg. D-8-29
Chargualaf, Preciosa S -pg. D-7-9
Chargualaf, Rafael -pg. D-13-34
Chargualaf, Ramon M -pg. D-8-13
Chargualaf, Ramon M -pg. D-8-28
Chargualaf, Ramon T -pg. D-8-28
Chargualaf, Rita C -pg. D-4-58
Chargualaf, Rita S -pg. D-11-26
Chargualaf, Rosa A -pg. D-9-17
Chargualaf, Rosa L -pg. D-11-27
Chargualaf, Rosa SN -pg. D-8-18
Chargualaf, Rosalia A -pg. D-9-17
Chargualaf, Rosalia C -pg. D-11-35
Chargualaf, Rosario S -pg. D-7-9
Chargualaf, Santiago T -pg. D-7-18
Chargualaf, Sergio -pg. D-3-25
Chargualaf, Vicente -pg. D-3-14
Chargualaf, Vicente A -pg. D-9-18
Chargualaf, Vicente C -pg. D-4-58
Chargualaf, Vicente C -pg. D-6-6
Chargualaf, Vicente C -pg. D-9-15
Chargualaf, Vicente SN -pg. D-8-28
Charguane, Francisco T -pg. D-11-34
Charguane, Maria C -pg. D-11-34
Charguiya, Rita B -pg. D-12-5
Charlasuro, Anthony -pg. D-13-15
Charsaguas, Concepcion S -pg. D-3-4
Chase, Donald W -pg. D-13-15
Chaves, Edward G -pg. D-13-41
Cheguina, Catalina S -pg. D-9-31
Cheguina, Francisco S -pg. D-9-31
Cheguina, Joaquina S -pg. D-9-31
Cheguina, Jose S -pg. D-9-35
Cheguina, Josefa S -pg. D-9-31
Cheguina, Maxima S -pg. D-9-31
Cheguina, Polocarpio A -pg. D-9-31
Cheguina, Regina S -pg. D-9-31
Cheguina, Vicente A -pg. D-9-37
Chiguina, Antonio M -pg. D-1-53
Chiguina, Enrique M -pg. D-7-24
Chiguina, Jesus M -pg. D-8-27
Chiguina, Jose Q -pg. D-5-19
Chiguina, Juan LG -pg. D-8-35
Chiguina, Juan M -pg. D-8-35
Chiguina, Julia LG -pg. D-8-35
Chiguina, Lagrimas LG -pg. D-8-35
Chiguina, Magdalena -pg. D-8-26
Chiguina, Marcelo M -pg. D-5-19

Chiguina, Maria N -pg. D-8-2
Chiguina, Maria P -pg. D-2-62
Chiguina, Maria Q -pg. D-5-19
Chiguina, Monica C -pg. D-8-26
Chiquina, Jesus D -pg. D-8-18
Chisinski, Alex -pg. D-13-45
Chiyska, Gordon S -pg. D-13-36
Chrickshank, Harold E -pg. D-13-10
Christian, Frank P -pg. D-13-5
Clache, George T -pg. D-13-22
Clapper, Daniel R -pg. D-13-5
Clark, Alfred B -pg. D-13-5
Clark, Francis S -pg. D-13-36
Clark, Gordon T -pg. D-1-47
Clark, Rodney A -pg. D-1-47
Clark, Ruth V -pg. D-1-47
Claveria, Francisco P -pg. D-2-74
Claveria, Juan A -pg. D-2-74
Claveria, Vicenta P -pg. D-2-74
Cleofas, Sixto C -pg. D-4-35
Cloughley, Constance J -pg. D-1-54
Cloughley, Janet W -pg. D-1-54
Cloughly, Sterling T -pg. D-13-44
Cobb, Lesley F -pg. D-13-10
Coffer, Albert R -pg. D-13-10
Collette, Edwin R -pg. D-13-22
Collier, Zadek -pg. D-13-40
Colner, Andy -pg. D-1-6
Colner, Concepcion U -pg. D-1-6
Colner, Frank U -pg. D-1-6
Colner, Howard U -pg. D-1-6
Colner, Mary U -pg. D-1-6
Colner, Ruth U -pg. D-1-6
Coluns, Ralph G -pg. D-13-5
Comado, Concepcion SN -pg. D-8-41
Comado, Guardalupe SN -pg. D-8-41
Comado, Juan P -pg. D-8-41
Comado, Juan SN -pg. D-8-41
Comado, Maria SN -pg. D-8-41
Comado, Prudencio SN -pg. D-8-41
Comado, Remedios SN -pg. D-8-41
Coman, Alex R -pg. D-13-19
Combs, Elmer G -pg. D-13-19
Comer, Ernest M -pg. D-13-5
Conant, Arnold M -pg. D-13-19
Concepcion, Ana A -pg. D-4-68
Concepcion, Ana B -pg. D-9-30
Concepcion, Ana C -pg. D-3-7
Concepcion, Ana C -pg. D-4-25
Concepcion, Ana C -pg. D-4-66
Concepcion, Ana L -pg. D-11-23
Concepcion, Ana Q -pg. D-10-31
Concepcion, Antonia C -pg. D-4-68
Concepcion, Antonia M -pg. D-3-5
Concepcion, Antonio -pg. D-13-28
Concepcion, Antonio D -pg. D-11-22
Concepcion, Antonio Q -pg. D-10-31
Concepcion, Asuncion P -pg. D-10-11
Concepcion, Atanacio A -pg. D-4-25

Concepcion, Balbino T -pg. D-11-20
Concepcion, Biatres C -pg. D-10-24
Concepcion, Carmen B -pg. D-9-16
Concepcion, Catalina P -pg. D-11-6
Concepcion, Clara D -pg. D-11-32
Concepcion, Consolacion H -pg. D-4-72
Concepcion, Cristina C -pg. D-10-24
Concepcion, Cristobal D -pg. D-11-38
Concepcion, Delfina D -pg. D-11-38
Concepcion, Dolores A -pg. D-4-16
Concepcion, Dolores C -pg. D-11-32
Concepcion, Eduviges D -pg. D-11-38
Concepcion, Engracia C -pg. D-10-24
Concepcion, Enrique A -pg. D-4-25
Concepcion, Enrique D -pg. D-11-38
Concepcion, Enrique P -pg. D-11-6
Concepcion, Enrique S -pg. D-11-5
Concepcion, Enrique T -pg. D-11-20
Concepcion, Enriqueta C -pg. D-12-8
Concepcion, Estela C -pg. D-3-5
Concepcion, Felicita A -pg. D-4-25
Concepcion, Felipe -pg. D-3-7
Concepcion, Francisco P -pg. D-11-6
Concepcion, Gertrudes S -pg. D-10-36
Concepcion, Gregorio Q -pg. D-10-31
Concepcion, Guadalupe A -pg. D-4-25
Concepcion, Hazel C -pg. D-4-66
Concepcion, Hinara L -pg. D-11-22
Concepcion, Inocencio P -pg. D-11-6
Concepcion, Jesus A -pg. D-4-68
Concepcion, Jesus A -pg. D-5-9
Concepcion, Jesus C -pg. D-10-25
Concepcion, Jesus LG -pg. D-4-66
Concepcion, Jesus P -pg. D-10-11
Concepcion, Jesus Q -pg. D-10-30
Concepcion, Jesus R -pg. D-4-104
Concepcion, Joaquin -pg. D-10-30
Concepcion, Joaquin C -pg. D-4-66
Concepcion, Joaquin Q -pg. D-10-31
Concepcion, Jose A -pg. D-4-68
Concepcion, Jose A -pg. D-5-9
Concepcion, Jose C -pg. D-10-36
Concepcion, Jose C -pg. D-13-34
Concepcion, Jose G -pg. D-3-5
Concepcion, Jose M -pg. D-3-7
Concepcion, Jose P -pg. D-10-11
Concepcion, Jose Q -pg. D-10-30
Concepcion, Jose R -pg. D-9-16
Concepcion, Jose T -pg. D-11-19
Concepcion, Josefa D -pg. D-11-19
Concepcion, Josefina H -pg. D-4-72
Concepcion, Juan -pg. D-13-22
Concepcion, Juan A -pg. D-4-25
Concepcion, Juan C -pg. D-4-25
Concepcion, Juan C -pg. D-4-66
Concepcion, Juan C -pg. D-13-34
Concepcion, Juan L -pg. D-11-23
Concepcion, Juan Q -pg. D-10-31
Concepcion, Juan S -pg. D-11-19

Concepcion, Juan T -pg. D-11-19
Concepcion, Juana P -pg. D-4-24
Concepcion, Juana P -pg. D-11-6
Concepcion, Julia A -pg. D-4-68
Concepcion, Magdalena C -pg. D-4-66
Concepcion, Manuel A -pg. D-4-68
Concepcion, Manuel A -pg. D-5-9
Concepcion, Manuel C -pg. D-4-72
Concepcion, Manuel C -pg. D-10-25
Concepcion, Manuel C -pg. D-13-28
Concepcion, Manuel Q -pg. D-10-31
Concepcion, Maria B -pg. D-9-16
Concepcion, Maria C -pg. D-2-42
Concepcion, Maria C -pg. D-4-66
Concepcion, Maria C -pg. D-10-24
Concepcion, Maria D -pg. D-11-38
Concepcion, Maria LG -pg. D-4-66
Concepcion, Maria Q -pg. D-10-30
Concepcion, Maria U -pg. D-4-104
Concepcion, Pedro A -pg. D-4-25
Concepcion, Ramon G -pg. D-7-24
Concepcion, Ramon R -pg. D-9-14
Concepcion, Rosa B -pg. D-9-16
Concepcion, Rosa G -pg. D-4-68
Concepcion, Rosa M -pg. D-10-5
Concepcion, Rosario A -pg. D-4-68
Concepcion, Rosario C -pg. D-4-66
Concepcion, Soledad T -pg. D-11-20
Concepcion, Susana A -pg. D-4-16
Concepcion, Teodoro D -pg. D-11-38
Concepcion, Teresa A -pg. D-4-25
Concepcion, Tomas A -pg. D-3-75
Concepcion, Tomas B -pg. D-9-16
Concepcion, Tomasa P -pg. D-10-11
Concepcion, Vicente H -pg. D-4-72
Concepcion, Vicente R -pg. D-4-104
Concepcion, Vicente U -pg. D-4-104
Conrad, Constant F -pg. D-13-15
Contreras, Vicente M -pg. D-10-10
Cook, Harvey M -pg. D-13-5
Cooper, Charles P -pg. D-13-40
Cooper, Milton H -pg. D-13-44
Cooper, Raymond M -pg. D-13-36
Coppersmith, Ora D -pg. D-13-41
Corine, William O -pg. D-13-15
Cortez, Felix -pg. D-13-22
Coryell, Fred -pg. D-13-45
Covington, Edward J -pg. D-13-44
Cox, Dolores B -pg. D-11-2
Cox, John W -pg. D-13-10
Cox, O.J. -pg. D-11-2
Cramtere, Kenneth B -pg. D-13-19
Cranit, John F -pg. D-13-10
Crawford, Ardere Y -pg. D-13-10
Crisostimo, Ambrosio P -pg. D-4-64
Crisostimo, Ana P -pg. D-4-121
Crisostimo, Angel P -pg. D-4-42
Crisostimo, Antonio P -pg. D-4-119
Crisostimo, Antonio P -pg. D-4-123

Crisostimo, Celestine P -pg. D-4-64
Crisostimo, Concepcion P -pg. D-4-119
Crisostimo, Concepcion R -pg. D-4-119
Crisostimo, Dolores -pg. D-4-25
Crisostimo, Dolores C -pg. D-4-118
Crisostimo, Dolores P -pg. D-4-29
Crisostimo, Dolores P -pg. D-4-64
Crisostimo, Estoquia C -pg. D-4-123
Crisostimo, Faustino C -pg. D-4-119
Crisostimo, Felecita A -pg. D-4-42
Crisostimo, Felicita P -pg. D-4-64
Crisostimo, Felomenia P -pg. D-4-29
Crisostimo, Francisco V -pg. D-4-29
Crisostimo, Jesus R -pg. D-4-119
Crisostimo, Joaquin P -pg. D-4-119
Crisostimo, Jose A -pg. D-4-3
Crisostimo, Jose P -pg. D-4-29
Crisostimo, Jose P -pg. D-4-64
Crisostimo, Jose T -pg. D-4-119
Crisostimo, Josefa A -pg. D-4-3
Crisostimo, Josefa P -pg. D-4-121
Crisostimo, Josefina V -pg. D-4-29
Crisostimo, Juan P -pg. D-4-29
Crisostimo, Juan P -pg. D-4-118
Crisostimo, Marcelo C -pg. D-4-120
Crisostimo, Maria A -pg. D-4-3
Crisostimo, Maria C -pg. D-4-123
Crisostimo, Maria P -pg. D-4-121
Crisostimo, Maria R -pg. D-4-119
Crisostimo, Maria T -pg. D-4-119
Crisostimo, Mariano P -pg. D-4-64
Crisostimo, Nicolasa A -pg. D-4-42
Crisostimo, Pacita V -pg. D-4-29
Crisostimo, Pedro -pg. D-4-3
Crisostimo, Pedro C -pg. D-4-123
Crisostimo, Primitiva V -pg. D-4-29
Crisostimo, Purification V -pg. D-4-29
Crisostimo, Ramona C -pg. D-4-123
Crisostimo, Teresa A -pg. D-4-42
Crisostimo, Vicenta P -pg. D-4-118
Crisostomo, Ana -pg. D-8-10
Crisostomo, Ana A -pg. D-2-35
Crisostomo, Ana C -pg. D-2-20
Crisostomo, Ana C -pg. D-2-66
Crisostomo, Ana G -pg. D-5-87
Crisostomo, Ana M -pg. D-11-36
Crisostomo, Ana P -pg. D-8-24
Crisostomo, Ana SN -pg. D-5-79
Crisostomo, Angel C -pg. D-5-83
Crisostomo, Angel M -pg. D-8-24
Crisostomo, Antonia F -pg. D-7-15
Crisostomo, Antonio C -pg. D-2-12
Crisostomo, Antonio C -pg. D-2-20
Crisostomo, Anunsacion P -pg. D-8-24
Crisostomo, Attemio R -pg. D-1-11
Crisostomo, Augustia -pg. D-1-18
Crisostomo, Brigida -pg. D-3-36
Crisostomo, Concepcion M -pg. D-11-36
Crisostomo, Concepcion SA -pg. D-5-17

Crisostomo, Delfina -pg. D-5-79
Crisostomo, Desiderio -pg. D-3-36
Crisostomo, Dionisio F -pg. D-2-66
Crisostomo, Dolores A -pg. D-2-35
Crisostomo, Dolores F -pg. D-2-66
Crisostomo, Dolores M -pg. D-11-36
Crisostomo, Doroteo SA -pg. D-5-17
Crisostomo, Elena M -pg. D-8-10
Crisostomo, Encarnacion -pg. D-5-90
Crisostomo, Felipe -pg. D-5-79
Crisostomo, Felix -pg. D-3-36
Crisostomo, Felix C -pg. D-5-79
Crisostomo, Francisco -pg. D-5-75
Crisostomo, Francisco -pg. D-5-83
Crisostomo, Francisco B -pg. D-2-26
Crisostomo, Francisco M -pg. D-11-36
Crisostomo, Francisco SA -pg. D-5-17
Crisostomo, Genaro M -pg. D-11-35
Crisostomo, German -pg. D-5-87
Crisostomo, Gregorio -pg. D-5-83
Crisostomo, Ignacia F -pg. D-2-66
Crisostomo, Ignacia M -pg. D-11-35
Crisostomo, Isabel M -pg. D-11-36
Crisostomo, Jesus -pg. D-5-80
Crisostomo, Jesus -pg. D-5-90
Crisostomo, Jesus -pg. D-8-10
Crisostomo, Jesus A -pg. D-2-26
Crisostomo, Jesus C -pg. D-2-13
Crisostomo, Jesus C -pg. D-5-90
Crisostomo, Jesus D -pg. D-5-75
Crisostomo, Jesus P -pg. D-3-36
Crisostomo, Jesus P -pg. D-8-24
Crisostomo, Joaquin A -pg. D-2-35
Crisostomo, Joaquin M -pg. D-2-35
Crisostomo, Joaquin M -pg. D-8-10
Crisostomo, Joaquin M -pg. D-8-16
Crisostomo, Joaquina P -pg. D-5-83
Crisostomo, Jose -pg. D-5-80
Crisostomo, Jose -pg. D-5-83
Crisostomo, Jose C -pg. D-5-82
Crisostomo, Jose C -pg. D-10-32
Crisostomo, Jose D -pg. D-2-66
Crisostomo, Jose LG -pg. D-8-16
Crisostomo, Jose M -pg. D-8-10
Crisostomo, Jose M -pg. D-11-36
Crisostomo, Jose R -pg. D-1-11
Crisostomo, Josefa D -pg. D-2-20
Crisostomo, Josefina C -pg. D-8-24
Crisostomo, Juan -pg. D-3-11
Crisostomo, Juan A -pg. D-2-35
Crisostomo, Juan B -pg. D-5-75
Crisostomo, Juan C -pg. D-11-23
Crisostomo, Juan P -pg. D-1-63
Crisostomo, Juan SA -pg. D-5-17
Crisostomo, Juan T -pg. D-7-15
Crisostomo, Juana S -pg. D-5-4
Crisostomo, Juana S -pg. D-5-4
Crisostomo, Lourdes -pg. D-5-87
Crisostomo, Lourdes S -pg. D-5-4

Crisostomo, Luisa G -pg. D-5-87
Crisostomo, Luisa R -pg. D-1-11
Crisostomo, Manuel -pg. D-8-10
Crisostomo, Manuela C -pg. D-2-20
Crisostomo, Margarita M -pg. D-11-36
Crisostomo, Maria -pg. D-3-36
Crisostomo, Maria A -pg. D-5-98
Crisostomo, Maria B -pg. D-2-26
Crisostomo, Maria C -pg. D-2-20
Crisostomo, Maria C -pg. D-5-75
Crisostomo, Maria C -pg. D-5-75
Crisostomo, Maria C -pg. D-5-82
Crisostomo, Maria F -pg. D-2-66
Crisostomo, Maria F -pg. D-2-66
Crisostomo, Maria LG -pg. D-8-16
Crisostomo, Maria M -pg. D-11-35
Crisostomo, Maria P -pg. D-8-24
Crisostomo, Maria R -pg. D-1-11
Crisostomo, Mariano -pg. D-5-75
Crisostomo, Mariano -pg. D-5-82
Crisostomo, Mariano B -pg. D-5-4
Crisostomo, Mecaila C -pg. D-2-12
Crisostomo, Miguel C -pg. D-1-63
Crisostomo, Nicolasa -pg. D-5-80
Crisostomo, Pedro C -pg. D-2-66
Crisostomo, Pedro LG -pg. D-8-16
Crisostomo, Pedro M -pg. D-8-10
Crisostomo, Pilar -pg. D-5-75
Crisostomo, Rafael C -pg. D-2-20
Crisostomo, Ramon J -pg. D-11-35
Crisostomo, Romana A -pg. D-5-87
Crisostomo, Rosa C -pg. D-3-10
Crisostomo, Rosa M -pg. D-8-10
Crisostomo, Rosalia -pg. D-5-80
Crisostomo, Rosalina -pg. D-5-90
Crisostomo, Sebastian F -pg. D-7-15
Crisostomo, Soledad -pg. D-3-36
Crisostomo, Soledad M -pg. D-11-35
Crisostomo, Teodoro -pg. D-5-79
Crisostomo, Tomas C -pg. D-2-20
Crisostomo, Vicente -pg. D-3-36
Crisostomo, Vicente C -pg. D-2-12
Crisostomo, Vicente C -pg. D-2-20
Crisostomo, Vicente C -pg. D-8-10
Crisostomo, Vicente F -pg. D-7-16
Crisostomo, Vicente LG -pg. D-8-16
Crisostomo, Vicente P -pg. D-1-11
Crisostomo, Vicente S -pg. D-5-4
Crisostomo, Vicente SA -pg. D-5-17
Cristobal, Adriano M -pg. D-4-43
Cristobal, Adriano U -pg. D-4-44
Cristobal, Carmen U -pg. D-4-43
Cristobal, Eduviges U -pg. D-4-44
Cristobal, Fe U -pg. D-4-44
Cristobal, George U -pg. D-4-44
Crorides, Lule Q -pg. D-13-22
Cross, Koltis C -pg. D-13-36
Crowley, Joseph F -pg. D-13-32
Crullena, Clemente -pg. D-13-22

Cruz, Guadalupe R -pg. D-11-24
Cruz, Adela C -pg. D-4-58
Cruz, Adela C -pg. D-5-8
Cruz, Adelaid C -pg. D-10-4
Cruz, Agnes A -pg. D-9-13
Cruz, Agustin -pg. D-3-69
Cruz, Agustin S -pg. D-5-65
Cruz, Agustina C -pg. D-10-18
Cruz, Albert F -pg. D-4-43
Cruz, Alejandro P -pg. D-4-91
Cruz, Alfonsina -pg. D-3-12
Cruz, Amable B -pg. D-4-24
Cruz, Amadeo Artemio A -pg. D-12-18
Cruz, Amparo T -pg. D-4-103
Cruz, Ana -pg. D-3-7
Cruz, Ana -pg. D-3-8
Cruz, Ana -pg. D-3-11
Cruz, Ana -pg. D-3-65
Cruz, Ana -pg. D-5-80
Cruz, Ana -pg. D-8-11
Cruz, Ana A -pg. D-2-11
Cruz, Ana A -pg. D-4-100
Cruz, Ana A -pg. D-9-13
Cruz, Ana A -pg. D-11-17
Cruz, Ana A -pg. D-11-21
Cruz, Ana B -pg. D-2-36
Cruz, Ana B -pg. D-3-10
Cruz, Ana B -pg. D-5-31
Cruz, Ana B -pg. D-5-46
Cruz, Ana B -pg. D-6-40
Cruz, Ana B -pg. D-10-11
Cruz, Ana B -pg. D-11-25
Cruz, Ana C -pg. D-3-8
Cruz, Ana C -pg. D-3-69
Cruz, Ana C -pg. D-4-3
Cruz, Ana C -pg. D-4-4
Cruz, Ana C -pg. D-4-23
Cruz, Ana C -pg. D-5-42
Cruz, Ana C -pg. D-6-20
Cruz, Ana C -pg. D-6-20
Cruz, Ana C -pg. D-9-12
Cruz, Ana C -pg. D-9-21
Cruz, Ana C -pg. D-10-18
Cruz, Ana D -pg. D-2-16
Cruz, Ana G -pg. D-1-50
Cruz, Ana G -pg. D-2-20
Cruz, Ana G -pg. D-4-35
Cruz, Ana G -pg. D-5-80
Cruz, Ana J -pg. D-6-15
Cruz, Ana M -pg. D-4-13
Cruz, Ana P -pg. D-4-126
Cruz, Ana P -pg. D-5-51
Cruz, Ana Q -pg. D-13-43
Cruz, Ana R -pg. D-1-7
Cruz, Ana R -pg. D-1-59
Cruz, Ana R -pg. D-2-84
Cruz, Ana R -pg. D-9-2
Cruz, Ana S -pg. D-2-55
Cruz, Ana S -pg. D-4-31

Cruz, Ana S -pg. D-6-17
Cruz, Ana S -pg. D-9-23
Cruz, Ana S -pg. D-10-21
Cruz, Ana T -pg. D-2-32
Cruz, Ana T -pg. D-2-32
Cruz, Ana T -pg. D-4-103
Cruz, Ana T -pg. D-6-8
Cruz, Ana T -pg. D-12-2
Cruz, Ana T -pg. D-12-18
Cruz, Ana U -pg. D-5-99
Cruz, Anacleto D -pg. D-4-44
Cruz, Andesina C -pg. D-5-8
Cruz, Andrea G -pg. D-2-20
Cruz, Andrea M -pg. D-4-71
Cruz, Angel F -pg. D-4-7
Cruz, Angela S -pg. D-10-36
Cruz, Angelina L -pg. D-4-77
Cruz, Angelina LG -pg. D-3-9
Cruz, Angustia R -pg. D-4-86
Cruz, Anparo -pg. D-3-32
Cruz, Antonia A -pg. D-4-15
Cruz, Antonia A -pg. D-4-34
Cruz, Antonia B -pg. D-4-117
Cruz, Antonia M -pg. D-5-76
Cruz, Antonia O -pg. D-6-34
Cruz, Antonia P -pg. D-1-18
Cruz, Antonia S -pg. D-4-11
Cruz, Antonia S -pg. D-4-31
Cruz, Antonio -pg. D-3-32
Cruz, Antonio -pg. D-3-35
Cruz, Antonio -pg. D-3-46
Cruz, Antonio -pg. D-3-55
Cruz, Antonio -pg. D-3-65
Cruz, Antonio -pg. D-5-71
Cruz, Antonio -pg. D-5-80
Cruz, Antonio A -pg. D-1-59
Cruz, Antonio B -pg. D-1-53
Cruz, Antonio B -pg. D-5-31
Cruz, Antonio B -pg. D-6-40
Cruz, Antonio B -pg. D-11-26
Cruz, Antonio C -pg. D-1-27
Cruz, Antonio C -pg. D-3-41
Cruz, Antonio C -pg. D-4-50
Cruz, Antonio C -pg. D-5-21
Cruz, Antonio C -pg. D-6-21
Cruz, Antonio C -pg. D-6-29
Cruz, Antonio C -pg. D-9-20
Cruz, Antonio D -pg. D-11-47
Cruz, Antonio G -pg. D-2-20
Cruz, Antonio G -pg. D-5-31
Cruz, Antonio I -pg. D-3-75
Cruz, Antonio LG -pg. D-4-102
Cruz, Antonio LG -pg. D-9-7
Cruz, Antonio P -pg. D-4-58
Cruz, Antonio Q -pg. D-5-80
Cruz, Antonio Q -pg. D-10-26
Cruz, Antonio Q -pg. D-11-26
Cruz, Antonio R -pg. D-1-59
Cruz, Antonio R -pg. D-4-4

Cruz, Antonio S -pg. D-10-21
Cruz, Antonio T -pg. D-4-20
Cruz, Antonio T -pg. D-4-103
Cruz, Apolanaria -pg. D-1-41
Cruz, Asuncion C -pg. D-4-4
Cruz, Asuncion N -pg. D-10-29
Cruz, Asuncion P -pg. D-1-18
Cruz, Asuncion T -pg. D-3-65
Cruz, Asuncion R -pg. D-4-85
Cruz, Augusto P -pg. D-1-18
Cruz, Aurelia -pg. D-3-46
Cruz, Baltazara S -pg. D-4-30
Cruz, Barcilisa -pg. D-5-80
Cruz, Bartola J -pg. D-6-18
Cruz, Beatrice T -pg. D-1-3
Cruz, Beatris T -pg. D-4-53
Cruz, Benita C -pg. D-9-19
Cruz, Benito S -pg. D-10-21
Cruz, Bernadita S -pg. D-4-11
Cruz, Bernardino L -pg. D-4-27
Cruz, Bruno F -pg. D-4-115
Cruz, Candelaria -pg. D-3-15
Cruz, Candelaria P -pg. D-4-91
Cruz, Candelaria T -pg. D-4-53
Cruz, Candelaria T -pg. D-6-8
Cruz, Candelario B -pg. D-4-85
Cruz, Caridad S -pg. D-10-21
Cruz, Caridad T -pg. D-11-16
Cruz, Carlos J -pg. D-5-29
Cruz, Carlos P -pg. D-4-2
Cruz, Carlos P -pg. D-13-27
Cruz, Carlos Q -pg. D-12-20
Cruz, Carlos T -pg. D-5-24
Cruz, Carlota K -pg. D-2-20
Cruz, Carmen -pg. D-5-68
Cruz, Carmen A -pg. D-3-41
Cruz, Carmen A -pg. D-4-50
Cruz, Carmen A -pg. D-11-16
Cruz, Carmen B -pg. D-10-11
Cruz, Carmen C -pg. D-3-46
Cruz, Carmen C -pg. D-6-21
Cruz, Carmen C -pg. D-9-20
Cruz, Carmen D -pg. D-6-8
Cruz, Carmen N -pg. D-4-4
Cruz, Carmen P -pg. D-1-19
Cruz, Carmen P -pg. D-8-14
Cruz, Carmen SN -pg. D-6-18
Cruz, Carmen SN -pg. D-6-18
Cruz, Catalina -pg. D-3-15
Cruz, Catalina -pg. D-3-42
Cruz, Catalina A -pg. D-9-10
Cruz, Catalina F -pg. D-2-12
Cruz, Cecilia -pg. D-3-9
Cruz, Cecilia -pg. D-3-46
Cruz, Cecilia B -pg. D-4-46
Cruz, Cecilia D -pg. D-3-40
Cruz, Clotilde -pg. D-3-11
Cruz, Clotilde S -pg. D-10-21
Cruz, Concepcion -pg. D-3-11

Cruz, Concepcion -pg. D-3-11
Cruz, Concepcion A -pg. D-2-25
Cruz, Concepcion C -pg. D-4-45
Cruz, Concepcion C -pg. D-4-80
Cruz, Concepcion C -pg. D-5-21
Cruz, Concepcion L -pg. D-4-27
Cruz, Concepcion LG -pg. D-4-61
Cruz, Concepcion P -pg. D-2-84
Cruz, Concepcion R -pg. D-12-3
Cruz, Concepcion SN -pg. D-4-75
Cruz, Consalacion C -pg. D-4-23
Cruz, Consolacion -pg. D-5-97
Cruz, Consolacion LG -pg. D-4-42
Cruz, Constantino -pg. D-3-46
Cruz, Cristina T -pg. D-7-12
Cruz, Cristina U -pg. D-11-7
Cruz, Cristobal LG -pg. D-11-2
Cruz, Cristobal Q -pg. D-12-3
Cruz, David M -pg. D-4-111
Cruz, David T -pg. D-5-44
Cruz, Delfina A -pg. D-4-100
Cruz, Delfina A -pg. D-9-10
Cruz, Delfina C -pg. D-4-80
Cruz, Delfina M -pg. D-4-71
Cruz, Delgadina S -pg. D-10-36
Cruz, Delores J -pg. D-6-15
Cruz, Delores LG -pg. D-11-6
Cruz, Delores S -pg. D-6-17
Cruz, Demetrio G -pg. D-1-49
Cruz, Dimas A -pg. D-9-13
Cruz, Dolores -pg. D-3-10
Cruz, Dolores -pg. D-5-97
Cruz, Dolores A -pg. D-1-59
Cruz, Dolores A -pg. D-9-10
Cruz, Dolores A -pg. D-10-6
Cruz, Dolores B -pg. D-3-10
Cruz, Dolores C -pg. D-3-69
Cruz, Dolores C -pg. D-4-42
Cruz, Dolores C -pg. D-5-36
Cruz, Dolores C -pg. D-6-20
Cruz, Dolores C -pg. D-9-19
Cruz, Dolores C -pg. D-9-20
Cruz, Dolores C -pg. D-11-10
Cruz, Dolores G -pg. D-1-24
Cruz, Dolores G -pg. D-4-93
Cruz, Dolores G -pg. D-9-11
Cruz, Dolores L -pg. D-4-27
Cruz, Dolores M -pg. D-2-49
Cruz, Dolores M -pg. D-5-4
Cruz, Dolores O -pg. D-4-18
Cruz, Dolores O -pg. D-6-34
Cruz, Dolores P -pg. D-3-15
Cruz, Dolores P -pg. D-4-58
Cruz, Dolores Q -pg. D-10-34
Cruz, Dolores R -pg. D-4-55
Cruz, Dolores T -pg. D-4-77
Cruz, Dolores T -pg. D-12-11
Cruz, Dolores W -pg. D-2-81
Cruz, Dometila Q -pg. D-12-3

Cruz, Dominga P -pg. D-2-46
Cruz, Dominga P -pg. D-4-2
Cruz, Domingo A -pg. D-4-4
Cruz, Donecio T -pg. D-1-43
Cruz, Eduardo -pg. D-3-8
Cruz, Edward C -pg. D-9-41
Cruz, Edward D -pg. D-1-50
Cruz, Edward R -pg. D-4-85
Cruz, Elena B -pg. D-10-11
Cruz, Elena C -pg. D-5-21
Cruz, Elena G -pg. D-2-40
Cruz, Elena T -pg. D-5-44
Cruz, Elizabeth T -pg. D-5-24
Cruz, Elude T -pg. D-5-24
Cruz, Emeterio -pg. D-3-8
Cruz, Emilia D -pg. D-10-7
Cruz, Emilia H -pg. D-10-33
Cruz, Emilia R -pg. D-4-85
Cruz, Emmanuel T -pg. D-5-44
Cruz, Encarnacio A -pg. D-11-31
Cruz, Encarnacion -pg. D-3-15
Cruz, Encarnacion C -pg. D-9-10
Cruz, Enes C -pg. D-11-25
Cruz, Engracia -pg. D-3-65
Cruz, Engracia C -pg. D-2-76
Cruz, Engracia D -pg. D-2-16
Cruz, Engracia S -pg. D-4-31
Cruz, Engranacion P -pg. D-4-91
Cruz, Enrique -pg. D-3-8
Cruz, Enrique -pg. D-13-22
Cruz, Enrique A -pg. D-11-9
Cruz, Enrique A -pg. D-12-11
Cruz, Enrique D -pg. D-6-40
Cruz, Enrique C -pg. D-4-50
Cruz, Enrique C -pg. D-11-33
Cruz, Enrique LG -pg. D-4-42
Cruz, Enrique M -pg. D-1-9
Cruz, Enrique P -pg. D-2-46
Cruz, Enrique R -pg. D-4-55
Cruz, Enrique T -pg. D-12-11
Cruz, Enriques N -pg. D-4-4
Cruz, Enriqueta T -pg. D-6-20
Cruz, Estella C -pg. D-5-8
Cruz, Estella R -pg. D-4-85
Cruz, Eufracia N -pg. D-4-11
Cruz, Eugene P -pg. D-13-32
Cruz, Eugenia A -pg. D-2-25
Cruz, Eugenio -pg. D-3-40
Cruz, Eulalia P -pg. D-3-55
Cruz, Felecita C -pg. D-4-35
Cruz, Felicidad C -pg. D-11-6
Cruz, Felicidad T -pg. D-4-95
Cruz, Felicita D -pg. D-1-50
Cruz, Felicita P -pg. D-11-46
Cruz, Felipe A -pg. D-5-38
Cruz, Felipe D -pg. D-2-49
Cruz, Felipe S -pg. D-9-24
Cruz, Felis R -pg. D-4-55
Cruz, Felix -pg. D-3-7

Cruz, Felix -pg. D-5-68
Cruz, Felix A -pg. D-2-11
Cruz, Felix A -pg. D-4-103
Cruz, Felix C -pg. D-1-53
Cruz, Felix C -pg. D-2-63
Cruz, Felix C -pg. D-5-95
Cruz, Felix D -pg. D-2-16
Cruz, Felix D -pg. D-8-32
Cruz, Felix F -pg. D-1-53
Cruz, Felix S -pg. D-6-38
Cruz, Felix S -pg. D-10-36
Cruz, Felix SN -pg. D-6-18
Cruz, Felix T -pg. D-4-103
Cruz, Fermina C -pg. D-5-21
Cruz, Fidela LG -pg. D-5-38
Cruz, Filomena C -pg. D-4-73
Cruz, Filomena Q -pg. D-5-49
Cruz, Filomenia C -pg. D-4-58
Cruz, Flora C -pg. D-6-29
Cruz, Flora LG -pg. D-11-6
Cruz, Florentina C -pg. D-9-19
Cruz, Francisca C -pg. D-4-68
Cruz, Francisca E -pg. D-9-13
Cruz, Francisca M -pg. D-4-71
Cruz, Francisca M -pg. D-5-49
Cruz, Francisca P -pg. D-3-49
Cruz, Francisca P -pg. D-5-51
Cruz, Francisca SN -pg. D-11-50
Cruz, Francisco -pg. D-3-6
Cruz, Francisco -pg. D-3-7
Cruz, Francisco -pg. D-3-11
Cruz, Francisco -pg. D-3-15
Cruz, Francisco -pg. D-3-69
Cruz, Francisco -pg. D-5-71
Cruz, Francisco A -pg. D-1-12
Cruz, Francisco A -pg. D-2-11
Cruz, Francisco B -pg. D-4-55
Cruz, Francisco B -pg. D-6-20
Cruz, Francisco C -pg. D-2-76
Cruz, Francisco C -pg. D-4-52
Cruz, Francisco C -pg. D-4-68
Cruz, Francisco C -pg. D-4-95
Cruz, Francisco C -pg. D-5-21
Cruz, Francisco C -pg. D-12-8
Cruz, Francisco D -pg. D-8-9
Cruz, Francisco G -pg. D-1-48
Cruz, Francisco G -pg. D-4-93
Cruz, Francisco G -pg. D-5-47
Cruz, Francisco J -pg. D-2-68
Cruz, Francisco J -pg. D-7-22
Cruz, Francisco LG -pg. D-4-116
Cruz, Francisco M -pg. D-1-18
Cruz, Francisco M -pg. D-4-111
Cruz, Francisco P -pg. D-1-18
Cruz, Francisco P -pg. D-2-46
Cruz, Francisco P -pg. D-4-45
Cruz, Francisco P -pg. D-8-14
Cruz, Francisco S -pg. D-5-34
Cruz, Francisco S -pg. D-10-14

Cruz, Francisco S -pg. D-10-21
Cruz, Francisco T -pg. D-1-43
Cruz, Francisco T -pg. D-4-20
Cruz, Francisco T -pg. D-4-53
Cruz, Francisco T -pg. D-4-99
Cruz, Francisco T -pg. D-5-29
Cruz, Francisco T -pg. D-6-18
Cruz, Francisco T -pg. D-12-2
Cruz, Franscico C -pg. D-9-25
Cruz, Froilan D -pg. D-11-2
Cruz, Gabriel S -pg. D-10-34
Cruz, Galo U -pg. D-11-7
Cruz, German -pg. D-3-65
Cruz, Geronimo D -pg. D-2-16
Cruz, Gertrudes C -pg. D-9-20
Cruz, Gertrudes T -pg. D-5-29
Cruz, Gloria -pg. D-3-65
Cruz, Gloria B -pg. D-12-20
Cruz, Gonsalo T -pg. D-12-2
Cruz, Gonzalo C -pg. D-6-20
Cruz, Gonzalo R -pg. D-9-2
Cruz, Gregorio A -pg. D-2-11
Cruz, Gregorio A -pg. D-10-6
Cruz, Gregorio B -pg. D-4-14
Cruz, Gregorio C -pg. D-5-42
Cruz, Gregorio Q -pg. D-5-94
Cruz, Gregorio S -pg. D-4-31
Cruz, Gregorio S -pg. D-11-4
Cruz, Gregorio T -pg. D-6-20
Cruz, Guadalup D -pg. D-1-50
Cruz, Guadalupe C -pg. D-11-4
Cruz, Guadalupe M -pg. D-11-23
Cruz, Guillermo H -pg. D-10-33
Cruz, Henry F -pg. D-4-43
Cruz, Henry M -pg. D-4-71
Cruz, Herman F -pg. D-4-7
Cruz, Hermanigildo G -pg. D-4-100
Cruz, Hinara C -pg. D-11-31
Cruz, Ignacia C -pg. D-3-69
Cruz, Ignacia C -pg. D-5-8
Cruz, Ignacia G -pg. D-1-47
Cruz, Ignacia H -pg. D-5-26
Cruz, Ignacia I -pg. D-4-81
Cruz, Ignacio -pg. D-5-68
Cruz, Ignacio A -pg. D-1-59
Cruz, Ignacio A -pg. D-4-100
Cruz, Ignacio A -pg. D-11-16
Cruz, Ignacio A -pg. D-11-21
Cruz, Ignacio B -pg. D-11-16
Cruz, Ignacio B -pg. D-11-21
Cruz, Ignacio C -pg. D-9-19
Cruz, Ignacio C -pg. D-9-20
Cruz, Ignacio G -pg. D-2-20
Cruz, Ignacio M -pg. D-3-12
Cruz, Ignacio M -pg. D-4-77
Cruz, Ignacio M -pg. D-4-126
Cruz, Ignacio S -pg. D-9-24
Cruz, Ignacio T -pg. D-1-42
Cruz, Ignacio T -pg. D-4-20

Cruz, Ignacio T -pg. D-4-95
Cruz, Ignasia C -pg. D-6-21
Cruz, Ingacio M -pg. D-5-8
Cruz, Isabel -pg. D-3-9
Cruz, Isabel -pg. D-3-11
Cruz, Isabel A -pg. D-9-13
Cruz, Isabel B -pg. D-12-20
Cruz, Isabel C -pg. D-4-3
Cruz, Isabel C -pg. D-9-12
Cruz, Isabel C -pg. D-11-12
Cruz, Isabel G -pg. D-1-47
Cruz, Isabel L -pg. D-2-83
Cruz, Isabel M -pg. D-1-34
Cruz, Isabel M -pg. D-4-112
Cruz, Isabel M -pg. D-12-20
Cruz, Isabel T -pg. D-1-57
Cruz, Isabel T -pg. D-5-44
Cruz, Jaime Q -pg. D-12-20
Cruz, Jesus -pg. D-3-8
Cruz, Jesus -pg. D-3-11
Cruz, Jesus -pg. D-3-32
Cruz, Jesus -pg. D-3-65
Cruz, Jesus -pg. D-3-70
Cruz, Jesus -pg. D-5-68
Cruz, Jesus A -pg. D-9-10
Cruz, Jesus A -pg. D-9-12
Cruz, Jesus A -pg. D-12-18
Cruz, Jesus B -pg. D-4-117
Cruz, Jesus B -pg. D-5-30
Cruz, Jesus B -pg. D-5-31
Cruz, Jesus B -pg. D-12-18
Cruz, Jesus C -pg. D-1-42
Cruz, Jesus C -pg. D-3-7
Cruz, Jesus C -pg. D-5-21
Cruz, Jesus C -pg. D-9-12
Cruz, Jesus C -pg. D-9-20
Cruz, Jesus C -pg. D-10-11
Cruz, Jesus C -pg. D-10-18
Cruz, Jesus C -pg. D-11-31
Cruz, Jesus D -pg. D-4-43
Cruz, Jesus E -pg. D-1-53
Cruz, Jesus F -pg. D-5-8
Cruz, Jesus G -pg. D-1-47
Cruz, Jesus G -pg. D-4-93
Cruz, Jesus G -pg. D-5-34
Cruz, Jesus H -pg. D-5-26
Cruz, Jesus I -pg. D-4-72
Cruz, Jesus LG -pg. D-4-52
Cruz, Jesus LG -pg. D-9-7
Cruz, Jesus M -pg. D-4-13
Cruz, Jesus M -pg. D-4-71
Cruz, Jesus O -pg. D-6-34
Cruz, Jesus P -pg. D-1-19
Cruz, Jesus P -pg. D-2-46
Cruz, Jesus P -pg. D-2-55
Cruz, Jesus P -pg. D-4-2
Cruz, Jesus P -pg. D-10-9
Cruz, Jesus Q -pg. D-6-11
Cruz, Jesus Q -pg. D-10-35

Cruz, Jesus R -pg. D-9-2
Cruz, Jesus S -pg. D-9-23
Cruz, Jesus S -pg. D-11-6
Cruz, Jesus T -pg. D-1-42
Cruz, Jesus T -pg. D-4-103
Cruz, Jesus T -pg. D-12-18
Cruz, Jesus V -pg. D-13-29
Cruz, Jesusa S -pg. D-10-21
Cruz, Joaquin A -pg. D-5-31
Cruz, Joaquin A -pg. D-9-13
Cruz, Joaquin B -pg. D-4-46
Cruz, Joaquin B -pg. D-4-78
Cruz, Joaquin B -pg. D-6-40
Cruz, Joaquin B -pg. D-11-4
Cruz, Joaquin C -pg. D-1-47
Cruz, Joaquin C -pg. D-4-57
Cruz, Joaquin C -pg. D-7-22
Cruz, Joaquin C -pg. D-10-8
Cruz, Joaquin C -pg. D-12-2
Cruz, Joaquin D -pg. D-4-24
Cruz, Joaquin G -pg. D-4-35
Cruz, Joaquin G -pg. D-4-92
Cruz, Joaquin G -pg. D-9-10
Cruz, Joaquin I -pg. D-11-6
Cruz, Joaquin LG -pg. D-2-10
Cruz, Joaquin LG -pg. D-4-61
Cruz, Joaquin M -pg. D-4-10
Cruz, Joaquin M -pg. D-4-113
Cruz, Joaquin M -pg. D-11-23
Cruz, Joaquin N -pg. D-4-4
Cruz, Joaquin O -pg. D-6-34
Cruz, Joaquin O -pg. D-12-3
Cruz, Joaquin P -pg. D-4-75
Cruz, Joaquin P -pg. D-7-11
Cruz, Joaquin Q -pg. D-6-11
Cruz, Joaquin R -pg. D-9-2
Cruz, Joaquin R -pg. D-11-24
Cruz, Joaquin R -pg. D-12-18
Cruz, Joaquin S -pg. D-4-11
Cruz, Joaquin S -pg. D-7-12
Cruz, Joaquin T -pg. D-1-42
Cruz, Joaquin T -pg. D-5-8
Cruz, Joaquin T -pg. D-5-24
Cruz, Joaquin T -pg. D-7-11
Cruz, Joaquin U -pg. D-11-7
Cruz, Joaquin G -pg. D-1-48
Cruz, Joaquina C -pg. D-2-63
Cruz, Joaquina D -pg. D-11-47
Cruz, Joaquina L -pg. D-4-42
Cruz, Joaquina T -pg. D-1-43
Cruz, Jose -pg. D-3-5
Cruz, Jose -pg. D-3-5
Cruz, Jose -pg. D-3-10
Cruz, Jose -pg. D-3-11
Cruz, Jose -pg. D-3-11
Cruz, Jose -pg. D-3-32
Cruz, Jose -pg. D-3-39
Cruz, Jose -pg. D-3-40
Cruz, Jose -pg. D-3-42

Cruz, Jose -pg. D-3-46
Cruz, Jose -pg. D-3-70
Cruz, Jose -pg. D-4-111
Cruz, Jose -pg. D-5-80
Cruz, Jose -pg. D-5-97
Cruz, Jose A -pg. D-2-11
Cruz, Jose A -pg. D-4-50
Cruz, Jose A -pg. D-4-53
Cruz, Jose A -pg. D-4-100
Cruz, Jose A -pg. D-4-104
Cruz, Jose A -pg. D-5-44
Cruz, Jose A -pg. D-6-40
Cruz, Jose A -pg. D-9-13
Cruz, Jose A -pg. D-11-46
Cruz, Jose A -pg. D-12-18
Cruz, Jose A -pg. D-12-21
Cruz, Jose A -pg. D-13-28
Cruz, Jose B -pg. D-2-36
Cruz, Jose B -pg. D-3-63
Cruz, Jose B -pg. D-4-117
Cruz, Jose B -pg. D-5-30
Cruz, Jose B -pg. D-5-31
Cruz, Jose C -pg. D-1-7
Cruz, Jose C -pg. D-1-27
Cruz, Jose C -pg. D-1-70
Cruz, Jose C -pg. D-2-63
Cruz, Jose C -pg. D-4-23
Cruz, Jose C -pg. D-4-52
Cruz, Jose C -pg. D-4-61
Cruz, Jose C -pg. D-4-71
Cruz, Jose C -pg. D-4-120
Cruz, Jose C -pg. D-5-21
Cruz, Jose C -pg. D-5-36
Cruz, Jose C -pg. D-5-60
Cruz, Jose C -pg. D-5-95
Cruz, Jose C -pg. D-6-20
Cruz, Jose C -pg. D-6-21
Cruz, Jose C -pg. D-9-12
Cruz, Jose C -pg. D-9-20
Cruz, Jose C -pg. D-10-19
Cruz, Jose C -pg. D-11-10
Cruz, Jose C -pg. D-11-40
Cruz, Jose C -pg. D-13-28
Cruz, Jose D -pg. D-8-11
Cruz, Jose D -pg. D-8-14
Cruz, Jose F -pg. D-1-27
Cruz, Jose F -pg. D-4-18
Cruz, Jose F -pg. D-5-8
Cruz, Jose F -pg. D-5-8
Cruz, Jose G -pg. D-1-47
Cruz, Jose G -pg. D-2-84
Cruz, Jose G -pg. D-4-68
Cruz, Jose G -pg. D-5-21
Cruz, Jose G -pg. D-5-34
Cruz, Jose I -pg. D-4-4
Cruz, Jose J -pg. D-7-22
Cruz, Jose L -pg. D-2-83
Cruz, Jose LG -pg. D-2-10
Cruz, Jose LG -pg. D-4-42

Cruz, Jose LG -pg. D-4-61
Cruz, Jose LG -pg. D-5-39
Cruz, Jose LG -pg. D-9-7
Cruz, Jose M -pg. D-3-8
Cruz, Jose M -pg. D-3-46
Cruz, Jose M -pg. D-3-69
Cruz, Jose M -pg. D-4-71
Cruz, Jose M -pg. D-4-102
Cruz, Jose M -pg. D-4-113
Cruz, Jose M -pg. D-5-25
Cruz, Jose M -pg. D-7-13
Cruz, Jose M -pg. D-9-23
Cruz, Jose M -pg. D-11-23
Cruz, Jose M -pg. D-12-20
Cruz, Jose M jr. -pg. D-3-69
Cruz, Jose N -pg. D-4-4
Cruz, Jose O -pg. D-4-18
Cruz, Jose O -pg. D-6-34
Cruz, Jose O -pg. D-12-3
Cruz, Jose P -pg. D-1-18
Cruz, Jose P -pg. D-2-67
Cruz, Jose P -pg. D-3-40
Cruz, Jose P -pg. D-4-2
Cruz, Jose P -pg. D-4-58
Cruz, Jose P -pg. D-4-126
Cruz, Jose P -pg. D-5-25
Cruz, Jose P -pg. D-5-51
Cruz, Jose P -pg. D-8-14
Cruz, Jose P -pg. D-9-11
Cruz, Jose P -pg. D-9-19
Cruz, Jose P -pg. D-10-9
Cruz, Jose P -pg. D-12-17
Cruz, Jose P -pg. D-13-22
Cruz, Jose Q -pg. D-4-120
Cruz, Jose Q -pg. D-5-25
Cruz, Jose Q -pg. D-5-68
Cruz, Jose Q -pg. D-6-11
Cruz, Jose Q -pg. D-10-27
Cruz, Jose Q -pg. D-11-31
Cruz, Jose Q -pg. D-13-28
Cruz, Jose R -pg. D-9-2
Cruz, Jose S -pg. D-2-81
Cruz, Jose S -pg. D-4-30
Cruz, Jose S -pg. D-4-31
Cruz, Jose S -pg. D-6-38
Cruz, Jose S -pg. D-10-21
Cruz, Jose S -pg. D-11-4
Cruz, Jose SN -pg. D-4-55
Cruz, Jose SN -pg. D-10-32
Cruz, Jose T -pg. D-1-42
Cruz, Jose T -pg. D-1-43
Cruz, Jose T -pg. D-1-57
Cruz, Jose T -pg. D-4-20
Cruz, Jose T -pg. D-4-78
Cruz, Jose T -pg. D-5-44
Cruz, Jose T -pg. D-12-11
Cruz, Josefa B -pg. D-12-20
Cruz, Josefa C -pg. D-5-2
Cruz, Josefa C -pg. D-5-25

Cruz, Josefa C -pg. D-5-39
Cruz, Josefa C -pg. D-9-12
Cruz, Josefa C -pg. D-11-25
Cruz, Josefa D -pg. D-3-5
Cruz, Josefa G -pg. D-9-11
Cruz, Josefa I -pg. D-4-73
Cruz, Josefa J -pg. D-6-15
Cruz, Josefa L -pg. D-2-83
Cruz, Josefa M -pg. D-1-34
Cruz, Josefa M -pg. D-4-50
Cruz, Josefa P -pg. D-5-2
Cruz, Josefa Q -pg. D-4-120
Cruz, Josefa Q -pg. D-5-65
Cruz, Josefa R -pg. D-9-2
Cruz, Josefa S -pg. D-2-32
Cruz, Josefa S -pg. D-4-31
Cruz, Josefa S -pg. D-10-21
Cruz, Josefa SN -pg. D-6-14
Cruz, Josefa U -pg. D-4-17
Cruz, Josefina -pg. D-3-11
Cruz, Josefina B -pg. D-5-30
Cruz, Josefina B -pg. D-10-14
Cruz, Josefina C -pg. D-1-27
Cruz, Josefina C -pg. D-4-3
Cruz, Josefina C -pg. D-9-19
Cruz, Josefina F -pg. D-4-7
Cruz, Josefina M -pg. D-4-111
Cruz, Josefina Q -pg. D-12-20
Cruz, Josefina S -pg. D-4-31
Cruz, Joseph -pg. D-3-40
Cruz, Joseph C -pg. D-11-12
Cruz, Juan -pg. D-3-5
Cruz, Juan -pg. D-3-11
Cruz, Juan -pg. D-3-32
Cruz, Juan -pg. D-3-42
Cruz, Juan -pg. D-3-55
Cruz, Juan -pg. D-3-65
Cruz, Juan -pg. D-5-49
Cruz, Juan -pg. D-5-96
Cruz, Juan -pg. D-10-2
Cruz, Juan A -pg. D-2-11
Cruz, Juan A -pg. D-3-32
Cruz, Juan A -pg. D-5-24
Cruz, Juan A -pg. D-9-10
Cruz, Juan A -pg. D-11-31
Cruz, Juan B -pg. D-2-81
Cruz, Juan B -pg. D-3-6
Cruz, Juan B -pg. D-4-31
Cruz, Juan B -pg. D-5-30
Cruz, Juan B -pg. D-5-31
Cruz, Juan B -pg. D-12-20
Cruz, Juan C -pg. D-3-64
Cruz, Juan C -pg. D-4-57
Cruz, Juan C -pg. D-4-58
Cruz, Juan C -pg. D-5-21
Cruz, Juan C -pg. D-5-42
Cruz, Juan C -pg. D-5-68
Cruz, Juan C -pg. D-9-10
Cruz, Juan C -pg. D-9-22

Cruz, Juan C -pg. D-10-14
Cruz, Juan C -pg. D-11-25
Cruz, Juan D -pg. D-6-8
Cruz, Juan F -pg. D-5-6
Cruz, Juan G -pg. D-1-24
Cruz, Juan G -pg. D-1-34
Cruz, Juan G -pg. D-2-20
Cruz, Juan G -pg. D-3-11
Cruz, Juan G -pg. D-4-93
Cruz, Juan I -pg. D-2-20
Cruz, Juan I -pg. D-10-39
Cruz, Juan I -pg. D-11-6
Cruz, Juan L -pg. D-3-51
Cruz, Juan LG -pg. D-1-53
Cruz, Juan LG -pg. D-4-32
Cruz, Juan LG -pg. D-4-61
Cruz, Juan LG -pg. D-11-6
Cruz, Juan LG -pg. D-12-4
Cruz, Juan M -pg. D-4-51
Cruz, Juan M -pg. D-4-51
Cruz, Juan M -pg. D-5-39
Cruz, Juan M -pg. D-5-49
Cruz, Juan M -pg. D-11-23
Cruz, Juan O -pg. D-4-18
Cruz, Juan O -pg. D-6-34
Cruz, Juan P -pg. D-4-2
Cruz, Juan P -pg. D-4-126
Cruz, Juan P -pg. D-5-51
Cruz, Juan P -pg. D-9-7
Cruz, Juan P -pg. D-9-22
Cruz, Juan Q -pg. D-10-26
Cruz, Juan Q -pg. D-10-34
Cruz, Juan R -pg. D-1-59
Cruz, Juan R -pg. D-4-85
Cruz, Juan R -pg. D-9-2
Cruz, Juan R -pg. D-11-24
Cruz, Juan S -pg. D-1-59
Cruz, Juan S -pg. D-4-11
Cruz, Juan S -pg. D-6-17
Cruz, Juan S -pg. D-6-38
Cruz, Juan S -pg. D-9-23
Cruz, Juan S -pg. D-10-33
Cruz, Juan SN -pg. D-1-9
Cruz, Juan SN -pg. D-10-4
Cruz, Juan T -pg. D-4-20
Cruz, Juan T -pg. D-5-24
Cruz, Juan T -pg. D-12-18
Cruz, Juan N -pg. D-4-4
Cruz, Juana C -pg. D-5-95
Cruz, Julia A -pg. D-4-50
Cruz, Julia D -pg. D-4-55
Cruz, Julia G -pg. D-9-11
Cruz, Julia M -pg. D-5-2
Cruz, Julia R -pg. D-4-86
Cruz, Julia S -pg. D-2-55
Cruz, Juliana C -pg. D-5-36
Cruz, Juliana F -pg. D-4-43
Cruz, Juliana G -pg. D-5-34
Cruz, Juliana R -pg. D-1-59

Cruz, Julita S -pg. D-11-4
Cruz, Justa S -pg. D-9-24
Cruz, Justo -pg. D-3-69
Cruz, Lagrimas N -pg. D-6-8
Cruz, Leocadio C -pg. D-8-10
Cruz, Leonora T -pg. D-4-20
Cruz, Leonsia C -pg. D-5-34
Cruz, Lorenzo -pg. D-5-97
Cruz, Lorenzo -pg. D-10-14
Cruz, Lorenzo B -pg. D-10-14
Cruz, Lorenzo G -pg. D-5-96
Cruz, Lorenzo Q -pg. D-12-20
Cruz, Lourdes -pg. D-5-97
Cruz, Lourdes A -pg. D-4-50
Cruz, Lourdes C -pg. D-11-7
Cruz, Lourdes J -pg. D-7-22
Cruz, Lourdes L -pg. D-4-27
Cruz, Lourdes R -pg. D-4-85
Cruz, Lucia I -pg. D-2-20
Cruz, Luis A -pg. D-4-80
Cruz, Luis C -pg. D-9-20
Cruz, Luis D -pg. D-6-21
Cruz, Luis M -pg. D-5-51
Cruz, Luis T -pg. D-13-30
Cruz, Luisa B -pg. D-12-20
Cruz, Luisa C -pg. D-4-49
Cruz, Luisa D -pg. D-8-10
Cruz, Luisa T -pg. D-2-21
Cruz, Luisa T -pg. D-4-20
Cruz, Luisa T -pg. D-5-24
Cruz, Lydia T -pg. D-5-24
Cruz, Macario -pg. D-3-10
Cruz, Magdalena -pg. D-3-11
Cruz, Magdalena C -pg. D-4-57
Cruz, Magdalena L -pg. D-4-27
Cruz, Magdalena M -pg. D-11-2
Cruz, Magdalena Q -pg. D-5-65
Cruz, Magdalena Q -pg. D-12-20
Cruz, Maicala P -pg. D-2-42
Cruz, Manuel -pg. D-10-6
Cruz, Manuel A -pg. D-4-13
Cruz, Manuel A -pg. D-11-31
Cruz, Manuel B -pg. D-4-125
Cruz, Manuel B -pg. D-12-3
Cruz, Manuel C -pg. D-2-25
Cruz, Manuel C -pg. D-2-76
Cruz, Manuel C -pg. D-2-76
Cruz, Manuel C -pg. D-3-15
Cruz, Manuel C -pg. D-5-2
Cruz, Manuel C -pg. D-5-21
Cruz, Manuel C -pg. D-5-71
Cruz, Manuel D -pg. D-2-16
Cruz, Manuel G -pg. D-2-20
Cruz, Manuel G -pg. D-4-93
Cruz, Manuel I -pg. D-4-3
Cruz, Manuel LG -pg. D-9-7
Cruz, Manuel R -pg. D-9-2
Cruz, Manuel S -pg. D-4-11
Cruz, Manuel S -pg. D-4-31

Cruz, Manuel S -pg. D-7-12
Cruz, Manuel S -pg. D-11-26
Cruz, Manuel S -pg. D-12-17
Cruz, Manuel T -pg. D-1-43
Cruz, Manuela C -pg. D-10-14
Cruz, Marcela A -pg. D-10-6
Cruz, Marcela Q -pg. D-10-26
Cruz, Marcela S -pg. D-6-38
Cruz, Marcela T -pg. D-5-95
Cruz, Margarita A -pg. D-9-12
Cruz, Margarita C -pg. D-4-52
Cruz, Margarita C -pg. D-4-78
Cruz, Margarita T -pg. D-5-29
Cruz, Maria -pg. D-3-6
Cruz, Maria -pg. D-3-8
Cruz, Maria -pg. D-3-11
Cruz, Maria -pg. D-3-11
Cruz, Maria -pg. D-3-15
Cruz, Maria -pg. D-3-32
Cruz, Maria -pg. D-3-40
Cruz, Maria -pg. D-3-42
Cruz, Maria -pg. D-3-65
Cruz, Maria -pg. D-4-35
Cruz, Maria A -pg. D-2-11
Cruz, Maria A -pg. D-3-7
Cruz, Maria A -pg. D-3-11
Cruz, Maria A -pg. D-3-75
Cruz, Maria A -pg. D-4-100
Cruz, Maria A -pg. D-4-104
Cruz, Maria A -pg. D-9-10
Cruz, Maria A -pg. D-9-10
Cruz, Maria A -pg. D-9-12
Cruz, Maria A -pg. D-10-6
Cruz, Maria A -pg. D-11-21
Cruz, Maria A -pg. D-11-21
Cruz, Maria A -pg. D-12-18
Cruz, Maria B -pg. D-2-36
Cruz, Maria B -pg. D-3-14
Cruz, Maria B -pg. D-3-40
Cruz, Maria B -pg. D-4-14
Cruz, Maria B -pg. D-4-117
Cruz, Maria B -pg. D-4-117
Cruz, Maria B -pg. D-5-30
Cruz, Maria B -pg. D-5-30
Cruz, Maria B -pg. D-5-31
Cruz, Maria B -pg. D-5-46
Cruz, Maria B -pg. D-9-10
Cruz, Maria B -pg. D-10-14
Cruz, Maria B -pg. D-11-25
Cruz, Maria B -pg. D-12-20
Cruz, Maria C -pg. D-2-63
Cruz, Maria C -pg. D-2-76
Cruz, Maria C -pg. D-4-27
Cruz, Maria C -pg. D-4-52
Cruz, Maria C -pg. D-4-68
Cruz, Maria C -pg. D-5-21
Cruz, Maria C -pg. D-5-21
Cruz, Maria C -pg. D-5-95
Cruz, Maria C -pg. D-9-11

Cruz, Maria C -pg. D-9-12
Cruz, Maria C -pg. D-9-20
Cruz, Maria C -pg. D-9-22
Cruz, Maria C -pg. D-9-25
Cruz, Maria C -pg. D-10-14
Cruz, Maria C -pg. D-10-19
Cruz, Maria C -pg. D-11-25
Cruz, Maria D -pg. D-3-6
Cruz, Maria D -pg. D-8-11
Cruz, Maria F -pg. D-5-8
Cruz, Maria G -pg. D-4-35
Cruz, Maria H -pg. D-5-26
Cruz, Maria H -pg. D-5-26
Cruz, Maria H -pg. D-10-33
Cruz, Maria I -pg. D-4-4
Cruz, Maria J -pg. D-6-14
Cruz, Maria J -pg. D-6-15
Cruz, Maria J -pg. D-7-22
Cruz, Maria L -pg. D-4-27
Cruz, Maria L -pg. D-11-48
Cruz, Maria LG -pg. D-4-61
Cruz, Maria LG -pg. D-4-102
Cruz, Maria M -pg. D-3-57
Cruz, Maria M -pg. D-4-13
Cruz, Maria M -pg. D-4-111
Cruz, Maria M -pg. D-7-13
Cruz, Maria M -pg. D-9-23
Cruz, Maria M -pg. D-10-39
Cruz, Maria N -pg. D-4-4
Cruz, Maria O -pg. D-4-18
Cruz, Maria O -pg. D-6-34
Cruz, Maria O -pg. D-12-3
Cruz, Maria O -pg. D-12-3
Cruz, Maria P pg. D-4-58
Cruz, Maria P -pg. D-5-51
Cruz, Maria P -pg. D-10-9
Cruz, Maria Q -pg. D-5-25
Cruz, Maria Q -pg. D-6-11
Cruz, Maria Q -pg. D-11-26
Cruz, Maria R -pg. D-1-59
Cruz, Maria R -pg. D-4-55
Cruz, Maria R -pg. D-4-119
Cruz, Maria R -pg. D-9-2
Cruz, Maria R -pg. D-9-2
Cruz, Maria R -pg. D-11-23
Cruz, Maria S -pg. D-2-32
Cruz, Maria S -pg. D-2-55
Cruz, Maria S -pg. D-4-31
Cruz, Maria S -pg. D-4-31
Cruz, Maria S -pg. D-4-31
Cruz, Maria S -pg. D-6-16
Cruz, Maria S -pg. D-6-38
Cruz, Maria S -pg. D-10-21
Cruz, Maria S -pg. D-4-11
Cruz, Maria SN -pg. D-1-9
Cruz, Maria SN -pg. D-4-75
Cruz, Maria SN -pg. D-11-50
Cruz, Maria T -pg. D-1-4
Cruz, Maria T -pg. D-2-21

Cruz, Maria T -pg. D-4-53
Cruz, Maria T -pg. D-5-44
Cruz, Maria T -pg. D-7-11
Cruz, Maria T -pg. D-8-9
Cruz, Maria T -pg. D-12-2
Cruz, Maria T -pg. D-12-11
Cruz, Maria U -pg. D-11-7
Cruz, Maria W -pg. D-4-50
Cruz, Maria Jr.? -pg. D-3-11
Cruz, Maria Lourdes Q -pg. D-12-3
Cruz, Mariano -pg. D-3-32
Cruz, Mariano A -pg. D-4-20
Cruz, Mariano C -pg. D-2-25
Cruz, Mariano C -pg. D-2-32
Cruz, Mariano C -pg. D-6-14
Cruz, Mariano L -pg. D-4-27
Cruz, Mariano M -pg. D-4-49
Cruz, Mariano M -pg. D-11-50
Cruz, Mariano S -pg. D-6-8
Cruz, Martina C -pg. D-9-22
Cruz, Matias T -pg. D-4-103
Cruz, Matilde -pg. D-5-97
Cruz, Matilde T -pg. D-1-3
Cruz, Miguel -pg. D-3-69
Cruz, Miguel C -pg. D-4-4
Cruz, Miguel J -pg. D-6-15
Cruz, Miguel L -pg. D-4-27
Cruz, Miguel M -pg. D-5-68
Cruz, Miguel P -pg. D-9-20
Cruz, Miguel Q -pg. D-10-34
Cruz, Misaericordia S -pg. D-4-125
Cruz, Natividad -pg. D-3-55
Cruz, Natividad pg. D-5-96
Cruz, Natividad -pg. D-5-97
Cruz, Natividad C -pg. D-4-52
Cruz, Natividad C -pg. D-5-39
Cruz, Natividad Q -pg. D-2-11
Cruz, Natividad S -pg. D-4-31
Cruz, Nicolas M -pg. D-2-13
Cruz, Nicolas M -pg. D-7-13
Cruz, Nicolasa B -pg. D-5-30
Cruz, Nicolasa M -pg. D-4-22
Cruz, Nicolasa T -pg. D-4-77
Cruz, Nicolasa T -pg. D-9-4
Cruz, Nieves G -pg. D-5-34
Cruz, Nieves M -pg. D-2-49
Cruz, Olimpia -pg. D-3-9
Cruz, Oliva T -pg. D-11-21
Cruz, Orelia T -pg. D-12-11
Cruz, Oscar -pg. D-3-8
Cruz, Pablo C -pg. D-9-20
Cruz, Paderno P -pg. D-2-83
Cruz, Paterno M -pg. D-13-26
Cruz, Paula G -pg. D-5-34
Cruz, Paulino G -pg. D-2-32
Cruz, Pedro -pg. D-3-15
Cruz, Pedro -pg. D-3-55
Cruz, Pedro -pg. D-5-80
Cruz, Pedro -pg. D-5-97

Cruz, Pedro B -pg. D-5-30
Cruz, Pedro C -pg. D-2-11
Cruz, Pedro C -pg. D-2-78
Cruz, Pedro C -pg. D-6-34
Cruz, Pedro G -pg. D-2-20
Cruz, Pedro G -pg. D-4-93
Cruz, Pedro G -pg. D-5-26
Cruz, Pedro G -pg. D-6-32
Cruz, Pedro H -pg. D-5-26
Cruz, Pedro I -pg. D-4-73
Cruz, Pedro LG -pg. D-9-8
Cruz, Pedro M -pg. D-4-51
Cruz, Pedro O -pg. D-6-34
Cruz, Pedro P -pg. D-3-40
Cruz, Pedro R -pg. D-1-59
Cruz, Pedro R -pg. D-12-3
Cruz, Pedro S -pg. D-2-32
Cruz, Pedro S -pg. D-5-30
Cruz, Pedro S -pg. D-10-21
Cruz, Pedro S -pg. D-13-29
Cruz, Pedro T -pg. D-12-2
Cruz, Perpetua C -pg. D-5-36
Cruz, Peter F -pg. D-4-43
Cruz, Pilar M -pg. D-7-13
Cruz, Preciosa Q -pg. D-11-40
Cruz, Quintina C -pg. D-4-4
Cruz, Rafael O -pg. D-6-34
Cruz, Ramon -pg. D-3-7
Cruz, Ramon C -pg. D-6-20
Cruz, Ramon C -pg. D-9-41
Cruz, Ramon M -pg. D-3-8
Cruz, Ramon P -pg. D-2-67
Cruz, Ramon P -pg. D-9-24
Cruz, Raymondo R -pg. D-4-55
Cruz, Raymundo C -pg. D-12-2
Cruz, Redosindo A -pg. D-5-46
Cruz, Regina -pg. D-3-39
Cruz, Regina A -pg. D-4-80
Cruz, Regina P -pg. D-4-91
Cruz, Regina S -pg. D-4-11
Cruz, Regina SN -pg. D-11-50
Cruz, Remedios C -pg. D-6-21
Cruz, Remedios LG -pg. D-2-10
Cruz, Rita -pg. D-3-6
Cruz, Rita B -pg. D-2-68
Cruz, Rita B -pg. D-11-25
Cruz, Rita D -pg. D-4-24
Cruz, Rita G -pg. D-4-92
Cruz, Rita G -pg. D-4-93
Cruz, Rita LG -pg. D-4-102
Cruz, Rita O -pg. D-12-3
Cruz, Rita P -pg. D-2-67
Cruz, Rita S -pg. D-4-31
Cruz, Rita T -pg. D-5-29
Cruz, Rita T -pg. D-6-8
Cruz, Rita W -pg. D-4-50
Cruz, Robert F -pg. D-4-43
Cruz, Roman J -pg. D-7-22
Cruz, Romana C -pg. D-10-14

Cruz, Rosa -pg. D-3-11
Cruz, Rosa -pg. D-3-12
Cruz, Rosa -pg. D-5-80
Cruz, Rosa A -pg. D-2-25
Cruz, Rosa A -pg. D-4-104
Cruz, Rosa A -pg. D-11-17
Cruz, Rosa A -pg. D-12-18
Cruz, Rosa B -pg. D-2-68
Cruz, Rosa C -pg. D-1-27
Cruz, Rosa C -pg. D-2-42
Cruz, Rosa C -pg. D-9-20
Cruz, Rosa C -pg. D-11-25
Cruz, Rosa D -pg. D-4-55
Cruz, Rosa D -pg. D-4-83
Cruz, Rosa G -pg. D-5-34
Cruz, Rosa J -pg. D-7-22
Cruz, Rosa LG -pg. D-3-12
Cruz, Rosa LG -pg. D-5-38
Cruz, Rosa M -pg. D-4-113
Cruz, Rosa R -pg. D-4-8
Cruz, Rosa R -pg. D-4-55
Cruz, Rosa S -pg. D-9-24
Cruz, Rosa S -pg. D-10-21
Cruz, Rosa T -pg. D-1-42
Cruz, Rosa T -pg. D-2-32
Cruz, Rosa T -pg. D-5-44
Cruz, Rosa T -pg. D-12-18
Cruz, Rosalia -pg. D-3-42
Cruz, Rosalia -pg. D-3-69
Cruz, Rosalia A -pg. D-4-100
Cruz, Rosalia A -pg. D-12-18
Cruz, Rosalia G -pg. D-1-47
Cruz, Rosalia M -pg. D-12-20
Cruz, Rosalia R -pg. D-9-2
Cruz, Rosalia R -pg. D-12-3
Cruz, Rosalia T -pg. D-6-8
Cruz, Rosaline F -pg. D-4-43
Cruz, Rosario -pg. D-3-11
Cruz, Rosario -pg. D-3-39
Cruz, Rosario -pg. D-3-63
Cruz, Rosario A -pg. D-2-11
Cruz, Rosario B -pg. D-4-117
Cruz, Rosario D -pg. D-3-6
Cruz, Rosario H -pg. D-5-26
Cruz, Rosario LG -pg. D-4-116
Cruz, Rosario O -pg. D-4-18
Cruz, Rosario Q -pg. D-5-25
Cruz, Rosario R -pg. D-3-3
Cruz, Rosario S -pg. D-4-31
Cruz, Rosario SN -pg. D-1-9
Cruz, Rosario T -pg. D-5-44
Cruz, Rosario T -pg. D-12-11
Cruz, Rosario C -pg. D-3-28
Cruz, Rufina C -pg. D-5-42
Cruz, Rufina T -pg. D-4-96
Cruz, Santiago A -pg. D-12-18
Cruz, Santiago C -pg. D-2-25
Cruz, Santiago C -pg. D-9-20
Cruz, Santiago LG -pg. D-12-20

Cruz, Saturnina B -pg. D-3-10
Cruz, Segundo -pg. D-3-42
Cruz, Serafin R -pg. D-10-29
Cruz, Serafina P -pg. D-1-18
Cruz, Silviestre C -pg. D-4-27
Cruz, Simeon B -pg. D-4-112
Cruz, Simona C -pg. D-6-21
Cruz, Simplicia M -pg. D-4-51
Cruz, Soledad C -pg. D-5-21
Cruz, Soledad C -pg. D-5-39
Cruz, Soledad P -pg. D-10-9
Cruz, Soledad Q -pg. D-10-27
Cruz, Soledad R -pg. D-4-55
Cruz, Soledad T -pg. D-4-99
Cruz, Susana L -pg. D-12-10
Cruz, Teodoro F -pg. D-4-43
Cruz, Teodoro S -pg. D-9-24
Cruz, Teordoro B -pg. D-3-10
Cruz, Teresa C -pg. D-2-16
Cruz, Teresa D -pg. D-1-50
Cruz, Teresa M -pg. D-3-46
Cruz, Teresita T -pg. D-1-3
Cruz, Tomas -pg. D-3-15
Cruz, Tomas A -pg. D-9-12
Cruz, Tomas B -pg. D-2-36
Cruz, Tomas C -pg. D-4-23
Cruz, Tomas C -pg. D-4-35
Cruz, Tomas E -pg. D-9-12
Cruz, Tomas F -pg. D-4-43
Cruz, Tomas I -pg. D-12-4
Cruz, Tomas L -pg. D-4-98
Cruz, Tomas Q -pg. D-10-26
Cruz, Tomas T -pg. D-4-20
Cruz, Tomas T -pg. D-5-24
Cruz, Tomas T -pg. D-7-11
Cruz, Tomas T -pg. D-12-11
Cruz, Tomasa C -pg. D-4-57
Cruz, Tomasa G -pg. D-4-93
Cruz, Trinidad -pg. D-5-71
Cruz, Trinidad A -pg. D-4-50
Cruz, Trinidad A -pg. D-11-44
Cruz, Trinidad M -pg. D-3-10
Cruz, Trinidad T -pg. D-1-43
Cruz, Urfia T -pg. D-6-20
Cruz, Venancio T -pg. D-9-2
Cruz, Veronica C -pg. D-5-36
Cruz, Vicenta C -pg. D-9-11
Cruz, Vicenta C -pg. D-9-20
Cruz, Vicenta LG -pg. D-5-38
Cruz, Vicenta M -pg. D-2-53
Cruz, Vicenta R -pg. D-1-59
Cruz, Vicenta R -pg. D-4-55
Cruz, Vicenta S -pg. D-9-24
Cruz, Vicenta M -pg. D-3-70
Cruz, Vicente -pg. D-3-7
Cruz, Vicente -pg. D-3-11
Cruz, Vicente -pg. D-3-39
Cruz, Vicente -pg. D-3-69
Cruz, Vicente -pg. D-3-70

Cruz, Vicente -pg. D-7-13
Cruz, Vicente A -pg. D-2-11
Cruz, Vicente A -pg. D-2-16
Cruz, Vicente A -pg. D-4-17
Cruz, Vicente A -pg. D-4-100
Cruz, Vicente B -pg. D-1-10
Cruz, Vicente B -pg. D-4-30
Cruz, Vicente B -pg. D-5-25
Cruz, Vicente B -pg. D-5-30
Cruz, Vicente B -pg. D-11-25
Cruz, Vicente C -pg. D-4-3
Cruz, Vicente C -pg. D-4-50
Cruz, Vicente C -pg. D-4-57
Cruz, Vicente C -pg. D-5-95
Cruz, Vicente C -pg. D-9-20
Cruz, Vicente C -pg. D-10-7
Cruz, Vicente C -pg. D-11-44
Cruz, Vicente G -pg. D-6-14
Cruz, Vicente G -pg. D-9-11
Cruz, Vicente G -pg. D-9-11
Cruz, Vicente LG -pg. D-3-32
Cruz, Vicente LG -pg. D-4-11
Cruz, Vicente M -pg. D-3-6
Cruz, Vicente M -pg. D-3-69
Cruz, Vicente M -pg. D-5-2
Cruz, Vicente M -pg. D-5-49
Cruz, Vicente M -pg. D-5-89
Cruz, Vicente M -pg. D-12-20
Cruz, Vicente P -pg. D-2-67
Cruz, Vicente P -pg. D-4-126
Cruz, Vicente Q -pg. D-11-26
Cruz, Vicente R -pg. D-4-55
Cruz, Vicente R -pg. D-9-2
Cruz, Vicente S -pg. D-5-36
Cruz, Vicente S -pg. D-10-21
Cruz, Vicente S -pg. D-11-13
Cruz, Vicente S -pg. D-12-20
Cruz, Vicente T -pg. D-6-8
Cruz, Vicente T -pg. D-6-16
Cruz, Vicente T -pg. D-12-2
Cruz, Vicente W -pg. D-2-81
Cruz, Victoria I -pg. D-12-4
Cruz, Vidal J -pg. D-5-42
Cruz, Vincente -pg. D-13-22
Culmer, Franklin RD -pg. D-13-5
Cummings, Wade C -pg. D-13-22
Curtis, John E -pg. D-13-46
Cushing, Alice R -pg. D-13-2
Cushing, Alice R -pg. D-13-2
Cushing, Edith E -pg. D-13-2
Cushing, Francis C -pg. D-13-2
Cushing, Francis C -pg. D-13-2
Cusseh, James I -pg. D-13-44
D'Angelo, Guisippe -pg. D-2-2
Dahl, Raymond M -pg. D-13-41
Daily, James T -pg. D-13-10
Daleyva, Noberto -pg. D-4-90
Daleyva, Vicente L -pg. D-4-90
Dalrymyle, Jess R -pg. D-13-5

Damian, Andres B -pg. D-1-70
Damian, Candido B -pg. D-13-31
Damian, Celestina B -pg. D-1-70
Damian, Consolacion C -pg. D-3-54
Damian, Constantine -pg. D-3-54
Damian, Damazo B -pg. D-11-3
Damian, Dorothy -pg. D-3-54
Damian, Elizabeth M -pg. D-11-3
Damian, Engracio B -pg. D-1-70
Damian, Florentino B -pg. D-1-70
Damian, Jose B -pg. D-3-53
Damian, Justo -pg. D-1-69
Damian, Katharine -pg. D-3-54
Damian, Maria R -pg. D-11-3
Damian, Norman -pg. D-3-54
Damian, Pacita R -pg. D-11-3
Damian, Petronila B -pg. D-1-69
Damian, Priscila B -pg. D-1-70
Damian, Sixta B -pg. D-1-70
Daneson, Kerafas G -pg. D-13-36
Daniels, Charles E -pg. D-13-33
Danio, Donald E -pg. D-13-19
Dannson, John S -pg. D-13-33
Darling, Harold N -pg. D-13-46
Darling, Janice R -pg. D-1-54
Darling, Richard O -pg. D-1-54
Darney, James W -pg. D-13-11
Darrio, George W -pg. D-13-36
Dave, Willian H Jr. -pg. D-13-15
Davidson, Arthur J -pg. D-13-40
Davis, Edward R -pg. D-13-10
Davis, Frank L -pg. D-3-31
Davis, James E -pg. D-13-5
Davis, Josefina C -pg. D-3-32
Davis, Lincoln R -pg. D-13-43
Davis, Oswen -pg. D-13-43
Davis, William J. Jr. -pg. D-13-5
Davison, George -pg. D-13-44
Dawson, George L -pg. D-11-13
Dawson, John S -pg. D-13-10
Dawson, Rosa L -pg. D-11-13
Day, Petronila U -pg. D-4-21
De Legaria, Gil -pg. D-9-8
De Castro, Crispulo -pg. D-13-22
De Jesus, Antonio P -pg. D-5-58
De Jesus, Antonio T -pg. D-5-51
De Jesus, Dolores P -pg. D-5-58
De Jesus, Felix S -pg. D-5-50
De Jesus, Gregorio T -pg. D-5-51
De Jesus, Ignacia T -pg. D-5-51
De Jesus, Jesus T -pg. D-5-51
De Jesus, Joaquin S -pg. D-5-52
De Jesus, Magdalena P -pg. D-5-58
De Jesus, Maria P -pg. D-5-58
De Jesus, Maria T -pg. D-5-51
De Jesus, Rosendo -pg. D-13-22
De Jesus, Vicente S -pg. D-5-58
De La Cruz, Antonio R -pg. D-11-46
De La Cruz, Beatrice R -pg. D-11-46

De La Cruz, Blas -pg. D-11-46
De La Cruz, Jose -pg. D-11-13
De La Cruz, Jose R -pg. D-11-46
De La Cruz, Natividad R -pg. D-11-46
De La Cruz, Nicolasa B -pg. D-11-13
De La Rosa, Agueda T -pg. D-5-10
De La Rosa, Antonia T -pg. D-5-10
De La Rosa, Carmen T -pg. D-5-10
De La Rosa, Felisita T -pg. D-5-10
De La Rosa, Francisco T -pg. D-5-10
De La Rosa, Ignacia T -pg. D-5-10
De La Rosa, Mariano R -pg. D-5-10
De La Torre, Apolonia A -pg. D-5-60
De La Torre, Felicita A -pg. D-5-60
De La Torre, Francisca -pg. D-5-60
De La Torre, Jesus A -pg. D-5-60
De La Torre, Jose A -pg. D-5-60
De La Torre, Juan A -pg. D-5-60
De La Torre, Juan A -pg. D-5-60
De La Torre, Juan A de -pg. D-5-60
De La Torre, Julia A -pg. D-5-60
De La Torre, Soledad A -pg. D-5-60
De Leon, Adela -pg. D-3-66
de Leon, Alzo Aspi -pg. D-11-18
de Leon, Ana D -pg. D-1-50
de Leon, Dolores A -pg. D-1-50
De Leon, Dolores C -pg. D-11-15
De Leon, Dolores P -pg. D-13-43
De Leon, Elisa -pg. D-3-66
De Leon, Elizabeth B -pg. D-2-66
de Leon, Francisca D -pg. D-1-50
de Leon, Francisca I -pg. D-1-50
De Leon, Francisca T -pg. D-9-13
De Leon, Francisco C -pg. D-11-15
De Leon, Francisco P -pg. D-11-15
De Leon, Francisco Q -pg. D-13-29
de Leon, Gregorio D -pg. D-1-50
de Leon, Jesus D -pg. D-1-50
De Leon, Joaquin I -pg. D-3-66
De Leon, Joaquin U -pg. D-2-66
de Leon, Jose M -pg. D-1-50
De Leon, Jose P -pg. D-9-13
de Leon, Juanita D -pg. D-1-50
De Leon, Julia -pg. D-3-66
De Leon, Maria -pg. D-3-66
De Leon, Menna M -pg. D-2-66
De Leon, Mercedes F -pg. D-2-66
de Leon, Tomas D -pg. D-1-50
De Los Santos, Guilermo -pg. D-13-22
de Tobes, Eliza C -pg. D-1-50
de Tobes, Juan C -pg. D-1-50
De Torres, Jose -pg. D-13-22
Deal, John D -pg. D-13-10
Dees, Julia I. L -pg. D-1-53
Dees, Louis L. D -pg. D-1-53
Dees, Pauline L -pg. D-1-53
Dees, Randal E -pg. D-13-31
Degracia, Ana T -pg. D-11-44
Degracia, Antonio A -pg. D-11-48

Degracia, Clemete A -pg. D-11-48
Degracia, Dolores T -pg. D-11-44
Degracia, Elena T -pg. D-11-44
Degracia, Esteban T -pg. D-11-44
Degracia, Francisco T -pg. D-11-44
Degracia, Gregorio A -pg. D-11-48
Degracia, Lorenzo A -pg. D-11-48
Degracia, Manuel B -pg. D-11-44
Degracia, Monica T -pg. D-11-44
Degracia, Petronila A -pg. D-11-48
Degracia, Rosa A -pg. D-11-48
DeHarber, Barbara D -pg. D-13-2
DeHarber, Grace H -pg. D-13-2
DeHarber, Helen S -pg. D-13-2
DeHarber, Louis G -pg. D-13-2
DeHarber, Pauline H -pg. D-13-2
Dejima, T -pg. D-3-41
Dela Torre, Francisco C -pg. D-5-59
Dela Torre, Gregorio A -pg. D-5-59
Dela Torre, Juan N -pg. D-13-34
Delgado, Alfonso M -pg. D-12-9
Delgado, Ana C -pg. D-1-64
Delgado, Ana M -pg. D-5-24
Delgado, Ana N -pg. D-8-5
Delgado, Ana S -pg. D-3-70
Delgado, Ana SN -pg. D-8-11
Delgado, Antonio -pg. D-3-70
Delgado, Antonio P -pg. D-8-13
Delgado, Beatrice -pg. D-8-13
Delgado, Carmen P -pg. D-8-13
Delgado, Concepcion T -pg. D-8-30
Delgado, Consolacion SN -pg. D-8-11
Delgado, Crispina M -pg. D-5-82
Delgado, Delfina SN -pg. D-8-11
Delgado, Dorotea -pg. D-3-70
Delgado, Enrique SN -pg. D-8-5
Delgado, Francisco C -pg. D-1-40
Delgado, Francisco D -pg. D-8-13
Delgado, Isabel C -pg. D-1-40
Delgado, Jesus C -pg. D-1-64
Delgado, Jesus M -pg. D-1-67
Delgado, Jesus M -pg. D-5-24
Delgado, Jose C -pg. D-1-64
Delgado, Jose D -pg. D-1-40
Delgado, Jose D -pg. D-8-6
Delgado, Jose M -pg. D-1-64
Delgado, Jose M -pg. D-8-30
Delgado, Jose SN -pg. D-8-11
Delgado, Josefa C -pg. D-1-40
Delgado, Josefa C -pg. D-8-30
Delgado, Juan -pg. D-3-70
Delgado, Juan F -pg. D-5-24
Delgado, Juan M -pg. D-8-30
Delgado, Julia P -pg. D-8-13
Delgado, Luis D -pg. D-2-5
Delgado, Manuel T -pg. D-8-30
Delgado, Maria C -pg. D-1-64
Delgado, Maria F -pg. D-8-8
Delgado, Maria SN -pg. D-8-11

Delgado, Mercedes C -pg. D-1-64
Delgado, Mercedes P -pg. D-8-13
Delgado, Nicolas M -pg. D-8-8
Delgado, Pedro M -pg. D-3-70
Delgado, Pedro M -pg. D-5-82
Delgado, Pedro T -pg. D-8-30
Delgado, Rita M -pg. D-5-24
Delgado, Rosa -pg. D-2-22
Delgado, Rosa P -pg. D-8-13
Delgado, Rosario C -pg. D-1-40
Delgado, Rosario F -pg. D-8-8
Delgado, Rufina F -pg. D-8-8
Delgado, Silvano M -pg. D-8-11
Delgado, Tomasa D -pg. D-8-6
Delgado, Vicente C -pg. D-1-64
Delia, John M -pg. D-13-19
Dell, George F -pg. D-13-22
Demapan, Manuel D -pg. D-11-26
Dembasher, Anna M -pg. D-4-51
Dembroker, Michael Z -pg. D-13-32
Demokesko, Lula M -pg. D-4-87
Dennen, William A -pg. D-13-15
Dennis, Edward D -pg. D-13-15
Derguan, Joseph O -pg. D-13-15
Desa, Josefa B -pg. D-1-31
Desa, Maria D -pg. D-1-31
Desa, Nieves L -pg. D-4-116
Devenport, William D -pg. D-13-34
Devin, Kenneth C -pg. D-13-5
Devore, David A -pg. D-13-10
Dexter, Arthur E -pg. D-13-36
Diaz, Adela B -pg. D-4-81
Diaz, Agustin T -pg. D-4-5
Diaz, Alejandro T -pg. D-4-5
Diaz, Alfonsina T -pg. D-1-3
Diaz, Alfred M -pg. D-10-2
Diaz, Amparo LG -pg. D-4-47
Diaz, Ana B -pg. D-4-81
Diaz, Ana C -pg. D-3-66
Diaz, Ana G -pg. D-4-11
Diaz, Ana P -pg. D-11-44
Diaz, Ana P -pg. D-11-44
Diaz, Andresina T -pg. D-11-16
Diaz, Antonia F -pg. D-10-2
Diaz, Antonio F -pg. D-4-81
Diaz, Antonio SN -pg. D-4-11
Diaz, Atanacio T -pg. D-4-5
Diaz, Cecilia T -pg. D-1-3
Diaz, Cecilio T -pg. D-4-5
Diaz, Concepcion -pg. D-5-90
Diaz, Concepcion C -pg. D-11-16
Diaz, Concepcion F -pg. D-11-17
Diaz, Concepcion L -pg. D-2-35
Diaz, Concepcion L -pg. D-11-33
Diaz, Consolacion B -pg. D-4-81
Diaz, Dolores LG -pg. D-4-47
Diaz, Dolores P -pg. D-11-44
Diaz, Doroteo D -pg. D-4-5
Diaz, Elizabeth M -pg. D-10-2

Diaz, Elpidia P -pg. D-11-44
Diaz, Engracia C -pg. D-11-6
Diaz, Felix L -pg. D-11-33
Diaz, Filomino C -pg. D-2-50
Diaz, Francisca P -pg. D-1-44
Diaz, Francisco -pg. D-5-90
Diaz, Francisco L -pg. D-2-35
Diaz, Francisco L -pg. D-11-33
Diaz, Francisco S -pg. D-4-81
Diaz, Grabiel T -pg. D-4-5
Diaz, Guadalupe C -pg. D-11-6
Diaz, Ignacia F -pg. D-4-81
Diaz, Ignacio F -pg. D-4-81
Diaz, Irene M -pg. D-10-2
Diaz, Isabel L -pg. D-11-33
Diaz, Jesus F -pg. D-4-81
Diaz, Joaquin C -pg. D-11-16
Diaz, Joaquin F -pg. D-4-81
Diaz, Joaquin M -pg. D-10-2
Diaz, Joaquin M -pg. D-11-33
Diaz, Joaquin T -pg. D-1-3
Diaz, Joaquin T -pg. D-1-3
Diaz, Joaquina T -pg. D-11-16
Diaz, John M -pg. D-10-2
Diaz, Jose C -pg. D-11-6
Diaz, Jose C -pg. D-11-17
Diaz, Jose D -pg. D-4-36
Diaz, Jose F -pg. D-10-2
Diaz, Joseph M -pg. D-10-2
Diaz, Juan B -pg. D-2-34
Diaz, Juan B -pg. D-5-90
Diaz, Juan C -pg. D-11-17
Diaz, Juan F -pg. D-4-81
Diaz, Juan M -pg. D-11-44
Diaz, Juan S -pg. D-4-81
Diaz, Juan T -pg. D-1-3
Diaz, Julia G -pg. D-4-12
Diaz, Justina F -pg. D-11-17
Diaz, Magdalena F -pg. D-11-17
Diaz, Magdalena M -pg. D-11-33
Diaz, Manuel C -pg. D-11-6
Diaz, Manuel P -pg. D-11-44
Diaz, Manuel T -pg. D-11-16
Diaz, Maria B -pg. D-4-81
Diaz, Maria F -pg. D-4-81
Diaz, Maria F -pg. D-10-2
Diaz, Maria G -pg. D-4-11
Diaz, Maria S -pg. D-4-81
Diaz, Maria T -pg. D-1-3
Diaz, Maria T -pg. D-4-5
Diaz, Mary D M -pg. D-10-2
Diaz, Natividad T -pg. D-4-5
Diaz, Nicolas T -pg. D-11-16
Diaz, Pedro C -pg. D-11-6
Diaz, Regina P -pg. D-11-45
Diaz, Rita F -pg. D-4-81
Diaz, Rosa B -pg. D-4-81
Diaz, Rosa C -pg. D-11-6
Diaz, Rosa C -pg. D-11-6

Diaz, Rosa L -pg. D-2-35
Diaz, Rosa L -pg. D-5-90
Diaz, Rosa LG -pg. D-4-47
Diaz, Tomasa C -pg. D-11-6
Diaz, Veronica -pg. D-5-90
Diaz, Veronica L -pg. D-2-35
Diaz, Vicente L -pg. D-11-33
Diaz, Vicente P -pg. D-11-44
Diaz, Vicente T -pg. D-4-5
Diaz, Vicente T -pg. D-11-16
Diaz, Zacarias G -pg. D-4-12
DiBaun, William G -pg. D-13-34
Dickson, Joseph W -pg. D-13-41
Diego, Agueda D -pg. D-8-4
Diego, Dolores D -pg. D-8-4
Diego, Dolores SN -pg. D-8-17
Diego, Edward S -pg. D-8-40
Diego, Enemesio SN -pg. D-8-4
Diego, Florentina D -pg. D-8-4
Diego, Francisco D -pg. D-8-4
Diego, Ignacia LG -pg. D-8-29
Diego, Jesus SN -pg. D-8-17
Diego, Joaquin SN -pg. D-8-17
Diego, Jose SN -pg. D-8-40
Diego, Juan N -pg. D-8-18
Diego, Juan N -pg. D-8-18
Diego, Juan S -pg. D-8-40
Diego, Juan SN -pg. D-8-17
Diego, Maria D -pg. D-8-4
Diego, Maria N -pg. D-8-18
Diego, Regina D -pg. D-8-4
Diego, Romauldo C -pg. D-8-17
Diego, Rosa S -pg. D-8-40
Diego, Rosa SN -pg. D-8-17
Diego, Rosalia N -pg. D-8-18
Diego, Tomas S -pg. D-8-40
Diego, Vicente C -pg. D-8-4
Diego, Vicente SN -pg. D-8-17
Digue, Alvin A -pg. D-13-5
Dillard, Charlie G -pg. D-13-36
Dillon, Lloyd A -pg. D-13-21
Dillon, Lydia M -pg. D-3-60
Dimapan, Antonia A -pg. D-12-2
Dimapan, Carmen C -pg. D-4-44
Dimapan, Ignacio A -pg. D-4-24
Dimapan, Jose C -pg. D-4-44
Dimapan, Mariano D -pg. D-4-24
Dimapan, Mercedes S -pg. D-4-125
Dimapan, Rosa C -pg. D-4-44
Dimapan, Rosario C -pg. D-4-44
Dimapan, Vicente A -pg. D-4-44
Dimapan, Vicente I -pg. D-12-2
Dinamore, Marie C -pg. D-1-55
Dinsmoore, Alfred -pg. D-13-44
Ditlerson, Raymond E -pg. D-13-15
Divera, Ana B -pg. D-2-80
Divera, Carmen B -pg. D-2-80
Divera, Donato B -pg. D-2-80
Divera, Francisca B -pg. D-2-80

Divera, Juan B -pg. D-2-80
Divera, Marcos A -pg. D-2-81
Divera, Nicolas A -pg. D-2-80
Divera, Rogelio B -pg. D-2-80
Dixon, Kenneth E -pg. D-13-5
Dobry, John H -pg. D-13-22
Dodson, James P -pg. D-13-41
Dodson, Vern -pg. D-13-11
Donato, Juan C -pg. D-13-22
Dooley, Florence B -pg. D-4-85
Dooley, Tevin F -pg. D-13-22
Dooley, Tevis C -pg. D-4-85
Dooley, William -pg. D-13-15
Dornbey, Francis P -pg. D-13-11
Dorrett, David A -pg. D-13-22
Dorsey, Oscar D -pg. D-13-22
Dorsine, Charle E -pg. D-13-11
Doty, Thomas W -pg. D-13-5
Dougherty, Gerald J -pg. D-13-36
Ducey, James A -pg. D-13-15
Duckett, Andrew J -pg. D-13-5
Dudley, Reese R -pg. D-13-36
Duenas, Agustin -pg. D-3-49
Duenas, Alfredo C -pg. D-1-22
Duenas, Ana -pg. D-3-26
Duenas, Ana -pg. D-5-74
Duenas, Ana B -pg. D-1-36
Duenas, Ana B -pg. D-4-42
Duenas, Ana C -pg. D-2-43
Duenas, Ana C -pg. D-2-57
Duenas, Ana F -pg. D-2-75
Duenas, Ana M -pg. D-5-69
Duenas, Ana M -pg. D-8-2
Duenas, Ana P -pg. D-8-3
Duenas, Ana S -pg. D-11-17
Duenas, Ana S -pg. D-11-18
Duenas, Antonia C -pg. D-2-57
Duenas, Antonia F -pg. D-2-62
Duenas, Antonia L -pg. D-4-95
Duenas, Antonia T -pg. D-4-115
Duenas, Antonio -pg. D-3-49
Duenas, Antonio B -pg. D-3-38
Duenas, Antonio C -pg. D-2-43
Duenas, Antonio F -pg. D-1-35
Duenas, Antonio M -pg. D-3-48
Duenas, Antonio S -pg. D-11-44
Duenas, Antonio T -pg. D-8-49
Duenas, Anunsacion T -pg. D-8-50
Duenas, Asuncion B -pg. D-2-26
Duenas, Asuncion P -pg. D-4-115
Duenas, Benita T -pg. D-8-49
Duenas, Bernardino F -pg. D-2-62
Duenas, Brigida SN -pg. D-8-7
Duenas, Carlos S -pg. D-10-34
Duenas, Carlos T -pg. D-8-50
Duenas, Carmelo S -pg. D-11-45
Duenas, Carmen A -pg. D-11-45
Duenas, Carmen C -pg. D-1-22
Duenas, Carmen C -pg. D-11-44

Duenas, Carmen LG -pg. D-5-74
Duenas, Cartina M -pg. D-8-27
Duenas, Catalina B -pg. D-1-36
Duenas, Catalina D -pg. D-8-31
Duenas, Catalina LG -pg. D-4-111
Duenas, Catalina Q -pg. D-11-11
Duenas, Celedonia L -pg. D-8-4
Duenas, Clemente -pg. D-5-74
Duenas, Clemente C -pg. D-5-74
Duenas, Concepcion C -pg. D-1-22
Duenas, Concepcion C -pg. D-1-22
Duenas, Concepcion E -pg. D-7-12
Duenas, Conchita F -pg. D-5-29
Duenas, Cristobal C -pg. D-1-22
Duenas, Delgadina T -pg. D-8-50
Duenas, Dolores C -pg. D-2-43
Duenas, Dolores F -pg. D-5-28
Duenas, Dolores LG -pg. D-4-112
Duenas, Dolores R -pg. D-5-87
Duenas, Dolores S -pg. D-2-32
Duenas, Dometila A -pg. D-1-36
Duenas, Dometrio S -pg. D-5-43
Duenas, Dominica M -pg. D-8-3
Duenas, Eduardo C -pg. D-1-22
Duenas, Elidia -pg. D-3-26
Duenas, Eliza C -pg. D-1-22
Duenas, Eliza C -pg. D-8-32
Duenas, Emelia B -pg. D-2-59
Duenas, Emelia C -pg. D-5-28
Duenas, Engracia B -pg. D-2-59
Duenas, Enrique A -pg. D-11-45
Duenas, Enrique D -pg. D-8-49
Duenas, Enrique F -pg. D-1-35
Duenas, Enriqueta M -pg. D-8-27
Duenas, Esperanza S -pg. D-5-43
Duenas, Esteban M -pg. D-8-3
Duenas, Estella C -pg. D-1-22
Duenas, Ester P -pg. D-8-3
Duenas, Eugenia -pg. D-3-48
Duenas, Felisa M -pg. D-3-7
Duenas, Fernando T -pg. D-8-46
Duenas, Flora P -pg. D-8-3
Duenas, Florencio Q -pg. D-5-28
Duenas, Francisca -pg. D-3-6
Duenas, Francisca L -pg. D-8-4
Duenas, Francisco A -pg. D-2-75
Duenas, Francisco B -pg. D-2-59
Duenas, Francisco C -pg. D-2-57
Duenas, Francisco C -pg. D-3-6
Duenas, Francisco D -pg. D-11-13
Duenas, Francisco F -pg. D-1-35
Duenas, Francisco M -pg. D-8-4
Duenas, Francisco M -pg. D-12-17
Duenas, Francisco Q -pg. D-5-17
Duenas, Francisco S -pg. D-10-34
Duenas, Francisco S -pg. D-11-17
Duenas, Francisco SN -pg. D-10-34
Duenas, Fredicinda M -pg. D-8-3
Duenas, Gonzalo D -pg. D-8-31

Duenas, Gregorio A -pg. D-1-35
Duenas, Gregorio D -pg. D-8-31
Duenas, Gregorio F -pg. D-1-36
Duenas, Guadalupe LG -pg. D-4-111
Duenas, Ignacia C -pg. D-11-28
Duenas, Ignacia LG -pg. D-4-111
Duenas, Ignacio B -pg. D-5-45
Duenas, Ignacio T -pg. D-4-115
Duenas, Ignacio T -pg. D-8-50
Duenas, Irene M -pg. D-4-55
Duenas, Isabel -pg. D-3-26
Duenas, Isabel B -pg. D-5-43
Duenas, Isabel C -pg. D-1-22
Duenas, Isabel LG -pg. D-4-111
Duenas, Isabel M -pg. D-8-27
Duenas, Isabel P -pg. D-3-26
Duenas, Jesus -pg. D-3-7
Duenas, Jesus -pg. D-11-11
Duenas, Jesus B -pg. D-2-11
Duenas, Jesus B -pg. D-2-59
Duenas, Jesus C -pg. D-13-32
Duenas, Jesus D -pg. D-8-31
Duenas, Jesus E -pg. D-5-42
Duenas, Jesus F -pg. D-1-36
Duenas, Jesus M -pg. D-8-27
Duenas, Jesus Q -pg. D-5-17
Duenas, Jesus S -pg. D-5-43
Duenas, Jesus S -pg. D-10-34
Duenas, Jesus SN -pg. D-8-7
Duenas, Jesus T -pg. D-8-7
Duenas, Joaquin -pg. D-3-26
Duenas, Joaquin A -pg. D-2-75
Duenas, Joaquin B -pg. D-1-36
Duenas, Joaquin B -pg. D-5-43
Duenas, Joaquin B -pg. D-11-23
Duenas, Joaquin D -pg. D-1-51
Duenas, Joaquin D -pg. D-2-26
Duenas, Joaquin F -pg. D-1-35
Duenas, Joaquina T -pg. D-8-31
Duenas, Jose -pg. D-3-7
Duenas, Jose A -pg. D-3-48
Duenas, Jose B -pg. D-2-8
Duenas, Jose B -pg. D-2-59
Duenas, Jose C -pg. D-1-22
Duenas, Jose C -pg. D-1-22
Duenas, Jose C -pg. D-2-56
Duenas, Jose C -pg. D-5-28
Duenas, Jose C -pg. D-8-32
Duenas, Jose C -pg. D-11-44
Duenas, Jose D -pg. D-8-31
Duenas, Jose F -pg. D-2-57
Duenas, Jose L -pg. D-11-17
Duenas, Jose LG -pg. D-4-111
Duenas, Jose M -pg. D-5-17
Duenas, Jose M -pg. D-8-27
Duenas, Jose P -pg. D-11-11
Duenas, Jose Q -pg. D-2-83
Duenas, Jose S -pg. D-5-43
Duenas, Jose S -pg. D-10-34

Duenas, Jose S -pg. D-11-17
Duenas, Jose SN -pg. D-8-7
Duenas, Jose T -pg. D-8-50
Duenas, Josefa B -pg. D-2-8
Duenas, Josefa B -pg. D-2-11
Duenas, Josefa B -pg. D-5-74
Duenas, Josefa D -pg. D-1-51
Duenas, Josefa S -pg. D-11-13
Duenas, Josefina -pg. D-3-26
Duenas, Josefina B -pg. D-1-36
Duenas, Juan -pg. D-5-74
Duenas, Juan B -pg. D-1-36
Duenas, Juan B -pg. D-2-59
Duenas, Juan B -pg. D-4-42
Duenas, Juan D -pg. D-1-51
Duenas, Juan D -pg. D-8-31
Duenas, Juan F -pg. D-1-36
Duenas, Juan F -pg. D-2-62
Duenas, Juan F -pg. D-4-111
Duenas, Juan M -pg. D-1-51
Duenas, Juan M -pg. D-5-45
Duenas, Juan M -pg. D-8-40
Duenas, Juan P -pg. D-11-11
Duenas, Juan Q -pg. D-5-17
Duenas, Juan R -pg. D-13-26
Duenas, Juan S -pg. D-2-28
Duenas, Juan T -pg. D-8-2
Duenas, Juan T -pg. D-8-27
Duenas, Juan T -pg. D-8-50
Duenas, Juana E -pg. D-5-17
Duenas, Juana T -pg. D-4-115
Duenas, Juanita F -pg. D-5-29
Duenas, Julia E -pg. D-4-95
Duenas, Julia P -pg. D-11-11
Duenas, Julian M -pg. D-5-17
Duenas, Julian S -pg. D-10-34
Duenas, Juliana R -pg. D-1-22
Duenas, Laura L -pg. D-8-4
Duenas, Lolita F -pg. D-5-29
Duenas, Lucy P -pg. D-11-11
Duenas, Luis P -pg. D-2-11
Duenas, Magdalena S -pg. D-5-46
Duenas, Manuel B -pg. D-5-43
Duenas, Manuel C -pg. D-5-28
Duenas, Manuel D -pg. D-5-46
Duenas, Manuel F -pg. D-1-36
Duenas, Manuel L -pg. D-5-29
Duenas, Manuel M -pg. D-4-55
Duenas, Manuel M -pg. D-8-3
Duenas, Manuel P -pg. D-8-3
Duenas, Manuel Q -pg. D-5-17
Duenas, Manuela F -pg. D-1-35
Duenas, Manuela S -pg. D-10-34
Duenas, Maria -pg. D-3-7
Duenas, Maria -pg. D-5-74
Duenas, Maria B -pg. D-4-42
Duenas, Maria B -pg. D-5-43
Duenas, Maria C -pg. D-2-43
Duenas, Maria C -pg. D-8-32

Duenas, Maria C -pg. D-8-32
Duenas, Maria D -pg. D-4-43
Duenas, Maria D -pg. D-8-31
Duenas, Maria D -pg. D-11-43
Duenas, Maria F -pg. D-2-62
Duenas, Maria G -pg. D-2-56
Duenas, Maria G -pg. D-11-39
Duenas, Maria L -pg. D-4-95
Duenas, Maria L -pg. D-8-4
Duenas, Maria LG -pg. D-4-111
Duenas, Maria P -pg. D-8-3
Duenas, Maria P -pg. D-11-11
Duenas, Maria Q -pg. D-5-17
Duenas, Maria Q -pg. D-11-11
Duenas, Maria Q -pg. D-11-11
Duenas, Maria S -pg. D-5-43
Duenas, Maria S -pg. D-10-34
Duenas, Maria SN -pg. D-3-48
Duenas, Maria SN -pg. D-8-7
Duenas, Maria SN -pg. D-11-17
Duenas, Mariano D -pg. D-10-36
Duenas, Marta L -pg. D-8-4
Duenas, Mary D -pg. D-2-83
Duenas, Mary J -pg. D-2-83
Duenas, Milagros A -pg. D-3-6
Duenas, Nicolasa C -pg. D-5-27
Duenas, Nicolasa P -pg. D-4-115
Duenas, Olympia B -pg. D-4-43
Duenas, Pedro A -pg. D-11-45
Duenas, Pedro B -pg. D-2-11
Duenas, Pedro B -pg. D-5-45
Duenas, Pedro L -pg. D-13-35
Duenas, Pedro LG -pg. D-4-111
Duenas, Pedro M -pg. D-8-27
Duenas, Pedro Q -pg. D-11-11
Duenas, Pedro S -pg. D-13-29
Duenas, Pedro T -pg. D-8-50
Duenas, Ramon C -pg. D-5-17
Duenas, Ramon C -pg. D-5-74
Duenas, Ramon D -pg. D-8-31
Duenas, Ramon Q -pg. D-5-27
Duenas, Ramon S -pg. D-11-17
Duenas, Ramon T -pg. D-8-31
Duenas, Remedios B -pg. D-1-36
Duenas, Remedios B -pg. D-4-42
Duenas, Remedios D -pg. D-1-51
Duenas, Rita B -pg. D-4-42
Duenas, Rita D -pg. D-8-31
Duenas, Rita F -pg. D-2-62
Duenas, Rita T -pg. D-8-49
Duenas, Roman L -pg. D-8-4
Duenas, Roman P -pg. D-4-115
Duenas, Rosa B -pg. D-2-59
Duenas, Rosa C -pg. D-3-7
Duenas, Rosa C -pg. D-8-32
Duenas, Rosa F -pg. D-5-17
Duenas, Rosalia C -pg. D-2-43
Duenas, Rosalina M -pg. D-8-2
Duenas, Rosario B -pg. D-4-42

Duenas, Rosario M -pg. D-8-3
Duenas, Rufina L -pg. D-4-95
Duenas, Santiago -pg. D-11-11
Duenas, Santiago S -pg. D-5-43
Duenas, Serafina S -pg. D-11-18
Duenas, Silvestre D -pg. D-8-31
Duenas, Soledad D -pg. D-11-28
Duenas, Supiana B -pg. D-8-49
Duenas, Teresa T -pg. D-8-31
Duenas, Tomasa E -pg. D-1-60
Duenas, Tomasa T -pg. D-8-49
Duenas, Veronica Q -pg. D-11-49
Duenas, Vicente -pg. D-3-49
Duenas, Vicente A -pg. D-1-36
Duenas, Vicente A -pg. D-11-48
Duenas, Vicente B -pg. D-1-36
Duenas, Vicente B -pg. D-2-59
Duenas, Vicente B -pg. D-4-42
Duenas, Vicente D -pg. D-1-51
Duenas, Vicente D -pg. D-8-31
Duenas, Vicente F -pg. D-2-62
Duenas, Vicente F -pg. D-2-75
Duenas, Vicente M -pg. D-3-7
Duenas, Vicente M -pg. D-8-27
Duenas, Vicente Q -pg. D-11-11
Duenas, Vicente T -pg. D-8-50
Duicid, Clarence R -pg. D-13-32
Dumapan, Pedro D -pg. D-5-98
Dumonal, Andresina Q -pg. D-11-38
Dumonal, Candelaria G. -pg. D-11-9
Dumonal, Jose G -pg. D-11-8
Dumonal, Maria Q -pg. D-11-38
Dumonal, Martin L -pg. D-11-8
Dumonal, Pedro G -pg. D-11-38
Dumonal, Rosa Q -pg. D-11-38
Dumonal, Rosalia Q -pg. D-11-38
Dungca, Adela -pg. D-3-37
Dungca, Antonia -pg. D-3-64
Dungca, Carmen -pg. D-3-38
Dungca, Concepcion -pg. D-3-34
Dungca, Concepcion -pg. D-3-37
Dungca, Constansia -pg. D-3-34
Dungca, Emilia Q -pg. D-3-64
Dungca, Esperanza -pg. D-3-37
Dungca, Felicita -pg. D-3-34
Dungca, Felicita -pg. D-3-37
Dungca, Felisberto -pg. D-3-64
Dungca, Felix -pg. D-3-37
Dungca, Felix G -pg. D-3-37
Dungca, Francisco -pg. D-3-34
Dungca, Jose -pg. D-3-34
Dungca, Jose -pg. D-3-38
Dungca, Josefina -pg. D-3-37
Dungca, Juan -pg. D-3-64
Dungca, Justo -pg. D-3-37
Dungca, Justo -pg. D-3-64
Dungca, Maria C -pg. D-3-37
Dungca, Teordoro G -pg. D-3-63
Dungca, Vicenta -pg. D-3-64

Durna, William H Jr. -pg. D-13-15
Dydasco, Ester M -pg. D-1-31
Dydasco, Felix T -pg. D-1-43
Dydasco, Gale M -pg. D-1-31
Dydasco, Gregorio T -pg. D-1-43
Dydasco, Jesus T -pg. D-13-27
Dydasco, Joaquin A -pg. D-2-16
Dydasco, Joaquin T -pg. D-1-43
Dydasco, Jose T -pg. D-1-43
Dydasco, Juan T -pg. D-1-43
Dydasco, Maria M -pg. D-1-31
Dydasco, Maria M -pg. D-1-31
Dydasco, Oscar M -pg. D-1-31
Dydasco, Rosa T -pg. D-1-43
Dydasco, Vicente A -pg. D-2-13
Dyer, Virgil R -pg. D-13-15
Easley, William P -pg. D-13-46
Eastham, Walter H -pg. D-13-5
Easton, Charlie H -pg. D-13-36
Eaton, Albert ? -pg. D-13-5
Eclavea, Antonio R -pg. D-1-26
Eclavea, Enrique R -pg. D-3-23
Eclavea, Lucio Q -pg. D-1-26
Eclavea, Tomasa R -pg. D-1-26
Edmondson, Harold D -pg. D-13-19
Edwards, Charles W -pg. D-10-32
Edwards, Edwin F -pg. D-10-32
Edwards, Francis D -pg. D-10-32
Edwards, Richard H -pg. D-10-32
Edwing, Alfred E -pg. D-13-33
Egbert, Willard E -pg. D-13-22
Egsnest, John J Jr -pg. D-13-40
Eintinis, Edonaldo -pg. D-13-15
Flatico, Juan A -pg. D-4-46
Elatico, Tomasa M -pg. D-4-46
Elliott, Concepcion M -pg. D-3-58
Elliott, Delia B -pg. D-3-58
Elliott, Hiram W -pg. D-3-58
Elliott, Hiram W -pg. D-3-58
Elliott, Joseph A -pg. D-3-58
Elliott, Lovie E -pg. D-3-58
Elliott, Marion J -pg. D-13-11
Elliott, Mary D -pg. D-3-58
Elliott, Nathaniel L -pg. D-13-45
Elliott, Richard C -pg. D-3-58
Elliott, Woodrow P -pg. D-3-58
Ellis, Augustine J -pg. D-13-11
Elson, Oscar E -pg. D-13-19
Ely, Harold M -pg. D-13-6
English, Floyd E -pg. D-13-33
Eochiliman, Charles -pg. D-13-11
Epstein, Esther B -pg. D-1-16
Epstein, Minna C -pg. D-1-17
Epstein, William I -pg. D-13-18
Erb, Clifford A -pg. D-13-6
Erickson, Albert -pg. D-13-36
Ernest, William B -pg. D-13-6
Eschilsman, Edna V -pg. D-11-10
Espenosa, Ana C -pg. D-1-67

Espenosa, Antonio C -pg. D-1-67
Espenosa, Barceliza C -pg. D-1-67
Espenosa, Joaquin C -pg. D-1-67
Espenosa, Jose C -pg. D-1-67
Espenosa, Juan C -pg. D-1-67
Espenosa, Maria C -pg. D-1-67
Espinosa, Ana M -pg. D-11-39
Espinosa, Ana T -pg. D-9-8
Espinosa, Carmen M -pg. D-9-6
Espinosa, Dolores B -pg. D-4-64
Espinosa, Dolores F -pg. D-1-66
Espinosa, Dolores M -pg. D-9-6
Espinosa, Domingo T -pg. D-9-8
Espinosa, Enemesia N -pg. D-9-9
Espinosa, Francisco B -pg. D-9-27
Espinosa, Francisco C -pg. D-5-87
Espinosa, Ignacia B -pg. D-9-26
Espinosa, Ignacia C -pg. D-9-12
Espinosa, Ignacio M -pg. D-9-6
Espinosa, Isidro B -pg. D-9-27
Espinosa, Jesus -pg. D-13-26
Espinosa, Jesus M -pg. D-9-6
Espinosa, Jesus M -pg. D-11-39
Espinosa, Joaquina B -pg. D-9-26
Espinosa, Joaquina M -pg. D-11-39
Espinosa, Jose M -pg. D-11-39
Espinosa, Jose T -pg. D-9-8
Espinosa, Josefina T -pg. D-9-8
Espinosa, Josephine E -pg. D-11-39
Espinosa, Maria M -pg. D-11-39
Espinosa, Pedro C -pg. D-9-8
Espinosa, Serafin N -pg. D-9-6
Espinosa, Tomasa M -pg. D-11-39
Espinosa, Vicente M -pg. D-9-6
Espinosa, Vicente M -pg. D-9-30
Espinosa, Vicente N -pg. D-9-26
Espinosa, William E -pg. D-11-39
Esteban, Carmen E -pg. D-5-46
Esteban, Felipe E -pg. D-5-45
Esteban, Jesus E -pg. D-5-45
Esteban, Lagrimas E -pg. D-5-46
Esteban, Maria E -pg. D-5-45
Esteban, Maria E -pg. D-5-45
Esteban, Natividad E -pg. D-5-46
Esteban, Pedro P -pg. D-5-45
Estrellas, Maria P -pg. D-7-20
Eueton, Nina C -pg. D-4-51
Eustaquio, Ana C -pg. D-3-68
Eustaquio, Angel B -pg. D-3-68
Eustaquio, Antonio B -pg. D-3-68
Eustaquio, Augusto -pg. D-3-69
Eustaquio, Carlos -pg. D-3-69
Eustaquio, Eduardo -pg. D-3-69
Eustaquio, Elena B -pg. D-3-68
Eustaquio, Felix B -pg. D-3-68
Eustaquio, Florencia B -pg. D-3-69
Eustaquio, Francisco C -pg. D-3-69
Eustaquio, Gregorio B -pg. D-3-68
Eustaquio, Jose B -pg. D-3-68

Eustaquio, Jose G -pg. D-3-68
Eustaquio, Josefina C -pg. D-3-55
Eustaquio, Reducinda G -pg. D-3-65
Eustaquio, Rosalia -pg. D-3-69
Eustaquio, Virginia -pg. D-3-69
Evangelista, Ana M -pg. D-1-4
Evangelista, Apolonio E -pg. D-1-4
Evangelista, Dolores T -pg. D-1-70
Evangelista, Jesus M -pg. D-1-4
Evangelista, Jesus T -pg. D-1-70
Evangelista, Jose M -pg. D-1-4
Evangelista, Jose T -pg. D-1-70
Evangelista, Josefa M -pg. D-1-4
Evangelista, Juan T -pg. D-1-70
Evangelista, Manuel T -pg. D-1-70
Evangelista, Pedro E -pg. D-1-70
Evangelista, Pedro T -pg. D-1-70
Evangelista, Rosa T -pg. D-1-70
Evangelista, Rosalia T -pg. D-1-70
Evangelista, Rosario T -pg. D-1-70
Evangelista, Vicente M -pg. D-1-4
Evaristo, Francisco -pg. D-5-97
Evaristo, Jesus L -pg. D-5-98
Evaristo, Joaquin -pg. D-5-97
Evaristo, Jose E -pg. D-5-97
Evaristo, Margarito -pg. D-5-97
Evaristo, Maria L -pg. D-5-97
Evaristo, Pedro -pg. D-5-97
Evelhoch, Calvin A -pg. D-13-40
Fairly, Marian B -pg. D-6-6
Faith, Dale -pg. D-13-40
Fall, Caroline W -pg. D-3-45
Fall, Fred W -pg. D-3-45
Fard, Daniel -pg. D-13-6
Farfan, Ignacio C -pg. D-1-35
Farfan, Jesus C -pg. D-1-34
Farfan, Jose C -pg. D-1-34
Farfan, Rosa C -pg. D-1-35
Farley, William T -pg. D-13-37
Farmer, Claude K -pg. D-13-46
Farrell, Antonia -pg. D-3-70
Farrell, Filomena -pg. D-3-70
Farrell, Joaquin -pg. D-3-70
Farrell, Maria A -pg. D-3-70
Faula, James M -pg. D-13-20
Fausto, Joaquina G -pg. D-3-23
Feelings, Antonio G -pg. D-13-37
Fegurgur, Alejandra N -pg. D-9-26
Fegurgur, Ana N -pg. D-9-26
Fegurgur, Carmen F -pg. D-9-27
Fegurgur, Cristina B -pg. D-9-4
Fegurgur, Dolores D -pg. D-5-90
Fegurgur, Dolores N -pg. D-9-4
Fegurgur, Dolores SN -pg. D-12-16
Fegurgur, Elena B -pg. D-9-4
Fegurgur, Enrique F -pg. D-4-18
Fegurgur, Enrique F -pg. D-12-16
Fegurgur, Eugenia N -pg. D-9-4
Fegurgur, Felix SN -pg. D-12-16

Fegurgur, Francisco B -pg. D-9-4
Fegurgur, Francisco J -pg. D-4-18
Fegurgur, Francisco N -pg. D-9-26
Fegurgur, Francisco SN -pg. D-12-16
Fegurgur, Francisco F -pg. D-4-9
Fegurgur, Isabel T -pg. D-4-9
Fegurgur, Isidro N -pg. D-9-26
Fegurgur, Jesus N -pg. D-9-26
Fegurgur, Jesus S -pg. D-9-32
Fegurgur, Jesus S -pg. D-11-35
Fegurgur, Joaquin N -pg. D-9-25
Fegurgur, Joaquin S -pg. D-11-35
Fegurgur, Jose F -pg. D-5-90
Fegurgur, Jose S -pg. D-9-32
Fegurgur, Manuela C -pg. D-9-25
Fegurgur, Maria S -pg. D-9-32
Fegurgur, Maria SN -pg. D-12-16
Fegurgur, Nicolas SN -pg. D-12-16
Fegurgur, Rita J -pg. D-4-18
Fegurgur, Rita S -pg. D-9-32
Fegurgur, Rosa A -pg. D-9-46
Fegurgur, Rosalia J -pg. D-4-18
Fegurgur, Rosauro C -pg. D-9-32
Fegurgur, Venancio N -pg. D-9-4
Fegurgur, Veronica S -pg. D-9-32
Feja, Francisco F -pg. D-5-39
Feja, Maria F -pg. D-5-39
Feja, Vicenta F -pg. D-5-39
Fejarang, Ana -pg. D-3-8
Fejarang, Angelina -pg. D-3-74
Fejarang, Anicia -pg. D-3-8
Fejarang, Gregorio -pg. D-3-8
Fejarang, Jesus -pg. D-3-74
Fejarang, Jesus M -pg. D-2-39
Fejarang, Joaquin C -pg. D-3-8
Fejarang, Jose -pg. D-3-8
Fejarang, Jose -pg. D-3-74
Fejarang, Jose M -pg. D-2-38
Fejarang, Jose P -pg. D-3-74
Fejarang, Juana C -pg. D-3-15
Fejarang, Laura -pg. D-3-74
Fejarang, Maria -pg. D-3-74
Fejarang, Maria -pg. D-3-74
Fejarang, Mercedes C -pg. D-3-8
Fejarang, Precila -pg. D-3-8
Fejarang, Rosa C -pg. D-3-8
Fejeran, Amanda P -pg. D-7-3
Fejeran, Ana B -pg. D-10-19
Fejeran, Ana C -pg. D-10-7
Fejeran, Ana C -pg. D-10-8
Fejeran, Andrea A -pg. D-7-9
Fejeran, Antonia C -pg. D-4-68
Fejeran, Antonio C -pg. D-10-16
Fejeran, Antonio S -pg. D-10-31
Fejeran, Barcelisa B -pg. D-10-19
Fejeran, Benigno C -pg. D-4-68
Fejeran, Caridad C -pg. D-10-7
Fejeran, Concepcion -pg. D-5-76
Fejeran, Concepcion I -pg. D-10-7

Fejeran, Concepcion T -pg. D-7-13
Fejeran, Consolacion SN -pg. D-7-3
Fejeran, Cristina C -pg. D-4-68
Fejeran, Delfina Q -pg. D-7-6
Fejeran, Dolores A -pg. D-8-28
Fejeran, Dolores C -pg. D-10-8
Fejeran, Dolores P -pg. D-7-7
Fejeran, Dolores S -pg. D-10-7
Fejeran, Dolores S -pg. D-10-31
Fejeran, Domingo S -pg. D-10-37
Fejeran, Domingo SN -pg. D-10-6
Fejeran, Edward S -pg. D-10-31
Fejeran, Encarnacion S -pg. D-10-37
Fejeran, Enrique C -pg. D-10-8
Fejeran, Enrique F -pg. D-4-56
Fejeran, Enrique P -pg. D-7-7
Fejeran, Enrique P -pg. D-13-29
Fejeran, Felicidad M -pg. D-5-70
Fejeran, Felix S -pg. D-10-19
Fejeran, Florencio P -pg. D-13-26
Fejeran, Francisca C -pg. D-4-67
Fejeran, Francisca C -pg. D-4-115
Fejeran, Francisco C -pg. D-4-67
Fejeran, Francisco C -pg. D-10-8
Fejeran, Francisco P -pg. D-7-7
Fejeran, Geronimo C -pg. D-4-68
Fejeran, Ignacio A -pg. D-7-9
Fejeran, Ignacio S -pg. D-10-31
Fejeran, Isidro S -pg. D-10-19
Fejeran, Jesus A -pg. D-8-28
Fejeran, Jesus B -pg. D-10-19
Fejeran, Jesus C -pg. D-4-115
Fejeran, Jesus C -pg. D-10-14
Fejeran, Jesus F -pg. D-7-20
Fejeran, Jesus I -pg. D-10-7
Fejeran, Jesus Q -pg. D-7-6
Fejeran, Jesus S -pg. D-10-6
Fejeran, Joaquin C -pg. D-4-67
Fejeran, Joaquin C -pg. D-4-68
Fejeran, Joaquin C -pg. D-10-31
Fejeran, Joaquin C -pg. D-13-29
Fejeran, Joaquin P -pg. D-4-67
Fejeran, Joaquin P -pg. D-13-29
Fejeran, Joaquin Q -pg. D-7-6
Fejeran, Joaquin R -pg. D-4-57
Fejeran, Joaquin S -pg. D-10-7
Fejeran, Joaquin T -pg. D-5-91
Fejeran, Jose A -pg. D-7-2
Fejeran, Jose C -pg. D-4-67
Fejeran, Jose C -pg. D-4-98
Fejeran, Jose C -pg. D-4-115
Fejeran, Jose C -pg. D-10-7
Fejeran, Jose C -pg. D-10-8
Fejeran, Jose LG -pg. D-8-28
Fejeran, Jose P -pg. D-7-3
Fejeran, Jose R -pg. D-5-74
Fejeran, Jose R -pg. D-10-19
Fejeran, Jose S -pg. D-4-67
Fejeran, Jose S -pg. D-10-7

Fejeran, Jose S -pg. D-10-31
Fejeran, Jose SN -pg. D-7-3
Fejeran, Josef C -pg. D-4-68
Fejeran, Juan A -pg. D-8-28
Fejeran, Juan B -pg. D-10-19
Fejeran, Juan C -pg. D-4-67
Fejeran, Juan C -pg. D-10-8
Fejeran, Juan LG -pg. D-8-24
Fejeran, Juan P -pg. D-4-67
Fejeran, Juan S -pg. D-7-9
Fejeran, Juan S -pg. D-10-6
Fejeran, Juan T -pg. D-7-13
Fejeran, Juana S -pg. D-10-37
Fejeran, Juliana C -pg. D-4-21
Fejeran, Justo -pg. D-13-34
Fejeran, Lucas S -pg. D-10-37
Fejeran, Luis A -pg. D-5-70
Fejeran, Luis C -pg. D-4-67
Fejeran, Magdalena C -pg. D-4-68
Fejeran, Magdalena R -pg. D-4-57
Fejeran, Manuel C -pg. D-4-68
Fejeran, Manuel S -pg. D-10-37
Fejeran, Manuel F -pg. D-4-26
Fejeran, Maria B -pg. D-10-19
Fejeran, Maria C -pg. D-4-67
Fejeran, Maria C -pg. D-4-115
Fejeran, Maria C -pg. D-4-120
Fejeran, Maria C -pg. D-10-7
Fejeran, Maria I -pg. D-10-7
Fejeran, Maria Q -pg. D-7-6
Fejeran, Maria R -pg. D-10-19
Fejeran, Maria S -pg. D-10-6
Fejeran, Maria S -pg. D-10-6
Fejeran, Martina T -pg. D-7-13
Fejeran, Miguel C -pg. D-10-8
Fejeran, Pedro A -pg. D-7-13
Fejeran, Pedro C -pg. D-4-68
Fejeran, Pedro R -pg. D-4-57
Fejeran, Pilar S -pg. D-10-37
Fejeran, Potenciana F -pg. D-4-26
Fejeran, Ramon C -pg. D-4-21
Fejeran, Ramon F -pg. D-4-26
Fejeran, Ramon G -pg. D-8-17
Fejeran, Ramona S -pg. D-10-37
Fejeran, Remedio T -pg. D-7-13
Fejeran, Remedios C -pg. D-4-21
Fejeran, Remedios C -pg. D-4-120
Fejeran, Rita LG -pg. D-4-117
Fejeran, Rosa B -pg. D-10-14
Fejeran, Rosa C -pg. D-4-68
Fejeran, Rosa C -pg. D-7-8
Fejeran, Rosa C -pg. D-7-8
Fejeran, Rosa Q -pg. D-7-6
Fejeran, Rosa SN -pg. D-7-3
Fejeran, Rosalia C -pg. D-4-68
Fejeran, Teresa M -pg. D-8-24
Fejeran, Tomas A -pg. D-8-28
Fejeran, Tomas P -pg. D-7-7
Fejeran, Tomas R -pg. D-10-19

Fejeran, Tomas S -pg. D-10-31
Fejeran, Vicenta P -pg. D-4-67
Fejeran, Vicente B -pg. D-10-19
Fejeran, Vicente C -pg. D-4-115
Fejeran, Vicente C -pg. D-4-120
Fejeran, Vicente Q -pg. D-7-6
Fejerang, Cerile A -pg. D-1-53
Fejerang, Francisco -pg. D-11-28
Fejerang, Ignacia N -pg. D-8-10
Fejerang, Maria M -pg. D-11-30
Feld, Ferne E -pg. D-4-116
Feldman, Joseph -pg. D-13-15
Felt, Theodoreo M -pg. D-13-27
Fender, Albert -pg. D-13-32
Ferguson, John C -pg. D-13-6
Feritan, Francis I -pg. D-13-3
Feritan, Francis I -pg. D-13-3
Feritan, Mary E -pg. D-13-3
Feritan, Michael E -pg. D-13-3
Fernandez, Agapito C -pg. D-10-2
Fernandez, Ana C -pg. D-2-63
Fernandez, Ana L -pg. D-5-33
Fernandez, Ana Q -pg. D-5-54
Fernandez, Ana SA -pg. D-5-21
Fernandez, Antonia SA -pg. D-5-21
Fernandez, Antonio O -pg. D-12-7
Fernandez, Carmen Q -pg. D-12-3
Fernandez, Consolacion L -pg. D-5-33
Fernandez, Engracia C -pg. D-10-2
Fernandez, Francisca C -pg. D-2-63
Fernandez, Francisco D -pg. D-13-26
Fernandez, Gonzalo L -pg. D-5-33
Fernandez, Isabel P -pg. D-12-7
Fernandez, Jesus L -pg. D-3-47
Fernandez, Jesus L -pg. D-5-32
Fernandez, Jesus L -pg. D-5-33
Fernandez, Jesus P -pg. D-12-7
Fernandez, Jesus Q -pg. D-12-7
Fernandez, Jesus SA -pg. D-5-22
Fernandez, Joaquina L -pg. D-5-32
Fernandez, Jose L -pg. D-5-21
Fernandez, Jose L -pg. D-5-33
Fernandez, Jose P -pg. D-12-7
Fernandez, Jose Q -pg. D-5-32
Fernandez, Juan C -pg. D-2-63
Fernandez, Juan L -pg. D-5-32
Fernandez, Maria L -pg. D-5-32
Fernandez, Maria P -pg. D-12-7
Fernandez, Maria Q -pg. D-12-7
Fernandez, Maria S -pg. D-3-48
Fernandez, Maria SA -pg. D-5-22
Fernandez, Mercedes Q -pg. D-12-7
Fernandez, Obdulia Q -pg. D-12-3
Fernandez, Paz L -pg. D-5-33
Fernandez, Roque O -pg. D-12-7
Fernandez, Santiago L -pg. D-5-33
Fernandez, Satunina -pg. D-1-26
Fernandez, Soledad L -pg. D-5-33
Fernandez, Soledad S -pg. D-3-48

Fernandez, Vicente C -pg. D-2-63
Fernandez, Vicente C -pg. D-10-2
Fernandez, Vicente L -pg. D-5-33
Filbins, Kenneth R -pg. D-13-23
Finian, Albert W -pg. D-13-37
Finkler, Frank S -pg. D-13-37
Finona, Ana F -pg. D-1-31
Finona, Antonia R -pg. D-1-31
Finona, Antonia T -pg. D-5-62
Finona, Antonio C -pg. D-10-37
Finona, Antonio F -pg. D-10-37
Finona, Beatres R -pg. D-1-31
Finona, Elena R -pg. D-1-31
Finona, Eliza T -pg. D-5-59
Finona, Engracia R -pg. D-1-31
Finona, Estella R -pg. D-1-31
Finona, Fidel T -pg. D-5-62
Finona, Francisco C -pg. D-10-36
Finona, Francisco G -pg. D-5-62
Finona, Ignacia T -pg. D-5-59
Finona, Jesus G -pg. D-1-46
Finona, Joaquin C -pg. D-10-37
Finona, Joaquin R -pg. D-1-31
Finona, Jose F -pg. D-10-37
Finona, Jose G -pg. D-5-59
Finona, Jose SN -pg. D-10-36
Finona, Jose T -pg. D-5-60
Finona, Jose T -pg. D-5-62
Finona, Manuel C -pg. D-10-37
Finona, Manuela C -pg. D-10-36
Finona, Maria R -pg. D-1-31
Finona, Maria SN -pg. D-10-36
Finona, Regina C -pg. D-10-36
Finona, Rita G -pg. D-1-46
Finona, Rosa R -pg. D-1-31
Finona, Rosalia T -pg. D-5-59
Finona, Teresa F -pg. D-10-37
Finona, Vicenta T -pg. D-5-60
Finona, Vicente T -pg. D-5-59
Finona, Victoria T -pg. D-5-59
Fischer, William F -pg. D-13-23
Fisher, George M -pg. D-13-15
Fitzgerald, George -pg. D-13-23
Flennils, Harold C -pg. D-13-20
Florence, Orion A -pg. D-13-6
Flores, Alfonsina SN -pg. D-8-16
Flores, Alfred G -pg. D-2-17
Flores, Alfred G -pg. D-5-75
Flores, Alfred SN -pg. D-8-16
Flores, Alice SN -pg. D-8-16
Flores, Amelia B -pg. D-8-33
Flores, Ana B -pg. D-4-94
Flores, Ana C -pg. D-1-41
Flores, Ana C -pg. D-2-13
Flores, Ana C -pg. D-2-28
Flores, Ana C -pg. D-2-28
Flores, Ana C -pg. D-2-65
Flores, Ana C -pg. D-2-83
Flores, Ana F -pg. D-2-40

Flores, Ana F -pg. D-2-40
Flores, Ana G -pg. D-2-77
Flores, Ana G -pg. D-4-88
Flores, Ana G -pg. D-5-3
Flores, Ana L -pg. D-4-7
Flores, Ana LG -pg. D-5-28
Flores, Ana P -pg. D-2-66
Flores, Ana SN -pg. D-1-32
Flores, Ana T -pg. D-2-55
Flores, Ana U -pg. D-5-11
Flores, Andrea C -pg. D-4-79
Flores, Angel G -pg. D-2-59
Flores, Annie M -pg. D-4-89
Flores, Antonia de L. -pg. D-1-44
Flores, Antonia G -pg. D-5-75
Flores, Antonia N -pg. D-4-120
Flores, Antonio C -pg. D-2-13
Flores, Antonio C -pg. D-2-13
Flores, Antonio F -pg. D-2-40
Flores, Antonio M -pg. D-4-101
Flores, Artemio LG -pg. D-5-28
Flores, Aurora G -pg. D-2-59
Flores, Barcelisa F -pg. D-4-80
Flores, Beatres C -pg. D-1-41
Flores, Beatrice T -pg. D-2-28
Flores, Beatris L -pg. D-4-12
Flores, Benigno LG -pg. D-2-35
Flores, Candelaria C -pg. D-1-27
Flores, Candelaria C -pg. D-5-70
Flores, Candelaria S -pg. D-8-46
Flores, Carlos C -pg. D-1-41
Flores, Carmen C -pg. D-2-66
Flores, Carmen C -pg. D-4-79
Flores, Carmen I -pg. D-5-12
Flores, Carmen M -pg. D-2-83
Flores, Carmen S -pg. D-1-44
Flores, Carmen SN -pg. D-8-9
Flores, Cecelia B -pg. D-1-43
Flores, Concepcion C -pg. D-2-28
Flores, Consuelo SN -pg. D-8-9
Flores, David de L. -pg. D-1-44
Flores, Delfina B -pg. D-8-33
Flores, Dolores A -pg. D-5-40
Flores, Dolores B -pg. D-8-33
Flores, Dolores C -pg. D-2-13
Flores, Dolores C -pg. D-4-120
Flores, Dolores D -pg. D-8-7
Flores, Dolores M -pg. D-2-35
Flores, Dolores R -pg. D-1-57
Flores, Dolores SN -pg. D-1-32
Flores, Edward -pg. D-5-98
Flores, Elizabeth de L. -pg. D-1-44
Flores, Emilia -pg. D-5-98
Flores, Emma SN -pg. D-8-16
Flores, Engracia C -pg. D-4-120
Flores, Enrique -pg. D-5-98
Flores, Enrique D -pg. D-1-10
Flores, Felisberto C -pg. D-4-94
Flores, Felix -pg. D-3-39

Flores, Felix U -pg. D-5-11
Flores, Filomina T -pg. D-2-28
Flores, Francisca -pg. D-1-20
Flores, Francisco C -pg. D-5-12
Flores, Francisco D -pg. D-1-10
Flores, Francisco F -pg. D-4-86
Flores, Francisco G -pg. D-2-59
Flores, Francisco G -pg. D-2-59
Flores, Francisco M -pg. D-5-12
Flores, Francisco N -pg. D-4-120
Flores, George -pg. D-5-98
Flores, George F -pg. D-4-87
Flores, George L -pg. D-4-12
Flores, Grace -pg. D-5-98
Flores, Gregorio L -pg. D-4-12
Flores, Gregorio M -pg. D-2-83
Flores, Gregorio SN -pg. D-8-16
Flores, Guadalupe B -pg. D-1-43
Flores, Guillerma C -pg. D-5-12
Flores, Guillermo de L. -pg. D-1-44
Flores, Guillermo S -pg. D-1-44
Flores, Helen SN -pg. D-8-16
Flores, Henry T -pg. D-2-19
Flores, Ida SN -pg. D-8-16
Flores, Ignacio C -pg. D-1-9
Flores, Ignacio F -pg. D-4-87
Flores, Ignacio G -pg. D-4-86
Flores, Ignacio T -pg. D-2-27
Flores, Isabel C -pg. D-2-13
Flores, Isabel F -pg. D-10-5
Flores, Isidro G -pg. D-2-59
Flores, Jesus A -pg. D-8-7
Flores, Jesus C -pg. D-2-66
Flores, Jesus F -pg. D-4-80
Flores, Jesus F -pg. D-5-75
Flores, Jesus G -pg. D-2-59
Flores, Jesus L -pg. D-4-12
Flores, Jesus M -pg. D-1-20
Flores, Jesus M -pg. D-2-83
Flores, Jesus P -pg. D-2-8
Flores, Joaquin -pg. D-2-75
Flores, Joaquin B -pg. D-1-3
Flores, Joaquin C -pg. D-1-41
Flores, Joaquin C -pg. D-4-120
Flores, Joaquin D -pg. D-4-120
Flores, Joaquin D -pg. D-8-33
Flores, Joaquin F -pg. D-2-40
Flores, Joaquin F -pg. D-4-86
Flores, Joaquin L -pg. D-4-12
Flores, Joaquin L -pg. D-13-33
Flores, Joaquin P -pg. D-2-66
Flores, Joaquin S -pg. D-2-52
Flores, Joaquin SN -pg. D-1-32
Flores, Joaquina G -pg. D-2-59
Flores, Joaquina G -pg. D-2-77
Flores, Joaquina G -pg. D-8-22
Flores, Joaquina SN -pg. D-2-75
Flores, Jose -pg. D-13-27
Flores, Jose A -pg. D-2-74

Flores, Jose A -pg. D-5-39
Flores, Jose A -pg. D-8-46
Flores, Jose B -pg. D-1-43
Flores, Jose B -pg. D-5-13
Flores, Jose C -pg. D-1-9
Flores, Jose C -pg. D-2-13
Flores, Jose C -pg. D-2-19
Flores, Jose C -pg. D-2-65
Flores, Jose C -pg. D-2-65
Flores, Jose C -pg. D-2-66
Flores, Jose D -pg. D-1-32
Flores, Jose D -pg. D-8-16
Flores, Jose de L. -pg. D-1-44
Flores, Jose F -pg. D-2-40
Flores, Jose F -pg. D-5-28
Flores, Jose F -pg. D-10-5
Flores, Jose G -pg. D-2-59
Flores, Jose G -pg. D-2-64
Flores, Jose G -pg. D-5-98
Flores, Jose L -pg. D-4-7
Flores, Jose L -pg. D-4-12
Flores, Jose LG -pg. D-2-27
Flores, Jose LG -pg. D-5-28
Flores, Jose M -pg. D-4-101
Flores, Jose M -pg. D-5-12
Flores, Jose R -pg. D-1-43
Flores, Jose S -pg. D-1-44
Flores, Jose SN -pg. D-1-32
Flores, Jose SN -pg. D-8-16
Flores, Josefa C -pg. D-1-9
Flores, Josefa C -pg. D-1-23
Flores, Josefa P -pg. D-2-66
Flores, Josefina F -pg. D-2-40
Flores, Josefina T -pg. D-8-7
Flores, Joseph -pg. D-5-98
Flores, Juan A -pg. D-1-7
Flores, Juan C -pg. D-1-9
Flores, Juan C -pg. D-1-41
Flores, Juan C -pg. D-2-65
Flores, Juan C -pg. D-4-120
Flores, Juan D -pg. D-8-9
Flores, Juan F -pg. D-4-7
Flores, Juan G -pg. D-1-41
Flores, Juan G -pg. D-2-77
Flores, Juan LG -pg. D-5-28
Flores, Juan M -pg. D-1-20
Flores, Juana LG -pg. D-5-28
Flores, Juana M -pg. D-4-89
Flores, Juana M -pg. D-4-101
Flores, Juaquina C -pg. D-1-9
Flores, Julia C -pg. D-5-12
Flores, Julia I -pg. D-5-12
Flores, Julian L -pg. D-4-12
Flores, Lagrimas R -pg. D-1-57
Flores, Leon D -pg. D-4-94
Flores, Leon L -pg. D-4-94
Flores, Lorenzo A -pg. D-5-70
Flores, Lorenzo L -pg. D-4-12
Flores, Lorenzo P -pg. D-13-29

Flores, Luis T -pg. D-2-28
Flores, Magarita -pg. D-5-70
Flores, Magdalena B -pg. D-2-75
Flores, Magdalena B -pg. D-5-13
Flores, Magdalena T -pg. D-2-19
Flores, Manuel A -pg. D-5-39
Flores, Manuel A -pg. D-5-71
Flores, Manuel B -pg. D-1-3
Flores, Manuel C -pg. D-2-28
Flores, Manuel D -pg. D-8-22
Flores, Manuel F -pg. D-4-7
Flores, Manuel G -pg. D-1-10
Flores, Manuel M -pg. D-1-20
Flores, Manuel P -pg. D-5-39
Flores, Manuel T -pg. D-1-20
Flores, Margarita C -pg. D-1-41
Flores, Maria A -pg. D-4-16
Flores, Maria B -pg. D-1-43
Flores, Maria B -pg. D-1-43
Flores, Maria B -pg. D-5-13
Flores, Maria B -pg. D-5-13
Flores, Maria C -pg. D-2-13
Flores, Maria C -pg. D-3-39
Flores, Maria C -pg. D-4-120
Flores, Maria F -pg. D-2-40
Flores, Maria F -pg. D-4-86
Flores, Maria G -pg. D-2-59
Flores, Maria G -pg. D-2-77
Flores, Maria G -pg. D-4-88
Flores, Maria L -pg. D-4-7
Flores, Maria L -pg. D-4-12
Flores, Maria LG -pg. D-4-101
Flores, Maria M -pg. D-4-89
Flores, Maria T -pg. D-5-70
Flores, Mariano S -pg. D-1-44
Flores, Martin G -pg. D-2-78
Flores, Natividad C -pg. D-2-13
Flores, Natividad G -pg. D-2-59
Flores, Nellie G -pg. D-2-59
Flores, Nicolasa C -pg. D-1-9
Flores, Nicolasa C -pg. D-1-41
Flores, Nieves AC -pg. D-4-103
Flores, Nieves C -pg. D-2-28
Flores, Nieves M -pg. D-4-103
Flores, Pedro B -pg. D-5-13
Flores, Pedro F -pg. D-4-87
Flores, Pedro G -pg. D-2-17
Flores, Pedro G -pg. D-2-59
Flores, Pedro G -pg. D-2-78
Flores, Pedro G -pg. D-2-83
Flores, Pedro G -pg. D-5-75
Flores, Pedro LG -pg. D-5-28
Flores, Pedro M -pg. D-2-83
Flores, Pedro T -pg. D-2-28
Flores, Prudencio C -pg. D-2-28
Flores, Prudencio D -pg. D-8-7
Flores, Quintina C -pg. D-2-28
Flores, Rafaela SN -pg. D-8-16
Flores, Ramon C -pg. D-2-28

Flores, Ramon G -pg. D-4-88
Flores, Ramona A -pg. D-10-15
Flores, Remedio F -pg. D-10-5
Flores, Remedios A -pg. D-4-101
Flores, Remedios B -pg. D-1-43
Flores, Remedios D -pg. D-1-10
Flores, Ricardo C -pg. D-4-94
Flores, Rita A -pg. D-10-15
Flores, Rita B -pg. D-1-3
Flores, Rita B -pg. D-8-33
Flores, Rita C -pg. D-1-9
Flores, Rita C -pg. D-4-79
Flores, Rita C -pg. D-5-12
Flores, Rita de L. -pg. D-1-44
Flores, Rita L -pg. D-4-12
Flores, Rita LG -pg. D-2-27
Flores, Rita T -pg. D-5-98
Flores, Rosa B -pg. D-5-13
Flores, Rosa C -pg. D-1-7
Flores, Rosa C -pg. D-2-65
Flores, Rosa G -pg. D-1-20
Flores, Rosa S -pg. D-2-52
Flores, Rosalia C -pg. D-1-41
Flores, Rosario C -pg. D-4-79
Flores, Rosario C -pg. D-5-12
Flores, Rosario F -pg. D-4-7
Flores, Rosario F -pg. D-4-86
Flores, Ruth de L. -pg. D-1-44
Flores, Sabino C -pg. D-4-103
Flores, Sergio D -pg. D-4-94
Flores, Socorro SN -pg. D-2-75
Flores, Susana F -pg. D-4-86
Flores, Tomasa C -pg. D-1-27
Flores, Tomasa C -pg. D-5-70
Flores, Trinidad A -pg. D-5-39
Flores, Vicenta C -pg. D-2-13
Flores, Vicenta C -pg. D-4-79
Flores, Vicente A -pg. D-5-40
Flores, Vicente A -pg. D-5-70
Flores, Vicente A -pg. D-5-71
Flores, Vicente A -pg. D-10-5
Flores, Vicente C -pg. D-2-28
Flores, Vicente C -pg. D-2-52
Flores, Vicente D -pg. D-8-7
Flores, Vicente LG -pg. D-2-27
Flores, Vicente M -pg. D-5-11
Flores, Vicente S -pg. D-3-39
Flores, Virgina -pg. D-5-98
Flores, Virginia A -pg. D-5-39
Flores, Virginia C -pg. D-2-28
Flores, William B -pg. D-8-33
Fodden, George G -pg. D-11-50
Fodden, Mildred J -pg. D-11-50
Folleon, Haskon -pg. D-13-26
Ford, Thomas -pg. D-13-23
Foster, Arthur B -pg. D-13-6
Foster, Frank R -pg. D-13-40
Foster, John C -pg. D-13-15
Fotes, Hosea D -pg. D-13-6

Fotheringham, Douglas E -pg. D-13-37
Fountain, James L -pg. D-13-15
Fox, Donald A -pg. D-13-34
Fradenburg, Lester W -pg. D-13-44
France, Cylde A -pg. D-13-6
Francis, Oliver T -pg. D-13-6
Francisco, Ana L -pg. D-5-72
Francisco, Angustia C -pg. D-5-72
Francisco, Antonio -pg. D-5-72
Francisco, Antonio C -pg. D-2-62
Francisco, Antonio C -pg. D-2-76
Francisco, Candelaria F -pg. D-1-23
Francisco, Carmen -pg. D-5-72
Francisco, Carmen C -pg. D-2-76
Francisco, Catalina T -pg. D-1-15
Francisco, Concepcion C -pg. D-2-62
Francisco, Dolores -pg. D-5-72
Francisco, Domingo -pg. D-2-76
Francisco, Efigenia C -pg. D-5-72
Francisco, Fidela T -pg. D-1-15
Francisco, Gracia S -pg. D-5-18
Francisco, Ignacia C -pg. D-2-76
Francisco, Ignacia C -pg. D-5-72
Francisco, Ignacio -pg. D-5-72
Francisco, Ignacio F -pg. D-1-22
Francisco, Jesus C -pg. D-1-15
Francisco, Jesus F -pg. D-1-23
Francisco, Joaquin S -pg. D-5-72
Francisco, Jose C -pg. D-2-62
Francisco, Jose C -pg. D-2-76
Francisco, Jose C -pg. D-5-72
Francisco, Jose F -pg. D-1-22
Francisco, Jose P -pg. D-1-22
Francisco, Josefa F -pg. D-1-23
Francisco, Josefa S -pg. D-5-18
Francisco, Juan -pg. D-5-72
Francisco, Juan C -pg. D-2-62
Francisco, Juana C -pg. D-2-62
Francisco, Maria -pg. D-5-72
Francisco, Maria C -pg. D-5-72
Francisco, Maria T -pg. D-1-15
Francisco, Maria T -pg. D-1-15
Francisco, Maria J C -pg. D-2-76
Francisco, Natividad -pg. D-5-72
Francisco, Nicolas P -pg. D-5-72
Francisco, Pedro C -pg. D-2-62
Francisco, Pedro C -pg. D-5-72
Francisco, Rita F -pg. D-1-22
Francisco, Rosa C -pg. D-2-76
Francisco, Rosario S -pg. D-5-18
Francisco, Teresa C -pg. D-2-62
Francisco, Vicente -pg. D-5-72
Francisco, Vicente S -pg. D-5-18
Francisco, Vicente T -pg. D-5-18
Franklin, Harold H -pg. D-13-46
Franklin, William J -pg. D-13-16
Franquez, Ana C -pg. D-1-39
Franquez, Ana I -pg. D-1-19
Franquez, Ana T -pg. D-1-42

Franquez, Antonia C -pg. D-1-46
Franquez, Carmen G -pg. D-1-19
Franquez, Emiliana P -pg. D-1-46
Franquez, Felicita M -pg. D-1-46
Franquez, Francisco G -pg. D-1-19
Franquez, George P -pg. D-11-27
Franquez, Isabel C -pg. D-1-39
Franquez, Jesus G -pg. D-1-19
Franquez, Jesus T -pg. D-13-27
Franquez, Joaquin I -pg. D-1-19
Franquez, Jose C -pg. D-1-46
Franquez, Jose I -pg. D-1-41
Franquez, Jose T -pg. D-1-42
Franquez, Josefa L -pg. D-1-20
Franquez, Josefina C -pg. D-1-46
Franquez, Lorenzo C -pg. D-1-46
Franquez, Luisa M -pg. D-3-52
Franquez, Manuel S -pg. D-3-52
Franquez, Manuel T -pg. D-1-42
Franquez, Maria C -pg. D-1-39
Franquez, Maria G -pg. D-1-19
Franquez, Maria P -pg. D-1-46
Franquez, Maria T -pg. D-1-42
Franquez, Maria T -pg. D-1-42
Franquez, Mercedes M -pg. D-1-47
Franquez, Patricia M -pg. D-1-46
Franquez, Pedro C -pg. D-1-39
Franquez, Pedro I -pg. D-1-39
Franquez, Pedro T -pg. D-13-32
Franquez, Remedios C -pg. D-1-46
Franquez, Remedios I -pg. D-1-19
Franquez, Remedios T -pg. D-1-42
Franquez, Rita C -pg. D-1-39
Franquez, Rita C -pg. D-1-46
Franquez, Rosalia P -pg. D-11-27
Franquez, Vicente I -pg. D-1-46
Freegord, Guadalupe B -pg. D-11-2
Freeman, Kenneth M -pg. D-13-46
Freeman, Thomas J -pg. D-13-23
French, [illegible] F -pg. D-13-20
French, Vernes H -pg. D-13-33
Fricke, Oliver E -pg. D-13-41
Fritz, George J -pg. D-13-16
Frontislan, Wiliiam L -pg. D-13-14
Fujikawa, Ana -pg. D-3-46
Fujikawa, Antonio -pg. D-3-46
Fujikawa, Antonio M -pg. D-3-46
Fujikawa, Dolores -pg. D-3-46
Fujikawa, Marcela -pg. D-3-46
Fujikawa, Maria SN -pg. D-3-46
Fulst, ? J -pg. D-13-16
Furst, Mildred E -pg. D-13-19
Fyman, Ara L -pg. D-13-23
Gabriel, Reginal L -pg. D-13-11
Gallagher, James A -pg. D-13-16
Gamboa, Antonio P -pg. D-7-22
Gamboa, Isabel P -pg. D-7-22
Gamboa, Isabel P -pg. D-7-22
Gamboa, Julia P -pg. D-7-22

Gamboa, Lorenzo P -pg. D-7-22
Gamboa, Vicente C -pg. D-7-22
Gamboa, Vicente P -pg. D-7-22
Gandeza, Aguilino A -pg. D-3-15
Gandeza, Isabel C -pg. D-3-16
Ganna, Herman -pg. D-13-37
Garcia, Adela -pg. D-3-65
Garcia, Ana F -pg. D-3-43
Garcia, Angela C -pg. D-3-33
Garcia, Antonina -pg. D-5-84
Garcia, Antonio LG -pg. D-5-84
Garcia, Antonio SN -pg. D-3-43
Garcia, Demetrio -pg. D-3-43
Garcia, Demetrio LG -pg. D-4-94
Garcia, Edward -pg. D-3-31
Garcia, Elizabeth -pg. D-3-31
Garcia, Esperanza -pg. D-3-33
Garcia, Florencio -pg. D-3-33
Garcia, Francisco -pg. D-3-31
Garcia, Francisco -pg. D-3-33
Garcia, Francisco -pg. D-3-43
Garcia, Francisco S -pg. D-1-35
Garcia, Gertrudes C -pg. D-5-84
Garcia, Gertrudes F -pg. D-7-8
Garcia, Gonzalo -pg. D-3-33
Garcia, Isabel -pg. D-3-43
Garcia, Jaime M -pg. D-13-27
Garcia, Jesus -pg. D-3-31
Garcia, Jesus -pg. D-3-33
Garcia, Jesus -pg. D-3-43
Garcia, Jesus C -pg. D-7-8
Garcia, Jesus F -pg. D-7-8
Garcia, Jose -pg. D-3-31
Garcia, Jose -pg. D-3-43
Garcia, Jose -pg. D-3-65
Garcia, Jose C -pg. D-3-32
Garcia, Jose F -pg. D-7-8
Garcia, Josefina -pg. D-3-31
Garcia, Juan -pg. D-3-31
Garcia, Juan -pg. D-3-43
Garcia, Juan -pg. D-3-65
Garcia, Juan -pg. D-5-84
Garcia, Juan A -pg. D-1-35
Garcia, Juan C -pg. D-5-84
Garcia, Juan SN -pg. D-3-31
Garcia, Justo -pg. D-3-33
Garcia, Lucia -pg. D-3-65
Garcia, Magdalena A -pg. D-3-32
Garcia, Maria -pg. D-3-31
Garcia, Maria -pg. D-3-43
Garcia, Maria E -pg. D-3-65
Garcia, Maria F -pg. D-7-8
Garcia, Maria S -pg. D-1-35
Garcia, Mariano -pg. D-3-33
Garcia, Mercedes -pg. D-5-84
Garcia, Nicolas -pg. D-3-43
Garcia, Rosa -pg. D-3-33
Garcia, Rosa M -pg. D-3-31
Garcia, Soledad F -pg. D-7-8

Garcia, Teresa T -pg. D-5-84
Garcia, Tomasa -pg. D-3-33
Garcia, Trinidad LG -pg. D-4-94
Garrido, Agueda A -pg. D-1-38
Garrido, Agustin S -pg. D-3-18
Garrido, Ana A -pg. D-1-38
Garrido, Ana A -pg. D-8-47
Garrido, Ana B -pg. D-4-58
Garrido, Ana C -pg. D-9-22
Garrido, Ana M -pg. D-8-41
Garrido, Ana T -pg. D-9-11
Garrido, Anselmo B -pg. D-4-58
Garrido, Anselmo M -pg. D-4-56
Garrido, Antonia B -pg. D-5-6
Garrido, Antonia M -pg. D-8-41
Garrido, Asuncion N -pg. D-9-8
Garrido, Beatris LG -pg. D-4-107
Garrido, Carmen -pg. D-3-16
Garrido, Carmen C -pg. D-9-22
Garrido, Carmen N -pg. D-9-8
Garrido, Carmen P -pg. D-8-46
Garrido, Clotilda A -pg. D-1-38
Garrido, Concepcion C -pg. D-9-7
Garrido, Concepcion M -pg. D-9-29
Garrido, Concepcion S -pg. D-8-46
Garrido, Concepcion S -pg. D-9-22
Garrido, Dolores M -pg. D-4-55
Garrido, Dolores M -pg. D-4-102
Garrido, Dolores M -pg. D-9-29
Garrido, Dorothea -pg. D-3-16
Garrido, Enrique B -pg. D-5-5
Garrido, Enrique M -pg. D-4-106
Garrido, Enrique S -pg. D-8-46
Garrido, Facundo B -pg. D-4-58
Garrido, Felicia B -pg. D-4-58
Garrido, Felix SN -pg. D-8-41
Garrido, Francisco B -pg. D-4-59
Garrido, Francisco C -pg. D-8-46
Garrido, Francisco C -pg. D-9-7
Garrido, Francisco L -pg. D-4-83
Garrido, Francisco LG -pg. D-4-107
Garrido, Gonzalo S -pg. D-1-69
Garrido, Guadalupe T -pg. D-9-11
Garrido, Ignacio C -pg. D-9-22
Garrido, Ignacio L -pg. D-1-52
Garrido, Ignacio S -pg. D-8-46
Garrido, Isabel G -pg. D-4-94
Garrido, James -pg. D-3-16
Garrido, Jesus -pg. D-3-16
Garrido, Jesus B -pg. D-5-6
Garrido, Jesus C -pg. D-3-18
Garrido, Jesus C -pg. D-5-30
Garrido, Jesus C -pg. D-9-7
Garrido, Jesus M -pg. D-4-102
Garrido, Jesus T -pg. D-2-5
Garrido, Jesusa S -pg. D-1-69
Garrido, Joaquin G -pg. D-5-38
Garrido, Joaquin M -pg. D-4-56
Garrido, Joaquin M -pg. D-4-102

Garrido, Joaquin N -pg. D-9-22
Garrido, Joaquina I -pg. D-5-97
Garrido, Joaquina P -pg. D-8-46
Garrido, Jose A -pg. D-1-38
Garrido, Jose B -pg. D-2-5
Garrido, Jose B -pg. D-5-6
Garrido, Jose C -pg. D-4-55
Garrido, Jose C -pg. D-9-7
Garrido, Jose C -pg. D-9-22
Garrido, Jose C -pg. D-9-29
Garrido, Jose G -pg. D-4-94
Garrido, Jose M -pg. D-4-56
Garrido, Jose M -pg. D-5-5
Garrido, Jose M -pg. D-9-30
Garrido, Jose P -pg. D-1-38
Garrido, Jose R -pg. D-11-12
Garrido, Jose S -pg. D-8-46
Garrido, Jose T -pg. D-9-11
Garrido, Joseph -pg. D-3-16
Garrido, Juan C -pg. D-4-58
Garrido, Juan M -pg. D-4-102
Garrido, Juan M -pg. D-8-41
Garrido, Juan M -pg. D-9-29
Garrido, Juan P -pg. D-8-46
Garrido, Juan R -pg. D-9-11
Garrido, Juan T -pg. D-2-5
Garrido, Leocadia C -pg. D-1-69
Garrido, Lila P -pg. D-2-50
Garrido, Louise M -pg. D-2-50
Garrido, Lourdes -pg. D-3-16
Garrido, Lucia B -pg. D-4-59
Garrido, Luis P -pg. D-2-50
Garrido, Luis P -pg. D-2-50
Garrido, Luisa B -pg. D-4-59
Garrido, Magdalena A -pg. D-1-38
Garrido, Magdalena P -pg. D-1-52
Garrido, Manuel B -pg. D-5-6
Garrido, Manuel G -pg. D-1-69
Garrido, Manuel T -pg. D-2-5
Garrido, Margarita B -pg. D-5-6
Garrido, Maria -pg. D-3-16
Garrido, Maria B -pg. D-5-5
Garrido, Maria C -pg. D-3-75
Garrido, Maria C -pg. D-5-30
Garrido, Maria C -pg. D-5-30
Garrido, Maria C -pg. D-9-22
Garrido, Maria G -pg. D-4-94
Garrido, Maria G -pg. D-4-94
Garrido, Maria LG -pg. D-4-107
Garrido, Maria R -pg. D-9-11
Garrido, Maria S -pg. D-1-69
Garrido, Maria S -pg. D-1-69
Garrido, Maria S -pg. D-8-46
Garrido, Maria T -pg. D-2-5
Garrido, Maria T -pg. D-2-50
Garrido, Maria T -pg. D-9-11
Garrido, Mariana M -pg. D-4-56
Garrido, Maximino T -pg. D-9-11
Garrido, Miguel C -pg. D-9-7

Garrido, Nicolas C -pg. D-9-22
Garrido, Nicolas N -pg. D-9-22
Garrido, Prudencio B -pg. D-5-6
Garrido, Ramon C -pg. D-9-7
Garrido, Ramon G -pg. D-9-22
Garrido, Raymond F -pg. D-2-50
Garrido, Roman LG -pg. D-4-107
Garrido, Rosa C -pg. D-9-7
Garrido, Rosa N -pg. D-11-28
Garrido, Rosalia S -pg. D-8-46
Garrido, Salomon -pg. D-3-67
Garrido, Simona B -pg. D-4-58
Garrido, Soledad T -pg. D-9-11
Garrido, Teodoro L -pg. D-4-83
Garrido, Teresa M -pg. D-8-41
Garrido, Tomas B -pg. D-4-59
Garrido, Tomas S -pg. D-9-23
Garrido, Trinidad A -pg. D-8-46
Garrido, Trinidad LG -pg. D-4-106
Garrido, Vicenta S -pg. D-3-16
Garrido, Vicenta T -pg. D-2-5
Garrido, Vicente -pg. D-3-16
Garrido, Vicente A -pg. D-8-47
Garrido, Vicente B -pg. D-5-30
Garrido, Vicente C -pg. D-9-22
Garrido, Vicente L -pg. D-4-83
Garrido, Vicente L -pg. D-8-46
Garrido, Victoriano B -pg. D-4-58
Garrido, Vincente -pg. D-13-27
Garrison, Andrew -pg. D-3-74
Garrison, Delila -pg. D-3-74
Garrison, Francisca J -pg. D-3-74
Garrison, Jose -pg. D-3-74
Garrison, Manuel -pg. D-3-74
Garrison, Maria -pg. D-3-74
Garrison, Tomas -pg. D-3-74
Gauew, Jessie J -pg. D-13-6
Gauidierg, Dan W -pg. D-13-37
Gay, Ana T -pg. D-4-30
Gay, Elizabeth L -pg. D-4-30
Gay, Elmer L -pg. D-4-30
Gay, Elmer L -pg. D-4-30
Gay, Emily L -pg. D-4-30
Gay, Emma L -pg. D-4-30
Gay, James K -pg. D-4-30
George, Felix P -pg. D-3-5
George, Jose M -pg. D-3-5
George, Josefa M -pg. D-3-5
George, Luisa L -pg. D-4-116
George, Pilar L -pg. D-4-116
George, Regina L -pg. D-4-116
George, Rosa L -pg. D-4-116
George, Rosario L -pg. D-4-116
George, Sara M -pg. D-3-5
George, Vicente -pg. D-4-116
Gibson, Arethea V -pg. D-10-8
Gibson, Charles C -pg. D-13-16
Gibson, Norman L -pg. D-10-9
Gibson, Norman M -pg. D-13-29

Gilpise, Robert E -pg. D-13-6
Glascott, Rubert -pg. D-13-41
Glenn, John S -pg. D-13-6
Goff, Alfard B -pg. D-13-40
Gofigan, Ana A -pg. D-9-37
Gofigan, Antonina A -pg. D-9-37
Gofigan, Francisca A -pg. D-9-36
Gofigan, Geronimo Q -pg. D-9-37
Gofigan, Grabiel Q -pg. D-9-37
Gofigan, Gregorio Q -pg. D-9-37
Gofigan, Joaquina A -pg. D-9-37
Gofigan, Jose Q -pg. D-9-36
Gofigan, Maria A -pg. D-9-37
Gofigan, Oliva A -pg. D-9-37
Gofigan, Ramon Q -pg. D-9-37
Gofigan, Vicenta Q -pg. D-9-37
Gogo, Amparo A -pg. D-5-89
Gogo, Ana -pg. D-5-89
Gogo, Ana C -pg. D-5-43
Gogo, Ana C -pg. D-5-82
Gogo, Asunsion C -pg. D-5-43
Gogo, Beatris S -pg. D-1-68
Gogo, Carmela Q -pg. D-5-83
Gogo, Catalina -pg. D-5-89
Gogo, Catalina C -pg. D-1-66
Gogo, Consolacion N -pg. D-1-67
Gogo, Consolacion S -pg. D-1-68
Gogo, Daniel G -pg. D-5-89
Gogo, Enrique C -pg. D-5-43
Gogo, Enrique S -pg. D-1-68
Gogo, Eugneia -pg. D-5-80
Gogo, Felicita -pg. D-5-78
Gogo, Felicita -pg. D-5-83
Gogo, Felix C -pg. D-5-43
Gogo, Felix C -pg. D-5-44
Gogo, Fidel C -pg. D-5-43
Gogo, Filomena A -pg. D-5-82
Gogo, Ignacio A -pg. D-5-89
Gogo, Isabel -pg. D-5-79
Gogo, Jesus -pg. D-5-79
Gogo, Jesus C -pg. D-5-43
Gogo, Jesus Q -pg. D-5-79
Gogo, Joaquin C -pg. D-5-43
Gogo, Joaquina C -pg. D-5-80
Gogo, Jose -pg. D-5-83
Gogo, Jose C -pg. D-1-66
Gogo, Jose C -pg. D-5-79
Gogo, Jose G -pg. D-5-78
Gogo, Josefa -pg. D-5-83
Gogo, Juan -pg. D-5-80
Gogo, Juan -pg. D-13-23
Gogo, Juan C -pg. D-5-43
Gogo, Juan G -pg. D-5-82
Gogo, Juan G -pg. D-5-82
Gogo, Juan S -pg. D-1-67
Gogo, Lourdes C -pg. D-1-66
Gogo, Margarita -pg. D-5-80
Gogo, Maria C -pg. D-1-66
Gogo, Maria S -pg. D-1-68

Gogo, Pedro -pg. D-5-82
Gogo, Pedro -pg. D-5-89
Gogo, Ramon G -pg. D-5-80
Gogo, Rosa R -pg. D-3-3
Gogo, Rosario C -pg. D-1-66
Gogo, Teodora G -pg. D-5-83
Gogo, Venancio G -pg. D-1-66
Gogo, Veronica -pg. D-5-82
Gogo, Veronica S -pg. D-1-68
Gogo, Vicente -pg. D-5-89
Gogo, Vicente G -pg. D-5-89
Gogo, Virginia S -pg. D-1-68
Gogue, Agustin SL -pg. D-5-95
Gogue, Ana -pg. D-5-80
Gogue, Ana Q -pg. D-5-78
Gogue, Ana SN -pg. D-12-16
Gogue, Antonia LG -pg. D-4-35
Gogue, Antonia S -pg. D-5-95
Gogue, Antonio -pg. D-5-78
Gogue, Antonio LG -pg. D-4-35
Gogue, Carmen G -pg. D-9-11
Gogue, Carmen P -pg. D-2-56
Gogue, Catalina SN -pg. D-12-16
Gogue, Clotilde -pg. D-5-78
Gogue, Delfina -pg. D-5-95
Gogue, Enrique W -pg. D-2-56
Gogue, Geronimo A -pg. D-8-22
Gogue, Gloria P -pg. D-11-31
Gogue, Gregorio P -pg. D-2-56
Gogue, Isabel -pg. D-9-11
Gogue, Isabel R -pg. D-11-32
Gogue, Jesus -pg. D-5-95
Gogue, Jesus G -pg. D-4-35
Gogue, Jesus Q -pg. D-5-78
Gogue, Joaquin G -pg. D-9-11
Gogue, Joaquina G -pg. D-5-80
Gogue, Joaquina G -pg. D-9-11
Gogue, Jose -pg. D-5-80
Gogue, Jose -pg. D-5-95
Gogue, Jose C -pg. D-4-35
Gogue, Jose G -pg. D-5-80
Gogue, Jose Q -pg. D-5-78
Gogue, Josefina -pg. D-5-95
Gogue, Juan -pg. D-5-80
Gogue, Juan A -pg. D-5-78
Gogue, Juan Q -pg. D-5-78
Gogue, Juana T -pg. D-5-83
Gogue, Magdalena -pg. D-5-95
Gogue, Maria -pg. D-5-95
Gogue, Maria -pg. D-9-11
Gogue, Maria A -pg. D-5-78
Gogue, Maria SN -pg. D-12-16
Gogue, Patricia P -pg. D-11-31
Gogue, Pedro -pg. D-5-80
Gogue, Pedro Q -pg. D-5-78
Gogue, Ramon -pg. D-5-78
Gogue, Ramona W -pg. D-2-17
Gogue, Rita -pg. D-5-81
Gogue, Rita A -pg. D-5-78

Gogue, Rita A -pg. D-13-43
Gogue, Rosa LG -pg. D-4-35
Gogue, Roy B -pg. D-11-32
Gogue, Tomas -pg. D-5-95
Gogue, Tomas SN -pg. D-12-16
Gogue, Vicenta A -pg. D-5-78
Gogue, Vicenta W -pg. D-2-81
Gogue, Vicente -pg. D-5-95
Gogue, Vicente -pg. D-5-95
Gogue, Vicente Q -pg. D-5-78
Gogue, Vicente R -pg. D-11-31
Gogue, Vicente T -pg. D-12-16
Gomabon, Ana B -pg. D-2-45
Gomabon, Jesus B -pg. D-2-45
Gomabon, Jose B -pg. D-2-45
Gomabon, Jose N -pg. D-2-44
Gomabon, Juan B -pg. D-2-45
Gomez, Jesus A -pg. D-2-32
Gomez, Jose -pg. D-5-32
Gomez, Jose C -pg. D-5-38
Gomez, Manuela C -pg. D-5-38
Gomez, Maria C -pg. D-2-32
Gomez, Rosa C -pg. D-5-38
Gomez, Silvestre J -pg. D-2-18
Gomez, Vincente S -pg. D-13-29
Gonzalo, Antonia N -pg. D-4-8
Gonzalo, Clotilde N -pg. D-4-8
Gonzalo, Josefina N -pg. D-4-8
Gonzalo, Pedro G -pg. D-4-8
Goodall, Jack W -pg. D-13-6
Goodman, Niel C -pg. D-13-44
Goodwin, Avea C -pg. D-4-86
Goodwin, Keith E -pg. D-13-33
Goodwin, Sula C -pg. D-1-54
Gormich, Paul F -pg. D-13-37
Gorouch, Wilbur P -pg. D-13-11
Gourley, William J -pg. D-13-11
Gove, William D -pg. D-13-20
Gracies, Wilbur B -pg. D-13-37
Graham, Grey M -pg. D-13-11
Grand, Alex A -pg. D-13-23
Grandy, Harry R -pg. D-13-33
Granson, Westen M -pg. D-13-11
Gravelle, Anna O -pg. D-13-4
Gravelle, Homer J -pg. D-13-4
Gray, William L -pg. D-13-6
Gregory, James C -pg. D-13-16
Gretuky, Tony -pg. D-13-25
Grey, Gustav C -pg. D-11-42
Grey, Nicolas C -pg. D-11-42
Grey, Paul -pg. D-11-42
Grey, Rosario C -pg. D-11-42
Grey, Wilhelmina C -pg. D-11-42
Grote, Nelis N -pg. D-13-6
Grover, Archie W -pg. D-13-42
Grugautren, William -pg. D-13-23
Guerrero, Amparo C -pg. D-3-15
Guerrero, Ana -pg. D-3-18
Guerrero, Ana -pg. D-5-76

Guerrero, Ana B -pg. D-2-23
Guerrero, Ana C -pg. D-5-74
Guerrero, Ana C -pg. D-10-39
Guerrero, Ana I -pg. D-2-81
Guerrero, Ana LG -pg. D-1-11
Guerrero, Ana M -pg. D-2-18
Guerrero, Ana Q -pg. D-6-40
Guerrero, Ana R -pg. D-1-8
Guerrero, Ana R -pg. D-2-41
Guerrero, Ana T -pg. D-4-70
Guerrero, Antonia -pg. D-3-15
Guerrero, Antonia B -pg. D-6-29
Guerrero, Antonia LG -pg. D-1-11
Guerrero, Antonia R -pg. D-2-41
Guerrero, Antonia R -pg. D-2-41
Guerrero, Antonina Q -pg. D-6-40
Guerrero, Antonio B -pg. D-2-23
Guerrero, Antonio C -pg. D-2-23
Guerrero, Antonio C -pg. D-2-28
Guerrero, Benabe Q -pg. D-6-40
Guerrero, Candaleria B -pg. D-2-24
Guerrero, Caridad M -pg. D-7-20
Guerrero, Carlos C -pg. D-2-23
Guerrero, Carmelo G -pg. D-6-19
Guerrero, Carmen -pg. D-3-18
Guerrero, Cesario P -pg. D-5-33
Guerrero, Concepcion B -pg. D-2-24
Guerrero, Concepcion M -pg. D-2-64
Guerrero, Concepcion Q -pg. D-6-40
Guerrero, Concepcion R -pg. D-2-41
Guerrero, Dolores -pg. D-3-64
Guerrero, Dolores M -pg. D-7-20
Guerrero, Dolores Q -pg. D-4-80
Guerrero, Dolores R -pg. D-2-41
Guerrero, Emperatris -pg. D-3-64
Guerrero, Enrique C -pg. D-2-23
Guerrero, Enrique P -pg. D-5-33
Guerrero, Felomena L -pg. D-7-20
Guerrero, Francisca -pg. D-5-74
Guerrero, Francisca LG -pg. D-1-11
Guerrero, Francisca O -pg. D-2-43
Guerrero, Francisca R -pg. D-1-8
Guerrero, Francisco B -pg. D-2-24
Guerrero, Francisco C -pg. D-2-23
Guerrero, Francisco C -pg. D-5-33
Guerrero, Francisco C -pg. D-5-74
Guerrero, Francisco G -pg. D-2-20
Guerrero, Francisco V -pg. D-1-8
Guerrero, Gregorio R -pg. D-2-41
Guerrero, Herminia -pg. D-3-15
Guerrero, Howard I -pg. D-2-81
Guerrero, Ignacia P -pg. D-5-36
Guerrero, Ignacio -pg. D-3-64
Guerrero, Ignacio B -pg. D-11-30
Guerrero, Ignacio LG -pg. D-3-64
Guerrero, Isabel -pg. D-5-74
Guerrero, Jesus -pg. D-3-15
Guerrero, Jesus -pg. D-3-64
Guerrero, Jesus -pg. D-5-74

Guerrero, Jesus B -pg. D-2-24
Guerrero, Jesus C -pg. D-2-23
Guerrero, Jesus L -pg. D-7-20
Guerrero, Jesus M -pg. D-2-18
Guerrero, Jesus M -pg. D-7-20
Guerrero, Jesus P -pg. D-5-33
Guerrero, Jesus P -pg. D-6-19
Guerrero, Jesus T -pg. D-4-70
Guerrero, Joaquin -pg. D-3-37
Guerrero, Joaquin -pg. D-3-37
Guerrero, Joaquin -pg. D-3-64
Guerrero, Joaquin -pg. D-5-74
Guerrero, Joaquin C -pg. D-2-23
Guerrero, Joaquin M -pg. D-2-64
Guerrero, Joaquin P -pg. D-6-40
Guerrero, Joaquin R -pg. D-1-8
Guerrero, Joaquin SN -pg. D-5-30
Guerrero, Joaquina M -pg. D-11-30
Guerrero, Joaquina R -pg. D-4-55
Guerrero, Jorge R -pg. D-1-8
Guerrero, Jose -pg. D-3-15
Guerrero, Jose -pg. D-3-64
Guerrero, Jose -pg. D-5-74
Guerrero, Jose B -pg. D-2-23
Guerrero, Jose B -pg. D-11-21
Guerrero, Jose C -pg. D-5-33
Guerrero, Jose C -pg. D-10-39
Guerrero, Jose D -pg. D-6-29
Guerrero, Jose M -pg. D-5-45
Guerrero, Jose M -pg. D-7-20
Guerrero, Jose P -pg. D-4-80
Guerrero, Jose P -pg. D-5-33
Guerrero, Jose Q -pg. D-6-40
Guerrero, Josefina -pg. D-3-37
Guerrero, Josefina P -pg. D-5-33
Guerrero, Juan -pg. D-3-37
Guerrero, Juan B -pg. D-2-23
Guerrero, Juan B -pg. D-2-23
Guerrero, Juan F -pg. D-1-11
Guerrero, Juan LG -pg. D-1-11
Guerrero, Juan M -pg. D-10-39
Guerrero, Juan P -pg. D-10-39
Guerrero, Juan T -pg. D-4-70
Guerrero, Julian M -pg. D-7-20
Guerrero, Lorenzo C -pg. D-3-18
Guerrero, Luisa C -pg. D-3-37
Guerrero, Manuel -pg. D-3-15
Guerrero, Manuel -pg. D-3-37
Guerrero, Manuel I -pg. D-2-81
Guerrero, Manuel M -pg. D-4-11
Guerrero, Maria -pg. D-3-15
Guerrero, Maria -pg. D-3-18
Guerrero, Maria -pg. D-5-74
Guerrero, Maria B -pg. D-2-24
Guerrero, Maria C -pg. D-2-23
Guerrero, Maria C -pg. D-5-76
Guerrero, Maria L -pg. D-2-20
Guerrero, Maria M -pg. D-2-18
Guerrero, Maria M -pg. D-11-30

Guerrero, Maria P -pg. D-5-33
Guerrero, Maria P -pg. D-6-19
Guerrero, Maria Q -pg. D-6-40
Guerrero, Maria R -pg. D-1-8
Guerrero, Maria R -pg. D-2-41
Guerrero, Mariano C -pg. D-5-76
Guerrero, Mariano C -pg. D-10-39
Guerrero, Matias D -pg. D-13-31
Guerrero, Maxima M -pg. D-11-30
Guerrero, Nicolas G -pg. D-2-20
Guerrero, Nicolas M -pg. D-2-81
Guerrero, Nicolasa C -pg. D-5-33
Guerrero, Nieves C -pg. D-2-20
Guerrero, Olimpia Q -pg. D-4-80
Guerrero, Oliva -pg. D-3-37
Guerrero, Pedro -pg. D-3-15
Guerrero, Pedro B -pg. D-2-43
Guerrero, Pedro B -pg. D-5-77
Guerrero, Pedro F -pg. D-3-15
Guerrero, Pedro LG -pg. D-1-11
Guerrero, Ramon -pg. D-3-37
Guerrero, Regina -pg. D-3-64
Guerrero, Regina P -pg. D-11-21
Guerrero, Rita -pg. D-3-64
Guerrero, Rita B -pg. D-2-24
Guerrero, Rita T -pg. D-4-70
Guerrero, Rosa I -pg. D-2-81
Guerrero, Rosa M -pg. D-11-30
Guerrero, Rosa Q -pg. D-6-40
Guerrero, Rosa R -pg. D-2-41
Guerrero, Rosa T -pg. D-3-64
Guerrero, Rosalia R -pg. D-1-8
Guerrero, Santiago -pg. D-3-64
Guerrero, Santiago I -pg. D-2-81
Guerrero, Silvestre L -pg. D-2-20
Guerrero, Soledad M -pg. D-2-18
Guerrero, Thomas M -pg. D-11-30
Guerrero, Venancio T -pg. D-4-70
Guerrero, Vicenta R -pg. D-1-8
Guerrero, Vicente -pg. D-5-76
Guerrero, Vicente B -pg. D-2-23
Guerrero, Vicente B -pg. D-2-24
Guerrero, Vicente C -pg. D-2-23
Guerrero, Vicente C -pg. D-4-70
Guerrero, Vicente LG -pg. D-2-23
Guerrero, Vicente M -pg. D-2-18
Guerrero, Vicente R -pg. D-5-15
Guerrero, Vicente S -pg. D-7-19
Guerrero, Virginia -pg. D-3-64
Guerrero, Jose G -pg. D-4-33
Guevara, Ana G -pg. D-1-67
Guevara, Enriqueta C -pg. D-1-40
Guevara, Fernando SN -pg. D-1-40
Guevara, Isabel C -pg. D-1-40
Guevara, Jesus C -pg. D-1-40
Guevara, Jose C -pg. D-1-40
Guevara, Juan D -pg. D-1-67
Guevara, Juan G -pg. D-1-67
Guevara, Maria C -pg. D-1-40

Guevara, Rosa C -pg. D-1-40
Guevara, Rosa SN -pg. D-2-3
Guevarra, Antonio C -pg. D-5-90
Guevarra, Elena F -pg. D-5-91
Guevarra, Eulalia -pg. D-5-90
Guevarra, Froilan -pg. D-5-90
Guevarra, Gregorio D -pg. D-5-91
Guevarra, Jose -pg. D-5-89
Guevarra, Maria -pg. D-5-91
Guevarra, Maria A -pg. D-5-89
Guevarra, Maria D -pg. D-5-90
Guevarra, Mariano -pg. D-5-90
Guevarra, Rita -pg. D-5-91
Guevarra, Vicente C -pg. D-5-89
Guevarra, Vincente A -pg. D-13-27
Guinn, George E Jr -pg. D-13-23
Guioco, Antonia S -pg. D-5-56
Guioco, Jesus D -pg. D-5-56
Guisara, Vibencio -pg. D-13-27
Guivara, Antonia A -pg. D-6-25
Guivara, Antonio G -pg. D-6-33
Guivara, Consolacion B -pg. D-6-33
Guivara, Jesus Q -pg. D-6-25
Guivara, Jose B -pg. D-6-33
Guivara, Jose P -pg. D-6-34
Guivara, Maria G -pg. D-6-33
Guivara, Soledad P -pg. D-6-34
Guivara, Vicente A -pg. D-6-25
Gullo, Albert -pg. D-13-42
Gumabon, A M -pg. D-2-15
Gumabon, Ariston G -pg. D-2-15
Gumabon, Carmen N -pg. D-2-15
Gumabon, Vicente N -pg. D-2-15
Gumataotao, Adela D -pg. D-11-14
Gumataotao, Adela D -pg. D-11-15
Gumataotao, Agustin -pg. D-3-4
Gumataotao, Albert D -pg. D-11-15
Gumataotao, Ana L -pg. D-5-40
Gumataotao, Ana S -pg. D-5-98
Gumataotao, Andres B -pg. D-11-20
Gumataotao, Antonia C -pg. D-5-38
Gumataotao, Antonio B -pg. D-11-14
Gumataotao, Antonio L -pg. D-5-40
Gumataotao, Antonio S -pg. D-4-124
Gumataotao, Atanacio T -pg. D-4-5
Gumataotao, Carlos I -pg. D-4-19
Gumataotao, Carlos L -pg. D-5-40
Gumataotao, Carmen S -pg. D-11-4
Gumataotao, Catalina T -pg. D-4-6
Gumataotao, Delores M -pg. D-11-27
Gumataotao, Dolores I -pg. D-4-19
Gumataotao, Emilia L -pg. D-5-40
Gumataotao, Emiliana C -pg. D-5-38
Gumataotao, Eulogio E -pg. D-4-18
Gumataotao, Felix I -pg. D-4-19
Gumataotao, Fermin G -pg. D-4-19
Gumataotao, Francisco -pg. D-3-4
Gumataotao, Francisco B -pg. D-11-50
Gumataotao, Francisco G -pg. D-4-19

INDEX
1930 Population Census of Guam: Transcribed

Gumataotao, Francisco G -pg. D-4-123
Gumataotao, Francisco L -pg. D-5-40
Gumataotao, Francisco M -pg. D-5-65
Gumataotao, George S -pg. D-11-4
Gumataotao, Guadalupe I -pg. D-4-19
Gumataotao, Ignacia C -pg. D-4-19
Gumataotao, Ignacio B -pg. D-3-4
Gumataotao, Isabel T -pg. D-4-5
Gumataotao, Joaquin D -pg. D-11-27
Gumataotao, Joaquin L -pg. D-5-40
Gumataotao, Jose C -pg. D-5-38
Gumataotao, Jose D -pg. D-11-14
Gumataotao, Jose L -pg. D-5-40
Gumataotao, Jose S -pg. D-1-69
Gumataotao, Jose T -pg. D-4-6
Gumataotao, Josefina D -pg. D-11-15
Gumataotao, Juan B -pg. D-11-20
Gumataotao, Juan C -pg. D-11-20
Gumataotao, Juan L -pg. D-5-40
Gumataotao, Juan P -pg. D-11-50
Gumataotao, Juan T -pg. D-4-6
Gumataotao, Juana D -pg. D-4-54
Gumataotao, Juana S -pg. D-1-69
Gumataotao, Lagrimas D -pg. D-11-15
Gumataotao, Leon D -pg. D-11-15
Gumataotao, Manuela G -pg. D-4-19
Gumataotao, Maria B -pg. D-11-20
Gumataotao, Maria C -pg. D-11-4
Gumataotao, Maria D -pg. D-11-14
Gumataotao, Maria I -pg. D-4-19
Gumataotao, Maria L -pg. D-5-40
Gumataotao, Maria P -pg. D-4-18
Gumataotao, Maria S -pg. D-11-4
Gumataotao, Mariano P -pg. D-11-50
Gumataotao, Nicolas D -pg. D-11-14
Gumataotao, Olimpia C -pg. D-5-38
Gumataotao, Oliva D -pg. D-11-15
Gumataotao, Oscar D -pg. D-11-15
Gumataotao, Paciano D -pg. D-4-19
Gumataotao, Pedro D -pg. D-11-15
Gumataotao, Rafael L -pg. D-5-40
Gumataotao, Ramona T -pg. D-4-5
Gumataotao, Rita L -pg. D-5-40
Gumataotao, Rita U -pg. D-3-4
Gumataotao, Soledad S -pg. D-4-124
Gumataotao, Stella M -pg. D-11-27
Gumataotao, Teresa B -pg. D-11-20
Gumataotao, Teresa G -pg. D-4-19
Gumataotao, Tomas LG -pg. D-5-38
Gumataotao, Vicente D -pg. D-11-15
Gumataotao, Vicente M -pg. D-3-20
Gumataotao, Vicente T -pg. D-4-6
Gunn, Anna R -pg. D-1-21
Gunn, Emmette Jr. F -pg. D-1-21
Gunn, Gloria L -pg. D-3-44
Gunn, Grace T -pg. D-3-44
Gunn, James D -pg. D-1-21
Gunn, Lititia M -pg. D-3-44
Gunn, Max C -pg. D-3-44

Gunn, Max C -pg. D-13-33
Gunn, Patricia A -pg. D-3-44
Gunnoc, Kenneth S -pg. D-13-16
Gurnan, Ermette F -pg. D-13-31
Gusbino, John R -pg. D-13-34
Gusukuma, Yaisuke -pg. D-10-15
Gutierres, Tomasa D -pg. D-3-31
Gutierrez, Agueda -pg. D-3-42
Gutierrez, Ana D -pg. D-4-12
Gutierrez, Angustia -pg. D-3-43
Gutierrez, Atanacio P -pg. D-4-14
Gutierrez, Atonia -pg. D-3-43
Gutierrez, Augusto -pg. D-3-43
Gutierrez, Carlos -pg. D-3-43
Gutierrez, Carlos D -pg. D-4-12
Gutierrez, Catalina M -pg. D-4-10
Gutierrez, Domingo M -pg. D-4-10
Gutierrez, Esiquiel N -pg. D-4-9
Gutierrez, Federico -pg. D-3-43
Gutierrez, Felecita D -pg. D-4-12
Gutierrez, Filomenia D -pg. D-4-12
Gutierrez, Ignacia M -pg. D-4-10
Gutierrez, Jane -pg. D-3-43
Gutierrez, Jesus T -pg. D-4-9
Gutierrez, Jose -pg. D-3-43
Gutierrez, Jose -pg. D-4-14
Gutierrez, Jose D -pg. D-4-12
Gutierrez, Juan D -pg. D-4-14
Gutierrez, Julia -pg. D-3-43
Gutierrez, Leonila -pg. D-4-14
Gutierrez, Luis N -pg. D-4-12
Gutierrez, Maria -pg. D-3-43
Gutierrez, Maria D -pg. D-4-12
Gutierrez, Maria M -pg. D-4-9
Gutierrez, Maria P -pg. D-4-14
Gutierrez, Maria T -pg. D-3-42
Gutierrez, Maria -pg. D-4-9
Gutierrez, Roland -pg. D-3-43
Gutierrez, Rosa D -pg. D-4-14
Gutierrez, Soledad -pg. D-4-14
Gutierrez, Tomas -pg. D-3-43
Gutierrez, Tomas C -pg. D-3-42
Gutierrez, Tomasa D -pg. D-4-12
Guzman, Adela M -pg. D-4-39
Guzman, Amanda P -pg. D-13-43
Guzman, Ana M -pg. D-3-38
Guzman, Ana M -pg. D-4-38
Guzman, Ana M -pg. D-4-39
Guzman, Ana P -pg. D-4-100
Guzman, Antonia C -pg. D-4-77
Guzman, Antonia C -pg. D-11-33
Guzman, Antonina -pg. D-3-39
Guzman, Antonio S -pg. D-11-27
Guzman, Caridad C -pg. D-4-80
Guzman, Dolores C -pg. D-3-39
Guzman, Dolores C -pg. D-11-27
Guzman, Edward -pg. D-3-39
Guzman, Edward P -pg. D-2-64
Guzman, Emiliana P -pg. D-3-24

Guzman, Enestina C -pg. D-11-27
Guzman, Esperanza C -pg. D-4-80
Guzman, Francisca M -pg. D-4-39
Guzman, Francisco C -pg. D-11-27
Guzman, Francisco D -pg. D-3-24
Guzman, Francisco L -pg. D-11-32
Guzman, Gonzalo M -pg. D-4-38
Guzman, Gregorio -pg. D-3-38
Guzman, Gregorio C -pg. D-11-27
Guzman, Guadalupe C -pg. D-11-27
Guzman, Isabel P -pg. D-2-64
Guzman, Jesus -pg. D-3-39
Guzman, Jesus C -pg. D-11-33
Guzman, Joaquin C -pg. D-4-38
Guzman, Joaquin C -pg. D-11-32
Guzman, Jose -pg. D-3-39
Guzman, Jose C -pg. D-11-33
Guzman, Jose M -pg. D-4-38
Guzman, Jose M -pg. D-4-100
Guzman, Jose P -pg. D-2-64
Guzman, Josefina -pg. D-3-39
Guzman, Juan -pg. D-3-24
Guzman, Juan -pg. D-3-39
Guzman, Juan A -pg. D-4-80
Guzman, Juan C -pg. D-7-24
Guzman, Juan G -pg. D-11-39
Guzman, Juan LG -pg. D-3-25
Guzman, Juan S -pg. D-11-19
Guzman, Julio M -pg. D-4-38
Guzman, Maria C -pg. D-11-32
Guzman, Maria C -pg. D-11-33
Guzman, Natividad -pg. D-3-39
Guzman, Norberto M -pg. D-4-39
Guzman, Pedro M -pg. D-4-39
Guzman, Petronila C -pg. D-11-27
Guzman, Pilar -pg. D-3-24
Guzman, Rita C -pg. D-4-80
Guzman, Silvia P -pg. D-2-64
Guzman, Trinidad C -pg. D-4-80
Guzman, Vicenta C -pg. D-11-19
Guzman, Vicente -pg. D-3-39
Hair, Robert R -pg. D-13-6
Hall, Claude W -pg. D-13-44
Hall, Francis J -pg. D-13-3
Hall, Lorene H -pg. D-13-3
Hall, Robert W -pg. D-13-3
Hall, Thurman F -pg. D-13-3
Hall, Virginia L -pg. D-13-3
Haller, Dolores U -pg. D-4-24
Haller, Fred -pg. D-4-24
Haller, Johnny F -pg. D-4-24
Hallsworth, Norman -pg. D-13-23
Hamamoto, Concepcion A -pg. D-11-51
Hamamoto, Dolores A -pg. D-11-51
Hamamoto, Francisco A -pg. D-11-51
Hamamoto, I -pg. D-11-51
Hamamoto, Jesus A -pg. D-11-51
Hamamoto, Jose A -pg. D-11-51
Hamamoto, Juanita A -pg. D-11-51

Hamamoto, Maria A -pg. D-11-51
Hamamoto, Maria A -pg. D-11-51
Hamilton, Byron C -pg. D-13-16
Hamrick, Edward C -pg. D-11-2
Hamrick, Magdalena C -pg. D-11-2
Handley, Henry A -pg. D-13-16
Hangels, William R -pg. D-13-16
Haniu, Asuncion B -pg. D-4-116
Haniu, Atanacio B -pg. D-3-66
Haniu, Concepcion C -pg. D-3-66
Haniu, Fidela B -pg. D-4-116
Haniu, Francisco -pg. D-3-66
Haniu, Jesus B -pg. D-4-116
Haniu, Jose B -pg. D-4-116
Haniu, Juan B -pg. D-4-116
Haniu, Maria B -pg. D-4-115
Haniu, Tidela B -pg. D-4-116
Hanna, Roert N -pg. D-13-42
Hansen, Carmen M -pg. D-11-39
Hansen, Martin F -pg. D-11-39
Haphayer, Raymond B -pg. D-13-11
Hara, Jesus -pg. D-3-52
Hara, Jose -pg. D-3-52
Hara, Jose M -pg. D-3-52
Hara, Manuel -pg. D-3-52
Hara, Maria -pg. D-3-52
Hara, Romona C -pg. D-3-52
Hardesty, Charles L -pg. D-13-42
Harding, Oscar L -pg. D-13-6
Hare, Agnes D -pg. D-1-54
Hare, Aloha D -pg. D-1-54
Hare, Theron S -pg. D-13-21
Harriet, John T. Jr. -pg. D-13-6
Harrison, Clifford A -pg. D-13-6
Harrison, N E -pg. D-11-50
Harrison, Paul H -pg. D-13-11
Harrison, Yan B -pg. D-13-6
Hart, Ana Q -pg. D-10-35
Hart, Caridad Q -pg. D-10-35
Hart, Guillermo M -pg. D-10-35
Hart, Jose Q -pg. D-10-35
Hart, Pedro Q -pg. D-10-35
Hart, Rosa Q -pg. D-10-35
Hart, Thomas M -pg. D-13-42
Hart, Vicente Q -pg. D-10-35
Hartley, George W -pg. D-13-23
Hasen, Margaret M -pg. D-3-47
Hasen, Margaret T -pg. D-3-47
Hasen, Owen P -pg. D-3-47
Hasen, Robert I -pg. D-3-47
Haskins, William R -pg. D-13-37
Hassig, Edwin F -pg. D-13-6
Hatoba, Rita M -pg. D-10-11
Hayes, May C -pg. D-11-50
Hays, James F -pg. D-13-18
Hazeltime, Laura V -pg. D-1-48
Hebern, Charles E -pg. D-13-16
Hefer, Roman -pg. D-13-23
Hefferon, Robert L -pg. D-13-23

Helman, Chester R -pg. D-13-16
Heng, James L -pg. D-13-6
Heraling, Wayne G -pg. D-13-16
Herdener, Leonard L -pg. D-13-46
Herideig, Wilbur E -pg. D-13-37
Herman, Albert -pg. D-13-37
Herminerl, Peter -pg. D-13-11
Hernandez, Ana F -pg. D-2-38
Hernandez, Asuncion Q -pg. D-2-77
Hernandez, Carmen B -pg. D-5-37
Hernandez, Catalina B -pg. D-2-45
Hernandez, Concepcion A -pg. D-5-52
Hernandez, Elisa Q -pg. D-2-77
Hernandez, Eugenio P -pg. D-10-23
Hernandez, Felix B -pg. D-2-45
Hernandez, Francisco B -pg. D-5-37
Hernandez, Ignacia B -pg. D-5-37
Hernandez, Ignacio E -pg. D-5-46
Hernandez, Joaquin B -pg. D-5-37
Hernandez, Joaquin F -pg. D-2-77
Hernandez, Joaquin N -pg. D-5-58
Hernandez, Joaquina Q -pg. D-2-77
Hernandez, Jose B -pg. D-5-63
Hernandez, Jose F -pg. D-2-38
Hernandez, Jose H -pg. D-2-64
Hernandez, Jose Q -pg. D-2-77
Hernandez, Juan H -pg. D-5-52
Hernandez, Juning B -pg. D-5-37
Hernandez, Manuel P -pg. D-2-45
Hernandez, Maria B -pg. D-5-36
Hernandez, Maria B -pg. D-5-37
Hernandez, Maria SN -pg. D-5-58
Hernandez, Maria T -pg. D-2-64
Hernandez, Ramon E -pg. D-5-36
Hernandez, Rosa B -pg. D-2-45
Hernandez, Rosario B -pg. D-5-37
Herrera, Carmen B -pg. D-6-16
Herrera, Carmen T -pg. D-6-20
Herrera, Felicidad B -pg. D-6-16
Herrera, Fransisco S -pg. D-6-16
Herrera, Guadalupe T -pg. D-6-20
Herrera, Jesus S -pg. D-13-29
Herrera, Jose S -pg. D-6-16
Herrera, Jose T -pg. D-6-20
Herrera, Manuel A -pg. D-7-24
Herrera, Maria T -pg. D-6-20
Herrera, Vicente T -pg. D-6-20
Herrero, Alfredo C -pg. D-1-63
Herrero, Alice W -pg. D-4-44
Herrero, Ana SN -pg. D-1-37
Herrero, Angel C -pg. D-1-63
Herrero, Beatris SN -pg. D-4-120
Herrero, Caridad C -pg. D-4-107
Herrero, Carlos C -pg. D-1-63
Herrero, Carlos P -pg. D-4-121
Herrero, Consuelo C -pg. D-1-62
Herrero, Dolores C -pg. D-1-62
Herrero, Edward C -pg. D-1-63
Herrero, Francisco L -pg. D-1-37

Herrero, Helen C -pg. D-4-44
Herrero, Henry A -pg. D-4-44
Herrero, Ingracia SN -pg. D-1-37
Herrero, Jose SN -pg. D-1-37
Herrero, Josefa SN -pg. D-1-37
Herrero, Juan SN -pg. D-1-37
Herrero, Julia C -pg. D-1-62
Herrero, Lillian J -pg. D-4-44
Herrero, Lillian J -pg. D-4-121
Herrero, Luis SN -pg. D-1-37
Herrero, Margarita SN -pg. D-4-120
Herrero, Maria C -pg. D-1-62
Herrero, Maria C -pg. D-1-62
Herrero, Regina SN -pg. D-4-120
Herrero, Rosa SN -pg. D-4-120
Herrero, Ruth L -pg. D-4-44
Herrero, Soledad SN -pg. D-1-37
Herrero, Tomas C -pg. D-1-62
Herrero, Vicente P -pg. D-4-44
Herrero, Vicente R -pg. D-4-120
Herwerdo, Ellis W -pg. D-13-37
Hess, Kenneth B -pg. D-13-11
Hiddiston, Heschel D -pg. D-13-11
Higaka, Tokichi -pg. D-4-99
Hill, Annette A -pg. D-13-4
Hill, James A -pg. D-13-4
Hind, Frederick S -pg. D-13-20
Hines, Adolfo C -pg. D-1-5
Hines, Arturo C -pg. D-1-5
Hines, Aurora C -pg. D-1-5
Hines, Bibiana C -pg. D-1-5
Hines, Cristobal C -pg. D-2-23
Hines, Eloisa C -pg. D-1-4
Hines, Fabian D -pg. D-1-4
Hines, Joaquina T -pg. D-2-23
Hines, Margarita T -pg. D-2-23
Hines, Maria C -pg. D-1-4
Hoff, Clarence C -pg. D-13-42
Hong Yee, Concepcion C -pg. D-13-43
Hong Yee, Jose -pg. D-3-75
Hong Yee, Rosa -pg. D-3-75
Hong Yee, Vicente A -pg. D-3-75
Hong-Yee, Francisco P -pg. D-1-11
Hong-Yee, Isabel P -pg. D-1-11
Hong-Yee, Jesus P -pg. D-1-11
Hong-Yee, Joaquin P -pg. D-1-11
Hong-Yee, Jose P -pg. D-1-11
Hong-Yee, Maria P -pg. D-1-11
Hong-Yee, Nieves P -pg. D-1-11
Hopper, Mildred C -pg. D-13-2
Hopper, Raymond E -pg. D-13-2
Hornsong, Florence J -pg. D-4-51
Hornsong, Ralph A -pg. D-4-51
Horton, Merton T -pg. D-13-44
Horvick, Paul I -pg. D-11-50
Horwell, Richard W -pg. D-13-20
Howell, Galen B -pg. D-13-42
Hudson, George E -pg. D-2-35
Hudson, Gregoria A -pg. D-2-35

Hudson, James E -pg. D-2-35
Hudson, James M -pg. D-2-35
Hudson, Mary O -pg. D-2-35
Hudson, Pearl E -pg. D-2-35
Hughes, Betty -pg. D-1-2
Hughes, Helen -pg. D-1-2
Hughes, Joaquina U -pg. D-1-2
Hughes, Maud -pg. D-1-2
Hughes, Rose B -pg. D-1-2
Hughes, Virginia -pg. D-1-2
Hughes, William R -pg. D-1-2
Hughes, William R jr. -pg. D-1-3
Hunt, Thomas D -pg. D-13-11
Huntise, George C -pg. D-13-11
Huntise, Warren J -pg. D-13-11
Hutchens, Frank C -pg. D-13-23
Hutchins, Harnes Q -pg. D-13-44
Ibanez, Candalera SN -pg. D-2-57
Ibanez, Cayetano C -pg. D-2-57
Ibanez, Clotilde SN -pg. D-2-57
Ibanez, Jesus SN -pg. D-2-57
Ibanez, Pedro SN -pg. D-2-57
Ibanez, Vicente SN -pg. D-2-57
Ibao, Fabian C -pg. D-5-74
Ibasco, Agnes S -pg. D-5-88
Ibasco, Rita C -pg. D-2-58
Ichida, Ana C -pg. D-3-29
Ichihara, Ana SM -pg. D-1-22
Ichihara, Dolores SM -pg. D-1-22
Ichihara, Francisco SM -pg. D-1-22
Ichihara, Jesus SM -pg. D-1-22
Ichihara, Joaquin SM -pg. D-1-22
Ichihara, Jose SM -pg. D-1-22
Ichihara, Juan SM -pg. D-1-22
Ichihara, Kamekichi -pg. D-1-22
Ichihara, Maria SM -pg. D-1-22
Iglesias, Ana LG -pg. D-5-61
Iglesias, Ana M -pg. D-10-33
Iglesias, Antonio -pg. D-13-35
Iglesias, Antonio A -pg. D-1-50
Iglesias, Carmen -pg. D-5-78
Iglesias, Cerefina G -pg. D-2-27
Iglesias, Consolacion -pg. D-5-78
Iglesias, Consolacion G -pg. D-5-78
Iglesias, Enrique T -pg. D-1-50
Iglesias, Francisco A -pg. D-2-27
Iglesias, Francisco Q -pg. D-10-33
Iglesias, Guadalupe C -pg. D-10-34
Iglesias, Isabel A -pg. D-1-50
Iglesias, Jesus A -pg. D-1-50
Iglesias, Jesus C -pg. D-1-63
Iglesias, Jose -pg. D-5-78
Iglesias, Jose C -pg. D-10-34
Iglesias, Jose G -pg. D-5-61
Iglesias, Jose Q -pg. D-10-33
Iglesias, Josefa A -pg. D-1-50
Iglesias, Juan -pg. D-5-78
Iglesias, Juan -pg. D-10-33
Iglesias, Juan T -pg. D-5-78

Iglesias, Juana I -pg. D-2-16
Iglesias, Julia C -pg. D-10-34
Iglesias, Luis G -pg. D-1-63
Iglesias, Magdalena -pg. D-10-33
Iglesias, Manuel C -pg. D-5-53
Iglesias, Maria A -pg. D-1-50
Iglesias, Maria C -pg. D-1-63
Iglesias, Maria C -pg. D-1-63
Iglesias, Maria P -pg. D-5-53
Iglesias, Oliva C -pg. D-1-63
Iglesias, Rosa -pg. D-5-78
Iglesias, Rosario P -pg. D-5-53
Iglesias, Tomas A -pg. D-1-50
Iglesias, Trinidad C -pg. D-10-34
Ignacio, Ana C -pg. D-4-4
Ignacio, Ana T -pg. D-7-20
Ignacio, Aniceto C -pg. D-10-9
Ignacio, Anisia J -pg. D-7-16
Ignacio, Antonio C -pg. D-10-9
Ignacio, Barbara C -pg. D-4-4
Ignacio, Celestina J -pg. D-7-16
Ignacio, Dolores P -pg. D-10-39
Ignacio, Engracia S -pg. D-4-95
Ignacio, Enrique M -pg. D-4-6
Ignacio, Enrique R -pg. D-7-16
Ignacio, Enrique T -pg. D-7-21
Ignacio, Enriqueta S -pg. D-4-95
Ignacio, Felipe C -pg. D-4-4
Ignacio, Felix T -pg. D-7-21
Ignacio, Filomena C -pg. D-4-87
Ignacio, Francisco C -pg. D-4-4
Ignacio, Francisco N -pg. D-2-80
Ignacio, Francisco P -pg. D-10-39
Ignacio, Francisco T -pg. D-4-51
Ignacio, Gregorio C -pg. D-11-33
Ignacio, Imperatris C -pg. D-4-21
Ignacio, Isabel C -pg. D-10-9
Ignacio, Jesus C -pg. D-4-4
Ignacio, Jesus C -pg. D-4-36
Ignacio, Jesus C -pg. D-8-48
Ignacio, Jesus N -pg. D-2-80
Ignacio, Jesus R -pg. D-5-24
Ignacio, Joaquin C -pg. D-10-9
Ignacio, Jose C -pg. D-10-39
Ignacio, Jose N -pg. D-2-80
Ignacio, Jose T -pg. D-11-8
Ignacio, Josefa J -pg. D-7-16
Ignacio, Josefina P -pg. D-10-39
Ignacio, Juan C -pg. D-10-9
Ignacio, Juan J -pg. D-7-16
Ignacio, Juan N -pg. D-2-81
Ignacio, Juan P -pg. D-10-39
Ignacio, Juana C -pg. D-4-4
Ignacio, Juana C -pg. D-10-9
Ignacio, Leonsio C -pg. D-4-36
Ignacio, Loreta C -pg. D-4-4
Ignacio, Luis C -pg. D-13-27
Ignacio, Luis T -pg. D-7-21
Ignacio, Manuel A -pg. D-10-39

Ignacio, Manuel C -pg. D-4-95
Ignacio, Manuel N -pg. D-2-80
Ignacio, Manuel P -pg. D-4-4
Ignacio, Marcela N -pg. D-2-80
Ignacio, Maria C -pg. D-4-4
Ignacio, Maria C -pg. D-4-34
Ignacio, Maria C -pg. D-10-9
Ignacio, Maria M -pg. D-4-6
Ignacio, Maria N -pg. D-2-80
Ignacio, Maria S -pg. D-4-95
Ignacio, Pedro A -pg. D-2-80
Ignacio, Pedro J -pg. D-7-16
Ignacio, Pedro N -pg. D-2-81
Ignacio, Rafael C -pg. D-4-4
Ignacio, Rafael P -pg. D-10-39
Ignacio, Ramon C -pg. D-4-79
Ignacio, Regina M -pg. D-4-6
Ignacio, Regina P -pg. D-10-39
Ignacio, Rita C -pg. D-4-4
Ignacio, Rita C -pg. D-10-39
Ignacio, Rosa A -pg. D-5-24
Ignacio, Rosa C -pg. D-4-36
Ignacio, Rosa C -pg. D-10-39
Ignacio, Santiago R -pg. D-10-40
Ignacio, Soledad J -pg. D-7-16
Ignacio, Tomas J -pg. D-7-16
Ignacio, Tomasa A -pg. D-4-79
Ignacio, Trinidad R -pg. D-6-40
Ignacio, Vicente A -pg. D-6-40
Ignasio, Jose R -pg. D-6-17
Imaizumi, Francisco -pg. D-5-85
Imaizumi, Jose -pg. D-5-85
Imaizumi, Jose S -pg. D-5-85
Imaizumi, Maria D -pg. D-5-85
Imaizumi, Pedro -pg. D-5-85
Imbuluzqueta, Cripsin -pg. D-1-56
Indalecio, Ana M -pg. D-4-54
Indalecio, Antonio M -pg. D-4-54
Indalecio, Ignacia M -pg. D-4-53
Indalecio, Juan I -pg. D-4-53
Indalecio, Maria M -pg. D-4-54
Indalecio, Vincete I -pg. D-13-29
Indelecio, Ana -pg. D-3-48
Indelecio, Belen M -pg. D-3-44
Indelecio, Carmen -pg. D-3-48
Indelecio, Catalina -pg. D-3-15
Indelecio, Dolores -pg. D-3-46
Indelecio, Dolores -pg. D-3-48
Indelecio, Emeteria -pg. D-3-15
Indelecio, Jose -pg. D-3-14
Indelecio, Jose -pg. D-3-48
Indelecio, Jose I -pg. D-3-44
Indelecio, Margarita R -pg. D-3-3
Indelecio, Pedro C -pg. D-3-14
Indelecio, Rita -pg. D-3-44
Indelecio, Rosa -pg. D-3-48
Indelecio, Rufina C -pg. D-3-14
Inks, Richard R -pg. D-13-16
Inouye, Ana S -pg. D-10-7

Inouye, Benedicta S -pg. D-10-8
Inouye, Joaquin S -pg. D-10-7
Inouye, Maria S -pg. D-10-8
Iriarte, Agustina D -pg. D-3-13
Iriarte, Ana -pg. D-3-20
Iriarte, Ana -pg. D-3-22
Iriarte, Ana R -pg. D-2-43
Iriarte, Ana S -pg. D-3-17
Iriarte, Ana T -pg. D-4-105
Iriarte, Antonio -pg. D-3-13
Iriarte, Antonio G -pg. D-4-105
Iriarte, Beatris -pg. D-3-23
Iriarte, Cristina -pg. D-3-20
Iriarte, Dolores -pg. D-3-13
Iriarte, Feliciana R -pg. D-2-43
Iriarte, Francisco -pg. D-3-20
Iriarte, Geronimo R -pg. D-2-43
Iriarte, Ignacia T -pg. D-3-19
Iriarte, Ignacio D -pg. D-3-17
Iriarte, Isabel R -pg. D-2-43
Iriarte, Jesus -pg. D-3-13
Iriarte, Jesus C -pg. D-3-18
Iriarte, Jesus R -pg. D-2-43
Iriarte, Joaquin R -pg. D-2-43
Iriarte, Jose -pg. D-3-13
Iriarte, Jose -pg. D-3-20
Iriarte, Jose C -pg. D-5-40
Iriarte, Jose R -pg. D-5-32
Iriarte, Juan -pg. D-3-20
Iriarte, Juan -pg. D-3-23
Iriarte, Juan C -pg. D-2-43
Iriarte, Juana -pg. D-3-13
Iriarte, Julia -pg. D-3-21
Iriarte, Lorenzo -pg. D-3-22
Iriarte, Margarita R -pg. D-2-43
Iriarte, Maria -pg. D-3-13
Iriarte, Maria -pg. D-3-17
Iriarte, Maria F -pg. D-3-23
Iriarte, Maria LG -pg. D-3-21
Iriarte, Maria R -pg. D-2-43
Iriarte, Natividad -pg. D-3-13
Iriarte, Natividad L -pg. D-5-46
Iriarte, Nicolas C -pg. D-3-13
Iriarte, Pedro C -pg. D-5-46
Iriarte, Pedro L -pg. D-5-46
Iriarte, Rosa -pg. D-3-22
Iriarte, Tomas -pg. D-3-13
Iriarte, Tomas -pg. D-3-23
Iriarte, Tomas D -pg. D-3-23
Iriarte, Vicente D -pg. D-3-21
Iriarte, Vicente L -pg. D-5-46
Isam, Roscoe W -pg. D-13-20
Isezaki, Ana P -pg. D-9-42
Isezaki, Carmen P -pg. D-9-42
Isezaki, Concepcion P -pg. D-9-42
Isezaki, Francisco M -pg. D-9-42
Isezaki, Joaquina M -pg. D-9-42
Isezaki, Jose P -pg. D-9-42
Isezaki, Josefina M -pg. D-9-42

Isezaki, Juan P -pg. D-9-42
Isezaki, Lucia M -pg. D-9-42
Isezaki, Marcelina P -pg. D-9-42
Isezaki, Maria P -pg. D-9-42
Isezaki, Rosa M -pg. D-9-42
Isezaki, Vicente -pg. D-9-42
Isezaki, William P -pg. D-9-42
Isezaki, Yokichi -pg. D-9-42
Ishizaki, Agueda P -pg. D-11-9
Ishizaki, Dolores P -pg. D-11-9
Ishizaki, Filomena P -pg. D-11-9
Ishizaki, Francisco -pg. D-11-9
Ishizaki, Irene P -pg. D-11-9
Ishizaki, Isabel P -pg. D-11-9
Ishizaki, Joaquin P -pg. D-11-9
Ishizaki, Maria P -pg. D-11-9
Ishizaki, Vicente P -pg. D-11-9
Ishizaki, Victoria P -pg. D-11-9
Isidro, Ursula A -pg. D-3-49
Israel, Otis A -pg. D-13-16
Ito, Genge -pg. D-1-21
Ito, Jesus S -pg. D-1-21
Ito, Vicente S -pg. D-1-21
Iwatsut, Carmen S -pg. D-3-30
Iwatsut, Jose -pg. D-3-30
Iwatsut, Juana -pg. D-3-30
Iwatsut, Severa -pg. D-3-30
Iwatsut, Tomas -pg. D-3-30
Jackson, Arthur K -pg. D-2-3
Jackson, Arthur W -pg. D-2-3
Jackson, Dolores K -pg. D-2-3
Jackson, Frank K -pg. D-2-4
Jackson, Henry K -pg. D-2-3
Jackson, Irene R -pg. D-2-4
Jackson, Rosie M -pg. D-2-4
Jackson, Steven M -pg. D-13-41
James, Concepcion B -pg. D-11-14
James, Frank B -pg. D-11-14
James, Gurnie -pg. D-13-16
James, Henry B -pg. D-11-14
James, Jose F -pg. D-11-10
James, Joseph B -pg. D-11-14
James, Mary B -pg. D-11-14
James, Pedro F -pg. D-4-77
James, William F -pg. D-11-14
James, Woodrow F -pg. D-5-29
Jarry, Benjamin F -pg. D-13-35
Jarvis, Thomas A -pg. D-13-37
Javier, Benito -pg. D-13-23
Javier, Dolores A -pg. D-3-45
Javier, Isabel -pg. D-3-45
Javier, Jose P -pg. D-5-97
Javier, Julia P -pg. D-3-73
Javier, Maria -pg. D-3-45
Javier, Mariquita -pg. D-5-97
Javier, Rosa P -pg. D-5-97
Jeffer, Larrus -pg. D-13-40
Jergenson, Tiels W -pg. D-13-20
Jesus, Ana B -pg. D-6-28

Jesus, Ana S -pg. D-6-5
Jesus, Angela C -pg. D-2-10
Jesus, Antonio C -pg. D-4-30
Jesus, Antonio LG -pg. D-7-2
Jesus, Carmen B -pg. D-6-28
Jesus, Concepcion L -pg. D-7-16
Jesus, Delfina S -pg. D-6-5
Jesus, Elias LG -pg. D-7-2
Jesus, Ernestina B -pg. D-6-27
Jesus, Felicita LG -pg. D-7-2
Jesus, Felix -pg. D-11-47
Jesus, Felix J -pg. D-6-2
Jesus, Fidel LG -pg. D-7-2
Jesus, Fidela LG -pg. D-7-2
Jesus, Francisca B -pg. D-6-27
Jesus, Francisco B -pg. D-6-28
Jesus, Francisco C -pg. D-4-30
Jesus, Francisco C -pg. D-7-6
Jesus, Guadalupe B -pg. D-4-30
Jesus, Guadalupe C -pg. D-7-6
Jesus, Joaquin B -pg. D-6-28
Jesus, Joaquin F -pg. D-7-6
Jesus, Joaquin L -pg. D-7-2
Jesus, Jose B -pg. D-6-28
Jesus, Jose C -pg. D-4-30
Jesus, Jose J -pg. D-6-2
Jesus, Josefa B -pg. D-4-30
Jesus, Josefa C -pg. D-4-30
Jesus, Josefa LG -pg. D-7-2
Jesus, Juan B -pg. D-4-30
Jesus, Juan B -pg. D-6-27
Jesus, Juana B -pg. D-6-28
Jesus, Lorenzo B -pg. D-6-28
Jesus, Lucas C -pg. D-7-6
Jesus, Lucas SN -pg. D-2-16
Jesus, Luis SN -pg. D-5-9
Jesus, Maria C -pg. D-2-16
Jesus, Maria H -pg. D-2-68
Jesus, Maria S -pg. D-6-5
Jesus, Marselo B -pg. D-6-27
Jesus, Nicolasa B -pg. D-6-28
Jesus, Ofemia LG -pg. D-7-2
Jesus, Pedro LG -pg. D-7-2
Jesus, Rosalia C -pg. D-4-30
Jesus, Vicenta C -pg. D-7-6
Jesus, Vicente B -pg. D-6-28
Jesus, Vicente B -pg. D-6-28
Jesus, Vicente C -pg. D-4-30
Johnson, Andrew -pg. D-3-72
Johnson, Francis -pg. D-3-72
Johnson, Hans -pg. D-13-45
Johnson, Ignacia P -pg. D-3-72
Johnson, Jesus -pg. D-3-72
Johnson, Joseph E -pg. D-13-11
Johnson, Juan -pg. D-3-72
Johnson, Leonisa -pg. D-3-72
Johnson, Olga -pg. D-3-72
Johnson, Patrick -pg. D-3-72
Johnston, Agueda I -pg. D-3-30

Johnston, Harbert I -pg. D-3-30
Johnston, James E -pg. D-13-42
Johnston, Joseph W -pg. D-3-30
Johnston, Marian A -pg. D-3-30
Johnston, Thomas I -pg. D-3-30
Johnston, William G -pg. D-3-30
Jone, George A -pg. D-13-23
Jones, Milburn K -pg. D-13-11
Jorgensen, Beatrice -pg. D-13-43
Jorgensen, Dorothy -pg. D-13-44
Jorgensen, Helen -pg. D-13-43
Jorgensen, Joan -pg. D-13-44
Jorgensen, Joyce -pg. D-13-44
Joses, Douglas -pg. D-3-58
Joses, Maurice -pg. D-3-58
Joses, Maurice -pg. D-13-18
Joses, Robert -pg. D-3-58
Juan, Camilo C -pg. D-5-44
Juan, ISabel M -pg. D-5-44
Julian, Delmar -pg. D-13-42
Julian, Marie E -pg. D-1-37
Julian, Vincent V -pg. D-13-26
Julian, Vivian M -pg. D-1-37
Kaminga, Catalina S -pg. D-5-94
Kaminga, John R -pg. D-5-94
Kamminga, David F -pg. D-1-52
Kamminga, Elvira S -pg. D-1-53
Kamminga, Felicidad T -pg. D-8-2
Kamminga, Felicitas SN -pg. D-10-22
Kamminga, Felix R -pg. D-10-22
Kamminga, Francisco R -pg. D-1-12
Kamminga, Frank F -pg. D-1-52
Kamminga, Gaily F -pg. D-1-52
Kamminga, Gaily R -pg. D-1-53
Kamminga, Gaily SN -pg. D-2-3
Kamminga, Gretje SN -pg. D-10-22
Kamminga, Henry F -pg. D-1-52
Kamminga, Henry SN -pg. D-2-3
Kamminga, Joaquina F -pg. D-1-52
Kamminga, Joaquina H -pg. D-1-52
Kamminga, Johannes F -pg. D-1-52
Kamminga, John S -pg. D-1-53
Kamminga, Jose -pg. D-1-52
Kamminga, Jose F -pg. D-1-52
Kamminga, Jose H -pg. D-2-3
Kamminga, Juana R -pg. D-10-22
Kamminga, Juana SN -pg. D-10-22
Kamminga, Lolkje H -pg. D-10-22
Kamminga, Lorenzo F -pg. D-1-52
Kamminga, Magdalena F -pg. D-1-52
Kamminga, Maria F -pg. D-1-52
Kamminga, Maria F -pg. D-1-52
Kamminga, Maria H -pg. D-10-22
Kamminga, Maria SN -pg. D-2-3
Kamminga, Pilar SN -pg. D-10-23
Kamminga, Remedios S -pg. D-1-53
Kamminga, Rita T -pg. D-1-12
Kamminga, Simon H -pg. D-8-2
Kamminga, Vicenta SN -pg. D-10-23

Kamminga, Virginia SN -pg. D-2-3
Kamo, Carmen C -pg. D-8-16
Kanagawa, Crecencia D -pg. D-2-32
Kanagawa, Lucio H -pg. D-2-31
Kanagawa, Pedro D -pg. D-2-32
Kanagawa, Rufina D -pg. D-2-32
Kearney, James F -pg. D-13-23
Keepfer, Lawrence H -pg. D-13-37
Kei, Eikichi -pg. D-4-90
Keith, Arley L -pg. D-13-40
Kellett, Wayne D -pg. D-13-11
Kellison, Edna M -pg. D-11-32
Kellison, Edward -pg. D-13-37
Kellison, Grace -pg. D-11-32
Kellison, Janet M -pg. D-11-32
Kelly, David H -pg. D-13-28
Kelly, Kenneth P -pg. D-13-11
Kennedy, Earnest E -pg. D-13-37
Kennedy, Paul B -pg. D-13-11
Kilroy, Lawrence C -pg. D-13-20
Kimball, Lloyd B -pg. D-13-33
Kina, Yoshinoku -pg. D-10-15
Kirisay, Debert W -pg. D-13-23
Kirmijama, Juan -pg. D-8-18
Kirmijama, Margarita -pg. D-8-18
Kirmijama, Maria M -pg. D-8-18
Kirmijama, Mariano -pg. D-8-18
Kirmijama, Rita M -pg. D-8-18
Klappholz, Henry E -pg. D-13-16
Klopz, Harvey F -pg. D-13-42
Kreiling, Howard F -pg. D-13-20
Kucharoki, Edmund -pg. D-13-12
Kuernmich, Robert H -pg. D-13-33
Kuhnz, Eugene S -pg. D-11-50
Kunkel, Edward T -pg. D-13-44
Kunkol, Edward K -pg. D-1-54
Kunkol, Elan M -pg. D-1-54
Kunkol, Helen E -pg. D-1-54
Kuokes, Henry L -pg. D-13-16
Kuoz, Joseph Q -pg. D-13-12
Kurokaw, Genro -pg. D-3-47
La Crosse, Rudoloph D -pg. D-13-23
Laguana, Agustin I -pg. D-10-38
Laguana, Ana I -pg. D-10-38
Laguana, Ana I -pg. D-10-38
Laguana, Ana S -pg. D-10-38
Laguana, Carlos C -pg. D-4-113
Laguana, Faustino C -pg. D-6-21
Laguana, Felicidad P -pg. D-4-113
Laguana, Felix S -pg. D-10-38
Laguana, Ignacia P -pg. D-4-113
Laguana, Ignacio I -pg. D-10-38
Laguana, Jesus C -pg. D-4-113
Laguana, Jesus I -pg. D-10-38
Laguana, Joaquina P -pg. D-4-113
Laguana, Jose C -pg. D-4-113
Laguana, Jose I -pg. D-1-53
Laguana, Jose P -pg. D-4-113
Laguana, Maria I -pg. D-10-38

Laguana, Ramon I -pg. D-10-38
Laguana, Rita C -pg. D-4-113
Laguana, Rosa I -pg. D-10-38
Laguana, Rosa P -pg. D-4-113
Laguana, Rosa S -pg. D-10-39
Laguana, Soledad P -pg. D-4-113
Laguana, Vicente P -pg. D-10-38
Laingot, Luis L -pg. D-13-21
Lamb, Hughey -pg. D-13-7
Lanais, George J -pg. D-13-37
Landes, Lester P -pg. D-13-7
Landmark, Elenora O -pg. D-1-35
Lanen, Leonard G -pg. D-13-12
Lang, Harry J -pg. D-13-33
Lang, vern -pg. D-13-12
Languridge, George C -pg. D-13-7
Lans, Walter R -pg. D-13-37
Lansdowne, Florence H -pg. D-1-35
Lansdowne, Herbert S -pg. D-13-26
Lansdowne, Jessie P -pg. D-1-35
Lansdowne, Kenneth R -pg. D-1-35
Laptap, Martina L -pg. D-2-29
Larry, Joseph McG -pg. D-13-33
Larson, Robert T -pg. D-13-44
Larwan, Nathan P -pg. D-13-12
Lason, Malcom W -pg. D-13-26
Lauren, Jack A -pg. D-13-39
Lawrence, John T. Jr. -pg. D-13-12
Lazaro, Antonia U -pg. D-4-21
Lazaro, Ernesto U -pg. D-4-21
Lazaro, Juan U -pg. D-4-17
Lazaro, Manuel R -pg. D-4-126
Le Gette, Curtis W -pg. D-13-3
Le Gette, Geraldine -pg. D-13-3
Lea, Luther B -pg. D-13-40
Leach, Orsin C -pg. D-13-40
Lebsock, Daniel R -pg. D-13-7
Lecadio, Antonia U -pg. D-4-35
Lecadio, Carmilita U -pg. D-4-35
Lecadio, Fermetiva U -pg. D-4-35
Leddy, Daniel B -pg. D-4-108
Leddy, Elsie B -pg. D-4-108
Leddy, Henry S -pg. D-4-118
Leddy, John B -pg. D-4-117
Leddy, Maria S -pg. D-4-117
Ledria, Harry F -pg. D-13-7
Ledwick, Thomas F -pg. D-13-42
Lee, Charles H -pg. D-13-12
Lee, Marjorie Jean -pg. D-3-33
Lee, Will G -pg. D-13-16
Leech, Lawrence E -pg. D-13-7
Leffo, George M -pg. D-13-7
Legaria, Eugenio de D -pg. D-6-3
Legg, Lawrence M -pg. D-13-20
Leon, Ana S -pg. D-3-50
Leon, Antonio C -pg. D-3-50
Leon, Asuncion C -pg. D-4-100
Leon, Asuncion C -pg. D-4-100
Leon, Enrique M -pg. D-4-116

Leon, Francisco C -pg. D-4-100
Leon, Juan C -pg. D-4-100
Leon, Juan M -pg. D-4-100
Leon, Juan M -pg. D-4-116
Leon, Lourdes M -pg. D-4-116
Leon Guerrero, Agapito C -pg. D-4-76
Leon Guerrero, Alejo B -pg. D-2-31
Leon Guerrero, Amparo C -pg. D-4-112
Leon Guerrero, Ana A -pg. D-1-57
Leon Guerrero, Ana A -pg. D-8-27
Leon Guerrero, Ana B -pg. D-1-56
Leon Guerrero, Ana B -pg. D-6-7
Leon Guerrero, Ana C -pg. D-2-49
Leon Guerrero, Ana C -pg. D-2-50
Leon Guerrero, Ana C -pg. D-4-17
Leon Guerrero, Ana C -pg. D-4-20
Leon Guerrero, Ana C -pg. D-4-37
Leon Guerrero, Ana C -pg. D-4-46
Leon Guerrero, Ana C -pg. D-4-46
Leon Guerrero, Ana C -pg. D-5-29
Leon Guerrero, Ana D -pg. D-8-13
Leon Guerrero, Ana de LG -pg. D-1-14
Leon Guerrero, Ana F -pg. D-4-5
Leon Guerrero, Ana L -pg. D-4-61
Leon Guerrero, Ana M -pg. D-4-76
Leon Guerrero, Ana M -pg. D-8-12
Leon Guerrero, Ana N -pg. D-4-43
Leon Guerrero, Ana P -pg. D-2-49
Leon Guerrero, Ana P -pg. D-4-105
Leon Guerrero, Ana R -pg. D-1-34
Leon Guerrero, Ana S -pg. D-1-15
Leon Guerrero, Ana S -pg. D-1-15
Leon Guerrero, Ana S -pg. D-3-22
Leon Guerrero, Ana S -pg. D-4-41
Leon Guerrero, Ana S -pg. D-4-65
Leon Guerrero, Angustia LG -pg. D-8-32
Leon Guerrero, Antonia A -pg. D-4-116
Leon Guerrero, Antonia B -pg. D-1-56
Leon Guerrero, Antonia F -pg. D-1-52
Leon Guerrero, Antonia F -pg. D-5-56
Leon Guerrero, Antonia R -pg. D-1-12
Leon Guerrero, Antonio C -pg. D-5-29
Leon Guerrero, Asuncion A -pg. D-5-11
Leon Guerrero, Balbino D -pg. D-2-56
Leon Guerrero, Balbino S -pg. D-1-12
Leon Guerrero, Baltazaar B -pg. D-6-7
Leon Guerrero, Baltazar B -pg. D-1-10
Leon Guerrero, Barsalisa C -pg. D-2-49
Leon Guerrero, Beatris LG -pg. D-4-75
Leon Guerrero, Benigno D -pg. D-5-24
Leon Guerrero, Bernarda C -pg. D-3-30
Leon Guerrero, Brigida S -pg. D-1-2
Leon Guerrero, Caridad A -pg. D-1-56
Leon Guerrero, Carlos B -pg. D-1-61
Leon Guerrero, Carlos C -pg. D-1-61
Leon Guerrero, Carlos S -pg. D-1-12
Leon Guerrero, Carlota T -pg. D-8-32
Leon Guerrero, Carmen A -pg. D-1-36
Leon Guerrero, Carmen A -pg. D-1-57

Leon Guerrero, Carmen B -pg. D-4-107
Leon Guerrero, Carmen C -pg. D-5-46
Leon Guerrero, Carmen C -pg. D-5-60
Leon Guerrero, Carmen D -pg. D-8-13
Leon Guerrero, Carmen G -pg. D-9-15
Leon Guerrero, Carmen P -pg. D-4-43
Leon Guerrero, Carmen T -pg. D-4-86
Leon Guerrero, Catalina -pg. D-3-22
Leon Guerrero, Cecelia B -pg. D-1-39
Leon Guerrero, Clotilde T -pg. D-2-52
Leon Guerrero, Concepcion B -pg. D-1-39
Leon Guerrero, Concepcion D -pg. D-2-56
Leon Guerrero, Concepcion I -pg. D-4-112
Leon Guerrero, Concepcion p -pg. D-4-108
Leon Guerrero, Concepcion T -pg. D-2-52
Leon Guerrero, Consolacion -pg. D-3-10
Leon Guerrero, Consolacion M -pg. D-8-12
Leon Guerrero, Delfina R -pg. D-4-82
Leon Guerrero, Delfina T -pg. D-2-52
Leon Guerrero, Dolores A -pg. D-1-36
Leon Guerrero, Dolores A -pg. D-8-28
Leon Guerrero, Dolores B -pg. D-3-10
Leon Guerrero, Dolores C -pg. D-4-20
Leon Guerrero, Dolores C -pg. D-4-74
Leon Guerrero, Dolores C -pg. D-4-112
Leon Guerrero, Dolores F -pg. D-1-51
Leon Guerrero, Dolores F -pg. D-5-56
Leon Guerrero, Dolores I -pg. D-4-112
Leon Guerrero, Dolores L -pg. D-5-18
Leon Guerrero, Dolores P -pg. D-4-105
Leon Guerrero, Dolores S -pg. D-4-41
Leon Guerrero, Dolores T -pg. D-2-10
Leon Guerrero, Dolores U -pg. D-4-123
Leon Guerrero, Dominga A -pg. D-8-28
Leon Guerrero, Efraim B -pg. D-6-7
Leon Guerrero, Eliza P -pg. D-4-108
Leon Guerrero, Elvira D -pg. D-5-24
Leon Guerrero, Emelia B -pg. D-2-31
Leon Guerrero, Emelia C -pg. D-2-47
Leon Guerrero, Encarnacion B -pg. D-6-7
Leon Guerrero, Enrique C -pg. D-2-47
Leon Guerrero, Ephraim C -pg. D-4-46
Leon Guerrero, Eriberto C -pg. D-4-37
Leon Guerrero, Esiquiel C -pg. D-4-76
Leon Guerrero, Estefania G -pg. D-9-15
Leon Guerrero, Ester B -pg. D-5-18
Leon Guerrero, Ester F -pg. D-1-56
Leon Guerrero, Eulelia A -pg. D-5-12
Leon Guerrero, Exsaperanza B -pg. D-1-56
Leon Guerrero, Faustino C -pg. D-4-20
Leon Guerrero, Felipe G -pg. D-4-82
Leon Guerrero, Felis P -pg. D-4-117
Leon Guerrero, Felis S -pg. D-4-41
Leon Guerrero, Felix B -pg. D-6-7
Leon Guerrero, Florencia S -pg. D-2-49
Leon Guerrero, Francisca B -pg. D-1-39
Leon Guerrero, Francisco -pg. D-3-6
Leon Guerrero, Francisco B -pg. D-2-31
Leon Guerrero, Francisco B -pg. D-2-47

Leon Guerrero, Francisco B -pg. D-2-73
Leon Guerrero, Francisco b -pg. D-4-107
Leon Guerrero, Francisco C -pg. D-1-61
Leon Guerrero, Francisco C -pg. D-4-76
Leon Guerrero, Francisco C -pg. D-5-29
Leon Guerrero, Francisco LG -pg. D-2-56
Leon Guerrero, Francisco R -pg. D-4-64
Leon Guerrero, Francisco S -pg. D-2-49
Leon Guerrero, Francisco S -pg. D-8-12
Leon Guerrero, Gertrudes P -pg. D-4-105
Leon Guerrero, Gloria C -pg. D-2-47
Leon Guerrero, Gonzalo A -pg. D-1-56
Leon Guerrero, Gonzalo B -pg. D-1-56
Leon Guerrero, Gregorio S -pg. D-1-2
Leon Guerrero, Ignacia -pg. D-3-29
Leon Guerrero, Ignacia B -pg. D-6-7
Leon Guerrero, Ignacia S -pg. D-4-64
Leon Guerrero, Ignacio C -pg. D-4-21
Leon Guerrero, Ignacio F -pg. D-2-10
Leon Guerrero, Ignacio G -pg. D-9-15
Leon Guerrero, Ignacio LG -pg. D-4-75
Leon Guerrero, Ignacio P -pg. D-4-43
Leon Guerrero, Ignacio S -pg. D-2-37
Leon Guerrero, Isabel B -pg. D-1-39
Leon Guerrero, Isabel C -pg. D-5-60
Leon Guerrero, Isabel D -pg. D-2-56
Leon Guerrero, Isabel D -pg. D-8-13
Leon Guerrero, Isabel T -pg. D-2-78
Leon Guerrero, Isidro C -pg. D-1-61
Leon Guerrero, James -pg. D-3-22
Leon Guerrero, Jesus -pg. D-3-56
Leon Guerrero, Jesus A -pg. D-8-28
Leon Guerrero, Jesus B -pg. D-6-7
Leon Guerrero, Jesus C -pg. D-5-29
Leon Guerrero, Jesus G -pg. D-3-75
Leon Guerrero, Jesus G -pg. D-9-15
Leon Guerrero, Jesus I -pg. D-4-112
Leon Guerrero, Jesus LG -pg. D-4-75
Leon Guerrero, Jesus N -pg. D-4-36
Leon Guerrero, Jesus P -pg. D-1-37
Leon Guerrero, Jesus P -pg. D-5-11
Leon Guerrero, Jesus R -pg. D-4-59
Leon Guerrero, Jesus S -pg. D-1-2
Leon Guerrero, Jesus S -pg. D-2-55
Leon Guerrero, Jesus U -pg. D-4-49
Leon Guerrero, Jesusa P -pg. D-4-52
Leon Guerrero, Joaquin A -pg. D-1-56
Leon Guerrero, Joaquin B -pg. D-1-56
Leon Guerrero, Joaquin B -pg. D-2-55
Leon Guerrero, Joaquin C -pg. D-1-56
Leon Guerrero, Joaquin C -pg. D-4-112
Leon Guerrero, Joaquin D -pg. D-8-13
Leon Guerrero, Joaquin I -pg. D-4-112
Leon Guerrero, Joaquin M -pg. D-8-12
Leon Guerrero, Joaquin N -pg. D-8-32
Leon Guerrero, Joaquin P -pg. D-2-48
Leon Guerrero, Joaquin P -pg. D-4-52
Leon Guerrero, Joaquin P -pg. D-4-105
Leon Guerrero, Joaquin P -pg. D-5-66

Leon Guerrero, Joaquin R -pg. D-2-40
Leon Guerrero, Joaquin S -pg. D-8-27
Leon Guerrero, Joaquin T -pg. D-4-86
Leon Guerrero, Joaquina A -pg. D-5-12
Leon Guerrero, Joaquina B -pg. D-2-31
Leon Guerrero, Joaquina S -pg. D-1-12
Leon Guerrero, Joaquina S -pg. D-2-49
Leon Guerrero, Jose -pg. D-3-29
Leon Guerrero, Jose -pg. D-3-44
Leon Guerrero, Jose -pg. D-3-56
Leon Guerrero, Jose A -pg. D-1-56
Leon Guerrero, Jose A -pg. D-5-24
Leon Guerrero, Jose C -pg. D-2-50
Leon Guerrero, Jose C -pg. D-3-6
Leon Guerrero, Jose C -pg. D-4-22
Leon Guerrero, Jose C -pg. D-4-46
Leon Guerrero, Jose C -pg. D-5-46
Leon Guerrero, Jose D -pg. D-4-126
Leon Guerrero, Jose D -pg. D-5-24
Leon Guerrero, Jose F -pg. D-4-46
Leon Guerrero, Jose G -pg. D-9-15
Leon Guerrero, Jose I -pg. D-4-112
Leon Guerrero, Jose M -pg. D-8-12
Leon Guerrero, Jose P -pg. D-2-49
Leon Guerrero, Jose P -pg. D-2-52
Leon Guerrero, Jose P -pg. D-4-52
Leon Guerrero, Jose P -pg. D-4-59
Leon Guerrero, Jose P -pg. D-4-105
Leon Guerrero, Jose P -pg. D-4-117
Leon Guerrero, Jose P -pg. D-5-66
Leon Guerrero, Jose R -pg. D-3-56
Leon Guerrero, Jose R -pg. D-4-59
Leon Guerrero, Jose S -pg. D-1-15
Leon Guerrero, Jose S -pg. D-2-49
Leon Guerrero, Jose S -pg. D-3-23
Leon Guerrero, Jose S -pg. D-4-64
Leon Guerrero, Josefa M -pg. D-8-12
Leon Guerrero, Josefa T -pg. D-2-38
Leon Guerrero, Josefina A -pg. D-1-56
Leon Guerrero, Josefina C -pg. D-5-29
Leon Guerrero, Josefina M -pg. D-4-76
Leon Guerrero, Josefina S -pg. D-1-12
Leon Guerrero, Juan -pg. D-3-6
Leon Guerrero, Juan -pg. D-3-18
Leon Guerrero, Juan -pg. D-3-23
Leon Guerrero, Juan -pg. D-5-17
Leon Guerrero, Juan B -pg. D-1-39
Leon Guerrero, Juan C -pg. D-4-20
Leon Guerrero, Juan C -pg. D-4-46
Leon Guerrero, Juan C -pg. D-5-18
Leon Guerrero, Juan C -pg. D-5-29
Leon Guerrero, Juan D -pg. D-2-56
Leon Guerrero, Juan L -pg. D-4-61
Leon Guerrero, Juan LG -pg. D-4-82
Leon Guerrero, Juan LG -pg. D-6-12
Leon Guerrero, Juan P -pg. D-4-43
Leon Guerrero, Juan P -pg. D-4-52
Leon Guerrero, Juan P -pg. D-4-117
Leon Guerrero, Juan S -pg. D-1-39

Leon Guerrero, Juan S -pg. D-2-49
Leon Guerrero, Juan T -pg. D-2-10
Leon Guerrero, Juan T -pg. D-3-29
Leon Guerrero, Juan U -pg. D-4-61
Leon Guerrero, Juan LG -pg. D-1-53
Leon Guerrero, Juana C -pg. D-2-49
Leon Guerrero, Juana C -pg. D-4-37
Leon Guerrero, Juaquina S -pg. D-1-15
Leon Guerrero, Justa B -pg. D-2-73
Leon Guerrero, Justo C -pg. D-4-46
Leon Guerrero, Justo T -pg. D-2-10
Leon Guerrero, Lagrimas P -pg. D-4-108
Leon Guerrero, Leon C -pg. D-6-7
Leon Guerrero, Leonia T -pg. D-2-10
Leon Guerrero, Linea A -pg. D-1-56
Leon Guerrero, Lorenzo A -pg. D-2-55
Leon Guerrero, Lorenzo C -pg. D-2-47
Leon Guerrero, Lourdes C -pg. D-4-20
Leon Guerrero, Lourdes P -pg. D-4-43
Leon Guerrero, Lourdes S -pg. D-1-12
Leon Guerrero, Luis T -pg. D-2-78
Leon Guerrero, Luisa A -pg. D-4-43
Leon Guerrero, Luisa U -pg. D-4-123
Leon Guerrero, Magdalena C -pg. D-1-61
Leon Guerrero, Magdalena L -pg. D-4-61
Leon Guerrero, Magdalena P -pg. D-2-52
Leon Guerrero, Magno P -pg. D-4-117
Leon Guerrero, Manuel -pg. D-3-23
Leon Guerrero, Manuel C -pg. D-2-49
Leon Guerrero, Manuel C -pg. D-4-20
Leon Guerrero, Manuel LG -pg. D-4-39
Leon Guerrero, Manuel LG -pg. D-4-75
Leon Guerrero, Margarita P -pg. D-4-117
Leon Guerrero, Maria -pg. D-1-2
Leon Guerrero, Maria -pg. D-3-6
Leon Guerrero, Maria -pg. D-3-23
Leon Guerrero, Maria -pg. D-3-44
Leon Guerrero, Maria -pg. D-3-56
Leon Guerrero, Maria A -pg. D-1-56
Leon Guerrero, Maria A -pg. D-3-23
Leon Guerrero, Maria A -pg. D-4-41
Leon Guerrero, Maria A -pg. D-5-12
Leon Guerrero, Maria A -pg. D-8-27
Leon Guerrero, Maria B -pg. D-1-39
Leon Guerrero, Maria B -pg. D-1-56
Leon Guerrero, Maria C -pg. D-2-47
Leon Guerrero, Maria C -pg. D-2-49
Leon Guerrero, Maria C -pg. D-4-20
Leon Guerrero, Maria C -pg. D-4-74
Leon Guerrero, Maria C -pg. D-4-112
Leon Guerrero, Maria C -pg. D-5-18
Leon Guerrero, Maria C -pg. D-5-46
Leon Guerrero, Maria C -pg. D-5-46
Leon Guerrero, Maria C -pg. D-5-60
Leon Guerrero, Maria C -pg. D-8-5
Leon Guerrero, Maria F -pg. D-1-51
Leon Guerrero, Maria F -pg. D-4-121
Leon Guerrero, Maria F -pg. D-5-56
Leon Guerrero, Maria G -pg. D-9-15

Leon Guerrero, Maria L -pg. D-2-40
Leon Guerrero, Maria L -pg. D-5-17
Leon Guerrero, Maria M -pg. D-3-56
Leon Guerrero, Maria M -pg. D-4-76
Leon Guerrero, Maria M -pg. D-8-12
Leon Guerrero, Maria P -pg. D-2-49
Leon Guerrero, Maria P -pg. D-4-52
Leon Guerrero, Maria P -pg. D-4-105
Leon Guerrero, Maria P -pg. D-4-108
Leon Guerrero, Maria R -pg. D-1-11
Leon Guerrero, Maria R -pg. D-4-117
Leon Guerrero, Maria S -pg. D-2-49
Leon Guerrero, Maria S -pg. D-2-55
Leon Guerrero, Maria T -pg. D-2-52
Leon Guerrero, Maria T -pg. D-2-52
Leon Guerrero, Maria U -pg. D-4-123
Leon Guerrero, Maria Q T -pg. D-2-52
Leon Guerrero, Mariana LG -pg. D-4-82
Leon Guerrero, Mariana M -pg. D-4-76
Leon Guerrero, Mariana P -pg. D-4-107
Leon Guerrero, Mariano -pg. D-3-23
Leon Guerrero, Mariano A -pg. D-5-12
Leon Guerrero, Mariano D -pg. D-8-13
Leon Guerrero, Mariano LG -pg. D-4-75
Leon Guerrero, Mariano R -pg. D-8-13
Leon Guerrero, Matias -pg. D-3-6
Leon Guerrero, Maximino G -pg. D-9-15
Leon Guerrero, Miguel A -pg. D-4-41
Leon Guerrero, Nicolasa C -pg. D-4-37
Leon Guerrero, Nicolasa R -pg. D-4-59
Leon Guerrero, Oliva L -pg. D-5-18
Leon Guerrero, Pedro -pg. D-3-6
Leon Guerrero, Pedro -pg. D-3-29
Leon Guerrero, Pedro -pg. D-3-56
Leon Guerrero, Pedro B -pg. D-2-73
Leon Guerrero, Pedro C -pg. D-4-37
Leon Guerrero, Pedro C -pg. D-4-76
Leon Guerrero, Pedro C -pg. D-5-18
Leon Guerrero, Pedro LG -pg. D-1-37
Leon Guerrero, Pedro P -pg. D-4-37
Leon Guerrero, Pedro P -pg. D-4-52
Leon Guerrero, Pedro R -pg. D-9-15
Leon Guerrero, Petra M -pg. D-8-12
Leon Guerrero, Ramon -pg. D-8-28
Leon Guerrero, Ramon B -pg. D-1-36
Leon Guerrero, Ramon C -pg. D-2-47
Leon Guerrero, Ramon G -pg. D-1-12
Leon Guerrero, Regina P -pg. D-4-43
Leon Guerrero, Remedios C -pg. D-4-17
Leon Guerrero, Rita C -pg. D-4-46
Leon Guerrero, Rita C -pg. D-4-76
Leon Guerrero, Rita P -pg. D-3-6
Leon Guerrero, Rita R -pg. D-1-34
Leon Guerrero, Rofina LG -pg. D-1-37
Leon Guerrero, Rosa -pg. D-3-6
Leon Guerrero, Rosa A -pg. D-8-28
Leon Guerrero, Rosa B -pg. D-6-7
Leon Guerrero, Rosa C -pg. D-4-74
Leon Guerrero, Rosa C -pg. D-5-18

Leon Guerrero, Rosa C -pg. D-5-46
Leon Guerrero, Rosa D -pg. D-8-13
Leon Guerrero, Rosa P -pg. D-4-43
Leon Guerrero, Rosa R -pg. D-3-6
Leon Guerrero, Rosa S -pg. D-4-41
Leon Guerrero, Rosa U -pg. D-4-123
Leon Guerrero, Rosalia S -pg. D-1-2
Leon Guerrero, Rosario -pg. D-3-56
Leon Guerrero, Rosario A -pg. D-8-27
Leon Guerrero, Rosario B -pg. D-2-56
Leon Guerrero, Rosario C -pg. D-2-49
Leon Guerrero, Rosario C -pg. D-4-37
Leon Guerrero, Rosario C -pg. D-4-76
Leon Guerrero, Rosario D -pg. D-8-13
Leon Guerrero, Rosario LG -pg. D-4-62
Leon Guerrero, Rosario S -pg. D-1-12
Leon Guerrero, Segundo P -pg. D-4-121
Leon Guerrero, Sibastian LG -pg. D-4-82
Leon Guerrero, Silvestre C -pg. D-1-56
Leon Guerrero, Soledad LG -pg. D-4-82
Leon Guerrero, Suzana I -pg. D-4-112
Leon Guerrero, Tomas B -pg. D-1-39
Leon Guerrero, Tomas LG -pg. D-4-75
Leon Guerrero, Tomas R -pg. D-4-82
Leon Guerrero, Tomasa P -pg. D-4-108
Leon Guerrero, Trinidad C -pg. D-2-49
Leon Guerrero, Vicenta C -pg. D-2-48
Leon Guerrero, Vicenta de LG -pg. D-1-14
Leon Guerrero, Vicenta N -pg. D-8-32
Leon Guerrero, Vicenta S -pg. D-1-15
Leon Guerrero, Vicenta SA -pg. D-3-23
Leon Guerrero, Vicenta T -pg. D-2-10
Leon Guerrero, Vicente -pg. D-3-56
Leon Guerrero, Vicente A -pg. D-4-76
Leon Guerrero, Vicente B -pg. D-2-31
Leon Guerrero, Vicente B -pg. D-5-46
Leon Guerrero, Vicente C -pg. D-1-56
Leon Guerrero, Vicente C -pg. D-2-31
Leon Guerrero, Vicente C -pg. D-2-47
Leon Guerrero, Vicente C -pg. D-2-49
Leon Guerrero, Vicente C -pg. D-4-20
Leon Guerrero, Vicente C -pg. D-4-46
Leon Guerrero, Vicente C -pg. D-5-60
Leon Guerrero, Vicente D -pg. D-4-126
Leon Guerrero, Vicente G -pg. D-9-15
Leon Guerrero, Vicente LG -pg. D-1-51
Leon Guerrero, Vicente LG -pg. D-5-56
Leon Guerrero, Vicente M -pg. D-4-76
Leon Guerrero, Vicente M -pg. D-8-5
Leon Guerrero, Vicente P -pg. D-2-49
Leon Guerrero, Vicente P -pg. D-3-44
Leon Guerrero, Vicente P -pg. D-5-60
Leon Guerrero, Vicente S -pg. D-1-15
Leon Guerrero, Vicente S -pg. D-4-64
Leon Guerrero, Vicente S -pg. D-8-32
Leon Guerrero, Victoria C -pg. D-2-47
Leon Guerrero, Virginia -pg. D-3-22
Leonard, Charles H -pg. D-13-12
Letechiers, Herbert G -pg. D-13-37

Levi, Robert D -pg. D-13-12
Lewi, Daniel P -pg. D-13-12
Lifon, Titiana L -pg. D-4-79
Limtiaco, Adela A -pg. D-7-7
Limtiaco, Ana A -pg. D-7-7
Limtiaco, Ana C -pg. D-7-16
Limtiaco, Ana SN -pg. D-7-2
Limtiaco, Ana T -pg. D-7-16
Limtiaco, Angela C -pg. D-7-16
Limtiaco, Antonia A -pg. D-7-7
Limtiaco, Antonia C -pg. D-7-16
Limtiaco, Antonio A -pg. D-7-16
Limtiaco, Antonio T -pg. D-7-7
Limtiaco, Aurora C -pg. D-11-36
Limtiaco, Catlina A -pg. D-7-16
Limtiaco, Cecilia C -pg. D-4-85
Limtiaco, Concepcion C -pg. D-4-85
Limtiaco, Delfina I -pg. D-4-34
Limtiaco, Dolores C -pg. D-7-16
Limtiaco, Dolores M -pg. D-11-36
Limtiaco, Dolores T -pg. D-7-2
Limtiaco, Francisco A -pg. D-4-34
Limtiaco, Francisco C -pg. D-7-16
Limtiaco, Gregorio I -pg. D-4-34
Limtiaco, Guillermo C -pg. D-7-16
Limtiaco, Ignacio M -pg. D-11-36
Limtiaco, Ignacio Q -pg. D-11-36
Limtiaco, Joaquin A -pg. D-4-85
Limtiaco, Joaquina A -pg. D-7-16
Limtiaco, Jose A -pg. D-7-16
Limtiaco, Jose L -pg. D-7-16
Limtiaco, Josefina SN -pg. D-7-2
Limtiaco, Juan A -pg. D-7-2
Limtiaco, Juan C -pg. D-7-16
Limtiaco, Juan I -pg. D-4-34
Limtiaco, Justina C -pg. D-11-36
Limtiaco, Magdalena T -pg. D-7-2
Limtiaco, Manuel C -pg. D-7-16
Limtiaco, Manuela C -pg. D-11-36
Limtiaco, Maria A -pg. D-7-7
Limtiaco, Maria A -pg. D-7-16
Limtiaco, Maria C -pg. D-3-50
Limtiaco, Maria T -pg. D-7-2
Limtiaco, Matilde SN -pg. D-7-2
Limtiaco, Pedro -pg. D-3-50
Limtiaco, Remedio T -pg. D-7-2
Limtiaco, Rosa A -pg. D-7-7
Limtiaco, Rosalinda -pg. D-3-50
Limtiaco, Santiago A -pg. D-7-2
Limtiaco, Stanley C -pg. D-11-36
Limtiaco, Ursula I -pg. D-4-34
Limtiaco, Vicente A -pg. D-7-7
Lindermare, Florence A -pg. D-13-19
Lindsey, Arthur W -pg. D-13-23
Linnelle, Bert S -pg. D-13-16
Lippold, John A -pg. D-13-12
Lizama, Agueda S -pg. D-11-27
Lizama, Agustin A -pg. D-11-47
Lizama, Ana -pg. D-5-70

Lizama, Ana Q -pg. D-7-17
Lizama, Ana Q -pg. D-10-33
Lizama, Ana S -pg. D-4-83
Lizama, Beatris Q -pg. D-7-17
Lizama, Benedicto F -pg. D-11-23
Lizama, Benita P -pg. D-5-14
Lizama, Bernadita C -pg. D-4-118
Lizama, Bernado P -pg. D-5-14
Lizama, Candelaria U -pg. D-11-13
Lizama, Caridad L -pg. D-4-13
Lizama, Caridad T -pg. D-6-19
Lizama, Carmelo L -pg. D-6-17
Lizama, Carmen A -pg. D-4-27
Lizama, Carmen S -pg. D-4-83
Lizama, Catalina P -pg. D-5-14
Lizama, Catalina S -pg. D-4-57
Lizama, Cecilia Q -pg. D-11-37
Lizama, Concepcion B -pg. D-4-98
Lizama, Concepcion C -pg. D-4-118
Lizama, Concepcion D -pg. D-1-46
Lizama, Concepcion S -pg. D-4-83
Lizama, Concepcion S -pg. D-6-18
Lizama, Constancio Q -pg. D-7-17
Lizama, Cristina C -pg. D-11-47
Lizama, Cristobal A -pg. D-4-27
Lizama, Daniel Q -pg. D-11-37
Lizama, Dolores C -pg. D-11-37
Lizama, Dolores C -pg. D-11-47
Lizama, Dolores P -pg. D-4-126
Lizama, Dolores P -pg. D-5-14
Lizama, Dolores S -pg. D-4-57
Lizama, Elloy LG -pg. D-11-8
Lizama, Emilia L -pg. D-4-13
Lizama, Felicita C -pg. D-11-7
Lizama, Felipe C -pg. D-4-27
Lizama, Felisa M -pg. D-2-46
Lizama, Felix F -pg. D-1-46
Lizama, Felix F -pg. D-11-27
Lizama, Felix L -pg. D-4-13
Lizama, Florencia C -pg. D-4-118
Lizama, Francisca P -pg. D-4-27
Lizama, Francisco -pg. D-5-70
Lizama, Francisco A -pg. D-4-14
Lizama, Francisco L -pg. D-2-46
Lizama, Francisco T -pg. D-12-19
Lizama, Gregorio P -pg. D-4-27
Lizama, Gregorio T -pg. D-6-19
Lizama, Gregorio T -pg. D-12-19
Lizama, Guadalupe C -pg. D-11-41
Lizama, Hipolito P -pg. D-5-14
Lizama, Ignacia -pg. D-5-70
Lizama, Ignacio C -pg. D-12-19
Lizama, Ignacio T -pg. D-4-98
Lizama, Jesus B -pg. D-4-98
Lizama, Jesus C -pg. D-11-41
Lizama, Jesus N -pg. D-7-21
Lizama, Jesus Q -pg. D-10-33
Lizama, Jesus S -pg. D-4-83
Lizama, Jesus T -pg. D-12-19

Lizama, Joaquin A -pg. D-6-18
Lizama, Joaquin Q -pg. D-10-33
Lizama, Joaquina C -pg. D-4-118
Lizama, Joaquina Q -pg. D-10-33
Lizama, Jose -pg. D-5-70
Lizama, Jose A -pg. D-4-14
Lizama, Jose B -pg. D-4-39
Lizama, Jose B -pg. D-4-98
Lizama, Jose C -pg. D-4-118
Lizama, Jose D -pg. D-11-37
Lizama, Jose F -pg. D-4-126
Lizama, Jose L -pg. D-7-24
Lizama, Jose P -pg. D-4-27
Lizama, Jose P -pg. D-4-57
Lizama, Jose Q -pg. D-1-54
Lizama, Jose Q -pg. D-7-17
Lizama, Jose S -pg. D-4-83
Lizama, Jose T -pg. D-6-19
Lizama, Jose T -pg. D-12-19
Lizama, Juan A -pg. D-4-14
Lizama, Juan C -pg. D-4-35
Lizama, Juan C -pg. D-4-118
Lizama, Juan C -pg. D-11-7
Lizama, Juan D -pg. D-11-27
Lizama, Juan L -pg. D-7-21
Lizama, Juan N -pg. D-4-103
Lizama, Juan P -pg. D-4-83
Lizama, Juan P -pg. D-4-126
Lizama, Juan Q -pg. D-11-37
Lizama, Juan S -pg. D-4-83
Lizama, Juan SN -pg. D-5-10
Lizama, Juliana P -pg. D-5-14
Lizama, Justo P -pg. D-5-14
Lizama, Lorenzo C -pg. D-4-27
Lizama, Lucia B -pg. D-4-98
Lizama, Luis A -pg. D-4-14
Lizama, Luisa G -pg. D-4-35
Lizama, Magdalena C -pg. D-3-6
Lizama, Manuel D -pg. D-11-27
Lizama, Manuel Q -pg. D-10-33
Lizama, Marcelina P -pg. D-5-14
Lizama, Marcelino B -pg. D-4-27
Lizama, Maria -pg. D-5-70
Lizama, Maria A -pg. D-4-14
Lizama, Maria B -pg. D-4-98
Lizama, Maria C -pg. D-11-41
Lizama, Maria LG -pg. D-11-7
Lizama, Maria M -pg. D-4-13
Lizama, Maria N -pg. D-4-103
Lizama, Maria P -pg. D-4-27
Lizama, Maria Q -pg. D-7-17
Lizama, Maria S -pg. D-4-57
Lizama, Maria S -pg. D-4-83
Lizama, Maria T -pg. D-6-19
Lizama, Maria T -pg. D-12-19
Lizama, Marta P -pg. D-4-126
Lizama, Milgaros Q -pg. D-7-17
Lizama, Pedro C -pg. D-13-27
Lizama, Pedro De Leon -pg. D-5-46

Lizama, Pedro L -pg. D-6-18
Lizama, Pedro T -pg. D-12-19
Lizama, Petronila P -pg. D-4-126
Lizama, Raymundo L -pg. D-4-41
Lizama, Regina T -pg. D-12-19
Lizama, Remedios C -pg. D-4-118
Lizama, Rita N -pg. D-4-8
Lizama, Rita P -pg. D-4-83
Lizama, Rita S -pg. D-4-57
Lizama, Roberto LG -pg. D-11-8
Lizama, Roduvico C -pg. D-7-17
Lizama, Rosa -pg. D-5-70
Lizama, Rosa A -pg. D-2-46
Lizama, Rosa D -pg. D-11-27
Lizama, Rosa Q -pg. D-10-33
Lizama, Rosa S -pg. D-4-83
Lizama, Rosalia D -pg. D-11-17
Lizama, Saturnina A -pg. D-4-27
Lizama, Simeon Q -pg. D-11-37
Lizama, Simon N -pg. D-4-103
Lizama, Soledad C -pg. D-11-13
Lizama, Soledad LG -pg. D-4-39
Lizama, Soledad Q -pg. D-10-33
Lizama, Teafela C -pg. D-6-17
Lizama, Thomas C -pg. D-11-8
Lizama, Tomas A -pg. D-4-14
Lizama, Trinidad DR -pg. D-5-70
Lizama, Urfia N -pg. D-7-21
Lizama, Vicenta A -pg. D-5-11
Lizama, Vicente -pg. D-10-33
Lizama, Vicente A -pg. D-3-6
Lizama, Vicente D -pg. D-11-41
Lizama, Vicente L -pg. D-4-8
Lizama, Vicente L -pg. D-4-13
Lizama, Vicente Q -pg. D-7-17
Lizama, Vicente Q -pg. D-10-33
Lizama, Vicente T -pg. D-6-19
Lizama, Victoria L -pg. D-2-46
Loftuard, Stepen A -pg. D-13-21
Long, Betty F -pg. D-4-82
Long, Emilia P -pg. D-4-82
Lorenzo, Fernando A -pg. D-7-3
Lorenzo, Matilde A -pg. D-7-3
Lorenzo, Rosa A -pg. D-7-3
Loresg, William H -pg. D-13-7
Lorighbaugh, Harry I -pg. D-13-7
Lucero, Maria M -pg. D-4-37
Lucero, Vicente M -pg. D-4-37
Ludweck, Joseph B -pg. D-13-7
Luedess, Fred -pg. D-13-39
Lujan, Ana C -pg. D-2-10
Lujan, Ana C -pg. D-4-17
Lujan, Ana F -pg. D-4-6
Lujan, Ana L -pg. D-4-118
Lujan, Andres C -pg. D-8-7
Lujan, Antonia C -pg. D-2-62
Lujan, Antonia C -pg. D-9-18
Lujan, Antonia C -pg. D-9-19
Lujan, Antonia LG -pg. D-5-27

Lujan, Antonio -pg. D-3-53
Lujan, Atanasio L -pg. D-4-76
Lujan, Brigida C -pg. D-2-10
Lujan, Carmen G -pg. D-5-11
Lujan, Carmen U -pg. D-3-53
Lujan, Catalina C -pg. D-1-15
Lujan, Concepcion C -pg. D-2-61
Lujan, Concepcion C -pg. D-2-61
Lujan, David LG -pg. D-5-27
Lujan, Dolores C -pg. D-1-70
Lujan, Dolores C -pg. D-4-17
Lujan, Dolores C -pg. D-9-18
Lujan, Dolores L -pg. D-5-35
Lujan, Dometrio E -pg. D-9-13
Lujan, Engracia G -pg. D-13-43
Lujan, Enrique -pg. D-3-53
Lujan, Enrique M -pg. D-5-28
Lujan, Florencia D -pg. D-2-61
Lujan, Francisco -pg. D-3-53
Lujan, Francisco C -pg. D-9-19
Lujan, Francisco G -pg. D-8-3
Lujan, Frankie F -pg. D-4-6
Lujan, Gloria T -pg. D-8-3
Lujan, Gregorio C -pg. D-4-17
Lujan, Ignacio C -pg. D-8-32
Lujan, Ignacio LG -pg. D-5-27
Lujan, Isabel C -pg. D-2-62
Lujan, Isabel L -pg. D-5-11
Lujan, Jesus A -pg. D-8-7
Lujan, Jesus C -pg. D-2-10
Lujan, Jesus G -pg. D-5-11
Lujan, Jesus S -pg. D-5-35
Lujan, Joaquin D -pg. D-3-36
Lujan, Joaquin E -pg. D-9-18
Lujan, Joaquin F -pg. D-4-6
Lujan, Joaquin M -pg. D-5-28
Lujan, Joaquin S -pg. D-5-35
Lujan, Joaquin SN -pg. D-2-61
Lujan, Jose A -pg. D-8-7
Lujan, Jose B -pg. D-8-7
Lujan, Jose C -pg. D-4-17
Lujan, Jose C -pg. D-9-13
Lujan, Jose C -pg. D-9-18
Lujan, Jose G -pg. D-2-61
Lujan, Jose G -pg. D-13-29
Lujan, Jose LG -pg. D-5-27
Lujan, Jose P -pg. D-4-17
Lujan, Jose S -pg. D-5-45
Lujan, Josefina LG -pg. D-5-27
Lujan, Juan C -pg. D-9-13
Lujan, Juan E -pg. D-9-12
Lujan, Juan M -pg. D-5-28
Lujan, Juan S -pg. D-5-35
Lujan, Laura C -pg. D-9-18
Lujan, Luis G -pg. D-4-91
Lujan, Luisa C -pg. D-4-17
Lujan, Luisa P -pg. D-3-66
Lujan, Magdalena -pg. D-3-36
Lujan, Manuel -pg. D-3-53

Lujan, Manuel M -pg. D-5-27
Lujan, Manuel N -pg. D-1-70
Lujan, Manuel O -pg. D-3-53
Lujan, Manuela E -pg. D-9-13
Lujan, Marcela C -pg. D-5-87
Lujan, Margarita -pg. D-3-36
Lujan, Maria -pg. D-3-36
Lujan, Maria -pg. D-3-53
Lujan, Maria A -pg. D-8-7
Lujan, Maria C -pg. D-2-61
Lujan, Maria C -pg. D-8-7
Lujan, Maria C -pg. D-8-7
Lujan, Maria C -pg. D-9-13
Lujan, Maria F -pg. D-4-6
Lujan, Maria F -pg. D-8-7
Lujan, Maria G -pg. D-5-38
Lujan, Maria M -pg. D-2-61
Lujan, Maria S -pg. D-5-28
Lujan, Maria T -pg. D-4-91
Lujan, Mariano LG -pg. D-4-6
Lujan, Nicolasa -pg. D-3-36
Lujan, Oliva M -pg. D-2-61
Lujan, Paz M -pg. D-5-28
Lujan, Paz S -pg. D-5-33
Lujan, Pedro C -pg. D-3-36
Lujan, Perpetuo -pg. D-3-36
Lujan, Ramona C -pg. D-3-36
Lujan, Rita C -pg. D-9-13
Lujan, Roman F -pg. D-4-6
Lujan, Rosa C -pg. D-1-68
Lujan, Rosa F -pg. D-4-7
Lujan, Rosa S -pg. D-5-35
Lujan, Rosa T -pg. D-9-12
Lujan, Rosario C -pg. D-2-62
Lujan, Rosario C -pg. D-4-17
Lujan, Rufina -pg. D-3-36
Lujan, Rufina C -pg. D-2-62
Lujan, Salvador C -pg. D-4-17
Lujan, Trinidad -pg. D-3-36
Lujan, Vicente C -pg. D-2-62
Lujan, Vicente C -pg. D-4-17
Lujan, Vicente N -pg. D-1-68
Lujan, Vicente R -pg. D-1-68
Lujan, Victor G -pg. D-5-38
Lujan, William -pg. D-3-53
Luna, Juan -pg. D-13-23
Lupa, Jose -pg. D-13-23
Lurhinas, Charles D -pg. D-13-12
Lurney, Merle F -pg. D-13-37
Lusk, Marjorie D -pg. D-4-39
Lusk, Truett C -pg. D-4-39
Lusk, Truett C -pg. D-13-33
Lusk, Virginia W -pg. D-4-40
Lusongco, Ana -pg. D-5-98
Lusongco, Antonio D -pg. D-5-98
Lusongco, Antonio M -pg. D-5-98
Lusongco, Dolores -pg. D-5-98
Lusongco, Joaquin -pg. D-5-98
Lusongco, Luis -pg. D-5-98

Lusongco, Maria T -pg. D-5-98
Lusongco, Rosa D -pg. D-5-98
Lyorght, John -pg. D-13-35
M[illegible], Victor H -pg. D-13-17
Maanao, Ana M -pg. D-4-104
Maanao, Antonia R -pg. D-4-28
Maanao, Dolores I -pg. D-4-104
Maanao, Dolores R -pg. D-4-28
Maanao, Francisca T -pg. D-7-21
Maanao, Gregorio I -pg. D-4-104
Maanao, Guadalupe R -pg. D-4-28
Maanao, Jose A -pg. D-6-34
Maanao, Jose I -pg. D-4-28
Maanao, Jose T -pg. D-7-21
Maanao, Manuel -pg. D-6-34
Maanao, Maria I -pg. D-4-104
Maanao, Ramona M -pg. D-7-19
Maanao, Rita T -pg. D-7-21
Maanao, Ruth T -pg. D-7-21
Maanao, Vicente A -pg. D-7-21
Mable, Sidney C -pg. D-13-42
Mace, John W -pg. D-13-12
Macias, Adela C -pg. D-4-107
Macias, Carmen C -pg. D-4-107
Macias, Enrique H -pg. D-4-107
Macias, Jose C -pg. D-4-107
Macias, Magdalena C -pg. D-4-107
Macos, Hernogenes -pg. D-13-35
Madrid, Jose M -pg. D-1-56
Maekawa, Aurelia D -pg. D-11-42
Mafnas, Agueda LG -pg. D-4-51
Mafnas, Ana A -pg. D-5-13
Mafnas, Ana B -pg. D-4-59
Mafnas, Ana C -pg. D-4-50
Mafnas, Ana F -pg. D-2-41
Mafnas, Ana L -pg. D-4-25
Mafnas, Ana Q -pg. D-10-18
Mafnas, Ana R -pg. D-4-53
Mafnas, Andres F -pg. D-2-41
Mafnas, Antonia A -pg. D-5-13
Mafnas, Antonia C -pg. D-4-50
Mafnas, Antonia LG -pg. D-4-51
Mafnas, Antonio A -pg. D-5-13
Mafnas, Antonio B -pg. D-4-59
Mafnas, Antonio C -pg. D-4-47
Mafnas, Antonio C -pg. D-4-54
Mafnas, Antonio L -pg. D-4-25
Mafnas, Antonio T -pg. D-11-42
Mafnas, Asuncion B -pg. D-4-59
Mafnas, Carmen C -pg. D-3-16
Mafnas, Carmen LG -pg. D-4-51
Mafnas, Concepcion A -pg. D-5-13
Mafnas, Consolacion T -pg. D-11-42
Mafnas, Dolores L -pg. D-4-25
Mafnas, Dominga C -pg. D-4-50
Mafnas, Elena A -pg. D-5-91
Mafnas, Elisa C -pg. D-12-8
Mafnas, Felecita M -pg. D-4-54
Mafnas, Filomenia R -pg. D-4-53

Mafnas, Francisco C -pg. D-4-48
Mafnas, Francisco C -pg. D-12-8
Mafnas, Francisco L -pg. D-4-25
Mafnas, Francisco LG -pg. D-4-51
Mafnas, Francisco R -pg. D-4-53
Mafnas, Geronimo C -pg. D-12-8
Mafnas, Ignacia LG -pg. D-4-51
Mafnas, Ignacia R -pg. D-4-53
Mafnas, Ignacio M -pg. D-1-54
Mafnas, Ignacio R -pg. D-4-53
Mafnas, Jesus -pg. D-3-16
Mafnas, Jesus F -pg. D-2-41
Mafnas, Joaquin C -pg. D-11-42
Mafnas, Joaquin C -pg. D-12-8
Mafnas, Joaquin R -pg. D-4-47
Mafnas, Joaquin R -pg. D-4-53
Mafnas, Joaqun F -pg. D-5-91
Mafnas, Jose -pg. D-3-16
Mafnas, Jose A -pg. D-5-13
Mafnas, Jose B -pg. D-4-59
Mafnas, Jose C -pg. D-4-25
Mafnas, Jose C -pg. D-4-48
Mafnas, Jose C -pg. D-4-53
Mafnas, Jose F -pg. D-5-58
Mafnas, Jose M -pg. D-4-51
Mafnas, Jose M -pg. D-4-54
Mafnas, Jose P -pg. D-3-16
Mafnas, Jose R -pg. D-4-51
Mafnas, Jose R -pg. D-4-53
Mafnas, Jose T -pg. D-11-42
Mafnas, Josefa A -pg. D-5-13
Mafnas, Juan C -pg. D-4-48
Mafnas, Juan C -pg. D-4-50
Mafnas, Juan C -pg. D-12-8
Mafnas, Juan T -pg. D-11-42
Mafnas, Juana T -pg. D-3-20
Mafnas, Lucia R -pg. D-4-54
Mafnas, Luis C -pg. D-5-58
Mafnas, Magdalena M -pg. D-4-54
Mafnas, Manuel P -pg. D-4-24
Mafnas, Manuel P -pg. D-5-85
Mafnas, Maria B -pg. D-4-59
Mafnas, Maria B -pg. D-4-59
Mafnas, Maria C -pg. D-4-47
Mafnas, Maria C -pg. D-4-50
Mafnas, Maria C -pg. D-12-8
Mafnas, Maria C -pg. D-12-8
Mafnas, Maria P -pg. D-3-25
Mafnas, Maria R -pg. D-4-53
Mafnas, Pricila -pg. D-3-17
Mafnas, Regina L -pg. D-4-25
Mafnas, Remedios M -pg. D-4-54
Mafnas, Rita LG -pg. D-4-51
Mafnas, Rosa A -pg. D-5-13
Mafnas, Rosa L -pg. D-4-25
Mafnas, Rosa R -pg. D-4-51
Mafnas, Rosa R -pg. D-4-54
Mafnas, Rosalia T -pg. D-11-42
Mafnas, Rosario C -pg. D-4-48

Mafnas, Rosario M -pg. D-5-76
Mafnas, Santiago C -pg. D-4-54
Mafnas, Serafin B -pg. D-12-7
Mafnas, Serafin C -pg. D-12-8
Mafnas, Silvestre C -pg. D-4-48
Mafnas, Tomasa L -pg. D-4-25
Mafnas, Trinidad C -pg. D-4-48
Mafnas, Venancio C -pg. D-3-20
Mafnas, Vicenta A -pg. D-5-13
Mafnas, Vicenta C -pg. D-4-25
Mafnas, Vicenta C -pg. D-12-8
Mafnas, Vicente -pg. D-3-16
Mafnas, Vicente B -pg. D-4-59
Mafnas, Vicente M -pg. D-5-13
Mafnas, Vicente M -pg. D-5-76
Mafnas, Vicente P -pg. D-4-59
Mafnas, Vicente R -pg. D-4-54
Mafnas, Ynes S -pg. D-10-18
Maguadog, Antonia C -pg. D-9-14
Maguadog, Jesus C -pg. D-9-23
Maguadog, Luis N -pg. D-9-23
Maguadog, Maria C -pg. D-9-23
Maguadog, Maria C -pg. D-9-23
Maguadog, Moises N -pg. D-9-14
Malcom, Walter L -pg. D-13-12
Malijan, Eliza M -pg. D-9-46
Malijan, Jose M -pg. D-9-46
Malijan, Luisa A -pg. D-9-42
Malijan, Rita A -pg. D-9-42
Malingle, Hershel L -pg. D-13-16
Manalisay, Alejandra B -pg. D-9-9
Manalisay, Ana C -pg. D-9-12
Manalisay, Asuncion C -pg. D-9-5
Manalisay, Beatriz T -pg. D-9-14
Manalisay, Carmen C -pg. D-9-12
Manalisay, Carmen C -pg. D-9-14
Manalisay, Felix C -pg. D-9-9
Manalisay, Francisco T -pg. D-9-38
Manalisay, Gregorio C -pg. D-9-2
Manalisay, Guardalupe C -pg. D-9-38
Manalisay, Isidro C -pg. D-9-14
Manalisay, Jesus C -pg. D-9-12
Manalisay, Joaquin C -pg. D-9-12
Manalisay, Jose C -pg. D-9-12
Manalisay, Jose C -pg. D-9-33
Manalisay, Juan C -pg. D-9-12
Manalisay, Juana A -pg. D-5-91
Manalisay, Julian C -pg. D-9-16
Manalisay, Manuel C -pg. D-9-12
Manalisay, Maria A -pg. D-9-2
Manalisay, Maria B -pg. D-9-14
Manalisay, Maria C -pg. D-9-12
Manalisay, Maria SN -pg. D-9-16
Manalisay, Nieves C -pg. D-9-14
Manalisay, Rita C -pg. D-9-5
Manalisay, Socorro C -pg. D-9-14
Manalisay, Soledad T -pg. D-9-33
Manalisay, Venancio C -pg. D-9-5
Manauhern, Florence A -pg. D-13-19

Manglona, Adela F -pg. D-2-53
Manglona, Adriano C -pg. D-4-28
Manglona, Ana F -pg. D-2-53
Manglona, Ana L -pg. D-4-29
Manglona, Antonio C -pg. D-4-28
Manglona, Bernadita C -pg. D-4-28
Manglona, Carmen L -pg. D-4-29
Manglona, Dolores C -pg. D-4-28
Manglona, Espreciosa M -pg. D-6-32
Manglona, Felix C -pg. D-4-29
Manglona, Francisco C -pg. D-4-28
Manglona, Gregorio L -pg. D-4-29
Manglona, Ignacio F -pg. D-2-53
Manglona, Inocencio C -pg. D-4-28
Manglona, Jesus M -pg. D-6-32
Manglona, Jose L -pg. D-4-30
Manglona, Juan M -pg. D-4-30
Manglona, Juan M -pg. D-6-32
Manglona, Juan S -pg. D-4-28
Manglona, Julia F -pg. D-2-53
Manglona, Leoncia M -pg. D-6-32
Manglona, Luisa L -pg. D-4-30
Manglona, Manuel M -pg. D-6-32
Manglona, Maria L -pg. D-4-29
Manglona, Maria S -pg. D-4-29
Manglona, Paulino S -pg. D-6-32
Manglona, Pedro M -pg. D-6-32
Manglona, Reymundo L -pg. D-4-29
Manglona, Rosario M -pg. D-4-30
Manglona, Rosita C -pg. D-4-28
Manglona, Susana S -pg. D-4-29
Manglona, Tomas M -pg. D-4-29
Manglona, Vicente F -pg. D-2-53
Manglona, Vicente S -pg. D-4-29
Manglona, Vicente S -pg. D-6-39
Manglona, Vincente -pg. D-13-35
Manglona, Virginia L -pg. D-4-30
Manibusan, Agueda C -pg. D-4-21
Manibusan, Agustin M -pg. D-5-10
Manibusan, Albert D -pg. D-2-39
Manibusan, Alice D -pg. D-2-39
Manibusan, Ana -pg. D-5-77
Manibusan, Ana A -pg. D-1-25
Manibusan, Ana A -pg. D-1-25
Manibusan, Ana A -pg. D-5-4
Manibusan, Ana C -pg. D-1-19
Manibusan, Ana C -pg. D-1-19
Manibusan, Ana C -pg. D-4-56
Manibusan, Ana C -pg. D-10-4
Manibusan, Ana F -pg. D-10-4
Manibusan, Ana L -pg. D-4-116
Manibusan, Ana M -pg. D-1-17
Manibusan, Ana M -pg. D-5-10
Manibusan, Aniceto Q -pg. D-5-77
Manibusan, Antonia C -pg. D-2-3
Manibusan, Antonia M -pg. D-4-96
Manibusan, Antonio B -pg. D-2-11
Manibusan, Antonio L -pg. D-5-59
Manibusan, Antonio M -pg. D-2-24

Manibusan, Antonio M -pg. D-13-28
Manibusan, Antonio P -pg. D-5-10
Manibusan, Antonio S -pg. D-5-4
Manibusan, Asuncion C -pg. D-4-57
Manibusan, Benigno C -pg. D-2-11
Manibusan, Carmen -pg. D-5-75
Manibusan, Carmen C -pg. D-1-29
Manibusan, Consalasion D -pg. D-2-39
Manibusan, Dolores B -pg. D-5-3
Manibusan, Dolores E -pg. D-2-67
Manibusan, Dolores M -pg. D-1-17
Manibusan, Dolores S -pg. D-5-88
Manibusan, Doroteo P -pg. D-5-3
Manibusan, Eduardo B -pg. D-2-11
Manibusan, Engracia C -pg. D-4-56
Manibusan, Felisa LG -pg. D-2-24
Manibusan, Felix -pg. D-5-77
Manibusan, Felix M -pg. D-4-116
Manibusan, Fidela C -pg. D-10-24
Manibusan, Filomena A -pg. D-5-4
Manibusan, Filomena T -pg. D-1-9
Manibusan, Francisca B -pg. D-4-117
Manibusan, Francisco B -pg. D-4-99
Manibusan, Francisco C -pg. D-10-24
Manibusan, Francisco M -pg. D-5-10
Manibusan, Francisco P -pg. D-5-3
Manibusan, Francisco Q -pg. D-5-61
Manibusan, Geronimo T -pg. D-3-28
Manibusan, Herminia C -pg. D-10-24
Manibusan, Ignacia A -pg. D-5-4
Manibusan, Ignacia C -pg. D-10-24
Manibusan, Ignacio DLG -pg. D-13-23
Manibusan, Ignacio Q -pg. D-5-75
Manibusan, Ignaica M -pg. D-5-4
Manibusan, Isabel A -pg. D-5-4
Manibusan, Isabel B -pg. D-4-99
Manibusan, Isabel C -pg. D-1-16
Manibusan, Jesus B -pg. D-2-11
Manibusan, Jesus C -pg. D-1-29
Manibusan, Jesus E -pg. D-4-64
Manibusan, Jesus L -pg. D-5-59
Manibusan, Jesus LG -pg. D-4-56
Manibusan, Jesus M -pg. D-2-3
Manibusan, Jesus P -pg. D-3-55
Manibusan, Jesus P -pg. D-5-10
Manibusan, Joaquin E -pg. D-4-64
Manibusan, Joaquin L -pg. D-4-116
Manibusan, Joaquin P -pg. D-1-29
Manibusan, Joaquin R -pg. D-5-88
Manibusan, Joaquin T -pg. D-2-24
Manibusan, Joaquina B -pg. D-2-11
Manibusan, John T -pg. D-2-39
Manibusan, Jose -pg. D-5-75
Manibusan, Jose A -pg. D-1-45
Manibusan, Jose A -pg. D-3-60
Manibusan, Jose A -pg. D-5-4
Manibusan, Jose B -pg. D-4-99
Manibusan, Jose C -pg. D-4-57
Manibusan, Jose C -pg. D-4-64

Manibusan, Jose C -pg. D-5-10
Manibusan, Jose D -pg. D-11-5
Manibusan, Jose G -pg. D-5-59
Manibusan, Jose G -pg. D-5-70
Manibusan, Jose L -pg. D-5-59
Manibusan, Jose M -pg. D-2-24
Manibusan, Jose M -pg. D-4-101
Manibusan, Jose M -pg. D-5-10
Manibusan, Jose P -pg. D-5-4
Manibusan, Jose Q -pg. D-13-23
Manibusan, Jose R -pg. D-4-97
Manibusan, Jose T -pg. D-5-3
Manibusan, Joseph D -pg. D-2-39
Manibusan, Juan A -pg. D-1-45
Manibusan, Juan A -pg. D-5-4
Manibusan, Juan B -pg. D-2-11
Manibusan, Juan C -pg. D-1-19
Manibusan, Juan C -pg. D-10-24
Manibusan, Juan E -pg. D-4-64
Manibusan, Juan M -pg. D-1-17
Manibusan, Juan M -pg. D-2-24
Manibusan, Juan M -pg. D-4-99
Manibusan, Juan P -pg. D-5-10
Manibusan, Juan R -pg. D-1-19
Manibusan, Juan SN -pg. D-10-4
Manibusan, Juan T -pg. D-4-21
Manibusan, Juana G -pg. D-4-97
Manibusan, Juana L -pg. D-5-59
Manibusan, Juana LG -pg. D-2-24
Manibusan, Juana M -pg. D-5-10
Manibusan, Julita B -pg. D-1-16
Manibusan, Julita E -pg. D-4-64
Manibusan, Justina E -pg. D-4-64
Manibusan, Lorenzo A -pg. D-1-45
Manibusan, Lorenzo SN -pg. D-1-45
Manibusan, Lourdes B -pg. D-2-11
Manibusan, Luis P -pg. D-1-25
Manibusan, Luis P -pg. D-1-54
Manibusan, Luis P -pg. D-5-93
Manibusan, Luisa C -pg. D-4-56
Manibusan, Magdalena M -pg. D-4-101
Manibusan, Manuel G -pg. D-5-59
Manibusan, Manuel SN -pg. D-10-24
Manibusan, Maria -pg. D-5-75
Manibusan, Maria A -pg. D-1-25
Manibusan, Maria B -pg. D-2-11
Manibusan, Maria B -pg. D-4-99
Manibusan, Maria C -pg. D-1-16
Manibusan, Maria C -pg. D-4-56
Manibusan, Maria C -pg. D-10-4
Manibusan, Maria C -pg. D-10-24
Manibusan, Maria C -pg. D-11-5
Manibusan, Maria E -pg. D-2-67
Manibusan, Maria E -pg. D-4-64
Manibusan, Maria M -pg. D-1-17
Manibusan, Maria M -pg. D-2-24
Manibusan, Maria M -pg. D-4-96
Manibusan, Maria M -pg. D-4-101
Manibusan, Maria M -pg. D-5-10

Manibusan, Maria P -pg. D-2-67
Manibusan, Maria P -pg. D-5-10
Manibusan, Maria SN -pg. D-10-4
Manibusan, Martina M -pg. D-4-97
Manibusan, Mary D -pg. D-2-39
Manibusan, Matias P -pg. D-5-10
Manibusan, Matilida C -pg. D-2-3
Manibusan, Mercedes -pg. D-5-88
Manibusan, Miguel C -pg. D-10-24
Manibusan, Modesta -pg. D-5-77
Manibusan, Nicolas C -pg. D-4-101
Manibusan, Nicolas L -pg. D-5-59
Manibusan, Nicolasa P -pg. D-5-3
Manibusan, Pedro A -pg. D-1-25
Manibusan, Pedro F -pg. D-4-97
Manibusan, Ramon P -pg. D-5-10
Manibusan, Regina A -pg. D-1-45
Manibusan, Regina L -pg. D-1-31
Manibusan, Regina L -pg. D-4-116
Manibusan, Rita P -pg. D-5-77
Manibusan, Rosa A -pg. D-1-25
Manibusan, Rosa C -pg. D-4-57
Manibusan, Rosa C -pg. D-10-4
Manibusan, Rosa P -pg. D-5-3
Manibusan, Rosa T -pg. D-1-9
Manibusan, Rosario -pg. D-5-88
Manibusan, Rosario L -pg. D-4-116
Manibusan, Rosario M -pg. D-5-10
Manibusan, Rufina LG -pg. D-2-24
Manibusan, Segundo P -pg. D-5-3
Manibusan, Soledad B -pg. D-4-99
Manibusan, Tomasa P -pg. D-5-3
Manibusan, Trinidad C -pg. D-1-29
Manibusan, Trinidad C -pg. D-4-21
Manibusan, Trinidad M -pg. D-1-17
Manibusan, Vicente C -pg. D-2-3
Manibusan, Vicente C -pg. D-4-57
Manibusan, Vicente C -pg. D-10-24
Manibusan, Vicente E -pg. D-2-67
Manibusan, Vicente P -pg. D-2-67
Manibusan, Vicente P -pg. D-5-10
Manibusan, Vicente T -pg. D-1-17
Manibusan, Victoria C -pg. D-10-24
Manibusan, Vincent H -pg. D-2-39
Manilisay, Ana A -pg. D-2-59
Manilisay, Dolores A -pg. D-2-59
Manilisay, Jesus A -pg. D-2-60
Manilisay, Jesus S -pg. D-2-59
Manilisay, Manuel A -pg. D-2-59
Manilisay, Maria A -pg. D-2-60
Manley, Albert P -pg. D-5-95
Manley, Albert R -pg. D-1-71
Manley, Asuncion R -pg. D-5-95
Manley, Concepcion L -pg. D-11-2
Manley, Enrique R -pg. D-1-71
Manley, Frank R -pg. D-1-71
Manley, Jose R -pg. D-1-71
Manley, Lilian -pg. D-5-95
Manley, Manuel R -pg. D-1-71

Manley, Vicenta -pg. D-5-95
Manley, Vicente -pg. D-5-95
Manley, William R -pg. D-1-71
Mansapit, Clemente B -pg. D-9-4
Mansapit, Cristobal M -pg. D-9-3
Mansapit, Felix C -pg. D-9-3
Mansapit, Felomenia M -pg. D-9-3
Mansapit, Gabriel M -pg. D-9-3
Mansapit, Jesus M -pg. D-9-3
Mansapit, Joaquin M -pg. D-9-3
Mansapit, Jose M -pg. D-9-23
Mansapit, Manuel N -pg. D-9-4
Mansapit, Maria M -pg. D-9-3
Mansapit, Nicolasa C -pg. D-9-4
Mansapit, Pedro N -pg. D-9-4
Mansapit, Santiago N -pg. D-9-4
Mansapit, Venancio N -pg. D-9-4
Mansapit, Vicente M -pg. D-9-3
Manse, Pack M -pg. D-13-42
Mantanona, Ana M -pg. D-8-27
Mantanona, Ana N -pg. D-8-25
Mantanona, Ana T -pg. D-8-35
Mantanona, Andrea C -pg. D-11-35
Mantanona, Angelina P -pg. D-8-31
Mantanona, Antonia P -pg. D-8-41
Mantanona, Antonio M -pg. D-8-47
Mantanona, Artemio T -pg. D-8-12
Mantanona, Ascension M -pg. D-8-48
Mantanona, Atanacio I -pg. D-12-9
Mantanona, Atanasio I -pg. D-1-41
Mantanona, Baldomero C -pg. D-8-8
Mantanona, Benito M -pg. D-12-19
Mantanona, Carmen I -pg. D-12-9
Mantanona, Carmen L -pg. D-8-9
Mantanona, Carmen P -pg. D-8-31
Mantanona, Carmen T -pg. D-1-41
Mantanona, Casiano A -pg. D-8-9
Mantanona, Cecilio C -pg. D-8-35
Mantanona, Consolacion T -pg. D-8-26
Mantanona, David T -pg. D-1-69
Mantanona, Dolores L -pg. D-8-9
Mantanona, Dolores M -pg. D-8-27
Mantanona, Domitilia M -pg. D-8-27
Mantanona, Ediviges T -pg. D-8-35
Mantanona, Eliza N -pg. D-8-25
Mantanona, Enrique T -pg. D-8-12
Mantanona, Felicita P -pg. D-8-31
Mantanona, Felicita S -pg. D-8-32
Mantanona, Felix T -pg. D-1-69
Mantanona, Filomena A -pg. D-8-46
Mantanona, Francisca N -pg. D-8-25
Mantanona, Francisco M -pg. D-8-26
Mantanona, Froilan A -pg. D-8-48
Mantanona, Genoveva M -pg. D-8-27
Mantanona, Genoveva T -pg. D-8-9
Mantanona, Ignacia M -pg. D-8-27
Mantanona, Ignacio L -pg. D-8-9
Mantanona, Isabel -pg. D-8-28
Mantanona, Issac C -pg. D-8-26

INDEX
1930 Population Census of Guam: Transcribed

Mantanona, Jesus C -pg. D-8-8
Mantanona, Jesus M -pg. D-8-8
Mantanona, Jesus N -pg. D-8-27
Mantanona, Jesus T -pg. D-8-9
Mantanona, Jesus T -pg. D-8-26
Mantanona, Jesus T -pg. D-8-35
Mantanona, Joaquina M -pg. D-8-8
Mantanona, Jose C -pg. D-8-28
Mantanona, Jose L -pg. D-8-9
Mantanona, Jose M -pg. D-8-8
Mantanona, Jose M -pg. D-8-12
Mantanona, Jose M -pg. D-8-26
Mantanona, Jose M -pg. D-8-27
Mantanona, Jose N -pg. D-8-27
Mantanona, Josefa M -pg. D-8-27
Mantanona, Juan M -pg. D-8-46
Mantanona, Juan P -pg. D-1-54
Mantanona, Juan P -pg. D-8-41
Mantanona, Juan T -pg. D-8-9
Mantanona, Luis C -pg. D-8-25
Mantanona, Manuel P -pg. D-8-32
Mantanona, Manuel P -pg. D-8-41
Mantanona, Manuela M -pg. D-8-26
Mantanona, Margarita L -pg. D-8-9
Mantanona, Margarita M -pg. D-8-8
Mantanona, Maria M -pg. D-8-8
Mantanona, Maria N -pg. D-8-25
Mantanona, Maria N -pg. D-8-27
Mantanona, Maria T -pg. D-8-12
Mantanona, Maria T -pg. D-8-26
Mantanona, Mariana C -pg. D-11-35
Mantanona, Martina M -pg. D-8-26
Mantanona, Milagro P -pg. D-8-41
Mantanona, Pedro M -pg. D-8-27
Mantanona, Petronila A -pg. D-8-46
Mantanona, Potenciana T -pg. D-8-33
Mantanona, Ramon M -pg. D-8-27
Mantanona, Remedios S -pg. D-8-32
Mantanona, Ricardo T -pg. D-8-12
Mantanona, Rita L -pg. D-8-9
Mantanona, Rita T -pg. D-1-69
Mantanona, Robert T -pg. D-8-33
Mantanona, Roman T -pg. D-8-12
Mantanona, Romen P -pg. D-8-31
Mantanona, Rosa M -pg. D-8-28
Mantanona, Sabina P -pg. D-8-31
Mantanona, Silvestre M -pg. D-8-33
Mantanona, Silvestre N -pg. D-8-26
Mantanona, Vicenta L -pg. D-1-13
Mantel, Edward T -pg. D-13-16
Mapleson, Joseph -pg. D-13-7
Marak, Joseph -pg. D-13-24
Marcelo, Julian C -pg. D-4-8
Mare, William H -pg. D-13-12
Marford, Jessie K -pg. D-13-35
Marguss, Feliz A -pg. D-13-12
Mariano, Amalia -pg. D-3-71
Mariano, Ana -pg. D-3-71
Mariano, Ana Q -pg. D-3-70

Mariano, Antonio -pg. D-3-71
Mariano, Candelaria F -pg. D-3-71
Mariano, Jesus -pg. D-3-71
Mariano, Jose -pg. D-3-71
Mariano, Juan -pg. D-3-71
Mariano, Juan Q -pg. D-3-71
Mariano, Maria -pg. D-3-71
Mariano, Nicolas -pg. D-3-71
Mariano, Vicente -pg. D-3-71
Marion, Eduardo B -pg. D-2-13
Marion, Henry L -pg. D-2-13
Marion, Jesus L -pg. D-2-13
Marion, Maria L -pg. D-2-13
Marion, Silvia L -pg. D-2-13
Marrion, Geronimo B -pg. D-2-39
Marrion, Lorenzo B -pg. D-2-79
Marrion, Maria M -pg. D-2-39
Marrion, Rita M -pg. D-2-39
Marsh, John A -pg. D-13-26
Marst, Dorothy B -pg. D-3-58
Marst, John Calvin -pg. D-3-58
Martin, Alexander Jr. -pg. D-13-31
Martin, Bird M -pg. D-13-16
Martin, Gilbert -pg. D-13-35
Martin, Laura B -pg. D-3-61
Martines, Carmen R -pg. D-8-45
Martines, Clemente R -pg. D-8-45
Martines, Jesus M -pg. D-8-45
Martines, Joaquin R -pg. D-8-45
Martines, Josefa R -pg. D-8-45
Martinez, Ana L -pg. D-3-27
Martinez, Ana N -pg. D-8-25
Martinez, Angel W -pg. D-8-36
Martinez, Angelina C -pg. D-4-17
Martinez, Antonia -pg. D-3-27
Martinez, Antonia C -pg. D-8-35
Martinez, Antonia F -pg. D-2-30
Martinez, Antonia I -pg. D-3-59
Martinez, Antonio K -pg. D-8-36
Martinez, Antonio P -pg. D-4-69
Martinez, Candelaria M -pg. D-8-8
Martinez, Caridad M -pg. D-4-33
Martinez, Carlina T -pg. D-8-49
Martinez, Carmen V -pg. D-2-39
Martinez, Carrie M -pg. D-4-114
Martinez, Charlie K -pg. D-8-36
Martinez, Concepcion C -pg. D-1-37
Martinez, Concepcion F -pg. D-2-64
Martinez, Concepcion P -pg. D-4-69
Martinez, Concepcion R? -pg. D-3-21
Martinez, Dolores LG -pg. D-4-96
Martinez, Dolores M -pg. D-8-8
Martinez, Eduviges P -pg. D-4-69
Martinez, Elena N -pg. D-8-25
Martinez, Emelia SA -pg. D-2-25
Martinez, Emilia K -pg. D-8-36
Martinez, Enrique M -pg. D-8-15
Martinez, Fidel C -pg. D-4-17
Martinez, Francisca M -pg. D-2-64

Martinez, Francisca P -pg. D-4-89
Martinez, Francisco M -pg. D-4-33
Martinez, Francisco SA -pg. D-2-25
Martinez, Francisco V -pg. D-2-29
Martinez, Grace J -pg. D-4-114
Martinez, Ignacio C -pg. D-2-64
Martinez, Inby K -pg. D-8-36
Martinez, Isabel SA -pg. D-2-25
Martinez, Isabel V -pg. D-2-28
Martinez, James K -pg. D-8-36
Martinez, Jesus F -pg. D-2-64
Martinez, Jesus M -pg. D-2-64
Martinez, Jesus N -pg. D-8-25
Martinez, Jesus P -pg. D-4-89
Martinez, Jesus SA -pg. D-2-25
Martinez, Jeus R -pg. D-8-25
Martinez, Joaquin P -pg. D-4-89
Martinez, Joaquin R -pg. D-8-49
Martinez, Joaquin SA -pg. D-2-25
Martinez, Joaquin T -pg. D-8-49
Martinez, Jose -pg. D-3-27
Martinez, Jose C -pg. D-4-17
Martinez, Jose F -pg. D-2-30
Martinez, Jose LG -pg. D-4-96
Martinez, Jose N -pg. D-8-25
Martinez, Jose P -pg. D-4-69
Martinez, Jose R -pg. D-8-8
Martinez, Jose T -pg. D-8-49
Martinez, Jose V -pg. D-2-28
Martinez, Josefina -pg. D-3-27
Martinez, Josefina V -pg. D-2-39
Martinez, Juan -pg. D-3-27
Martinez, Juan C -pg. D-4-69
Martinez, Juan M -pg. D-4-33
Martinez, Juan P -pg. D-4-69
Martinez, Juan P -pg. D-4-96
Martinez, Juan V -pg. D-2-39
Martinez, Juana LG -pg. D-4-96
Martinez, Juana P -pg. D-4-89
Martinez, Julia C -pg. D-4-17
Martinez, Lourdes C -pg. D-1-37
Martinez, Lucy R -pg. D-4-114
Martinez, Luis -pg. D-3-27
Martinez, Manuel C -pg. D-4-38
Martinez, Manuel P -pg. D-4-89
Martinez, Manuel R -pg. D-8-35
Martinez, Margarita M -pg. D-4-33
Martinez, Maria -pg. D-3-27
Martinez, Maria F -pg. D-2-30
Martinez, Maria F -pg. D-2-64
Martinez, Maria LG -pg. D-4-96
Martinez, Maria M -pg. D-8-8
Martinez, Maria M -pg. D-8-25
Martinez, Maria M -pg. D-10-11
Martinez, Maria N -pg. D-8-25
Martinez, Maria R -pg. D-4-33
Martinez, Maria T -pg. D-3-27
Martinez, Mariano C -pg. D-5-30
Martinez, Marino C -pg. D-5-75

Martinez, May R -pg. D-4-114
Martinez, Melchor V -pg. D-4-114
Martinez, Nieves P -pg. D-4-69
Martinez, Oliva M -pg. D-5-52
Martinez, Pedro -pg. D-3-27
Martinez, Pedro -pg. D-3-27
Martinez, Ramon C -pg. D-2-30
Martinez, Regina C -pg. D-8-35
Martinez, Remedios C -pg. D-4-17
Martinez, Rita C -pg. D-4-114
Martinez, Rita LG -pg. D-4-96
Martinez, Rita M -pg. D-8-25
Martinez, Rita P -pg. D-4-69
Martinez, Rosa -pg. D-3-27
Martinez, Rosa P -pg. D-4-89
Martinez, Rosalina C -pg. D-8-15
Martinez, Susana B -pg. D-10-12
Martinez, Teordora V -pg. D-2-28
Martinez, Trinidad SN -pg. D-4-38
Martinez, Vicente B -pg. D-4-114
Martinez, Vicente C -pg. D-2-39
Martinez, Vicente LG -pg. D-4-96
Martinez, Vicente M -pg. D-5-51
Martinez, Vicente P -pg. D-1-37
Martinez, Vicente V -pg. D-2-39
Mason, Sidney E -pg. D-13-12
Masterton, Amy C -pg. D-3-56
Masterton, George W -pg. D-13-31
Masterton, Nancy -pg. D-3-57
Masterton, William B -pg. D-3-56
Mata, Ana M -pg. D-9-9
Mata, Carmen M -pg. D-9-9
Mata, Francisco M -pg. D-9-9
Mata, Ignacio M -pg. D-9-9
Mata, Jesus M -pg. D-9-9
Mata, Joaquin M -pg. D-9-9
Mata, Jose M -pg. D-9-9
Mata, Juan M -pg. D-9-9
Mata, Martina M -pg. D-9-9
Mata, Milagro M -pg. D-9-9
Mata, Rosa M -pg. D-9-9
Mata, Vicente M -pg. D-11-10
Matagulay, Ana S -pg. D-6-14
Matagulay, Carmen S -pg. D-6-14
Matagulay, Flora S -pg. D-6-14
Matagulay, Juan C -pg. D-6-14
Matagulay, Maria S -pg. D-6-14
Matanane, Ana B -pg. D-2-60
Matanane, Ana Q -pg. D-5-49
Matanane, Benedicto -pg. D-3-16
Matanane, Carlos -pg. D-3-16
Matanane, Carlos A -pg. D-5-45
Matanane, Carmen SN -pg. D-5-42
Matanane, Catalina -pg. D-3-24
Matanane, Catalina Q -pg. D-5-50
Matanane, Dolores B -pg. D-2-60
Matanane, Eduardo -pg. D-3-24
Matanane, Eugenia B -pg. D-2-61
Matanane, Felicita Q -pg. D-5-50

Matanane, Felisa C -pg. D-4-74
Matanane, Francisco -pg. D-3-16
Matanane, Francisco C -pg. D-4-74
Matanane, Ignacia -pg. D-3-24
Matanane, Jesus -pg. D-3-16
Matanane, Jesus -pg. D-3-24
Matanane, Jesus C -pg. D-4-74
Matanane, Jose -pg. D-3-16
Matanane, Jose -pg. D-13-35
Matanane, Jose A -pg. D-5-45
Matanane, Jose C -pg. D-5-45
Matanane, Jose M -pg. D-5-44
Matanane, Josefa Q -pg. D-5-50
Matanane, Juan -pg. D-3-24
Matanane, Juan C -pg. D-3-4
Matanane, Juan M -pg. D-5-42
Matanane, Magdalena C -pg. D-3-4
Matanane, Manuel M -pg. D-5-49
Matanane, Maria A -pg. D-3-16
Matanane, Maria C -pg. D-11-37
Matanane, Maria Q -pg. D-5-50
Matanane, Nicolasa A -pg. D-5-45
Matanane, Rita L -pg. D-5-44
Matanane, Rosa C -pg. D-4-74
Matanane, Tomas -pg. D-3-4
Matanane, Tomas -pg. D-3-16
Matanane, Vicente A -pg. D-5-45
Matanane, Vicente Q -pg. D-5-50
Matanane, Victorina -pg. D-3-24
Mateo, Antonio C -pg. D-5-87
Mateo, Gregorio SN -pg. D-2-77
Mateo, Jose C -pg. D-5-87
Mateo, Juan SN -pg. D-2-77
Mateo, Maria -pg. D-5-87
Mateo, Maria R -pg. D-5-87
Mateo, Maria SN -pg. D-2-77
Mateo, Miguel -pg. D-5-87
Mateo, Pedro C -pg. D-2-77
Mateo, Pedro SN -pg. D-2-77
Mateo, Ramon SN -pg. D-2-77
Mateo, Rosa SN -pg. D-2-77
Mateo, Rosa SN -pg. D-2-77
Materne, Ana P -pg. D-4-23
Materne, Ana Q -pg. D-8-40
Materne, Andres D -pg. D-4-55
Materne, Antonio M -pg. D-4-56
Materne, Antonio M -pg. D-4-68
Materne, Clementina C -pg. D-4-56
Materne, Dolores C -pg. D-4-56
Materne, Dolores C -pg. D-4-56
Materne, Domingo M -pg. D-4-7
Materne, Eduvigis M -pg. D-4-56
Materne, Francisca M -pg. D-4-7
Materne, Francisca M -pg. D-5-10
Materne, Francisco M -pg. D-4-7
Materne, Ines S -pg. D-8-46
Materne, Inez M -pg. D-4-7
Materne, Joaquin P -pg. D-4-22
Materne, Jose C -pg. D-4-56

Materne, Jose P -pg. D-4-69
Materne, Jose S -pg. D-8-40
Materne, Josefa P -pg. D-4-68
Materne, Juan M -pg. D-4-7
Materne, Luis M -pg. D-4-7
Materne, Manuel D -pg. D-5-75
Materne, Margarita M -pg. D-4-7
Materne, Maria S -pg. D-4-7
Materne, Mariana P -pg. D-4-22
Materne, Mariano M -pg. D-4-22
Materne, Mercedes M -pg. D-4-7
Materne, Pedro D -pg. D-5-75
Materne, Petronilla M -pg. D-4-7
Materne, Pontinciana -pg. D-4-7
Materne, Teresa M -pg. D-4-7
Matheson, Douglas G -pg. D-13-42
Matias, Leonardo P -pg. D-4-90
Matsumiya, Antonio M -pg. D-10-9
Matsumiya, Jesus M -pg. D-10-9
Matsumiya, Joaquin M -pg. D-10-9
Matsumiya, Jose M -pg. D-10-9
Matsumiya, Josefina M -pg. D-10-9
Matsumiya, Rafael Z -pg. D-10-9
Matsumiya, Tomas M -pg. D-10-9
Matterson, Wiston C -pg. D-13-21
Matteson, Clyde Q -pg. D-13-26
Maxwell, Walter G -pg. D-13-24
May, Harold V -pg. D-13-12
May, Luella H -pg. D-4-47
Mayhew, Barbara -pg. D-3-31
Mayhew, Carolyn -pg. D-3-31
Mayhew, Eileen S -pg. D-3-31
Mayhew, Harold -pg. D-3-31
Mayhew, Maria D -pg. D-3-31
Mayhew, Thomas -pg. D-3-31
Mayhew, Thomas E -pg. D-3-31
Mayo, Concepcion L -pg. D-4-73
Mayor, Felipe -pg. D-13-24
McAllister, William R -pg. D-13-32
McAvory, Harry M -pg. D-13-12
McBride, George T -pg. D-13-21
McBurnie, Herbert C -pg. D-13-37
McCan, James H -pg. D-13-16
McCann, Frank -pg. D-5-11
McCann, Marvel F -pg. D-5-11
McCann, Rita A -pg. D-5-11
McChicken, Herbert S -pg. D-13-20
McClain, John B -pg. D-13-24
McCord, Constance E -pg. D-3-60
McCord, Pearle E -pg. D-3-60
McCormack, John A -pg. D-13-18
McCormick, Betty G -pg. D-3-73
McCormick, Joana A -pg. D-3-73
McCormick, Margaret M -pg. D-3-73
McCullough, F -pg. D-11-18
McCullough, Florence T -pg. D-11-18
McCullough, Thomas L -pg. D-13-39
McDenneth, Wilbur J -pg. D-13-7
McDonald, Catherine C -pg. D-3-73

McDonald, Charles H -pg. D-3-73
McDonald, Dolores M -pg. D-3-73
McDonald, Elizabeth A -pg. D-3-73
McDonald, Elmer E -pg. D-13-37
McDonald, Francis -pg. D-3-73
McDonald, James B -pg. D-3-73
McDonald, John F -pg. D-3-73
McDonald, Josephine F -pg. D-3-73
McDonald, Mary I -pg. D-3-73
McDonald, Veronica -pg. D-3-73
McElligott, Les M -pg. D-13-35
McGann, Catherine W -pg. D-1-10
McGann, James Jr. H -pg. D-1-10
McGretty, Ann -pg. D-1-7
McIslen, Meret L -pg. D-13-16
McKinley, Rufus W -pg. D-13-7
McKinney, Alfie E Jr -pg. D-13-45
McLean, Elsa N -pg. D-1-31
McLean, James W -pg. D-13-29
Mcleit, Clifford J -pg. D-13-7
McNeely, Thomas W -pg. D-13-17
McNeil, Earnest -pg. D-13-7
McNitt, Wesley D -pg. D-13-17
McOdeum, Earnest D -pg. D-13-7
McWilliams, Garland L -pg. D-13-7
Meadows, John H -pg. D-13-12
Medockers, Carl W -pg. D-13-12
Megofna, Ana P -pg. D-10-21
Megofna, Antonio G -pg. D-5-58
Megofna, Carmen C -pg. D-10-24
Megofna, Juan A -pg. D-2-31
Megofna, Manuel F -pg. D-4-78
Megofna, Rita F -pg. D-4-78
Melendez, Franz B -pg. D-13-31
Melingan, Harold H -pg. D-13-46
Mendiola, Ana -pg. D-3-18
Mendiola, Ana -pg. D-3-29
Mendiola, Ana -pg. D-3-40
Mendiola, Ana C -pg. D-4-8
Mendiola, Ana F -pg. D-4-39
Mendiola, Ana G -pg. D-11-36
Mendiola, Ana M -pg. D-4-35
Mendiola, Ana M -pg. D-5-61
Mendiola, Ana N -pg. D-2-61
Mendiola, Ana P -pg. D-3-18
Mendiola, Ana Q -pg. D-11-31
Mendiola, Ana Q -pg. D-13-43
Mendiola, Ana S -pg. D-3-32
Mendiola, Ana S -pg. D-11-26
Mendiola, Andres -pg. D-3-17
Mendiola, Antonia A -pg. D-5-62
Mendiola, Antonia B -pg. D-5-92
Mendiola, Antonia M -pg. D-4-35
Mendiola, Antonia P -pg. D-5-7
Mendiola, Antonia P -pg. D-5-7
Mendiola, Antonia T -pg. D-7-5
Mendiola, Antonio C -pg. D-3-52
Mendiola, Antonio C -pg. D-4-83
Mendiola, Antonio P -pg. D-1-4

Mendiola, Antonio Q -pg. D-4-39
Mendiola, Antonio R -pg. D-11-31
Mendiola, Augusto C -pg. D-6-4
Mendiola, Barbara S -pg. D-6-20
Mendiola, Beatrice S -pg. D-11-26
Mendiola, Benedicta M -pg. D-11-31
Mendiola, Benigno C -pg. D-1-19
Mendiola, Brigida F -pg. D-4-39
Mendiola, Candelaria P -pg. D-7-17
Mendiola, Carlos C -pg. D-4-87
Mendiola, Carmela S -pg. D-7-10
Mendiola, Carmen -pg. D-3-41
Mendiola, Carmen C -pg. D-10-20
Mendiola, Carmen M -pg. D-5-61
Mendiola, Catalina -pg. D-3-54
Mendiola, Catalino Q -pg. D-11-36
Mendiola, Celia P -pg. D-7-17
Mendiola, Cesario -pg. D-3-18
Mendiola, Clotilde C -pg. D-4-8
Mendiola, Concepcion M -pg. D-4-36
Mendiola, Concepcion M -pg. D-4-38
Mendiola, Concepcion S -pg. D-2-43
Mendiola, Concepcion U -pg. D-11-7
Mendiola, Consolacion G -pg. D-3-52
Mendiola, Consolascion S -pg. D-11-26
Mendiola, Consolasion F -pg. D-1-19
Mendiola, Dolores LG -pg. D-11-40
Mendiola, Dolores Q -pg. D-11-31
Mendiola, Elena T -pg. D-7-17
Mendiola, Elias C -pg. D-4-8
Mendiola, Eliza C -pg. D-4-8
Mendiola, Eliza S -pg. D-4-73
Mendiola, Engracia -pg. D-3-17
Mendiola, Engracia -pg. D-3-54
Mendiola, Enrique -pg. D-3-41
Mendiola, Enrique C -pg. D-4-8
Mendiola, Felicidad -pg. D-3-32
Mendiola, Felipa C -pg. D-6-19
Mendiola, Fidela T -pg. D-7-17
Mendiola, Filomena U -pg. D-1-4
Mendiola, Filomina C -pg. D-2-30
Mendiola, Francisca -pg. D-3-54
Mendiola, Francisca -pg. D-5-99
Mendiola, Francisco -pg. D-3-17
Mendiola, Francisco -pg. D-3-40
Mendiola, Francisco A -pg. D-11-41
Mendiola, Francisco C -pg. D-4-3
Mendiola, Francisco G -pg. D-2-61
Mendiola, Francisco N -pg. D-2-61
Mendiola, Francisco P -pg. D-1-4
Mendiola, Francisco P -pg. D-2-66
Mendiola, Francisco P -pg. D-5-7
Mendiola, Francisco U -pg. D-11-40
Mendiola, Francisco U -pg. D-13-29
Mendiola, Gabriel S -pg. D-6-4
Mendiola, Geronimo C -pg. D-11-35
Mendiola, Geronimo R -pg. D-6-5
Mendiola, Gloria A -pg. D-1-65
Mendiola, Gonzalo -pg. D-3-40

Mendiola, Gregorio G -pg. D-11-36
Mendiola, Guadalupe M -pg. D-11-31
Mendiola, Guadalupe T -pg. D-7-17
Mendiola, Ignacia G -pg. D-6-4
Mendiola, Ignacio -pg. D-3-17
Mendiola, Ignacio -pg. D-3-18
Mendiola, Ignacio C -pg. D-1-68
Mendiola, Ignacio C -pg. D-4-83
Mendiola, Ignacio G -pg. D-6-4
Mendiola, Ignacio Q -pg. D-11-27
Mendiola, Ignacio Q -pg. D-11-31
Mendiola, Ignacio R -pg. D-6-4
Mendiola, Ignacio S -pg. D-2-43
Mendiola, Ignacio S -pg. D-11-26
Mendiola, Isabel -pg. D-3-52
Mendiola, Isabel A -pg. D-11-41
Mendiola, Isabel C -pg. D-4-83
Mendiola, Isidro M -pg. D-5-61
Mendiola, Jesus -pg. D-3-18
Mendiola, Jesus -pg. D-3-41
Mendiola, Jesus -pg. D-3-54
Mendiola, Jesus -pg. D-3-54
Mendiola, Jesus A -pg. D-3-40
Mendiola, Jesus A -pg. D-5-62
Mendiola, Jesus B -pg. D-4-93
Mendiola, Jesus C -pg. D-3-19
Mendiola, Jesus C -pg. D-4-3
Mendiola, Jesus G -pg. D-11-36
Mendiola, Jesus LG -pg. D-11-40
Mendiola, Jesus M -pg. D-4-36
Mendiola, Jesus M -pg. D-4-104
Mendiola, Jesus P -pg. D-4-73
Mendiola, Jesus P -pg. D-5-58
Mendiola, Jesus Q -pg. D-7-17
Mendiola, Jesus S -pg. D-4-73
Mendiola, Jesus S -pg. D-7-23
Mendiola, Jesusa -pg. D-5-99
Mendiola, Joaquin -pg. D-3-41
Mendiola, Joaquin B -pg. D-1-3
Mendiola, Joaquin L -pg. D-7-3
Mendiola, Joaquin M -pg. D-5-62
Mendiola, Joaquin M -pg. D-11-40
Mendiola, Joaquin P -pg. D-3-75
Mendiola, Joaquin P -pg. D-7-17
Mendiola, Joaquin S -pg. D-7-10
Mendiola, Joaquina -pg. D-3-41
Mendiola, Joaquina A -pg. D-1-65
Mendiola, Joaquina C -pg. D-11-35
Mendiola, Joaquina G -pg. D-6-4
Mendiola, Joaquina M -pg. D-11-31
Mendiola, Jose -pg. D-3-18
Mendiola, Jose -pg. D-3-54
Mendiola, Jose A -pg. D-13-32
Mendiola, Jose B -pg. D-4-93
Mendiola, Jose C -pg. D-3-41
Mendiola, Jose C -pg. D-3-54
Mendiola, Jose C -pg. D-4-83
Mendiola, Jose F -pg. D-1-20
Mendiola, Jose F -pg. D-7-20

Mendiola, Jose G -pg. D-2-43
Mendiola, Jose G -pg. D-11-36
Mendiola, Jose H -pg. D-5-62
Mendiola, Jose L -pg. D-4-112
Mendiola, Jose M -pg. D-1-67
Mendiola, Jose M -pg. D-5-58
Mendiola, Jose P -pg. D-7-17
Mendiola, Jose Q -pg. D-7-17
Mendiola, Jose S -pg. D-4-113
Mendiola, Josefa C -pg. D-3-28
Mendiola, Josefa U -pg. D-11-7
Mendiola, Juan -pg. D-3-40
Mendiola, Juan -pg. D-3-40
Mendiola, Juan -pg. D-3-54
Mendiola, Juan -pg. D-3-54
Mendiola, Juan A -pg. D-5-62
Mendiola, Juan B -pg. D-4-93
Mendiola, Juan B -pg. D-5-37
Mendiola, Juan C -pg. D-3-17
Mendiola, Juan C -pg. D-4-73
Mendiola, Juan C -pg. D-4-104
Mendiola, Juan C -pg. D-5-99
Mendiola, Juan C -pg. D-7-10
Mendiola, Juan C -pg. D-10-20
Mendiola, Juan C -pg. D-11-35
Mendiola, Juan F -pg. D-4-39
Mendiola, Juan G -pg. D-11-36
Mendiola, Juan H -pg. D-4-73
Mendiola, Juan L -pg. D-1-69
Mendiola, Juan L -pg. D-3-40
Mendiola, Juan M -pg. D-4-36
Mendiola, Juan M -pg. D-4-105
Mendiola, Juan M -pg. D-11-31
Mendiola, Juan N -pg. D-2-61
Mendiola, Juan P pg. D-4-3
Mendiola, Juan P -pg. D-5-7
Mendiola, Juan P -pg. D-5-61
Mendiola, Juan Q -pg. D-11-31
Mendiola, Juan S -pg. D-4-98
Mendiola, Juan U -pg. D-11-7
Mendiola, Juan Q -pg. D-6-19
Mendiola, Juana P -pg. D-5-58
Mendiola, Julia -pg. D-3-41
Mendiola, Julia C -pg. D-4-73
Mendiola, Julian C -pg. D-4-8
Mendiola, Juliana C -pg. D-4-83
Mendiola, Juliana G -pg. D-1-69
Mendiola, Juliana M -pg. D-4-37
Mendiola, Justo D P -pg. D-7-17
Mendiola, Laura G -pg. D-6-4
Mendiola, Leonardo -pg. D-3-17
Mendiola, Lina C -pg. D-6-4
Mendiola, Lorenzo M -pg. D-5-61
Mendiola, Lourdes -pg. D-3-54
Mendiola, Lucia -pg. D-3-19
Mendiola, Luis S -pg. D-11-26
Mendiola, Magdalena H -pg. D-4-73
Mendiola, Magdalena M -pg. D-4-38
Mendiola, Magdalena M -pg. D-4-73

Mendiola, Magdalena S -pg. D-4-73
Mendiola, Manuel B -pg. D-5-58
Mendiola, Manuel F -pg. D-11-19
Mendiola, Manuel P -pg. D-3-18
Mendiola, Manuel Q -pg. D-11-31
Mendiola, Manuel S -pg. D-7-20
Mendiola, Margarita F -pg. D-4-39
Mendiola, Margarita M -pg. D-13-43
Mendiola, Maria -pg. D-3-18
Mendiola, Maria -pg. D-3-28
Mendiola, Maria -pg. D-3-40
Mendiola, Maria -pg. D-3-54
Mendiola, Maria A -pg. D-3-75
Mendiola, Maria A -pg. D-11-41
Mendiola, Maria B -pg. D-4-93
Mendiola, Maria B -pg. D-5-92
Mendiola, Maria C -pg. D-1-66
Mendiola, Maria C -pg. D-3-40
Mendiola, Maria C -pg. D-3-54
Mendiola, Maria C -pg. D-4-3
Mendiola, Maria C -pg. D-4-83
Mendiola, Maria E -pg. D-5-99
Mendiola, Maria F -pg. D-3-19
Mendiola, Maria F -pg. D-4-39
Mendiola, Maria G -pg. D-6-4
Mendiola, Maria G -pg. D-6-4
Mendiola, Maria G -pg. D-11-36
Mendiola, Maria I -pg. D-4-87
Mendiola, Maria M -pg. D-4-8
Mendiola, Maria M -pg. D-4-73
Mendiola, Maria M -pg. D-10-9
Mendiola, Maria M -pg. D-10-12
Mendiola, Maria P -pg. D-1-4
Mendiola, Maria P -pg. D-2-73
Mendiola, Maria P -pg. D-5-7
Mendiola, Maria P -pg. D-5-58
Mendiola, Maria Q -pg. D-11-31
Mendiola, Maria R -pg. D-3-17
Mendiola, Maria S -pg. D-2-43
Mendiola, Maria U -pg. D-11-7
Mendiola, Mariano -pg. D-3-41
Mendiola, Mariano -pg. D-5-7
Mendiola, Mariano C -pg. D-3-41
Mendiola, Mariano R -pg. D-11-7
Mendiola, Martina -pg. D-3-28
Mendiola, Martina S -pg. D-11-26
Mendiola, Miguela M -pg. D-11-12
Mendiola, Nieves R -pg. D-2-35
Mendiola, Pablo -pg. D-3-17
Mendiola, Paula L -pg. D-4-112
Mendiola, Paz C -pg. D-10-20
Mendiola, Pedro C -pg. D-10-20
Mendiola, Pedro M -pg. D-4-8
Mendiola, Pedro P -pg. D-1-4
Mendiola, Pedro P -pg. D-7-17
Mendiola, Pilar C -pg. D-4-3
Mendiola, Pilar P -pg. D-7-17
Mendiola, Polonia F -pg. D-10-12
Mendiola, Precentacion C -pg. D-10-20

Mendiola, Precilia P -pg. D-5-7
Mendiola, Preciosa G -pg. D-11-36
Mendiola, Priscilla F -pg. D-4-39
Mendiola, Quintino M -pg. D-2-19
Mendiola, Regina S -pg. D-6-20
Mendiola, Regino Q -pg. D-11-12
Mendiola, Rita -pg. D-3-29
Mendiola, Rita C -pg. D-3-54
Mendiola, Rita M -pg. D-5-61
Mendiola, Rita Q -pg. D-4-112
Mendiola, Rosa -pg. D-3-29
Mendiola, Rosa -pg. D-5-99
Mendiola, Rosa C -pg. D-1-66
Mendiola, Rosa C -pg. D-4-3
Mendiola, Rosa F -pg. D-1-20
Mendiola, Rosa F -pg. D-7-20
Mendiola, Rosa M -pg. D-4-104
Mendiola, Rosa M -pg. D-4-105
Mendiola, Rosa Q -pg. D-11-31
Mendiola, Rosa S -pg. D-4-73
Mendiola, Rosalia C -pg. D-6-4
Mendiola, Rosario M -pg. D-4-35
Mendiola, Rufina P -pg. D-3-18
Mendiola, Saturnino Q -pg. D-11-31
Mendiola, Serafina P -pg. D-5-7
Mendiola, Sergio M -pg. D-4-105
Mendiola, Severa SN -pg. D-7-23
Mendiola, Soledad P -pg. D-1-4
Mendiola, Stella A -pg. D-11-41
Mendiola, Teresa C -pg. D-4-3
Mendiola, Thomas U -pg. D-11-7
Mendiola, Tomas -pg. D-3-18
Mendiola, Tomas F -pg. D-4-39
Mendiola, Tomas S -pg. D-4-73
Mendiola, Tomas S -pg. D-6-20
Mendiola, Trinidad M -pg. D-10-12
Mendiola, Ursula A -pg. D-5-62
Mendiola, Usurla A -pg. D-3-40
Mendiola, Venancio P -pg. D-4-93
Mendiola, Veronica -pg. D-3-41
Mendiola, Vicenta B -pg. D-4-93
Mendiola, Vicente -pg. D-3-18
Mendiola, Vicente B -pg. D-2-36
Mendiola, Vicente C -pg. D-11-29
Mendiola, Vicente F -pg. D-1-20
Mendiola, Vicente G -pg. D-1-69
Mendiola, Vicente L -pg. D-4-112
Mendiola, Vicente M -pg. D-5-62
Mendiola, Vicente M -pg. D-10-12
Mendiola, Vicente N -pg. D-2-61
Mendiola, Vicente O -pg. D-6-20
Mendiola, Vicente P -pg. D-1-4
Mendiola, Virginia C -pg. D-4-73
Mendiola, Virginia N -pg. D-2-61
Mendiola, Ynes C -pg. D-10-20
Mendosa, Ana M -pg. D-5-38
Meno, Ana B -pg. D-8-43
Meno, Ana C -pg. D-8-5
Meno, Ana L -pg. D-8-6

Meno, Ana LG -pg. D-8-22
Meno, Ana M -pg. D-8-23
Meno, Ana N -pg. D-8-26
Meno, Ana T -pg. D-8-23
Meno, Angel C -pg. D-9-27
Meno, Antonia C -pg. D-8-23
Meno, Antonia C -pg. D-8-26
Meno, Antonia M -pg. D-9-17
Meno, Antonio -pg. D-5-66
Meno, Antonio M -pg. D-9-17
Meno, Antonio N -pg. D-2-5
Meno, Antonio N -pg. D-8-5
Meno, Asuncion C -pg. D-8-34
Meno, Asuncion Q -pg. D-9-27
Meno, Candelaria LG -pg. D-8-22
Meno, Candelaria P -pg. D-8-6
Meno, Candelaria Q -pg. D-8-42
Meno, Carlos C -pg. D-8-20
Meno, Carmen C -pg. D-5-60
Meno, Carmen C -pg. D-7-20
Meno, Carmen C -pg. D-8-14
Meno, Cevera C -pg. D-9-17
Meno, Concepcion L -pg. D-8-6
Meno, Concepcion L -pg. D-8-7
Meno, Concepcion M -pg. D-8-23
Meno, Consolacion -pg. D-5-66
Meno, Consolacion M -pg. D-7-20
Meno, Consolacion N -pg. D-8-26
Meno, Cornelia C -pg. D-8-33
Meno, Dolores -pg. D-5-66
Meno, Dolores -pg. D-9-27
Meno, Edividis LG -pg. D-8-22
Meno, Efraim C -pg. D-8-14
Meno, Eliza C -pg. D-8-5
Meno, Encarncion M -pg. D-8-33
Meno, Engracia T -pg. D-8-18
Meno, Enrique C -pg. D-8-19
Meno, Enriqueta C -pg. D-8-5
Meno, Esteban C -pg. D-8-19
Meno, Fedela C -pg. D-8-19
Meno, Felipe M -pg. D-9-30
Meno, Felipe N -pg. D-8-3
Meno, Felipe Q -pg. D-8-19
Meno, Felix M -pg. D-8-23
Meno, Felix P -pg. D-2-21
Meno, Feliza T -pg. D-8-23
Meno, Florentina C -pg. D-8-14
Meno, Francisca P -pg. D-2-21
Meno, Francisco -pg. D-5-66
Meno, Francisco D -pg. D-8-6
Meno, Francisco M -pg. D-7-20
Meno, Genoveva C -pg. D-8-5
Meno, Genoveva N -pg. D-8-5
Meno, Geronimo M -pg. D-9-17
Meno, Geronimo SN -pg. D-8-23
Meno, Gregorio C -pg. D-8-14
Meno, Ignacio P -pg. D-2-21
Meno, Isabel P -pg. D-2-21
Meno, Isidro M -pg. D-5-60

Meno, Isidro T -pg. D-7-23
Meno, Jesus C -pg. D-8-5
Meno, Jesus C -pg. D-8-33
Meno, Jesus L -pg. D-8-6
Meno, Jesus LG -pg. D-8-22
Meno, Jesus M -pg. D-7-20
Meno, Jesus N -pg. D-8-26
Meno, Jesus P -pg. D-2-21
Meno, Jesus Q -pg. D-8-42
Meno, Jesus Q -pg. D-9-27
Meno, Joaquin C -pg. D-8-34
Meno, Joaquin C -pg. D-8-35
Meno, Joaquin L -pg. D-8-6
Meno, Joaquin LG -pg. D-8-23
Meno, Joaquin T -pg. D-8-35
Meno, Joaquina M -pg. D-9-30
Meno, Jose B -pg. D-5-45
Meno, Jose C -pg. D-8-23
Meno, Jose C -pg. D-8-30
Meno, Jose C -pg. D-8-34
Meno, Jose D -pg. D-8-5
Meno, Jose J -pg. D-12-19
Meno, Jose L -pg. D-8-6
Meno, Jose LG -pg. D-8-22
Meno, Jose M -pg. D-2-15
Meno, Jose M -pg. D-7-20
Meno, Jose M -pg. D-8-23
Meno, Jose M -pg. D-8-43
Meno, Jose M -pg. D-9-30
Meno, Jose N -pg. D-8-13
Meno, Jose P -pg. D-2-21
Meno, Jose T -pg. D-8-13
Meno, Jose T -pg. D-8-35
Meno, Josefa B -pg. D-2-15
Meno, Josefina A -pg. D-8-24
Meno, Juan LG -pg. D-8-23
Meno, Juan M -pg. D-5-66
Meno, Juan M -pg. D-8-23
Meno, Juan P -pg. D-8-14
Meno, Juan T -pg. D-8-23
Meno, Juana A -pg. D-8-24
Meno, Juana C -pg. D-8-19
Meno, Justa -pg. D-5-66
Meno, Justina LG -pg. D-8-22
Meno, Lorenso Q -pg. D-8-42
Meno, Lourdes A -pg. D-8-24
Meno, Manuel C -pg. D-8-6
Meno, Manuel L -pg. D-8-7
Meno, Manuela P -pg. D-8-3
Meno, Margarita C -pg. D-8-19
Meno, Margarita C -pg. D-8-33
Meno, Margarita T -pg. D-8-35
Meno, Maria -pg. D-9-27
Meno, Maria A -pg. D-8-24
Meno, Maria B -pg. D-2-45
Meno, Maria B -pg. D-8-43
Meno, Maria B -pg. D-8-43
Meno, Maria C -pg. D-8-23
Meno, Maria C -pg. D-8-33

Meno, Maria G -pg. D-2-16
Meno, Maria L -pg. D-8-6
Meno, Maria LG -pg. D-8-22
Meno, Maria M -pg. D-8-23
Meno, Maria M -pg. D-8-32
Meno, Maria N -pg. D-2-5
Meno, Maria P -pg. D-5-66
Meno, Maria P -pg. D-8-6
Meno, Maria P -pg. D-8-6
Meno, Maria T -pg. D-8-35
Meno, Matilda T -pg. D-7-23
Meno, Natividad C -pg. D-8-19
Meno, Natividad T -pg. D-7-23
Meno, Nicolasa G -pg. D-2-16
Meno, Patrona C -pg. D-8-14
Meno, Pedro C -pg. D-7-23
Meno, Prudencio C -pg. D-8-14
Meno, Quintin -pg. D-13-24
Meno, Ramon LG -pg. D-8-22
Meno, Ramon M -pg. D-8-30
Meno, Ramon M -pg. D-8-43
Meno, Ramon P -pg. D-8-6
Meno, Ramon T -pg. D-8-35
Meno, Regina M -pg. D-8-23
Meno, Regino C -pg. D-8-33
Meno, Rita C -pg. D-12-19
Meno, Rita P -pg. D-8-6
Meno, Roman C -pg. D-8-19
Meno, Rosa C -pg. D-8-19
Meno, Rosa T -pg. D-8-35
Meno, Rosario C -pg. D-8-30
Meno, Sabina M -pg. D-7-20
Meno, Sebastian N -pg. D-8-22
Meno, Soledad P -pg. D-8-3
Meno, Teodora C -pg. D-9-17
Meno, Tomas G -pg. D-2-16
Meno, Tomas T -pg. D-9-25
Meno, Ursula N -pg. D-8-26
Meno, Vicenta M -pg. D-7-20
Meno, Vicenta P -pg. D-2-21
Meno, Vicente -pg. D-5-66
Meno, Vicente C -pg. D-8-8
Meno, Vicente C -pg. D-8-42
Meno, Vicente G -pg. D-2-16
Meno, Vicente L -pg. D-8-7
Meno, Vicente M -pg. D-2-21
Meno, Vicente M -pg. D-8-19
Meno, Vicente P -pg. D-8-6
Meno, Vicente T -pg. D-8-23
Meno, Vicitacion C -pg. D-10-4
Meno, Vinancio C -pg. D-8-26
Meno, Virginia P -pg. D-8-6
Mensoto, Pedro -pg. D-13-24
Merfalen, Antonio M -pg. D-4-41
Merfalen, Joaquin P -pg. D-4-41
Merfalen, Jose M -pg. D-4-41
Merfalen, Josefina M -pg. D-4-41
Merfalen, Lourdes M -pg. D-4-41
Merfalen, Manuel M -pg. D-4-42

Merfalen, Maria M -pg. D-4-41
Merfalen, Pedro M -pg. D-4-41
Merfalen, Vicente M -pg. D-4-41
Mesa, Adriano C -pg. D-4-125
Mesa, Alfonsina P -pg. D-6-33
Mesa, Alfredo LG -pg. D-1-5
Mesa, Ana -pg. D-3-31
Mesa, Ana C -pg. D-1-52
Mesa, Ana C -pg. D-4-34
Mesa, Ana M -pg. D-3-30
Mesa, Ana P -pg. D-4-45
Mesa, Ana P -pg. D-4-123
Mesa, Ana P -pg. D-6-33
Mesa, Ana R -pg. D-5-32
Mesa, Andres C -pg. D-4-65
Mesa, Antonia C -pg. D-4-27
Mesa, Antonia M -pg. D-4-56
Mesa, Antonia P -pg. D-2-81
Mesa, Antonia W -pg. D-1-12
Mesa, Antonio -pg. D-3-31
Mesa, Antonio C -pg. D-1-52
Mesa, Antonio LG -pg. D-1-5
Mesa, Antonio M -pg. D-4-54
Mesa, Antonio T -pg. D-4-54
Mesa, Beatrice LG -pg. D-1-5
Mesa, Benigno R -pg. D-4-102
Mesa, Candelaria -pg. D-3-27
Mesa, Candelaria F -pg. D-4-119
Mesa, Carmen I -pg. D-3-30
Mesa, Carmen M -pg. D-4-110
Mesa, Carridad M -pg. D-8-20
Mesa, Concepcion -pg. D-3-27
Mesa, Consolacion M -pg. D-4-6
Mesa, Consolacion S -pg. D-5-37
Mesa, Crisostimo F -pg. D-4-119
Mesa, Delores C -pg. D-13-43
Mesa, Dolores A -pg. D-4-50
Mesa, Dolores C -pg. D-2-8
Mesa, Dolores C -pg. D-3-12
Mesa, Dolores LG -pg. D-1-5
Mesa, Dolores R -pg. D-4-102
Mesa, Dolores R -pg. D-5-32
Mesa, Edward C -pg. D-1-52
Mesa, Edwardo C -pg. D-4-91
Mesa, Eloterio F -pg. D-4-119
Mesa, Emilia P -pg. D-4-60
Mesa, Engracia S -pg. D-4-59
Mesa, Enrique A -pg. D-4-34
Mesa, Enrique P -pg. D-6-33
Mesa, Esther M -pg. D-2-77
Mesa, Felis P -pg. D-4-45
Mesa, Felix C -pg. D-6-32
Mesa, Fernando LG -pg. D-1-5
Mesa, Francisca R -pg. D-1-42
Mesa, Francisco -pg. D-3-12
Mesa, Francisco -pg. D-3-27
Mesa, Francisco G -pg. D-4-91
Mesa, Francisco M -pg. D-8-20
Mesa, Francisco P -pg. D-6-33

Mesa, Geronimo R -pg. D-3-26
Mesa, Gloria -pg. D-3-12
Mesa, Gloria -pg. D-3-27
Mesa, Gonzales P -pg. D-6-32
Mesa, Herminia P -pg. D-4-54
Mesa, Ignacio C -pg. D-4-27
Mesa, Ignacio M -pg. D-4-25
Mesa, Isabel M -pg. D-4-6
Mesa, Jesus B -pg. D-4-34
Mesa, Jesus C -pg. D-2-7
Mesa, Jesus C -pg. D-4-6
Mesa, Jesus G -pg. D-1-52
Mesa, Jesus LG -pg. D-1-5
Mesa, Jesus P -pg. D-4-60
Mesa, Jesus P -pg. D-6-33
Mesa, Jesus U -pg. D-2-9
Mesa, Jesusa LG -pg. D-1-5
Mesa, Joaquin C -pg. D-2-9
Mesa, Joaquin C -pg. D-4-50
Mesa, Joaquin M -pg. D-2-76
Mesa, Joaquin M -pg. D-4-24
Mesa, Joaquin P -pg. D-6-33
Mesa, Jose -pg. D-3-27
Mesa, Jose C -pg. D-2-8
Mesa, Jose C -pg. D-2-8
Mesa, Jose G -pg. D-1-5
Mesa, Jose LG -pg. D-1-5
Mesa, Jose M -pg. D-2-77
Mesa, Jose M -pg. D-4-6
Mesa, Jose M -pg. D-4-56
Mesa, Jose M -pg. D-4-56
Mesa, Jose M -pg. D-5-31
Mesa, Jose M -pg. D-6-33
Mesa, Jose M -pg. D-13-31
Mesa, Jose P -pg. D-4-45
Mesa, Jose P -pg. D-6-33
Mesa, Jose P -pg. D-8-20
Mesa, Jose R -pg. D-1-42
Mesa, Jose R -pg. D-3-30
Mesa, Jose S -pg. D-1-13
Mesa, Jose T -pg. D-4-25
Mesa, Jose T -pg. D-4-34
Mesa, Jose U -pg. D-2-9
Mesa, Jose W -pg. D-1-12
Mesa, Josefa C -pg. D-4-65
Mesa, Josefina C -pg. D-4-34
Mesa, Josefina R -pg. D-1-42
Mesa, Juan C -pg. D-4-27
Mesa, Juan C -pg. D-4-119
Mesa, Juan C -pg. D-13-29
Mesa, Juan D -pg. D-4-65
Mesa, Juan F -pg. D-4-60
Mesa, Juan LG -pg. D-1-5
Mesa, Juan M -pg. D-4-50
Mesa, Juan M -pg. D-6-32
Mesa, Juan P -pg. D-4-60
Mesa, Juan R -pg. D-1-42
Mesa, Juana C -pg. D-2-7
Mesa, Juana G -pg. D-10-11

Mesa, Juana P -pg. D-4-54
Mesa, Juliana B -pg. D-1-13
Mesa, Luis C -pg. D-5-37
Mesa, Manuel P -pg. D-4-45
Mesa, Manuel R -pg. D-5-32
Mesa, Marcial F -pg. D-4-119
Mesa, Margarita M -pg. D-2-77
Mesa, Margarita M -pg. D-4-110
Mesa, Maria -pg. D-3-12
Mesa, Maria -pg. D-3-26
Mesa, Maria -pg. D-3-30
Mesa, Maria B -pg. D-4-24
Mesa, Maria B -pg. D-4-34
Mesa, Maria C -pg. D-4-65
Mesa, Maria C -pg. D-4-65
Mesa, Maria G -pg. D-10-11
Mesa, Maria L -pg. D-4-102
Mesa, Maria M -pg. D-2-77
Mesa, Maria P -pg. D-4-123
Mesa, Maria P -pg. D-6-33
Mesa, Maria R -pg. D-5-32
Mesa, Maria R -pg. D-10-22
Mesa, Maria SA -pg. D-5-31
Mesa, Maria U -pg. D-2-9
Mesa, Maria U -pg. D-2-9
Mesa, Mariano C -pg. D-1-42
Mesa, Matilde M -pg. D-10-11
Mesa, Nicolasa -pg. D-3-30
Mesa, Paciencia L -pg. D-4-102
Mesa, Pedro C -pg. D-4-65
Mesa, Rafael P -pg. D-4-45
Mesa, Ramon M -pg. D-5-74
Mesa, Remedios P -pg. D-4-123
Mesa, Rita C -pg. D-6-32
Mesa, Rita M -pg. D-2-77
Mesa, Rita P -pg. D-4-123
Mesa, Rosa -pg. D-3-27
Mesa, Rosa -pg. D-5-27
Mesa, Rosa B -pg. D-4-34
Mesa, Rosa F -pg. D-2-9
Mesa, Rosa T -pg. D-4-25
Mesa, Rosalia M -pg. D-4-110
Mesa, Rosalia P -pg. D-6-33
Mesa, Rosalia R -pg. D-4-71
Mesa, Rosario C -pg. D-4-91
Mesa, Rosario S -pg. D-4-59
Mesa, Rufina A -pg. D-3-31
Mesa, Sisto A -pg. D-4-50
Mesa, Soledad -pg. D-3-27
Mesa, Susana B -pg. D-4-125
Mesa, Teresita C -pg. D-1-52
Mesa, Tomas E -pg. D-2-8
Mesa, Tomas P -pg. D-6-33
Mesa, Tomas R -pg. D-4-102
Mesa, Tomasa C -pg. D-6-32
Mesa, Tomasa M -pg. D-2-77
Mesa, Vicenta F -pg. D-3-26
Mesa, Vicente -pg. D-3-27
Mesa, Vicente B -pg. D-1-12

Mesa, Vicente C -pg. D-4-91
Mesa, Vicente C -pg. D-6-32
Mesa, Vicente L -pg. D-4-102
Mesa, Vicente LG -pg. D-1-5
Mesa, Vicente M -pg. D-4-27
Mesa, Vicente M -pg. D-4-45
Mesa, Vicente M -pg. D-4-59
Mesa, Vicente M -pg. D-8-20
Mesa, Vicente P -pg. D-4-54
Mesa, Vicente R -pg. D-4-102
Mesa, Vicente S -pg. D-3-12
Mesa, William C -pg. D-1-52
Messick, John E -pg. D-13-33
Metzinrsou, Lawarence M -pg. D-13-7
Meza, Dolores SN -pg. D-11-19
Meza, Francisco P -pg. D-11-50
Midyette, Robert S -pg. D-13-24
Migofna, Ana A -pg. D-2-38
Migofna, Anastasio M -pg. D-2-38
Migofna, Ignacio A -pg. D-2-38
Migofna, Jose A -pg. D-2-38
Migofna, Vicente A -pg. D-2-38
Mihen, John Jr -pg. D-13-37
Mikelson, Paul B -pg. D-13-46
Milies, Burlie H -pg. D-13-7
Miller, Elizabeth R -pg. D-3-53
Miller, Jay F -pg. D-13-18
Miller, Loran L -pg. D-3-53
Miller, Margaret H -pg. D-1-52
Miller, Ruth C -pg. D-3-53
Miller, Thornton C -pg. D-13-31
Millinchamp, Henry -pg. D-5-38
Millinchamp, Julia M -pg. D-3-45
Millinchamp, Rita A -pg. D-3-45
Miner, Baldomero P -pg. D-2-33
Miner, Clara A -pg. D-1-59
Miner, Joaquina A -pg. D-1-59
Miner, Jose A -pg. D-13-33
Miner, Leoniza A -pg. D-1-59
Miner, Maria B -pg. D-2-33
Miner, Timoteo B -pg. D-2-33
Misara, Rosa M -pg. D-4-6
Miteno, Arthur W -pg. D-13-7
Mix, Carl -pg. D-13-44
Miyasaki, Dolores SN -pg. D-1-60
Miyasaki, Maria SN -pg. D-1-60
Miyasaki, Pedro SN -pg. D-1-60
Miyasaki, Rita SN -pg. D-1-60
Miyasaki, Tornogoro -pg. D-1-60
Monnito, Edward E -pg. D-13-24
Monsier, Irene -pg. D-4-87
Monsier, Ogla M -pg. D-4-87
Montales, Eduardo -pg. D-4-122
Moody, Harry W -pg. D-13-17
Moore, Carl P -pg. D-13-26
Moore, David D -pg. D-13-12
Moore, Linwood J -pg. D-13-12
Moore, Loyd F -pg. D-13-17
Morcilla, Vicente C -pg. D-2-50

Morcillas, Dorotea P -pg. D-4-118
Morcillas, Jesus D -pg. D-4-118
Morcillas, Jose P -pg. D-4-118
Morcillas, Maria P -pg. D-4-118
Moreland, Ira H -pg. D-13-17
Morgan, Donald E -pg. D-13-12
Morgan, T G -pg. D-13-44
Morien, Trimmon O -pg. D-13-7
Morita, Joaquin A -pg. D-7-4
Morita, Jose A -pg. D-7-4
Morris, Robert A -pg. D-13-33
Morrison, Ted R -pg. D-13-17
Morrone, Luther T -pg. D-13-17
Morwich, John J -pg. D-13-7
Mosick, Joseph W -pg. D-13-37
Mowers, Gordon E -pg. D-13-38
Mulford, James A -pg. D-11-38
Mullaby, Patrick A -pg. D-13-12
Mullahey, Mary A -pg. D-11-50
Mullahey, Thomas F -pg. D-11-50
Mullahey, Thomas Jr -pg. D-11-50
Mullaly, Eugene L -pg. D-13-3
Mullaly, Evelyn H -pg. D-13-3
Mullaly, Patricia V -pg. D-13-3
Mullenax, William D -pg. D-13-17
Muna, Ana G -pg. D-1-48
Muna, Ana G -pg. D-4-26
Muna, Ana G -pg. D-4-26
Muna, Ana M -pg. D-5-12
Muna, Ana P -pg. D-6-23
Muna, Antonia P -pg. D-4-111
Muna, Antonio C -pg. D-5-14
Muna, Asuncion S -pg. D-6-27
Muna, Carmen P -pg. D-6-23
Muna, Cesera S -pg. D-6-27
Muna, Clara M -pg. D-10-38
Muna, Cristina S -pg. D-6-27
Muna, Dolores F -pg. D-1-48
Muna, Evelyna P -pg. D-4-111
Muna, Felicita -pg. D-2-16
Muna, Felicita D -pg. D-2-82
Muna, Felix G -pg. D-5-12
Muna, Flora G -pg. D-4-11
Muna, Florensia S -pg. D-6-27
Muna, Florentino S -pg. D-6-37
Muna, Francisco D -pg. D-2-82
Muna, Genoveva G -pg. D-4-11
Muna, Gregorio D -pg. D-2-82
Muna, Gregorio D -pg. D-6-27
Muna, Ignacia M -pg. D-5-12
Muna, Ignacio D -pg. D-2-82
Muna, Isabel S -pg. D-6-27
Muna, Jesus D -pg. D-2-82
Muna, Jesus M -pg. D-5-12
Muna, Joaquin M -pg. D-10-38
Muna, Joaquin F -pg. D-1-48
Muna, Jose C -pg. D-4-11
Muna, Jose C -pg. D-4-26
Muna, Jose D -pg. D-2-82

Muna, Jose M -pg. D-10-38
Muna, Jose P -pg. D-2-82
Muna, Josefa S -pg. D-6-27
Muna, Juan -pg. D-4-111
Muna, Juan D -pg. D-1-48
Muna, Juan F -pg. D-1-48
Muna, Juana B -pg. D-6-29
Muna, Magdalena M -pg. D-10-38
Muna, Manuel M -pg. D-10-38
Muna, Maria C -pg. D-4-20
Muna, Maria G -pg. D-4-11
Muna, Maria M -pg. D-5-12
Muna, Maria S -pg. D-6-27
Muna, Maria T -pg. D-1-48
Muna, Norberto P -pg. D-4-111
Muna, Pedro S -pg. D-6-27
Muna, Pilar P -pg. D-4-111
Muna, Ramon M -pg. D-10-38
Muna, Rosa G -pg. D-1-48
Muna, Rufina C -pg. D-10-38
Muna, Saturnina G -pg. D-4-26
Muna, Tomas P -pg. D-4-111
Muna, Tomasa G -pg. D-4-26
Muna, Vicenta -pg. D-3-38
Muna, Vicenta C -pg. D-4-26
Muna, Vicente F -pg. D-4-20
Muna, Vicente T -pg. D-1-48
Munoz, Adela -pg. D-3-51
Munoz, Alejandro SR -pg. D-7-14
Munoz, Ana T -pg. D-5-3
Munoz, Antonio -pg. D-3-62
Munoz, Candelaria C -pg. D-3-63
Munoz, Clotilde -pg. D-3-51
Munoz, Clotilde F -pg. D-4-67
Munoz, Dolores S -pg. D-11-20
Munoz, Elena G -pg. D-5-5
Munoz, Francisco -pg. D-3-63
Munoz, Francisco C -pg. D-11-20
Munoz, Gregorio S -pg. D-11-20
Munoz, Hernando -pg. D-3-51
Munoz, Isabel -pg. D-3-62
Munoz, Isabel -pg. D-3-63
Munoz, Isabel S -pg. D-11-20
Munoz, Isabel T -pg. D-5-3
Munoz, Jesus -pg. D-3-62
Munoz, Jesus F -pg. D-4-67
Munoz, Jesusa -pg. D-3-51
Munoz, Joaquin -pg. D-3-63
Munoz, Joaquin F -pg. D-4-67
Munoz, Joaquin I -pg. D-4-67
Munoz, Joaquina -pg. D-3-62
Munoz, Jose C -pg. D-3-62
Munoz, Jose C -pg. D-3-63
Munoz, Jose F -pg. D-3-51
Munoz, Jose F -pg. D-4-67
Munoz, Jose I -pg. D-5-5
Munoz, Josefa F -pg. D-4-67
Munoz, Juan -pg. D-3-62
Munoz, Juan C -pg. D-3-51

Munoz, Manuel C -pg. D-5-3
Munoz, Manuela C -pg. D-7-14
Munoz, Maria C -pg. D-3-62
Munoz, Maria T -pg. D-5-3
Munoz, Maria T -pg. D-5-3
Munoz, Ramon -pg. D-3-62
Munoz, Regina F -pg. D-3-51
Munoz, Rosa -pg. D-3-62
Munoz, Rosa C -pg. D-7-14
Munoz, Rosa I -pg. D-3-62
Munoz, Vcente C -pg. D-7-14
Munoz, Vicente -pg. D-3-51
Munoz, Vicente C -pg. D-3-62
Murphree, Carmen -pg. D-3-30
Murphree, George M -pg. D-3-30
Murray, Ida R -pg. D-12-11
Murray, Wallace J -pg. D-13-17
Myers, Clem Q -pg. D-13-24
Myers, Guadalupe S -pg. D-11-41
Mylas, Walter R -pg. D-13-13
Naburn, Albert -pg. D-13-24
Naburn, Francisco S -pg. D-10-37
Namauleg, Ana P -pg. D-7-23
Namauleg, Antonio E -pg. D-1-65
Namauleg, Catalina P -pg. D-7-23
Namauleg, Dolores Q -pg. D-9-34
Namauleg, Gregorio E -pg. D-1-65
Namauleg, Jesus E -pg. D-1-65
Namauleg, Joaquin N -pg. D-1-65
Namauleg, Maria E -pg. D-1-65
Namauleg, Maria N -pg. D-4-36
Namauleg, Maria T -pg. D-4-11
Namauleg, Mariano G -pg. D-4-36
Namauleg, Pedro C -pg. D-13-24
Namauleg, Rosa E -pg. D-1-65
Nangauta, Antonia C -pg. D-9-26
Nangauta, Jose N -pg. D-9-26
Nangauta, Juan T -pg. D-9-26
Nangauta, Julian C -pg. D-9-5
Nangauta, Lucia N -pg. D-9-26
Nangauta, Luis N -pg. D-9-26
Nangauta, Mariano C -pg. D-9-26
Nangauta, Soledad N -pg. D-9-16
Nangauta, Vicente N -pg. D-9-26
Nanguata, Antonio Q -pg. D-9-6
Nanguata, Concepcion T -pg. D-9-6
Nanguata, Isabel Q -pg. D-9-28
Nanguata, Joaquin T -pg. D-9-6
Nanguata, Magdalena Q -pg. D-9-6
Nanguata, Patricio N -pg. D-9-28
Nanguata, Vicente T -pg. D-9-6
Napute, Albert M -pg. D-8-45
Napute, Dolores M -pg. D-8-45
Napute, Jesus T -pg. D-8-45
Napute, Joaquin M -pg. D-8-45
Napute, Juan M -pg. D-8-45
Napute, Pedro M -pg. D-8-45
Naputi, Ana B -pg. D-2-15
Naputi, Ana B -pg. D-2-15

Naputi, Ana C -pg. D-8-19
Naputi, Ana F -pg. D-8-17
Naputi, Antonia A -pg. D-9-7
Naputi, Antonia F -pg. D-8-17
Naputi, Antonia T -pg. D-8-23
Naputi, Antonio C -pg. D-8-25
Naputi, Antonio T -pg. D-8-34
Naputi, Asuncion B -pg. D-2-15
Naputi, Brigida B -pg. D-2-15
Naputi, Carmela T -pg. D-9-23
Naputi, Carmen D -pg. D-8-6
Naputi, Carmen M -pg. D-8-11
Naputi, Carmen M -pg. D-8-19
Naputi, Catalina B -pg. D-2-15
Naputi, Clotilde SN -pg. D-8-10
Naputi, Concepcion F -pg. D-8-17
Naputi, Concepcion M -pg. D-8-11
Naputi, Consolacion M -pg. D-8-19
Naputi, Cristobal F -pg. D-8-17
Naputi, Dolores M -pg. D-8-25
Naputi, Dolores T -pg. D-9-23
Naputi, Elerio F -pg. D-3-46
Naputi, Elminia N -pg. D-8-11
Naputi, Enrique A -pg. D-9-8
Naputi, Enrique P -pg. D-8-18
Naputi, Francisco F -pg. D-8-17
Naputi, Herman N -pg. D-8-10
Naputi, Jesus A -pg. D-9-8
Naputi, Jesus B -pg. D-2-15
Naputi, Jesus C -pg. D-8-19
Naputi, Jesus N -pg. D-2-15
Naputi, Jesus T -pg. D-8-34
Naputi, Joaquin A -pg. D-9-30
Naputi, Joaquin B -pg. D-2-15
Naputi, Joaquin T -pg. D-8-25
Naputi, Jose A -pg. D-9-7
Naputi, Jose A -pg. D-9-16
Naputi, Jose B -pg. D-2-15
Naputi, Jose C -pg. D-8-19
Naputi, Jose C -pg. D-8-25
Naputi, Jose M -pg. D-8-11
Naputi, Jose R -pg. D-2-18
Naputi, Jose SN -pg. D-8-34
Naputi, Josefa R -pg. D-2-18
Naputi, Juan A -pg. D-9-9
Naputi, Juan D -pg. D-8-25
Naputi, Juan F -pg. D-8-17
Naputi, Juan F -pg. D-9-8
Naputi, Juan T -pg. D-8-11
Naputi, Juan T -pg. D-8-34
Naputi, Leonardo N -pg. D-8-11
Naputi, Lorenzo E -pg. D-9-6
Naputi, Lorenzo N -pg. D-9-9
Naputi, Lucas D -pg. D-8-34
Naputi, Lucas T -pg. D-8-10
Naputi, Magdalena SN -pg. D-8-10
Naputi, Manuel P -pg. D-8-10
Naputi, Marcela SN -pg. D-8-34
Naputi, Maria B -pg. D-2-15

Naputi, Maria C -pg. D-8-19
Naputi, Maria F -pg. D-8-17
Naputi, Maria F -pg. D-9-8
Naputi, Maria M -pg. D-8-11
Naputi, Maria M -pg. D-8-18
Naputi, Maria N -pg. D-9-9
Naputi, Maria T -pg. D-8-12
Naputi, Narcisa A -pg. D-9-7
Naputi, Nicolasa D -pg. D-8-5
Naputi, Pio C -pg. D-8-18
Naputi, Remedios M -pg. D-8-11
Naputi, Remedios T -pg. D-8-34
Naputi, Rita D -pg. D-8-25
Naputi, Rita F -pg. D-9-8
Naputi, Rosa B -pg. D-2-15
Naputi, Rosa P -pg. D-8-10
Naputi, Rosalia B -pg. D-2-15
Naputi, Sebastian M -pg. D-8-11
Naputi, Simona A -pg. D-9-7
Naputi, Teresa D -pg. D-8-6
Naputi, Tomasa F -pg. D-9-30
Naputi, Vicente D -pg. D-8-6
Naputi, Vicente F -pg. D-9-8
Naputi, Vicente P -pg. D-8-17
Naputi, Vicente T -pg. D-8-6
Narly, Wayne -pg. D-13-40
Narpen, Edward T A -pg. D-13-7
Nateo, Pete M -pg. D-13-8
Naune, Ernie -pg. D-13-6
Nauta, Ana M -pg. D-10-24
Nauta, Antonia C -pg. D-4-2
Nauta, Antonia M -pg. D-10-24
Nauta, Antonio T -pg. D-4-2
Nauta, Carmen M -pg. D-10-24
Nauta, Carmen T -pg. D-4-10
Nauta, Emilia S -pg. D-4-67
Nauta, Eulogio M -pg. D-10-24
Nauta, Felicidad C -pg. D-4-2
Nauta, Felicita T -pg. D-10-24
Nauta, Felix Q -pg. D-10-25
Nauta, Francisca T -pg. D-4-10
Nauta, Francisco N -pg. D-4-11
Nauta, Francisco S -pg. D-4-67
Nauta, Jesus M -pg. D-4-10
Nauta, Jesus Q -pg. D-10-25
Nauta, Jesus S -pg. D-4-67
Nauta, Joaquin N -pg. D-4-66
Nauta, Joaquin S -pg. D-4-67
Nauta, Joaquin T -pg. D-4-10
Nauta, Joaquina Q -pg. D-10-25
Nauta, Jose N -pg. D-10-24
Nauta, Jose Q -pg. D-10-25
Nauta, Jose S -pg. D-4-67
Nauta, Juan Q -pg. D-10-25
Nauta, Juan S -pg. D-4-67
Nauta, Juan T -pg. D-4-10
Nauta, Lucia Q -pg. D-10-25
Nauta, Manuel Q -pg. D-10-25
Nauta, Maria N -pg. D-7-19

Nauta, Maria Q -pg. D-10-25
Nauta, Maria Q -pg. D-10-25
Nauta, Maria T -pg. D-4-10
Nauta, Maria T -pg. D-4-10
Nauta, Mariano N -pg. D-10-25
Nauta, Martina Q -pg. D-10-25
Nauta, Paulina T -pg. D-4-10
Nauta, Pedro Q -pg. D-10-25
Nauta, Pedro S -pg. D-4-67
Nauta, Pedro T -pg. D-4-10
Nauta, Rita M -pg. D-10-24
Nauta, Rita Q -pg. D-10-25
Nauta, Rosario S -pg. D-4-67
Nauta, Vincente Q -pg. D-13-29
Navarro, Agnes -pg. D-5-81
Navarro, Angela T -pg. D-5-81
Navarro, Dionisio M -pg. D-5-82
Navarro, Francisca -pg. D-5-81
Navarro, Isabel -pg. D-5-81
Navarro, Lucas M -pg. D-5-81
Navarro, Manuela Q -pg. D-5-82
Navarro, Maria Q -pg. D-5-83
Navarro, Mariano M -pg. D-5-86
Navarro, Pedro -pg. D-5-81
Navarro, Vicenta -pg. D-5-81
Neaves, Roscol B -pg. D-13-8
Nededoc, Agnes M -pg. D-6-23
Nededoc, Ana C -pg. D-6-21
Nededoc, Ana M -pg. D-6-23
Nededoc, Ana T -pg. D-6-28
Nededoc, Andres C -pg. D-6-24
Nededoc, Bastian T -pg. D-6-28
Nededoc, Candelaria C -pg. D-6-24
Nededoc, Carmen C -pg. D-6-21
Nededoc, Carmen T -pg. D-6-28
Nededoc, Cristina S -pg. D-6-18
Nededoc, Dolores R -pg. D-6-15
Nededoc, Dolores T -pg. D-6-12
Nededoc, Emilio C -pg. D-6-21
Nededoc, Enrique C -pg. D-6-21
Nededoc, Feliza C -pg. D-6-28
Nededoc, Francisco C -pg. D-6-21
Nededoc, Jesus A -pg. D-6-28
Nededoc, Jesus T -pg. D-6-31
Nededoc, Joaquin C -pg. D-6-24
Nededoc, Joaquin P -pg. D-6-38
Nededoc, Jose C -pg. D-6-21
Nededoc, Jose N -pg. D-6-23
Nededoc, Jose S -pg. D-6-18
Nededoc, Juan M -pg. D-6-23
Nededoc, Juan P -pg. D-6-12
Nededoc, Juan S -pg. D-6-15
Nededoc, Juan T -pg. D-6-12
Nededoc, Juan T -pg. D-6-31
Nededoc, Juana T -pg. D-6-28
Nededoc, Maria C -pg. D-6-24
Nededoc, Maria T -pg. D-6-31
Nededoc, Matea R -pg. D-6-15
Nededoc, Nicolasa C -pg. D-6-24

Nededoc, Pedro P -pg. D-6-18
Nededoc, Pedro T -pg. D-6-28
Nededoc, Rita T -pg. D-6-12
Nededoc, Roque N -pg. D-6-15
Nededoc, Theadora C -pg. D-6-23
Nededoc, Tomas C -pg. D-6-24
Nededoc, Vicente P -pg. D-6-31
Nededoc, Vicente S -pg. D-6-24
Nededog, Antonia P -pg. D-11-47
Nededog, Beatrice N -pg. D-10-29
Nededog, Enrique P -pg. D-11-47
Nededog, Felix P -pg. D-13-29
Nededog, Ignacio P -pg. D-11-47
Nededog, Juan N -pg. D-11-47
Nededog, Magdalena P -pg. D-11-47
Nededog, Nicolasa N -pg. D-1-20
Nededog, Veronica P -pg. D-11-47
Nego, Jose R -pg. D-5-15
Nego, Maria R -pg. D-5-15
Nego, Rosa R -pg. D-5-15
Nego, Vicente R -pg. D-5-15
Nelson, Ana G -pg. D-1-37
Nelson, Catherine C -pg. D-4-16
Nelson, Claude L -pg. D-13-33
Nelson, Edward A -pg. D-13-20
Nelson, Edward R -pg. D-1-37
Nelson, Florence -pg. D-4-16
Nelson, George E -pg. D-5-54
Nelson, Henry -pg. D-4-16
Nelson, J E -pg. D-5-54
Nelson, J E Jr. -pg. D-5-54
Nelson, Maxwell -pg. D-13-38
Nelson, May M -pg. D-5-54
Nelson, Peter M -pg. D-4-16
Nelson, Peter M -pg. D-4-16
Nelson, Potenciana F -pg. D-5-54
Nelson, Rosie E -pg. D-5-54
Neri, Victor -pg. D-13-24
Nerona, Maria G -pg. D-2-3
Neuneann, Elmer G -pg. D-13-17
Newby, Homer C -pg. D-13-44
Nicheo, Mack -pg. D-13-41
Ninaisen, Antonio S -pg. D-2-72
Ninaisen, Dolores S -pg. D-2-72
Ninaisen, Francisca N -pg. D-2-61
Ninaisen, Maria -pg. D-1-18
Ninaisen, Maria S -pg. D-2-72
Ninete, Ana C -pg. D-1-68
Ninete, Antonio P -pg. D-1-62
Ninete, Gregorio C -pg. D-1-68
Ninete, Guillerma M -pg. D-1-62
Ninete, Ignacio C -pg. D-1-68
Ninete, Ignacio C -pg. D-1-68
Ninete, Ignacio M -pg. D-1-62
Ninete, Jesus P -pg. D-1-62
Ninete, Joaquin C -pg. D-1-62
Ninete, Joaquin P -pg. D-1-62
Ninete, Jose C -pg. D-1-62
Ninete, Maria C -pg. D-1-68

Ninete, Maria C -pg. D-1-68
Ninete, Maria M -pg. D-1-62
Ninete, Maria P -pg. D-1-62
Ninete, Pedro P -pg. D-1-62
Ninete, Rosalia P -pg. D-1-62
Ninete, Rosario M -pg. D-1-62
Ninete, Segundo M -pg. D-1-62
Ninete, Vicente P -pg. D-1-62
Niny, Charles R -pg. D-13-7
Nixon, Ivery -pg. D-13-38
Nka, Shinsuke -pg. D-10-15
Noda, Barcilisa P -pg. D-11-31
Noda, Noaichi -pg. D-3-38
Norana, June H -pg. D-13-19
Norrie, Frank J -pg. D-13-8
Notley, Emilia M -pg. D-3-45
Notley, Grace T -pg. D-3-45
Notley, William H -pg. D-3-45
Nreinu, Henry -pg. D-13-7
Nudiamer, William R -pg. D-13-17
Nunn, Clarence -pg. D-13-42
O'Briant, Paul J -pg. D-13-8
O'Brien, Otto T -pg. D-13-38
O'Leary, William C -pg. D-13-13
Oakes, George E -pg. D-13-38
Oats, Clive -pg. D-13-17
Ocampo, Dolores G -pg. D-4-101
Ocampo, Macario -pg. D-13-24
Ocampo, Peta A -pg. D-10-18
Ochai, Alfonsina B -pg. D-4-90
Ochai, Alfred B -pg. D-4-89
Ochai, Artemio B -pg. D-4-89
Ochai, Concepcion B -pg. D-4-89
Ochai, Francisco B -pg. D-4-90
Ochai, German B -pg. D-4-89
Ochai, Gonzalo B -pg. D-4-89
Ochai, Jose B -pg. D-4-89
Ochai, Jose B -pg. D-4-89
Ochai, Juan B -pg. D-4-90
Ochai, Maria B -pg. D-4-89
Ochai, Soledad B -pg. D-4-89
Oconner, Antonia U -pg. D-4-97
Ogo, Ana O -pg. D-12-14
Ogo, Ana T -pg. D-8-49
Ogo, Antonia M -pg. D-5-4
Ogo, Antonia O -pg. D-12-14
Ogo, Eseqiel O -pg. D-12-2
Ogo, Esperansa O -pg. D-12-2
Ogo, Francisco A -pg. D-4-27
Ogo, Francisco M -pg. D-12-2
Ogo, Isabel O -pg. D-12-2
Ogo, Jesus O -pg. D-12-2
Ogo, Joaquin O -pg. D-12-21
Ogo, Joaquina O -pg. D-12-14
Ogo, Jose T -pg. D-5-4
Ogo, Juan O -pg. D-4-98
Ogo, Juan O -pg. D-4-99
Ogo, Juan O -pg. D-8-18
Ogo, Magdalena O -pg. D-12-2

Ogo, Manuel G -pg. D-4-21
Ogo, Manuel L -pg. D-4-41
Ogo, Maria F -pg. D-5-41
Ogo, Maria M -pg. D-5-4
Ogo, Maria O -pg. D-12-14
Ogo, Pedro M -pg. D-5-4
Ogo, Pedro O -pg. D-12-14
Ogo, Ramona O -pg. D-4-98
Ogo, Rita A -pg. D-12-15
Ogo, Rosa D -pg. D-4-21
Ogo, Rufina T -pg. D-3-12
Ogo, Teodora O -pg. D-12-14
Ogo, Ulita D -pg. D-4-21
Ogo, Vicenta D -pg. D-4-21
Ogo, Vicente J -pg. D-12-14
Ogoen, Quentin M -pg. D-13-38
Ojeda, Antonia -pg. D-3-68
Ojeda, Carmen -pg. D-3-68
Ojeda, Carmen C -pg. D-2-57
Ojeda, Consolacion C -pg. D-2-57
Ojeda, Elias -pg. D-3-68
Ojeda, Emilia T -pg. D-3-12
Ojeda, Eugenia -pg. D-3-68
Ojeda, Felicidad -pg. D-3-68
Ojeda, Felicita -pg. D-3-68
Ojeda, Francisco M -pg. D-5-42
Ojeda, Francisco T -pg. D-3-13
Ojeda, Juan M -pg. D-2-75
Ojeda, Maria -pg. D-3-68
Ojeda, Maria C -pg. D-2-57
Ojeda, Pedro SN -pg. D-2-75
Ojeda, Rosa SN -pg. D-2-75
Ojeda, Rosalia J -pg. D-3-68
Ojeda, Tressie -pg. D-3-68
Ojeda, Vicente -pg. D-3-68
Oka, Antonio T -pg. D-3-38
Okada, Carlos -pg. D-3-34
Okada, Edmond -pg. D-3-34
Okada, Edward -pg. D-3-34
Okada, Francisco -pg. D-3-34
Okada, Gregorio -pg. D-3-34
Okada, Jesus -pg. D-3-34
Okada, Jose S -pg. D-3-34
Okada, Juan -pg. D-3-34
Okada, Oscar -pg. D-3-34
Okada, Rosa -pg. D-11-27
Okada, Vicenta S -pg. D-3-34
Okiyama, Ana G -pg. D-4-37
Okiyama, Carmen G -pg. D-4-37
Okiyama, Francisco K -pg. D-6-5
Okiyama, Jacoba G -pg. D-4-37
Okiyama, Jesus -pg. D-3-49
Okiyama, Jesus C -pg. D-6-5
Okiyama, Jose C -pg. D-4-38
Okiyama, Jose G -pg. D-4-37
Okiyama, Maria -pg. D-3-49
Okiyama, Maria C -pg. D-6-5
Okiyama, Maria G -pg. D-4-37
Okizaki, Jesus M -pg. D-10-11

Okizaki, Joaquin M -pg. D-10-11
Okizaki, Joaquina B -pg. D-10-11
Okizaki, Rita M -pg. D-10-11
Olaiz, Joaquin P Z -pg. D-1-56
Oleson, John W -pg. D-13-38
Oliva, Frank D -pg. D-13-24
Olive, Concepcion T -pg. D-5-29
Olive, Euell Francis -pg. D-5-29
Olive, Euella T -pg. D-5-29
Olive, Franklin T -pg. D-5-29
Olive, Robert H B -pg. D-13-20
Olive, Ruth T -pg. D-5-30
Onedera, Ana S -pg. D-5-45
Onidera, Agueda S -pg. D-12-17
Onidera, Carmen S -pg. D-12-17
Onidera, Juan J -pg. D-12-17
Onidera, Juan S -pg. D-12-17
Onidera, Maria S -pg. D-12-17
Onidera, Maria S -pg. D-12-17
Onquit, Arcadio -pg. D-13-24
Oracion, Maria C -pg. D-4-39
Orfet, Russell J -pg. D-13-8
Oroso, Ana C -pg. D-2-79
Oroso, Delfina -pg. D-3-40
Oroso, George -pg. D-3-40
Oroso, Juan -pg. D-3-40
Oroso, Vicente -pg. D-3-40
Ortan, Frank F -pg. D-13-38
Osborn, Oscar E -pg. D-13-17
Osborne, Burton F -pg. D-13-42
Osone, Fudentura -pg. D-4-86
Ovlasa, John J -pg. D-13-38
Paat, Fidel E -pg. D-13-24
Pablo, Agueda D -pg. D-4-24
Pablo, Alfonso G -pg. D-4-115
Pablo, Ana N -pg. D-3-23
Pablo, Ana V -pg. D-5-42
Pablo, Angelina C -pg. D-5-8
Pablo, Angustia M -pg. D-4-23
Pablo, Antonia -pg. D-5-76
Pablo, Antonia C -pg. D-5-38
Pablo, Antonia T -pg. D-8-43
Pablo, Antonio A -pg. D-4-45
Pablo, Antonio E -pg. D-2-17
Pablo, Antonio P -pg. D-4-99
Pablo, Antonio P -pg. D-8-39
Pablo, Antonio T -pg. D-8-43
Pablo, Benjamin A -pg. D-8-42
Pablo, Concepcion B -pg. D-2-17
Pablo, Concepcion C -pg. D-5-8
Pablo, Concepcion M -pg. D-4-23
Pablo, Dolores A -pg. D-4-23
Pablo, Dolores B -pg. D-8-39
Pablo, Dolores F -pg. D-5-76
Pablo, Elena A -pg. D-8-42
Pablo, Emelia R -pg. D-2-18
Pablo, Engracia T -pg. D-8-43
Pablo, Exequiel S -pg. D-5-24
Pablo, Felicidad A -pg. D-4-23

Pablo, Felicita V -pg. D-5-42
Pablo, Felix P -pg. D-7-24
Pablo, Francisco -pg. D-5-76
Pablo, Getrudes B -pg. D-2-17
Pablo, Gregorio B -pg. D-8-39
Pablo, Ignacio P -pg. D-4-115
Pablo, Isabel -pg. D-5-76
Pablo, Jacinto A -pg. D-4-24
Pablo, Jesus B -pg. D-2-17
Pablo, Jesus P -pg. D-5-15
Pablo, Jesus P -pg. D-8-43
Pablo, Jesus T -pg. D-8-43
Pablo, Joaquin -pg. D-3-24
Pablo, Joaquin A -pg. D-8-48
Pablo, Joaquin B -pg. D-8-39
Pablo, Joaquin P -pg. D-5-37
Pablo, Joaquin V -pg. D-5-42
Pablo, Jose A -pg. D-4-115
Pablo, Jose A -pg. D-8-39
Pablo, Jose B -pg. D-2-18
Pablo, Jose C -pg. D-1-47
Pablo, Jose C -pg. D-4-23
Pablo, Jose C -pg. D-5-8
Pablo, Jose C -pg. D-5-37
Pablo, Jose M -pg. D-4-23
Pablo, Jose P -pg. D-8-39
Pablo, Jose P -pg. D-8-43
Pablo, Jose P -pg. D-8-46
Pablo, Jose T -pg. D-8-43
Pablo, Josefa P -pg. D-8-39
Pablo, Josefina M -pg. D-4-23
Pablo, Juan C -pg. D-5-8
Pablo, Juan C -pg. D-5-37
Pablo, Juan D -pg. D-4-24
Pablo, Juan P -pg. D-1-47
Pablo, Juan P -pg. D-5-76
Pablo, Juan P -pg. D-8-40
Pablo, Juan SN -pg. D-8-43
Pablo, Lorenzo -pg. D-5-76
Pablo, Lorenzo D -pg. D-5-8
Pablo, Magdalena B -pg. D-2-17
Pablo, Manuel C -pg. D-5-8
Pablo, Manuela C -pg. D-5-8
Pablo, Maria -pg. D-3-24
Pablo, Maria B -pg. D-2-18
Pablo, Maria B -pg. D-2-18
Pablo, Maria P -pg. D-1-47
Pablo, Maria P -pg. D-2-62
Pablo, Maria P -pg. D-5-14
Pablo, Maria P -pg. D-8-39
Pablo, Maria V -pg. D-5-42
Pablo, Mariano A -pg. D-8-39
Pablo, Rafael P -pg. D-8-39
Pablo, Ramon A -pg. D-8-42
Pablo, Remedios P -pg. D-2-62
Pablo, Rosa A -pg. D-8-42
Pablo, Rosa G -pg. D-4-115
Pablo, Rosario R -pg. D-2-17
Pablo, Serafin A -pg. D-8-42

Pablo, Soledad D -pg. D-4-24
Pablo, Soledad P -pg. D-8-39
Pablo, Tomas B -pg. D-8-39
Pablo, Vicente B -pg. D-8-39
Pablo, Vicente C -pg. D-5-8
Pablo, Vicente R -pg. D-2-17
Padeson, Dolores W -pg. D-2-62
Palacios, Antonio S -pg. D-2-5
Palacios, Carlos B -pg. D-4-109
Palacios, Francisca C -pg. D-1-10
Palacios, Francisco C -pg. D-1-10
Palacios, Jose C -pg. D-1-10
Palacios, Jose T -pg. D-1-10
Palacios, Josefina C -pg. D-1-10
Palacios, Juan T -pg. D-5-3
Palacios, Maria C -pg. D-1-10
Palacios, Maria C -pg. D-1-10
Palacios, Maria T -pg. D-1-10
Palacios, Rosa B -pg. D-4-109
Palomo, Ana -pg. D-5-69
Palomo, Ana C -pg. D-2-57
Palomo, Ana C -pg. D-2-66
Palomo, Ana R -pg. D-5-35
Palomo, Antonia -pg. D-5-79
Palomo, Antonio R -pg. D-2-7
Palomo, Asuncion A -pg. D-5-23
Palomo, Asuncion M -pg. D-2-7
Palomo, Carmen C -pg. D-2-66
Palomo, Carmen C -pg. D-6-36
Palomo, Cecilia C -pg. D-4-2
Palomo, Clotilde P -pg. D-2-52
Palomo, Concepcion M -pg. D-1-4
Palomo, Consolacion -pg. D-5-69
Palomo, Enrique C -pg. D-6-36
Palomo, Estofonia C -pg. D-4-2
Palomo, Francisca T G -pg. D-2-17
Palomo, Francisco C -pg. D-4-2
Palomo, Francisco C -pg. D-5-27
Palomo, Francisco D -pg. D-5-27
Palomo, Gabina A -pg. D-5-23
Palomo, Gertrudes T -pg. D-4-2
Palomo, Gregorio P -pg. D-5-79
Palomo, Ignacio C -pg. D-5-69
Palomo, Ignacio C -pg. D-6-36
Palomo, Ignacio D -pg. D-2-17
Palomo, Ignacio T -pg. D-4-2
Palomo, Irene L -pg. D-1-13
Palomo, Isabel T -pg. D-5-79
Palomo, Jesus -pg. D-5-69
Palomo, Jesus LG -pg. D-1-13
Palomo, Jesus R -pg. D-5-35
Palomo, Joaquin B -pg. D-1-4
Palomo, Joaquin L -pg. D-1-13
Palomo, Joaquin M -pg. D-1-4
Palomo, Joaquina M -pg. D-1-4
Palomo, Jose -pg. D-5-69
Palomo, Jose -pg. D-5-69
Palomo, Jose -pg. D-5-79
Palomo, Jose C -pg. D-2-66

Palomo, Jose C -pg. D-2-66
Palomo, Jose G -pg. D-2-17
Palomo, Jose L -pg. D-1-13
Palomo, Jose T -pg. D-4-2
Palomo, Juan -pg. D-5-69
Palomo, Juan A -pg. D-5-30
Palomo, Juan D -pg. D-5-30
Palomo, Luis P -pg. D-2-52
Palomo, Manuel A -pg. D-5-23
Palomo, Maria -pg. D-5-79
Palomo, Maria C -pg. D-2-66
Palomo, Maria C -pg. D-4-2
Palomo, Maria C -pg. D-5-27
Palomo, Maria C -pg. D-5-27
Palomo, Maria C -pg. D-6-36
Palomo, Maria G -pg. D-2-17
Palomo, Maria L -pg. D-1-13
Palomo, Maria M -pg. D-1-4
Palomo, Maria P -pg. D-2-52
Palomo, Maria SM -pg. D-5-69
Palomo, Oliva -pg. D-5-70
Palomo, Patricia C -pg. D-6-36
Palomo, Pedro C -pg. D-4-2
Palomo, Pedro G -pg. D-6-36
Palomo, Ramon C -pg. D-5-69
Palomo, Rita D -pg. D-5-30
Palomo, Rita L -pg. D-1-13
Palomo, Rita LG -pg. D-2-52
Palomo, Roman -pg. D-5-70
Palomo, Silvestre G -pg. D-2-17
Palomo, Teresa N -pg. D-5-69
Palomo, Tomas C -pg. D-6-36
Palomo, Vicenta S -pg. D-4-2
Palomo, Vicente -pg. D-5-69
Palomo, Vicente A -pg. D-5-35
Palomo, Vicente C -pg. D-2-57
Palomo, Vicente D -pg. D-5-30
Palomo, Vicente G -pg. D-2-17
Palomo, Vicente M -pg. D-1-4
Palomo, Vicente P -pg. D-2-52
Palomo, Vicente R -pg. D-5-35
Palting, Alejo -pg. D-3-34
Palting, Florencia -pg. D-3-34
Palting, Francisco -pg. D-3-34
Palting, Margarito -pg. D-3-34
Palting, Pancracio -pg. D-3-34
Palting, Pancracio R -pg. D-3-34
Palting, Soledad D -pg. D-3-34
Palumbo, Carmine -pg. D-13-32
Palumbo, Theena C -pg. D-1-48
Pangelinan, Alfonso C -pg. D-5-96
Pangelinan, Alfonso M -pg. D-5-51
Pangelinan, Alvina -pg. D-5-97
Pangelinan, Amparo B -pg. D-5-52
Pangelinan, Ana -pg. D-3-39
Pangelinan, Ana -pg. D-5-96
Pangelinan, Ana G -pg. D-1-7
Pangelinan, Ana M -pg. D-5-51
Pangelinan, Ana P -pg. D-4-63

Pangelinan, Ana P -pg. D-4-65
Pangelinan, Ana P -pg. D-4-121
Pangelinan, Ana Q -pg. D-11-27
Pangelinan, Ana R -pg. D-1-44
Pangelinan, Ana S -pg. D-4-47
Pangelinan, Andrea S -pg. D-11-21
Pangelinan, Antonia -pg. D-3-4
Pangelinan, Antonia B -pg. D-1-49
Pangelinan, Antonia B -pg. D-12-10
Pangelinan, Antonio C -pg. D-5-96
Pangelinan, Antonio I -pg. D-5-49
Pangelinan, Antonio M -pg. D-5-51
Pangelinan, Antonio N -pg. D-4-55
Pangelinan, Antonio T -pg. D-4-97
Pangelinan, Antonio U -pg. D-2-48
Pangelinan, Barbara I -pg. D-5-49
Pangelinan, Barcelisa B -pg. D-5-7
Pangelinan, Bartola -pg. D-5-94
Pangelinan, Benancio U -pg. D-2-40
Pangelinan, Benedicto S -pg. D-11-21
Pangelinan, Benita C -pg. D-4-29
Pangelinan, Candelaria -pg. D-5-96
Pangelinan, Carmen A -pg. D-1-30
Pangelinan, Carmen Q -pg. D-5-64
Pangelinan, Carmen R -pg. D-4-37
Pangelinan, Carment T -pg. D-2-70
Pangelinan, Catalina C -pg. D-2-44
Pangelinan, Catalina C -pg. D-5-48
Pangelinan, Concepcion L -pg. D-4-124
Pangelinan, Concepcion M -pg. D-5-11
Pangelinan, Consolacion B -pg. D-1-49
Pangelinan, Consuelo E -pg. D-1-66
Pangelinan, Cristina S -pg. D-11-21
Pangelinan, Delfin -pg. D-5-97
Pangelinan, Delfina T -pg. D-5-62
Pangelinan, Dolores C -pg. D-1-32
Pangelinan, Dolores G -pg. D-5-89
Pangelinan, Dolores Q -pg. D-5-50
Pangelinan, Doroteo L -pg. D-4-18
Pangelinan, Elena D -pg. D-1-11
Pangelinan, Elmenijildia M -pg. D-12-11
Pangelinan, Emeterio P -pg. D-4-121
Pangelinan, Emilia S -pg. D-11-21
Pangelinan, Emilio P -pg. D-5-94
Pangelinan, Enrique A -pg. D-1-30
Pangelinan, Enrique LG -pg. D-5-65
Pangelinan, Enrique P -pg. D-5-97
Pangelinan, Erotida E -pg. D-1-66
Pangelinan, Eufrasia P -pg. D-4-63
Pangelinan, Felix Q -pg. D-11-27
Pangelinan, Felix U -pg. D-13-29
Pangelinan, Francisca B -pg. D-1-49
Pangelinan, Francisca B -pg. D-12-8
Pangelinan, Francisca L -pg. D-4-18
Pangelinan, Francisca L -pg. D-4-125
Pangelinan, Francisco -pg. D-5-64
Pangelinan, Francisco B -pg. D-1-49
Pangelinan, Francisco B -pg. D-12-10
Pangelinan, Francisco C -pg. D-4-125

INDEX
1930 Population Census of Guam: Transcribed

Pangelinan, Francisco D -pg. D-4-18
Pangelinan, Francisco G -pg. D-1-24
Pangelinan, Francisco M -pg. D-5-11
Pangelinan, Francisco P -pg. D-4-121
Pangelinan, Francisco S -pg. D-11-21
Pangelinan, Francisco T -pg. D-9-4
Pangelinan, Guido B -pg. D-2-44
Pangelinan, Henry C -pg. D-1-32
Pangelinan, Henry S -pg. D-1-32
Pangelinan, Ignacia G -pg. D-1-24
Pangelinan, Ignacia R -pg. D-4-37
Pangelinan, Ignacio -pg. D-3-57
Pangelinan, Ignacio D -pg. D-3-39
Pangelinan, Ignacio R -pg. D-2-63
Pangelinan, Irene R -pg. D-4-102
Pangelinan, Isabel C -pg. D-5-49
Pangelinan, Jesus -pg. D-5-64
Pangelinan, Jesus C -pg. D-5-49
Pangelinan, Jesus G -pg. D-4-63
Pangelinan, Jesus L -pg. D-4-125
Pangelinan, Jesus Q -pg. D-12-21
Pangelinan, Jesus R -pg. D-4-29
Pangelinan, Jesus R -pg. D-4-37
Pangelinan, Jesus S -pg. D-5-64
Pangelinan, Jesus T -pg. D-5-62
Pangelinan, Jesusa C -pg. D-4-29
Pangelinan, Jesusa P -pg. D-4-63
Pangelinan, Jesusa S -pg. D-4-47
Pangelinan, Joaquin -pg. D-3-17
Pangelinan, Joaquin -pg. D-3-39
Pangelinan, Joaquin A -pg. D-7-24
Pangelinan, Joaquin B -pg. D-1-49
Pangelinan, Joaquin B -pg. D-2-55
Pangelinan, Joaquin B -pg. D-5-7
Pangelinan, Joaquin C -pg. D-4-96
Pangelinan, Joaquin P -pg. D-3-17
Pangelinan, Joaquin P -pg. D-4-63
Pangelinan, Joaquin T -pg. D-2-40
Pangelinan, Joaquina R -pg. D-1-45
Pangelinan, Jose -pg. D-3-39
Pangelinan, Jose -pg. D-3-57
Pangelinan, Jose -pg. D-5-64
Pangelinan, Jose A -pg. D-3-7
Pangelinan, Jose B -pg. D-1-49
Pangelinan, Jose B -pg. D-2-55
Pangelinan, Jose B -pg. D-5-7
Pangelinan, Jose B -pg. D-5-52
Pangelinan, Jose B -pg. D-12-10
Pangelinan, Jose C -pg. D-1-49
Pangelinan, Jose C -pg. D-4-36
Pangelinan, Jose C -pg. D-4-124
Pangelinan, Jose C -pg. D-5-48
Pangelinan, Jose C -pg. D-11-33
Pangelinan, Jose C -pg. D-12-12
Pangelinan, Jose De Leon -pg. D-5-50
Pangelinan, Jose G -pg. D-1-30
Pangelinan, Jose G -pg. D-5-96
Pangelinan, Jose I -pg. D-5-49
Pangelinan, Jose I -pg. D-5-64

Pangelinan, Jose M -pg. D-4-36
Pangelinan, Jose M -pg. D-5-4
Pangelinan, Jose M -pg. D-12-11
Pangelinan, Jose O -pg. D-12-8
Pangelinan, Jose R -pg. D-1-44
Pangelinan, Jose S -pg. D-11-21
Pangelinan, Jose T -pg. D-5-62
Pangelinan, Jose U -pg. D-5-62
Pangelinan, Josefa -pg. D-5-97
Pangelinan, Josefa B -pg. D-2-55
Pangelinan, Josefa C -pg. D-4-125
Pangelinan, Josefa C -pg. D-5-48
Pangelinan, Josefa Q -pg. D-5-6
Pangelinan, Juan -pg. D-5-94
Pangelinan, Juan -pg. D-13-24
Pangelinan, Juan A -pg. D-3-7
Pangelinan, Juan B -pg. D-12-8
Pangelinan, Juan B -pg. D-12-9
Pangelinan, Juan L -pg. D-4-18
Pangelinan, Juan M -pg. D-4-36
Pangelinan, Juan M -pg. D-4-36
Pangelinan, Juan M -pg. D-5-11
Pangelinan, Juan P -pg. D-4-90
Pangelinan, Juan Q -pg. D-5-50
Pangelinan, Juan S -pg. D-4-47
Pangelinan, Juan S -pg. D-5-52
Pangelinan, Juan SN -pg. D-5-11
Pangelinan, Juana B -pg. D-5-6
Pangelinan, Juana R -pg. D-1-44
Pangelinan, Julia M -pg. D-4-36
Pangelinan, Juliana G -pg. D-5-89
Pangelinan, Laura S -pg. D-11-21
Pangelinan, Lino T -pg. D-4-96
Pangelinan, Lorenzo L -pg. D-4-124
Pangelinan, Luis P -pg. D-11-33
Pangelinan, Luisa C -pg. D-3-4
Pangelinan, Luisa L -pg. D-4-125
Pangelinan, Magdalena -pg. D-3-17
Pangelinan, Magdalena -pg. D-3-39
Pangelinan, Magdalena B -pg. D-2-55
Pangelinan, Magdalena C -pg. D-5-49
Pangelinan, Manuel B -pg. D-1-10
Pangelinan, Manuel P -pg. D-3-19
Pangelinan, Manuel P -pg. D-5-56
Pangelinan, Manuel R -pg. D-5-49
Pangelinan, Manuela B -pg. D-5-52
Pangelinan, Margarita A -pg. D-1-30
Pangelinan, Margarita M -pg. D-4-36
Pangelinan, Maria -pg. D-3-17
Pangelinan, Maria -pg. D-3-39
Pangelinan, Maria -pg. D-3-57
Pangelinan, Maria -pg. D-5-94
Pangelinan, Maria A -pg. D-1-30
Pangelinan, Maria A -pg. D-5-94
Pangelinan, Maria B -pg. D-5-6
Pangelinan, Maria B -pg. D-6-39
Pangelinan, Maria B -pg. D-12-10
Pangelinan, Maria B -pg. D-12-20
Pangelinan, Maria C -pg. D-4-122

Pangelinan, Maria C -pg. D-4-123
Pangelinan, Maria C -pg. D-5-48
Pangelinan, Maria C -pg. D-5-56
Pangelinan, Maria C -pg. D-5-96
Pangelinan, Maria D -pg. D-4-125
Pangelinan, Maria G -pg. D-4-63
Pangelinan, Maria G -pg. D-5-96
Pangelinan, Maria L -pg. D-4-18
Pangelinan, Maria M -pg. D-5-11
Pangelinan, Maria P -pg. D-4-63
Pangelinan, Maria P -pg. D-4-121
Pangelinan, Maria P -pg. D-5-5
Pangelinan, Maria R -pg. D-2-63
Pangelinan, Maria S -pg. D-1-33
Pangelinan, Maria S -pg. D-11-21
Pangelinan, Maria T -pg. D-4-96
Pangelinan, Maria T -pg. D-4-123
Pangelinan, Maria T -pg. D-5-62
Pangelinan, Maria T -pg. D-9-3
Pangelinan, Maria U -pg. D-2-40
Pangelinan, Matias M -pg. D-5-6
Pangelinan, Matilde -pg. D-3-17
Pangelinan, Natividad L -pg. D-4-18
Pangelinan, Nicolas B -pg. D-1-49
Pangelinan, Nicolas P -pg. D-4-63
Pangelinan, Nicolasa A -pg. D-1-7
Pangelinan, Nieves C -pg. D-12-10
Pangelinan, Nieves LG -pg. D-5-65
Pangelinan, Pedro A -pg. D-1-30
Pangelinan, Pedro B -pg. D-12-10
Pangelinan, Pedro C -pg. D-12-9
Pangelinan, Pedro I -pg. D-5-49
Pangelinan, Pedro M -pg. D-5-11
Pangelinan, Pedro P -pg. D-4-63
Pangelinan, Pedro R -pg. D-12-10
Pangelinan, Pedro S -pg. D-11-27
Pangelinan, Perpetua S -pg. D-4-47
Pangelinan, Pricilia E -pg. D-1-66
Pangelinan, Regina M -pg. D-5-51
Pangelinan, Regina T -pg. D-5-62
Pangelinan, Rita -pg. D-3-39
Pangelinan, Rita A -pg. D-2-70
Pangelinan, Rita C -pg. D-4-29
Pangelinan, Rita L -pg. D-4-124
Pangelinan, Rosa C -pg. D-5-48
Pangelinan, Rosa LG -pg. D-5-64
Pangelinan, Rosa M -pg. D-4-36
Pangelinan, Rosa R -pg. D-4-102
Pangelinan, Rosalia -pg. D-3-17
Pangelinan, Rosalia I -pg. D-5-49
Pangelinan, Rosalia L -pg. D-4-125
Pangelinan, Rosalia P -pg. D-4-63
Pangelinan, Rosario -pg. D-5-96
Pangelinan, Rosario L -pg. D-4-125
Pangelinan, Rufina C -pg. D-11-33
Pangelinan, Rufina G -pg. D-5-96
Pangelinan, Salvador L -pg. D-4-18
Pangelinan, Serafina L -pg. D-4-18
Pangelinan, Serafina S -pg. D-11-21

Pangelinan, Silvino D -pg. D-5-5
Pangelinan, Tomas -pg. D-3-17
Pangelinan, Tomas M -pg. D-13-31
Pangelinan, Tomas P -pg. D-4-47
Pangelinan, Tomas S -pg. D-4-47
Pangelinan, Valentino E -pg. D-1-66
Pangelinan, Valeria L -pg. D-4-124
Pangelinan, Veronica B -pg. D-12-8
Pangelinan, Vicente -pg. D-3-39
Pangelinan, Vicente -pg. D-5-96
Pangelinan, Vicente A -pg. D-1-30
Pangelinan, Vicente B -pg. D-12-10
Pangelinan, Vicente De Leon -pg. D-5-52
Pangelinan, Vicente G -pg. D-5-89
Pangelinan, Vicente M -pg. D-4-36
Pangelinan, Vicente P -pg. D-5-89
Pangelinan, Vicente Q -pg. D-5-48
Pangelinan, Vicente R -pg. D-2-63
Pangelinan, Vicente S -pg. D-5-51
Pangelinan, Vicente T -pg. D-1-24
Pangelinan, Vicente T -pg. D-5-77
Pangelinan, Vicente U -pg. D-2-48
Pangilinan, Ana F -pg. D-12-15
Pangilinan, Carlos F -pg. D-12-15
Pangilinan, Francisco F -pg. D-12-15
Pangilinan, Jesus R -pg. D-12-17
Pangilinan, Jose C -pg. D-12-15
Pangilinan, Magdalena F -pg. D-12-15
Pangilinan, Maria F -pg. D-12-15
Parish, Paul I -pg. D-13-42
Parker, Chester D -pg. D-13-26
Parker, Dorothy C -pg. D-4-19
Parker, Edith M -pg. D-4-19
Parker, Herbert N -pg. D-13-41
Parker, Joan I -pg. D-4-19
Parker, Nance -pg. D-4-19
Parker, Patricia A -pg. D-4-19
Parrott, George C -pg. D-13-17
Pasich, Steven -pg. D-13-24
Patnade, Frederick O -pg. D-13-13
Patterson, Milan H -pg. D-13-13
Patton, Diamond -pg. D-13-13
Paulino, Alejandro LG -pg. D-8-4
Paulino, Ana L -pg. D-8-20
Paulino, Ana LG -pg. D-8-5
Paulino, Ana M -pg. D-8-35
Paulino, Ana N -pg. D-8-32
Paulino, Ana R -pg. D-1-42
Paulino, Ana SN -pg. D-8-3
Paulino, Angela L -pg. D-8-10
Paulino, Augusto C -pg. D-8-9
Paulino, Bernabe C -pg. D-1-54
Paulino, Bernabe R -pg. D-1-42
Paulino, Carmen D -pg. D-8-14
Paulino, Carmen L -pg. D-8-20
Paulino, Carmen N -pg. D-8-32
Paulino, Carmen SN -pg. D-8-2
Paulino, Cleto C -pg. D-8-11
Paulino, Concepcion L -pg. D-8-10

Paulino, Concepcion T -pg. D-8-2
Paulino, Cristobal R -pg. D-1-42
Paulino, Damiana C -pg. D-8-30
Paulino, Dolores -pg. D-8-32
Paulino, Felomena T -pg. D-8-2
Paulino, Francisco D -pg. D-8-30
Paulino, Francisco LG -pg. D-8-4
Paulino, Francisco SN -pg. D-8-3
Paulino, Ines L -pg. D-8-10
Paulino, Jesus D -pg. D-8-20
Paulino, Jesus LG -pg. D-8-4
Paulino, Jesus M -pg. D-8-24
Paulino, Joaquin L -pg. D-8-20
Paulino, Joaquina T -pg. D-8-2
Paulino, Jose A -pg. D-8-2
Paulino, Jose C -pg. D-8-35
Paulino, Jose LG -pg. D-8-4
Paulino, Jose SN -pg. D-8-2
Paulino, Josefa D -pg. D-8-30
Paulino, Josefina SN -pg. D-8-2
Paulino, Juan C -pg. D-8-24
Paulino, Juan F -pg. D-8-2
Paulino, Juan L -pg. D-8-10
Paulino, Juan M -pg. D-8-24
Paulino, Juan N -pg. D-8-10
Paulino, Julia LG -pg. D-8-11
Paulino, Juliana D -pg. D-8-20
Paulino, Leocadio C -pg. D-8-4
Paulino, Leonardo SN -pg. D-8-3
Paulino, Lourdes P -pg. D-8-10
Paulino, Manuel A -pg. D-8-2
Paulino, Manuel C -pg. D-8-9
Paulino, Manuel LG -pg. D-8-11
Paulino, Manuel T -pg. D-8-2
Paulino, Manuel T -pg. D-8-9
Paulino, Margarita L -pg. D-8-10
Paulino, Margarita LG -pg. D-8-11
Paulino, Maria C -pg. D-8-9
Paulino, Maria LG -pg. D-8-4
Paulino, Maria LG -pg. D-8-11
Paulino, Maria Q -pg. D-8-35
Paulino, Maria R -pg. D-1-42
Paulino, Maria SN -pg. D-8-2
Paulino, Maria SN -pg. D-8-2
Paulino, Maria SN -pg. D-8-2
Paulino, Mariano T -pg. D-8-2
Paulino, Nicolas C -pg. D-8-30
Paulino, Nicolas D -pg. D-8-30
Paulino, Pedro LG -pg. D-8-11
Paulino, Ramon T -pg. D-8-2
Paulino, Regina M -pg. D-8-35
Paulino, Rosa M -pg. D-8-24
Paulino, Rosalia SN -pg. D-8-2
Paulino, Santiago N -pg. D-8-20
Paulino, Teresa D -pg. D-8-30
Paulino, Tomas M -pg. D-8-24
Paulino, Tomas SN -pg. D-8-3
Paulino, Trinidad R -pg. D-1-42
Paulino, Trinidad SN -pg. D-8-2

Paulino, Vicente D -pg. D-8-30
Paulino, Vicente LG -pg. D-8-11
Paulino, Vicente N -pg. D-8-32
Paulino, Vicente T -pg. D-8-3
Payne, Dolores S -pg. D-2-78
Payne, Ignacia S -pg. D-2-78
Payne, Joseph S -pg. D-2-78
Payne, Patrick A -pg. D-2-78
Payne, Rosa S -pg. D-2-78
Payne, Tomas S -pg. D-2-78
Peacock, John F -pg. D-13-38
Pearson, James C W -pg. D-13-40
Peeples, Monroe T -pg. D-13-8
Pelas, Leon -pg. D-13-24
Pellecani, Ana R -pg. D-4-92
Pellecani, Rafael R -pg. D-4-92
Pellecani, Romulo R -pg. D-4-92
Penrose, Joseph R -pg. D-13-45
Peraira, Bernadita C -pg. D-4-111
Peraira, Genoveva P -pg. D-4-111
Peraira, Ignacio C -pg. D-4-111
Peraira, Jesus C -pg. D-4-111
Peraira, Juan C -pg. D-4-124
Peraira, Juana P -pg. D-4-124
Peraira, Manuel S -pg. D-4-111
Peraira, Maria P -pg. D-4-124
Peraira, Rita C -pg. D-4-111
Pereda, Ana C -pg. D-5-9
Pereda, Ana P -pg. D-4-65
Pereda, Antonia F -pg. D-5-55
Pereda, Antonio P -pg. D-4-65
Pereda, Antonio S -pg. D-1-36
Pereda, Asuncion P -pg. D-4-65
Pereda, Asuncion P -pg. D-4-65
Pereda, Catalina C -pg. D-5-9
Pereda, Concepcion LG -pg. D-1-36
Pereda, Cristina F -pg. D-5-55
Pereda, Diana F -pg. D-5-55
Pereda, Felicita C -pg. D-5-9
Pereda, Fidela C -pg. D-4-71
Pereda, Francisco C -pg. D-4-71
Pereda, Gertrudes C -pg. D-5-9
Pereda, Grabiel P -pg. D-5-9
Pereda, Ignacio F -pg. D-5-55
Pereda, Ignacio P -pg. D-4-65
Pereda, Isabel P -pg. D-4-65
Pereda, Jesus P -pg. D-4-65
Pereda, Jesus S -pg. D-4-65
Pereda, Joaquin LG -pg. D-1-36
Pereda, Jose B -pg. D-5-7
Pereda, Jose B -pg. D-5-54
Pereda, Jose P -pg. D-4-65
Pereda, Josefa B -pg. D-5-7
Pereda, Josefa B -pg. D-5-7
Pereda, Juan C -pg. D-4-71
Pereda, Juan C -pg. D-5-9
Pereda, Juan LG -pg. D-1-36
Pereda, Juan P -pg. D-4-65
Pereda, Juan P -pg. D-4-65

Pereda, Juan S -pg. D-5-7
Pereda, Luisa LG -pg. D-1-36
Pereda, Manuel P -pg. D-4-65
Pereda, Margarita C -pg. D-3-26
Pereda, Margarita C -pg. D-4-71
Pereda, Maria LG -pg. D-1-36
Pereda, Maria P -pg. D-4-65
Pereda, Maria P -pg. D-4-65
Pereda, Maria P -pg. D-4-65
Pereda, Natividad C -pg. D-4-71
Pereda, Pedro C -pg. D-5-9
Pereda, Rosa C -pg. D-4-71
Pereda, Rosa C -pg. D-4-71
Pereda, Rosa C -pg. D-5-9
Pereda, Rosa C -pg. D-5-9
Pereda, Vicente P -pg. D-4-65
Pereda, Vicente S -pg. D-4-65
Peredo, Ana B -pg. D-12-10
Peredo, Ana C -pg. D-3-50
Peredo, Ana T -pg. D-2-34
Peredo, Antonia -pg. D-3-54
Peredo, Antonia G -pg. D-2-56
Peredo, Antonio -pg. D-3-50
Peredo, Baldomero T -pg. D-2-34
Peredo, Beatrice P -pg. D-2-34
Peredo, Camilo J -pg. D-12-10
Peredo, Carmen -pg. D-3-50
Peredo, Dominga T -pg. D-2-34
Peredo, Emilia -pg. D-3-54
Peredo, Enrique -pg. D-3-54
Peredo, Fernando -pg. D-3-54
Peredo, Francisco B -pg. D-12-10
Peredo, Francisco P -pg. D-5-73
Peredo, Genoveva -pg. D-3-54
Peredo, Ignacio M -pg. D-3-75
Peredo, Joaquin B -pg. D-12-10
Peredo, Joaquin G -pg. D-2-56
Peredo, Joaquina -pg. D-3-50
Peredo, Jose C -pg. D-3-54
Peredo, Jose T -pg. D-2-34
Peredo, Juan B -pg. D-12-10
Peredo, Margarita -pg. D-3-54
Peredo, Maria -pg. D-3-50
Peredo, Mercedes -pg. D-3-50
Peredo, Nicomedes C -pg. D-8-24
Peredo, Pedro -pg. D-3-50
Peredo, Pedro B -pg. D-12-10
Peredo, Remedios -pg. D-3-50
Pereira, Amalia D -pg. D-5-15
Pereira, Dolores D -pg. D-5-15
Pereira, Ignacio D -pg. D-5-15
Pereira, Jose D -pg. D-5-15
Pereira, Lucia D -pg. D-5-15
Pereira, Ramon C -pg. D-5-15
Perez, Albert -pg. D-5-91
Perez, Alejandra SA -pg. D-5-41
Perez, Alejandro B -pg. D-11-9
Perez, Alfreda C -pg. D-2-7
Perez, Amanda L -pg. D-4-62

Perez, Amelia -pg. D-3-35
Perez, Ana -pg. D-3-23
Perez, Ana A -pg. D-4-15
Perez, Ana B -pg. D-2-79
Perez, Ana B -pg. D-5-77
Perez, Ana B -pg. D-11-28
Perez, Ana C -pg. D-2-69
Perez, Ana C -pg. D-2-69
Perez, Ana C -pg. D-11-11
Perez, Ana LG -pg. D-3-36
Perez, Ana M -pg. D-3-22
Perez, Ana M -pg. D-11-26
Perez, Ana M -pg. D-11-29
Perez, Ana P -pg. D-11-9
Perez, Ana S -pg. D-2-37
Perez, Ana S -pg. D-10-20
Perez, Ana T -pg. D-5-53
Perez, Ana T -pg. D-5-54
Perez, Angel -pg. D-4-58
Perez, Antonia C -pg. D-2-16
Perez, Antonia M -pg. D-11-26
Perez, Antonia S -pg. D-2-16
Perez, Antonia SA -pg. D-5-41
Perez, Antonio -pg. D-3-23
Perez, Antonio -pg. D-3-35
Perez, Antonio -pg. D-3-36
Perez, Antonio -pg. D-11-19
Perez, Antonio -pg. D-11-28
Perez, Antonio B -pg. D-4-78
Perez, Antonio C -pg. D-11-26
Perez, Antonio D -pg. D-1-14
Perez, Antonio D -pg. D-11-22
Perez, Antonio F -pg. D-2-75
Perez, Antonio F -pg. D-5-8
Perez, Antonio LG -pg. D-3-35
Perez, Antonio N -pg. D-11-28
Perez, Antonio P -pg. D-2-79
Perez, Antonio R -pg. D-13-35
Perez, Antonio S -pg. D-2-83
Perez, Asuncion C -pg. D-2-69
Perez, Asuncion SN -pg. D-11-19
Perez, Atanasio T -pg. D-1-20
Perez, Bacilia C -pg. D-10-8
Perez, Beatrice T -pg. D-1-20
Perez, Beatriz S -pg. D-10-20
Perez, Benancio C -pg. D-2-7
Perez, Bernadita P -pg. D-5-58
Perez, Brigida T -pg. D-1-20
Perez, Candaleria B -pg. D-2-79
Perez, Candelario S D -pg. D-1-14
Perez, Carmen D -pg. D-1-20
Perez, Carmen L -pg. D-5-69
Perez, Carmen P -pg. D-5-8
Perez, Catalina B -pg. D-12-9
Perez, Cecilia -pg. D-3-35
Perez, Celia D -pg. D-1-14
Perez, Cesario B -pg. D-4-75
Perez, Clotilde -pg. D-3-35
Perez, Clotilde -pg. D-5-83

Perez, Clotilde T -pg. D-5-54
Perez, Concepcion -pg. D-3-14
Perez, Concepcion -pg. D-3-35
Perez, Concepcion -pg. D-5-69
Perez, Concepcion A -pg. D-4-7
Perez, Concepcion B -pg. D-2-79
Perez, Concepcion C -pg. D-11-41
Perez, Concepcion D -pg. D-1-14
Perez, Concepcion P -pg. D-4-105
Perez, Concepcion P -pg. D-5-8
Perez, Concepcion S -pg. D-1-11
Perez, Conelio E -pg. D-1-31
Perez, Daniel L -pg. D-1-49
Perez, Daniel T -pg. D-1-21
Perez, David T -pg. D-1-20
Perez, Delfina -pg. D-3-23
Perez, Delgadina -pg. D-3-22
Perez, Delores -pg. D-3-35
Perez, Dolores A -pg. D-2-7
Perez, Dolores C -pg. D-11-11
Perez, Dolores F -pg. D-1-14
Perez, Dolores L -pg. D-4-62
Perez, Dolores P -pg. D-5-58
Perez, Donna S -pg. D-10-20
Perez, Dorotea -pg. D-3-35
Perez, Dorothea C -pg. D-1-49
Perez, Dorothy P -pg. D-11-21
Perez, Eduardo C -pg. D-2-7
Perez, Edward -pg. D-5-91
Perez, Eliza -pg. D-3-14
Perez, Elizabeth P -pg. D-4-126
Perez, Elizabeth P -pg. D-11-22
Perez, Eloy L -pg. D-11-41
Perez, Emaculada A -pg. D-4-15
Perez, Emelia T -pg. D-5-54
Perez, Emiia S -pg. D-3-3
Perez, Emilia -pg. D-3-34
Perez, Emilia -pg. D-5-69
Perez, Emiliana -pg. D-3-25
Perez, Emiliana F -pg. D-1-14
Perez, Emiliana R -pg. D-4-101
Perez, Encarnacion C -pg. D-10-8
Perez, Engracia -pg. D-3-22
Perez, Enriqueta G -pg. D-1-16
Perez, Ernesto -pg. D-3-35
Perez, Eulogia C -pg. D-1-49
Perez, Evelyn P -pg. D-11-22
Perez, Felicita T -pg. D-5-54
Perez, Felipe C -pg. D-2-69
Perez, Felipe C -pg. D-4-58
Perez, Felisa S -pg. D-3-51
Perez, Felix I -pg. D-3-35
Perez, Francisca -pg. D-3-35
Perez, Francisca D -pg. D-4-44
Perez, Francisco -pg. D-3-22
Perez, Francisco A -pg. D-4-15
Perez, Francisco D -pg. D-2-14
Perez, Francisco F -pg. D-1-14
Perez, Francisco L -pg. D-11-41

Perez, Francisco LG -pg. D-4-92
Perez, Francisco M -pg. D-3-24
Perez, Francisco P -pg. D-5-63
Perez, Francisco T -pg. D-5-54
Perez, Frank -pg. D-3-58
Perez, Frank SA -pg. D-2-70
Perez, Galo M -pg. D-11-26
Perez, Gerado C -pg. D-1-49
Perez, Gloria -pg. D-3-23
Perez, Gracia A -pg. D-2-75
Perez, Gregorio -pg. D-3-14
Perez, Gregorio -pg. D-3-36
Perez, Gregorio -pg. D-5-91
Perez, Gregorio B -pg. D-11-9
Perez, Gregorio D -pg. D-1-14
Perez, Gregorio D -pg. D-1-16
Perez, Gregorio F -pg. D-5-91
Perez, Gregorio G -pg. D-1-16
Perez, Gregorio G -pg. D-5-41
Perez, Gregorio M -pg. D-11-26
Perez, Gregorio M -pg. D-11-29
Perez, Gregorio S -pg. D-2-83
Perez, Gregorio T -pg. D-2-27
Perez, Gregorio T -pg. D-5-54
Perez, Helena D -pg. D-1-14
Perez, Honoria -pg. D-3-24
Perez, Ignacia C -pg. D-11-16
Perez, Ignacia Q -pg. D-2-71
Perez, Ignacio -pg. D-3-22
Perez, Ignacio -pg. D-5-69
Perez, Ignacio C -pg. D-2-69
Perez, Ignacio M -pg. D-11-29
Perez, Ingracia B -pg. D-4-78
Perez, Isabel -pg. D-3-35
Perez, Isabel T -pg. D-1-20
Perez, Ismael C -pg. D-4-71
Perez, Jesus -pg. D-3-23
Perez, Jesus -pg. D-3-24
Perez, Jesus -pg. D-3-35
Perez, Jesus -pg. D-5-83
Perez, Jesus B -pg. D-4-78
Perez, Jesus C -pg. D-2-14
Perez, Jesus C -pg. D-2-37
Perez, Jesus C -pg. D-11-11
Perez, Jesus F -pg. D-2-13
Perez, Jesus F -pg. D-10-36
Perez, Jesus F -pg. D-13-32
Perez, Jesus M -pg. D-2-67
Perez, Jesus M -pg. D-13-31
Perez, Jesus P -pg. D-2-82
Perez, Jesus S -pg. D-1-14
Perez, Jesus S -pg. D-2-37
Perez, Jesus S -pg. D-2-83
Perez, Jesus S -pg. D-3-3
Perez, Jesus S -pg. D-10-20
Perez, Jesus T -pg. D-5-54
Perez, Joaquin -pg. D-3-24
Perez, Joaquin A -pg. D-4-15
Perez, Joaquin C -pg. D-2-7

Perez, Joaquin C -pg. D-3-22
Perez, Joaquin C -pg. D-3-51
Perez, Joaquin C -pg. D-4-71
Perez, Joaquin D -pg. D-11-21
Perez, Joaquin F -pg. D-1-14
Perez, Joaquin F -pg. D-2-27
Perez, Joaquin S -pg. D-4-78
Perez, Joaquina -pg. D-3-34
Perez, John -pg. D-3-58
Perez, Jose -pg. D-3-14
Perez, Jose -pg. D-3-35
Perez, Jose -pg. D-5-69
Perez, Jose -pg. D-5-91
Perez, Jose -pg. D-11-41
Perez, Jose A -pg. D-13-27
Perez, Jose B -pg. D-2-70
Perez, Jose C -pg. D-2-14
Perez, Jose C -pg. D-2-69
Perez, Jose C -pg. D-4-71
Perez, Jose F -pg. D-1-14
Perez, Jose F -pg. D-4-62
Perez, Jose G -pg. D-5-83
Perez, Jose L -pg. D-11-41
Perez, Jose LG -pg. D-3-35
Perez, Jose M -pg. D-1-14
Perez, Jose M -pg. D-2-71
Perez, Jose M -pg. D-11-29
Perez, Jose P -pg. D-2-67
Perez, Jose P -pg. D-2-82
Perez, Jose P -pg. D-5-8
Perez, Jose R -pg. D-4-101
Perez, Jose R -pg. D-13-29
Perez, Jose S -pg. D-3-14
Perez, Jose S -pg. D-3-52
Perez, Jose S -pg. D-13-27
Perez, Jose SA -pg. D-5-41
Perez, Jose T -pg. D-2-27
Perez, Jose T -pg. D-5-54
Perez, Jose T -pg. D-9-10
Perez, Jose S D -pg. D-1-14
Perez, Josefa -pg. D-3-35
Perez, Josefa A -pg. D-3-58
Perez, Josefa C -pg. D-2-7
Perez, Josefa C -pg. D-2-14
Perez, Josefa C -pg. D-2-19
Perez, Josefa G -pg. D-5-83
Perez, Josefa P -pg. D-2-7
Perez, Josefa S -pg. D-2-83
Perez, Josefa SA -pg. D-5-41
Perez, Josefina -pg. D-3-14
Perez, Josefina -pg. D-3-35
Perez, Josefina C -pg. D-2-7
Perez, Joseph P -pg. D-11-22
Perez, Juan -pg. D-3-14
Perez, Juan -pg. D-3-25
Perez, Juan -pg. D-5-69
Perez, Juan -pg. D-5-91
Perez, Juan -pg. D-10-8
Perez, Juan C -pg. D-4-71

Perez, Juan C -pg. D-5-69
Perez, Juan C -pg. D-11-29
Perez, Juan D -pg. D-1-14
Perez, Juan D -pg. D-2-75
Perez, Juan D -pg. D-4-91
Perez, Juan F -pg. D-1-14
Perez, Juan LG -pg. D-2-7
Perez, Juan M -pg. D-11-29
Perez, Juan N -pg. D-11-28
Perez, Juan P -pg. D-2-82
Perez, Juan P -pg. D-5-3
Perez, Juan Q -pg. D-13-29
Perez, Juan R -pg. D-4-101
Perez, Juan S -pg. D-10-20
Perez, Juan T -pg. D-5-54
Perez, Juan T -pg. D-13-29
Perez, Juana B -pg. D-4-78
Perez, Julia A -pg. D-4-15
Perez, Juliana F -pg. D-3-5
Perez, Laura S -pg. D-2-37
Perez, Lourdes -pg. D-3-25
Perez, Luis C -pg. D-2-82
Perez, Luis S -pg. D-2-83
Perez, Magdalena -pg. D-3-23
Perez, Magdalena C -pg. D-2-81
Perez, Maira -pg. D-5-91
Perez, Manuel -pg. D-3-14
Perez, Manuel -pg. D-3-35
Perez, Manuel -pg. D-4-58
Perez, Manuel A -pg. D-4-15
Perez, Manuel B -pg. D-2-67
Perez, Manuel F -pg. D-5-53
Perez, Manuel T -pg. D-5-2
Perez, Manuel T -pg. D-5-54
Perez, Manuela C -pg. D-4-70
Perez, Margarita D -pg. D-2-13
Perez, Margarita S -pg. D-2-83
Perez, Maria -pg. D-3-14
Perez, Maria -pg. D-3-24
Perez, Maria -pg. D-3-35
Perez, Maria -pg. D-3-58
Perez, Maria -pg. D-5-69
Perez, Maria A -pg. D-4-15
Perez, Maria A -pg. D-5-83
Perez, Maria C -pg. D-1-49
Perez, Maria C -pg. D-2-7
Perez, Maria C -pg. D-3-5
Perez, Maria C -pg. D-4-71
Perez, Maria C -pg. D-10-20
Perez, Maria C -pg. D-11-16
Perez, Maria C -pg. D-11-28
Perez, Maria C -pg. D-11-48
Perez, Maria D -pg. D-2-13
Perez, Maria F -pg. D-1-14
Perez, Maria G -pg. D-1-16
Perez, Maria L -pg. D-4-62
Perez, Maria L -pg. D-11-41
Perez, Maria P -pg. D-2-82
Perez, Maria P -pg. D-4-126

Perez, Maria P -pg. D-5-8
Perez, Maria Q -pg. D-2-71
Perez, Maria Q -pg. D-2-71
Perez, Maria S -pg. D-2-37
Perez, Maria S -pg. D-2-37
Perez, Maria S -pg. D-10-20
Perez, Maria T -pg. D-1-20
Perez, Maria T -pg. D-2-27
Perez, Maria T -pg. D-5-54
Perez, Maria C. T -pg. D-2-27
Perez, Mariano C -pg. D-3-39
Perez, Mariano C -pg. D-11-19
Perez, Mariano T -pg. D-2-16
Perez, Matias LG -pg. D-2-7
Perez, Maxima B -pg. D-2-79
Perez, Mergilda M -pg. D-2-67
Perez, Nicolasa P -pg. D-3-35
Perez, Nieves L -pg. D-4-57
Perez, Norberto P -pg. D-4-126
Perez, Oligario C -pg. D-4-64
Perez, Oliva -pg. D-3-25
Perez, Oliva B -pg. D-4-78
Perez, Patricia SN -pg. D-11-19
Perez, Pedro -pg. D-3-23
Perez, Pedro -pg. D-3-35
Perez, Pedro C -pg. D-5-58
Perez, Pedro M -pg. D-11-29
Perez, Pedro A -pg. D-4-15
Perez, Pedro LG -pg. D-4-15
Perez, Pilar P -pg. D-5-8
Perez, Pilar S D -pg. D-1-14
Perez, Ramona P -pg. D-5-8
Perez, Remedio C -pg. D-2-7
Perez, Remedio D -pg. D-1-14
Perez, Remedius B -pg. D-11-9
Perez, Remedios LG -pg. D-4-92
Perez, Rita B -pg. D-2-67
Perez, Rita B -pg. D-2-79
Perez, Rita D -pg. D-3-14
Perez, Rita F -pg. D-10-36
Perez, Rita S -pg. D-2-37
Perez, Rita S -pg. D-10-20
Perez, Rosa -pg. D-3-52
Perez, Rosa -pg. D-5-91
Perez, Rosa A -pg. D-4-15
Perez, Rosa C -pg. D-1-49
Perez, Rosa C -pg. D-2-14
Perez, Rosa I -pg. D-3-34
Perez, Rosa L -pg. D-11-41
Perez, Rosa M -pg. D-11-29
Perez, Rosa Q -pg. D-2-71
Perez, Rosa R -pg. D-4-101
Perez, Rosa T -pg. D-2-27
Perez, Rosalia C -pg. D-3-24
Perez, Rosalia SN -pg. D-11-19
Perez, Rosalina C -pg. D-4-71
Perez, Rosalina I -pg. D-4-104
Perez, Rosario -pg. D-5-91
Perez, Rosario A -pg. D-4-7

Perez, Rosario A -pg. D-4-15
Perez, Rosario C -pg. D-2-69
Perez, Rosario C -pg. D-11-41
Perez, Rosario E -pg. D-5-91
Perez, Rosario L -pg. D-4-62
Perez, Santiago SN -pg. D-11-19
Perez, Santiago T -pg. D-11-11
Perez, Segundo B -pg. D-4-78
Perez, Sergio -pg. D-5-91
Perez, Soledad R -pg. D-4-101
Perez, Stella P -pg. D-11-22
Perez, Teresita B -pg. D-4-78
Perez, Teresita LG -pg. D-4-92
Perez, Theodoro C -pg. D-1-49
Perez, Tomas -pg. D-3-35
Perez, Tomas -pg. D-5-91
Perez, Tomas S -pg. D-3-3
Perez, Tomasa -pg. D-5-91
Perez, Tomasa C -pg. D-11-8
Perez, Tomasa F -pg. D-4-76
Perez, Tomasa S -pg. D-5-63
Perez, Ursula B -pg. D-11-28
Perez, Veronica SA -pg. D-2-70
Perez, Vicente -pg. D-3-35
Perez, Vicente -pg. D-5-83
Perez, Vicente B -pg. D-2-19
Perez, Vicente B -pg. D-4-126
Perez, Vicente B -pg. D-5-77
Perez, Vicente B -pg. D-11-28
Perez, Vicente C -pg. D-1-49
Perez, Vicente C -pg. D-11-41
Perez, Vicente D -pg. D-2-75
Perez, Vicente F -pg. D-1-14
Perez, Vicente F -pg. D-2-83
Perez, Vicente G -pg. D-1-16
Perez, Vicente M -pg. D-4-101
Perez, Vicente P -pg. D-2-71
Perez, Vicente S -pg. D-2-37
Perez, Vicente S -pg. D-10-20
Perez, Vicente T -pg. D-5-54
Perez, Victor P -pg. D-11-21
Perez, Victoria -pg. D-3-23
Perez, Victoria T -pg. D-2-27
Perez, Victoria T -pg. D-9-11
Perez, Virginia B -pg. D-11-9
Perez, Virginia P -pg. D-11-21
Perez, Walter -pg. D-3-58
Perkins, Hugh E -pg. D-13-26
Perkins, Travis T -pg. D-13-24
Perrett, Glenn J -pg. D-13-40
Perry, William R -pg. D-13-13
Petalii, Anthony -pg. D-13-13
Peteria, Lester L -pg. D-13-8
Peters, Edward T -pg. D-13-8
Peterson, Annie -pg. D-3-45
Peterson, Meabel -pg. D-3-44
Peterson, Rufina C -pg. D-3-44
Peterson, William C -pg. D-13-40
Petros, Ana C -pg. D-10-10

Petros, Antonio C -pg. D-10-10
Petros, Baltazar C -pg. D-10-10
Petros, Gregorio C -pg. D-10-10
Petros, Jesus C -pg. D-10-10
Petros, Joaquin C -pg. D-10-10
Petros, Jose C -pg. D-10-10
Petros, Josefa C -pg. D-10-10
Petros, Lorenzo M -pg. D-10-10
Petros, Magdalena C -pg. D-10-10
Petros, Pedro C -pg. D-10-10
Petros, Rosa C -pg. D-10-10
Petros, Vicente C -pg. D-10-10
Petterson, Gorden P -pg. D-13-13
Phillips, Dorothy M -pg. D-4-56
Phillips, Earl -pg. D-13-44
Phillips, Edgar -pg. D-13-33
Phillips, Edward A -pg. D-4-56
Pickens, Harry A -pg. D-13-46
Pinaula, Ana -pg. D-8-12
Pinaula, Antonio C -pg. D-2-63
Pinaula, Enrique LG -pg. D-11-21
Pinaula, Feliciana C -pg. D-2-63
Pinaula, Jesus P -pg. D-9-42
Pinaula, Jose P -pg. D-6-27
Pinaula, Maria A -pg. D-8-13
Pinaula, Miguel T -pg. D-11-11
Pinaula, Natividad A -pg. D-8-12
Pinaula, Vicente A -pg. D-8-12
Pinaula, Vicente P -pg. D-9-42
Pineda, Ana LG -pg. D-6-21
Pineda, Dolores C -pg. D-6-21
Pineda, Dolores LG -pg. D-6-21
Pineda, Jose C -pg. D-6-21
Pineda, Juan LG -pg. D-6-21
Pineda, Manuel C -pg. D-6-21
Pineda, Maxine LG -pg. D-6-21
Plachta, Helen K -pg. D-13-2
Plachta, Jacob F -pg. D-13-2
Plachta, Robert A -pg. D-13-2
Ploke, John F -pg. D-13-20
Pludre, Joseph F -pg. D-13-24
Pocaigue, Ana B -pg. D-2-24
Pocaigue, Antonia B -pg. D-2-24
Pocaigue, Dolores O -pg. D-12-6
Pocaigue, Domingo P -pg. D-12-6
Pocaigue, Francisco P -pg. D-2-24
Pocaigue, Jesusa O -pg. D-12-6
Pocaigue, Jose O -pg. D-12-6
Pocaigue, Maria O -pg. D-12-6
Pocaigue, Maria P -pg. D-12-11
Pocaigue, Paz O -pg. D-12-7
Pocaigue, Pedro P -pg. D-12-11
Pocaigue, Rafael O -pg. D-12-6
Pocaigue, Rita O -pg. D-12-6
Pocaigue, Rosabela B -pg. D-2-24
Pollock, James R -pg. D-13-17
Pollock, Verl D -pg. D-13-8
Poole, David L -pg. D-13-24
Porter, Frederick E -pg. D-13-18

Portusach, Antonia M -pg. D-4-82
Portusach, Magdalena M -pg. D-4-82
Portusach, Maria M -pg. D-4-82
Powell, Meriem C Jr -pg. D-13-40
Pralt, Parnell -pg. D-13-13
Presignand, William E -pg. D-13-34
Price, Harry C -pg. D-13-17
Price, Jimmie D -pg. D-13-24
Probst, Francis A -pg. D-3-52
Probst, Maria C -pg. D-3-52
Probst, Wesley O -pg. D-3-52
Pubet, Wlesey O -pg. D-13-35
Punzalan, Antonia -pg. D-2-14
Punzalan, Antonio A -pg. D-2-14
Punzalan, Bernardo -pg. D-13-33
Punzalan, Emelia A -pg. D-2-14
Punzalan, Jose A -pg. D-2-14
Punzalan, Nieves A -pg. D-2-14
Qualls, Charles E -pg. D-13-38
Quan, Alejandro C -pg. D-11-23
Quan, Antonio C -pg. D-11-23
Quan, Concepcion C -pg. D-11-23
Quan, Delfina C -pg. D-11-23
Quan, Engracia C -pg. D-11-23
Quan, Gregorio C -pg. D-11-23
Quan, Johnny C -pg. D-11-23
Quan, Maria D -pg. D-11-23
Quan, Olin Juan -pg. D-11-23
Quan, Regina C -pg. D-11-23
Quan, Regino C -pg. D-11-23
Quan, Rosalia C -pg. D-11-23
Quenga, Agustin C -pg. D-10-7
Quenga, Ana C -pg. D-6-26
Quenga, Ana M -pg. D-10-23
Quenga, Ana S -pg. D-10-7
Quenga, Ana S -pg. D-10-31
Quenga, Ana SN -pg. D-10-29
Quenga, Angustia SN -pg. D-10-29
Quenga, Antonia C -pg. D-10-27
Quenga, Antonia M -pg. D-10-23
Quenga, Antonio -pg. D-10-13
Quenga, Antonio C -pg. D-10-29
Quenga, Barbara T -pg. D-10-28
Quenga, Barceliza S -pg. D-10-13
Quenga, Carlos SN -pg. D-10-29
Quenga, Carolina SN -pg. D-10-28
Quenga, Celestina SN -pg. D-10-29
Quenga, Cevera C -pg. D-10-28
Quenga, Consolacion C -pg. D-10-27
Quenga, Cristobal C -pg. D-10-7
Quenga, Dolores C -pg. D-10-23
Quenga, Dolores C -pg. D-10-28
Quenga, Dolores T -pg. D-10-28
Quenga, Enrique C -pg. D-10-23
Quenga, Felix C -pg. D-10-28
Quenga, Felix M -pg. D-10-23
Quenga, Francisca M -pg. D-10-23
Quenga, Francisco T -pg. D-10-23
Quenga, Isabel S -pg. D-5-50

Quenga, Isabel S -pg. D-10-13
Quenga, Jaime S -pg. D-10-31
Quenga, Jesus C -pg. D-10-28
Quenga, Jesus T -pg. D-10-32
Quenga, Joaquin -pg. D-10-27
Quenga, Joaquina SN -pg. D-10-29
Quenga, Jose C -pg. D-10-27
Quenga, Jose C -pg. D-10-32
Quenga, Jose M -pg. D-10-23
Quenga, Jose S -pg. D-10-7
Quenga, Jose SN -pg. D-10-31
Quenga, Jose T -pg. D-10-28
Quenga, Josefa C -pg. D-10-7
Quenga, Josefina C -pg. D-10-28
Quenga, Josefina S -pg. D-5-50
Quenga, Juan B -pg. D-10-7
Quenga, Juan C -pg. D-6-26
Quenga, Juan SN -pg. D-5-50
Quenga, Juana C -pg. D-10-7
Quenga, Juana G -pg. D-10-27
Quenga, Justo S -pg. D-10-31
Quenga, Lorenzo T -pg. D-10-28
Quenga, Lourdes SN -pg. D-10-29
Quenga, Magdalena B -pg. D-10-27
Quenga, Magdalena H -pg. D-10-23
Quenga, Magdalena S -pg. D-10-7
Quenga, Manuel C -pg. D-10-23
Quenga, Manuel SN -pg. D-10-28
Quenga, Manuel SN -pg. D-10-29
Quenga, Manuel T -pg. D-10-28
Quenga, Maria B -pg. D-10-27
Quenga, Maria M -pg. D-10-23
Quenga, Maria S -pg. D-10-7
Quenga, Maria S -pg. D-10-13
Quenga, Maria SN -pg. D-10-29
Quenga, Maria SN -pg. D-10-29
Quenga, Maria T -pg. D-10-28
Quenga, Maria T -pg. D-10-28
Quenga, Matilde M -pg. D-10-23
Quenga, Matilde S -pg. D-10-32
Quenga, Mercedes H -pg. D-10-23
Quenga, Milagro SN -pg. D-10-28
Quenga, Natividad SN -pg. D-10-29
Quenga, Pedro B -pg. D-10-27
Quenga, Pilar C -pg. D-10-7
Quenga, Regina T -pg. D-10-32
Quenga, Rosalia C -pg. D-10-28
Quenga, Rufina C -pg. D-10-23
Quenga, Sebastian C -pg. D-10-28
Quenga, Silvino T -pg. D-10-28
Quenga, Soledad C -pg. D-10-23
Quenga, Teodoro SN -pg. D-10-29
Quenga, Teresita S -pg. D-10-31
Quenga, Vicenta B -pg. D-10-27
Quenga, Vicenta T -pg. D-10-28
Quenga, Vicente C -pg. D-10-28
Quenga, Vicente Q -pg. D-10-19
Quenga, Vicente SN -pg. D-10-28
Quenga, Vicente SN -pg. D-10-29

Quenga, William S -pg. D-10-31
Quichocho, Ana -pg. D-3-62
Quichocho, Ana -pg. D-5-67
Quichocho, Ana D -pg. D-12-15
Quichocho, Ana P -pg. D-12-10
Quichocho, Ana Q -pg. D-3-73
Quichocho, Ana T -pg. D-7-13
Quichocho, Antonia -pg. D-3-73
Quichocho, Antonio C -pg. D-5-73
Quichocho, Beatrice L -pg. D-2-71
Quichocho, Beatrice Q -pg. D-2-9
Quichocho, Bernadita T -pg. D-7-13
Quichocho, Carmela N -pg. D-1-65
Quichocho, Carmen -pg. D-5-73
Quichocho, Carmen B -pg. D-2-71
Quichocho, Concepcion S -pg. D-5-73
Quichocho, Consolacion Q -pg. D-10-32
Quichocho, Dolores F -pg. D-2-78
Quichocho, Dolores I -pg. D-12-13
Quichocho, Emeterio S -pg. D-2-74
Quichocho, Engracia T -pg. D-4-79
Quichocho, Esperansa -pg. D-3-73
Quichocho, Felicita -pg. D-5-65
Quichocho, Felipe A -pg. D-5-73
Quichocho, Francisca N -pg. D-1-65
Quichocho, Francisco -pg. D-5-66
Quichocho, Francisco -pg. D-5-67
Quichocho, Francisco Q -pg. D-2-9
Quichocho, Ignacia T -pg. D-1-48
Quichocho, Ignacio C -pg. D-12-4
Quichocho, Ignacio Q -pg. D-10-30
Quichocho, Ignacio T -pg. D-4-79
Quichocho, Isabel L -pg. D-2-71
Quichocho, Isabel S -pg. D-2-74
Quichocho, Isabel T -pg. D-4-79
Quichocho, Jesus -pg. D-5-66
Quichocho, Jesus C -pg. D-1-62
Quichocho, Jesus C -pg. D-12-4
Quichocho, Jesus I -pg. D-12-13
Quichocho, Jesus L -pg. D-2-71
Quichocho, Jesus P -pg. D-3-75
Quichocho, Jesus P -pg. D-5-66
Quichocho, Jesus Q -pg. D-1-62
Quichocho, Jesus Q -pg. D-2-71
Quichocho, Jesus Q -pg. D-12-8
Quichocho, Jesus S -pg. D-5-73
Quichocho, Jesusa Q -pg. D-2-8
Quichocho, Joaquin D -pg. D-12-4
Quichocho, Joaquin L -pg. D-12-16
Quichocho, Joaquin N -pg. D-5-61
Quichocho, Joaquin S -pg. D-2-74
Quichocho, Joaquina C -pg. D-1-62
Quichocho, Joaquina Q -pg. D-2-9
Quichocho, Joaquina T -pg. D-5-66
Quichocho, Jose -pg. D-3-62
Quichocho, Jose -pg. D-3-73
Quichocho, Jose -pg. D-5-65
Quichocho, Jose -pg. D-5-73
Quichocho, Jose C -pg. D-12-20

Quichocho, Jose G -pg. D-2-44
Quichocho, Jose I -pg. D-12-13
Quichocho, Jose N -pg. D-1-65
Quichocho, Jose P -pg. D-2-74
Quichocho, Jose P -pg. D-12-10
Quichocho, Jose Q -pg. D-2-30
Quichocho, Jose Q -pg. D-2-44
Quichocho, Jose Q -pg. D-10-26
Quichocho, Jose R -pg. D-2-71
Quichocho, Jose R -pg. D-2-71
Quichocho, Jose S -pg. D-2-74
Quichocho, Jose T -pg. D-4-79
Quichocho, Josefa -pg. D-5-67
Quichocho, Josefa C -pg. D-12-4
Quichocho, Josefa G -pg. D-2-44
Quichocho, Josefa Q -pg. D-1-19
Quichocho, Josefa S -pg. D-5-73
Quichocho, Juan -pg. D-3-73
Quichocho, Juan I -pg. D-12-13
Quichocho, Juan L -pg. D-2-71
Quichocho, Juan P -pg. D-12-13
Quichocho, Juan S -pg. D-5-73
Quichocho, Juan T -pg. D-4-79
Quichocho, Juan T -pg. D-7-13
Quichocho, Juana R -pg. D-5-67
Quichocho, Juana S -pg. D-2-74
Quichocho, Julia C -pg. D-1-62
Quichocho, Lorenzo -pg. D-3-73
Quichocho, Lourdes G -pg. D-2-44
Quichocho, Manuel -pg. D-5-73
Quichocho, Manuel I -pg. D-12-13
Quichocho, Manuel P -pg. D-3-64
Quichocho, Manuel T -pg. D-5-66
Quichocho, Maria -pg. D-5-65
Quichocho, Maria -pg. D-5-65
Quichocho, Maria -pg. D-5-66
Quichocho, Maria B -pg. D-2-71
Quichocho, Maria C -pg. D-5-73
Quichocho, Maria I -pg. D-12-13
Quichocho, Maria L -pg. D-2-71
Quichocho, Maria P -pg. D-3-62
Quichocho, Maria P -pg. D-12-9
Quichocho, Maria P -pg. D-12-10
Quichocho, Maria P -pg. D-12-20
Quichocho, Maria Q -pg. D-5-66
Quichocho, Maria S -pg. D-5-73
Quichocho, Maria T -pg. D-4-79
Quichocho, Maria T -pg. D-7-13
Quichocho, Mariano Q -pg. D-5-61
Quichocho, Miguel Q -pg. D-5-67
Quichocho, Natividad P -pg. D-12-20
Quichocho, Nicolas -pg. D-5-65
Quichocho, Nicolas B -pg. D-2-71
Quichocho, Nicolas G -pg. D-5-65
Quichocho, Nicolasa Q -pg. D-5-65
Quichocho, Ofracia T -pg. D-7-13
Quichocho, Patrocinio -pg. D-3-62
Quichocho, Pedro -pg. D-5-73
Quichocho, Pedro N -pg. D-1-65

Quichocho, Rafael Q -pg. D-1-58
Quichocho, Rita -pg. D-3-73
Quichocho, Rosa -pg. D-5-65
Quichocho, Rosa -pg. D-5-65
Quichocho, Rosa -pg. D-5-66
Quichocho, Rosa G -pg. D-2-44
Quichocho, Rosa G -pg. D-5-66
Quichocho, Rosa L -pg. D-2-56
Quichocho, Rosa P -pg. D-2-30
Quichocho, Rosa T -pg. D-7-13
Quichocho, Rosalia -pg. D-5-67
Quichocho, Rosario -pg. D-5-65
Quichocho, Rosario -pg. D-5-66
Quichocho, Rosario P -pg. D-12-10
Quichocho, Rosario T -pg. D-4-79
Quichocho, Rosario T -pg. D-7-13
Quichocho, Rufina L -pg. D-2-71
Quichocho, Soledad A -pg. D-11-40
Quichocho, Soledad P -pg. D-12-10
Quichocho, Teodoro -pg. D-5-66
Quichocho, Teodoro -pg. D-5-66
Quichocho, Tomas T -pg. D-4-79
Quichocho, Tomasa C -pg. D-1-44
Quichocho, Trinidad I -pg. D-12-13
Quichocho, Trinidad Q -pg. D-5-66
Quichocho, Veronica I -pg. D-12-13
Quichocho, Vicenta G -pg. D-2-71
Quichocho, Vicente -pg. D-5-65
Quichocho, Vicente -pg. D-5-66
Quichocho, Vicente Q -pg. D-5-66
Quichocho, Vicente S -pg. D-2-74
Quichocho?, Juan -pg. D-13-27
Quidachay, Adela T -pg. D-9-46
Quidachay, Amanda Q -pg. D-8-35
Quidachay, Ana A -pg. D-10-15
Quidachay, Ana A -pg. D-12-16
Quidachay, Ana B -pg. D-6-27
Quidachay, Ana P -pg. D-12-7
Quidachay, Ana T -pg. D-12-14
Quidachay, Ana T -pg. D-12-16
Quidachay, Ana V -pg. D-5-83
Quidachay, Andrea A -pg. D-10-15
Quidachay, Andrea R -pg. D-8-41
Quidachay, Angela T -pg. D-8-31
Quidachay, Antonio B -pg. D-1-64
Quidachay, Antonio T -pg. D-12-14
Quidachay, Baldovino A -pg. D-5-92
Quidachay, Barcelisa -pg. D-5-92
Quidachay, Barsalisa Q -pg. D-2-76
Quidachay, Caridad B -pg. D-6-27
Quidachay, Carmen -pg. D-3-5
Quidachay, Delgadina M -pg. D-9-38
Quidachay, Delgadina S -pg. D-12-7
Quidachay, Dolores P -pg. D-12-7
Quidachay, Dolores S -pg. D-12-7
Quidachay, Emilia T -pg. D-12-15
Quidachay, Enriqueta T -pg. D-9-36
Quidachay, Feliciana SN -pg. D-5-86
Quidachay, Florensia B -pg. D-6-27

Quidachay, Francisco -pg. D-13-27
Quidachay, Francisco P -pg. D-12-7
Quidachay, Francisco R -pg. D-8-41
Quidachay, Francisco T -pg. D-9-39
Quidachay, Isabel T -pg. D-1-64
Quidachay, Jesus -pg. D-5-92
Quidachay, Jesus A -pg. D-3-67
Quidachay, Jesus B -pg. D-5-34
Quidachay, Jesus C -pg. D-5-65
Quidachay, Jesus Q -pg. D-8-31
Quidachay, Jesus T -pg. D-1-64
Quidachay, Jesus T -pg. D-12-16
Quidachay, Joaquin I -pg. D-9-46
Quidachay, Joaquin P -pg. D-12-7
Quidachay, Joaquina C -pg. D-5-32
Quidachay, Jose -pg. D-5-86
Quidachay, Jose D -pg. D-8-37
Quidachay, Jose I -pg. D-6-27
Quidachay, Jose L -pg. D-12-16
Quidachay, Jose P -pg. D-12-7
Quidachay, Jose Q -pg. D-8-31
Quidachay, Jose T -pg. D-9-46
Quidachay, Juan -pg. D-3-5
Quidachay, Juan B -pg. D-6-27
Quidachay, Juan M -pg. D-12-14
Quidachay, Juan Q -pg. D-5-14
Quidachay, Juan R -pg. D-8-41
Quidachay, Juan R -pg. D-9-46
Quidachay, Juan SN -pg. D-5-86
Quidachay, Juan T -pg. D-1-64
Quidachay, Luisa SN -pg. D-5-86
Quidachay, Manuel Q -pg. D-13-27
Quidachay, Manuela S -pg. D-9-46
Quidachay, Margarita Q -pg. D-6-14
Quidachay, Maria -pg. D-3-5
Quidachay, Maria A -pg. D-5-92
Quidachay, Maria B -pg. D-6-27
Quidachay, Maria I -pg. D-9-46
Quidachay, Maria M -pg. D-9-38
Quidachay, Maria Q -pg. D-6-14
Quidachay, Maria Q -pg. D-8-31
Quidachay, Maria R -pg. D-8-37
Quidachay, Maria T -pg. D-1-64
Quidachay, Maria T -pg. D-10-26
Quidachay, Mariano G -pg. D-6-14
Quidachay, Mariano P -pg. D-12-7
Quidachay, Pilar -pg. D-5-92
Quidachay, Preciosa T -pg. D-9-39
Quidachay, Prudencio T -pg. D-9-46
Quidachay, Ramon D -pg. D-9-38
Quidachay, Ramon P -pg. D-12-7
Quidachay, Ramona SN -pg. D-3-5
Quidachay, Remedio B -pg. D-1-64
Quidachay, Rita S -pg. D-12-7
Quidachay, Rosa A -pg. D-10-15
Quidachay, Rosa Q -pg. D-6-14
Quidachay, Rosa R -pg. D-8-37
Quidachay, Sara Q -pg. D-6-14
Quidachay, Teodosia A -pg. D-10-15

Quidachay, Teresa B -pg. D-6-27
Quidachay, Timoteo Q -pg. D-2-75
Quidachay, Timoteo Q -pg. D-5-3
Quidachay, Trindad R -pg. D-8-37
Quidachay, Trinidad T -pg. D-1-64
Quidachay, Veronica Q -pg. D-2-75
Quidachay, Vicenta -pg. D-2-17
Quidachay, Vicenta Q -pg. D-2-76
Quidachay, Vicente -pg. D-5-86
Quidachay, Vicente B -pg. D-1-64
Quidachay, Vicente P -pg. D-12-7
Quidachay, Vicente Q -pg. D-8-41
Quidachay, Vicente T -pg. D-9-22
Quidagua, Dolores C -pg. D-9-25
Quidagua, Felix C -pg. D-9-25
Quidagua, Ignacio T -pg. D-9-14
Quidagua, Jesus C -pg. D-9-25
Quidagua, Jose C -pg. D-9-25
Quidagua, Maria -pg. D-9-14
Quidagua, Maria C -pg. D-9-25
Quidagua, Maria C -pg. D-9-25
Quidagua, Pedro C -pg. D-9-25
Quidagua, Vicente C -pg. D-9-25
Quifunas, Clotilde T -pg. D-12-13
Quifunas, Felicita T -pg. D-12-13
Quifunas, Jose C -pg. D-12-13
Quifunas, Jose T -pg. D-12-13
Quifunas, Lourdes T -pg. D-12-13
Quifunas, Manuel A -pg. D-12-13
Quifunas, Manuel T -pg. D-12-13
Quifunas, Maria T -pg. D-12-13
Quifunas, Pedro T -pg. D-12-13
Quinata, Adela M -pg. D-9-33
Quinata, Agnes S -pg. D-9-44
Quinata, Aleho LG -pg. D-8-47
Quinata, Amparo A -pg. D-9-38
Quinata, Ana A -pg. D-9-34
Quinata, Ana A -pg. D-9-34
Quinata, Ana A -pg. D-9-39
Quinata, Ana C -pg. D-3-75
Quinata, Ana LG -pg. D-8-47
Quinata, Ana M -pg. D-9-40
Quinata, Ana Q -pg. D-9-43
Quinata, Ana S -pg. D-9-38
Quinata, Anastacia T -pg. D-9-35
Quinata, Anastacio T -pg. D-9-46
Quinata, Andina S -pg. D-9-38
Quinata, Antonia A -pg. D-9-41
Quinata, Antonia B -pg. D-9-39
Quinata, Antonio A -pg. D-9-35
Quinata, Antonio A -pg. D-9-38
Quinata, Antonio A -pg. D-10-29
Quinata, Antonio A -pg. D-13-29
Quinata, Antonio M -pg. D-9-31
Quinata, Antonio V -pg. D-9-45
Quinata, Asunsion C -pg. D-4-84
Quinata, Automina S -pg. D-9-38
Quinata, Bardovino M -pg. D-9-37
Quinata, Beatriz A -pg. D-9-41

Quinata, Beatriz A -pg. D-9-41
Quinata, Cayetano A -pg. D-8-47
Quinata, Cevera T -pg. D-9-36
Quinata, Conchita A -pg. D-9-41
Quinata, Daniel -pg. D-3-12
Quinata, Daniel B -pg. D-9-39
Quinata, Dolores A -pg. D-9-34
Quinata, edro I -pg. D-9-40
Quinata, Eduardo Q -pg. D-9-45
Quinata, Engracia A -pg. D-9-41
Quinata, Engracia M -pg. D-10-30
Quinata, Engracia M -pg. D-11-29
Quinata, Enrique C -pg. D-4-84
Quinata, Eugenio A -pg. D-11-30
Quinata, Eulogracia D -pg. D-9-37
Quinata, Faustino A -pg. D-9-33
Quinata, Faustino M -pg. D-9-33
Quinata, Feliciana T -pg. D-11-48
Quinata, Felicita A -pg. D-9-45
Quinata, Felisa S -pg. D-13-42
Quinata, Francisco A -pg. D-9-38
Quinata, Francisco B -pg. D-9-39
Quinata, Francisco D -pg. D-9-38
Quinata, Francisco LG -pg. D-8-47
Quinata, Francisco M -pg. D-9-39
Quinata, Grabiela A -pg. D-9-38
Quinata, Gregorio M -pg. D-10-30
Quinata, Guillerma M -pg. D-9-40
Quinata, Hermanigildo Q -pg. D-9-34
Quinata, Hilarion A -pg. D-9-44
Quinata, Ignacio A -pg. D-9-41
Quinata, Ignacio A -pg. D-9-41
Quinata, Isabel B -pg. D-9-39
Quinata, Isabel LG -pg. D-8-47
Quinata, Jacinto Q -pg. D-5-99
Quinata, Jesus A -pg. D-9-33
Quinata, Jesus B -pg. D-9-39
Quinata, Jesus S -pg. D-9-38
Quinata, Jesus S -pg. D-9-41
Quinata, Jesus S -pg. D-9-44
Quinata, Jesus T -pg. D-9-36
Quinata, Joaquin A -pg. D-9-46
Quinata, Joaquin C -pg. D-4-84
Quinata, Joaquin M -pg. D-9-40
Quinata, Joaquin S -pg. D-9-38
Quinata, Joaquina A -pg. D-9-46
Quinata, Joaquina T -pg. D-9-36
Quinata, Jose -pg. D-3-11
Quinata, Jose A -pg. D-9-34
Quinata, Jose A -pg. D-9-41
Quinata, Jose B -pg. D-9-39
Quinata, Jose C -pg. D-4-83
Quinata, Jose M -pg. D-9-40
Quinata, Jose M -pg. D-10-30
Quinata, Jose S -pg. D-9-38
Quinata, Jose S -pg. D-9-41
Quinata, Jose S -pg. D-9-44
Quinata, Jose SN -pg. D-9-41
Quinata, Jose T -pg. D-9-36

Quinata, Jose V -pg. D-4-83
Quinata, Josefina A -pg. D-9-41
Quinata, Josefina C -pg. D-4-83
Quinata, Josefina S -pg. D-9-38
Quinata, Josepha S -pg. D-9-44
Quinata, Juan A -pg. D-9-37
Quinata, Juan Q -pg. D-9-43
Quinata, Juan Q -pg. D-9-43
Quinata, Lucia T -pg. D-3-11
Quinata, Lucia T -pg. D-11-48
Quinata, Lucio M -pg. D-11-48
Quinata, Luis A -pg. D-9-39
Quinata, Luisa S -pg. D-11-48
Quinata, Lydia S -pg. D-9-38
Quinata, Magdalena T -pg. D-9-37
Quinata, Margarita S -pg. D-9-38
Quinata, Maria A -pg. D-9-33
Quinata, Maria A -pg. D-9-34
Quinata, Maria A -pg. D-9-34
Quinata, Maria A -pg. D-9-41
Quinata, Maria A -pg. D-9-41
Quinata, Maria LG -pg. D-8-47
Quinata, Maria M -pg. D-10-30
Quinata, Maria Q -pg. D-9-43
Quinata, Maria Q -pg. D-9-45
Quinata, Maria Q -pg. D-9-45
Quinata, Maria Q -pg. D-9-45
Quinata, Maria S -pg. D-9-44
Quinata, Mariano A -pg. D-9-34
Quinata, Mariano LG -pg. D-8-47
Quinata, Mariano S -pg. D-11-48
Quinata, Miguel A -pg. D-9-38
Quinata, Nicolasa M -pg. D-10-30
Quinata, Nieves A -pg. D-9-46
Quinata, Pansy -pg. D-3-11
Quinata, Ramon A -pg. D-9-34
Quinata, Rita A -pg. D-9-46
Quinata, Rita C -pg. D-4-83
Quinata, Roman LG -pg. D-8-47
Quinata, Rosa C -pg. D-4-83
Quinata, Rosabela B -pg. D-9-39
Quinata, Teresa A -pg. D-9-38
Quinata, Tomas -pg. D-3-11
Quinata, Trinidad A -pg. D-9-34
Quinata, Vicenta M -pg. D-9-37
Quinata, Vicente A -pg. D-9-34
Quinata, Vicente A -pg. D-9-38
Quinata, Vicente A -pg. D-9-46
Quinata, Vicente M -pg. D-9-33
Quinata, Vicente Q -pg. D-9-45
Quinata, Vicente T -pg. D-9-33
Quinata, Vicente T -pg. D-9-36
Quinata, Victoria LG -pg. D-8-47
Quinataotao, Virginia N -pg. D-13-43
Quinene, Ana A -pg. D-9-15
Quinene, Ana C -pg. D-9-22
Quinene, Ana F -pg. D-9-11
Quinene, Ana R -pg. D-9-14
Quinene, Cerilo F -pg. D-9-15

Quinene, Dometrio Q -pg. D-9-28
Quinene, Jesus R -pg. D-9-14
Quinene, Jose B -pg. D-11-6
Quinene, Jose C -pg. D-9-22
Quinene, Jose Q -pg. D-9-27
Quinene, Jose Q -pg. D-9-28
Quinene, Jose R -pg. D-9-14
Quinene, Josefa -pg. D-9-28
Quinene, Josefa -pg. D-9-28
Quinene, Librada C -pg. D-9-22
Quinene, Lutilde -pg. D-9-28
Quinene, Maria -pg. D-9-28
Quinene, Maria C -pg. D-9-22
Quinene, Pedro G -pg. D-9-14
Quinene, Santiago G -pg. D-9-28
Quinene, Silvestre R -pg. D-9-14
Quinene, Vicente F -pg. D-9-22
Quinene, Vicente R -pg. D-9-14
Quinian, Mark G -pg. D-13-13
Quintanilla, Albert C -pg. D-11-34
Quintanilla, Alfonsina D -pg. D-8-29
Quintanilla, Ana B -pg. D-11-24
Quintanilla, Ana C -pg. D-6-31
Quintanilla, Ana F -pg. D-1-66
Quintanilla, Ana G -pg. D-10-5
Quintanilla, Ana Q -pg. D-11-12
Quintanilla, Andrecina G -pg. D-10-5
Quintanilla, Andres L -pg. D-6-19
Quintanilla, Aniceto SN -pg. D-8-29
Quintanilla, Antonia C -pg. D-2-36
Quintanilla, Antonia P -pg. D-11-37
Quintanilla, Antonio A -pg. D-11-30
Quintanilla, Antonio P -pg. D-11-42
Quintanilla, Antonio SN -pg. D-11-24
Quintanilla, Beatrice P -pg. D-11-37
Quintanilla, Benabe N -pg. D-6-19
Quintanilla, Caridad P -pg. D-11-41
Quintanilla, Carlos C -pg. D-2-36
Quintanilla, Carmen B -pg. D-11-24
Quintanilla, Carmen C -pg. D-2-36
Quintanilla, Carmen C -pg. D-6-31
Quintanilla, Carmen SN -pg. D-11-24
Quintanilla, Catalina A -pg. D-11-30
Quintanilla, Catalina D -pg. D-8-29
Quintanilla, Clara M -pg. D-2-36
Quintanilla, Deonicia R -pg. D-11-38
Quintanilla, Dolores C -pg. D-1-59
Quintanilla, Dolores M -pg. D-11-47
Quintanilla, Dolores W -pg. D-11-35
Quintanilla, Edward A -pg. D-11-30
Quintanilla, Emelia C -pg. D-2-36
Quintanilla, Emeterio R -pg. D-8-22
Quintanilla, Engracia C -pg. D-11-36
Quintanilla, Felicita C -pg. D-1-59
Quintanilla, Felix B -pg. D-11-25
Quintanilla, Felix C -pg. D-11-28
Quintanilla, Francisca C -pg. D-2-36
Quintanilla, Francisca C -pg. D-11-34
Quintanilla, Francisca Q -pg. D-11-37

Quintanilla, Francisco C -pg. D-11-34
Quintanilla, Francisco C -pg. D-11-37
Quintanilla, Francisco R -pg. D-11-38
Quintanilla, Francisco T -pg. D-2-36
Quintanilla, Gertrudes R -pg. D-11-38
Quintanilla, Gonzalo M -pg. D-2-36
Quintanilla, Gregorio C -pg. D-1-59
Quintanilla, Guillermo B -pg. D-11-24
Quintanilla, Ignacia D -pg. D-8-29
Quintanilla, Ignacio C -pg. D-11-29
Quintanilla, Ignacio R -pg. D-11-41
Quintanilla, Jesus C -pg. D-6-31
Quintanilla, Jesus D -pg. D-5-35
Quintanilla, Jesus L -pg. D-11-47
Quintanilla, Jesus P -pg. D-11-42
Quintanilla, Jesus SN -pg. D-8-22
Quintanilla, Jesusa P -pg. D-11-42
Quintanilla, Joaquin P -pg. D-11-24
Quintanilla, Joaquin R -pg. D-11-37
Quintanilla, Joaquin SN -pg. D-1-51
Quintanilla, Jose B -pg. D-11-12
Quintanilla, Jose C -pg. D-2-36
Quintanilla, Jose C -pg. D-11-24
Quintanilla, Jose C -pg. D-11-29
Quintanilla, Jose C -pg. D-11-36
Quintanilla, Jose C -pg. D-11-36
Quintanilla, Jose G -pg. D-10-5
Quintanilla, Jose L -pg. D-11-25
Quintanilla, Jose R -pg. D-6-31
Quintanilla, Jose SN -pg. D-8-22
Quintanilla, Jose SN -pg. D-11-24
Quintanilla, Josefa T -pg. D-11-25
Quintanilla, Josefina SN -pg. D-11-24
Quintanilla, Juan C -pg. D-2-11
Quintanilla, Juan C -pg. D-6-31
Quintanilla, Juan D -pg. D-8-29
Quintanilla, Juan G -pg. D-10-6
Quintanilla, Juan P -pg. D-2-83
Quintanilla, Juan R -pg. D-11-30
Quintanilla, Juan S -pg. D-5-35
Quintanilla, Juan L -pg. D-6-19
Quintanilla, Julita C -pg. D-6-31
Quintanilla, Ladislao P -pg. D-11-37
Quintanilla, Lucia S -pg. D-5-35
Quintanilla, Luis C -pg. D-11-37
Quintanilla, Luis P -pg. D-11-37
Quintanilla, Luisa M -pg. D-11-47
Quintanilla, Manuel -pg. D-10-5
Quintanilla, Manuel C -pg. D-11-28
Quintanilla, Manuel P -pg. D-2-14
Quintanilla, Manuel P -pg. D-5-50
Quintanilla, Manuela SN -pg. D-8-22
Quintanilla, Manuela T -pg. D-11-25
Quintanilla, Maria C -pg. D-2-35
Quintanilla, Maria C -pg. D-11-29
Quintanilla, Maria D -pg. D-8-29
Quintanilla, Maria G -pg. D-2-12
Quintanilla, Maria L -pg. D-6-19
Quintanilla, Maria M -pg. D-2-36

Quintanilla, Maria S -pg. D-5-35
Quintanilla, Maria SN -pg. D-8-22
Quintanilla, Milagro C -pg. D-11-28
Quintanilla, Olimpia C -pg. D-2-36
Quintanilla, Rita R -pg. D-11-38
Quintanilla, Rosa W -pg. D-11-35
Quintanilla, Rosario A -pg. D-11-30
Quintanilla, Soledad T -pg. D-11-25
Quintanilla, Stella A -pg. D-11-30
Quintanilla, Trinidad C -pg. D-11-34
Quintanilla, Vicente C -pg. D-2-35
Quintanilla, Vicente C -pg. D-11-38
Quintanilla, Vicente G -pg. D-10-6
Quintanilla, Vicente P -pg. D-11-37
Quitano, Ana LG -pg. D-6-25
Quitano, Barlola LG -pg. D-6-25
Quitano, Emilia S -pg. D-6-11
Quitano, Guillelmo LG -pg. D-6-25
Quitano, Hil LG -pg. D-6-25
Quitano, Juan C -pg. D-5-23
Quitano, Juana S -pg. D-6-11
Quitano, Maria C -pg. D-6-10
Quitano, Maria LG -pg. D-6-25
Quitano, Ramon S -pg. D-6-11
Quitano, Redibiso S -pg. D-6-25
Quitano, Rita LG -pg. D-6-25
Quitano, Tomas C -pg. D-6-10
Quitano, Vicente LG -pg. D-6-25
Quitaro, Agustin P -pg. D-12-5
Quitaro, Antonia B -pg. D-12-5
Quitaro, Jesus B -pg. D-12-5
Quitaro, Jose B -pg. D-12-5
Quitaro, Juan B -pg. D-12-5
Quitaro, Maria B -pg. D-12-5
Quitaro, Ramon B -pg. D-12-5
Quitaro, Soledad B -pg. D-12-5
Quitonguico, Engracia T -pg. D-2-75
Quitonguico, Pedro C -pg. D-4-5
Quitugua, Adela C -pg. D-4-22
Quitugua, Ana C -pg. D-4-21
Quitugua, Ana C -pg. D-10-18
Quitugua, Ana F -pg. D-7-17
Quitugua, Ana Q -pg. D-11-37
Quitugua, Ana S -pg. D-10-19
Quitugua, Ana SN -pg. D-1-27
Quitugua, Ana SN -pg. D-5-56
Quitugua, Ana T -pg. D-2-58
Quitugua, Antonia A -pg. D-10-16
Quitugua, Antonia C -pg. D-10-8
Quitugua, Antonia C -pg. D-10-18
Quitugua, Antonio -pg. D-10-16
Quitugua, Antonio M -pg. D-13-35
Quitugua, Carlos C -pg. D-10-18
Quitugua, Catalina S -pg. D-7-10
Quitugua, Clementina S -pg. D-7-10
Quitugua, Concepcion C -pg. D-4-22
Quitugua, Concepcion F -pg. D-7-17
Quitugua, Dolores C -pg. D-10-8
Quitugua, Dolores G -pg. D-4-39

Quitugua, Dolores M -pg. D-4-113
Quitugua, Dolores SN -pg. D-10-34
Quitugua, Dometrio T -pg. D-7-12
Quitugua, Eliza F -pg. D-7-17
Quitugua, Engracia T -pg. D-7-12
Quitugua, Enrique R -pg. D-13-29
Quitugua, Felicidad S -pg. D-10-18
Quitugua, Felomina T -pg. D-2-58
Quitugua, Francisca -pg. D-5-87
Quitugua, Francisco A -pg. D-6-37
Quitugua, Francisco A -pg. D-10-16
Quitugua, Francisco B -pg. D-1-27
Quitugua, Francisco B -pg. D-5-56
Quitugua, Francisco Q -pg. D-10-15
Quitugua, Francisco T -pg. D-7-12
Quitugua, Fred C -pg. D-10-18
Quitugua, Gregorio T -pg. D-7-12
Quitugua, Guadalupe A -pg. D-6-37
Quitugua, Henry F -pg. D-7-18
Quitugua, Honoria M -pg. D-1-46
Quitugua, Ignacia C -pg. D-5-87
Quitugua, Ignacio P -pg. D-1-46
Quitugua, Isabel S -pg. D-10-18
Quitugua, Jesus C -pg. D-10-8
Quitugua, Jesus F -pg. D-7-18
Quitugua, Jesus T -pg. D-7-12
Quitugua, Joaquin A -pg. D-1-51
Quitugua, Joaquin C -pg. D-4-21
Quitugua, Joaquin G -pg. D-4-39
Quitugua, Joaquin J -pg. D-4-39
Quitugua, Joaquin P -pg. D-1-46
Quitugua, Joaquin R -pg. D-4-113
Quitugua, Joaquin T -pg. D-7-12
Quitugua, Jose -pg. D-10-16
Quitugua, Jose -pg. D-11-35
Quitugua, Jose A -pg. D-1-46
Quitugua, Jose A -pg. D-6-37
Quitugua, Jose C -pg. D-10-8
Quitugua, Jose C -pg. D-10-8
Quitugua, Jose D -pg. D-2-71
Quitugua, Jose P -pg. D-1-46
Quitugua, Jose P -pg. D-2-71
Quitugua, Jose Q -pg. D-2-19
Quitugua, Jose Q -pg. D-7-12
Quitugua, Jose S -pg. D-7-10
Quitugua, Jose SN -pg. D-1-27
Quitugua, Jose SN -pg. D-5-56
Quitugua, Josefa C -pg. D-4-32
Quitugua, Josefa D -pg. D-2-58
Quitugua, Josefina A -pg. D-6-37
Quitugua, Josefina M -pg. D-1-46
Quitugua, Juan -pg. D-2-14
Quitugua, Juan C -pg. D-4-21
Quitugua, Juan C -pg. D-10-8
Quitugua, Juan G -pg. D-4-39
Quitugua, Juan P -pg. D-2-71
Quitugua, Juan Q -pg. D-7-17
Quitugua, Juan S -pg. D-5-87
Quitugua, Juan S -pg. D-7-10

Quitugua, Juan T -pg. D-2-58
Quitugua, Juana Q -pg. D-7-19
Quitugua, Magdalena A -pg. D-7-6
Quitugua, Magdalena I -pg. D-2-19
Quitugua, Manuel C -pg. D-5-32
Quitugua, Maria A -pg. D-6-37
Quitugua, Maria A -pg. D-6-37
Quitugua, Maria A -pg. D-10-16
Quitugua, Maria C -pg. D-2-77
Quitugua, Maria D -pg. D-2-37
Quitugua, Maria D -pg. D-2-58
Quitugua, Maria F -pg. D-7-17
Quitugua, Maria I -pg. D-2-19
Quitugua, Maria P -pg. D-1-46
Quitugua, Maria P -pg. D-2-71
Quitugua, Maria P -pg. D-2-71
Quitugua, Maria Q -pg. D-10-34
Quitugua, Maria S -pg. D-5-74
Quitugua, Miguel T -pg. D-7-12
Quitugua, Milagro A -pg. D-10-16
Quitugua, Milagro P -pg. D-1-46
Quitugua, Natividad C -pg. D-4-22
Quitugua, Natividad S -pg. D-10-19
Quitugua, Pedro M -pg. D-1-46
Quitugua, Pedro P -pg. D-3-4
Quitugua, Pedro R -pg. D-7-7
Quitugua, Pedro T -pg. D-7-12
Quitugua, Ramon F -pg. D-7-18
Quitugua, Ramon Q -pg. D-10-18
Quitugua, Rita A -pg. D-10-16
Quitugua, Rita F -pg. D-7-18
Quitugua, Rita M -pg. D-4-113
Quitugua, Rita S -pg. D-7-10
Quitugua, Roberto T -pg. D-7-12
Quitugua, Rosa A -pg. D-7-6
Quitugua, Rosa S -pg. D-10-18
Quitugua, Rosa T -pg. D-2-59
Quitugua, Rosa T -pg. D-7-12
Quitugua, Rosalia A -pg. D-10-16
Quitugua, Rosario J -pg. D-4-39
Quitugua, Rufino -pg. D-5-87
Quitugua, Silvestre SN -pg. D-1-27
Quitugua, Silvestre SN -pg. D-5-57
Quitugua, Teofila SN -pg. D-5-57
Quitugua, Theofila SN -pg. D-1-27
Quitugua, Vicenta C -pg. D-2-77
Quitugua, Vicente -pg. D-4-39
Quitugua, Vicente A -pg. D-2-37
Quitugua, Vicente C -pg. D-4-21
Quitugua, Vicente C -pg. D-10-8
Quitugua, Vicente D -pg. D-2-58
Quitugua, Vicente P -pg. D-1-46
Quitugua, Vicente Q -pg. D-2-58
Quitugua, Vicente Q -pg. D-4-22
Quitugua, Vicente Q -pg. D-4-32
Rabago, Enrique C -pg. D-11-46
Rabago, Jose C -pg. D-11-46
Rabago, Jose J -pg. D-11-46
Rabago, Josefa C -pg. D-11-46

Rabago, Juan C -pg. D-11-46
Rabago, Natividad J -pg. D-11-46
Rabago, Vicente J -pg. D-11-46
Rabon, Antonia B -pg. D-5-5
Rabon, Jesus B -pg. D-5-5
Rabon, Jesus LG -pg. D-5-4
Rabon, Joaquin C -pg. D-5-4
Rabon, Jose C -pg. D-5-5
Rabon, Jose LG -pg. D-5-4
Rabon, Luisa LG -pg. D-5-4
Rabon, Nicolasa C -pg. D-5-9
Ramirez, Ana T -pg. D-4-77
Ramirez, Catalina T -pg. D-4-77
Ramirez, Emilia T -pg. D-4-77
Ramirez, Florencio T -pg. D-4-77
Ramirez, Jesus B -pg. D-4-77
Ramirez, Jose T -pg. D-4-77
Ramirez, Josefina T -pg. D-4-77
Ramirez, Maria T -pg. D-4-77
Ramirez, Maria T -pg. D-4-77
Ramos, Alejandro T -pg. D-2-68
Ramos, Juan H -pg. D-13-32
Ramos, Maria T -pg. D-2-68
Ramos, Rosa T -pg. D-2-68
Ramos, Trinidad T -pg. D-2-68
Ramstetin, Julian A -pg. D-13-42
Randolph, George H -pg. D-13-17
Rapolla, Angelina Q -pg. D-10-26
Rapolla, Antonia Q -pg. D-10-25
Rapolla, Antonio C -pg. D-10-26
Rapolla, Caridad T -pg. D-7-4
Rapolla, Carlos T -pg. D-7-4
Rapolla, Carmela R -pg. D-10-26
Rapolla, Catlina SN -pg. D-7-10
Rapolla, Consolacion SN -pg. D-7-10
Rapolla, Enrique C -pg. D-7-10
Rapolla, Francisca SN -pg. D-7-10
Rapolla, Francisco T -pg. D-7-4
Rapolla, Juan C -pg. D-7-4
Rapolla, Juan Q -pg. D-10-26
Rapolla, Lorenzo C -pg. D-10-25
Rapolla, Maria Q -pg. D-10-26
Rapolla, Maria SN -pg. D-7-10
Rapolla, Maria T -pg. D-7-4
Rapolla, Natividad T -pg. D-7-4
Rapolla, Ramon SN -pg. D-7-10
Rapolla, Rosalia T -pg. D-7-4
Rapolla, Santiago T -pg. D-7-4
Rapolla, Tomas Q -pg. D-10-26
Rapolla, Vicenta T -pg. D-7-4
Rapolla, Vicente T -pg. D-7-4
Rasni, Orval -pg. D-13-17
Ratcliff, Arson B -pg. D-13-40
Rathbories, Ray M -pg. D-13-8
Ratiles, Charles W -pg. D-13-24
Rayburn, Lloyd D -pg. D-13-13
Reames, Wm. L -pg. D-13-44
Rebb, Albert S -pg. D-13-8
Rediens, John A -pg. D-13-46

Reid, William E -pg. D-13-8
Reinnardt, Shierford M -pg. D-13-25
Reiter, Harold W -pg. D-13-8
Reiter, Henry G -pg. D-13-8
Rena, Edward M -pg. D-13-13
Renelles, Clyde E -pg. D-13-17
Respecio, Ambrosio D -pg. D-4-61
Respecio, Ana D -pg. D-4-61
Respecio, Jose D -pg. D-4-61
Respecio, Roman D -pg. D-4-61
Respicio, Luisa C -pg. D-4-57
Retas, Wayne E -pg. D-13-40
Retz, George I -pg. D-13-17
Reyes, Ana D -pg. D-5-2
Reyes, Ana D -pg. D-8-17
Reyes, Ana M -pg. D-4-32
Reyes, Ana M -pg. D-4-106
Reyes, Ana S -pg. D-11-3
Reyes, Ana SA -pg. D-2-47
Reyes, Andres B -pg. D-6-36
Reyes, Angelina A -pg. D-4-54
Reyes, Antonio C -pg. D-9-28
Reyes, Antonio P -pg. D-4-76
Reyes, Antonio T -pg. D-1-60
Reyes, Artemio T -pg. D-11-8
Reyes, Atelana T -pg. D-8-41
Reyes, Barcelisa Q -pg. D-4-112
Reyes, Benita G -pg. D-3-60
Reyes, Carmelo -pg. D-3-69
Reyes, Carmen A -pg. D-6-17
Reyes, Carmen C -pg. D-4-50
Reyes, Carmen M -pg. D-7-24
Reyes, Catalina Q -pg. D-4-112
Reyes, Cecilia M -pg. D-9-17
Reyes, Cisilo B -pg. D-6-17
Reyes, Concepcion M -pg. D-4-106
Reyes, Concepcion P -pg. D-11-42
Reyes, Concepcion S -pg. D-11-3
Reyes, Consolacion C -pg. D-6-36
Reyes, Consuelo SA -pg. D-2-47
Reyes, Delfina T -pg. D-11-8
Reyes, Dolores G -pg. D-3-44
Reyes, Dolores M -pg. D-7-24
Reyes, Dolores P -pg. D-11-42
Reyes, Dolores T -pg. D-4-76
Reyes, Dolores T -pg. D-9-5
Reyes, Edwardo D -pg. D-8-17
Reyes, Elvina C -pg. D-6-36
Reyes, Enrique C -pg. D-6-36
Reyes, Enrique C -pg. D-9-28
Reyes, Enrique P -pg. D-8-48
Reyes, Estafania C -pg. D-6-36
Reyes, Estefania S -pg. D-11-3
Reyes, Felicita C -pg. D-6-36
Reyes, Fermin B -pg. D-1-60
Reyes, Francisca B -pg. D-1-60
Reyes, Francisca P -pg. D-8-48
Reyes, Francisca T -pg. D-9-5
Reyes, Francisco C -pg. D-4-115

Reyes, Francisco G -pg. D-1-61
Reyes, Francisco L -pg. D-4-112
Reyes, Francisco Q -pg. D-4-112
Reyes, Francisco SA -pg. D-2-9
Reyes, Geronmio -pg. D-3-69
Reyes, Gonzalo C -pg. D-6-36
Reyes, Guadalupe M -pg. D-4-32
Reyes, Guadalupe T -pg. D-4-76
Reyes, Helena M -pg. D-4-106
Reyes, Henry M -pg. D-7-24
Reyes, Ignacia A -pg. D-4-54
Reyes, Ignacio A -pg. D-9-16
Reyes, Ignacio C -pg. D-4-32
Reyes, Ignacio C -pg. D-6-36
Reyes, Ignacio C -pg. D-9-17
Reyes, Ignacio G -pg. D-1-60
Reyes, Ignacio M -pg. D-4-32
Reyes, Ignacio M -pg. D-4-112
Reyes, Ignacio M -pg. D-9-16
Reyes, Isabel S -pg. D-9-15
Reyes, Isabel SA -pg. D-2-9
Reyes, Jesus -pg. D-3-60
Reyes, Jesus A -pg. D-6-17
Reyes, Jesus C -pg. D-4-50
Reyes, Jesus P -pg. D-4-100
Reyes, Jesus Q -pg. D-4-6
Reyes, Jesus R -pg. D-2-9
Reyes, Jesus R -pg. D-7-24
Reyes, Jesus S -pg. D-11-3
Reyes, Jesus S M -pg. D-7-24
Reyes, Joaquin A -pg. D-9-17
Reyes, Joaquin C -pg. D-6-36
Reyes, Joaquin C -pg. D-9-28
Reyes, Joaquin P -pg. D-11-29
Reyes, Joaquin SA -pg. D-2-46
Reyes, Jose -pg. D-3-69
Reyes, Jose A -pg. D-6-2
Reyes, Jose A -pg. D-9-15
Reyes, Jose B -pg. D-6-36
Reyes, Jose C -pg. D-6-36
Reyes, Jose C -pg. D-9-28
Reyes, Jose E -pg. D-4-106
Reyes, Jose M -pg. D-4-54
Reyes, Jose M -pg. D-4-106
Reyes, Jose M -pg. D-9-5
Reyes, Jose M -pg. D-9-16
Reyes, Jose P -pg. D-8-48
Reyes, Jose P -pg. D-11-42
Reyes, Jose Q -pg. D-4-6
Reyes, Jose R -pg. D-1-40
Reyes, Jose R -pg. D-8-48
Reyes, Jose S -pg. D-11-3
Reyes, Jose SA -pg. D-2-46
Reyes, Jose SN -pg. D-6-17
Reyes, Jose T -pg. D-9-5
Reyes, Jose T -pg. D-11-49
Reyes, Josefa M -pg. D-4-112
Reyes, Josefina M -pg. D-9-16
Reyes, Joseph M -pg. D-7-24

Reyes, Juan -pg. D-1-10
Reyes, Juan C -pg. D-8-41
Reyes, Juan G -pg. D-8-17
Reyes, Juan M -pg. D-9-17
Reyes, Juan P -pg. D-4-50
Reyes, Juan P -pg. D-8-48
Reyes, Juan SA -pg. D-2-47
Reyes, Julia M -pg. D-7-24
Reyes, Julia T -pg. D-1-60
Reyes, Laurion C -pg. D-11-8
Reyes, Lorenza M -pg. D-4-106
Reyes, Lorenzo M -pg. D-9-28
Reyes, Lourdes C -pg. D-6-36
Reyes, Lourdes P -pg. D-8-48
Reyes, Luis C -pg. D-4-50
Reyes, Luis SA -pg. D-1-45
Reyes, Luis SA -pg. D-2-9
Reyes, Luis T -pg. D-11-42
Reyes, Magdalena C -pg. D-6-17
Reyes, Manuel M -pg. D-4-112
Reyes, Manuel M -pg. D-12-17
Reyes, Manuela M -pg. D-1-61
Reyes, Margarita C -pg. D-9-28
Reyes, Margarita M -pg. D-4-32
Reyes, Maria A -pg. D-4-54
Reyes, Maria B -pg. D-1-60
Reyes, Maria C -pg. D-1-42
Reyes, Maria C -pg. D-4-115
Reyes, Maria C -pg. D-6-36
Reyes, Maria C -pg. D-6-36
Reyes, Maria M -pg. D-4-106
Reyes, Maria P -pg. D-8-48
Reyes, Maria P -pg. D-8-48
Reyes, Maria S -pg. D-4-80
Reyes, Maria S -pg. D-4-100
Reyes, Maria S -pg. D-9-15
Reyes, Maria S -pg. D-11-3
Reyes, Maria SA -pg. D-2-9
Reyes, Maria T -pg. D-1-60
Reyes, Maria T -pg. D-9-5
Reyes, Maria S -pg. D-6-2
Reyes, Mariano G -pg. D-1-61
Reyes, Mariano R -pg. D-2-46
Reyes, May A -pg. D-6-17
Reyes, Miguel C -pg. D-6-36
Reyes, Nicolas M -pg. D-9-16
Reyes, Nicolasa M -pg. D-4-112
Reyes, Nicolasa SA -pg. D-2-46
Reyes, Ramon A -pg. D-9-15
Reyes, Ramon R -pg. D-6-40
Reyes, Remundo M -pg. D-7-24
Reyes, Rita Q -pg. D-1-40
Reyes, Rita S -pg. D-9-15
Reyes, Roberto M -pg. D-7-24
Reyes, Rosa M -pg. D-9-16
Reyes, Rosa P -pg. D-11-42
Reyes, Rosa S -pg. D-9-15
Reyes, Rosalia A -pg. D-6-17
Reyes, Rosalia T -pg. D-4-76

Reyes, Rosario C -pg. D-11-8
Reyes, Rosario R -pg. D-1-58
Reyes, Rosario T -pg. D-1-60
Reyes, Rosario T -pg. D-11-8
Reyes, Rufina -pg. D-3-69
Reyes, Ruth C -pg. D-4-50
Reyes, Salome P -pg. D-11-42
Reyes, Soledad M -pg. D-11-29
Reyes, Teresa C -pg. D-9-28
Reyes, Teresa C -pg. D-9-28
Reyes, Teresa C -pg. D-11-25
Reyes, Thomas C -pg. D-11-25
Reyes, Tomas A -pg. D-6-17
Reyes, Trinidad P -pg. D-11-42
Reyes, Vicente B -pg. D-1-60
Reyes, Vicente C -pg. D-1-42
Reyes, Vicente C -pg. D-5-2
Reyes, Vicente C -pg. D-9-28
Reyes, Vicente G -pg. D-1-60
Reyes, Vicente Q -pg. D-4-6
Reynolds, Jack A -pg. D-13-17
Reynolds, Jacqueline J -pg. D-4-87
Reynolds, Madeline J -pg. D-4-87
Rice, Ana D -pg. D-11-6
Rice, Ana M -pg. D-11-6
Rice, Clarence R -pg. D-13-17
Rice, James H -pg. D-11-6
Rice, Thomas J -pg. D-11-6
Rich, Otto W -pg. D-13-8
Richards, William S -pg. D-13-8
Richardson, W R -pg. D-13-40
Richison, Catherin F -pg. D-3-47
Richison, Earl F -pg. D-3-47
Richison, Warren C -pg. D-3-47
Rider, Ervin R -pg. D-13-13
Rieniaore, Earl -pg. D-13-18
Rios, Agnes -pg. D-3-5
Rios, Agueda S -pg. D-10-22
Rios, Albert LG -pg. D-4-62
Rios, Alfred -pg. D-3-5
Rios, Ana G -pg. D-5-47
Rios, Ana L -pg. D-13-43
Rios, Antonia LG -pg. D-4-62
Rios, Antonia S -pg. D-10-22
Rios, Beatris -pg. D-3-5
Rios, Brigido A -pg. D-4-85
Rios, Elizabeth LG -pg. D-4-62
Rios, Emeliana G -pg. D-5-47
Rios, Enrique LG -pg. D-5-47
Rios, Ermina -pg. D-3-5
Rios, Felipe R -pg. D-10-21
Rios, Francisca G -pg. D-5-47
Rios, Helen LG -pg. D-4-62
Rios, Jesus S -pg. D-10-22
Rios, Jose LG -pg. D-4-62
Rios, Jose S -pg. D-10-22
Rios, Josefa LG -pg. D-4-85
Rios, Joseph LG -pg. D-4-62
Rios, Juan S -pg. D-10-22

Rios, Lagrimas S -pg. D-10-22
Rios, Maria -pg. D-3-5
Rios, Maria LG -pg. D-4-85
Rios, Maria S -pg. D-10-22
Rios, Rita S -pg. D-10-22
Rios, Rosa -pg. D-10-22
Rios, Tomasa S -pg. D-3-5
Rios, Vicente LG -pg. D-3-5
Ripple, Louis McC -pg. D-13-42
Risch, Harold F -pg. D-13-8
Rivera, Adela S -pg. D-6-18
Rivera, Amalia SA -pg. D-5-40
Rivera, Ana B -pg. D-6-3
Rivera, Ana L -pg. D-5-55
Rivera, Ana M -pg. D-4-88
Rivera, Ana R -pg. D-2-60
Rivera, Ana S -pg. D-6-18
Rivera, Ana T -pg. D-5-15
Rivera, Andres G -pg. D-5-62
Rivera, Antonia T -pg. D-5-15
Rivera, Antonio D -pg. D-6-3
Rivera, Antonio R -pg. D-2-2
Rivera, Antonio S -pg. D-6-22
Rivera, Asfriro U -pg. D-2-53
Rivera, Asuncion A -pg. D-2-6
Rivera, Asuncion S -pg. D-6-22
Rivera, Asuncion U -pg. D-2-53
Rivera, Beatice R -pg. D-5-56
Rivera, Beatriz R -pg. D-5-87
Rivera, Candelaria T -pg. D-5-15
Rivera, Carmen A -pg. D-2-6
Rivera, Carmen A -pg. D-8-21
Rivera, Catalina SN -pg. D-2-44
Rivera, Celedonia A -pg. D-8-21
Rivera, Delores LG -pg. D-6-24
Rivera, Delores S -pg. D-6-30
Rivera, Dolores A -pg. D-8-21
Rivera, Dolores R -pg. D-5-56
Rivera, Dolores T -pg. D-5-15
Rivera, Elisabal A -pg. D-2-6
Rivera, Felix D -pg. D-6-18
Rivera, Florencia G -pg. D-1-68
Rivera, Francisca T -pg. D-5-15
Rivera, Francisco A -pg. D-8-21
Rivera, Francisco U -pg. D-2-53
Rivera, Francisco S -pg. D-6-22
Rivera, Fransisca LG -pg. D-6-24
Rivera, Gonzalo SA -pg. D-5-40
Rivera, Gregorio S -pg. D-6-30
Rivera, Guadalupe B -pg. D-6-3
Rivera, Ignacio G -pg. D-1-68
Rivera, Ignacio R -pg. D-2-60
Rivera, Ignacio SN -pg. D-2-44
Rivera, Isabel R -pg. D-1-19
Rivera, Isabel R -pg. D-2-60
Rivera, Jesus LG -pg. D-6-24
Rivera, Jesus R -pg. D-1-19
Rivera, Jesus R -pg. D-2-60
Rivera, Jesus S -pg. D-6-30

Rivera, Joaquin A -pg. D-8-21
Rivera, Joaquin D -pg. D-6-24
Rivera, Joaquin LG -pg. D-2-60
Rivera, Joaquin R -pg. D-5-55
Rivera, Joaquin U -pg. D-5-40
Rivera, Jose A -pg. D-2-6
Rivera, Jose A -pg. D-8-21
Rivera, Jose G -pg. D-5-15
Rivera, Jose LG -pg. D-8-21
Rivera, Jose R -pg. D-2-60
Rivera, Jose S -pg. D-6-18
Rivera, Jose SA -pg. D-5-40
Rivera, Jose SN -pg. D-2-44
Rivera, Jose T -pg. D-5-15
Rivera, Jose U -pg. D-2-6
Rivera, Jose S -pg. D-6-22
Rivera, Josefa A -pg. D-2-6
Rivera, Juan D -pg. D-6-30
Rivera, Juan G -pg. D-1-68
Rivera, Juan R -pg. D-2-60
Rivera, Juan SA -pg. D-5-40
Rivera, Juan SN -pg. D-1-67
Rivera, Juan T -pg. D-5-15
Rivera, Juan U -pg. D-2-53
Rivera, Juana A -pg. D-2-6
Rivera, Leocaldo U -pg. D-2-53
Rivera, Loreta R -pg. D-2-2
Rivera, Magdalena A -pg. D-2-6
Rivera, Manuel G -pg. D-3-41
Rivera, Manuel R -pg. D-2-60
Rivera, Manuel SN -pg. D-5-40
Rivera, Manuela U -pg. D-2-54
Rivera, Marcelina M -pg. D-4-88
Rivera, Maria A -pg. D-8-21
Rivera, Maria G -pg. D-4-84
Rivera, Maria M -pg. D-3-41
Rivera, Maria R -pg. D-2-60
Rivera, Maria R -pg. D-5-87
Rivera, Maria S -pg. D-6-30
Rivera, Maria SN -pg. D-2-44
Rivera, Maria SN -pg. D-2-44
Rivera, Maria T -pg. D-5-15
Rivera, Maria S -pg. D-6-22
Rivera, Mariano G -pg. D-5-56
Rivera, Martin B -pg. D-6-3
Rivera, Miguel SN -pg. D-2-44
Rivera, Natividad S -pg. D-6-18
Rivera, Pedro A -pg. D-8-21
Rivera, Pilar R -pg. D-5-56
Rivera, Remedios R -pg. D-5-56
Rivera, Remedios S -pg. D-6-22
Rivera, Ros G -pg. D-1-67
Rivera, Rosa A -pg. D-2-6
Rivera, Rosa S -pg. D-6-30
Rivera, Rosa U -pg. D-5-40
Rivera, Soledad S -pg. D-6-18
Rivera, Tomas S -pg. D-6-22
Rivera, Vicente B -pg. D-6-3
Rivera, Vicente S -pg. D-6-18

Rivera, Vicente U -pg. D-2-54
Roales, Tracy H -pg. D-13-8
Robert, Carl H -pg. D-13-17
Robert, Charley -pg. D-13-45
Robert, Maurice K -pg. D-13-35
Robert, Raymond R -pg. D-13-25
Robert, Wiley D -pg. D-13-34
Roberto, Agustin -pg. D-5-99
Roberto, Amparo G -pg. D-1-28
Roberto, Ana -pg. D-5-99
Roberto, Ana D -pg. D-4-106
Roberto, Ana G -pg. D-1-28
Roberto, Anastacia D -pg. D-4-106
Roberto, Andres A -pg. D-3-57
Roberto, Antonio G -pg. D-1-28
Roberto, Bernice M -pg. D-4-94
Roberto, Clara D -pg. D-3-57
Roberto, Concepcion D -pg. D-2-81
Roberto, Concepcion R -pg. D-4-110
Roberto, Cristina B -pg. D-5-99
Roberto, Daniel B -pg. D-3-57
Roberto, Dolores A -pg. D-4-110
Roberto, Dolores C -pg. D-3-57
Roberto, Emelia D -pg. D-2-82
Roberto, Emma S -pg. D-4-94
Roberto, Enrique B -pg. D-4-88
Roberto, Eulalia B -pg. D-4-110
Roberto, Federica C -pg. D-3-57
Roberto, Felipe -pg. D-5-99
Roberto, Felix S -pg. D-4-88
Roberto, Francisca G -pg. D-1-28
Roberto, Francisco R -pg. D-4-110
Roberto, Francisco S -pg. D-1-28
Roberto, Gregorio G -pg D-1-28
Roberto, Hazel M -pg. D-4-94
Roberto, Ignacio T -pg. D-3-57
Roberto, Ignatius I -pg. D-3-57
Roberto, Isabel B -pg. D-4-88
Roberto, Isabel R -pg. D-4-88
Roberto, Jesus R -pg. D-4-106
Roberto, Jesus R -pg. D-4-110
Roberto, Jose -pg. D-3-57
Roberto, Jose -pg. D-3-57
Roberto, Jose -pg. D-5-99
Roberto, Jose C -pg. D-1-68
Roberto, Jose G -pg. D-1-28
Roberto, Josefina R -pg. D-4-110
Roberto, Juan -pg. D-5-99
Roberto, Juan A -pg. D-4-110
Roberto, Juan B -pg. D-5-47
Roberto, Juan R -pg. D-4-106
Roberto, Lidia M -pg. D-1-68
Roberto, Lorensa A -pg. D-3-57
Roberto, Luis D -pg. D-4-106
Roberto, Luisa B -pg. D-4-88
Roberto, Manuel B -pg. D-2-81
Roberto, Margarita P -pg. D-3-57
Roberto, Maria A -pg. D-3-57
Roberto, Maria A -pg. D-10-29

Roberto, Maria B -pg. D-4-12
Roberto, Maria B -pg. D-4-110
Roberto, Maria D -pg. D-4-106
Roberto, Maria D -pg. D-4-106
Roberto, Mary M -pg. D-3-57
Roberto, Matilde I -pg. D-3-57
Roberto, Mercedes B -pg. D-4-94
Roberto, Mercedes D -pg. D-4-106
Roberto, Pedro G -pg. D-1-28
Roberto, Simon K -pg. D-10-22
Roberto, Simona D -pg. D-4-106
Roberto, Sixta D -pg. D-4-106
Roberto, Thomas J -pg. D-3-57
Roberto, Vicenta M -pg. D-1-68
Roberto, Vicente -pg. D-5-99
Roberto, Wallace H -pg. D-4-94
Roberto, William A -pg. D-3-57
Rodrigez, Carmen R -pg. D-12-4
Rodrigez, Maria R -pg. D-12-3
Rodrigez, Vicente M -pg. D-12-3
Rodrigues, Ana R -pg. D-2-30
Rodriguez, Ana -pg. D-5-96
Rodriguez, Antonia R -pg. D-5-96
Rodriguez, Dolores B -pg. D-5-96
Rodriguez, Jesus -pg. D-5-96
Rodriguez, Jose -pg. D-5-96
Rodriguez, Lucas S -pg. D-5-96
Rodriguez, Maria -pg. D-5-96
Rodriguez, Ramon -pg. D-5-96
Rodriguez, Vicente -pg. D-5-96
Rojas, Ana I -pg. D-3-3
Rojas, Ana M -pg. D-5-44
Rojas, Ana S -pg. D-7-3
Rojas, Antonia LG -pg. D-1-6
Rojas, Antonia S -pg. D-7-3
Rojas, Antonio C -pg. D-7-22
Rojas, Asuncion LG -pg. D-1-6
Rojas, Bonita R -pg. D-3-3
Rojas, Candelaria -pg. D-3-10
Rojas, Carmen -pg. D-3-3
Rojas, Carmen LG -pg. D-1-6
Rojas, Concepcion -pg. D-3-10
Rojas, Concepcion C -pg. D-5-71
Rojas, Delores -pg. D-3-10
Rojas, Dolores -pg. D-3-2
Rojas, Enrique -pg. D-5-72
Rojas, Francisca C -pg. D-5-88
Rojas, Francisco -pg. D-3-2
Rojas, Francisco A -pg. D-1-6
Rojas, Ignacio R -pg. D-4-63
Rojas, Isabel -pg. D-3-3
Rojas, Isabel -pg. D-3-10
Rojas, Jesus LG -pg. D-4-76
Rojas, Joaquin C -pg. D-3-2
Rojas, Joaquin I -pg. D-3-3
Rojas, Joaquin R -pg. D-4-48
Rojas, Jose -pg. D-5-72
Rojas, Jose C -pg. D-5-88
Rojas, Jose R -pg. D-4-62

Rojas, Jose S -pg. D-3-3
Rojas, Juan C -pg. D-3-10
Rojas, Juan R -pg. D-7-3
Rojas, Juan S -pg. D-7-3
Rojas, Juana -pg. D-3-10
Rojas, Manuel C -pg. D-3-3
Rojas, Manuel S -pg. D-7-22
Rojas, Margarita -pg. D-3-2
Rojas, Maria -pg. D-3-2
Rojas, Maria -pg. D-3-2
Rojas, Maria -pg. D-5-72
Rojas, Maria LG -pg. D-1-6
Rojas, Maria M -pg. D-4-48
Rojas, Maria R -pg. D-3-3
Rojas, Mariano R -pg. D-4-64
Rojas, Nieves C -pg. D-5-71
Rojas, Pedro -pg. D-3-2
Rojas, Pedro A -pg. D-5-71
Rojas, Pedro R -pg. D-5-44
Rojas, Pedro S -pg. D-7-3
Rojas, Ramon S -pg. D-7-3
Rojas, Rosa -pg. D-5-72
Rojas, Vergenia LG -pg. D-1-6
Rojas, Vicente T -pg. D-5-88
Rollins, James Q -pg. D-13-38
Rolnicko, Doris R -pg. D-13-3
Rolnicko, Janet D -pg. D-13-3
Rolnicko, Walter O -pg. D-13-3
Rolnicko, Walter O -pg. D-13-3
Romero, Rita G -pg. D-1-58
Ronguillo, Maicela M -pg. D-3-63
Root, Ana I -pg. D-3-36
Root, Doroty -pg. D-3-36
Root, James E Jr -pg. D-13-21
Root, Joe -pg. D-3-36
Rosa, Emilio G -pg. D-4-18
Rosa, Felipe R -pg. D-4-18
Rosa, Felisa LG -pg. D-4-59
Rosa, Joaquin R -pg. D-4-55
Rosa, Jose G -pg. D-4-18
Rosa, Josefa J -pg. D-4-18
Rosa, Manuel M -pg. D-4-59
Rosa, Maria R -pg. D-4-59
Rosa, Oliva LG -pg. D-4-59
Rosa, Rita LG -pg. D-4-59
Rosa, Rita M -pg. D-4-59
Rosa, Teodora T -pg. D-12-11
Rosa, Teresa G -pg. D-4-18
Rosao, Charles -pg. D-13-42
Rosario, Ana A -pg. D-6-40
Rosario, Ana C -pg. D-1-64
Rosario, Ana LG -pg. D-1-48
Rosario, Ana P -pg. D-5-26
Rosario, Ana T -pg. D-2-2
Rosario, Ana T -pg. D-2-2
Rosario, Antonio C -pg. D-5-36
Rosario, Antonio T -pg. D-5-49
Rosario, Antonio T -pg. D-5-63
Rosario, Barbara M -pg. D-2-18

Rosario, Brigida C -pg. D-4-86
Rosario, Carlina F -pg. D-3-45
Rosario, Carlos R -pg. D-4-85
Rosario, Carmen S -pg. D-1-19
Rosario, Consuelo A -pg. D-2-30
Rosario, Daisy SA -pg. D-5-63
Rosario, Delfina A -pg. D-4-87
Rosario, Dolores -pg. D-3-31
Rosario, Dolores -pg. D-3-46
Rosario, Dolores A -pg. D-2-30
Rosario, Dolores A -pg. D-3-4
Rosario, Dolores M -pg. D-2-18
Rosario, Dolores M -pg. D-2-30
Rosario, Dolores P -pg. D-5-56
Rosario, Dolores T -pg. D-5-49
Rosario, Domingo C -pg. D-1-16
Rosario, Domingo C -pg. D-4-86
Rosario, Domingo R -pg. D-4-85
Rosario, Elizabeth -pg. D-3-46
Rosario, Engracia C -pg. D-4-86
Rosario, Esperanza T -pg. D-5-49
Rosario, Francisco A -pg. D-4-87
Rosario, Francisco A -pg. D-5-56
Rosario, Francisco C -pg. D-1-26
Rosario, Francisco C -pg. D-1-26
Rosario, Francisco C -pg. D-4-86
Rosario, Francisco R -pg. D-4-85
Rosario, George G -pg. D-5-37
Rosario, Gregorio P -pg. D-5-26
Rosario, Gregorio S -pg. D-1-19
Rosario, Guadalupe F -pg. D-3-3
Rosario, Guadalupe S -pg. D-1-38
Rosario, Helen T -pg. D-2-2
Rosario, Ignacio A -pg. D-5-37
Rosario, Ignacio L -pg. D-1-59
Rosario, Ignacio P -pg. D-1-54
Rosario, Jesus C -pg. D-1-16
Rosario, Jesus C -pg. D-1-64
Rosario, Jesus C -pg. D-5-95
Rosario, Jesus P -pg. D-5-26
Rosario, Jesus R -pg. D-2-30
Rosario, Joaquin C -pg. D-1-59
Rosario, Joaquin C -pg. D-4-87
Rosario, Joaquin P -pg. D-5-26
Rosario, Joaquina B -pg. D-2-58
Rosario, Joaquina R -pg. D-2-71
Rosario, Jose -pg. D-3-27
Rosario, Jose -pg. D-13-28
Rosario, Jose A -pg. D-3-4
Rosario, Jose A -pg. D-4-87
Rosario, Jose B -pg. D-4-85
Rosario, Jose B -pg. D-5-26
Rosario, Jose C -pg. D-1-26
Rosario, Jose C -pg. D-4-86
Rosario, Jose G -pg. D-5-38
Rosario, Jose P -pg. D-5-26
Rosario, Jose R -pg. D-4-85
Rosario, Jose R -pg. D-8-37
Rosario, Jose S -pg. D-2-30

Rosario, Jose T -pg. D-5-49
Rosario, Josefa C -pg. D-1-16
Rosario, Josefina A -pg. D-2-30
Rosario, Juan A -pg. D-5-76
Rosario, Juan B -pg. D-5-36
Rosario, Juan C -pg. D-3-3
Rosario, Juan M -pg. D-2-18
Rosario, Juan R -pg. D-2-30
Rosario, Juan T -pg. D-5-49
Rosario, Julia M -pg. D-2-18
Rosario, Juliana B -pg. D-2-18
Rosario, Lourdes -pg. D-3-46
Rosario, Lourdes P -pg. D-5-26
Rosario, Lucia C -pg. D-4-86
Rosario, Lucille R -pg. D-4-85
Rosario, Luisa -pg. D-3-3
Rosario, Luisa LG -pg. D-1-48
Rosario, Magdalena A -pg. D-4-87
Rosario, Magdalena C -pg. D-1-16
Rosario, Manuel -pg. D-3-27
Rosario, Manuel B -pg. D-3-3
Rosario, Manuel L -pg. D-1-59
Rosario, Manuel T -pg. D-2-2
Rosario, Maria -pg. D-3-27
Rosario, Maria A -pg. D-4-87
Rosario, Maria C -pg. D-1-26
Rosario, Maria C -pg. D-1-26
Rosario, Maria C -pg. D-1-64
Rosario, Maria C -pg. D-5-36
Rosario, Maria C -pg. D-5-36
Rosario, Maria C -pg. D-5-95
Rosario, Maria G -pg. D-5-37
Rosario, Maria M -pg. D-2-18
Rosario, Maria P -pg. D-2-30
Rosario, Maria P -pg. D-5-26
Rosario, Maria R -pg. D-4-85
Rosario, Maria S -pg. D-1-19
Rosario, Maria T -pg. D-5-77
Rosario, Miguel R -pg. D-4-85
Rosario, Milagro L -pg. D-1-59
Rosario, Pedro C -pg. D-1-16
Rosario, Pedro C -pg. D-5-64
Rosario, Pedro T -pg. D-2-2
Rosario, Priscilla M -pg. D-1-38
Rosario, Remedios R -pg. D-1-16
Rosario, Rosa L -pg. D-1-59
Rosario, Rosa M -pg. D-2-30
Rosario, Rosa S -pg. D-3-27
Rosario, Rosalia -pg. D-3-27
Rosario, Rosaline -pg. D-3-46
Rosario, Rufina T -pg. D-2-2
Rosario, Sara -pg. D-3-45
Rosario, Silvestre C -pg. D-1-59
Rosario, Soledad G -pg. D-5-37
Rosario, Soledad SA -pg. D-5-63
Rosario, Sylvia J -pg. D-1-38
Rosario, Teresa G -pg. D-1-59
Rosario, Terza C -pg. D-1-16
Rosario, Tomas R -pg. D-4-85

Rosario, Trudis C -pg. D-1-26
Rosario, Vicenta A -pg. D-4-87
Rosario, Vicenta C -pg. D-2-30
Rosario, Vicenta R -pg. D-4-85
Rosario, Vicente A -pg. D-4-87
Rosario, Vicente B -pg. D-1-54
Rosario, Vicente C -pg. D-1-26
Rosario, Vicente C -pg. D-1-64
Rosario, Vicente F -pg. D-1-26
Rosario, Vicente LG -pg. D-1-48
Rosario, Vicente Q -pg. D-2-30
Rosario, Vincente -pg. D-13-32
Rosemeice, Vernon W -pg. D-13-42
Rosendo, Manuel H -pg. D-5-98
Rothessnel, Ella M -pg. D-13-19
Roughton, Clifford -pg. D-13-46
Routridge, Shurl W -pg. D-13-13
Rowley, Milagros C -pg. D-3-59
Rowley, W W -pg. D-3-59
Rowls, Julian -pg. D-13-24
Rual, Dorn -pg. D-13-25
Rudbern, Stanley H B -pg. D-13-20
Rufio, Robert G -pg. D-13-34
Rupley, Carmen S -pg. D-4-106
Rupley, Juan SA -pg. D-4-105
Rupley, Magdalena A -pg. D-4-106
Rupley, Maria S -pg. D-4-105
Rupley, Prisciliana S -pg. D-4-106
Rupley, Santiago I -pg. D-4-106
Rusnelhart, Leland -pg. D-13-17
Rusnold, Clarence E -pg. D-13-34
Russell, Carl W -pg. D-13-40
Russell, Cyril R -pg. D-13-41
Russell, Harry M -pg. D-13-41
Russell, Mayton -pg. D-13-13
Russell, Ruby -pg. D-13-19
Ruth, James W -pg. D-5-75
Sablan, Alfred C -pg. D-6-2
Sablan, Alfred C -pg. D-11-39
Sablan, Aliandro B -pg. D-6-7
Sablan, Amalia B -pg. D-5-53
Sablan, Amalia R -pg. D-2-4
Sablan, Ana A -pg. D-4-122
Sablan, Ana B -pg. D-5-53
Sablan, Ana C -pg. D-2-65
Sablan, Ana C -pg. D-5-39
Sablan, Ana G -pg. D-2-51
Sablan, Ana I -pg. D-10-39
Sablan, Ana M -pg. D-11-5
Sablan, Ana P -pg. D-2-5
Sablan, Ana P -pg. D-2-73
Sablan, Ana P -pg. D-4-125
Sablan, Ana P -pg. D-6-11
Sablan, Ana R -pg. D-2-4
Sablan, Ana S -pg. D-1-2
Sablan, Ana S -pg. D-10-15
Sablan, Ana S -pg. D-11-39
Sablan, Andrea M -pg. D-11-5
Sablan, Andrea S -pg. D-11-13

Sablan, Andres SN -pg. D-11-19
Sablan, Angel A -pg. D-4-33
Sablan, Antonia LG -pg. D-2-54
Sablan, Antonio C -pg. D-4-114
Sablan, Antonio C -pg. D-13-29
Sablan, Antonio D -pg. D-5-53
Sablan, Antonio G -pg. D-1-66
Sablan, Antonio LG -pg. D-2-54
Sablan, Antonio Q -pg. D-2-8
Sablan, Antonio Q -pg. D-6-10
Sablan, Antonio R -pg. D-2-4
Sablan, Artemio C -pg. D-6-2
Sablan, Asuncion -pg. D-3-18
Sablan, Asuncion B -pg. D-2-42
Sablan, Asuncion G -pg. D-2-42
Sablan, Augusto S -pg. D-1-2
Sablan, Brigida Q -pg. D-6-10
Sablan, Candelaria C -pg. D-4-115
Sablan, Carlos T -pg. D-4-33
Sablan, Carmen -pg. D-3-70
Sablan, Carmen C -pg. D-4-114
Sablan, Carmen LG -pg. D-2-54
Sablan, Carmen S -pg. D-11-39
Sablan, Carolina G -pg. D-5-81
Sablan, Cecelia S -pg. D-1-9
Sablan, Cecilio S -pg. D-6-10
Sablan, Concepcion M -pg. D-3-52
Sablan, Cristina B -pg. D-5-53
Sablan, Cristobal LG -pg. D-2-54
Sablan, Daniel B -pg. D-6-7
Sablan, Diana S -pg. D-1-9
Sablan, Diego S -pg. D-6-6
Sablan, Dolores A -pg. D-3-17
Sablan, Dolores B -pg. D-11-2
Sablan, Dolores D -pg. D-2-18
Sablan, Dolores LG -pg. D-2-54
Sablan, Dolores P -pg. D-4-126
Sablan, Dolores Q -pg. D-6-10
Sablan, Dolores S -pg. D-10-15
Sablan, Dolores T -pg. D-4-33
Sablan, Dolores T -pg. D-4-113
Sablan, Dolores T -pg. D-11-29
Sablan, Dorothea S -pg. D-1-9
Sablan, Efiginia B -pg. D-1-2
Sablan, Elena B -pg. D-6-20
Sablan, Elena S -pg. D-11-20
Sablan, Emelia R -pg. D-2-4
Sablan, Emerenciana A -pg. D-4-33
Sablan, Emilia C -pg. D-4-115
Sablan, Emiliana S -pg. D-1-9
Sablan, Emiliana SN -pg. D-11-19
Sablan, Emma T -pg. D-4-113
Sablan, Engracia C -pg. D-5-39
Sablan, Enrique -pg. D-13-30
Sablan, Enrique B -pg. D-2-4
Sablan, Enrique C -pg. D-4-114
Sablan, Enrique C -pg. D-6-2
Sablan, Enrique P -pg. D-11-24
Sablan, Entropia E -pg. D-2-42

Sablan, Epifanio B -pg. D-2-4
Sablan, Estefania E -pg. D-11-39
Sablan, Eugenia T -pg. D-4-33
Sablan, Eulogio I -pg. D-10-39
Sablan, Felicita B -pg. D-2-4
Sablan, Felicita C -pg. D-5-39
Sablan, Felipa N G -pg. D-1-66
Sablan, Felisa D -pg. D-2-18
Sablan, Felix S -pg. D-1-2
Sablan, Florentina -pg. D-5-81
Sablan, Francisca C -pg. D-5-39
Sablan, Francisco A -pg. D-3-17
Sablan, Francisco B -pg. D-2-4
Sablan, Francisco B -pg. D-6-7
Sablan, Francisco C -pg. D-4-122
Sablan, Francisco C -pg. D-5-39
Sablan, Francisco C -pg. D-6-22
Sablan, Francisco C -pg. D-13-30
Sablan, Francisco M -pg. D-11-5
Sablan, Francisco P -pg. D-11-24
Sablan, Francisco S -pg. D-1-2
Sablan, Francisco S -pg. D-11-13
Sablan, Francisco S -pg. D-11-18
Sablan, Francisco S -pg. D-11-37
Sablan, Francisco SN -pg. D-11-19
Sablan, Francisco T -pg. D-4-114
Sablan, Francisco U -pg. D-11-45
Sablan, Grabiela S -pg. D-3-17
Sablan, Gregorio G -pg. D-1-66
Sablan, Gregorio S -pg. D-1-2
Sablan, Guadalupe P -pg. D-11-24
Sablan, Guadalupi B -pg. D-6-7
Sablan, Guilliermo D -pg. D-4-114
Sablan, Harvey J -pg. D-2-42
Sablan, Honorato A -pg. D-13-30
Sablan, Illuminada A -pg. D-4-33
Sablan, Isabel -pg. D-3-18
Sablan, Isabel C -pg. D-4-122
Sablan, Isabel R -pg. D-2-4
Sablan, Jaime Q -pg. D-6-10
Sablan, Jesus -pg. D-3-68
Sablan, Jesus -pg. D-5-81
Sablan, Jesus C -pg. D-5-39
Sablan, Jesus C -pg. D-6-20
Sablan, Jesus D -pg. D-2-4
Sablan, Jesus G -pg. D-1-66
Sablan, Jesus L -pg. D-4-125
Sablan, Jesus P -pg. D-2-5
Sablan, Jesus P -pg. D-4-126
Sablan, Jesus P -pg. D-11-24
Sablan, Jesus Q -pg. D-2-8
Sablan, Jesus S -pg. D-10-15
Sablan, Jesus T -pg. D-11-29
Sablan, Jesusa P -pg. D-11-24
Sablan, Joaq. P -pg. D-2-5
Sablan, Joaquin A -pg. D-11-10
Sablan, Joaquin B -pg. D-11-2
Sablan, Joaquin C -pg. D-11-24
Sablan, Joaquin D -pg. D-2-4

Sablan, Joaquin P -pg. D-4-126
Sablan, Joaquin R -pg. D-2-65
Sablan, Joaquin S -pg. D-10-15
Sablan, Joaquin S -pg. D-11-18
Sablan, John S -pg. D-4-114
Sablan, Jose -pg. D-3-18
Sablan, Jose A -pg. D-3-68
Sablan, Jose A -pg. D-4-122
Sablan, Jose B -pg. D-2-4
Sablan, Jose B -pg. D-2-8
Sablan, Jose C -pg. D-1-66
Sablan, Jose C -pg. D-2-65
Sablan, Jose C -pg. D-4-122
Sablan, Jose C -pg. D-11-29
Sablan, Jose G -pg. D-3-70
Sablan, Jose L -pg. D-4-33
Sablan, Jose M -pg. D-13-31
Sablan, Jose P -pg. D-2-5
Sablan, Jose P -pg. D-4-126
Sablan, Jose P -pg. D-5-56
Sablan, Jose P -pg. D-13-30
Sablan, Jose S -pg. D-10-15
Sablan, Jose S -pg. D-11-18
Sablan, Jose S -pg. D-11-18
Sablan, Jose S -pg. D-11-39
Sablan, Jose S -pg. D-13-25
Sablan, Jose T -pg. D-4-114
Sablan, Josefa B -pg. D-2-4
Sablan, Josefa C -pg. D-6-3
Sablan, Josefa D -pg. D-2-18
Sablan, Josefa S -pg. D-11-18
Sablan, Josefina S -pg. D-1-9
Sablan, Juan -pg. D-5-81
Sablan, Juan A -pg. D-4-122
Sablan, Juan B -pg. D-2-42
Sablan, Juan D -pg. D-11-20
Sablan, Juan P -pg. D-2-73
Sablan, Juan P -pg. D-6-11
Sablan, Juan R -pg. D-6-11
Sablan, Juan S -pg. D-1-2
Sablan, Juan S -pg. D-11-18
Sablan, Juan S -pg. D-11-39
Sablan, Juan S -pg. D-11-39
Sablan, Juan T -pg. D-11-29
Sablan, Juan U -pg. D-11-45
Sablan, Juana S -pg. D-11-13
Sablan, Juanita T -pg. D-4-113
Sablan, Lino S -pg. D-2-54
Sablan, Lorenzo A -pg. D-3-18
Sablan, Lourdes A -pg. D-4-33
Sablan, Lourdes B -pg. D-5-53
Sablan, Lourdes S -pg. D-11-18
Sablan, Luis C -pg. D-11-5
Sablan, Magdalena T -pg. D-4-33
Sablan, Manuel -pg. D-5-81
Sablan, Manuel C -pg. D-1-9
Sablan, Manuel C -pg. D-4-122
Sablan, Manuel D -pg. D-2-5
Sablan, Manuel I -pg. D-10-39

Sablan, Manuel L -pg. D-4-125
Sablan, Manuel S -pg. D-11-18
Sablan, Manuela B -pg. D-2-4
Sablan, Manuela B -pg. D-5-53
Sablan, Manuela S -pg. D-6-22
Sablan, Marcial A -pg. D-4-33
Sablan, Margarita R -pg. D-2-4
Sablan, Margarita T -pg. D-4-33
Sablan, Maria -pg. D-3-17
Sablan, Maria -pg. D-5-81
Sablan, Maria A -pg. D-4-33
Sablan, Maria B -pg. D-2-4
Sablan, Maria B -pg. D-5-53
Sablan, Maria B -pg. D-6-7
Sablan, Maria B -pg. D-6-20
Sablan, Maria B -pg. D-6-20
Sablan, Maria B -pg. D-11-2
Sablan, Maria C -pg. D-2-65
Sablan, Maria C -pg. D-2-65
Sablan, Maria C -pg. D-3-68
Sablan, Maria C -pg. D-3-70
Sablan, Maria C -pg. D-4-122
Sablan, Maria C -pg. D-5-39
Sablan, Maria C -pg. D-11-39
Sablan, Maria G -pg. D-1-66
Sablan, Maria L -pg. D-2-42
Sablan, Maria LG -pg. D-2-54
Sablan, Maria P -pg. D-2-5
Sablan, Maria S -pg. D-1-2
Sablan, Maria S -pg. D-1-35
Sablan, Maria S -pg. D-10-15
Sablan, Maria S -pg. D-11-37
Sablan, Maria SN -pg. D-11-19
Sablan, Maria T -pg. D-4-33
Sablan, Maria T -pg. D-4-113
Sablan, Maria T -pg. D-11-29
Sablan, Maria U -pg. D-11-45
Sablan, Mariano C -pg. D-2-65
Sablan, Marta R -pg. D-2-4
Sablan, Martina S -pg. D-10-15
Sablan, Matilde S -pg. D-1-2
Sablan, Mecaila S -pg. D-11-18
Sablan, Natividad C -pg. D-2-65
Sablan, Natividad C -pg. D-4-122
Sablan, Nicolas B -pg. D-5-53
Sablan, Nicolas Q -pg. D-6-10
Sablan, Nicolas S -pg. D-6-18
Sablan, Nicolasa S -pg. D-10-14
Sablan, Nivest L -pg. D-4-125
Sablan, Patricia S -pg. D-1-9
Sablan, Pedro B -pg. D-2-42
Sablan, Pedro B -pg. D-5-53
Sablan, Pedro C -pg. D-4-122
Sablan, Pedro LG -pg. D-2-54
Sablan, Pedro P -pg. D-1-2
Sablan, Pedro P -pg. D-11-45
Sablan, Pedro R -pg. D-3-52
Sablan, Peter T -pg. D-4-114
Sablan, Placida I -pg. D-10-39

Sablan, Potenciana -pg. D-3-18
Sablan, Preciousa -pg. D-3-18
Sablan, Rafael C -pg. D-3-58
Sablan, Ramon -pg. D-3-52
Sablan, Ramon D -pg. D-4-113
Sablan, Ramon R -pg. D-2-4
Sablan, Ramon T -pg. D-4-114
Sablan, Ramon U -pg. D-11-45
Sablan, Raymond G -pg. D-1-19
Sablan, Regina C -pg. D-4-122
Sablan, Remedios R -pg. D-2-4
Sablan, Remedios S -pg. D-6-22
Sablan, Rita C -pg. D-4-122
Sablan, Roque S -pg. D-10-15
Sablan, Rosa B -pg. D-5-53
Sablan, Rosa C -pg. D-4-122
Sablan, Rosa G -pg. D-1-19
Sablan, Rosa P -pg. D-2-5
Sablan, Rosa P -pg. D-6-11
Sablan, Rosa S -pg. D-11-18
Sablan, Rosalia C -pg. D-6-2
Sablan, Rosalia T -pg. D-4-33
Sablan, Rosalie R -pg. D-2-4
Sablan, Rosario G -pg. D-4-33
Sablan, Rosita C -pg. D-6-3
Sablan, Rowley C -pg. D-6-3
Sablan, Santiago T -pg. D-4-113
Sablan, Segundo S -pg. D-1-2
Sablan, Silvia G -pg. D-1-66
Sablan, Soledad T -pg. D-4-33
Sablan, Susana P -pg. D-5-16
Sablan, Sylvestre A -pg. D-11-10
Sablan, Telesforo S -pg. D-5-81
Sablan, Teresita SN -pg. D-11-19
Sablan, Theresa P -pg. D-1-9
Sablan, Thomas C -pg. D-11-39
Sablan, Thomas P -pg. D-11-5
Sablan, Tomasa Q -pg. D-2-8
Sablan, Trinidad S -pg. D-10-15
Sablan, Vicenta B -pg. D-2-4
Sablan, Vicenta C -pg. D-5-16
Sablan, Vicenta D -pg. D-2-18
Sablan, Vicenta LG -pg. D-2-54
Sablan, Vicente A -pg. D-11-10
Sablan, Vicente B -pg. D-2-4
Sablan, Vicente B -pg. D-5-53
Sablan, Vicente C -pg. D-4-122
Sablan, Vicente C -pg. D-5-39
Sablan, Vicente D -pg. D-6-3
Sablan, Vicente P -pg. D-3-17
Sablan, Vicente P -pg. D-11-24
Sablan, Vicente R -pg. D-2-51
Sablan, Vicente S -pg. D-10-15
Sablan, Vicente S -pg. D-11-18
Sablan, Vicente S -pg. D-11-39
Sablan, Vicente T -pg. D-11-29
Sablan, Vicente U -pg. D-11-39
Sablan, Virginia C -pg. D-6-2
Sacramento, Angel N -pg. D-4-36

Sacramento, Francisca N -pg. D-4-36
Safford, Siollo? -pg. D-13-8
Sagcisa, Arnol -pg. D-13-8
Sage, Edward V -pg. D-13-13
Sahagon, Ana R -pg. D-8-42
Sahagon, Esperansa P -pg. D-8-48
Sahagon, Magdalena Q -pg. D-2-31
Sahagon, Magdalena Q -pg. D-5-22
Sahagon, Manuel C -pg. D-8-42
Sahagon, Maria Q -pg. D-5-22
Sahagon, Olimpia T -pg. D-8-41
Sahagon, Tenacio R -pg. D-8-41
Sahagon, Vicente R -pg. D-8-48
Sahagun, Francisco Q -pg. D-7-24
Sakai, Ana F -pg. D-4-79
Sakai, Felix F -pg. D-4-79
Sakai, Matilde F -pg. D-4-79
Sakai, Rita F -pg. D-4-79
Sakai, Tomas F -pg. D-4-79
Sakai, Utaro -pg. D-4-79
Sakakibara, Benjamin P -pg. D-4-14
Sakakibara, Carmen P -pg. D-4-14
Sakakibara, Concepcion P -pg. D-4-14
Sakakibara, Florence P -pg. D-4-14
Sakakibara, Frank P -pg. D-4-14
Sakakibara, June P -pg. D-4-14
Sakakibara, Millan P -pg. D-4-14
Salas, Adela -pg. D-3-32
Salas, Agapito -pg. D-13-27
Salas, Agapito S -pg. D-5-63
Salas, Agueda B -pg. D-4-40
Salas, Albina -pg. D-3-67
Salas, Alicia S -pg. D-8-47
Salas, Ana -pg. D-3-3
Salas, Ana A -pg. D-4-10
Salas, Ana A -pg. D-6-24
Salas, Ana A -pg. D-7-14
Salas, Ana B -pg. D-1-37
Salas, Ana C -pg. D-2-26
Salas, Ana C -pg. D-4-66
Salas, Ana D -pg. D-2-43
Salas, Ana F -pg. D-10-16
Salas, Ana I -pg. D-10-20
Salas, Ana M -pg. D-3-12
Salas, Ana M -pg. D-6-23
Salas, Ana SN -pg. D-1-32
Salas, Angel J -pg. D-7-14
Salas, Angelina Q -pg. D-10-27
Salas, Antonia F -pg. D-10-16
Salas, Antonia R -pg. D-6-7
Salas, Antonio -pg. D-3-62
Salas, Antonio C -pg. D-10-27
Salas, Antonio C -pg. D-10-35
Salas, Antonio D -pg. D-4-66
Salas, Antonio LG -pg. D-4-40
Salas, Antonio M -pg. D-6-23
Salas, Antonio P -pg. D-4-45
Salas, Antonio Q -pg. D-3-70
Salas, Antonio Q -pg. D-4-123

Salas, Antonio R -pg. D-6-7
Salas, Antonio SN -pg. D-1-35
Salas, Antonio U -pg. D-4-48
Salas, Atanacio -pg. D-3-66
Salas, Auria G -pg. D-4-72
Salas, Barcelisa I -pg. D-10-21
Salas, Bartola SN -pg. D-1-32
Salas, Benigno D -pg. D-3-12
Salas, Brigida A -pg. D-7-14
Salas, Candelaria S -pg. D-8-47
Salas, Caridad B -pg. D-6-34
Salas, Carlos -pg. D-3-67
Salas, Carmen A -pg. D-4-10
Salas, Carmen A -pg. D-6-24
Salas, Catalina -pg. D-3-63
Salas, Catalina J -pg. D-7-14
Salas, Cecilia LG -pg. D-6-38
Salas, Cecilio M -pg. D-10-16
Salas, Cecilio S -pg. D-3-67
Salas, Celestina T -pg. D-5-96
Salas, Clotilde -pg. D-3-65
Salas, Clotilde LG -pg. D-4-57
Salas, Clotilde S -pg. D-2-5
Salas, Concepcion -pg. D-3-20
Salas, Concepcion P -pg. D-3-32
Salas, Concepcion P -pg. D-4-45
Salas, Consolacion F -pg. D-2-34
Salas, Delfina C -pg. D-6-34
Salas, Dionicio -pg. D-3-65
Salas, Dolores A -pg. D-4-10
Salas, Dolores I -pg. D-10-20
Salas, Dolores LG -pg. D-6-38
Salas, Dolores M -pg. D-3-66
Salas, Dolores S -pg. D-1-90
Salas, Domingo C -pg. D-5-50
Salas, Dorotea S -pg. D-2-5
Salas, Elias SN -pg. D-1-33
Salas, Elpidia S -pg. D-2-5
Salas, Emeterio G -pg. D-4-72
Salas, Emeterio S -pg. D-3-2
Salas, Encarnacion B -pg. D-4-40
Salas, Engracia -pg. D-3-70
Salas, Enrique A -pg. D-4-10
Salas, Enrique S -pg. D-4-47
Salas, Esperanza S -pg. D-4-47
Salas, Estella B -pg. D-4-40
Salas, Eufrosina -pg. D-3-66
Salas, Evelyn T -pg. D-2-19
Salas, Facundo C -pg. D-13-25
Salas, Felicidad B -pg. D-11-14
Salas, Felista C -pg. D-2-26
Salas, Felix -pg. D-3-12
Salas, Felix -pg. D-3-20
Salas, Felix -pg. D-3-66
Salas, Felix B -pg. D-2-26
Salas, Felix B -pg. D-5-52
Salas, Felix S -pg. D-4-47
Salas, Felix S -pg. D-8-44
Salas, Feliza J -pg. D-7-14

Salas, Francisco B -pg. D-6-34
Salas, Francisco C -pg. D-4-66
Salas, Francisco C -pg. D-6-9
Salas, Francisco P -pg. D-4-45
Salas, Francisco P -pg. D-5-53
Salas, Francisco Q -pg. D-3-3
Salas, Francisco S -pg. D-1-37
Salas, Francisco S -pg. D-2-5
Salas, Francisco S -pg. D-6-38
Salas, Francisco S -pg. D-8-47
Salas, Frank A -pg. D-7-14
Salas, Fransisco S -pg. D-6-26
Salas, Galo L -pg. D-3-32
Salas, Genoveva F -pg. D-3-68
Salas, Geraldo S -pg. D-2-5
Salas, Guadalupe B -pg. D-6-34
Salas, Guardalupe S -pg. D-8-48
Salas, Guilliermo A -pg. D-4-10
Salas, Herman A -pg. D-7-14
Salas, Ignacia -pg. D-3-2
Salas, Ignacio C -pg. D-10-35
Salas, Ignacio N -pg. D-4-11
Salas, Ignacio Q -pg. D-1-36
Salas, Isabel C -pg. D-4-66
Salas, Isabel SN -pg. D-7-18
Salas, Javier D -pg. D-2-26
Salas, Jesus -pg. D-3-32
Salas, Jesus -pg. D-3-65
Salas, Jesus A -pg. D-4-10
Salas, Jesus C -pg. D-2-26
Salas, Jesus C -pg. D-10-35
Salas, Jesus F -pg. D-3-40
Salas, Jesus F -pg. D-10-16
Salas, Jesus J -pg. D-7-14
Salas, Jesus L -pg. D-3-66
Salas, Jesus M -pg. D-5-6
Salas, Jesus M -pg. D-6-23
Salas, Jesus P -pg. D-5-53
Salas, Jesus Q -pg. D-13-31
Salas, Jesus S -pg. D-8-47
Salas, Jesus SN -pg. D-1-32
Salas, Jesus T -pg. D-4-11
Salas, Joaquin -pg. D-3-63
Salas, Joaquin -pg. D-3-66
Salas, Joaquin -pg. D-3-70
Salas, Joaquin C -pg. D-5-14
Salas, Joaquin F -pg. D-10-16
Salas, Joaquin J -pg. D-7-14
Salas, Joaquin LG -pg. D-6-38
Salas, Joaquin Q -pg. D-3-62
Salas, Joaquin S -pg. D-6-7
Salas, Joaquin S -pg. D-10-35
Salas, Joaquin SN -pg. D-1-33
Salas, Joaquina A -pg. D-6-9
Salas, Joaquina T -pg. D-4-70
Salas, Jose -pg. D-2-5
Salas, Jose -pg. D-3-2
Salas, Jose -pg. D-3-3
Salas, Jose -pg. D-3-12

Salas, Jose -pg. D-3-63
Salas, Jose -pg. D-3-65
Salas, Jose -pg. D-5-96
Salas, Jose A -pg. D-6-9
Salas, Jose B -pg. D-10-21
Salas, Jose B -pg. D-11-14
Salas, Jose C -pg. D-1-32
Salas, Jose C -pg. D-2-26
Salas, Jose C -pg. D-4-66
Salas, Jose C -pg. D-5-52
Salas, Jose C -pg. D-10-35
Salas, Jose D -pg. D-3-63
Salas, Jose F -pg. D-10-16
Salas, Jose G -pg. D-4-72
Salas, Jose I -pg. D-4-9
Salas, Jose I -pg. D-10-20
Salas, Jose J -pg. D-7-14
Salas, Jose LG -pg. D-6-38
Salas, Jose M -pg. D-5-6
Salas, Jose M -pg. D-6-23
Salas, Jose M -pg. D-10-20
Salas, Jose P -pg. D-5-50
Salas, Jose Q -pg. D-3-65
Salas, Jose S -pg. D-3-67
Salas, Jose S -pg. D-5-73
Salas, Jose S -pg. D-6-24
Salas, Jose S -pg. D-7-19
Salas, Jose S -pg. D-8-48
Salas, Jose S -pg. D-10-35
Salas, Jose SN -pg. D-4-96
Salas, Josefa -pg. D-3-20
Salas, Josefa B -pg. D-2-26
Salas, Josefa C -pg. D-10-35
Salas, Josefa F -pg. D-3-63
Salas, Josefa M -pg. D-3-2
Salas, Josefa S -pg. D-8-47
Salas, Josefina B -pg. D-1-37
Salas, Josefina S -pg. D-8-47
Salas, Juan -pg. D-3-62
Salas, Juan A -pg. D-4-10
Salas, Juan A -pg. D-4-123
Salas, Juan A -pg. D-6-24
Salas, Juan B -pg. D-5-52
Salas, Juan B -pg. D-10-21
Salas, Juan C -pg. D-10-35
Salas, Juan J -pg. D-5-96
Salas, Juan M -pg. D-5-6
Salas, Juan M -pg. D-6-23
Salas, Juan P -pg. D-4-45
Salas, Juan P -pg. D-5-50
Salas, Juan P -pg. D-5-53
Salas, Juan S -pg. D-2-79
Salas, Juan S -pg. D-3-75
Salas, Juan S -pg. D-4-48
Salas, Juan S -pg. D-4-90
Salas, Juan S -pg. D-5-73
Salas, Juan S -pg. D-6-25
Salas, Juan S -pg. D-8-48
Salas, Juan U -pg. D-4-48

Salas, Juana -pg. D-5-41
Salas, Juana B -pg. D-10-21
Salas, Julita B -pg. D-11-14
Salas, Lorenzo P -pg. D-8-48
Salas, Lucas S -pg. D-5-41
Salas, Lucia M -pg. D-6-23
Salas, Lucia Q -pg. D-10-27
Salas, Luis SN -pg. D-3-12
Salas, Luisa B -pg. D-11-14
Salas, Luisa S -pg. D-3-67
Salas, Magdalena -pg. D-3-70
Salas, Magdalena A -pg. D-4-10
Salas, Magdalena C -pg. D-10-35
Salas, Magdalena Q -pg. D-5-14
Salas, Magdalena U -pg. D-4-48
Salas, Manuel B -pg. D-11-14
Salas, Manuel F -pg. D-6-34
Salas, Manuel J -pg. D-7-14
Salas, Manuela C -pg. D-3-70
Salas, Manuela M -pg. D-5-6
Salas, Manuela S -pg. D-6-16
Salas, Manuela SN -pg. D-1-32
Salas, Marcela C -pg. D-10-35
Salas, Margarita S -pg. D-8-48
Salas, Maria -pg. D-3-2
Salas, Maria -pg. D-3-63
Salas, Maria -pg. D-3-65
Salas, Maria B -pg. D-4-40
Salas, Maria B -pg. D-5-52
Salas, Maria B -pg. D-10-21
Salas, Maria B -pg. D-11-14
Salas, Maria C -pg. D-3-3
Salas, Maria C -pg. D-10-35
Salas, Maria F -pg. D-1-61
Salas, Maria F -pg. D-2-34
Salas, Maria F -pg. D-3-20
Salas, Maria F -pg. D-10-16
Salas, Maria I -pg. D-10-20
Salas, Maria I -pg. D-10-21
Salas, Maria J -pg. D-7-14
Salas, Maria LG -pg. D-6-38
Salas, Maria M -pg. D-4-10
Salas, Maria M -pg. D-5-6
Salas, Maria P -pg. D-4-45
Salas, Maria P -pg. D-5-53
Salas, Maria Q -pg. D-4-61
Salas, Maria S -pg. D-1-37
Salas, Maria S -pg. D-6-26
Salas, Maria S -pg. D-8-47
Salas, Maria Y -pg. D-3-52
Salas, Mariano SN -pg. D-5-6
Salas, Martina C -pg. D-10-35
Salas, Matilde -pg. D-3-67
Salas, Mercedes -pg. D-3-20
Salas, Mercedes S -pg. D-1-37
Salas, Miguel -pg. D-3-32
Salas, Miguel -pg. D-3-65
Salas, Miguel S -pg. D-4-90
Salas, Nicolas Q -pg. D-1-61

Salas, Nicolasa J -pg. D-7-14
Salas, Nicolasa L -pg. D-4-72
Salas, Nieves A -pg. D-4-123
Salas, Otelia S -pg. D-2-5
Salas, Patricia S -pg. D-4-47
Salas, Pedro C -pg. D-4-61
Salas, Pedro C -pg. D-4-61
Salas, Pedro C -pg. D-5-73
Salas, Pedro LG -pg. D-6-38
Salas, Pedro P -pg. D-5-52
Salas, Pedro Q -pg. D-4-61
Salas, Pedro S -pg. D-8-48
Salas, Pedro T -pg. D-4-11
Salas, Petronilia J -pg. D-7-14
Salas, Pilar S -pg. D-3-66
Salas, Providenia -pg. D-3-67
Salas, Rafaela -pg. D-3-67
Salas, Ramon C -pg. D-4-40
Salas, Ramon C -pg. D-5-74
Salas, Ramon S -pg. D-4-46
Salas, Ramona LG -pg. D-3-65
Salas, Regina -pg. D-3-70
Salas, Regina S -pg. D-2-43
Salas, Remedios -pg. D-3-70
Salas, Reymunda F -pg. D-2-34
Salas, Ricardo -pg. D-3-65
Salas, Rita A -pg. D-4-96
Salas, Rita C -pg. D-4-66
Salas, Rita P -pg. D-5-50
Salas, Rita P -pg. D-10-20
Salas, Roberto A -pg. D-7-14
Salas, Romeo C -pg. D-6-22
Salas, Rosa A -pg. D-6-9
Salas, Rosa B -pg. D-4-40
Salas, Rosa B -pg. D-5-52
Salas, Rosa C -pg. D-1-35
Salas, Rosa C -pg. D-4-61
Salas, Rosa C -pg. D-5-74
Salas, Rosa F -pg. D-10-16
Salas, Rosa P -pg. D-4-45
Salas, Rosa S -pg. D-4-46
Salas, Rosa S -pg. D-10-35
Salas, Rosa T -pg. D-4-11
Salas, Rosalia S -pg. D-6-26
Salas, Rosario -pg. D-3-62
Salas, Rosario -pg. D-3-70
Salas, Rosario B -pg. D-5-52
Salas, Rosario B -pg. D-6-34
Salas, Salvador -pg. D-3-67
Salas, Sergio S -pg. D-2-5
Salas, Silvia U -pg. D-4-48
Salas, Simplicia -pg. D-3-66
Salas, Simplicia -pg. D-3-67
Salas, Soledad A -pg. D-4-10
Salas, Soledad B -pg. D-6-35
Salas, Soledad B -pg. D-10-21
Salas, Soledad C -pg. D-3-62
Salas, Soledad M -pg. D-6-23
Salas, Soledad S -pg. D-6-22

Salas, Susana C -pg. D-3-62
Salas, Teresa C -pg. D-10-35
Salas, Theresa SN -pg. D-1-32
Salas, Tomas -pg. D-3-12
Salas, Tomasa -pg. D-3-65
Salas, Trinidad -pg. D-3-20
Salas, Trinidad LG -pg. D-6-38
Salas, Trinidad LG -pg. D-11-8
Salas, Ursula S -pg. D-4-101
Salas, Vicenta A -pg. D-4-96
Salas, Vicente -pg. D-3-3
Salas, Vicente -pg. D-3-20
Salas, Vicente A -pg. D-4-10
Salas, Vicente B -pg. D-6-35
Salas, Vicente C -pg. D-4-66
Salas, Vicente C -pg. D-6-7
Salas, Vicente M -pg. D-6-23
Salas, Vicente M -pg. D-10-21
Salas, Vicente S -pg. D-3-20
Salas, Vicente S -pg. D-6-34
Salas, Vinancio A -pg. D-4-10
Salas, Vincente -pg. D-13-35
Salas, Virginia -pg. D-3-20
Salas, William -pg. D-3-62
Salatesrio, W -pg. D-13-18
Saloaga, Cristina C -pg. D-11-34
Salubnamnam, Faustina S -pg. D-6-22
Salubnamnam, Juan T -pg. D-6-22
Saluboramnam, Ana B -pg. D-6-25
Saluboramnam, Consolasion B -pg. D-6-25
Saluboramnam, Maria B -pg. D-6-25
Saluboramnam, Vicente T -pg. D-6-25
San Agustin, Alberto S -pg. D-2-23
San Agustin, Alejandro C -pg. D-2-6
San Agustin, Ana B -pg. D-2-2
San Agustin, Ana C -pg. D-4-121
San Agustin, Ana C -pg. D-5-42
San Agustin, Antonia C -pg. D-5-26
San Agustin, Arturo C -pg. D-5-31
San Agustin, Asuncion B -pg. D-2-2
San Agustin, Asuncion SA -pg. D-2-29
San Agustin, Candido S -pg. D-3-32
San Agustin, Caridad R -pg. D-5-28
San Agustin, Carlos SA -pg. D-2-25
San Agustin, Carmen B -pg. D-2-2
San Agustin, Dolores B -pg. D-2-2
San Agustin, Dolores B -pg. D-2-2
San Agustin, Dolores E -pg. D-2-6
San Agustin, Dolores L -pg. D-2-75
San Agustin, Dolores M -pg. D-5-35
San Agustin, Eduardo SA -pg. D-2-29
San Agustin, Eliza D -pg. D-5-25
San Agustin, Enrique Q -pg. D-7-23
San Agustin, Faustino SA -pg. D-5-38
San Agustin, Francisco C -pg. D-5-18
San Agustin, Francisco C -pg. D-5-26
San Agustin, Francisco S -pg. D-2-34
San Agustin, George S -pg. D-2-23
San Agustin, Gertrudes C -pg. D-5-42

San Agustin, Gonzalo C -pg. D-5-18
San Agustin, Gregorio C -pg. D-5-42
San Agustin, Ignacio C -pg. D-5-42
San Agustin, Isabel R -pg. D-5-28
San Agustin, Isabel S -pg. D-2-33
San Agustin, Jesus R -pg. D-5-28
San Agustin, Jesus SN -pg. D-2-6
San Agustin, Jesusa C -pg. D-5-32
San Agustin, Joaquin C -pg. D-2-39
San Agustin, Joaquin C -pg. D-5-26
San Agustin, Joaquina SA -pg. D-2-29
San Agustin, John -pg. D-3-32
San Agustin, Jose C -pg. D-1-54
San Agustin, Jose C -pg. D-5-18
San Agustin, Jose D -pg. D-5-31
San Agustin, Jose E -pg. D-5-28
San Agustin, Jose H -pg. D-2-6
San Agustin, Jose P -pg. D-5-31
San Agustin, Jose SA -pg. D-2-6
San Agustin, Jose SA -pg. D-2-25
San Agustin, Josefa B -pg. D-2-2
San Agustin, Josefa B -pg. D-2-2
San Agustin, Josefa M -pg. D-5-25
San Agustin, Josefa M -pg. D-5-38
San Agustin, Josefina R -pg. D-5-28
San Agustin, Juan B -pg. D-2-2
San Agustin, Juan C -pg. D-2-23
San Agustin, Juan C -pg. D-4-121
San Agustin, Juan C -pg. D-5-42
San Agustin, Juan R -pg. D-5-28
San Agustin, Juan S -pg. D-2-33
San Agustin, Juana C -pg. D-2-25
San Agustin, Lourdes C -pg. D-5-75
San Agustin, Lucia C -pg. D-2-56
San Agustin, Magdalena R -pg. D-2-60
San Agustin, Manuel C -pg. D-5-18
San Agustin, Maria -pg. D-3-32
San Agustin, Maria B -pg. D-2-2
San Agustin, Maria C -pg. D-5-18
San Agustin, Maria D -pg. D-2-29
San Agustin, Maria L -pg. D-2-39
San Agustin, Maria P -pg. D-5-31
San Agustin, Maria Q -pg. D-5-31
San Agustin, Maria R -pg. D-5-28
San Agustin, Maria S -pg. D-2-23
San Agustin, Maria S -pg. D-2-33
San Agustin, Maria S -pg. D-2-33
San Agustin, Mariano C -pg. D-5-26
San Agustin, Mariano R -pg. D-5-28
San Agustin, Mariano SN -pg. D-2-6
San Agustin, Miguel E -pg. D-2-33
San Agustin, Miguel S -pg. D-2-33
San Agustin, Modesta S -pg. D-2-34
San Agustin, Olimpia M -pg. D-5-35
San Agustin, Patricia S -pg. D-2-23
San Agustin, Pedro M -pg. D-5-38
San Agustin, Pedro S -pg. D-2-23
San Agustin, Pedro S -pg. D-2-33
San Agustin, Pedro SA -pg. D-2-2

San Agustin, Ramon B -pg. D-2-2
San Agustin, Ramon P -pg. D-5-31
San Agustin, Ramon S -pg. D-5-35
San Agustin, Remedio B -pg. D-2-2
San Agustin, Reymunda S -pg. D-2-34
San Agustin, Rita S -pg. D-2-33
San Agustin, Rosa C -pg. D-2-25
San Agustin, Rosa C -pg. D-5-31
San Agustin, Rosa M -pg. D-5-39
San Agustin, Rosario B -pg. D-2-2
San Agustin, Rosario SA -pg. D-2-29
San Agustin, Susana P -pg. D-5-31
San Agustin, Ursula SA -pg. D-2-29
San Agustin, Vicente B -pg. D-2-2
San Agustin, Vicente D -pg. D-5-25
San Agustin, Vicente M -pg. D-5-39
San Agustin, Victor M -pg. D-5-38
San Agustin, Victoria SA -pg. D-2-29
San Agustin, Virginia S -pg. D-2-34
San Luis, Maria A -pg. D-5-95
San Miguel, Ana Q -pg. D-5-70
San Miguel, Angustia -pg. D-5-85
San Miguel, Antonia C -pg. D-5-85
San Miguel, Concepcion -pg. D-5-85
San Miguel, Delfina -pg. D-5-69
San Miguel, Delfina S -pg. D-11-24
San Miguel, Felipe -pg. D-5-69
San Miguel, Fidela -pg. D-5-69
San Miguel, Jose C -pg. D-5-85
San Miguel, Jose M -pg. D-1-40
San Miguel, Juan -pg. D-5-85
San Miguel, Juan Q -pg. D-11-24
San Miguel, Justa S -pg. D-11-24
San Miguel, Manuel Q -pg. D-5-69
San Miguel, Maria -pg. D-5-85
San Miguel, Rosario -pg. D-5-85
San Miguel, Sylvia S -pg. D-11-24
San Miguel, Tomasa S -pg. D-11-24
San Miguel, Trinidad -pg. D-5-70
San Miguel, Vicenta B -pg. D-1-40
San Nicolas, Adela C -pg. D-5-22
San Nicolas, Adela P -pg. D-10-3
San Nicolas, Adela T -pg. D-1-64
San Nicolas, Agustin M -pg. D-8-9
San Nicolas, Alfredo -pg. D-8-21
San Nicolas, Alfredo C -pg. D-1-9
San Nicolas, Amali A -pg. D-5-2
San Nicolas, Amelia P -pg. D-2-57
San Nicolas, Ana -pg. D-3-48
San Nicolas, Ana A -pg. D-2-58
San Nicolas, Ana A -pg. D-5-2
San Nicolas, Ana C -pg. D-6-16
San Nicolas, Ana C -pg. D-8-8
San Nicolas, Ana C -pg. D-9-6
San Nicolas, Ana C -pg. D-9-8
San Nicolas, Ana C -pg. D-10-13
San Nicolas, Ana D -pg. D-1-21
San Nicolas, Ana G -pg. D-1-38
San Nicolas, Ana P -pg. D-1-7

San Nicolas, Ana S -pg. D-7-22
San Nicolas, Ana S -pg. D-8-38
San Nicolas, Ana T -pg. D-1-41
San Nicolas, Ana T -pg. D-6-31
San Nicolas, Angelina M -pg. D-8-21
San Nicolas, Antoino F -pg. D-10-3
San Nicolas, Antonia C -pg. D-6-16
San Nicolas, Antonia C -pg. D-8-15
San Nicolas, Antonia F -pg. D-8-15
San Nicolas, Antonia LG -pg. D-8-16
San Nicolas, Antonia T -pg. D-11-25
San Nicolas, Antonio B -pg. D-6-22
San Nicolas, Antonio C -pg. D-8-17
San Nicolas, Antonio D -pg. D-13-30
San Nicolas, Antonio E -pg. D-9-20
San Nicolas, Antonio G -pg. D-2-43
San Nicolas, Antonio L -pg. D-7-5
San Nicolas, Antonio M -pg. D-5-50
San Nicolas, Antonio P -pg. D-8-17
San Nicolas, Antonio S -pg. D-10-5
San Nicolas, Antonio SN -pg. D-2-68
San Nicolas, Antonio SN -pg. D-7-20
San Nicolas, Antonio SN -pg. D-8-38
San Nicolas, Antonio SN -pg. D-9-25
San Nicolas, Asuncion M -pg. D-7-19
San Nicolas, Asuncion T -pg. D-9-25
San Nicolas, Atanacio C -pg. D-5-22
San Nicolas, Aurelia M -pg. D-8-21
San Nicolas, Barbara C -pg. D-4-20
San Nicolas, Barceliza C -pg. D-6-22
San Nicolas, Beatres T -pg. D-1-41
San Nicolas, Beatrice C -pg. D-2-16
San Nicolas, Beatris C -pg. D-4-119
San Nicolas, Beatris C -pg. D-7-20
San Nicolas, Beatris M -pg. D-4-110
San Nicolas, Benancio S -pg. D-8-38
San Nicolas, Benita -pg. D-2-44
San Nicolas, Candido A -pg. D-5-2
San Nicolas, Carlos -pg. D-3-25
San Nicolas, Carmelo C -pg. D-6-3
San Nicolas, Carmen C -pg. D-4-119
San Nicolas, Carmen C -pg. D-6-3
San Nicolas, Carmen C -pg. D-8-16
San Nicolas, Carmen G -pg. D-12-15
San Nicolas, Carmen L -pg. D-2-80
San Nicolas, Carmen M -pg. D-7-19
San Nicolas, Carmen P -pg. D-10-3
San Nicolas, Carmen R -pg. D-3-74
San Nicolas, Carmen S -pg. D-8-38
San Nicolas, Catalina C -pg. D-8-8
San Nicolas, Catlina P -pg. D-10-4
San Nicolas, Cecilia M -pg. D-4-37
San Nicolas, Concepcion C -pg. D-1-63
San Nicolas, Concepcion C -pg. D-8-16
San Nicolas, Concepcion C -pg. D-9-6
San Nicolas, Concepcion M -pg. D-6-17
San Nicolas, Concepcion S -pg. D-8-38
San Nicolas, Concepcion SN -pg. D-2-79
San Nicolas, Conelia T -pg. D-1-41

San Nicolas, Consalacion C -pg. D-4-119
San Nicolas, Consalacion C -pg. D-4-119
San Nicolas, Consolacion -pg. D-5-86
San Nicolas, Consolacion C -pg. D-10-13
San Nicolas, Consolacion S -pg. D-7-21
San Nicolas, Consuelo C -pg. D-9-6
San Nicolas, Cristina G -pg. D-6-15
San Nicolas, Cristobal S -pg. D-8-38
San Nicolas, David S -pg. D-6-38
San Nicolas, Delgadina C -pg. D-2-68
San Nicolas, Dolores -pg. D-3-48
San Nicolas, Dolores C -pg. D-1-38
San Nicolas, Dolores C -pg. D-5-22
San Nicolas, Dolores M -pg. D-3-25
San Nicolas, Dolores M -pg. D-5-85
San Nicolas, Dolores N -pg. D-8-22
San Nicolas, Dolores P -pg. D-10-4
San Nicolas, Dolores T -pg. D-4-24
San Nicolas, Dominga A -pg. D-3-48
San Nicolas, Elias C -pg. D-2-44
San Nicolas, Elias N -pg. D-8-21
San Nicolas, Elizabeth C -pg. D-5-22
San Nicolas, Elizabeth M -pg. D-8-21
San Nicolas, Emilia -pg. D-3-75
San Nicolas, Enrique C -pg. D-2-68
San Nicolas, Enrique C -pg. D-6-3
San Nicolas, Enrique R -pg. D-1-38
San Nicolas, Enrique S -pg. D-8-38
San Nicolas, Ettmina G -pg. D-1-39
San Nicolas, Eugenio -pg. D-3-12
San Nicolas, Eugenio I -pg. D-2-27
San Nicolas, Eugenio M -pg. D-4-37
San Nicolas, Eugenio V -pg. D-3-12
San Nicolas, Felicita C -pg. D-7-20
San Nicolas, Felicita L -pg. D-1-37
San Nicolas, Felipe C -pg. D-6-3
San Nicolas, Felipe T -pg. D-8-14
San Nicolas, Felipe U -pg. D-4-37
San Nicolas, Felix -pg. D-3-4
San Nicolas, Felix C -pg. D-6-16
San Nicolas, Felix E -pg. D-9-6
San Nicolas, Felix P -pg. D-2-58
San Nicolas, Felomena E -pg. D-9-8
San Nicolas, Fidela C -pg. D-2-68
San Nicolas, Filomeno T -pg. D-7-5
San Nicolas, Florencio A -pg. D-13-30
San Nicolas, Francisca C -pg. D-5-21
San Nicolas, Francisca M -pg. D-4-37
San Nicolas, Francisca S -pg. D-8-38
San Nicolas, Francisco -pg. D-3-4
San Nicolas, Francisco -pg. D-3-12
San Nicolas, Francisco -pg. D-3-75
San Nicolas, Francisco A -pg. D-6-31
San Nicolas, Francisco A -pg. D-7-19
San Nicolas, Francisco C -pg. D-5-22
San Nicolas, Francisco C -pg. D-6-22
San Nicolas, Francisco C -pg. D-8-29
San Nicolas, Francisco C -pg. D-9-8
San Nicolas, Francisco G -pg. D-1-38

San Nicolas, Francisco I -pg. D-2-27
San Nicolas, Francisco P -pg. D-10-3
San Nicolas, Francisco T -pg. D-8-24
San Nicolas, Froilan -pg. D-9-7
San Nicolas, Gabriela C -pg. D-7-5
San Nicolas, Geronimo C -pg. D-13-27
San Nicolas, Geronmio T -pg. D-8-24
San Nicolas, Gertrudes P -pg. D-10-4
San Nicolas, Gregorio A -pg. D-7-19
San Nicolas, Gregorio P -pg. D-10-3
San Nicolas, Gregorio S -pg. D-4-75
San Nicolas, Guadalupe T -pg. D-1-41
San Nicolas, Guillermo F -pg. D-10-3
San Nicolas, Herman D -pg. D-2-44
San Nicolas, Hilario SN -pg. D-5-20
San Nicolas, Ignacia A -pg. D-5-2
San Nicolas, Ignacia P -pg. D-8-17
San Nicolas, Ignacia S -pg. D-7-22
San Nicolas, Ignacio -pg. D-3-4
San Nicolas, Ignacio A -pg. D-5-85
San Nicolas, Ignacio G -pg. D-12-15
San Nicolas, Ignacio LG -pg. D-8-15
San Nicolas, Isabel C -pg. D-4-119
San Nicolas, Isabel C -pg. D-8-14
San Nicolas, Isabel P -pg. D-1-7
San Nicolas, Isabel P -pg. D-1-45
San Nicolas, Isabel S -pg. D-8-38
San Nicolas, Jacinto P -pg. D-2-57
San Nicolas, Jesus -pg. D-3-25
San Nicolas, Jesus -pg. D-3-48
San Nicolas, Jesus -pg. D-11-12
San Nicolas, Jesus A -pg. D-10-29
San Nicolas, Jesus A -pg. D-12-16
San Nicolas, Jesus B -pg. D-9-6
San Nicolas, Jesus C -pg. D-8-16
San Nicolas, Jesus C -pg. D-10-5
San Nicolas, Jesus C -pg. D-10-13
San Nicolas, Jesus F -pg. D-8-15
San Nicolas, Jesus M -pg. D-7-19
San Nicolas, Jesus S -pg. D-5-50
San Nicolas, Jesus S -pg. D-9-20
San Nicolas, Jesus T -pg. D-1-41
San Nicolas, Jesus T -pg. D-8-24
San Nicolas, Joaquin -pg. D-1-37
San Nicolas, Joaquin -pg. D-3-48
San Nicolas, Joaquin A -pg. D-12-16
San Nicolas, Joaquin C -pg. D-1-63
San Nicolas, Joaquin C -pg. D-6-16
San Nicolas, Joaquin C -pg. D-10-13
San Nicolas, Joaquin F -pg. D-8-15
San Nicolas, Joaquin G -pg. D-5-20
San Nicolas, Joaquin I -pg. D-2-27
San Nicolas, Joaquin L -pg. D-8-9
San Nicolas, Joaquin L -pg. D-10-3
San Nicolas, Joaquin P -pg. D-13-30
San Nicolas, Joaquin S -pg. D-10-33
San Nicolas, Joaquin T -pg. D-9-6
San Nicolas, Joaquina -pg. D-3-75
San Nicolas, Joaquina C -pg. D-2-43

San Nicolas, Joaquina C -pg. D-8-16
San Nicolas, Joaquina S -pg. D-9-20
San Nicolas, Jose -pg. D-3-48
San Nicolas, Jose -pg. D-5-85
San Nicolas, Jose A -pg. D-10-29
San Nicolas, Jose B -pg. D-6-38
San Nicolas, Jose C -pg. D-1-7
San Nicolas, Jose C -pg. D-1-63
San Nicolas, Jose C -pg. D-3-74
San Nicolas, Jose C -pg. D-5-22
San Nicolas, Jose C -pg. D-6-16
San Nicolas, Jose C -pg. D-7-5
San Nicolas, Jose C -pg. D-8-7
San Nicolas, Jose C -pg. D-10-13
San Nicolas, Jose D -pg. D-5-50
San Nicolas, Jose F -pg. D-1-54
San Nicolas, Jose F -pg. D-8-15
San Nicolas, Jose G -pg. D-1-38
San Nicolas, Jose G -pg. D-5-21
San Nicolas, Jose G -pg. D-12-15
San Nicolas, Jose L -pg. D-7-5
San Nicolas, Jose L -pg. D-8-9
San Nicolas, Jose M -pg. D-8-22
San Nicolas, Jose M -pg. D-12-16
San Nicolas, Jose R -pg. D-3-71
San Nicolas, Jose S -pg. D-5-50
San Nicolas, Jose S -pg. D-6-15
San Nicolas, Jose S -pg. D-6-38
San Nicolas, Jose S -pg. D-7-21
San Nicolas, Jose S -pg. D-9-20
San Nicolas, Jose SN -pg. D-5-71
San Nicolas, Jose T -pg. D-1-63
San Nicolas, Jose T -pg. D-4-25
San Nicolas, Josefa A -pg. D-6-40
San Nicolas, Josefa C -pg. D-2-68
San Nicolas, Josefa C -pg. D-10-5
San Nicolas, Josefa M -pg. D-8-15
San Nicolas, Josefa M -pg. D-8-29
San Nicolas, Josefa S -pg. D-4-6
San Nicolas, Josefina A -pg. D-9-24
San Nicolas, Josefina C -pg. D-1-9
San Nicolas, Josefina C -pg. D-4-120
San Nicolas, Josefina C -pg. D-10-5
San Nicolas, Josefina T -pg. D-8-24
San Nicolas, Juan -pg. D-3-75
San Nicolas, Juan A -pg. D-9-24
San Nicolas, Juan A -pg. D-10-29
San Nicolas, Juan A -pg. D-12-16
San Nicolas, Juan A -pg. D-13-31
San Nicolas, Juan C -pg. D-4-20
San Nicolas, Juan C -pg. D-6-3
San Nicolas, Juan C -pg. D-7-5
San Nicolas, Juan C -pg. D-8-8
San Nicolas, Juan C -pg. D-9-6
San Nicolas, Juan G -pg. D-6-15
San Nicolas, Juan M -pg. D-8-21
San Nicolas, Juan P -pg. D-1-7
San Nicolas, Juan P -pg. D-10-3
San Nicolas, Juan R -pg. D-1-12

San Nicolas, Juan S -pg. D-2-44
San Nicolas, Juan S -pg. D-4-75
San Nicolas, Juan S -pg. D-9-8
San Nicolas, Juan S -pg. D-9-20
San Nicolas, Juan SN -pg. D-2-69
San Nicolas, Juana -pg. D-3-48
San Nicolas, Juana SN -pg. D-11-13
San Nicolas, Juana T -pg. D-9-25
San Nicolas, Julian M -pg. D-4-37
San Nicolas, Juliana -pg. D-3-5
San Nicolas, Lourdes P -pg. D-2-57
San Nicolas, Lucas L -pg. D-8-9
San Nicolas, Luciano C -pg. D-8-30
San Nicolas, Luis -pg. D-3-71
San Nicolas, Luis A -pg. D-5-2
San Nicolas, Luis S -pg. D-5-22
San Nicolas, Luisa M -pg. D-8-22
San Nicolas, Lunisia C -pg. D-6-22
San Nicolas, Magdalena -pg. D-3-75
San Nicolas, Magdalena B -pg. D-4-15
San Nicolas, Magdalena G -pg. D-12-15
San Nicolas, Magdalena L -pg. D-10-3
San Nicolas, Magdalena S -pg. D-4-75
San Nicolas, Manuel C -pg. D-8-16
San Nicolas, Manuel LG -pg. D-8-15
San Nicolas, Manuel P -pg. D-10-4
San Nicolas, Manuel U -pg. D-10-13
San Nicolas, Manuela T -pg. D-1-41
San Nicolas, Margarita -pg. D-1-9
San Nicolas, Margarita C -pg. D-7-5
San Nicolas, Maria -pg. D-3-25
San Nicolas, Maria -pg. D-3-75
San Nicolas, Maria -pg. D-5-85
San Nicolas, Maria A -pg. D 7 19
San Nicolas, Maria A -pg. D-9-24
San Nicolas, Maria A -pg. D-10-29
San Nicolas, Maria A -pg. D-12-16
San Nicolas, Maria C -pg. D-1-25
San Nicolas, Maria C -pg. D-1-63
San Nicolas, Maria C -pg. D-1-63
San Nicolas, Maria C -pg. D-2-16
San Nicolas, Maria C -pg. D-4-20
San Nicolas, Maria C -pg. D-7-5
San Nicolas, Maria C -pg. D-7-20
San Nicolas, Maria C -pg. D-8-8
San Nicolas, Maria C -pg. D-9-8
San Nicolas, Maria C -pg. D-9-8
San Nicolas, Maria C -pg. D-10-5
San Nicolas, Maria D -pg. D-1-21
San Nicolas, Maria D -pg. D-2-13
San Nicolas, Maria D -pg. D-2-44
San Nicolas, Maria F -pg. D-8-15
San Nicolas, Maria G -pg. D-4-48
San Nicolas, Maria G -pg. D-5-20
San Nicolas, Maria G -pg. D-6-15
San Nicolas, Maria G -pg. D-12-15
San Nicolas, Maria L -pg. D-7-5
San Nicolas, Maria L -pg. D-10-3
San Nicolas, Maria M -pg. D-3-71

San Nicolas, Maria M -pg. D-4-89
San Nicolas, Maria M -pg. D-8-21
San Nicolas, Maria M -pg. D-8-29
San Nicolas, Maria M -pg. D-9-8
San Nicolas, Maria M -pg. D-12-16
San Nicolas, Maria P -pg. D-1-7
San Nicolas, Maria P -pg. D-1-7
San Nicolas, Maria P -pg. D-2-57
San Nicolas, Maria S -pg. D-6-38
San Nicolas, Maria S -pg. D-7-21
San Nicolas, Maria S -pg. D-8-38
San Nicolas, Maria S -pg. D-13-43
San Nicolas, Maria SN -pg. D-9-25
San Nicolas, Maria T -pg. D-1-41
San Nicolas, Maria T -pg. D-8-24
San Nicolas, Maria T -pg. D-9-7
San Nicolas, Maria C -pg. D-6-22
San Nicolas, Maria Magdalena S -pg. D-6-38
San Nicolas, Mariano C -pg. D-8-15
San Nicolas, Mariano R -pg. D-11-25
San Nicolas, Martina L -pg. D-8-9
San Nicolas, Mattina G -pg. D-1-38
San Nicolas, Maxima S -pg. D-10-7
San Nicolas, Nicolasa A -pg. D-9-24
San Nicolas, Nicolasa S -pg. D-10-33
San Nicolas, Nicolasa SN -pg. D-5-89
San Nicolas, Nicolasa T -pg. D-8-24
San Nicolas, Nieves C -pg. D-2-80
San Nicolas, Olimpia -pg. D-3-12
San Nicolas, Olimpia -pg. D-3-75
San Nicolas, Paula SN -pg. D-2-75
San Nicolas, Pedro -pg. D-3-75
San Nicolas, Pedro -pg. D-5-86
San Nicolas, Pedro C -pg. D-8-8
San Nicolas, Pedro C -pg. D-9-8
San Nicolas, Pedro D -pg. D-2-44
San Nicolas, Pedro S -pg. D-9-20
San Nicolas, Pedro C -pg. D-4-15
San Nicolas, Pilar T -pg. D-9-25
San Nicolas, Quintin M -pg. D-8-29
San Nicolas, Rafael P -pg. D-8-17
San Nicolas, Ramon T -pg. D-8-24
San Nicolas, Ramona C -pg. D-9-6
San Nicolas, Ramona C -pg. D-11-13
San Nicolas, Redusindo A -pg. D-5-2
San Nicolas, Regina D -pg. D-1-21
San Nicolas, Remedios T -pg. D-1-41
San Nicolas, Rita -pg. D-3-48
San Nicolas, Rita A -pg. D-7-19
San Nicolas, Rita A -pg. D-9-24
San Nicolas, Rita P -pg. D-3-4
San Nicolas, Rosa -pg. D-3-75
San Nicolas, Rosa A -pg. D-10-29
San Nicolas, Rosa C -pg. D-2-16
San Nicolas, Rosa C -pg. D-4-119
San Nicolas, Rosa C -pg. D-7-20
San Nicolas, Rosa C -pg. D-8-8
San Nicolas, Rosa C -pg. D-8-14
San Nicolas, Rosa D -pg. D-2-44

San Nicolas, Rosa L -pg. D-10-3
San Nicolas, Rosa M -pg. D-4-37
San Nicolas, Rosa P -pg. D-1-7
San Nicolas, Rosa T -pg. D-6-31
San Nicolas, Rosalia -pg. D-3-25
San Nicolas, Rosalia C -pg. D-7-5
San Nicolas, Rosaria S -pg. D-9-20
San Nicolas, Rosario C -pg. D-8-14
San Nicolas, Rosario D -pg. D-2-44
San Nicolas, Rosina G -pg. D-6-15
San Nicolas, Rufina P -pg. D-10-3
San Nicolas, Rufino C -pg. D-8-16
San Nicolas, Seferina C -pg. D-8-8
San Nicolas, Segundo P -pg. D-8-17
San Nicolas, Silvia I -pg. D-2-27
San Nicolas, Soledad -pg. D-3-48
San Nicolas, Soledad G -pg. D-12-15
San Nicolas, Soledad M -pg. D-12-16
San Nicolas, Solidad M -pg. D-8-21
San Nicolas, Solidad M -pg. D-8-29
San Nicolas, Tomas C -pg. D-10-14
San Nicolas, Tomas G -pg. D-6-15
San Nicolas, Tomasa A -pg. D-7-19
San Nicolas, Tomasa M -pg. D-8-29
San Nicolas, Tomasa S -pg. D-8-38
San Nicolas, Trinidad M -pg. D-3-14
San Nicolas, Trinidad S -pg. D-8-38
San Nicolas, Vicenta -pg. D-3-71
San Nicolas, Vicenta C -pg. D-1-9
San Nicolas, Vicenta C -pg. D-7-5
San Nicolas, Vicenta C -pg. D-8-15
San Nicolas, Vicenta T -pg. D-2-69
San Nicolas, Vicenta T -pg. D-3-12
San Nicolas, Vicente -pg. D-5-85
San Nicolas, Vicente A -pg. D-12-15
San Nicolas, Vicente B -pg. D-4-30
San Nicolas, Vicente C -pg. D-4-20
San Nicolas, Vicente C -pg. D-7-5
San Nicolas, Vicente C -pg. D-8-15
San Nicolas, Vicente C -pg. D-9-8
San Nicolas, Vicente C -pg. D-9-24
San Nicolas, Vicente F -pg. D-6-17
San Nicolas, Vicente F -pg. D-7-5
San Nicolas, Vicente G -pg. D-5-20
San Nicolas, Vicente G -pg. D-12-15
San Nicolas, Vicente L -pg. D-1-38
San Nicolas, Vicente M -pg. D-6-16
San Nicolas, Vicente S -pg. D-1-41
San Nicolas, Vicente S -pg. D-9-20
San Nicolas, Vicente T -pg. D-1-41
San Nicolas, Vicente T -pg. D-4-119
San Nicolas, Vicente T -pg. D-7-19
San Nicolas, Vicente U -pg. D-5-2
San Nicolas, Victoria C -pg. D-2-44
San Nicolas, Victoria G -pg. D-12-15
San Nicolas, Victorina C -pg. D-10-5
Sanchez, Adriano C -pg. D-2-32
Sanchez, Alejo S -pg. D-9-42
Sanchez, Amparo G -pg. D-11-48

Sanchez, Amparo S -pg. D-9-43
Sanchez, Ana C -pg. D-2-22
Sanchez, Ana Q -pg. D-9-40
Sanchez, Angelina S -pg. D-9-43
Sanchez, Antonia C -pg. D-2-32
Sanchez, Antonia S -pg. D-9-42
Sanchez, Antonio A -pg. D-9-35
Sanchez, Antonio C -pg. D-2-32
Sanchez, Antonio S -pg. D-9-41
Sanchez, Brigida C -pg. D-2-23
Sanchez, Candido A -pg. D-2-22
Sanchez, Candido S -pg. D-2-31
Sanchez, Caridad A -pg. D-11-16
Sanchez, Carmela S -pg. D-11-15
Sanchez, Carmen S -pg. D-11-16
Sanchez, Ceriaco C -pg. D-2-22
Sanchez, Ciraco -pg. D-2-31
Sanchez, Clara Q -pg. D-9-31
Sanchez, Dolores C -pg. D-2-22
Sanchez, Elena Q -pg. D-9-31
Sanchez, Eliza S -pg. D-11-42
Sanchez, Emeteria A -pg. D-2-22
Sanchez, Emilia Q -pg. D-9-41
Sanchez, Emiliana C -pg. D-9-35
Sanchez, Engracia C -pg. D-2-22
Sanchez, Estokia S -pg. D-11-15
Sanchez, Eulogio C -pg. D-2-32
Sanchez, Francisco C -pg. D-2-22
Sanchez, Francisco C -pg. D-2-32
Sanchez, Francisco Q -pg. D-9-43
Sanchez, Francisco Q -pg. D-9-44
Sanchez, Francisco Q -pg. D-9-45
Sanchez, Francisco S -pg. D-9-45
Sanchez, Gloria C -pg. D-2-22
Sanchez, Ignacia S -pg. D-2-31
Sanchez, Ignacio Q -pg. D-11-32
Sanchez, Ignacio S -pg. D-9-42
Sanchez, Inrique Q -pg. D-9-34
Sanchez, Isabel C -pg. D-2-22
Sanchez, Isabel G -pg. D-11-32
Sanchez, Jesus Q -pg. D-9-40
Sanchez, Jesus S -pg. D-9-35
Sanchez, Joaquin A -pg. D-9-44
Sanchez, Joaquin Q -pg. D-9-41
Sanchez, Joaquin Q -pg. D-9-41
Sanchez, Joaquina A -pg. D-9-44
Sanchez, Jose A -pg. D-9-44
Sanchez, Jose Q -pg. D-9-40
Sanchez, Jose S -pg. D-9-42
Sanchez, Jose S -pg. D-11-15
Sanchez, Jose T -pg. D-13-27
Sanchez, Josefa S -pg. D-11-13
Sanchez, Juan A -pg. D-9-44
Sanchez, Juan C -pg. D-11-32
Sanchez, Juan Q -pg. D-9-40
Sanchez, Juanita C -pg. D-2-32
Sanchez, Julia C -pg. D-2-32
Sanchez, Justo A -pg. D-9-44
Sanchez, Laura A -pg. D-11-15

Sanchez, Lorenzo Q -pg. D-11-48
Sanchez, Lucas A -pg. D-9-35
Sanchez, Manuel C -pg. D-11-32
Sanchez, Manuel Q -pg. D-9-31
Sanchez, Manuel S -pg. D-5-89
Sanchez, Maria C -pg. D-2-22
Sanchez, Maria Q -pg. D-9-40
Sanchez, Milagro Q -pg. D-9-41
Sanchez, Moises Q -pg. D-9-40
Sanchez, Nicolas D -pg. D-9-40
Sanchez, Oliva Q -pg. D-9-41
Sanchez, Pablo -pg. D-13-28
Sanchez, Pedro C -pg. D-2-32
Sanchez, Pedro Q -pg. D-9-31
Sanchez, Priscilla S -pg. D-9-42
Sanchez, Ralph S -pg. D-9-42
Sanchez, Ricardo S -pg. D-2-31
Sanchez, Rosario Q -pg. D-9-40
Sanchez, Ruperta S -pg. D-2-31
Sanchez, Salvador A -pg. D-9-45
Sanchez, Segundo C -pg. D-2-22
Sanchez, Simon A -pg. D-2-32
Sanchez, Susana Q -pg. D-9-40
Sanchez, Teodora Q -pg. D-9-31
Sanchez, Teodoro S -pg. D-11-42
Sanchez, Trudes T -pg. D-9-34
Sanchez, Vicenta F -pg. D-11-48
Sanchez, Vicente Q -pg. D-9-45
Sanchez, Vicente S -pg. D-11-15
Sanchez, Virginia Q -pg. D-9-45
Sanguesa, Francisco J -pg. D-1-56
Sannils, Arturo -pg. D-13-25
Santa, Wayne W -pg. D-13-9
Santee, Lester H -pg. D-13-13
Santiago, Ana A -pg. D-9-45
Santiago, Ana C -pg. D-9-36
Santiago, Ana T -pg. D-9-43
Santiago, Asuncion A -pg. D-9-33
Santiago, Carmen C -pg. D-9-36
Santiago, Consolacion C -pg. D-9-23
Santiago, Dolores C -pg. D-9-36
Santiago, Domingo D -pg. D-9-33
Santiago, Eduvigis A -pg. D-9-45
Santiago, Felipe M -pg. D-9-23
Santiago, Francisca Q -pg. D-5-50
Santiago, Francisco S -pg. D-9-41
Santiago, Gregorio C -pg. D-9-24
Santiago, Gregorio S -pg. D-9-23
Santiago, Hilarion A -pg. D-9-33
Santiago, Jesus A -pg. D-9-45
Santiago, Joaquin C -pg. D-9-36
Santiago, Jose A -pg. D-9-33
Santiago, Jose C -pg. D-9-24
Santiago, Jose C -pg. D-9-36
Santiago, Jose Q -pg. D-5-50
Santiago, Jose Q -pg. D-9-36
Santiago, Josefa C -pg. D-9-24
Santiago, Juan Q -pg. D-9-45
Santiago, Juana C -pg. D-9-24

Santiago, Juana S -pg. D-9-23
Santiago, Juliana T -pg. D-9-43
Santiago, Justo Q -pg. D-9-43
Santiago, Marcela Q -pg. D-9-36
Santiago, Maria A -pg. D-9-33
Santiago, Maria S -pg. D-9-41
Santiago, Maria T -pg. D-9-43
Santiago, Maria T -pg. D-9-43
Santiago, Mariano C -pg. D-9-36
Santiago, Petra A -pg. D-9-33
Santiago, Rita T -pg. D-9-43
Santiago, Simon Q -pg. D-9-36
Santiago, Teresa Q -pg. D-9-36
Santiago, Vicente C -pg. D-9-24
Santiago, Vicente Q -pg. D-9-41
Santos, Abraham L -pg. D-11-35
Santos, Adela M -pg. D-8-38
Santos, Agapita T -pg. D-4-107
Santos, Agustin S -pg. D-11-40
Santos, Alejandra L -pg. D-11-35
Santos, Alejandro L -pg. D-11-33
Santos, Alfonsina R -pg. D-2-79
Santos, Amelia C -pg. D-6-13
Santos, Amparo C -pg. D-10-14
Santos, Amparo D -pg. D-2-37
Santos, Amparo S -pg. D-2-84
Santos, Ana A -pg. D-3-41
Santos, Ana A -pg. D-4-82
Santos, Ana A -pg. D-10-36
Santos, Ana B -pg. D-7-6
Santos, Ana B -pg. D-11-3
Santos, Ana B -pg. D-11-7
Santos, Ana B -pg. D-11-11
Santos, Ana B -pg. D-12-20
Santos, Ana C -pg. D-1-67
Santos, Ana C -pg. D-2-34
Santos, Ana C -pg. D-4-117
Santos, Ana D -pg. D-10-2
Santos, Ana L -pg. D-4-46
Santos, Ana M -pg. D-5-3
Santos, Ana N -pg. D-10-39
Santos, Ana Q -pg. D-10-33
Santos, Ana R -pg. D-3-3
Santos, Ana R -pg. D-11-46
Santos, Ana S -pg. D-2-32
Santos, Ana S -pg. D-4-26
Santos, Ana S -pg. D-5-36
Santos, Ana S -pg. D-10-9
Santos, Ana SN -pg. D-5-6
Santos, Ana SN -pg. D-10-14
Santos, Ana T -pg. D-2-54
Santos, Angel B -pg. D-2-34
Santos, Angela S -pg. D-5-26
Santos, Angela S -pg. D-5-36
Santos, Angelina -pg. D-3-69
Santos, Angelina C -pg. D-10-13
Santos, Aniceto D -pg. D-11-49
Santos, Antonia B -pg. D-9-14
Santos, Antonia C -pg. D-5-25

Santos, Antonia C -pg. D-10-13
Santos, Antonia C -pg. D-10-17
Santos, Antonia M -pg. D-10-11
Santos, Antonia Q -pg. D-10-28
Santos, Antonia S -pg. D-4-26
Santos, Antonia S -pg. D-7-5
Santos, Antonia S -pg. D-11-5
Santos, Antonina Q -pg. D-10-34
Santos, Antonio B -pg. D-11-46
Santos, Antonio C -pg. D-5-53
Santos, Antonio C -pg. D-10-14
Santos, Antonio D -pg. D-2-37
Santos, Antonio M -pg. D-11-48
Santos, Antonio Q -pg. D-10-34
Santos, Antonio R -pg. D-2-79
Santos, Antonio S -pg. D-7-4
Santos, Antonio S -pg. D-10-12
Santos, Antonio S -pg. D-11-4
Santos, Antonio U -pg. D-8-40
Santos, Asuncion C -pg. D-4-75
Santos, Aurelia H -pg. D-11-47
Santos, Barbara B -pg. D-10-34
Santos, Beatris B -pg. D-7-6
Santos, Benito Q -pg. D-11-38
Santos, Blas -pg. D-13-35
Santos, Carlos -pg. D-3-71
Santos, Carlos M -pg. D-4-42
Santos, Carmelo A -pg. D-4-44
Santos, Carmen P -pg. D-5-92
Santos, Carmen S -pg. D-11-4
Santos, Catalina C -pg. D-10-13
Santos, Catalina D -pg. D-11-48
Santos, Catalina L -pg. D-11-22
Santos, Catalina T -pg. D-1-39
Santos, Cecilia D -pg. D-11-49
Santos, Cintia B -pg. D-5-19
Santos, Clemente G -pg. D-4-75
Santos, Clementina R -pg. D-3-21
Santos, Clotilde P -pg. D-10-38
Santos, Concepcion C -pg. D-11-38
Santos, Concepcion L -pg. D-11-33
Santos, Concepcion S -pg. D-11-4
Santos, Conchita A -pg. D-10-36
Santos, Crisanta T -pg. D-1-39
Santos, Crispin M -pg. D-4-42
Santos, Cristobal R -pg. D-3-21
Santos, Delfin -pg. D-3-49
Santos, Delfina S -pg. D-11-4
Santos, Dolores -pg. D-5-64
Santos, Dolores A -pg. D-4-82
Santos, Dolores B -pg. D-7-8
Santos, Dolores C -pg. D-1-67
Santos, Dolores C -pg. D-4-117
Santos, Dolores C -pg. D-10-12
Santos, Dolores C -pg. D-10-13
Santos, Dolores M -pg. D-9-30
Santos, Dolores Q -pg. D-5-50
Santos, Dolores Q -pg. D-11-38
Santos, Dolores S -pg. D-5-20

Santos, Dolores SN -pg. D-10-14
Santos, Dolores T -pg. D-1-39
Santos, Dolores T -pg. D-4-107
Santos, Eliza N -pg. D-10-40
Santos, Eliza Q -pg. D-5-20
Santos, Emilasia C -pg. D-4-75
Santos, Emiliana Q -pg. D-11-43
Santos, Emilio T -pg. D-5-20
Santos, Emilio V -pg. D-7-24
Santos, Enrique B -pg. D-7-6
Santos, Enrique C -pg. D-10-13
Santos, Enrique S -pg. D-2-54
Santos, Enrique S -pg. D-4-110
Santos, Enrique S -pg. D-10-13
Santos, Enrique S -pg. D-11-5
Santos, Esiquel A -pg. D-4-71
Santos, Estela -pg. D-3-49
Santos, Esther S -pg. D-10-12
Santos, Eugenio T -pg. D-4-107
Santos, Evergista C -pg. D-4-101
Santos, Faustina C -pg. D-4-44
Santos, Faustina D -pg. D-2-37
Santos, Felecita G -pg. D-4-101
Santos, Felicidad B -pg. D-4-108
Santos, Felicidad G -pg. D-4-101
Santos, Felicidad S -pg. D-11-4
Santos, Felis T -pg. D-11-46
Santos, Felisiano T -pg. D-4-107
Santos, Felix -pg. D-5-92
Santos, Felix B -pg. D-4-108
Santos, Felix C -pg. D-4-102
Santos, Felix S -pg. D-4-101
Santos, Filomena Q -pg. D-1-26
Santos, Flora S -pg. D-11-5
Santos, Florence B -pg. D-11-7
Santos, Florencia S -pg. D-10-13
Santos, Florencio M -pg. D-1-18
Santos, Francisca M -pg. D-10-17
Santos, Francisca S -pg. D-5-20
Santos, Francisco -pg. D-3-71
Santos, Francisco A -pg. D-10-33
Santos, Francisco B -pg. D-5-19
Santos, Francisco B -pg. D-7-8
Santos, Francisco C -pg. D-4-117
Santos, Francisco F -pg. D-3-71
Santos, Francisco G -pg. D-4-75
Santos, Francisco G -pg. D-4-80
Santos, Francisco I -pg. D-4-80
Santos, Francisco I -pg. D-8-40
Santos, Francisco M -pg. D-4-22
Santos, Francisco P -pg. D-5-19
Santos, Francisco Q -pg. D-1-26
Santos, Francisco Q -pg. D-10-34
Santos, Francisco S -pg. D-2-84
Santos, Francisco S -pg. D-5-20
Santos, Francisco T -pg. D-5-20
Santos, Francisco V -pg. D-5-19
Santos, Froilan T -pg. D-1-54
Santos, Fructuoso -pg. D-3-71

Santos, Gabina Q -pg. D-10-28
Santos, Geronimo P -pg. D-4-107
Santos, Gertrudes B -pg. D-7-6
Santos, Gertrudes C -pg. D-5-64
Santos, Gertrudes T -pg. D-2-54
Santos, Gervasio I -pg. D-4-117
Santos, Gil C -pg. D-4-101
Santos, Gil M -pg. D-11-40
Santos, Glafira -pg. D-3-49
Santos, Gonzalo Q -pg. D-8-40
Santos, Gregorio B -pg. D-2-34
Santos, Gregorio C -pg. D-1-28
Santos, Gregorio C -pg. D-10-14
Santos, Guadalupe -pg. D-5-92
Santos, Guadalupe L -pg. D-11-3
Santos, Guadalupe L -pg. D-11-33
Santos, Guadalupe S -pg. D-10-13
Santos, Guadalupe S -pg. D-11-5
Santos, Helen M -pg. D-10-17
Santos, Henry M -pg. D-1-18
Santos, Herbert -pg. D-5-92
Santos, Idelfonso -pg. D-3-49
Santos, Ignacia -pg. D-3-71
Santos, Ignacia M -pg. D-1-18
Santos, Ignacio -pg. D-3-71
Santos, Ignacio A -pg. D-5-26
Santos, Ignacio C -pg. D-11-38
Santos, Ignacio D -pg. D-11-49
Santos, Ignacio Q -pg. D-1-26
Santos, Ignacio Q -pg. D-10-9
Santos, Ignacio S -pg. D-10-13
Santos, Ignacio S -pg. D-10-36
Santos, Ines P -pg. D-5-88
Santos, Isabel B -pg. D-5-2
Santos, Isabel C -pg. D-6-13
Santos, Isabel C -pg. D-11-27
Santos, Isabel H -pg. D-11-46
Santos, Isabel P -pg. D-10-38
Santos, Isabel R -pg. D-11-46
Santos, Isabel S -pg. D-7-4
Santos, Jaime -pg. D-3-2
Santos, Jane S -pg. D-5-26
Santos, Jesus -pg. D-3-71
Santos, Jesus -pg. D-5-64
Santos, Jesus A -pg. D-7-7
Santos, Jesus B -pg. D-2-29
Santos, Jesus B -pg. D-5-2
Santos, Jesus B -pg. D-13-30
Santos, Jesus C -pg. D-1-28
Santos, Jesus C -pg. D-1-67
Santos, Jesus C -pg. D-10-2
Santos, Jesus D -pg. D-2-37
Santos, Jesus D -pg. D-11-49
Santos, Jesus G -pg. D-2-39
Santos, Jesus G -pg. D-4-101
Santos, Jesus M -pg. D-8-38
Santos, Jesus M -pg. D-11-40
Santos, Jesus Q -pg. D-2-12
Santos, Jesus Q -pg. D-5-20

Santos, Jesus R -pg. D-1-17
Santos, Jesus R -pg. D-2-79
Santos, Jesus R -pg. D-11-46
Santos, Jesus S -pg. D-4-26
Santos, Jesus S -pg. D-4-104
Santos, Jesus S -pg. D-5-26
Santos, Jesus S -pg. D-10-9
Santos, Jesus S -pg. D-11-28
Santos, Jesus SN -pg. D-1-54
Santos, Jesus SN -pg. D-10-14
Santos, Jesus T -pg. D-1-39
Santos, Jesus T -pg. D-2-54
Santos, Jesus T -pg. D-4-107
Santos, Jesus V -pg. D-2-39
Santos, Jesus V -pg. D-5-19
Santos, Jesusa N -pg. D-10-40
Santos, Joaquin -pg. D-13-25
Santos, Joaquin B -pg. D-5-6
Santos, Joaquin C -pg. D-5-19
Santos, Joaquin D -pg. D-12-20
Santos, Joaquin G -pg. D-2-39
Santos, Joaquin G -pg. D-4-80
Santos, Joaquin Q -pg. D-13-30
Santos, Joaquin Q -pg. D-13-32
Santos, Joaquin S -pg. D-4-26
Santos, Joaquin S -pg. D-10-34
Santos, Joaquin T -pg. D-1-39
Santos, Joaquin U -pg. D-3-3
Santos, Joaquin V -pg. D-5-20
Santos, Joaquina C -pg. D-10-29
Santos, Joaquina R -pg. D-2-79
Santos, Joaquina S -pg. D-1-8
Santos, Joaquina T -pg. D-5-20
Santos, John H -pg. D-10-17
Santos, Jose -pg. D-5-64
Santos, Jose -pg. D-11-3
Santos, Jose A -pg. D-4-88
Santos, Jose A -pg. D-4-117
Santos, Jose B -pg. D-2-34
Santos, Jose B -pg. D-3-21
Santos, Jose B -pg. D-4-108
Santos, Jose B -pg. D-7-8
Santos, Jose B -pg. D-11-11
Santos, Jose C -pg. D-4-40
Santos, Jose C -pg. D-8-48
Santos, Jose C -pg. D-9-30
Santos, Jose C -pg. D-10-12
Santos, Jose C -pg. D-10-13
Santos, Jose C -pg. D-10-25
Santos, Jose C -pg. D-13-25
Santos, Jose D -pg. D-2-37
Santos, Jose D L -pg. D-10-25
Santos, Jose G -pg. D-4-108
Santos, Jose I -pg. D-10-15
Santos, Jose L -pg. D-11-33
Santos, Jose L -pg. D-11-33
Santos, Jose M -pg. D-1-18
Santos, Jose M -pg. D-4-42
Santos, Jose M -pg. D-8-38

Santos, Jose P -pg. D-10-38
Santos, Jose Q -pg. D-4-80
Santos, Jose Q -pg. D-5-20
Santos, Jose Q -pg. D-5-64
Santos, Jose Q -pg. D-10-33
Santos, Jose R -pg. D-1-8
Santos, Jose R -pg. D-2-79
Santos, Jose R -pg. D-4-40
Santos, Jose S -pg. D-2-2
Santos, Jose S -pg. D-4-109
Santos, Jose S -pg. D-5-19
Santos, Jose S -pg. D-5-20
Santos, Jose S -pg. D-5-36
Santos, Jose S -pg. D-10-9
Santos, Jose S -pg. D-10-34
Santos, Jose S -pg. D-11-5
Santos, Jose S -pg. D-11-35
Santos, Jose S -pg. D-11-38
Santos, Jose S -pg. D-13-30
Santos, Jose T -pg. D-1-28
Santos, Jose T -pg. D-1-39
Santos, Jose T -pg. D-2-54
Santos, Jose V -pg. D-3-49
Santos, Jose V -pg. D-5-19
Santos, Josefa B -pg. D-3-9
Santos, Josefa B -pg. D-5-2
Santos, Josefa B -pg. D-7-8
Santos, Josefa I -pg. D-4-80
Santos, Josefina -pg. D-3-9
Santos, Josefina D -pg. D-4-22
Santos, Joseph S -pg. D-11-5
Santos, Juan -pg. D-3-2
Santos, Juan -pg. D-5-64
Santos, Juan -pg. D-5-92
Santos, Juan -pg. D-5-92
Santos, Juan -pg. D-7-8
Santos, Juan B -pg. D-7-6
Santos, Juan C -pg. D-1-67
Santos, Juan C -pg. D-2-12
Santos, Juan C -pg. D-4-40
Santos, Juan C -pg. D-5-45
Santos, Juan C -pg. D-5-45
Santos, Juan C -pg. D-7-4
Santos, Juan C -pg. D-10-39
Santos, Juan D -pg. D-2-37
Santos, Juan G -pg. D-2-39
Santos, Juan G -pg. D-4-75
Santos, Juan M -pg. D-3-74
Santos, Juan M -pg. D-5-3
Santos, Juan M -pg. D-8-38
Santos, Juan M -pg. D-10-12
Santos, Juan N -pg. D-5-92
Santos, Juan P -pg. D-4-82
Santos, Juan P -pg. D-5-37
Santos, Juan P -pg. D-10-39
Santos, Juan Q -pg. D-5-20
Santos, Juan R -pg. D-11-46
Santos, Juan S -pg. D-2-84
Santos, Juan S -pg. D-5-22

Santos, Juan S -pg. D-5-88
Santos, Juan S -pg. D-10-9
Santos, Juan V -pg. D-2-37
Santos, Juana A -pg. D-7-10
Santos, Juana B -pg. D-2-26
Santos, Juana B -pg. D-4-108
Santos, Juana C -pg. D-6-13
Santos, Juana M -pg. D-5-3
Santos, Juana M -pg. D-8-38
Santos, Juana S -pg. D-11-39
Santos, Juana T -pg. D-5-23
Santos, Julia C -pg. D-10-17
Santos, Julia Q -pg. D-5-20
Santos, Juliana C -pg. D-5-45
Santos, Julita T -pg. D-1-39
Santos, Justo N -pg. D-5-92
Santos, Leonardo T -pg. D-11-39
Santos, Leonida -pg. D-3-71
Santos, Leonila D -pg. D-2-37
Santos, Lorenzo C -pg. D-5-75
Santos, Lorenzo C -pg. D-10-13
Santos, Lourdes C -pg. D-2-12
Santos, Lourdes I -pg. D-4-80
Santos, Lucy L -pg. D-10-25
Santos, Luis A -pg. D-2-79
Santos, Luis A -pg. D-5-19
Santos, Luis C -pg. D-2-12
Santos, Luis C -pg. D-10-13
Santos, Luis C -pg. D-11-22
Santos, Luis Q -pg. D-8-40
Santos, Luis Q -pg. D-11-43
Santos, Luisa G -pg. D-3-69
Santos, Magdalena C -pg. D-10-13
Santos, Magdalena I -pg. D-4-80
Santos, Magdalena J -pg. D-5-92
Santos, Magdalena Q -pg. D-4-80
Santos, Magdalena S -pg. D-11-28
Santos, Manuel A -pg. D-7-6
Santos, Manuel C -pg. D-1-28
Santos, Manuel C -pg. D-4-117
Santos, Manuel C -pg. D-10-21
Santos, Manuel C -pg. D-11-32
Santos, Manuel F -pg. D-10-29
Santos, Manuel L -pg. D-5-53
Santos, Manuel M -pg. D-3-2
Santos, Manuel S -pg. D-10-26
Santos, Manuel T -pg. D-2-54
Santos, Manuel S -pg. D-4-26
Santos, Marcos U -pg. D-4-75
Santos, Maria -pg. D-3-9
Santos, Maria A -pg. D-7-7
Santos, Maria A -pg. D-11-47
Santos, Maria B -pg. D-5-2
Santos, Maria B -pg. D-5-19
Santos, Maria B -pg. D-7-6
Santos, Maria B -pg. D-11-2
Santos, Maria C -pg. D-2-12
Santos, Maria C -pg. D-4-40
Santos, Maria C -pg. D-4-101

Santos, Maria C -pg. D-4-102
Santos, Maria C -pg. D-6-13
Santos, Maria C -pg. D-10-13
Santos, Maria G -pg. D-2-39
Santos, Maria G -pg. D-2-39
Santos, Maria H -pg. D-11-46
Santos, Maria I -pg. D-4-80
Santos, Maria I -pg. D-8-40
Santos, Maria L -pg. D-10-25
Santos, Maria L -pg. D-11-33
Santos, Maria LG -pg. D-4-117
Santos, Maria M -pg. D-4-42
Santos, Maria M -pg. D-10-12
Santos, Maria M -pg. D-10-15
Santos, Maria P -pg. D-4-69
Santos, Maria P -pg. D-10-38
Santos, Maria P -pg. D-11-32
Santos, Maria Q -pg. D-8-40
Santos, Maria R -pg. D-1-28
Santos, Maria R -pg. D-5-52
Santos, Maria S -pg. D-1-3
Santos, Maria S -pg. D-3-2
Santos, Maria S -pg. D-4-104
Santos, Maria S -pg. D-4-109
Santos, Maria S -pg. D-5-19
Santos, Maria S -pg. D-5-26
Santos, Maria S -pg. D-5-36
Santos, Maria S -pg. D-7-4
Santos, Maria S -pg. D-7-8
Santos, Maria S -pg. D-11-4
Santos, Maria S -pg. D-11-5
Santos, Maria SN -pg. D-10-14
Santos, Maria U -pg. D-4-75
Santos, Maria V pg. D 5 19
Santos, Mariano B -pg. D-11-7
Santos, Mariano C -pg. D-5-2
Santos, Martha B -pg. D-11-11
Santos, Martin M -pg. D-7-7
Santos, Martina L -pg. D-11-3
Santos, Martina S -pg. D-10-12
Santos, Matilde Q -pg. D-10-28
Santos, Mercedes G -pg. D-3-9
Santos, Mercedez C -pg. D-5-45
Santos, Miguel C -pg. D-1-28
Santos, Miguel G -pg. D-11-4
Santos, Miguel S -pg. D-7-4
Santos, Milagro C -pg. D-1-28
Santos, Natividad C -pg. D-10-12
Santos, Nicolas C -pg. D-10-12
Santos, Nicolas F -pg. D-3-71
Santos, Nicolas S -pg. D-1-8
Santos, Nicolas S -pg. D-2-84
Santos, Nicolas S -pg. D-5-73
Santos, Nicolas SN -pg. D-7-2
Santos, Nicolasa S -pg. D-10-12
Santos, Nicolasa SN -pg. D-10-14
Santos, Paz T -pg. D-4-107
Santos, Pedro A -pg. D-10-28
Santos, Pedro B -pg. D-5-19

Santos, Pedro C -pg. D-1-28
Santos, Pedro C -pg. D-4-117
Santos, Pedro C -pg. D-10-25
Santos, Pedro M -pg. D-2-37
Santos, Pedro M -pg. D-5-3
Santos, Pedro Q -pg. D-11-33
Santos, Pedro R -pg. D-1-28
Santos, Pedro S -pg. D-5-22
Santos, Pedro S -pg. D-5-25
Santos, Pedro S -pg. D-11-5
Santos, Presentacion -pg. D-3-2
Santos, Rafael -pg. D-3-9
Santos, Ramon C -pg. D-5-20
Santos, Ramon S -pg. D-9-24
Santos, Ramon SN -pg. D-10-14
Santos, Ramona D -pg. D-8-38
Santos, Raquel R -pg. D-3-21
Santos, Regina B -pg. D-7-8
Santos, Regina C -pg. D-10-12
Santos, Regina S -pg. D-5-22
Santos, Remedios C -pg. D-1-67
Santos, Rita A -pg. D-7-7
Santos, Rita B -pg. D-4-108
Santos, Rita C -pg. D-2-34
Santos, Rita Q -pg. D-11-43
Santos, Rita SN -pg. D-10-14
Santos, Rita T -pg. D-4-107
Santos, Rita T -pg. D-5-20
Santos, Romaldo G -pg. D-4-75
Santos, Roque S -pg. D-6-13
Santos, Roque T -pg. D-4-107
Santos, Rosa -pg. D-5-64
Santos, Rosa B -pg. D-7-6
Santos, Rosa C -pg. D-4-71
Santos, Rosa C -pg. D-10-25
Santos, Rosa F -pg. D-7-2
Santos, Rosa L -pg. D-11-33
Santos, Rosa M -pg. D-3-49
Santos, Rosa M -pg. D-5-3
Santos, Rosa M -pg. D-11-40
Santos, Rosa S -pg. D-1-8
Santos, Rosa S -pg. D-4-109
Santos, Rosa V -pg. D-5-19
Santos, Rosa V -pg. D-5-70
Santos, Rosalia B -pg. D-7-8
Santos, Rosalia S -pg. D-11-16
Santos, Rosalia SN -pg. D-10-14
Santos, Rosario -pg. D-5-64
Santos, Rosario C -pg. D-4-117
Santos, Rosario S -pg. D-5-26
Santos, Rosita S -pg. D-11-5
Santos, Rtia B -pg. D-7-6
Santos, Samson T -pg. D-4-107
Santos, Santiago B -pg. D-7-8
Santos, Santiago C -pg. D-13-30
Santos, Santiago S -pg. D-5-22
Santos, Saturnina B -pg. D-7-8
Santos, Segundo B -pg. D-1-39
Santos, Silvia C -pg. D-4-71

Santos, Soledad B -pg. D-7-6
Santos, Soledad S -pg. D-5-5
Santos, Soledad S -pg. D-10-21
Santos, Soledad S -pg. D-10-33
Santos, Soledad SN -pg. D-5-92
Santos, Stella S -pg. D-11-5
Santos, Susana S -pg. D-7-5
Santos, Teodora B -pg. D-5-2
Santos, Teresa C -pg. D-10-25
Santos, Teresa D -pg. D-12-20
Santos, Teresa M -pg. D-11-40
Santos, Thomas Q -pg. D-11-43
Santos, Tiburcio A -pg. D-10-12
Santos, Tom H T -pg. D-2-54
Santos, Tomas R -pg. D-3-21
Santos, Tomas S -pg. D-5-20
Santos, Tomasa I -pg. D-4-80
Santos, Tomasa T -pg. D-2-54
Santos, Trinidad S -pg. D-5-19
Santos, Ursula B -pg. D-3-21
Santos, Veronica M -pg. D-4-42
Santos, Vicenta C -pg. D-2-12
Santos, Vicenta R -pg. D-2-79
Santos, Vicente -pg. D-3-9
Santos, Vicente A -pg. D-7-8
Santos, Vicente A -pg. D-10-14
Santos, Vicente C -pg. D-1-27
Santos, Vicente C -pg. D-2-12
Santos, Vicente C -pg. D-10-25
Santos, Vicente D -pg. D-11-49
Santos, Vicente M -pg. D-5-64
Santos, Vicente S -pg. D-5-20
Santos, Vicente S -pg. D-10-34
Santos, Vicente S -pg. D-11-4
Santos, Vicente SN -pg. D-1-54
Santos, Vicente U -pg. D-8-38
Santos, Vidal S -pg. D-11-5
Santos, Vincente C -pg. D-13-30
Santos, Virginia S -pg. D-10-12
Santos, Wenseslao -pg. D-3-71
Santos, Ynes C -pg. D-10-13
Sargent, Annette -pg. D-1-10
Sargent, Sara K -pg. D-1-10
Sargent, Willard S -pg. D-13-18
Sarmiento, Carmen B -pg. D-11-16
Sarmiento, Daniel B -pg. D-11-16
Sarmiento, Juan -pg. D-13-25
Sarmiento, Juan B -pg. D-11-16
Sarmiento, Luisa B -pg. D-11-16
Sarmiento, Maria B -pg. D-11-16
Sarmiento, Soledad B -pg. D-11-16
Sarp, Orlan R -pg. D-13-8
Sartorina, Claude X -pg. D-13-8
Sawada, Akira -pg. D-4-90
Sawada, Haruko -pg. D-4-90
Sawada, Isamu -pg. D-4-90
Sawada, Kaneskisa -pg. D-4-90
Sawada, Kazuko -pg. D-4-90
Sawada, Nao -pg. D-4-90

Sawada, Taiko -pg. D-4-90
Sawers, John P. Jr. -pg. D-13-13
Sawyer, Paul F -pg. D-13-45
Sayama, Asuncion M -pg. D-8-3
Sayama, Jesus B -pg. D-2-30
Sayama, Jesus S -pg. D-2-29
Sayama, Joaquina B -pg. D-2-29
Sayama, Jose B -pg. D-2-29
Sayama, Maria B -pg. D-2-29
Sayama, Pedro B -pg. D-2-29
Sayama, Rosario B -pg. D-2-29
Sayama, Ursula B -pg. D-2-30
Sayre, Francis M -pg. D-13-41
Scasoldeo, Adolp R -pg. D-13-38
Schaisun, Emil C -pg. D-13-42
Scharff, Antonia F -pg. D-10-6
Scharff, Bafter -pg. D-10-6
Scharff, Charles E -pg. D-10-6
Scharff, Earnest -pg. D-10-6
Scharff, Ferdinand E -pg. D-10-6
Scharff, Ferdinand G E -pg. D-10-6
Scharff, George H -pg. D-10-6
Scharff, Herman A -pg. D-10-6
Scharff, Menar -pg. D-10-6
Scheid, Peter A -pg. D-13-3
Scheid, Robert F -pg. D-13-3
Scheid, Wanda C -pg. D-13-3
Schell, Charlie W -pg. D-13-32
Schell, Pearl I -pg. D-3-45
Scheuberg, Fred -pg. D-13-35
Schieder, Harry A -pg. D-13-18
Schiflerie, Elmers A -pg. D-13-25
Schira, Shokichi -pg. D-10-15
Schocueckei, Raymond J -pg. D-13-8
Schuam, Emilia G -pg. D-4-33
Scolar, Earl F -pg. D-13-38
Scott, Claude H -pg. D-13-38
Scott, James R -pg. D-13-18
Scott, James R jr. -pg. D-1-3
Scott, Sarah M -pg. D-1-3
Scurry, Valto -pg. D-13-44
Sealey, Armon Q -pg. D-13-13
Seimiya, Antonia A -pg. D-7-4
Seimiya, Crispina A -pg. D-7-4
Seimiya, Fidel T -pg. D-7-4
Seimiya, Juan A -pg. D-7-4
Sgambelluri, Adolfo C -pg. D-2-63
Sgambelluri, Belta C -pg. D-2-63
Sgambelluri, Hector C -pg. D-2-63
Sgambelluri, Joaquina C -pg. D-2-63
Sgambelluri, John C -pg. D-2-63
Sgambelluri, Josefina C -pg. D-2-63
Sgambelluri, Laura C -pg. D-2-63
Sgambelluri, Marcelo -pg. D-2-63
Sgambelluri, Rafael C -pg. D-2-63
Sgambelluri, Vicenta C -pg. D-2-63
Sharkey, William P -pg. D-13-32
Shefveland, Carle Q -pg. D-13-38
Sheidleo, Glenn D -pg. D-13-8

Shepherd, James E -pg. D-13-45
Sheridan, Bernard W -pg. D-13-20
Sherman, Jessi M -pg. D-3-45
Sherman, Joseph -pg. D-3-45
Sherman, Peter W -pg. D-3-45
Shimizu, Ambrosio T -pg. D-4-108
Shimizu, Ana S -pg. D-2-80
Shimizu, Carmen T -pg. D-3-47
Shimizu, Concepcion S -pg. D-2-80
Shimizu, Jesus -pg. D-3-47
Shimizu, Jesusa S -pg. D-2-80
Shimizu, Joaquin -pg. D-3-47
Shimizu, Joaquin T -pg. D-2-80
Shimizu, Jose I -pg. D-10-3
Shimizu, Jose K -pg. D-3-47
Shimizu, Josefina SN -pg. D-10-3
Shimizu, Joseph S -pg. D-2-80
Shimizu, Joseph SN -pg. D-10-3
Shimizu, Maria SN -pg. D-10-3
Shimizu, Matilde SN -pg. D-10-3
Shimoda, Juana C -pg. D-1-69
Shinohara, Carmen T -pg. D-3-28
Shinohara, Cecilia -pg. D-3-28
Shinohara, Gil -pg. D-3-28
Shinohara, Takehama -pg. D-3-28
Shipley, R V -pg. D-13-44
Shoeman, Kenneth M -pg. D-13-44
Sholing, Juan P -pg. D-2-45
Sholing, Magdalena P -pg. D-2-45
Sholing, Rita P -pg. D-2-45
Side, Samuel H -pg. D-13-18
Siegrint, Laura M -pg. D-13-4
Siegrint, Mariore T -pg. D-13-4
Siegrint, Norma D -pg. D-13-4
Siegrint, Norman B -pg. D-13-4
Siegrint, Warren H -pg. D-13-4
Sigenza, Joaquina -pg. D-13-43
Siguenza, Ana -pg. D-5-85
Siguenza, Ana B -pg. D-12-9
Siguenza, Ana B -pg. D-12-9
Siguenza, Ana T -pg. D-13-43
Siguenza, Carmen G -pg. D-5-85
Siguenza, Carmen M -pg. D-1-45
Siguenza, Carmen M -pg. D-1-45
Siguenza, Concepcion B -pg. D-12-9
Siguenza, Concepcion T -pg. D-2-74
Siguenza, Consolacion C -pg. D-1-45
Siguenza, Dolores C -pg. D-1-49
Siguenza, Dolores C -pg. D-1-49
Siguenza, Dolores S -pg. D-1-45
Siguenza, Ejinio B -pg. D-12-9
Siguenza, Emilia C -pg. D-1-45
Siguenza, Felipe T -pg. D-5-88
Siguenza, Felix N -pg. D-4-16
Siguenza, Fidela C -pg. D-1-45
Siguenza, Gregorio C -pg. D-1-49
Siguenza, Jesus C -pg. D-1-49
Siguenza, Jesus M -pg. D-1-45
Siguenza, Jesus S -pg. D-13-30

Siguenza, Joaquin S -pg. D-7-8
Siguenza, Joaquin T -pg. D-12-9
Siguenza, Jose -pg. D-5-88
Siguenza, Jose -pg. D-13-28
Siguenza, Jose B -pg. D-12-9
Siguenza, Jose C -pg. D-1-49
Siguenza, Jose P -pg. D-1-34
Siguenza, Jose T -pg. D-2-74
Siguenza, Jose T -pg. D-5-85
Siguenza, Josefina C -pg. D-1-45
Siguenza, Juan C -pg. D-1-34
Siguenza, Juan C -pg. D-1-49
Siguenza, Luis M -pg. D-1-45
Siguenza, Maria -pg. D-5-88
Siguenza, Maria C -pg. D-1-34
Siguenza, Maria C -pg. D-1-49
Siguenza, Nicolasa SN -pg. D-5-88
Siguenza, Ofemia -pg. D-5-85
Siguenza, Oliva C -pg. D-1-45
Siguenza, Pedro C -pg. D-1-45
Siguenza, Remedios M -pg. D-1-45
Siguenza, Rosa M -pg. D-1-45
Siguenza, Soledad D -pg. D-4-16
Siguenza, Vicente C -pg. D-1-49
Siguenza, Vicente S -pg. D-1-48
Silverthorn, Marie A -pg. D-13-45
Silverthorn, Mervin H -pg. D-13-45
Silverthorn, Mervin H Jr -pg. D-13-45
Silverthorn, Robert S -pg. D-13-45
Silverthorn, Russell L -pg. D-13-45
Simmons, Clyde O -pg. D-13-20
Simpson, [illegible] -pg. D-13-20
Simpson, Elvia H -pg. D-1-48
Simpson, Kenneth -pg. D-13-46
Simpson, Kirkpatrick -pg. D-1-48
Simpson, Lewis G -pg. D-13-13
Simpson, Millard C -pg. D-13-13
Siongco, Ana T -pg. D-5-52
Siongco, Ana T -pg. D-5-52
Siongco, Asuncion T -pg. D-5-52
Siongco, Jacinto P -pg. D-5-52
Siongco, Jesus T -pg. D-5-52
Siongco, Jose T -pg. D-5-52
Siongco, Vicente T -pg. D-5-52
Sipingco, Ignacia L -pg. D-5-59
Sitrelria, Frank P -pg. D-13-18
Skolasku, Lawrence P -pg. D-13-8
Slaughter, John B -pg. D-13-9
Smith, Edit N -pg. D-13-2
Smith, Gary B -pg. D-13-39
Smith, James A -pg. D-13-41
Smith, Paul -pg. D-13-13
Smith, Perry R -pg. D-13-2
Smith, Shirley A -pg. D-13-2
Smith, William C -pg. D-13-45
Snatl, Claude V -pg. D-13-9
Sneirki, Ben R -pg. D-13-25
Snider, Henry J -pg. D-13-38
Sococo, Gregorio U -pg. D-4-49

Sococo, Margarita U -pg. D-4-49
Sococo, Peter U -pg. D-4-49
Sococo, Rosa U -pg. D-4-49
Socoro, Jose -pg. D-13-25
Sohenberg, Netty V -pg. D-3-53
Soke, John M -pg. D-13-20
Soriano, Andrea SN -pg. D-11-13
Soriano, Enrique S -pg. D-3-44
Soriano, Jesus -pg. D-3-44
Soriano, Jose -pg. D-3-44
Soriano, Jose M -pg. D-11-13
Soriano, Lucia -pg. D-3-44
Soriano, Rita G -pg. D-3-44
Soriano, Vicente M -pg. D-11-13
Sorravos, Harland W -pg. D-13-38
Sosico, Dominga N -pg. D-2-81
Sosico, Jesus N -pg. D-2-81
Sosico, Jose N -pg. D-2-81
Sosico, Maria N -pg. D-2-81
Specker, Agne L -pg. D-13-3
Specker, Walter E -pg. D-13-3
Speer, Ana M -pg. D-11-25
Speese, George N -pg. D-13-39
Spice, Lloyd C -pg. D-13-9
Spicer, Dorothy M -pg. D-3-44
Sprague, Adelbert T -pg. D-13-41
Sridder, Clarence F -pg. D-13-18
Startovant, Wlmer M -pg. D-13-9
Staskey, Ornill R -pg. D-13-18
Sternberg, Carmen G -pg. D-3-67
Sternberg, George -pg. D-3-67
Sternberg, Jesus -pg. D-3-67
Sternberg, John -pg. D-3-67
Steter, [illegible] F -pg. D-13-18
Stewart, Lawrence LT -pg. D-13-25
Stewart, Leon R -pg. D-13-13
Stockman, David C -pg. D-3-58
Stockman, Edith M -pg. D-3-58
Stockman, Winifred M -pg. D-3-58
Stone, Carlo W -pg. D-13-9
Stone, Ewell B -pg. D-13-38
Stoughton, Charles E -pg. D-13-41
Straight, Jack H -pg. D-13-38
Stram, Henry A -pg. D-13-13
Strauch, Henry E -pg. D-13-25
Stuart, James A -pg. D-13-18
Stuart, James Jr. A -pg. D-1-47
Stuart, Jerome C -pg. D-1-47
Stuart, Sarah C -pg. D-1-47
Stuart, Thomas R -pg. D-1-47
Suarez, Ana M -pg. D-1-51
Suarez, Antonio C -pg. D-1-51
Suarez, Antonio D -pg. D-1-51
Suarez, Francisco M -pg. D-1-51
Suarez, Guadalupe M -pg. D-1-51
Suarez, Maria A -pg. D-1-51
Suarez, Rosa M -pg. D-1-51
Suarez, Teresa M -pg. D-1-51
Sudo, Ana B -pg. D-12-6

Sudo, Carmen B -pg. D-12-6
Sudo, Dolroes B -pg. D-12-6
Sudo, Ereni B -pg. D-12-6
Sudo, Felicita B -pg. D-12-6
Sudo, Gregorio -pg. D-12-6
Sudo, Jose B -pg. D-12-6
Sudo, Margarita B -pg. D-12-6
Sudo, Maria B -pg. D-12-6
Sudo, Rosa B -pg. D-12-6
Sugiyama, Josefina M -pg. D-8-3
Sullivan, Frank J -pg. D-13-39
Sullivan, Russell H -pg. D-13-21
Suriano, Carmen S -pg. D-9-18
Suriano, Dolores A -pg. D-9-18
Suriano, Geronmo S -pg. D-9-18
Suriano, Ignacio M -pg. D-9-18
Suriano, Joaquin M -pg. D-9-18
Suriano, Jose M -pg. D-9-21
Suriano, Jose S -pg. D-9-15
Suriano, Juan M -pg. D-9-18
Suriano, Lucia M -pg. D-9-18
Suriano, Maria Q -pg. D-9-21
Suriano, Patricio S -pg. D-9-18
Suriano, Rosa M -pg. D-9-18
Suriano, Trinidad Q -pg. D-9-21
Suriano, Vicente S -pg. D-9-18
Susuico, Benigno C -pg. D-5-63
Susuico, Ignacio -pg. D-5-63
Susuico, Josefa C -pg. D-5-63
Sutton, John A -pg. D-13-38
Suzuki, Ana C -pg. D-4-90
Suzuki, Rosita C -pg. D-4-90
Suzuki, Sngekichi -pg. D-3-47
Suzuki, Trusajo -pg. D-4-90
Sweeney, Paul -pg. D-13-38
Swift, Edwin O -pg. D-13-4
Swift, Mable A -pg. D-13-4
Sy-Pingco, Julia L -pg. D-2-46
Sy-Pingco, Virginia L -pg. D-2-46
Tackett, Clifford G -pg. D-13-9
Taeanao, Carmelo M -pg. D-11-47
Taeanao, Dolores C -pg. D-11-47
Taeanao, Francisco C -pg. D-11-47
Taeanao, Jesus C -pg. D-11-47
Taeanao, Joaquina C -pg. D-11-47
Taguacta, Carlina T -pg. D-5-55
Taguacta, Jesus B -pg. D-5-55
Taguacta, Joaquin B -pg. D-2-8
Taguacta, Jose B -pg. D-2-7
Taguacta, Jose T -pg. D-5-55
Taguacta, Manuel R -pg. D-2-7
Taguacta, Manuel T -pg. D-5-55
Taguacta, Maria T -pg. D-5-55
Taguacta, Mariano B -pg. D-2-7
Taguacta, Nicolasa T -pg. D-5-55
Taguacta, Pedro SA -pg. D-2-8
Taguacta, Rosa B -pg. D-2-7
Taguacta, Rosa SA -pg. D-2-8
Taguacta, Rosa T -pg. D-5-55

Taianao, Concepcion M -pg. D-6-2
Taianao, Guadalupe M -pg. D-6-17
Taianao, Ignacia M -pg. D-6-2
Taianao, Joaquin M -pg. D-6-18
Taianao, Vicente M -pg. D-6-18
Taienao, Antonio R -pg. D-10-22
Taienao, Guadalupe Y -pg. D-10-17
Taienao, Juan M -pg. D-10-17
Taijeran, Ana Q -pg. D-4-6
Taijeran, Jose -pg. D-4-6
Taijeron, Andresinia T -pg. D-8-42
Taijeron, Antonia A -pg. D-9-26
Taijeron, Antonia C -pg. D-3-9
Taijeron, Antonia S -pg. D-4-20
Taijeron, Antonio LG -pg. D-4-62
Taijeron, Antonio S -pg. D-9-18
Taijeron, Antonio S -pg. D-9-27
Taijeron, Asuncion -pg. D-3-10
Taijeron, Barbara J -pg. D-7-2
Taijeron, Bernardino C -pg. D-3-10
Taijeron, Candelaria S -pg. D-9-18
Taijeron, Carlos -pg. D-3-9
Taijeron, Carmen C -pg. D-9-27
Taijeron, Carmen M -pg. D-3-10
Taijeron, Eliza S -pg. D-5-34
Taijeron, Emma T -pg. D-9-27
Taijeron, Enrique T -pg. D-5-24
Taijeron, Felipe T -pg. D-8-50
Taijeron, Felisa G -pg. D-9-8
Taijeron, Francisco -pg. D-3-9
Taijeron, Francisco T -pg. D-9-12
Taijeron, Geronimo C -pg. D-5-34
Taijeron, Henry -pg. D-3-10
Taijeron, Isidro S -pg. D-5-34
Taijeron, Jesus -pg. D-3-20
Taijeron, Jesus D -pg. D-9-27
Taijeron, Jesus P -pg. D-3-9
Taijeron, Jesus T -pg. D-8-50
Taijeron, Joaquin -pg. D-3-20
Taijeron, Joaquin P -pg. D-3-9
Taijeron, Jose -pg. D-3-20
Taijeron, Jose B -pg. D-9-26
Taijeron, Jose D -pg. D-9-27
Taijeron, Jose LG -pg. D-4-62
Taijeron, Jose S -pg. D-5-34
Taijeron, Jose T -pg. D-8-50
Taijeron, Jose T -pg. D-9-26
Taijeron, Juan -pg. D-3-9
Taijeron, Juan -pg. D-3-9
Taijeron, Juan -pg. D-3-20
Taijeron, Juliana LG -pg. D-4-62
Taijeron, Lucia T -pg. D-8-50
Taijeron, Maria -pg. D-3-10
Taijeron, Maria B -pg. D-9-26
Taijeron, Maria D -pg. D-9-27
Taijeron, Maria S -pg. D-3-9
Taijeron, Maria S -pg. D-5-34
Taijeron, Maria S -pg. D-5-34
Taijeron, Maria T -pg. D-4-9

Taijeron, Maria T -pg. D-8-50
Taijeron, Mariano B -pg. D-9-18
Taijeron, Mariano G -pg. D-9-18
Taijeron, Mercedes LG -pg. D-4-62
Taijeron, Olimpia S -pg. D-5-34
Taijeron, Pedro -pg. D-3-10
Taijeron, Pedro T -pg. D-8-50
Taijeron, Preciardo S -pg. D-5-34
Taijeron, Ramon LG -pg. D-4-62
Taijeron, Ramona -pg. D-3-9
Taijeron, Remedios T -pg. D-8-50
Taijeron, Rosario -pg. D-3-20
Taijeron, Rufina Q -pg. D-4-17
Taijeron, Silvano T -pg. D-4-17
Taijeron, Vicente -pg. D-3-9
Taijeron, Vicente C -pg. D-9-16
Taijeron, Vicente P -pg. D-3-10
Taijeron, Vicente T -pg. D-8-50
Taijeron, Victoria -pg. D-3-10
Taijeto, Celestina B -pg. D-4-104
Taijeto, Jesus B -pg. D-4-104
Taijeto, Maria B -pg. D-4-104
Taijito, Francisco S -pg. D-7-18
Taijito, Jose T -pg. D-7-18
Taijito, Juan S -pg. D-7-18
Taijito, Magdalena S -pg. D-7-18
Taijito, Mamerto -pg. D-5-58
Taijito, Maria S -pg. D-7-18
Taijito, Mariano T -pg. D-7-7
Taijito, Maristela T -pg. D-7-18
Taijito, Soledad S -pg. D-7-18
Taijito, Vicenta S -pg. D-7-18
Taijto, Antonio T -pg. D-7-12
Taijto, Maria A -pg. D-7-12
Taimanglo, Alfredo M -pg. D-8-12
Taimanglo, Ana J -pg. D-3-20
Taimanglo, Ana M -pg. D-8-31
Taimanglo, Ana M -pg. D-10-17
Taimanglo, Ana O -pg. D-4-2
Taimanglo, Bartola A -pg. D-5-82
Taimanglo, Beatrice -pg. D-8-18
Taimanglo, Blas T -pg. D-8-31
Taimanglo, Clara M -pg. D-8-26
Taimanglo, Concepcion T -pg. D-8-49
Taimanglo, Cornelia -pg. D-8-18
Taimanglo, Dolores M -pg. D-8-13
Taimanglo, Dolores M -pg. D-8-26
Taimanglo, Dolores Q -pg. D-12-21
Taimanglo, Dolores T -pg. D-8-34
Taimanglo, Esperanza M -pg. D-8-32
Taimanglo, Felix Q -pg. D-12-21
Taimanglo, Francisco M -pg. D-8-32
Taimanglo, Gertrudes M -pg. D-8-12
Taimanglo, Gregorio Q -pg. D-12-21
Taimanglo, Guadalupe C -pg. D-5-82
Taimanglo, Guadalupe C -pg. D-8-28
Taimanglo, Guadalupe N -pg. D-8-29
Taimanglo, Ignacio M -pg. D-8-12
Taimanglo, Ingracia Q -pg. D-1-12

Taimanglo, Isidoro C -pg. D-8-29
Taimanglo, Jesus C -pg. D-8-13
Taimanglo, Joaquin C -pg. D-5-83
Taimanglo, Joaquin C -pg. D-8-18
Taimanglo, Joaquin M -pg. D-8-12
Taimanglo, Joaquin T -pg. D-1-54
Taimanglo, Jose C -pg. D-8-13
Taimanglo, Jose DLR -pg. D-5-82
Taimanglo, Jose M -pg. D-8-12
Taimanglo, Jose M -pg. D-10-17
Taimanglo, Jose N -pg. D-8-29
Taimanglo, Jose P -pg. D-8-42
Taimanglo, Jose T -pg. D-5-82
Taimanglo, Jose T -pg. D-8-2
Taimanglo, Jose T -pg. D-8-26
Taimanglo, Jose T -pg. D-8-34
Taimanglo, Josefa T -pg. D-8-49
Taimanglo, Josefina T -pg. D-8-49
Taimanglo, Juan C -pg. D-8-12
Taimanglo, Juan M -pg. D-8-13
Taimanglo, Juan M -pg. D-10-17
Taimanglo, Manuel N -pg. D-8-29
Taimanglo, Maria C -pg. D-8-13
Taimanglo, Maria P -pg. D-8-42
Taimanglo, Maria Q -pg. D-12-21
Taimanglo, Mariano C -pg. D-8-42
Taimanglo, Mariano T -pg. D-4-5
Taimanglo, Miguel M -pg. D-8-26
Taimanglo, Pedro A -pg. D-5-82
Taimanglo, Rita T -pg. D-4-5
Taimanglo, Silvino C -pg. D-8-49
Taimanglo, Soledad SN -pg. D-12-16
Taimanglo, Solidad N -pg. D-8-29
Taimanglo, Teodoro Q -pg. D-12-21
Taimanglo, Vicenta M -pg. D-10-17
Taimanglo, Vicente M -pg. D-10-17
Taimanglo, Victurino T -pg. D-8-26
Taimanglo, Vincente T -pg. D-13-25
Tainatongo, Catlina SN -pg. D-9-16
Tainatongo, Cerilo T -pg. D-9-22
Tainatongo, Concepcion T -pg. D-9-17
Tainatongo, Dolores B -pg. D-9-17
Tainatongo, Greorio SN -pg. D-9-17
Tainatongo, Ignacio SN -pg. D-9-16
Tainatongo, Jesus T -pg. D-9-17
Tainatongo, Josefa SN -pg. D-9-16
Tainatongo, Ramon M -pg. D-9-22
Tainatongo, Vicente M -pg. D-9-28
Tainatongo, Vicente T -pg. D-9-17
Tainatongo, Victorina T -pg. D-9-22
Taisague, Antonia S -pg. D-5-73
Taisague, Felisa C -pg. D-4-113
Taisague, Isabel S -pg. D-5-73
Taisague, Joaquin C -pg. D-5-72
Taisague, Juan S -pg. D-5-73
Taisague, Manuela O -pg. D-5-73
Taisague, Maria -pg. D-5-78
Taisague, Maria O -pg. D-5-73
Taisague, Maria O -pg. D-5-73

Taisague, Rosa S -pg. D-5-73
Taisague, Rosalia T -pg. D-4-113
Taisague, Vicenta G -pg. D-5-78
Taisague, Vicente S -pg. D-5-73
Taisipig, Ana T -pg. D-12-13
Taisipig, Antonia T -pg. D-12-14
Taisipig, Balbino T -pg. D-12-14
Taisipig, Carmen T -pg. D-12-14
Taisipig, Dolores T -pg. D-12-14
Taisipig, Gregorio M -pg. D-12-13
Taisipig, Gregorio T -pg. D-12-14
Taisipig, Herminia T -pg. D-12-14
Taisipig, Jesus T -pg. D-7-24
Taisipig, Jose T -pg. D-12-14
Taisipig, Juan T -pg. D-12-14
Taisipig, Rosa T -pg. D-12-14
Taison, Ana T -pg. D-4-97
Taison, Ana T -pg. D-4-97
Taison, Antonio T -pg. D-4-97
Taison, Maria T -pg. D-4-97
Taison, Roman T -pg. D-4-97
Taison, Rosalia T -pg. D-4-97
Taison, Sococo T -pg. D-4-97
Taitague, Agueda C -pg. D-7-15
Taitague, Alminla M -pg. D-8-33
Taitague, Amalia D -pg. D-8-14
Taitague, Ana B -pg. D-6-39
Taitague, Ana C -pg. D-6-12
Taitague, Angelina T -pg. D-8-33
Taitague, Antonia D -pg. D-7-21
Taitague, Antonia M -pg. D-8-14
Taitague, Baldobino B -pg. D-8-46
Taitague, Baldovino M -pg. D-8-33
Taitague, Candida B -pg. D-6-38
Taitague, Catalina C -pg. D-7-15
Taitague, Catalina T -pg. D-8-46
Taitague, Daniel N -pg. D-8-15
Taitague, David T -pg. D-8-15
Taitague, Delfina B -pg. D-6-39
Taitague, Domingo C -pg. D-6-12
Taitague, Edna M -pg. D-8-14
Taitague, Edward M -pg. D-8-33
Taitague, Espreciosa U -pg. D-8-49
Taitague, Felix B -pg. D-8-49
Taitague, Francisco M -pg. D-8-14
Taitague, Francisco P -pg. D-6-33
Taitague, Gonzalo M -pg. D-8-33
Taitague, Grace M -pg. D-8-14
Taitague, Gregorio D -pg. D-4-43
Taitague, Henry D -pg. D-8-22
Taitague, Ignacia Q -pg. D-8-22
Taitague, Ignacio C -pg. D-6-33
Taitague, Inocensio C -pg. D-6-38
Taitague, Jesus N -pg. D-8-22
Taitague, Jose C -pg. D-7-15
Taitague, Jose D -pg. D-8-14
Taitague, Jose M -pg. D-8-33
Taitague, Jose N -pg. D-8-15
Taitague, Jose Q -pg. D-8-22

Taitague, Josefa Q -pg. D-6-33
Taitague, Josefa Q -pg. D-11-20
Taitague, Josefa U -pg. D-8-49
Taitague, Josefina N -pg. D-8-15
Taitague, Joseph M -pg. D-8-14
Taitague, Juan D -pg. D-8-33
Taitague, Lorenzo N -pg. D-8-15
Taitague, Lourdes M -pg. D-8-14
Taitague, Magdalena B -pg. D-8-49
Taitague, Maria B -pg. D-6-39
Taitague, Maria B -pg. D-8-49
Taitague, Maria C -pg. D-7-15
Taitague, Maria N -pg. D-8-15
Taitague, Ramon T -pg. D-8-33
Taitague, Rosalia P -pg. D-6-33
Taitague, Rosalina N -pg. D-8-15
Taitague, Rosario D -pg. D-8-14
Taitague, Saturnina M -pg. D-8-33
Taitague, Susana P -pg. D-6-33
Taitague, Tomas B -pg. D-6-38
Taitague, Tomas M -pg. D-8-33
Taitague, Vicente Q -pg. D-6-33
Taitague, Victuriano L -pg. D-8-49
Taitajgue, Delfina B -pg. D-9-9
Taitano, Agustin S -pg. D-4-49
Taitano, Alfred F -pg. D-2-9
Taitano, Alfred J -pg. D-5-70
Taitano, Amanda D -pg. D-11-51
Taitano, Amparo M -pg. D-4-19
Taitano, Ana -pg. D-3-37
Taitano, Ana B -pg. D-4-48
Taitano, Ana D -pg. D-11-51
Taitano, Ana G -pg. D-4-70
Taitano, Ana G -pg. D-7-14
Taitano, Ana L -pg. D-4-45
Taitano, Ana M -pg. D-4-29
Taitano, Ana P -pg. D-4-46
Taitano, Ana Q -pg. D-5-53
Taitano, Ana S -pg. D-7-5
Taitano, Andrea G -pg. D-3-36
Taitano, Angel R -pg. D-1-19
Taitano, Antonia B -pg. D-4-48
Taitano, Antonia F -pg. D-7-11
Taitano, Antonio -pg. D-5-86
Taitano, Antonio C -pg. D-1-27
Taitano, Antonio C -pg. D-1-57
Taitano, Antonio M -pg. D-4-44
Taitano, Antonio R -pg. D-1-25
Taitano, Artemio -pg. D-3-33
Taitano, Arthur F -pg. D-2-10
Taitano, Barbina S -pg. D-7-5
Taitano, Barcelisa -pg. D-5-68
Taitano, Carlos F -pg. D-4-32
Taitano, Carlos P -pg. D-4-46
Taitano, Carmen LG -pg. D-7-18
Taitano, Carmen P -pg. D-2-9
Taitano, Carmen P -pg. D-11-38
Taitano, Carmen T -pg. D-7-12
Taitano, Catalina -pg. D-2-19

Taitano, Catalina C -pg. D-1-15
Taitano, Catalina F -pg. D-4-32
Taitano, Catherine A -pg. D-2-19
Taitano, Concepcion C -pg. D-1-59
Taitano, Concepcion L -pg. D-4-45
Taitano, Concepcion P -pg. D-4-86
Taitano, Concepcion R -pg. D-5-86
Taitano, Concepcion T -pg. D-5-48
Taitano, Concepcion T -pg. D-5-48
Taitano, David A -pg. D-2-19
Taitano, David C -pg. D-1-57
Taitano, David F -pg. D-5-54
Taitano, Dolores G -pg. D-11-38
Taitano, Dolores LG -pg. D-7-18
Taitano, Dolores P -pg. D-4-46
Taitano, Dolores S -pg. D-3-33
Taitano, Dolores T -pg. D-4-105
Taitano, Edward P -pg. D-1-57
Taitano, Emilia -pg. D-3-37
Taitano, Emilia B -pg. D-7-12
Taitano, Esther F -pg. D-4-32
Taitano, Faustina C -pg. D-1-27
Taitano, Felibetto M -pg. D-4-29
Taitano, Felicita L -pg. D-4-45
Taitano, Felicita LG -pg. D-7-18
Taitano, Francisca -pg. D-3-33
Taitano, Francisco -pg. D-3-33
Taitano, Francisco -pg. D-3-37
Taitano, Francisco -pg. D-13-35
Taitano, Francisco L -pg. D-4-45
Taitano, Francisco S -pg. D-10-33
Taitano, Francisco W -pg. D-4-51
Taitano, Frank F -pg. D-4-32
Taitano, George -pg. D-5-70
Taitano, George F -pg. D-2-10
Taitano, Gregorio p -pg. D-4-86
Taitano, Guilliermo T -pg. D-4-105
Taitano, Henry F -pg. D-4-32
Taitano, Henry O -pg. D-3-33
Taitano, Herminia -pg. D-5-71
Taitano, Herminia F -pg. D-2-10
Taitano, Isabel F -pg. D-8-46
Taitano, Jesus -pg. D-5-68
Taitano, Jesus D -pg. D-11-51
Taitano, Jesus LG -pg. D-7-18
Taitano, Jesus M -pg. D-1-25
Taitano, Jesus R -pg. D-1-25
Taitano, Jesusa M -pg. D-4-51
Taitano, Joaquin -pg. D-13-25
Taitano, Joaquin B -pg. D-4-49
Taitano, Joaquin F -pg. D-4-49
Taitano, Joaquin G -pg. D-4-70
Taitano, Joaquin G -pg. D-5-68
Taitano, Joaquin L -pg. D-4-45
Taitano, Joaquin P -pg. D-4-46
Taitano, Joaquin R -pg. D-2-30
Taitano, Joaquina M -pg. D-2-30
Taitano, John -pg. D-4-32
Taitano, John F -pg. D-4-32

Taitano, Jose -pg. D-5-68
Taitano, Jose -pg. D-5-86
Taitano, Jose B -pg. D-4-49
Taitano, Jose C -pg. D-1-27
Taitano, Jose C -pg. D-1-57
Taitano, Jose G -pg. D-11-38
Taitano, Jose I -pg. D-3-33
Taitano, Jose LG -pg. D-7-18
Taitano, Jose M -pg. D-3-33
Taitano, Jose M -pg. D-3-36
Taitano, Jose M -pg. D-4-51
Taitano, Jose P -pg. D-4-86
Taitano, Jose S -pg. D-5-46
Taitano, Jose S -pg. D-7-5
Taitano, Jose SN -pg. D-4-46
Taitano, Josefina -pg. D-3-33
Taitano, Josefina B -pg. D-4-48
Taitano, Joseph F -pg. D-4-32
Taitano, Juan -pg. D-5-68
Taitano, Juan B -pg. D-4-48
Taitano, Juan C -pg. D-1-15
Taitano, Juan L -pg. D-4-45
Taitano, Juan M -pg. D-1-15
Taitano, Juan M -pg. D-5-74
Taitano, Juan P -pg. D-4-46
Taitano, Juan S -pg. D-4-49
Taitano, Juan W -pg. D-4-105
Taitano, Juana -pg. D-3-33
Taitano, Julita T -pg. D-4-105
Taitano, Justo G -pg. D-7-14
Taitano, Laura I -pg. D-8-46
Taitano, Leonicio -pg. D-5-87
Taitano, Liberato -pg. D-3-37
Taitano, Lila B -pg. D-3-33
Taitano, Lillian A -pg. D-2-19
Taitano, Luis -pg. D-13-25
Taitano, Luis S -pg. D-13-27
Taitano, Luisa S -pg. D-4-49
Taitano, Luke A -pg. D-2-19
Taitano, Madalena C -pg. D-1-42
Taitano, Magdalena B -pg. D-4-49
Taitano, Magdalena P -pg. D-4-86
Taitano, Magdalena S -pg. D-4-49
Taitano, Manuel B -pg. D-5-86
Taitano, Manuel B -pg. D-7-11
Taitano, Manuel C -pg. D-5-48
Taitano, Manuel G -pg. D-5-53
Taitano, Manuel Q -pg. D-5-53
Taitano, Manuel T -pg. D-7-12
Taitano, Manuela L -pg. D-4-44
Taitano, Manuela LG -pg. D-7-18
Taitano, Marcelina P -pg. D-4-86
Taitano, Maria -pg. D-5-68
Taitano, Maria B -pg. D-4-48
Taitano, Maria B -pg. D-4-48
Taitano, Maria C -pg. D-1-27
Taitano, Maria C -pg. D-5-68
Taitano, Maria D -pg. D-11-51
Taitano, Maria L -pg. D-4-45

Taitano, Maria LG -pg. D-7-18
Taitano, Maria M -pg. D-2-30
Taitano, Maria M -pg. D-7-12
Taitano, Maria P -pg. D-4-86
Taitano, Maria P -pg. D-11-42
Taitano, Maria S -pg. D-5-46
Taitano, Maria T -pg. D-4-105
Taitano, Mariano -pg. D-3-37
Taitano, Mariano B -pg. D-1-26
Taitano, Matias T -pg. D-7-13
Taitano, Matilde S -pg. D-5-46
Taitano, Miguel A -pg. D-2-19
Taitano, Miguel C -pg. D-1-57
Taitano, Miguel C -pg. D-13-27
Taitano, Monica M -pg. D-4-86
Taitano, Nieves S -pg. D-4-23
Taitano, Pedro G -pg. D-7-14
Taitano, Pedro M -pg. D-4-49
Taitano, Pedro M -pg. D-4-51
Taitano, Percy E -pg. D-3-33
Taitano, Pero M -pg. D-3-33
Taitano, Rafael P -pg. D-4-46
Taitano, Ramon -pg. D-5-86
Taitano, Ramon P -pg. D-4-46
Taitano, Ramon SN -pg. D-2-9
Taitano, Regina D -pg. D-11-51
Taitano, Richard F -pg. D-4-32
Taitano, Rita -pg. D-3-37
Taitano, Rita C -pg. D-1-57
Taitano, Rita L -pg. D-4-45
Taitano, Rita M -pg. D-4-51
Taitano, Rita P -pg. D-3-33
Taitano, Rita T -pg. D-4-105
Taitano, Robert -pg. D-5-70
Taitano, Robert F -pg. D-2-9
Taitano, Rosa -pg. D-3-33
Taitano, Rosa G -pg. D-13-43
Taitano, Rosa L -pg. D-4-45
Taitano, Rosa M -pg. D-1-25
Taitano, Rosario F -pg. D-4-32
Taitano, Rosario F -pg. D-4-32
Taitano, Rosario L -pg. D-4-45
Taitano, Rosario T -pg. D-4-105
Taitano, Severa F -pg. D-7-12
Taitano, Sixta T -pg. D-4-105
Taitano, Teddy -pg. D-5-71
Taitano, Teodoro F -pg. D-7-11
Taitano, Tomasa M -pg. D-4-51
Taitano, Trinidad C -pg. D-1-27
Taitano, Trinidad P -pg. D-4-46
Taitano, Vicente G -pg. D-4-70
Taitano, Vicente M -pg. D-2-19
Taitano, Vicente M -pg. D-2-30
Taitano, Vicente S -pg. D-11-51
Taitano, Vicente T -pg. D-5-48
Taitinfong, Ana B -pg. D-2-9
Taitinfong, Ana B -pg. D-2-60
Taitinfong, Ana C -pg. D-2-3
Taitinfong, Ana C -pg. D-2-79

Taitinfong, Barbara B -pg. D-2-60
Taitinfong, Dominga A -pg. D-2-11
Taitinfong, Felisa C -pg. D-2-3
Taitinfong, Felix S -pg. D-2-3
Taitinfong, Francisco B -pg. D-2-79
Taitinfong, Guadalupe C -pg. D-2-79
Taitinfong, Ignacio B -pg. D-2-60
Taitinfong, Jesus B -pg. D-2-60
Taitinfong, Joaquin B -pg. D-2-60
Taitinfong, Jose B -pg. D-2-9
Taitinfong, Jose C -pg. D-2-79
Taitinfong, Jose de L -pg. D-2-79
Taitinfong, Jose SN -pg. D-2-9
Taitinfong, Josefa C -pg. D-2-3
Taitinfong, Juan S -pg. D-2-18
Taitinfong, Juana -pg. D-2-34
Taitinfong, Maria B -pg. D-2-60
Taitinfong, Maria C -pg. D-2-79
Taitinfong, Maria D -pg. D-2-9
Taitinfong, Mariano B -pg. D-2-60
Taitinfong, Rafael C -pg. D-2-3
Taitinfong, Romona S -pg. D-2-19
Taitinfong, Rosa B -pg. D-2-9
Taitinfong, Rosa C -pg. D-2-3
Taitinfong, Teresa T -pg. D-2-18
Taitinfong, Vicente B -pg. D-2-60
Taitinfong, Vicente De L -pg. D-2-60
Taitingfon, Carmen -pg. D-3-29
Taitingfon, Gabriela C -pg. D-3-29
Taitingfon, Ignacio -pg. D-3-29
Taitingfon, Isabel -pg. D-3-29
Taitingfon, Magdalena -pg. D-3-29
Taitingfon, Rita -pg. D-3-29
Taitingfong, Ana T -pg. D-12-14
Taitingfong, Angelina A -pg. D-12-12
Taitingfong, Antonia Q -pg. D-12-7
Taitingfong, Carmen A -pg. D-12-12
Taitingfong, Catalina B -pg. D-12-12
Taitingfong, Concepcion A -pg. D-12-12
Taitingfong, Concepcion de LG -pg. D-1-15
Taitingfong, Daniel C -pg. D-12-11
Taitingfong, Francisca B -pg. D-12-12
Taitingfong, Francisco A -pg. D-12-12
Taitingfong, Grabiela Q -pg. D-12-7
Taitingfong, Isabel A -pg. D-12-12
Taitingfong, Joaquin S -pg. D-2-2
Taitingfong, Jose B -pg. D-12-12
Taitingfong, Jose de LG -pg. D-1-15
Taitingfong, Juan C -pg. D-1-58
Taitingfong, Juan C -pg. D-5-88
Taitingfong, Juan C -pg. D-12-7
Taitingfong, Juan S -pg. D-4-47
Taitingfong, Magdalena S -pg. D-4-47
Taitingfong, Manuel C -pg. D-12-12
Taitingfong, Manuel T -pg. D-5-72
Taitingfong, Maria A -pg. D-12-12
Taitingfong, Maria C -pg. D-1-58
Taitingfong, Maria de LG -pg. D-1-14
Taitingfong, Rafael de LG -pg. D-1-15

Taitingfong, Ramon B -pg. D-12-12
Taitingfong, Ramon C -pg. D-1-14
Taitingfong, Ramon de LG -pg. D-1-15
Taitingfong, Rosa B -pg. D-12-11
Taitingfong, Rosa C -pg. D-12-12
Taitingfong, Rosalia A -pg. D-12-12
Taitingfong, Vicente S -pg. D-5-88
Tajalle, Ana M -pg. D-10-37
Tajalle, Andrea C -pg. D-7-13
Tajalle, Antonio A -pg. D-9-32
Tajalle, Concepcion G -pg. D-2-17
Tajalle, Consolacion M -pg. D-10-37
Tajalle, Dolores M -pg. D-10-37
Tajalle, Dolores T -pg. D-9-24
Tajalle, Dolores T -pg. D-9-25
Tajalle, Enrique T -pg. D-9-31
Tajalle, Felisa Q -pg. D-9-34
Tajalle, Felix -pg. D-13-25
Tajalle, Felix M -pg. D-10-37
Tajalle, Francisco M -pg. D-10-37
Tajalle, Gregoria C -pg. D-9-25
Tajalle, Jesus A -pg. D-9-32
Tajalle, Joaquina C -pg. D-10-12
Tajalle, Jose A -pg. D-9-32
Tajalle, Jose C -pg. D-9-24
Tajalle, Jose G -pg. D-2-17
Tajalle, Jose T -pg. D-9-24
Tajalle, Juan A -pg. D-9-32
Tajalle, Juan C -pg. D-10-37
Tajalle, Juan S -pg. D-10-12
Tajalle, Justo C -pg. D-2-17
Tajalle, Manuel C -pg. D-10-37
Tajalle, Maria -pg. D-11-35
Tajalle, Maria G -pg. D-2-17
Tajalle, Maria M -pg. D-10-37
Tajalle, Miguel S -pg. D-10-12
Tajalle, Milagro A -pg. D-9-31
Tajalle, Petronilia M -pg. D-10-37
Tajalle, Regina T -pg. D-9-25
Tajalle, Rita T -pg. D-9-12
Tajalle, Rufina M -pg. D-10-37
Tajalle, Soledad S -pg. D-10-12
Tajalle, Tomas S -pg. D-10-12
Tajalle, Vicente S -pg. D-10-12
Takai, Arezo V -pg. D-2-17
Takai, Francisca F -pg. D-2-17
Takano, Carlos SN -pg. D-1-21
Takano, Dolores SN -pg. D-1-21
Takano, Jesus SN -pg. D-1-21
Takano, Jose SN -pg. D-1-21
Takano, Josefina SN -pg. D-1-21
Takano, Luis SN -pg. D-1-21
Takano, Rosario SN -pg. D-1-21
Takano, Vicente K -pg. D-1-21
Takano, Vicente SN -pg. D-1-21
Talavera, Antonio Q -pg. D-2-82
Talavera, Concepcion P -pg. D-2-82
Talavera, Dolores P -pg. D-2-82
Talavera, Jesus P -pg. D-2-82

Talavera, Jose Q -pg. D-2-82
Talavera, Manuel M -pg. D-2-82
Talavera, Maria P -pg. D-2-82
Talbott, Ralph -pg. D-13-38
Talehart, Claude N -pg. D-13-6
Tanaka, Asuncion S -pg. D-1-3
Tanaka, Carmen S -pg. D-1-3
Tanaka, Emeterio S -pg. D-1-3
Tanaka, Jesus S -pg. D-1-3
Tanaka, Remedios S -pg. D-1-3
Tanaka, Rosa S -pg. D-1-3
Tanaka, Rosalia S -pg. D-1-3
Tanaka, Tomas S -pg. D-1-3
Taparan, Nicomede -pg. D-13-25
Tass, John A -pg. D-2-83
Tass, Maria A -pg. D-2-83
Tayama, Jose M -pg. D-8-3
Tayama, Jose S -pg. D-8-3
Taylor, Edgar -pg. D-13-9
Taylor, Robert L -pg. D-13-45
Teagne, Ralph -pg. D-13-38
Techaira, Erminia LG -pg. D-2-36
Techaira, Gregorio LG -pg. D-2-37
Techaira, Isabel LG -pg. D-2-36
Techaira, Jesus C -pg. D-2-37
Techaira, Joaquina LG -pg. D-2-37
Techaira, Mafada C -pg. D-2-37
Techaira, Manuel D -pg. D-2-36
Techaira, Manuel LG -pg. D-2-37
Techaira, Maria LG -pg. D-2-36
Techaira, Maria LG -pg. D-2-36
Techaira, Ramon LG -pg. D-2-36
Techaira, Remedio LG -pg. D-2-36
Tedpaogo, Ana C -pg. D-9-13
Tedpaogo, Angelina D -pg. D-8-13
Tedpaogo, Angelina D -pg. D-9-27
Tedpaogo, Carmen D -pg. D-9-27
Tedpaogo, Dolores C -pg. D-9-16
Tedpaogo, Eugenio G -pg. D-9-13
Tedpaogo, Felicita C -pg. D-9-13
Tedpaogo, Felipe D -pg. D-9-27
Tedpaogo, Gabriela A -pg. D-9-17
Tedpaogo, Ignacio E -pg. D-9-17
Tedpaogo, Jesus C -pg. D-9-13
Tedpaogo, Joaquin C -pg. D-9-13
Tedpaogo, Jose C -pg. D-9-13
Tedpaogo, Jose E -pg. D-9-3
Tedpaogo, Juan C -pg. D-9-16
Tedpaogo, Julia C -pg. D-9-16
Tedpaogo, Manuela D -pg. D-9-27
Tedpaogo, Mariano C -pg. D-9-16
Tedpaogo, Nicolasa A -pg. D-1-60
Tedpaogo, Vicenta C -pg. D-9-13
Tedpaogo, Vicente B -pg. D-9-3
Tedpaogo, Vicente C -pg. D-9-16
Tedtaotao, Angela T -pg. D-8-5
Tedtaotao, Antonio -pg. D-5-86
Tedtaotao, Dolores C -pg. D-8-5
Tedtaotao, Dolores C -pg. D-8-26

Tedtaotao, Gregorio T -pg. D-5-86
Tedtaotao, Jesus -pg. D-5-86
Tedtaotao, Jose C -pg. D-2-52
Tedtaotao, Juan T -pg. D-8-5
Tedtaotao, Lucas -pg. D-5-86
Tedtaotao, Magdalena T -pg. D-8-5
Tedtaotao, Manuel T -pg. D-5-86
Tedtaotao, Marcelina T -pg. D-5-81
Tedtaotao, Maria C -pg. D-8-26
Tedtaotao, Maria T -pg. D-8-5
Tedtaotao, Pedro M -pg. D-8-5
Tedtaotao, Rita T -pg. D-5-81
Tedtaotao, Robert C -pg. D-8-26
Tedtaotao, Rosa A -pg. D-5-86
Tedtaotao, Rosa T -pg. D-8-5
Tedtaotao, Rosalina M -pg. D-5-86
Tedtaotao, Rosario T -pg. D-8-5
Tedtaotao, Salvador -pg. D-5-86
Tenison, Dale -pg. D-3-46
Tenorio, Adela T -pg. D-2-38
Tenorio, Amanda G -pg. D-4-13
Tenorio, Ana -pg. D-5-81
Tenorio, Ana M -pg. D-1-69
Tenorio, Ana M -pg. D-8-44
Tenorio, Ana M -pg. D-8-45
Tenorio, Ana Q -pg. D-5-16
Tenorio, Ana T -pg. D-1-44
Tenorio, Ana T -pg. D-2-38
Tenorio, Andresina S -pg. D-5-21
Tenorio, Angel M -pg. D-1-69
Tenorio, Antonia D -pg. D-5-71
Tenorio, Antonia S -pg. D-5-21
Tenorio, Antonio P -pg. D-2-45
Tenorio, Antonio S -pg. D-5-21
Tenorio, Atanacio T -pg. D-4-13
Tenorio, Catalina T -pg. D-2-45
Tenorio, Clotilde -pg. D-3-20
Tenorio, Concepcion T -pg. D-2-45
Tenorio, Damiana SN -pg. D-5-31
Tenorio, Delfina -pg. D-3-19
Tenorio, Delfina -pg. D-5-84
Tenorio, Delfina T -pg. D-1-43
Tenorio, Dolores -pg. D-5-84
Tenorio, Dolores A -pg. D-5-21
Tenorio, Dolores SN -pg. D-5-30
Tenorio, Dolores T -pg. D-2-45
Tenorio, Dolores T -pg. D-2-45
Tenorio, Emliana T -pg. D-5-85
Tenorio, Encarnacion G -pg. D-4-13
Tenorio, Engracia T -pg. D-5-16
Tenorio, Enrgracia C -pg. D-5-61
Tenorio, Enrique G -pg. D-4-13
Tenorio, Enrique G -pg. D-5-84
Tenorio, Florencia M -pg. D-1-69
Tenorio, Francisco -pg. D-5-84
Tenorio, Francisco I -pg. D-5-85
Tenorio, Francisco R -pg. D-5-16
Tenorio, Francisco SN -pg. D-5-30
Tenorio, Francisco T -pg. D-4-13

Tenorio, Gonzalo -pg. D-3-19
Tenorio, Gregorio G -pg. D-5-84
Tenorio, Gregorio S -pg. D-5-21
Tenorio, Honoria -pg. D-3-19
Tenorio, Ignacia P -pg. D-11-31
Tenorio, Ignacia T -pg. D-12-8
Tenorio, Ignacio T -pg. D-1-10
Tenorio, Jesus -pg. D-13-25
Tenorio, Jesus B -pg. D-2-38
Tenorio, Jesus F -pg. D-5-72
Tenorio, Jesus N -pg. D-4-102
Tenorio, Jesus Q -pg. D-5-16
Tenorio, Jesus T -pg. D-2-45
Tenorio, Jesus T -pg. D-4-13
Tenorio, Jesusa -pg. D-5-71
Tenorio, Joaquin -pg. D-3-38
Tenorio, Joaquin G -pg. D-4-13
Tenorio, Joaquin Q -pg. D-5-61
Tenorio, Joaquin S -pg. D-5-15
Tenorio, Jose -pg. D-3-19
Tenorio, Jose A -pg. D-5-21
Tenorio, Jose B -pg. D-5-20
Tenorio, Jose G -pg. D-4-13
Tenorio, Jose M -pg. D-1-69
Tenorio, Jose M -pg. D-5-3
Tenorio, Jose M -pg. D-5-84
Tenorio, Jose Q -pg. D-5-71
Tenorio, Jose SN -pg. D-5-31
Tenorio, Jose T -pg. D-2-38
Tenorio, Jose T -pg. D-3-19
Tenorio, Josefa B -pg. D-5-19
Tenorio, Juan B -pg. D-4-34
Tenorio, Juan C -pg. D-0-44
Tenorio, Juan G -pg. D-4-13
Tenorio, Juan G -pg. D-4-102
Tenorio, Juan Q -pg. D-5-16
Tenorio, Juan S -pg. D-5-21
Tenorio, Juan SN -pg. D-5-31
Tenorio, Juan T -pg. D-12-8
Tenorio, Juana Q -pg. D-5-16
Tenorio, Juana S -pg. D-5-71
Tenorio, Julia B -pg. D-4-34
Tenorio, Leonardo C -pg. D-5-62
Tenorio, Leonardo C -pg. D-8-44
Tenorio, Lourdes L -pg. D-4-105
Tenorio, Lucia C -pg. D-8-44
Tenorio, Luis C -pg. D-4-88
Tenorio, Luis SN -pg. D-5-31
Tenorio, Magdalena T -pg. D-12-2
Tenorio, Manuel N -pg. D-1-69
Tenorio, Manuel T -pg. D-5-64
Tenorio, Maria -pg. D-5-84
Tenorio, Maria A -pg. D-5-81
Tenorio, Maria B -pg. D-4-34
Tenorio, Maria B -pg. D-5-84
Tenorio, Maria C -pg. D-5-61
Tenorio, Maria G -pg. D-4-102
Tenorio, Maria G -pg. D-5-84
Tenorio, Maria M -pg. D-8-45

Tenorio, Maria Q -pg. D-5-16
Tenorio, Maria Q -pg. D-5-71
Tenorio, Maria SN -pg. D-5-31
Tenorio, Maria T -pg. D-2-38
Tenorio, Maria T -pg. D-2-45
Tenorio, Mercedes -pg. D-5-64
Tenorio, Miguel R -pg. D-4-34
Tenorio, Natividad C -pg. D-5-84
Tenorio, Natividad N -pg. D-5-64
Tenorio, Oliva -pg. D-3-19
Tenorio, Oliva Q -pg. D-3-28
Tenorio, Pedro C -pg. D-8-44
Tenorio, Pedro M -pg. D-8-45
Tenorio, Pilajia A -pg. D-1-43
Tenorio, Ramona Q -pg. D-5-16
Tenorio, Regina -pg. D-5-84
Tenorio, Remedios -pg. D-5-64
Tenorio, Ricardo -pg. D-5-84
Tenorio, Rita G -pg. D-4-13
Tenorio, Roberto SN -pg. D-5-31
Tenorio, Rosa -pg. D-5-71
Tenorio, Rosa G -pg. D-3-19
Tenorio, Rosa G -pg. D-4-13
Tenorio, Rosa T -pg. D-3-38
Tenorio, Rosario -pg. D-5-84
Tenorio, Rosario -pg. D-5-84
Tenorio, Rosario B -pg. D-4-34
Tenorio, Sederino SN -pg. D-5-31
Tenorio, Teresa -pg. D-5-64
Tenorio, Teresa M -pg. D-8-45
Tenorio, Tomas -pg. D-5-71
Tenorio, Tomasa -pg. D-3-20
Tenorio, Tomasa SN -pg. D-5-30
Tenorio, Vicente -pg. D-3-19
Tenorio, Vicente B -pg. D-5-30
Tenorio, Vicente G -pg. D-5-81
Tenorio, Vicente S -pg. D-3-38
Terbure, Ernest W -pg. D-13-31
Terhune, John A -pg. D-13-26
Terlaje, Amalia T -pg. D-10-24
Terlaje, Antonia -pg. D-3-67
Terlaje, Antonia T -pg. D-4-11
Terlaje, Augusto -pg. D-3-67
Terlaje, Carmela A -pg. D-10-27
Terlaje, Carmen -pg. D-3-67
Terlaje, Carmen S -pg. D-3-28
Terlaje, Consuelo F -pg. D-13-43
Terlaje, Dolores A -pg. D-10-27
Terlaje, Dolores S -pg. D-7-22
Terlaje, Felisa C -pg. D-4-41
Terlaje, Felix A -pg. D-7-22
Terlaje, Francisco C -pg. D-4-41
Terlaje, Francisco J -pg. D-3-67
Terlaje, Francisco T -pg. D-4-38
Terlaje, Francisco T -pg. D-7-2
Terlaje, Gabriela A -pg. D-10-27
Terlaje, Gregorio C -pg. D-4-41
Terlaje, Ignacia T -pg. D-7-7
Terlaje, Isabel C -pg. D-4-41

Terlaje, Jesus -pg. D-3-28
Terlaje, Jesus A -pg. D-10-27
Terlaje, Jesus A -pg. D-10-27
Terlaje, Jesus C -pg. D-4-41
Terlaje, Jesus S -pg. D-4-5
Terlaje, Joaquin T -pg. D-7-2
Terlaje, Jose C -pg. D-7-13
Terlaje, Jose F -pg. D-3-28
Terlaje, Jose I -pg. D-4-41
Terlaje, Josefa F -pg. D-7-13
Terlaje, Josefa S -pg. D-4-5
Terlaje, Josefina -pg. D-3-67
Terlaje, Juan S -pg. D-4-5
Terlaje, Juan T -pg. D-7-7
Terlaje, Luis A -pg. D-3-28
Terlaje, Luis A -pg. D-10-27
Terlaje, Magdalena A -pg. D-7-2
Terlaje, Manuel C -pg. D-10-27
Terlaje, Manuela T -pg. D-7-7
Terlaje, Maria -pg. D-3-28
Terlaje, Maria -pg. D-3-67
Terlaje, Maria C -pg. D-4-41
Terlaje, Maria G -pg. D-4-11
Terlaje, Maria S -pg. D-3-67
Terlaje, Mercedes A -pg. D-10-27
Terlaje, Miguel A -pg. D-10-27
Terlaje, Pedro -pg. D-3-28
Terlaje, Pedro -pg. D-3-67
Terlaje, Precila -pg. D-3-28
Terlaje, Rosalia S -pg. D-4-5
Terlaje, Rosario -pg. D-3-28
Terlaje, Saturnina S -pg. D-4-38
Terlaje, Teresa S -pg. D-4-38
Terlaje, Tomas -pg. D-3-67
Terlaje, Vicente -pg. D-3-28
Terlaje, Vincente B -pg. D-13-30
Terlaji, Antonio B -pg. D-6-23
Terlaji, Antonio R -pg. D-6-2
Terlaji, Baldovino A -pg. D-6-27
Terlaji, Concepcion B -pg. D-6-23
Terlaji, Francisco R -pg. D-6-2
Terlaji, Joaquin B -pg. D-6-23
Terlaji, Joaquin R -pg. D-6-2
Terlaji, Joaquina A -pg. D-6-27
Terlaji, Jose B -pg. D-6-27
Terlaji, Juan R -pg. D-6-2
Terlaji, Magdalena M -pg. D-6-40
Terlaji, Maria A -pg. D-6-27
Terlaji, Maria C -pg. D-6-23
Terlaji, Maria R -pg. D-6-2
Terlaji, Rebustiano B -pg. D-6-23
Terlaji, Rosalia B -pg. D-6-23
Terlaji, Vicenta A -pg. D-6-34
Terlaji, Vicente R -pg. D-6-2
Teronend, Arthur M -pg. D-13-21
Tertaotao, Antonia C -pg. D-4-62
Tertaotao, Jesus A -pg. D-3-51
Teubner, Leysa M -pg. D-4-32
Teubner, Maryane F -pg. D-4-32

Teubner, Raymond -pg. D-4-32
Theodorsin, Orel G -pg. D-13-18
Thetford, William D -pg. D-13-41
Thomas, Francis E -pg. D-10-8
Thomas, Hurley A -pg. D-13-30
Thomas, Hurley K -pg. D-10-8
thomas, Luther W -pg. D-13-20
Thomas, William A -pg. D-13-9
Thomas, William B -pg. D-13-32
Thompson, Alvin L -pg. D-3-43
Thompson, Alvin L -pg. D-3-43
Thompson, George B -pg. D-13-38
Thompson, Ralph C -pg. D-3-43
Thompson, Rober Jr. -pg. D-13-14
Thompson, Rosa G -pg. D-3-43
Thompson, Thomas R -pg. D-13-13
Throsser, Wiley J -pg. D-13-9
Tichaira, Dolores -pg. D-5-65
Tichaira, Jose -pg. D-5-65
Tichaira, Juan D -pg. D-5-65
Tichaira, Manuel -pg. D-5-65
Tichaira, Manuela G -pg. D-5-65
Tichaira, Pedro -pg. D-5-65
Tichaira, Vicente -pg. D-5-65
Tickle, Patrick H -pg. D-13-39
Tinkler, Harold J -pg. D-13-14
Tiquiengco, Enrique B -pg. D-5-57
Todela, Jose P -pg. D-5-56
Todela, Jose P -pg. D-5-56
Tolentino, Felicita D -pg. D-11-40
Tolentino, Florencia D -pg. D-11-40
Tolentino, Joaquin T -pg. D-11-40
Tolentino, Maria D -pg. D-11-40
Tolentino, Maria L -pg. D-13-43
Tolentino, Matilde D -pg. D-11-40
Tolentino, Maximo L -pg. D-4-25
Tolentino, Rosalia D -pg. D-11-40
Tolentino, Tomasa DG -pg. D-11-40
Tolle, James B -pg. D-13-14
Toner, Martin J -pg. D-13-9
Topasna, Agueda -pg. D-3-24
Topasna, Amadeo A -pg. D-9-44
Topasna, Ana I -pg. D-9-35
Topasna, Ana LG -pg. D-3-24
Topasna, Antonia -pg. D-3-24
Topasna, Antonia Q -pg. D-9-43
Topasna, Candido T -pg. D-11-9
Topasna, Dolores A -pg. D-9-35
Topasna, Dolores C -pg. D-9-44
Topasna, Eucebio Q -pg. D-9-35
Topasna, Feliciana P -pg. D-9-44
Topasna, Felipe A -pg. D-9-35
Topasna, Felix T -pg. D-11-5
Topasna, Francisca I -pg. D-9-34
Topasna, Francisco -pg. D-3-24
Topasna, Francisco A -pg. D-9-35
Topasna, Francisco Q -pg. D-9-35
Topasna, Gregorio A -pg. D-9-35
Topasna, Isabel I -pg. D-9-35

Topasna, Isabel Q -pg. D-9-43
Topasna, Isidoro E -pg. D-9-43
Topasna, Jaime A -pg. D-9-35
Topasna, Jesus A -pg. D-3-52
Topasna, Jesus T -pg. D-9-12
Topasna, Joaquin C -pg. D-9-44
Topasna, Jose A -pg. D-9-35
Topasna, Jose I -pg. D-9-35
Topasna, Jose Q -pg. D-9-34
Topasna, Jose Q -pg. D-9-43
Topasna, Josefina I -pg. D-9-34
Topasna, Juan E -pg. D-9-39
Topasna, Juan Q -pg. D-9-35
Topasna, Juan Q -pg. D-9-43
Topasna, Juan Q -pg. D-9-43
Topasna, Julian I -pg. D-9-34
Topasna, Maria I -pg. D-9-34
Topasna, Maria T -pg. D-9-39
Topasna, Paterno -pg. D-3-24
Topasna, Pedro A -pg. D-9-43
Topasna, Petronila A -pg. D-9-35
Topasna, Rafael E -pg. D-9-36
Topasna, Rafael I -pg. D-11-5
Topasna, Resurecion Q -pg. D-9-43
Topasna, Rita I -pg. D-9-35
Topasna, Roman A -pg. D-9-35
Topasna, Rosalia -pg. D-3-24
Topasna, Rosalia Q -pg. D-9-43
Topasna, Soledad Q -pg. D-9-35
Topasna, Ursula A -pg. D-9-35
Topasna, Valentina C -pg. D-9-44
Torre, Amparo SN -pg. D-2-13
Torre, Ana U -pg. D-2-72
Torre, Benjamin C -pg. D-4-2
Torre, Consolacion C -pg. D-2-24
Torre, Dolores C -pg. D-4-2
Torre, Esperanza U -pg. D-2-73
Torre, Felicidad U -pg. D-2-72
Torre, Grabela T -pg. D-2-29
Torre, Gregorio SN -pg. D-2-13
Torre, Isabel U -pg. D-2-73
Torre, Jesus C -pg. D-2-13
Torre, Joaquin B -pg. D-2-72
Torre, Joaquin C -pg. D-4-2
Torre, Jose C -pg. D-2-29
Torre, Jose T -pg. D-2-29
Torre, Jose U -pg. D-2-72
Torre, Josefa A -pg. D-2-84
Torre, Juan C -pg. D-4-2
Torre, Juan U -pg. D-2-72
Torre, Luis C -pg. D-4-2
Torre, Luis SN -pg. D-2-13
Torre, Magdalena C -pg. D-4-3
Torre, Maria C -pg. D-4-2
Torre, Maria U -pg. D-2-73
Torre, Rosa N -pg. D-4-3
Torre, Rosa U -pg. D-2-72
Torre, Rosalia C -pg. D-4-2
Torre, Rosario T -pg. D-2-29

Torre, Vicenta U -pg. D-2-72
Torres, Ana -pg. D-3-50
Torres, Ana -pg. D-3-55
Torres, Ana C -pg. D-4-26
Torres, Ana E -pg. D-1-57
Torres, Ana P -pg. D-1-17
Torres, Ana P -pg. D-2-73
Torres, Ana P -pg. D-3-26
Torres, Anselmo T -pg. D-2-52
Torres, Antonia -pg. D-3-38
Torres, Antonia B -pg. D-4-77
Torres, Antonio C -pg. D-3-47
Torres, Antonio C -pg. D-4-77
Torres, Antonio C -pg. D-5-41
Torres, Antonio M -pg. D-3-26
Torres, Antonio P -pg. D-1-17
Torres, Antonio P -pg. D-6-15
Torres, Antonio U -pg. D-4-91
Torres, Asuncion -pg. D-3-50
Torres, Asuncion I -pg. D-9-21
Torres, Barbara C -pg. D-10-10
Torres, Beatrice -pg. D-5-54
Torres, Beatrice Q -pg. D-6-39
Torres, Beatriz M -pg. D-9-21
Torres, Caridad C -pg. D-3-47
Torres, Carmen C -pg. D-5-40
Torres, Carmen I -pg. D-3-28
Torres, Concepcion -pg. D-3-38
Torres, Concepcion C -pg. D-3-26
Torres, Concepcion C -pg. D-3-38
Torres, Concepcion C -pg. D-3-47
Torres, Concepcion C -pg. D-4-24
Torres, Concepcion E -pg. D-1-57
Torres, Consolacion N -pg. D-1-20
Torres, Daniel U -pg. D-10-30
Torres, Delfina M -pg. D-4-19
Torres, Dolores A -pg. D-5-41
Torres, Dolores B -pg. D-2-60
Torres, Dolores C -pg. D-5-41
Torres, Dolores H -pg. D-1-28
Torres, Dolores H -pg. D-1-28
Torres, Dolores P -pg. D-1-17
Torres, Dolores W -pg. D-3-6
Torres, Edward -pg. D-3-38
Torres, Engracia M -pg. D-9-21
Torres, Esteban U -pg. D-10-30
Torres, Felisa -pg. D-3-6
Torres, Felisita Q -pg. D-6-39
Torres, Felix C -pg. D-1-12
Torres, Felix H -pg. D-1-28
Torres, Felix H -pg. D-12-19
Torres, Flora E -pg. D-1-57
Torres, Francisco -pg. D-3-38
Torres, Francisco C -pg. D-1-12
Torres, Francisco C -pg. D-4-24
Torres, Francisco M -pg. D-4-19
Torres, Francisco P -pg. D-6-6
Torres, Francisco U -pg. D-10-30
Torres, Gregorio M -pg. D-4-110

Torres, Gregorio P -pg. D-1-17
Torres, Guadalupe Q -pg. D-6-39
Torres, Guadalupe U -pg. D-4-91
Torres, Helen U -pg. D-4-91
Torres, Ignacia C -pg. D-4-24
Torres, Ignacio E -pg. D-1-57
Torres, Ignacio R -pg. D-3-6
Torres, Ignasia P -pg. D-6-15
Torres, Isabel A -pg. D-5-41
Torres, Jesus C -pg. D-4-90
Torres, Jesus C -pg. D-5-41
Torres, Jesus C -pg. D-10-10
Torres, Jesus F -pg. D-3-38
Torres, Jesus H -pg. D-1-28
Torres, Jesus N -pg. D-1-20
Torres, Jesus P -pg. D-6-15
Torres, Jesus P -pg. D-11-50
Torres, Jesus T -pg. D-2-52
Torres, Jesus T -pg. D-8-2
Torres, Jesus U -pg. D-10-30
Torres, Joaquin -pg. D-10-30
Torres, Joaquin C -pg. D-10-10
Torres, Joaquin N -pg. D-4-32
Torres, Joaquina -pg. D-3-38
Torres, Joaquina P -pg. D-1-17
Torres, Jose -pg. D-3-38
Torres, Jose A -pg. D-1-53
Torres, Jose A -pg. D-5-41
Torres, Jose A -pg. D-13-31
Torres, Jose C -pg. D-1-12
Torres, Jose C -pg. D-3-55
Torres, Jose C -pg. D-4-25
Torres, Jose C -pg. D-4-26
Torres, Jose C -pg. D-5-49
Torres, Jose E -pg. D-1-57
Torres, Jose H -pg. D-5-41
Torres, Jose I -pg. D-9-21
Torres, Jose L -pg. D-5-40
Torres, Jose LG -pg. D-2-73
Torres, Jose M -pg. D-1-12
Torres, Jose M -pg. D-4-19
Torres, Jose M -pg. D-9-21
Torres, Jose P -pg. D-1-17
Torres, Jose P -pg. D-13-30
Torres, Jose U -pg. D-1-52
Torres, Jose U -pg. D-10-30
Torres, Josefa -pg. D-3-50
Torres, Josefa A -pg. D-4-110
Torres, Josefa B -pg. D-4-77
Torres, Josefa C -pg. D-3-47
Torres, Josefa D -pg. D-3-27
Torres, Josefina C -pg. D-4-24
Torres, Josefina H -pg. D-1-28
Torres, Josefina P -pg. D-1-29
Torres, Juan -pg. D-3-38
Torres, Juan C -pg. D-4-26
Torres, Juan C -pg. D-5-49
Torres, Juan D -pg. D-5-49
Torres, Juan E -pg. D-1-17

Torres, Juan G -pg. D-2-27
Torres, Juan LG -pg. D-2-60
Torres, Juan M -pg. D-3-38
Torres, Juan P -pg. D-6-15
Torres, Juan U -pg. D-4-91
Torres, Juan M -pg. D-4-19
Torres, Juana M -pg. D-4-19
Torres, Juana T -pg. D-2-52
Torres, Juana T -pg. D-5-54
Torres, Julia C -pg. D-4-26
Torres, Juliana P -pg. D-3-60
Torres, Lope -pg. D-3-38
Torres, Lourdes S -pg. D-9-23
Torres, Luis C -pg. D-3-47
Torres, Luis E -pg. D-1-20
Torres, Luis E -pg. D-1-57
Torres, Luis H -pg. D-1-29
Torres, Luis H -pg. D-12-19
Torres, Luis LG -pg. D-1-57
Torres, Luis N -pg. D-1-20
Torres, Manuel F -pg. D-5-54
Torres, Maria -pg. D-3-26
Torres, Maria C -pg. D-1-12
Torres, Maria C -pg. D-1-12
Torres, Maria C -pg. D-10-10
Torres, Maria G -pg. D-3-38
Torres, Maria H -pg. D-1-28
Torres, Maria M -pg. D-9-21
Torres, Maria N -pg. D-1-20
Torres, Maria P -pg. D-1-29
Torres, Maria P -pg. D-3-50
Torres, Maria P -pg. D-3-60
Torres, Maria P -pg. D-6-15
Torres, Maria P -pg. D-9-10
Torres, Maria R -pg. D-3-6
Torres, Maria U -pg. D-4-90
Torres, Maria U -pg. D-10-30
Torres, Maria O U -pg. D-10-30
Torres, Mariano T -pg. D-2-27
Torres, Maxima G -pg. D-2-27
Torres, Natividad C -pg. D-6-6
Torres, Pedro -pg. D-3-50
Torres, Pilar -pg. D-3-38
Torres, Ramon A -pg. D-1-53
Torres, Remedio N -pg. D-1-20
Torres, Ricardo -pg. D-3-38
Torres, Rita -pg. D-3-50
Torres, Rosa A -pg. D-1-52
Torres, Rosa P -pg. D-3-60
Torres, Rosa T -pg. D-2-52
Torres, Rosalia C -pg. D-4-26
Torres, Rosalia T -pg. D-5-54
Torres, Tomas C -pg. D-4-24
Torres, Tomas M -pg. D-4-19
Torres, Tomas N -pg. D-1-20
Torres, Tomas P -pg. D-6-16
Torres, Tomasa C -pg. D-3-47
Torres, Trinidad B -pg. D-4-77
Torres, Trinidad C -pg. D-5-49

Torres, Trinidad P -pg. D-2-70
Torres, Ursula U -pg. D-10-30
Torres, Vicenta Q -pg. D-4-32
Torres, Vicente A -pg. D-1-28
Torres, Vicente A -pg. D-5-41
Torres, Vicente C -pg. D-3-47
Torres, Vicente C -pg. D-4-24
Torres, Vicente C -pg. D-4-26
Torres, Vicente G -pg. D-4-24
Torres, Vicente M -pg. D-3-46
Torres, Vicente N -pg. D-4-19
Torres, Vicente P -pg. D-2-73
Totten, Charles R -pg. D-13-39
Toves, Agueda T -pg. D-4-26
Toves, Agustin S -pg. D-2-51
Toves, Alejandro B -pg. D-2-38
Toves, Amanda F -pg. D-1-18
Toves, Amparo C -pg. D-11-17
Toves, Ana A -pg. D-4-49
Toves, Ana B -pg. D-2-38
Toves, Ana C -pg. D-2-38
Toves, Ana D -pg. D-4-3
Toves, Ana M -pg. D-8-35
Toves, Ana M -pg. D-12-19
Toves, Ana N -pg. D-2-64
Toves, Ana Q -pg. D-2-19
Toves, Ana S -pg. D-4-96
Toves, Ana S -pg. D-5-79
Toves, Ana T -pg. D-8-49
Toves, Ann Q -pg. D-1-47
Toves, Antonio D -pg. D-4-3
Toves, Antonio F -pg. D-1-18
Toves, Antonio LG -pg. D-2-19
Toves, Antonio Q -pg. D-12-13
Toves, Authur B -pg. D-11-17
Toves, Candaleria H -pg. D-2-64
Toves, Carmen A -pg. D-4-49
Toves, Carmen F -pg. D-2-22
Toves, Concepcion F -pg. D-2-22
Toves, Consolacion A -pg. D-11-51
Toves, Dolores S -pg. D-2-51
Toves, Dometro M -pg. D-12-19
Toves, Elias B -pg. D-2-38
Toves, Felix -pg. D-5-97
Toves, Felix U -pg. D-5-89
Toves, Florence M -pg. D-11-17
Toves, Francisca S -pg. D-2-51
Toves, Francisco A -pg. D-4-49
Toves, Francisco Q -pg. D-5-70
Toves, Frank E -pg. D-11-17
Toves, Gregorio -pg. D-3-19
Toves, Harry A -pg. D-11-51
Toves, Inez M -pg. D-4-38
Toves, Isabel G -pg. D-5-79
Toves, Isabel M -pg. D-4-38
Toves, Isidro F -pg. D-12-13
Toves, Jesus A -pg. D-4-49
Toves, Jesus B -pg. D-5-61
Toves, Jesus C -pg. D-2-38

Toves, Jesus F -pg. D-2-22
Toves, Jesus M -pg. D-12-19
Toves, Jesus Q -pg. D-5-61
Toves, Jesus S -pg. D-2-51
Toves, Jesus T -pg. D-2-50
Toves, Joaquin C -pg. D-1-47
Toves, Joaquin M -pg. D-12-19
Toves, John A -pg. D-11-51
Toves, Jose A -pg. D-4-49
Toves, Jose B -pg. D-2-21
Toves, Jose B -pg. D-2-64
Toves, Jose C -pg. D-2-22
Toves, Jose D -pg. D-4-3
Toves, Jose F -pg. D-2-22
Toves, Jose G -pg. D-5-79
Toves, Jose M -pg. D-4-38
Toves, Jose Q -pg. D-11-17
Toves, Jose S -pg. D-2-51
Toves, Jose T -pg. D-1-34
Toves, Jose T -pg. D-4-26
Toves, Jose U -pg. D-5-97
Toves, Josefa H -pg. D-2-64
Toves, Josefina F -pg. D-2-22
Toves, Joseph G -pg. D-11-17
Toves, Juan -pg. D-3-19
Toves, Juan A -pg. D-2-12
Toves, Juan A -pg. D-4-49
Toves, Juan B -pg. D-2-64
Toves, Juan C -pg. D-4-38
Toves, Juan G -pg. D-4-49
Toves, Juan G -pg. D-12-19
Toves, Juan Q -pg. D-1-47
Toves, Juan Q -pg. D-2-19
Toves, Juan T -pg. D-11-51
Toves, Juana F -pg. D-3-19
Toves, Julia M -pg. D-4-38
Toves, Kenneth B -pg. D-11-17
Toves, Leonila Q -pg. D-12-13
Toves, Magdalena A -pg. D-4-34
Toves, Magdalena D -pg. D-4-3
Toves, Manuela Q -pg. D-5-61
Toves, Manuela T -pg. D-2-50
Toves, Maria -pg. D-3-19
Toves, Maria A -pg. D-4-49
Toves, Maria B -pg. D-2-51
Toves, Maria C -pg. D-2-51
Toves, Maria C -pg. D-5-97
Toves, Maria D -pg. D-4-3
Toves, Maria M -pg. D-4-38
Toves, Maria M -pg. D-4-38
Toves, Maria M -pg. D-12-19
Toves, Maria Q -pg. D-5-61
Toves, Maria Q -pg. D-5-61
Toves, Maria S -pg. D-1-48
Toves, Maria S -pg. D-2-51
Toves, Maria S -pg. D-5-90
Toves, Maria T -pg. D-8-43
Toves, Maria T -pg. D-8-49
Toves, Matilde Q -pg. D-5-61

Toves, Nicolas C -pg. D-2-51
Toves, Olimpia Q -pg. D-12-13
Toves, Pedro I -pg. D-4-3
Toves, Pedro L -pg. D-3-19
Toves, Pedro M -pg. D-12-19
Toves, Pedro T -pg. D-2-50
Toves, Pedro T -pg. D-2-51
Toves, Ramon S -pg. D-5-79
Toves, Ramon T -pg. D-8-49
Toves, Ramona M -pg. D-4-38
Toves, Rita G -pg. D-4-26
Toves, Rita M -pg. D-12-19
Toves, Rita Q -pg. D-2-19
Toves, Rosa D -pg. D-4-3
Toves, Rosa Q -pg. D-12-13
Toves, Rosa R -pg. D-1-18
Toves, Rosalia M -pg. D-4-38
Toves, Rosario M -pg. D-4-38
Toves, Rosario T -pg. D-8-49
Toves, Sergio B -pg. D-2-38
Toves, Teodoro M -pg. D-4-38
Toves, Teodosia B -pg. D-2-38
Toves, Teresa Q -pg. D-1-47
Toves, Tomas S -pg. D-2-51
Toves, Ursula S -pg. D-2-51
Toves, Vicenta G -pg. D-12-19
Toves, Vicente A -pg. D-4-49
Towner, Emilia L -pg. D-4-15
Towner, William A -pg. D-4-16
Towner, William H -pg. D-4-15
Townsend, Jack T -pg. D-3-44
Townsend, John W -pg. D-13-9
Townsend, Nietta -pg. D-3-44
Tracy, Albert H -pg. D-13-9
Treltas, Antonia T -pg. D-7-11
Treltas, Bartola C -pg. D-7-13
Treltas, Jose A -pg. D-7-13
Treltas, Rosalia C -pg. D-7-13
Treltas, Vicente C -pg. D-7-13
Tremclay, Albert J -pg. D-13-39
Troy, John J -pg. D-13-20
Troy, Ruth M -pg. D-1-36
Tuck, Byron H -pg. D-13-42
Tuncap, Angel -pg. D-4-9
Tuncap, Caridad P -pg. D-4-13
Tuncap, Celedonia T -pg. D-4-9
Tuncap, Clemente N -pg. D-4-9
Tuncap, Concepcion -pg. D-4-8
Tuncap, Delfina T -pg. D-4-9
Tuncap, Dolores -pg. D-4-8
Tuncap, Enrique T -pg. D-4-9
Tuncap, Felecita D -pg. D-4-36
Tuncap, Florentina T -pg. D-4-9
Tuncap, Gonzalo P -pg. D-4-13
Tuncap, Jesus T -pg. D-4-9
Tuncap, Jesus T -pg. D-4-9
Tuncap, Joaquin N -pg. D-4-12
Tuncap, Jose P -pg. D-4-13
Tuncap, Juan N -pg. D-7-24

Tuncap, Manuel P -pg. D-4-13
Tuncap, Maria -pg. D-4-8
Tuncap, Maria P -pg. D-4-13
Tuncap, Rita D -pg. D-4-36
Tuncap, Rosa T -pg. D-4-9
Turner, Francis M -pg. D-11-25
Turner, Herschell -pg. D-13-14
Turner, John C -pg. D-13-39
Twentey, Louis C -pg. D-13-32
Ty-Quiongco, Francisco B -pg. D-12-20
Tydingco, Antonia A -pg. D-6-16
Tydingco, Antonio C -pg. D-7-22
Tydingco, Carlos M -pg. D-7-22
Tydingco, Carlos P -pg. D-7-10
Tydingco, Dolores A -pg. D-7-15
Tydingco, Dolores C -pg. D-7-22
Tydingco, Dolores L -pg. D-7-10
Tydingco, Francisca L -pg. D-7-10
Tydingco, Helen C -pg. D-7-10
Tydingco, Jose A -pg. D-7-15
Tydingco, Jose C -pg. D-7-15
Tydingco, Juan A -pg. D-7-15
Tydingco, Manuel A -pg. D-7-10
Tydingco, Maria A -pg. D-7-15
Tydingco, Pedro A -pg. D-7-15
Tydingco, Rosa S -pg. D-6-22
Tydingco, Rufina A -pg. D-7-15
Tydingco, Ruth S -pg. D-7-10
Tydingco, Severa P -pg. D-7-11
Tydingco, Vicente -pg. D-7-10
Tyquiengco, Agustina B -pg. D-9-28
Tyquiengco, Antonio M -pg. D-9-4
Tyquiengco, Gregorio B -pg. D-9-4
Tyquiengco, Jesus N -pg. D-9-7
Tyquiengco, Joaquin B -pg. D-9-28
Tyquiengco, Jose N -pg. D-9-7
Tyquiengco, Lorenzo B -pg. D-9-29
Tyquiengco, Lourdes T -pg. D-9-29
Tyquiengco, Maria A -pg. D-9-27
Tyquiengco, Maria N -pg. D-9-7
Tyquiengco, Milagro T -pg. D-9-29
Tyquiengco, Nicolasa M -pg. D-9-4
Tyquiengco, Petronila T -pg. D-9-3
Tyquiengco, Rosa T -pg. D-9-3
Tyquiengco, Rosa T -pg. D-9-29
Tyquiengco, Rosario B -pg. D-9-27
Tyquiengco, Vicente B -pg. D-9-3
Tyquiengco, Vicente B -pg. D-9-4
Ulloa, Amanda R -pg. D-5-98
Ulloa, Ana C -pg. D-2-21
Ulloa, Ana C -pg. D-2-28
Ulloa, Ana S -pg. D-11-16
Ulloa, Carmen A -pg. D-2-47
Ulloa, David S -pg. D-3-53
Ulloa, Elena R -pg. D-8-45
Ulloa, Elizabeth A -pg. D-3-53
Ulloa, Esther M -pg. D-3-53
Ulloa, Evelyn R -pg. D-3-53
Ulloa, Francisco I -pg. D-1-69

Ulloa, Francisco J -pg. D-6-2
Ulloa, Gaspat U -pg. D-6-2
Ulloa, Genoveba J -pg. D-6-2
Ulloa, Gregorio S -pg. D-11-16
Ulloa, Ignacio A -pg. D-2-47
Ulloa, Jesus A -pg. D-2-47
Ulloa, Jesus C -pg. D-2-21
Ulloa, Joaquin I -pg. D-5-94
Ulloa, Joaquin U -pg. D-5-94
Ulloa, Joaquina C -pg. D-2-21
Ulloa, Joaquina G -pg. D-11-45
Ulloa, Josefina A -pg. D-2-47
Ulloa, Juan D -pg. D-11-15
Ulloa, Juan LG -pg. D-2-28
Ulloa, Juan Q -pg. D-13-27
Ulloa, Juan S -pg. D-11-15
Ulloa, Juan U -pg. D-5-40
Ulloa, Julia A -pg. D-2-47
Ulloa, Lourdes C -pg. D-2-21
Ulloa, Lucy -pg. D-3-53
Ulloa, Manuel F -pg. D-3-52
Ulloa, Marcelo U -pg. D-2-47
Ulloa, Maria A -pg. D-2-47
Ulloa, Maria A -pg. D-3-53
Ulloa, Maria C -pg. D-2-21
Ulloa, Maria F -pg. D-3-53
Ulloa, Maria R -pg. D-8-45
Ulloa, Maria S -pg. D-11-15
Ulloa, Mariano C -pg. D-2-21
Ulloa, Mariano D -pg. D-11-45
Ulloa, Paul I -pg. D-3-53
Ulloa, Roman C -pg. D-1-69
Ulloa, Rosa G -pg. D-11-15
Ulloa, Rosa N -pg. D-3-44
Ulloa, Rosa R -pg. D-8-45
Ulloa, Rosalia A -pg. D-2-47
Ulloa, Soledad R -pg. D-8-45
Ulloa, Teresa C -pg. D-1-69
Ulloa, Teresa R -pg. D-8-45
Ulloa, Tomas A -pg. D-2-47
Ulloa, Vicente C -pg. D-2-21
Ulloa, Vicente C -pg. D-11-13
Ulloa, Vicente R -pg. D-8-45
Ulloa, Vicente S -pg. D-11-16
Ulloa, Vicente U -pg. D-8-45
Ulloa, Vituriano S -pg. D-11-15
Uncangco, Ana S -pg. D-4-121
Uncangco, Baldomero C -pg. D-4-121
Uncangco, Concepcion S -pg. D-4-122
Uncangco, Eduardo S -pg. D-4-122
Uncangco, Jesus Q -pg. D-4-122
Uncangco, Jesus S -pg. D-4-122
Uncangco, Jose Q -pg. D-4-122
Uncangco, Jose S -pg. D-4-122
Uncangco, Magdalena S -pg. D-4-122
Uncangco, Maria Q -pg. D-4-122
Uncangco, Maria S -pg. D-4-122
Uncango, Elias -pg. D-5-67
Uncango, Francisco G -pg. D-4-123

Uncango, Gregorio -pg. D-5-67
Uncango, Guadalupe G -pg. D-4-123
Uncango, Isabel S -pg. D-5-67
Uncango, Jose G -pg. D-5-67
Uncango, Juana -pg. D-5-67
Uncango, Maria -pg. D-5-67
Uncango, Maria G -pg. D-4-123
Uncango, Maria G -pg. D-4-123
Uncango, Prescilla -pg. D-5-67
Uncango, Vicenta -pg. D-5-67
Uncango, Vicenta G -pg. D-4-123
Uncango, Vicente G -pg. D-4-123
Unchangco, Carmen L -pg. D-4-103
Unchangco, Jose M -pg. D-4-104
Unchangco, Pedro L -pg. D-4-103
Unchangco, Rosa L -pg. D-4-104
Unchangco, Rosa M -pg. D-4-104
Unchangco, Vicente P -pg. D-4-104
Underwood, Ana M -pg. D-3-59
Underwood, Betty R -pg. D-3-59
Underwood, Carmen E -pg. D-3-59
Underwood, Dolores A -pg. D-3-59
Underwood, James H -pg. D-3-58
Underwood, James L -pg. D-3-59
Underwood, John J -pg. D-3-59
Underwood, Raymond F -pg. D-3-59
Underwood, Rita E -pg. D-3-59
Ungacta, Ana C -pg. D-4-96
Ungacta, Antonio -pg. D-5-67
Ungacta, Antonio C -pg. D-4-96
Ungacta, Domingo P -pg. D-4-96
Ungacta, Domingo P -pg. D-5-67
Ungacta, Felix U -pg. D-4-44
Ungacta, Juan C -pg. D-4-96
Ungacta, Maria C -pg. D-4-96
Ungacta, Maria C -pg. D-4-96
Ungacta, Miguel C -pg. D-4-96
Ungacta, Nocolasa S -pg. D-4-61
Ungacta, Servino C -pg. D-4-96
Unpingco, Ana R -pg. D-4-61
Unpingco, Consuelo R -pg. D-4-62
Unpingco, Eliza A -pg. D-1-58
Unpingco, Felipe A -pg. D-10-30
Unpingco, Francisco R -pg. D-4-103
Unpingco, Gloria R -pg. D-1-58
Unpingco, Jesus -pg. D-3-21
Unpingco, Jesus A -pg. D-13-30
Unpingco, Jesus R -pg. D-4-62
Unpingco, Jose -pg. D-3-21
Unpingco, Jose A -pg. D-13-30
Unpingco, Jose R -pg. D-4-62
Unpingco, Joseph M -pg. D-4-103
Unpingco, Juan M -pg. D-4-103
Unpingco, Juan R -pg. D-1-58
Unpingco, Juan R -pg. D-13-27
Unpingco, Maria R -pg. D-4-61
Unpingco, Pedro -pg. D-3-21
Unpingco, Pedro S -pg. D-4-61
Unpingco, Remedios -pg. D-3-21

Unpingco, Ricardo M -pg. D-4-103
Unpingco, Rita M -pg. D-4-103
Unpingco, Rosa M -pg. D-3-21
Unpingco, Venancio -pg. D-3-21
Unpingco, Vicente M -pg. D-4-62
Unsiog, Clemente U -pg. D-10-38
Unsiog, Francisca J -pg. D-10-38
Unsiog, Joaquin J -pg. D-10-37
Unsiog, Maria U -pg. D-10-38
Unsiok, Agustin N -pg. D-11-48
Unsiok, Ana N -pg. D-11-48
Unsiok, Benefacio J -pg. D-11-48
Unsiok, Carmelo N -pg. D-11-47
Unsiok, Jose N -pg. D-11-48
Unsiok, Maria N -pg. D-11-48
Unsiok, Rosa N -pg. D-11-48
Unsiok, Sisto -pg. D-11-47
Untalan, Agustin DL -pg. D-4-40
Untalan, Ana F -pg. D-2-69
Untalan, Ana P -pg. D-2-57
Untalan, Antonia L -pg. D-4-44
Untalan, Antonia LG -pg. D-4-22
Untalan, Antonio DL -pg. D-4-40
Untalan, Beatrice F -pg. D-2-69
Untalan, Bonifacio F -pg. D-2-69
Untalan, Carlota F -pg. D-2-69
Untalan, Delfina L -pg. D-4-44
Untalan, Dolores -pg. D-3-66
Untalan, Emeliana P -pg. D-2-21
Untalan, Enrique LG -pg. D-4-40
Untalan, Estella B -pg. D-4-109
Untalan, Fidela M -pg. D-1-5
Untalan, Francisco C -pg. D-4-34
Untalan, Gil -pg. D-3-66
Untalan, Grillermo F -pg. D-2-69
Untalan, Guadalupe LG -pg. D-4-22
Untalan, Higinio C -pg. D-4-34
Untalan, Ignacia M -pg. D-1-5
Untalan, Isabel -pg. D-3-29
Untalan, Jesus -pg. D-3-29
Untalan, Jesus B -pg. D-2-69
Untalan, Jesus M -pg. D-1-5
Untalan, Jesus P -pg. D-2-7
Untalan, Jesus R -pg. D-2-78
Untalan, Joaquin G -pg. D-13-30
Untalan, Joaquin P -pg. D-13-30
Untalan, Jose -pg. D-3-66
Untalan, Jose C -pg. D-3-29
Untalan, Jose L -pg. D-3-66
Untalan, Jose LG -pg. D-4-22
Untalan, Jose M -pg. D-1-5
Untalan, Jose P -pg. D-2-78
Untalan, Jose T -pg. D-2-7
Untalan, Josefa -pg. D-3-29
Untalan, Josefina F -pg. D-2-69
Untalan, Josefina H -pg. D-3-66
Untalan, Juan -pg. D-3-66
Untalan, Juan M -pg. D-1-5
Untalan, Juan R -pg. D-2-78

Untalan, Juan T -pg. D-2-7
Untalan, Juana C -pg. D-4-34
Untalan, Leonisa B -pg. D-4-109
Untalan, Lourdes DL -pg. D-4-40
Untalan, Lourdes F -pg. D-2-69
Untalan, Luis B -pg. D-1-5
Untalan, Luis P -pg. D-2-57
Untalan, Manuel M -pg. D-1-5
Untalan, Maria -pg. D-3-29
Untalan, Maria B -pg. D-4-107
Untalan, Maria D -pg. D-2-22
Untalan, Maria F -pg. D-2-69
Untalan, Maria M -pg. D-1-5
Untalan, Modesta DL -pg. D-4-40
Untalan, Oliva R -pg. D-2-78
Untalan, Pedro -pg. D-3-66
Untalan, Pedro C -pg. D-4-22
Untalan, Pedro LG -pg. D-4-22
Untalan, Pedro P -pg. D-2-21
Untalan, Rita -pg. D-3-29
Untalan, Rita LG -pg. D-4-22
Untalan, Rita M -pg. D-1-6
Untalan, Rita T -pg. D-2-7
Untalan, Roque M -pg. D-2-45
Untalan, Rosa B -pg. D-4-107
Untalan, Rosa B -pg. D-4-108
Untalan, Rosa DL -pg. D-4-40
Untalan, Rosalia -pg. D-4-40
Untalan, Rosalia M -pg. D-2-45
Untalan, Rosario L -pg. D-4-44
Untalan, Rosario S -pg. D-4-40
Untalan, Serafina LG -pg. D-4-22
Untalan, Tomas F -pg. D-2-69
Untalan, Trinidad R -pg. D-2-78
Untalan, Vicente M -pg. D-1-5
Untalan, Vicente P -pg. D-4-108
Untalan, Virginia DL -pg. D-4-40
Uson, Jose A -pg. D-5-17
Uson, Juan A -pg. D-5-17
Uson, Maria A -pg. D-5-17
Uson, Ramon A -pg. D-5-17
Uson, Ramon G -pg. D-5-17
Uson, Rosalia A -pg. D-5-17
Uson, Teresa A -pg. D-5-17
Uson, Vicente A -pg. D-5-17
Uyehara, Tarusho -pg. D-10-15
Uyeno, Unichich -pg. D-12-21
Valenzuela, Ana LG -pg. D-4-63
Valenzuela, Francisco LG -pg. D-4-63
Valenzuela, Ignacio P -pg. D-4-63
Valenzuela, Isabel LG -pg. D-4-63
Vallandingham, Howard H -pg. D-13-9
Van Dejveker, Henry P -pg. D-13-18
Van Meter, Brigida C -pg. D-11-12
Van Meter, Consolacion C -pg. D-11-12
Van Meter, Juan C -pg. D-11-12
Van Oleck, Florin G -pg. D-13-39
Van Valey, Howard A -pg. D-13-20
Vandeberg, Marten A -pg. D-13-32

Vandenberg, Sidney R -pg. D-10-32
Vanghan, Maria D -pg. D-3-53
Vanghan, Wallace L -pg. D-3-53
Vanson, Ove P O -pg. D-13-26
Vazques, Aina -pg. D-3-46
Vazques, Jesus -pg. D-3-46
Vazques, Loreta -pg. D-3-46
Velanzuela, Antonia S -pg. D-4-57
Velanzuela, Francisco S -pg. D-4-57
Velanzuela, Joaquin C -pg. D-4-57
Velanzuela, Jose S -pg. D-4-57
Velanzuela, Regina S -pg. D-4-57
Velardi, Concepcion C -pg. D-4-114
Velardi, Pilar C -pg. D-4-114
Velardi, Rafaela C -pg. D-4-114
Velardi, Ruth C -pg. D-4-114
Velardi, Simon -pg. D-4-114
Velasco, Jose A -pg. D-4-34
Velasco, Sebastian -pg. D-13-31
Venesiano, Ana G -pg. D-1-7
Venesiano, Enrique G -pg. D-1-7
Venesiano, Patrick G -pg. D-1-7
Venesiano, Rosa G -pg. D-1-7
Vera, Roman M -pg. D-1-56
Verlardo, Evelyn C -pg. D-1-12
Villaflor, Lorenzo -pg. D-13-25
Villagomez, Ana A -pg. D-2-67
Villagomez, Antonia U -pg. D-1-29
Villagomez, Artemio A -pg. D-2-67
Villagomez, Carlos U -pg. D-1-30
Villagomez, Concepcion T -pg. D-5-5
Villagomez, Delfin U -pg. D-1-29
Villagomez, Delfina A -pg. D-2-68
Villagomez, Elena C -pg. D-1-47
Villagomez, Felicita -pg. D-3-24
Villagomez, Felix A -pg. D-2-68
Villagomez, Francisco A -pg. D-2-68
Villagomez, Francisco T -pg. D-5-5
Villagomez, Gregorio T -pg. D-5-5
Villagomez, Ignacio A -pg. D-2-68
Villagomez, Jesus U -pg. D-7-24
Villagomez, Joaquina G -pg. D-5-61
Villagomez, Jorge U -pg. D-1-30
Villagomez, Jose C -pg. D-1-29
Villagomez, Jose C -pg. D-5-72
Villagomez, Jose Q -pg. D-4-77
Villagomez, Jose T -pg. D-5-5
Villagomez, Jose U -pg. D-1-30
Villagomez, Jose V -pg. D-2-67
Villagomez, Josefa T -pg. D-5-5
Villagomez, Juan A -pg. D-2-68
Villagomez, Juan C -pg. D-5-5
Villagomez, Juan T -pg. D-5-5
Villagomez, Juan U -pg. D-1-30
Villagomez, Juan V -pg. D-5-61
Villagomez, Juana C -pg. D-1-47
Villagomez, Manuel G -pg. D-5-61
Villagomez, Maria C -pg. D-1-47
Villagomez, Maria T -pg. D-5-5

Villagomez, Prudencio U -pg. D-1-29
Villagomez, Rosa C -pg. D-1-47
Villagomez, Rosabella T -pg. D-5-5
Villagomez, Ruperto A -pg. D-2-68
Villorin, Silvestre -pg. D-13-25
Villova, Marcel D -pg. D-8-18
Vinluan?, Juanita D -pg. D-11-17
Vugent, David G Jr -pg. D-13-45
Vulte, Elizabeth -pg. D-1-21
Vulte, Nelson T -pg. D-13-14
Wackman, Donald T -pg. D-13-28
Waddle, Robert H -pg. D-13-18
Waidner, Charle M -pg. D-13-32
Waidner, Pauline -pg. D-1-54
Walker, Charles W -pg. D-13-41
Walker, Edmund -pg. D-13-14
Wallace, Guy A -pg. D-13-41
Wallise, Eugene R -pg. D-13-18
Walten, George D -pg. D-13-25
Walters, Adolfo S -pg. D-11-26
Walters, Alfonsina S -pg. D-11-25
Walters, Frederick E -pg. D-13-14
Walters, Jose A -pg. D-11-25
Walton, Eugene L -pg. D-1-16
Walton, Genevieve V -pg. D-1-7
Walton, George E -pg. D-13-32
Walton, Marie F -pg. D-1-16
Warblur, James D -pg. D-13-14
Ward, Edward M -pg. D-13-39
Ward, John C -pg. D-13-33
Warhol, Alexander -pg. D-13-39
Watson, Ann L -pg. D-1-21
Watson, Charles F -pg. D-13-25
Watson, Charles L -pg. D-1-21
Watson, Clarence O -pg. D-13-39
Watson, Mary E -pg. D-1-21
Weaber, Walter H -pg. D-13-14
Wells, Otto B -pg. D-13-45
West, Garfield H -pg. D-13-18
Whating, Chester -pg. D-13-9
Whitaker, Albert L -pg. D-13-14
White, Ana LG -pg. D-2-72
White, Ana P -pg. D-2-81
White, Antonia C -pg. D-2-72
White, Antonio LG -pg. D-2-72
White, Dolores C -pg. D-2-72
White, Eduardo LG -pg. D-2-72
White, Emelia A -pg. D-2-70
White, Horace G -pg. D-13-14
White, Jesus LG -pg. D-2-72
White, Joaquin LG -pg. D-2-72
White, Jose F -pg. D-2-70
White, Jose LG -pg. D-2-72
White, Jose W -pg. D-2-72
White, Juan C -pg. D-2-72
White, Juan F -pg. D-2-72
White, Justo LG -pg. D-2-72
White, Lourdes A -pg. D-2-70
White, Maria C -pg. D-2-72

White, Maria F -pg. D-2-56
White, Maria LG -pg. D-2-72
White, Oliva A -pg. D-2-70
White, Pedro A -pg. D-2-70
White, Rafaela P -pg. D-2-81
White, Ramon LG -pg. D-2-72
White, Rosa A -pg. D-2-70
White, Tomasa A -pg. D-2-70
White, William P -pg. D-2-56
White, William T -pg. D-13-44
Whitehead, Harry A -pg. D-13-14
Wightman, Robert R -pg. D-13-14
Wigle, David W -pg. D-13-46
Wigle, Iva SN -pg. D-1-54
Wilares, Peter J -pg. D-13-14
Wilbrun, Richmond W -pg. D-13-9
Wilhelm, Vincent R -pg. D-13-9
William, Kenneth C -pg. D-13-46
Williams, David I -pg. D-13-39
Williams, Ralph H -pg. D-13-39
Williams, William H -pg. D-13-26
Williamson, Wesley E -pg. D-13-41
Williford, Elijah C -pg. D-13-14
Willson, Leo Q -pg. D-13-26
Wilson, Alan B -pg. D-13-18
Wilson, Ellen M -pg. D-11-32
Wilson, James C -pg. D-13-39
Wilson, Mabel S -pg. D-11-32
Wilson, Maria -pg. D-3-45
Wilson, Robert L -pg. D-13-9
Winert, Josejain -pg. D-13-26
Wisley, Amalia S -pg. D-11-28
Wisley, Benito A -pg. D-11-34
Wisley, Dolores T -pg. D-11-28
Wisley, Elias A -pg. D-11-34
Wisley, Feliza A -pg. D-11-34
Wisley, Ignacio T -pg. D-11-28
Wisley, Jose S -pg. D-11-28
Wisley, Jose T -pg. D-11-28
Wisley, Juan D -pg. D-11-34
Wisley, Juan S -pg. D-11-28
Wisley, Mariano T -pg. D-11-33
Wisley, Remedio A -pg. D-11-34
Wisley, Rita A -pg. D-11-34
Wisley, Vicente D -pg. D-11-34
Wolford, Alfred C -pg. D-2-58
Wolford, Arthur C -pg. D-2-58
Wolford, Catalina C -pg. D-2-58
Wolford, Charlie C -pg. D-2-58
Wolford, Maria C -pg. D-2-58
Wolford, Robert C -pg. D-2-58
Womack, Edgar -pg. D-1-7
Womack, Francisca -pg. D-1-7
Womack, Leonarda -pg. D-1-7
Womack, Magdalena -pg. D-1-7
Won Pat, Antonio B -pg. D-11-19
Won Pat, Vicente B -pg. D-11-4
Wong-Pat, Ignacio -pg. D-3-44
Wongpat, Francisco B -pg. D-4-110

Wood, Anne S -pg. D-1-51
Wood, Laurance A -pg. D-13-9
Wood, Murrel D -pg. D-13-33
Wood, Robert W -pg. D-13-9
Wood, Samuel H -pg. D-13-39
Woodcock, Ronald O -pg. D-13-42
Woolsey, Kenneth A -pg. D-13-39
Worthington, Ralph -pg. D-13-9
Wright, Clayton W -pg. D-13-39
Wusstig, Antonia C -pg. D-5-48
Wusstig, Dolores C -pg. D-5-48
Wusstig, Eliza C -pg. D-5-48
Wusstig, Ernesto C -pg. D-5-48
Wusstig, Felix C -pg. D-5-48
Wusstig, George E -pg. D-5-48
Wusstig, Gloria C -pg. D-5-48
Wusstig, Juan C -pg. D-5-48
Wusstig, Lourdes C -pg. D-5-48
Wusstig, Luisa C -pg. D-5-48
Wusstig, Manuel C -pg. D-5-48
Wusstig, Maria C -pg. D-5-48
Wusstig, Naomi C -pg. D-5-48
Wyatt, James R -pg. D-13-9
Yabot, Silvens -pg. D-13-26
Yamaguchi, Ana A -pg. D-7-9
Yamaguchi, Isabel A -pg. D-7-9
Yamaguchi, Juan -pg. D-7-9
Yamaguchi, Juan A -pg. D-7-9
Yamaguchi, Manuel A -pg. D-7-9
Yamaguchi, Maria A -pg. D-7-9
Yamaguchi, Melinciana A -pg. D-7-9
Yamaguchi, Rosalia A -pg. D-7-9
Yamaguchi, Trinidad A -pg. D-7-9
Yamaguchi, Visitacion A -pg. D-7-9
Yamanaka, Alfonsina B -pg. D-10-4
Yamanaka, Ana B -pg. D-10-4
Yamanaka, Camilo U -pg. D-10-4
Yamanaka, Carmen B -pg. D-10-4
Yamanaka, Catalina M -pg. D-8-39
Yamanaka, Concepcion B -pg. D-10-4
Yamanaka, Diego -pg. D-8-39
Yamanaka, Francisco M -pg. D-8-39
Yamanaka, Jesus B -pg. D-10-5
Yamanaka, Jesus M -pg. D-8-39
Yamanaka, Jose B -pg. D-10-4
Yamanaka, Josefina M -pg. D-3-47
Yamanaka, Josefina M -pg. D-8-39
Yamanaka, Juan M -pg. D-8-39
Yamanaka, Magdalena B -pg. D-10-5
Yamanaka, Maria B -pg. D-10-4
Yamanaka, Maria M -pg. D-8-39
Yamanaka, Paula B -pg. D-10-4
Yamanaka, Rosa B -pg. D-10-4
Yamanaka, Rosa M -pg. D-8-39
Yamane, Soiyei -pg. D-10-15
Yamasaki, Antonio -pg. D-5-99
Yamasaki, Ignacio -pg. D-5-99
Yamasaki, Ignacio B -pg. D-5-69
Yamasaki, Pilar T -pg. D-5-99

Yamasaki, Vicenta -pg. D-5-99
Yamasaki, Vicenta T -pg. D-2-44
Yamashita, Concepcion C -pg. D-10-10
Yamashita, Felicitas C -pg. D-10-10
Yamashita, Jesus C -pg. D-10-10
Yamashita, Jose C -pg. D-10-10
Yamashita, Jose Q -pg. D-5-20
Yamashita, Luis C -pg. D-10-10
Yamashita, Maria C -pg. D-10-10
Yamashita, Raymundo H -pg. D-10-10
Yamashita, Remedios Q -pg. D-5-20
Ybay, Tomas -pg. D-13-26
Yienis, Herbert L -pg. D-13-14
Ylibana, Simmons -pg. D-13-14
Yokoi, Agueda Q -pg. D-2-14
Yokoi, Emelia Q -pg. D-2-14
Yokoi, Francisco Q -pg. D-2-14
Yokoi, Gertrudes Q -pg. D-2-14
Yokoi, Jose Q -pg. D-2-14
Yokoi, Jose T -pg. D-2-14
Yokoi, Juan Q -pg. D-2-14
Yokoi, Maria Q -pg. D-2-14
Yoshida, Concepcion a -pg. D-10-36
Yoshida, Dolores M -pg. D-10-36
Yoshida, Enrique A -pg. D-10-36
Yoshida, Jesus M -pg. D-10-36
Yoshida, Jose M -pg. D-10-36
Yoshida, Jose T -pg. D-10-36
Yoshida, Juan A -pg. D-4-42
Yoshida, Manuel M -pg. D-10-36
Yoshida, Rita H -pg. D-4-42
Yoshida, Rosa H -pg. D-4-42
Yoshida, Shitaro -pg. D-2-14
Young, Francis W -pg. D-13-14
Young, Otis F -pg. D-13-14
Zafra, Angustia E -pg. D-3-58
Zafra, Oliva C -pg. D-1-12
Zamora, Doroteo C -pg. D-3-75
Zamora, Juana C -pg. D-7-4
Zamora, Martin A -pg. D-4-8
Zamora, Pedro C -pg. D-7-4
Zamora, Rosita C -pg. D-7-4
Zamora, Ursula C -pg. D-7-4
Zerdick, Enor L -pg. D-13-14
Zilvach, William C -pg. D-11-50

www.ingramcontent.com/pod-product-compliance
Lightning Source LLC
Chambersburg PA
CBHW080253030426
42334CB00023BA/2801